VOYAGES
IN ENGLISH
GRAMMAR AND WRITING

3

Patricia Healey, I.H.M.
B.A., Immaculata University
M.A., Temple University
20 years teaching; 20 years in administration

Irene Kervick, I.H.M.
B.A., Immaculata University
M.A., Villanova University
46 years teaching

Anne B. McGuire, I.H.M.
B.A., Immaculata University
M.A., Villanova University
M.A., Immaculata University
16 years teaching; 14 years as elementary principal; 10 years staff development

Adrienne Saybolt, I.H.M.
B.A., Immaculata University
Pennsylvania State Board of Education, professional certification
M.A., St. John's University
40 years teaching

LOYOLA**PRESS.**

Art and Photography Acknowledgments

When there is more than one picture on a page, credits are supplied in sequence, left to right, top to bottom. Page positions are abbreviated as follows: **(t)** top, **(c)** center, **(b)** bottom, **(l)** left, **(r)** right.

Photos and illustrations not acknowledged are either owned by Loyola Press or from royalty-free sources including but not limited to Alamy, Art Resource, Big Stock, Bridgeman, Corbis/Veer, Dreamstime, Fotosearch, Getty Images, Northwind Images, Photoedit, Smithsonian, Wikipedia. Loyola Press has made every effort to locate the copyright holders for the cited works used in this publication and to make full acknowledgment for their use. In the case of any omissions, the Publisher will be pleased to make suitable acknowledgments in future editions.

Frontmatter: vii(bl) Phil Martin Photography.

iStockphoto, Frontmatter: iii, iv, vi, vii **Section 1:** 9, 10, 11, 15, 21, 26 **Section 2:** 32, 33, 36–39, 44–49 **Section 3:** 57, 58, 65, 66, 68, 69 **Section 4:** 75, 77, 79, 80, 82, 85, 86–88, 92, 104 **Section 5:** 113, 114, 116, 117, 120, 122, 124–126 **Section 6:** 137, 138, 142, 143, 152, 153, 156 **Section 7:** 167, 169, 171, 178, 182 **Section 8:** 187, 199, 202, 206, 207 **Chapter 1:** 210, 211, 222, 225, 226, 233, 235, 236, 238, 239, 241, 243, 247 **Chapter 2:** 248, 249, 251, 252, 260, 261, 267, 268 **Chapter 3:** 286, 287, 290, 292, 293, 303, 309, 311–313, 318 **Chapter 4:** 325, 327–330, 332, 333, 335, 338, 340, 341, 343–345, 349 **Chapter 5:** 362, 375, 379, 383, 385 **Chapter 6:** 400, 401, 402, 403, 413–415, 420 429, 433, 437 **Chapter 7:** 438, 440, 443, 451, 457, 462, 463 **Chapter 8:** 479, 481, 485, 492 493, 496, 502

Jupiterimages Unlimited, Frontmatter: iii–vii **Section 1:** 12–15, 17, 18, 19, 20, 22, 23 **Section 2:** 28, 29, 31, 35–37, 40–44, 52 **Section 3:** 54–56, 60–63, 66, 67 **Section 4:** 74, 76, 78, 80, 81, 83, 84, 86–91, 93–105, 108 **Section 5:** 110–112, 114–125, 127–130, 134 **Section 6:** 136, 138–142, 144–152, 156 **Section 7:** 158, 160–167, 170–179 **Section 8:** 184–186, 189–201, 203–205

Section 2: 30, Time & Life Pictures/Getty Images. **Section 3: 59(b)** Bettmann/Corbis. **Section 7: 159,** Herb Scharfman/Bettmann/Corbis. **Chapter 1: 219** Anni Betts. **237** Claire Joyce. **Chapter 2: 257(bl)** Greg Kuepfer. **270** Anni Betts. **Chapter 4: 331(t)** Anni Betts. **337** Bettmann/Corbis. **346** Anni Betts. **351(l)** Phil Martin Photography. **353(l)** Phil Martin Photography. **355(r)** Phil Martin Photography. **357(b)** Phil Martin Photography. **Chapter 5: 391** Anni Betts. **393** Anni Betts. **395** Anni Betts. **397** Anni Betts. **Chapter 7: 454** Anni Betts. **469(t)** Anni Betts. **Chapter 8: 487** Anni Betts. **499** President of the United States John Fitzgerald Kennedy, 1961–1963. Portrait photograph distributed by the White House.

Loyola Press has made every effort to locate the copyright holders for the cited works used in this publication and to make full acknowledgment for their use. In the case of any omissions, the publisher will be pleased to make suitable acknowledgments in future editions.

Acknowledgments continue on page T-535.

Cover Design: Think Book Works   Cover Artist: Pablo Bernasconi
Interior Design: Becca Taylor Gay/Loyola Press
Art Director: Judine O'Shea/Loyola Press
Editor: Maria Mondragón/Loyola Press

ISBN-13: 978-0-8294-2822-3
ISBN-10: 0-8294-2822-4

LOYOLA PRESS.
3441 N. Ashland Avenue
Chicago, Illinois 60657
(800) 621-1008
www.loyolapress.com

RRD / China / 04-10 / 1st Printing

Contents

Introduction	**Welcome to *Voyages in English***	OV-1
	Program Overview	OV-2
	How to Use This Program	OV-20

PART 1 Grammar

	Sentences Teacher Preparation	1a–1b
Section 1	**Sentences**	**1**
1.1	Sentences	2
1.2	Statements and Questions	4
1.3	Question Words	6
1.4	Commands	8
1.5	Exclamations	10
1.6	Kinds of Sentences	12
1.7	Subjects	14
1.8	Predicates	16
1.9	Combining Subjects and Predicates	18
1.10	Combining Sentences	20
1.11	Run-on Sentences	22
	Sentence Review	**24**
	Sentence Challenge	**26**
	Nouns Teacher Preparation	27a–27b
Section 2	**Nouns**	**27**
2.1	Nouns	28
2.2	Common and Proper Nouns	30
2.3	Singular and Plural Nouns	32
2.4	More Plural Nouns	34
2.5	Irregular Plural Nouns	36
2.6	Singular Possessive Nouns	38
2.7	Plural Possessive Nouns	40
2.8	Irregular Plural Possessive Nouns	42
2.9	Collective Nouns	44
2.10	Nouns as Subjects	46
2.11	Words Used as Nouns *and* as Verbs	48
	Noun Review	**50**
	Noun Challenge	**52**

Pronouns Teacher Preparation   53a–53b

Section 3   **Pronouns**   **53**

3.1	Pronouns	54
3.2	Subject Pronouns	56
3.3	Object Pronouns	58
3.4	Possessive Pronouns	60
3.5	Possessive Adjectives	62
3.6	Agreement of Pronouns and Verbs	64
3.7	*I* and *Me*	66
3.8	Compound Subjects and Objects	68
	Pronoun Review	**70**
	Pronoun Challenge	**72**

Verbs Teacher Preparation   73a–73b

Section 4   **Verbs**   **73**

4.1	Action Verbs	74
4.2	Being Verbs	76
4.3	Helping Verbs	78
4.4	Principal Parts of Verbs	80
4.5	Regular and Irregular Verbs	82
4.6	*Bring, Buy, Come,* and *Sit*	84
4.7	*Eat, Go,* and *See*	86
4.8	*Take, Tear,* and *Write*	88
4.9	Simple Present Tense	90
4.10	Simple Past Tense	92
4.11	Future Tense with *Will*	94
4.12	Future Tense with *Going To*	96
4.13	Present Progressive Tense	98
4.14	Past Progressive Tense	100
4.15	*Is* and *Are, Was* and *Were*	102
4.16	Contractions with *Not*	104
	Verb Review	**106**
	Verb Challenge	**108**

Adjectives Teacher Preparation   109a–109b

Section 5   **Adjectives**   **109**

5.1	Identifying Adjectives	110
5.2	Adjectives Before Nouns	112
5.3	Subject Complements	114
5.4	Compound Subject Complements	116
5.5	Adjectives That Compare	118
5.6	Irregular Adjectives That Compare	120
5.7	Adjectives That Tell How Many	122
5.8	Articles	124
5.9	Demonstrative Adjectives	126
5.10	Proper Adjectives	128
5.11	Nouns Used as Adjectives	130
	Adjective Review	**132**
	Adjective Challenge	**134**

Adverbs and Conjunctions Teacher Preparation   135a–135b

Section 6   **Adverbs and Conjunctions**   **135**

6.1	Adverbs	136
6.2	Adverbs That Tell When or How Often	138
6.3	Adverbs That Tell Where	140
6.4	Adverbs That Tell How	142
6.5	Negative Words	144
6.6	*Good* and *Well*	146
6.7	*To, Too,* and *Two*	148
6.8	*Their* and *There*	150
6.9	Coordinating Conjunctions	152
	Adverb and Conjunction Review	**154**
	Adverb and Conjunction Challenge	**156**

Punctuation and Capitalization Teacher Preparation   157a–157b

Section 7   **Punctuation and Capitalization**   **157**

7.1	End Punctuation	158
7.2	Capitalization	160
7.3	Abbreviations	162
7.4	Personal Titles and Initials	164
7.5	Titles of Books and Poems	166
7.6	Commas in a Series	168
7.7	Commas in Direct Address	170
7.8	Commas in Compound Sentences	172
7.9	Apostrophes	174
7.10	Addresses	176
7.11	Direct Quotations	178
	Punctuation and Capitalization Review	**180**
	Punctuation and Capitalization Challenge	**182**

Diagramming Teacher Preparation   183a–183b

Section 8   **Diagramming**   **183**

8.1	Subjects and Predicates	184
8.2	Possessives	186
8.3	Adjectives	188
8.4	Adverbs	190
8.5	Adjectives as Subject Complements	192
8.6	Compound Subjects	194
8.7	Compound Predicates	196
8.8	Compound Subject Complements	198
8.9	Compound Sentences	200
8.10	Diagramming Practice	202
8.11	More Diagramming Practice	204
	Diagramming Review	**206**
	Diagramming Challenge	**208**

PART 2 Written and Oral Communication

		Personal Narratives Teacher Preparation	210a–210b
Chapter 1		**Personal Narratives**	**210**
Lesson 1		What Makes a Good Personal Narrative?	212
Lesson 2		Beginning, Middle, and Ending	216
Lesson 3		*Writing Skills:* Strong Verbs	220
Lesson 4		*Word Study:* Colorful Adjectives	224
Lesson 5		*Study Skills:* Dictionary	228
Lesson 6		*Speaking and Listening Skills:* Oral Personal Narratives	232
		Writer's Workshop: Personal Narratives	**236**
		Rubrics	247y–247z

		How-to Articles Teacher Preparation	248a–248b
Chapter 2		**How-to Articles**	**248**
Lesson 1		What Makes a Good How-to Article?	250
Lesson 2		Parts of a How-to Article	254
Lesson 3		*Study Skills:* Dictionary Meanings	258
Lesson 4		*Writing Skills:* The Four Kinds of Sentences	262
Lesson 5		*Word Study:* Compound Words	266
Lesson 6		*Speaking and Listening Skills:* How-to Talks	270
		Writer's Workshop: How-to Articles	**274**
		Rubrics	285y–285z

		Descriptions Teacher Preparation	286a–286b
Chapter 3		**Descriptions**	**286**
Lesson 1		What Makes a Good Description?	288
Lesson 2		Writing a Description	292
Lesson 3		*Writing Skills:* Sensory Words	296
Lesson 4		*Study Skills:* Five-Senses Chart	300
Lesson 5		*Word Study:* Synonyms	304
Lesson 6		*Speaking and Listening Skills:* Oral Descriptions	308
		Writer's Workshop: Descriptions	**312**
		Rubrics	323y–323z

Personal Letters Teacher Preparation   **324a–324b**

Chapter 4   **Personal Letters**   **324**

Lesson 1   What Makes a Good Personal Letter?   326
Lesson 2   The Body of a Personal Letter   330
Lesson 3   *Literacy Skills:* Personal E-Mails   334
Lesson 4   *Writing Skills:* Compound Subjects   338
Lesson 5   *Word Study:* Antonyms   342
Lesson 6   *Speaking and Listening Skills:* Telephone Conversations 346
            Writer's Workshop: Personal Letters   **350**
            Rubrics   **361y–361z**

Book Reports Teacher Preparation   **362a–362b**

Chapter 5   **Book Reports**   **362**

Lesson 1   What Makes a Good Book Report?   364
Lesson 2   Character and Plot   368
Lesson 3   *Study Skills:* Parts of a Book   372
Lesson 4   *Writing Skills:* Compound Predicates   376
Lesson 5   *Word Study:* Prefixes   380
Lesson 6   *Speaking and Listening Skills:* Oral Book Reports   384
            Writer's Workshop: Book Reports   **388**
            Rubrics   **399y–399z**

Persuasive Writing Teacher Preparation   **400a–400b**

Chapter 6   **Persuasive Writing**   **400**

Lesson 1   What Makes Good Persuasive Writing?   402
Lesson 2   Beginning, Middle, and Ending   406
Lesson 3   *Study Skills:* Idea Webs   410
Lesson 4   *Writing Skills:* Compound Sentences   414
Lesson 5   *Word Study:* Suffixes   418
Lesson 6   *Speaking and Listening Skills:* Persuasive Speeches   422
            Writer's Workshop: Persuasive Writing   **426**
            Rubrics   **437y–437z**

Creative Writing: Realistic Fiction
Teacher Preparation   **438a–438b**

Chapter 7   **Creative Writing: Realistic Fiction**   **438**

Lesson 1   What Makes Good Realistic Fiction?   440
Lesson 2   Characters   444
Lesson 3   *Writing Skills:* Dialogue   448
Lesson 4   *Word Study:* Contractions   452
Lesson 5   *Writing Poetry:* Lines That Rhyme   456
Lesson 6   *Speaking and Listening Skills:* Skits   460
            Writer's Workshop: Realistic Fiction   **464**
            Rubrics   **475y–475z**

	Research Reports Teacher Preparation	476a–476b
Chapter 8	**Research Reports**	**476**
Lesson 1	What Makes a Good Research Report?	478
Lesson 2	Facts and Notes	482
Lesson 3	*Study Skills:* Library Skills	486
Lesson 4	*Writing Skills:* Revising Sentences	490
Lesson 5	*Word Study:* Homophones	494
Lesson 6	*Speaking and Listening Skills:* Oral Biographies	498
	Writer's Workshop: Research Reports	**502**
	Rubrics	513y–513z

Proofreading Marks	**514**
Grammar and Mechanics Handbook	**515**
Index	**530**
Acknowledgments	**T-535**
Scope and Sequence	**T-536**
Proofreading Marks	**inside back cover**
Writing Traits	**inside back cover**

Welcome to *Voyages in English*, a core English language arts curriculum that has been an outstanding success in elementary and middle schools since 1942. From the time of first publication, *Voyages in English* (*Voyages*) has focused on providing students with the tools necessary to become articulate communicators of the English language. For over 65 years, those who wrote, published, and used *Voyages* for classroom instruction never abandoned the belief that communication skills are crucial for opportunities and success in education and eventually in employment.

With these expectations in mind, *Voyages* has advanced the best values of the past to meet the demands of communication in the twenty-first century. The curriculum meets the following goals:

- **Enable children to master grammar** through direct instruction, rigorous practice, written application, and ongoing assessment.

- **Guide children to experience, explore, and improve their writing** through the in-depth study of unique writing genres, writing skill lessons, and the implementation of the writing process.

- **Give children the speaking and writing practice and tools they need** to communicate with clarity, accuracy, and ease.

- **Provide children and teachers with opportunities to use technology** as a means to learn, assess, apply new skills, and communicate outside the school setting.

- **Provide master and novice teachers with support and straightforward, practical lesson plans** that can be presented with confidence.

When learning is presented as a positive opportunity and a challenging adventure, children respond. *Voyages in English* subscribes to this idea, just as previous editions have. Regular, consistent use of *Voyages* helps create successful communicators in school and—eventually—in society. So welcome to *Voyages in English: Grammar and Writing*—enjoy the journey!

COMPLETE AND COMPREHENSIVE

Voyages in English: Grammar and Writing for grades 3 through 8 fully prepares students to become literate masters of the written and spoken word. The components and lessons in this program are the result of decades of research and practice by experts in the field of grammar and writing. The result—better writers, readers, listeners, and speakers as well as happy teachers, principals, and parents!

Student Editions

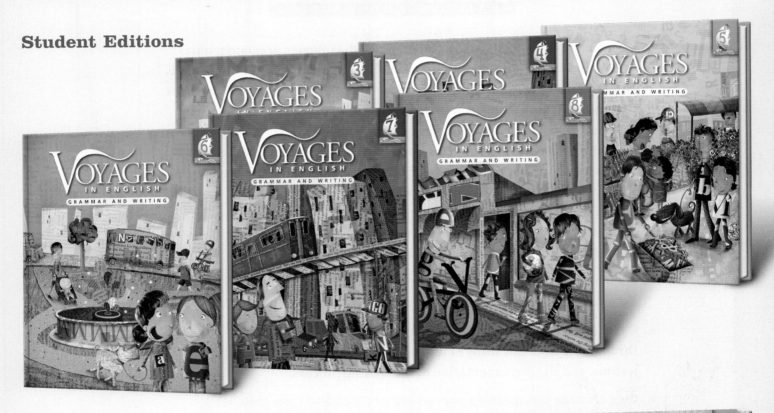

Teacher Editions

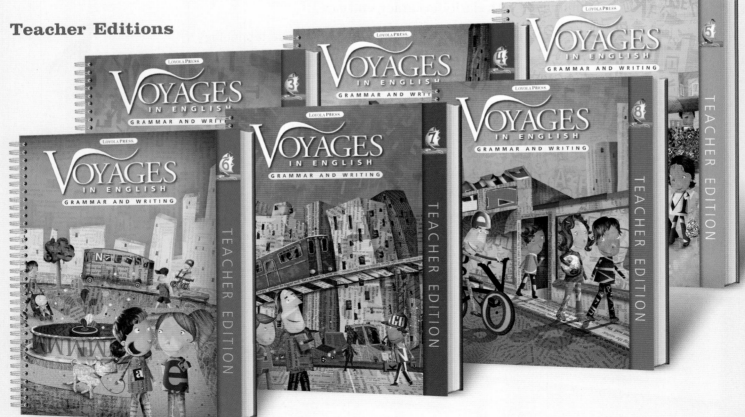

Practice Books
Grades 3–8

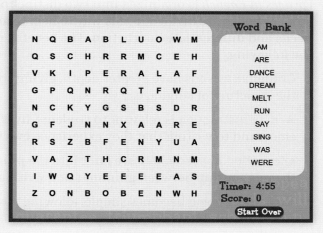

										Word Bank
N	Q	B	A	B	L	U	O	W	M	AM
Q	S	C	H	R	R	M	C	E	H	ARE
V	K	I	P	E	R	A	L	A	F	DANCE
G	P	Q	N	R	Q	T	F	W	D	DREAM
N	C	K	Y	G	S	B	S	D	R	MELT
G	F	J	N	N	X	A	A	R	E	RUN
R	S	Z	B	F	E	N	Y	U	A	SAY
V	A	Z	T	H	C	R	M	N	M	SING
I	W	Q	Y	E	E	E	E	A	S	WAS
Z	O	N	B	O	B	E	N	W	H	WERE

Timer: 4:55
Score: 0
Start Over

Additional Student Practice
www.voyagesinenglish.com

Assessment Books
Grades 3–8

Optional Customizable Assessment
Grades 3–8

ExamView® Assessment Suite Test Generator

Additional Teacher Support
www.voyagesinenglish.com

TWO CORE PARTS—ONE COHESIVE PROGRAM

Voyages in English is organized into two distinct parts: grammar and writing. The student books are divided in this way to help teachers tailor lesson plans to student needs and differentiate instruction. The benefits of this type of organization include the following:

- **Grammar lessons** have greater depth, giving students the tools needed to learn the structure of language.

- **Writing instruction** is relevant to students' lives, to the literature they read and enjoy, and to writing that they experience every day.

- **Integration opportunities** are built into the program, allowing teachers to show the relationship between grammar and writing.

- **Flexible planning** becomes simple, allowing for adaptations based on students' developmental levels.

- **Long-range and thematic planning** is effortless, allowing teachers to cover required standards.

PART I: GRAMMAR
The Structure of Language

- Parts of speech
- Usage
- Mechanics
- Agreement
- Punctuation/capitalization

PART II: WRITTEN AND ORAL COMMUNICATION
Written Expression

- Traits of effective writing
- Genre characteristics
- Sentence structure
- Word and study skills
- Seven-step writing process

INTEGRATION OPPORTUNITIES

Throughout the program, ample integration opportunities are built in to provide a systematic review of essential concepts.

Part I: Grammar
Writing Integration

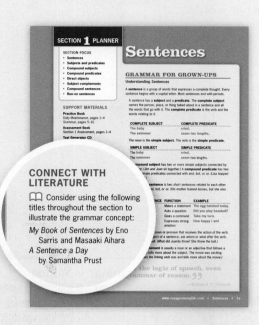

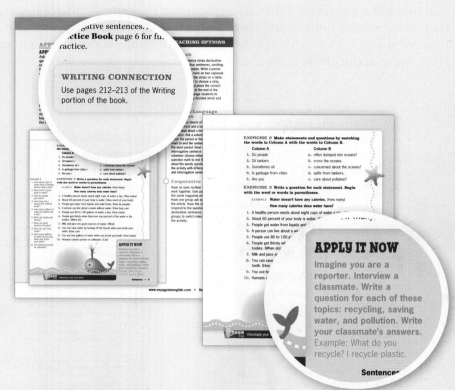

WRITING CONNECTION

Use pages 212–213 of the Writing portion of the book.

CONNECT WITH LITERATURE

Consider using the following titles throughout the section to illustrate the grammar concept:

My Book of Sentences by Eno Sarris and Masaaki Aihara
A Sentence a Day by Samantha Prust

APPLY IT NOW

Imagine you are a reporter. Interview a classmate. Write a question for each of these topics: recycling, saving water, and pollution. Write your classmate's answers. Example: What do you recycle? I recycle plastic.

Part II: Written and Oral Communication
Grammar Integration

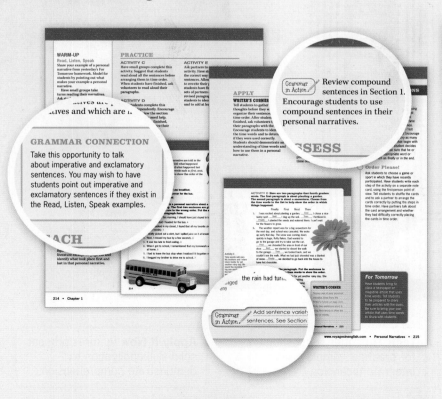

GRAMMAR CONNECTION

Take this opportunity to talk about imperative and exclamatory sentences. You may wish to have students point out imperative and exclamatory sentences if they exist in the Read, Listen, Speak examples.

Grammar in Action. Review compound sentences in Section 1. Encourage students to use compound sentences in their personal narratives.

Grammar in Action. Add sentence variety sentences. See Section

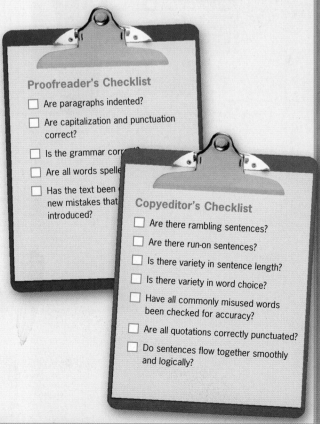

Proofreader's Checklist

☐ Are paragraphs indented?

☐ Are capitalization and punctuation correct?

☐ Is the grammar correct?

☐ Are all words spelled

☐ Has the text been new mistakes that introduced?

Copyeditor's Checklist

☐ Are there rambling sentences?

☐ Are there run-on sentences?

☐ Is there variety in sentence length?

☐ Is there variety in word choice?

☐ Have all commonly misused words been checked for accuracy?

☐ Are all quotations correctly punctuated?

☐ Do sentences flow together smoothly and logically?

Program Overview

STUDENT EDITION: GRAMMAR

An excellent education in the acquisition and application of language has never been exclusively about memorizing parts of speech in isolation or diagramming a sentence as an end in itself. Because of this, *Voyages in English* takes grammar further, helping students become polished, articulate, and intelligent communicators.

The grammar portion of the Student Edition focuses on the needs of the students and in building their confidence so that when they speak, others listen, and when they write, others understand their message and want to read more. In other words, *Voyages in English* has what it takes to help students succeed: more practice, more rigor, more application, more integration.

Thorough explanations and clear examples are provided for every grammar topic.

Ample practice ensures skill mastery.

Grammar in Action features challenge students to spot the importance of grammar in real-life writing.

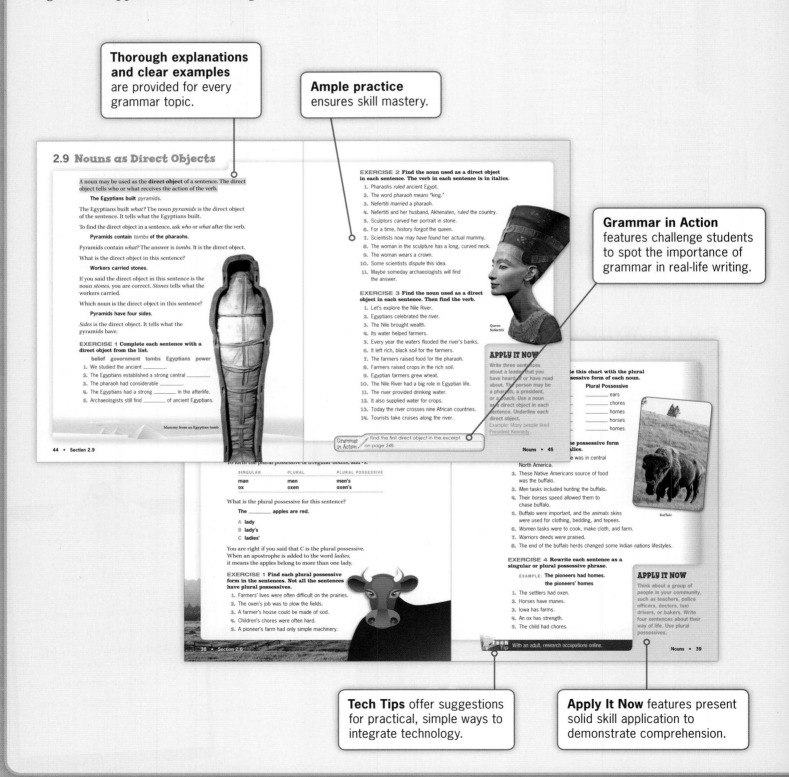

Tech Tips offer suggestions for practical, simple ways to integrate technology.

Apply It Now features present solid skill application to demonstrate comprehension.

A **Grammar Review** for every grammar section helps build student confidence and offers two full pages that can be used as review or informal assessment.

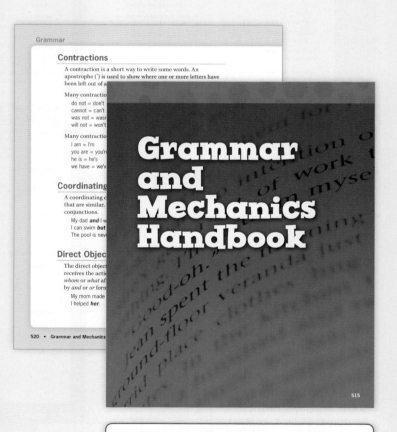

Noun Review

2.1 Find the nouns in each sentence.

1. Walruses are clumsy on land.
2. In the water, these animals are fast swimmers.
3. Their tusks are used to keep enemies away.
4. This animal lives in the area of the Arctic Ocean.

2.2 Find the nouns in each sentence. Tell whether each is a common or proper noun.

5. George Washington Carver was born a slave.
6. The former slave went to school and earned two degrees.
7. Carver created mo...

12. A person is considered an omnivore because humans eat plants and animals.

2.4 Complete each sentence with the plural form of the noun in parentheses.

13. The librarian read nursery rhymes and folktales to the _____. (child)
14. Tell us the story of the three blind _____. (mouse)
15. Little Bo Peep lost many of her _____. (sheep)
16. Jack had nimble _____. (foot)

2.5 Complete each sentence with the singular possessive form of the noun in parentheses.

17. _____ favorite animal is the sea turtle. (Eva)
18. A _____ nest is built by digging a hole in the sand. (female)
19. The _____ eggs are the size of table tennis balls. (turtle)
20. Predators threaten a _____ survival. (hatchling)
21. A _____ instinct is to head toward the moonlight and the sea. (baby)

2.6 Complete each sentence with the plural possessive form of the noun in parentheses.

22. John Sutter tried to keep quiet the discovery of gold. (workers)
23. _____ thoughts turned to gold. (Americans)
24. Many _____ choice was to travel by train. (men)
25. Most _____ dreams did not come true. (miners)

2.7 Find the collective noun in each sentence.

26. The herd of cattle grazes on the grass.
27. A flock of seagulls flew over the boat.
28. Out of the woods ran a pack of wild dogs.
29. A litter of kittens was playing.
30. Around the lemonade flew a swarm of bees.

2.8 Find the simple subject in each sentence.

31. Abe Lincoln lived in a log cabin.
32. Log cabins were practical in the 1800s.
33. Pioneers built them from available materials.
34. Timber was plentiful in those days.

35. Some homes are still built from logs.

2.9 Find the direct object in each sentence.

36. Clouds cover Venus.
37. The planets reflect sunlight.
38. Jupiter has several moons.
39. Rings of ice and rock orbit Saturn.
40. Astronauts gathered information about space.

2.10 Find the subject complement in each sentence.

41. Orlando is a city in Florida.
42. Florida is a southern state.
43. The first stop on our trip was Miami.
44. Disney World was another destination.
45. The Everglades is a home for alligators.

2.11 Tell if each italicized word is a noun or a verb.

46. My sister *plants* seeds in pots.
47. My sister and I water the *plants*.
48. This plant *blossoms* in the spring.
49. This plant has white *blossoms*.

Tech Tip Go to www.voyagesinenglish.com for more activities.

Nouns • 51

Noun Challenge

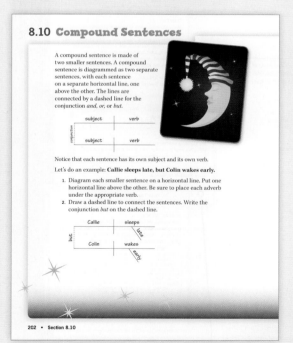

Read the paragraph and answer the questions.

1. Newfoundlands are dogs that are famous for rescuing people in distress. 2. They can swim and reach people in trouble in the water. 3. One dog named Star carried a rope out to a boat in trouble. 4. A crowd on shore then pulled the craft to safety. 5. The passengers' lives were saved. 6. More recently a dog named Boo jumped into a rushing river to save a drowning man. 7. The man was not able to shout for help, but the dog sensed the man was in trouble. 8. The dog hadn't been trained for rescue work, so the story is even more amazing. 9. A Newfoundland is a special breed. 10. The dog's webbed feet make it a good swimmer. 11. Its strong body is a powerhouse. 12. It swims the breaststroke rather than the dog paddle. 13. These dogs will dive into really deep water and can swim through high waves. 14. Clubs exist for Newfoundland owners.

1. Which noun is the subject of sentence 1?
2. Find the common nouns and the proper nouns in sentence 3.
3. Find a collective noun in sentence 4.
4. In sentence 4 what noun is the direct object?
5. In sentence 5 what is the singular possessive of passengers' lives?
6. In sentence 8 how is dog used?
7. In sentence 9 what noun is the subject complement?
8. What kind of noun is dog's in sentence 10?
9. In sentence 10 what is the singular form of feet?
10. How is powerhouse used in sentence 11?
11. What noun is the subject of sentence 13?
12. In sentence 13 is water used as a noun or as a verb?
13. How is clubs used in sentence 14?
14. In sentence 14 what kind of noun is clubs?

52 • Noun Challenge

A **Grammar Challenge** follows each Grammar Review to extend the learning or offer another opportunity for informal assessment.

8.10 Compound Sentences

A compound sentence is made of two smaller sentences. A compound sentence is diagrammed as two separate sentences, with each sentence on a separate horizontal line, one above the other. The lines are connected by a dashed line for the conjunction *and, or,* or *but.*

subject	verb
subject	verb

conjunction

Notice that each sentence has its own subject and its own verb.

Let's do an example: **Callie sleeps late, but Colin wakes early.**

1. Diagram each smaller sentence on a horizontal line. Put one horizontal line above the other. Be sure to place each adverb under the appropriate verb.
2. Draw a dashed line to connect the sentences. Write the conjunction *but* on the dashed line.

Callie	sleeps	late
Colin	wakes	early

but

202 • Section 8.10

Sentence Diagramming at every grade level helps students analyze, visualize, and unlock the English language.

Grammar

Contractions

A contraction is a short way to write some words. An apostrophe (') is used to show where one or more letters have been left out of a...

Many contraction...
do not = don't
cannot = can't
was not = wasn...
will not = won't

Many contraction...
I am = I'm
you are = you're
he is = he's
we have = we'v...

Coordinating...

A coordinating c... that are similar... conjunctions.

My dad **and** I w...
I can swim **but**...
The pool is neve...

Direct Object...

The direct objec... receives the actio... *whom* or *what* af... by *and* or *or* for...

My mom made...
I helped **her**.

520 • Grammar and Mechanics...

Grammar and Mechanics Handbook

515

The **Grammar and Mechanics Handbook** provides a quick reference tool for grammar, usage, and mechanics topics.

Program Overview

TEACHER EDITION: GRAMMAR

The core values and competencies that fortify *Voyages in English* have always been focused on high-level instruction that challenges the most able of students and supports those who struggle. Therefore, the Teacher Edition of *Voyages in English* is crafted with an easy-to-use, flexible format that includes support for teachers of all experience levels who serve children at all levels of development.

Background and Planning Support

An **at-a-glance skills list** provides focus for each grammar section.

Clear and straightforward grammar essentials provide all the background teachers need to teach the grammar topic.

Common Errors features alert teachers to errors students often make and advise how to correct them.

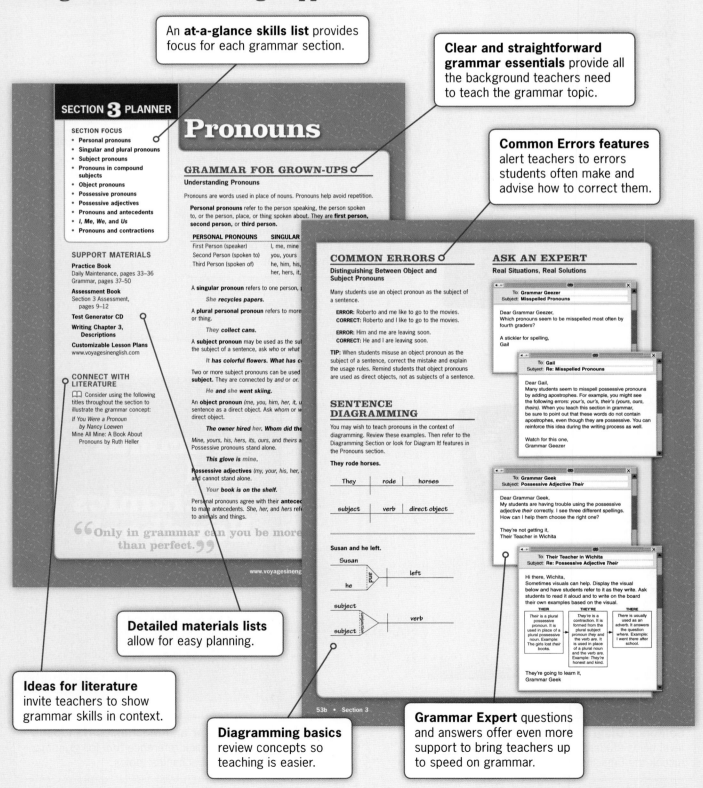

Detailed materials lists allow for easy planning.

Ideas for literature invite teachers to show grammar skills in context.

Diagramming basics review concepts so teaching is easier.

Grammar Expert questions and answers offer even more support to bring teachers up to speed on grammar.

Instruction

An **easy four-step teaching approach** is implemented in every lesson: Teach, Practice, Apply, Assess.

Teaching Options allow teachers to tailor instruction to student needs through **Reteach, Multiple Intelligences, English-Language Learners,** and **Diagram It!**

Daily Maintenance features help maintain proficiency in grammatical concepts that have already been taught and assessed.

Diagram It! features highlight sentence diagramming opportunities throughout the year.

Writing Connections help teachers transition easily and naturally between the writing and grammar sections.

Warm-Ups offer relevant, practical ideas for introducing each grammar concept in a way students can understand.

Systematic, direct instruction is provided for each grammar concept.

3.1 Personal Pronouns: Part I

OBJECTIVES
- To identify a personal pronoun as a word used in place of a noun
- To identify personal pronouns in sentences

 Maintenance

Assign **Practice Book** page 33, Section 3.1. After students finish,
1. Give immediate feedback.
2. Review concepts as needed.
3. Model the correct answer.

Pages 4–5 of the **Answer Key** contain tips for Daily Maintenance.

WARM-UP

Toss a ball to a student. Ask a volunteer to describe what happened. *(Ms. Smith tossed a ball to Emily.)* Have another volunteer describe what happened without using your name. *(You tossed the ball to Emily.)* Ask another volunteer to repeat the sentence without using the student's name. *(Ms. Smith tossed the ball to her.)* Finally, ask students to repeat the sentence without using the word *ball.* *(Ms. Smith gave it to Emily.)* Discuss the part of speech *(noun)* of each replaced word.

Read from a piece of writing that the class is currently reading. Emphasize the personal pronouns.

TEACH 1

Write the following paragraph on the board:

King Arthur was the king of Camelot. Some people believe that King Arthur really existed. King Arthur lived in a castle. King Arthur led the Knights of the Round Table.

Encourage students to listen closely as you read aloud the paragraph. Ask if students heard anything awkward or repetitive

in the paragraph. *(King Arthur is repeated many times.)*

Ask how students might change the paragraph to make it sound smoother. Discuss where words like the ones from the Warm-Up *(pronouns)* might be used. Have a volunteer read aloud the paragraph, replacing *King Arthur* with pronouns.

Have volunteers read aloud about personal pronouns, pausing after the chart, example sentences, and example paragraphs. Emphasize that personal pronouns take the place of nouns and help avoid repeating nouns and can make writing sound smoother.

PRACTICE 2

EXERCISE 1
Remind students that pronouns can improve the way sentences read and the way they sound. Ask volunteers to share their answers with the class.

EXERCISE 2
Complete item 1 with the class. Show how you used the list of personal pronouns to help determine the correct pronoun. Ask partners to exchange their answers.

EXERCISE 3
Have students rewrite the sentences, using pronouns. Invite volunteers to write their revised sentences on the board.

APPLY 3

APPLY IT NOW
Name different periods in history, such as the Middle Ages or the Renaissance. Have volunteers write their sentence pairs on the board. Students should be able to identify a personal pronoun as a word used in place of a noun

TeachTip Create a class spreadsheet of historical Web sites.

ASSESS 4

Note which students had difficulty identifying a personal pronoun as a word used in place of a noun, as well as identifying personal pronouns in sentences. Assign **Practice Book** page 37 for further practice.

WRITING CONNECTION
Use pages 286–287 of the Writing portion of the book. Be sure to point out pronouns in the literature excerpt and the student model.

TEACHING OPTIONS

Reteach
Write on the board the following sentence pairs:

Camelot was Arthur's castle.
_____ was Arthur's castle.

Lancelot was a famous knight.
_____ was a famous knight.

Knights were known for their bravery.
_____ were known for their bravery.

Have a volunteer read aloud the first sentence. Then have the student replace the underlined word with the correct pronoun and read aloud the completed sentence. Continue with the remaining sentence pairs.

Cooperative Learning
Have partners review the sentences in Exercise 1. Ask students to circle nouns that were not replaced by pronouns. Discuss that not every noun needs to be replaced by a pronoun. Point out that a pronoun should be used when a noun is repeated in more than one sentence. Emphasize that if a group of sentences had only pronouns, the reader wouldn't know what the sentences were about.

Meeting Individual Needs
Intrapersonal Invite students to spend five minutes writing about a recent event they attended, such as a sporting event or a birthday party. When students are finished, have them underline in their writing all of the personal pronouns they used. Encourage students to make sure all of the pronouns are used correctly.

Diagram It!
To practice these concepts in the context of diagramming, turn to Section 8.1.

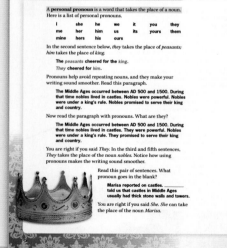

3.1 Personal Pronouns: Part I

A **personal pronoun** is a word that takes the place of a noun. Here is a list of personal pronouns.

I	she	he	we	it	you	they
me	her	him	us	its	yours	them
mine	hers	his		ours		

In the second sentence below, *they* takes the place of *peasants; him* takes the place of *king.*

The *peasants* cheered for the *king.*
They cheered for *him.*

Pronouns help avoid repeating nouns, and they make your writing sound smoother. Read this paragraph.

The Middle Ages occurred between AD 500 and 1500. During that time nobles lived in castles. Nobles were powerful. Nobles were under a king's rule. Nobles promised to serve their king and country.

Now read the paragraph with pronouns. What are they?

The Middle Ages occurred between AD 500 and 1500. During that time nobles lived in castles. They were powerful. Nobles were under a king's rule. They promised to serve their king and country.

You are right if you said *They.* In the third and fifth sentences, *They* takes the place of the noun *nobles.* Notice how using pronouns makes the writing sound smoother.

Read this pair of sentences. What pronoun goes in the blank?

Marisa reported on castles. _____ told us that castles in Middle Ages usually had thick stone walls and towers.

You are right if you said *She. She* can take the place of the noun *Marisa.*

APPLY IT NOW
Write four sentences about a period of history that interests you. Rewrite each sentence, using a pronoun to replace the noun.
Example: Castles were made from stone.
They were made from stone.

Pronouns • 55

STUDENT EDITION: WRITING

Writing Lessons

A truly excellent writing program always sets its sights on lifetime communication competence. *Voyages in English* is rooted in its tradition of excellence by helping students employ writing concepts, skills, and strategies that have stood the test of time.

Easy-to-follow, practical explanations and examples make writing relevant and engaging.

Link features demonstrate a writing concept or skill within the context of real-life writing or literary works.

Grammar in Action features offer grammar application that happens naturally within the context of writing.

Ample practice encourages writing mastery.

Tech Tips provide simple, natural ways to integrate technology in the classroom or at home.

Writer's Corner experiences offer skill application for each writing concept.

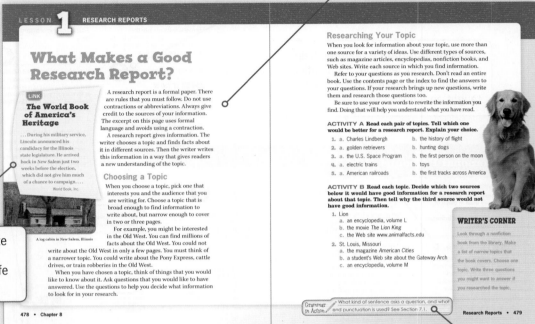

Writer's Workshop

In the span of one year, students work through a seven-step writing process to develop and publish eight written pieces that span eight distinct writing genres, including research reports. The systematic and evolutionary development of each piece sets in motion the goal of producing reflective, creative, critical, and articulate communicators.

The seven-step writing process mirrors the process often used by professional writers:

- Prewriting
- Drafting
- Content editing
- Revising
- Copyediting
- Proofreading
- Publishing

Complete coverage of writing skills and the writing process can increase standardized test-taking success.

Step-by-step practice is led by a model student.

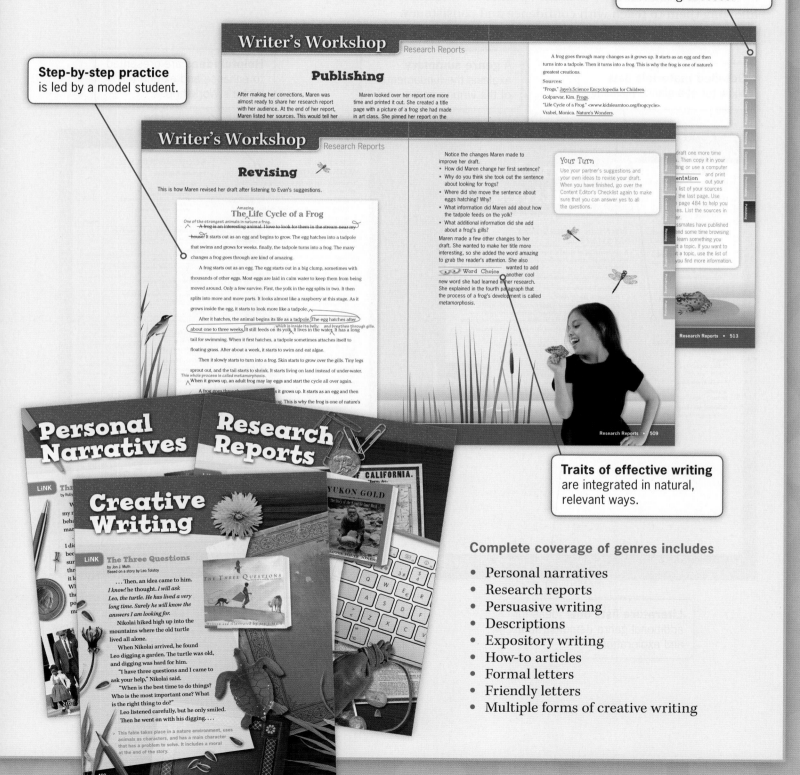

Traits of effective writing are integrated in natural, relevant ways.

Complete coverage of genres includes

- Personal narratives
- Research reports
- Persuasive writing
- Descriptions
- Expository writing
- How-to articles
- Formal letters
- Friendly letters
- Multiple forms of creative writing

TEACHER EDITION: WRITING

Since all students deserve a strong, interesting, and challenging curriculum with high-level results, *Voyages in English* not only raises the bar for expected outcomes but also provides strong and consistent instructional steps and support for teachers. A clear, easy-to-follow format gives new teachers and seasoned professionals the tools and confidence they need to guide students.

Background and Planning Support

In the Genre Planner, teachers are provided with clear definitions of the elements and characteristics of the specific writing genres they will present, allowing them to teach with confidence and consistency.

Detailed materials lists allow for at-a-glance planning.

A **genre summary** explains the fundamentals of the writing genre.

Helpful ideas are presented to enhance and extend the Writer's Workshop.

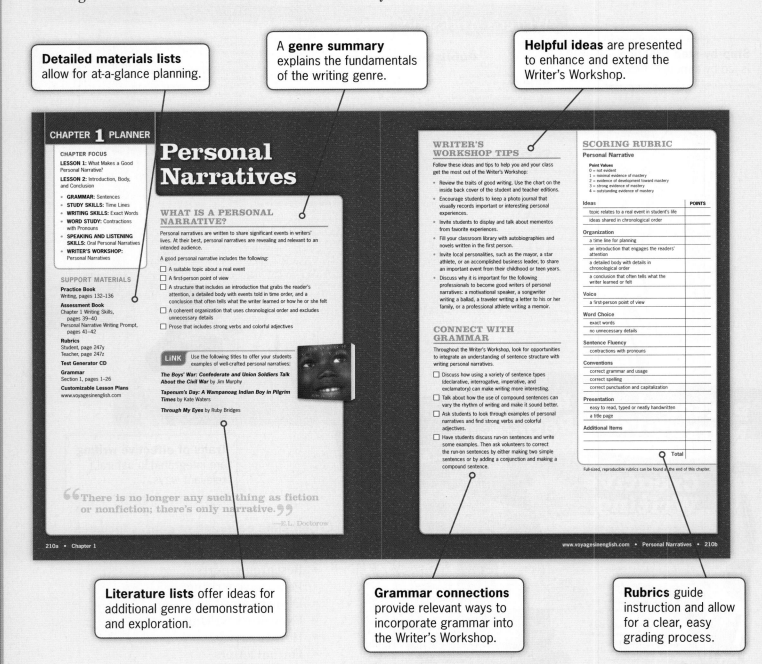

Literature lists offer ideas for additional genre demonstration and exploration.

Grammar connections provide relevant ways to incorporate grammar into the Writer's Workshop.

Rubrics guide instruction and allow for a clear, easy grading process.

Instruction

Read, Listen, Speak features offer small-group discussion of the writing assignment.

Systematic, direct instruction is provided for each topic.

A **simple four-step teaching approach:** Teach, Practice, Apply, Assess

Activities in a variety of learning styles: **Reteach, Multiple Intelligences,** and **English-Language Learners**

LESSON 1   What Makes a Good Personal Narrative?

OBJECTIVES
- To understand the characteristics of a personal narrative
- To understand and use time order in a personal narrative

WARM-UP
Read, Listen, Speak
Share your family member's personal narrative from yesterday's For Tomorrow homework. Model for students by pointing out the characteristics of a personal narrative in your story.
Have small groups retell the narratives they heard from family members. Ask students to point out in each example one characteristic that shows it is a personal narrative.

GRAMMAR CONNECTION
Take this opportunity to talk about the definition of a sentence, complete subjects and complete predicates, declarative sentences, and interrogative sentences. You may also wish to have students point out complete sentences, complete subjects, complete predicates, declarative sentences, and interrogative sentences if they exist in the Read, Listen, Speak examples.

TEACH ①
Have a volunteer read aloud the first paragraph. Reinforce that a personal narrative is a true story, not fiction.
Read aloud the section Topic. Ask students to name some topics that would make good personal narratives, such as a day at a museum, a family canoe trip, or a championship soccer game.
Have a volunteer read aloud the section Audience. Ask students to name other ways that personal narratives might change, depending on the audience.

Invite a volunteer to read aloud the section Point of View. Explain that all types of writing use a point of view. Ask volunteers to say a sentence using the first-person point of view. (*I spent the summer in Maine. My dog won first prize in the dog show.*)

LINK Have a volunteer read aloud the excerpt from *Through My Eyes*. Guide students to identify the topic (*starting a new school*). Guide students to discuss how the author feels about starting a new school and why. (*She was unhappy because she wouldn't be going to school with her friends.*)

PRACTICE ②

ACTIVITY A
Have partners complete this activity. When they have finished, invite volunteers to share their answers with the class.

ACTIVITY B
After students have completed the activity, have volunteers change items 3 and 13 to make them good personal narratives. Challenge students to list additional topics that would not make good personal narratives and explain why.

APPLY ③

WRITER'S CORNER
Suggest that students list as topics exciting or interesting things that they have done recently. Ask students to identify the audience that might be appropriate for each topic. When students have finished, ask volunteers to share their work with the class. Students should demonstrate an understanding of the characteristics of a personal narrative.

ASSESS ④
Note which students had difficulty understanding the characteristics of a personal narrative. Use the Reteach option with those students who need additional reinforcement.

TEACHING OPTIONS

Reteach
Ask students to draw a picture of an important or exciting event in their lives. Have volunteers share their stories with the class. As each student tells his or her story, write on the board the main events. Then ask students to retell their personal narratives.

Narrative Notions
Have small groups use a classroom or an online encyclopedia or other references to research events in the lives of famous people. Tell students to write short summaries of personal narratives that each famous person might write. Offer examples such as the following:

George Washington: We were all very cold at Valley Forge.

Sandra Day O'Connor: I was the first female Justice of the Supreme Court of the United States.

Nelson Mandela: I was in the sunlight for the first time in 27 years.

English-Language Learners
Invite English-language learners to do the brainstorming activity in their primary language so that they can focus their energy on generating ideas instead of choosing words and spelling words correctly. When students have finished, ask them to translate their ideas into English.

For Tomorrow
Ask students to find any kind of narrative to bring to class. Tell students to be prepared to share what they have found. Bring a personal narrative to class to share with students.

(Sample student page, left)

LESSON ①   PERSONAL NARRATIVES

What Makes a Good Personal Narrative?

LINK
Through My Eyes

On Sunday, November 13, my mother told me I would start at a new school the next day. She hinted there could be something unusual about it, but she didn't explain. . . . All I remember thinking that night was that I wouldn't be going to school with my friends anymore, and I wasn't happy about that.

Ruby Bridges

A narrative is a story. A personal narrative is a true story about something that happened to the writer. It could be a journal entry about the first day of school. It could be a letter describing an exciting trip. Ruby Bridges wrote her personal narrative *Through My Eyes*, sharing her experience in Louisiana in the 1960s. Here are some ideas for what makes a good personal narrative.

Topic
Anything that really happened to you can be a good topic for a personal narrative. It should be something you remember clearly. The topic might be something funny, exciting, or unusual.

Audience
The people who will read your story are your audience. Think of them when you choose your topic. Your friends might want to hear how you beat the newest video game. Your grandparents might be more interested in hearing about a family trip.

A student hugs a stand-up display of Ruby Bridges.

212 • Chapter 1

(Sample student page, right)

Point of View
Point of view shows who is telling the story. In your personal narrative, you are telling the story. This is called the first-person point of view. Use words such as *I, me, my, we,* and *our.*

Activity A
1. It actually happened to the writer.
2. It would interest her audience.
3. her peers
4. first person
5. *me, I, we, us, my*
6. Claire and her family went to adopt a puppy. Each family member played with and had his or her own experience with the puppies. The family finally chose one puppy.
7. Answers will vary.

ACTIVITY A Read the personal narrative on page 211 and answer these questions.
1. How can you tell that this is a personal narrative?
2. Why do you think the writer chose this topic?
3. Who is the audience of this narrative?
4. What is the point of view of this narrative?
5. What words are used to show the point of view?
6. What are the main events in the narrative?
7. What are the most interesting details?

Activity B
1. yes
2. yes
3. no
4. yes
5. no
6. no
7. yes
8. yes
9. yes
10. yes
11. yes
12. no
13. no
14. no
15. no

ACTIVITY B Decide which topics would make good personal narratives.
1. the day I found a $20 bill
2. my first piano recital
3. my brother's trip to the zoo
4. a train ride I'll never forget
5. the day I was born
6. what I'd do if I were an astronaut
7. my unlucky day at the beach
8. a boring afternoon
9. my summer vacation to the Grand Canyon
10. when I broke my arm
11. my first trip in an airplane
12. the day of the big snowstorm
13. how to build a bird house
14. my plans for college
15. the most helpful person I know

WRITER'S CORNER
Write three things that happened to you that would make good personal narratives.

Link offers ways that popular writing can be used as a model.

Grammar Connections allow seamless integration between writing and grammar.

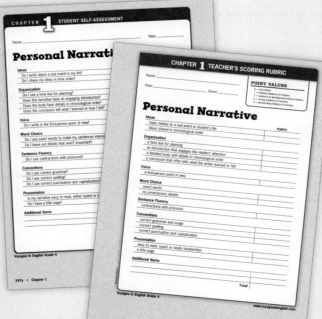

CHAPTER 1 STUDENT SELF-ASSESSMENT

Name _____ Date _____

Personal Narrative

Ideas
Do I write about a real event in my life?
Do I share my ideas in time order?

Organization
Do I use a time line for planning?
Does the narrative have an engaging introduction?
Does the body have details in chronological order?
Does the conclusion tell what I learned or how I felt?

Voice
Do I write in the first-person point of view?

Word Choice
Do I use exact words to make my sentences interes...
Do I leave out details that aren't important?

Sentence Fluency
Do I use contractions with pronouns?

Conventions
Do I use correct grammar?
Do I use correct spelling?
Do I use correct punctuation and capitalization?

Presentation
Is my narrative easy to read, either typed or n...
Do I have a title page?

Additional Items

Voyages in English Grade 4

247y • Chapter 1

CHAPTER 1 TEACHER'S SCORING RUBRIC

Name _____
Date _____ Score _____

POINT VALUES
0 = not evident
1 = minimal evidence of mastery
2 = evidence of development toward mastery
3 = strong evidence of mastery
4 = outstanding evidence of mastery

Personal Narrative

	POINTS
Ideas	
topic relates to a real event in student's life	
ideas shared in chronological order	
Organization	
a time line for planning	
an introduction that engages the readers' attention	
a detailed body with details in chronological order	
a conclusion that offers tells what the writer learned or felt	
Voice	
a first-person point of view	
Word Choice	
exact words	
no unnecessary details	
Sentence Fluency	
contractions with pronouns	
Conventions	
correct grammar and usage	
correct spelling	
correct punctuation and capitalization	
Presentation	
easy to read, typed or neatly handwritten	
a title page	
Additional Items	
Total	

Voyages in English Grade 4

www.voyagesinenglish.com • Personal Narratives • 247z

For Tomorrow features provide practical writing assignments and additional practice for homework or in-class study.

Rubrics

The Teacher Editions provide reproducible rubrics for students and teachers.

PRACTICE BOOK: PRACTICE MAKES PERFECT

Research shows that the more exposure and practice students have using newly introduced skills, the more likely they are to internalize and master them. That's why *Voyages in English* provides ample opportunity for additional practice.

Grammar Section Practice

Each grammar section of the Practice Book begins with Daily Maintenance opportunities that are described in each Teacher Edition lesson. Every grammar topic receives at least one page of additional practice.

Easy-to-understand directions

Plenty of practice

A **clear explanation** of the grammar skill

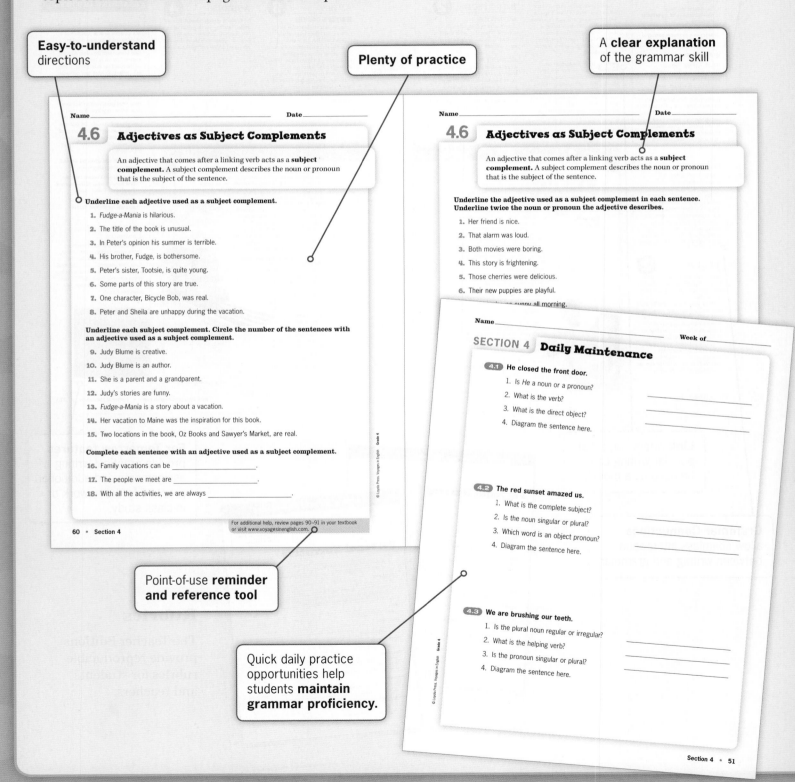

Name_____ Date_____

4.6 Adjectives as Subject Complements

An adjective that comes after a linking verb acts as a **subject complement.** A subject complement describes the noun or pronoun that is the subject of the sentence.

Underline each adjective used as a subject complement.

1. *Fudge-a-Mania* is hilarious.
2. The title of the book is unusual.
3. In Peter's opinion his summer is terrible.
4. His brother, Fudge, is bothersome.
5. Peter's sister, Tootsie, is quite young.
6. Some parts of this story are true.
7. One character, Bicycle Bob, was real.
8. Peter and Sheila are unhappy during the vacation.

Underline each subject complement. Circle the number of the sentences with an adjective used as a subject complement.

9. Judy Blume is creative.
10. Judy Blume is an author.
11. She is a parent and a grandparent.
12. Judy's stories are funny.
13. *Fudge-a-Mania* is a story about a vacation.
14. Her vacation to Maine was the inspiration for this book.
15. Two locations in the book, Oz Books and Sawyer's Market, are real.

Complete each sentence with an adjective used as a subject complement.

16. Family vacations can be _____.
17. The people we meet are _____.
18. With all the activities, we are always _____.

For additional help, review pages 90–91 in your textbook or visit www.voyagesinenglish.com.

60 • Section 4

Name_____ Date_____

4.6 Adjectives as Subject Complements

An adjective that comes after a linking verb acts as a **subject complement.** A subject complement describes the noun or pronoun that is the subject of the sentence.

Underline the adjective used as a subject complement in each sentence. Underline twice the noun or pronoun the adjective describes.

1. Her friend is nice.
2. That alarm was loud.
3. Both movies were boring.
4. This story is frightening.
5. Those cherries were delicious.
6. Their new puppies are playful.

Name_____ Week of_____

SECTION 4 Daily Maintenance

4.1 He closed the front door.
1. Is *He* a noun or a pronoun?
2. What is the verb? _____
3. What is the direct object? _____
4. Diagram the sentence here.

4.2 The red sunset amazed us.
1. What is the complete subject?
2. Is the noun singular or plural? _____
3. Which word is an object pronoun? _____
4. Diagram the sentence here.

4.3 We are brushing our teeth.
1. Is the plural noun regular or irregular? _____
2. What is the helping verb? _____
3. Is the pronoun singular or plural? _____
4. Diagram the sentence here.

Section 4 • 51

Point-of-use reminder and reference tool

Quick daily practice opportunities help students **maintain grammar proficiency.**

Writing Chapter Practice

The writing portion of the Practice Book is in one-to-one correspondence with the Student Edition and the Teacher Edition.

Clear directions

A **concise definition** of the lesson topic

Targeted practice

Handy reference for review

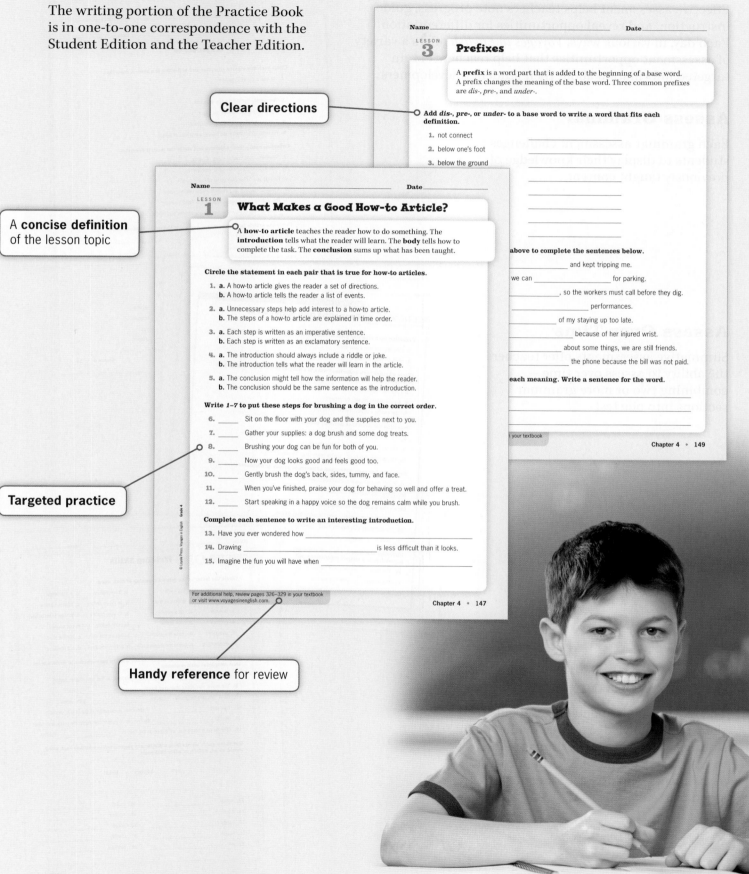

Name_____ Date_____

LESSON 3

Prefixes

A **prefix** is a word part that is added to the beginning of a base word. A prefix changes the meaning of the base word. Three common prefixes are *dis-*, *pre-*, and *under-*.

Add *dis-*, *pre-*, or *under-* to a base word to write a word that fits each definition.

1. not connect _____
2. below one's foot _____
3. below the ground _____

_____ above to complete the sentences below.

_____ and kept tripping me.

_____ we can _____ for parking.

_____, so the workers must call before they dig.

_____ performances.

_____ of my staying up too late.

_____ because of her injured wrist.

_____ about some things, we are still friends.

_____ the phone because the bill was not paid.

____ each meaning. Write a sentence for the word.

_____

_____

n your textbook

Chapter 4 • 149

Name_____ Date_____

LESSON 1

What Makes a Good How-to Article?

A **how-to article** teaches the reader how to do something. The **introduction** tells what the reader will learn. The **body** tells how to complete the task. The **conclusion** sums up what has been taught.

Circle the statement in each pair that is true for how-to articles.

1. **a.** A how-to article gives the reader a set of directions.
   b. A how-to article tells the reader a list of events.

2. **a.** Unnecessary steps help add interest to a how-to article.
   b. The steps of a how-to article are explained in time order.

3. **a.** Each step is written as an imperative sentence.
   b. Each step is written as an exclamatory sentence.

4. **a.** The introduction should always include a riddle or joke.
   b. The introduction tells what the reader will learn in the article.

5. **a.** The conclusion might tell how the information will help the reader.
   b. The conclusion should be the same sentence as the introduction.

Write *1–7* to put these steps for brushing a dog in the correct order.

6. _____ Sit on the floor with your dog and the supplies next to you.
7. _____ Gather your supplies: a dog brush and some dog treats.
8. _____ Brushing your dog can be fun for both of you.
9. _____ Now your dog looks good and feels good too.
10. _____ Gently brush the dog's back, sides, tummy, and face.
11. _____ When you've finished, praise your dog for behaving so well and offer a treat.
12. _____ Start speaking in a happy voice so the dog remains calm while you brush.

Complete each sentence to write an interesting introduction.

13. Have you ever wondered how _____
14. Drawing _____ is less difficult than it looks.
15. Imagine the fun you will have when _____

© Loyola Press, Voyages in English Grade 4

For additional help, review pages 326–329 in your textbook or visit www.voyagesinenglish.com

Chapter 4 • 147

ASSESSMENT BOOK: THE KEY TO INFORMED INSTRUCTION

Effective assessment helps teachers note progress, guide instruction, and reveal opportunities for differentiation. Each day, in various ways, *Voyages in English* offers a variety of assessment opportunities that help teachers obtain targeted information about their students' development.

Assess Grammar

Each grammar assessment challenges students to display their knowledge of previously taught content.

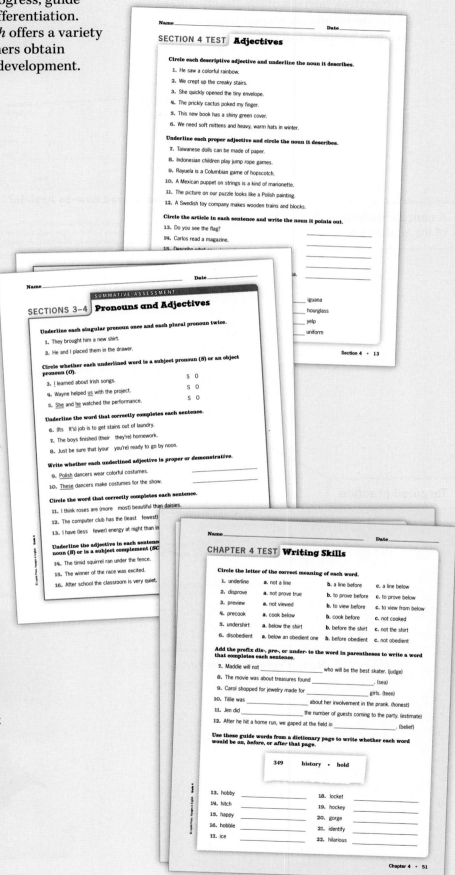

Assess Over Time

Summative assessments offer teachers the ability to assess over time—combining two or more grammar sections into one test.

Assess Writing

The writing assessments ask students to show their knowledge of specifically taught skills as well as use the writing process to craft a written piece. Writing-process assessments help prepare students for standardized tests.

Assess According to Class Needs
ExamView® Assessment Suite Test Generator

Today's teachers need flexibility to customize assessment to meet the needs of all students, offer assessment in a variety of formats, and analyze results quickly and easily. Therefore, *Voyages in English* is proud to offer the ExamView® Assessment Suite Test Generator, "a complete toolset in three seamless applications."

Voyages in English Test Generator is available for separate purchase. With this CD, teachers can build comprehensive tests with the Test Generator, administer customized tests with the Test Player, and analyze results with the Test Manager.

Each grade-level CD provides teachers with the following:

- Preformatted yet customizable assessments that correspond with the Assessment Book while offering 25% new test items for each test

- Alignment to key national and state standards

- The ability to save questions in Question Banks for compilation into multiple study guides and assessments

- Wide variety of question-selection methods and question types

- Question-scrambling capability for multiple test versions and secure test conditions

- Multiple test-delivery methods: printed, LAN, or export the test as an HTML file to be manually posted to a Web site

- Grade assessments through a variety of scanning methods, track progress, and generate reports

- On-screen help

Contact your sales representative at **800-621-1008** for more information or visit us online at **www.voyagesinenglish.com**.

Program Overview

STUDENTS: TECHNOLOGY INTEGRATION

In the Book

Students are invited to communicate, collaborate, research, and problem-solve using technology. Online resources and digital tools are suggested to enhance writing and reinforce grammar topic application.

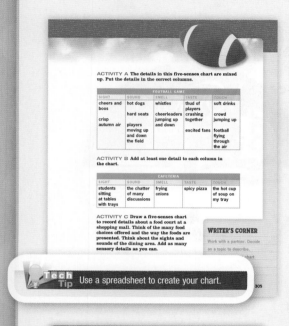

Students explore ways to publish their work using technology.

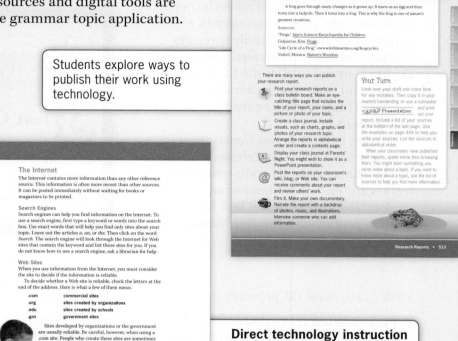

Tech Tips invite students to creatively apply their grammar skills, using a variety of technologies.

Direct technology instruction embedded into student lessons

On the Web

Find additional opportunities for students to strengthen and polish their grammar and writing skills at www.voyagesinenglish.com.

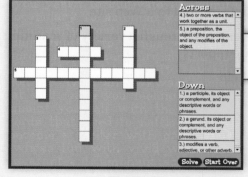

Interactive games for more practice

Grammar and Mechanics Handbook for at-home use

Additional writing activities expand learning.

TEACHERS: TECHNOLOGY INTEGRATION

In the Book

Easy, practical tips allow teachers to make technology a natural part of the language-arts classroom.

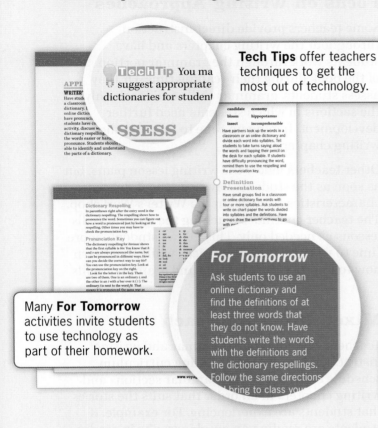

Tech Tips offer teachers techniques to get the most out of technology.

For Tomorrow

Ask students to use an online dictionary and find the definitions of at least three words that they do not know. Have students write the words with the definitions and the dictionary respellings. Follow the same directions and bring to class your...

Many **For Tomorrow** activities invite students to use technology as part of their homework.

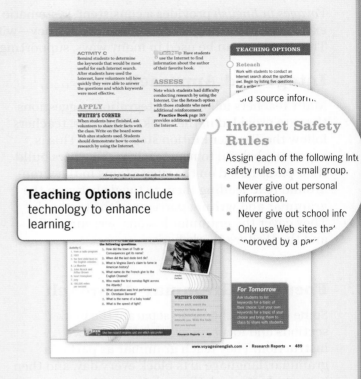

Teaching Options include technology to enhance learning.

Internet Safety Rules

Assign each of the following Internet safety rules to a small group.

- Never give out personal information.
- Never give out school info...
- Only use Web sites that... approved by a par...

For the Computer

Optional ExamView® Assessment Suite Test Generator (see page OV-17)

On the Web

Plenty of online support, including professional development and planning.

Research document explains how *Voyages* is based and anchored in research.

Ask An Expert provides additional teacher background to common questions.

Lesson Plan Charts show how to integrate the grammar and writing sections.

CREATING A PLAN THAT WORKS FOR YOU

Voyages in English provides a consistent, systematic teaching plan for student success and excellence in writing and grammar proficiency—with room for individual adaptation. The program can be used in many ways, supporting each teacher's personal style.

Integrated Approach

Many teachers follow the integration suggestions that are provided in the book. To do this, teachers follow the Teacher Edition step by step. This is especially helpful to new teachers. Teachers build their plans based on the suggestions in the wraparound text, leading them to toggle between the grammar and writing portions of the textbook. They cover the grammar lessons, writing skills, and the Writer's Workshops.

Focus on Grammar Approach

Some teachers choose to separate the book sections and focus on grammar for direct instruction. They teach grammar as part of a grammar/language arts block every day, and then have students work through the writing portion of the book at a different time, such as during reading time as seatwork. They may also choose to teach writing less often than grammar.

Focus on Writing Approaches

Some teachers provide direct instruction throughout the writing chapters and have students work through the grammar portion of the book during their reading time. Or they assess students' grammar skills and teach only the sections in which students need further development, freeing up time to focus on the writing chapters.

Other teachers follow the writing lesson plans, but as soon as the students have a grasp of the genre characteristics, they begin the Writer's Workshop. The teacher continues teaching the writing skills lessons as needed only. This allows students more time to work on their final piece while they learn how to improve their writing and grammar skills.

Mixed-Order Approach

Teachers who integrate grammar and writing instruction into their set reading curriculum schedule often teach the grammar sections and writing chapters in an order that suits the stories that students are experiencing. For example, if students are reading an autobiography in reading class, teachers may choose to have students experience the personal narrative writing chapter and the pronouns grammar section.

LESSON PLANS FOR THE INTEGRATED APPROACH

If you choose to implement the integrated approach, then use the following as a guide for how each grammar section and writing chapter work together.

Grade 3

Grammar	Writing
Sentences	Personal Narratives
Nouns	How-to Articles
Pronouns	Descriptions
Verbs	Personal Letters
Adjectives	Book Reports
Adverbs and Conjunctions	Persuasive Writing
Punctuation and Capitalization	Creative Writing
Diagramming	Research Reports

Grade 4

Grammar	Writing
Sentences	Personal Narratives
Nouns	Formal Letters
Pronouns	Descriptions
Adjectives	How-to Articles
Verbs	Persuasive Writing
Adverbs and Conjunctions	Creative Writing
Punctuation and Capitalization	Expository Writing
Diagramming	Research Reports

Grade 5

Grammar	Writing
Nouns	Personal Narratives
Pronouns	How-to Articles
Adjectives	Business Letters
Verbs	Descriptions
Adverbs	Book Reports
Prepositions, Conjunctions, and Interjections	Creative Writing
Sentences	Persuasive Writing
Punctuation and Capitalization Diagramming	Research Reports

Grade 6

Grammar	Writing
Nouns	Personal Narratives
Pronouns	How-to Articles
Adjectives	Descriptions
Verbs	Persuasive Writing
Adverbs	Expository Writing
Sentences	Business Letters
Conjunctions, Interjections, Punctuation, and Capitalization	Creative Writing
Diagramming	Research Reports

Grade 7

Grammar	Writing
Nouns Adjectives	Personal Narratives
Pronouns	Business Letters
Verbs	How-to Articles
Verbals	Descriptions
Adverbs Prepositions	Book Reviews
Sentences	Creative Writing
Conjunctions and Interjections Punctuation and Capitalization	Expository Writing
Diagramming	Research Reports

Grade 8

Grammar	Writing
Nouns Adjectives	Personal Narratives
Pronouns	How-to Articles
Verbs	Business Letters
Verbals	Descriptions
Adverbs Prepositions	Expository Writing
Sentences	Persuasive Writing
Conjunctions and Interjections Punctuation and Capitalization	Creative Writing
Diagramming	Research Reports

How to Use This Program

LESSON PLANNING MADE EASY

Each grammar section provides a developmentally appropriate study of a part of speech that includes grammar lessons with ample practice, a review lesson, and a challenge lesson. The Writing Connection that culminates each grammar lesson leads to the writing portion of the book to create an opportunity for integration between the two main parts. Each writing chapter in *Voyages in English* is a study of a single genre—a chapter opener, six lessons, and the genre's Writer's Workshop. Here are the main instructional elements for each grammar section and writing chapter.

PART I: GRAMMAR

- Daily Maintenance
- Warm-Up
- Practice
- Review
- Challenge

PART II: WRITTEN AND ORAL COMMUNICATION

- Literature excerpt
- Student model
- Genre lessons
- Writing skills lessons
- Writer's Workshops

If You Teach Grammar and Writing Three Days a Week,

- condense *Voyages* into a three-day-a-week plan.
- complete two of the activities and exercises shown in each grammar section and writing page span.

	Monday	Wednesday	Friday
GRAMMAR	**1.1** Sentences **1.2** Declarative & Interrogative Sentences	**1.3** Imperative & Exclamatory Sentences	**1.4** Complete Subjects & Predicates
WRITING	**Personal Narratives** Introducing the Genre, pp. 210–211	What Makes a Good Personal Narrative?, pp. 212–215	Introductions and Conclusions, pp. 216–219

If You Teach Grammar and Writing Every Day,

- apply this five-day-a-week plan throughout the program.
- complete all the activities and exercises shown in each grammar section and writing page span.

	Monday	Tuesday	Wednesday	Thursday	Friday
	Day 1	**Day 2**	**Day 3**	**Day 4**	**Day 5**
GRAMMAR	**1.1** Sentences	**1.2** Declarative & Interrogative Sentences	**1.3** Imperative & Exclamatory Sentences	**1.4** Complete Subjects & Predicates	**1.5** Simple Subjects & Predicates
WRITING	**Personal Narratives** Introducing the Genre pp. 210–211 Reading the excerpt and student model	What Makes a Good Personal Narrative?, pp. 212–213	What Makes a Good Personal Narrative?, pp. 214–215	Introduction, Body, & Conclusion, pp. 216–217	Introduction, Body, & Conclusion, pp. 218–219
	Day 6	**Day 7**	**Day 8**	**Day 9**	**Day 10**
GRAMMAR	**1.6** Compound Subjects	**1.7** Compound Predicates	**1.8** Direct Objects	**1.9** Subject Complements	**1.10** Compound Sentences
WRITING	Study Skills: Time Lines, pp. 220–221	Study Skills: Time Lines, pp. 222–223	Writing Skills: Exact Words, pp. 224–225	Writing Skills: Exact Words, pp. 226–227	Word Study: Contractions with Pronouns, pp. 228–229
	Day 11	**Day 12**	**Day 13**	**Day 14**	**Day 15**
GRAMMAR	**1.11** Run-on Sentences	Sentence Review	Sentence Challenge	Sentence Assessment	—
WRITING	Word Study: Contractions with Pronouns, pp. 230–231	Speaking & Listening Skills: Oral Personal Narrative, pp. 232–233	Speaking & Listening Skills: Oral Personal Narrative, pp. 234–235 Writing Skills Assessment	—	Writer's Workshop Prewriting, pp. 236–237
	Day 16	**Day 17**	**Day 18**	**Day 19**	**Day 20**
WRITING	Writer's Workshop Drafting, pp. 238–239	Writer's Workshop Content Editing, pp. 240–241	Writer's Workshop Revising, pp. 242–243	Writer's Workshop Copyediting and Proofreading, pp. 244–245	Writer's Workshop Publishing, pp. 246–247 Genre Assessment

Go to www.voyagesinenglish.com to find sample lesson plans for the whole year— one for each grammar section and writing chapter in the program.

INTRODUCING THE PROGRAM ON DAY ONE

Warm-Up

As a class, work together to write a three-sentence "text message" about a favorite book. Challenge students to use common text abbreviations, such as *LOL,* and convey the message in as few words and letters as possible. Write student ideas on the chalkboard. Read aloud the message two ways: literally and as it is intended. Together, note the differences in how the message sounds.

Explain to students that as technology moves us away from using standard English grammar and writing, it is even more important to learn, master, and use them correctly. Tell students that using grammar and writing correctly will help them be better readers, writers, listeners, and speakers as well as better students and workers when they are adults.

Teach

Guide students on a book walk through the textbook. Review the Table of Contents and the book's organization and contents. Explain that students will be using *Voyages in English* in their journey to master English grammar and writing.

Practice

Provide students with a minute or two to review the book's contents. Tour the room, pointing out interesting book features to individual students.

Apply

Have students go on their first *Voyages in English* scavenger hunt. Ask students to find features such as a grammar lesson, writing lesson, Writer's Workshop, Link, Grammar in Action, and Tech Tip. Award points or prizes to the students who are first to find the features.

Assess

Ask students the following questions: *Why is it important to study grammar and writing? What is one thing we will be learning this year? Which skill or topic might be most challenging for you? What do you think will be easiest to learn?*

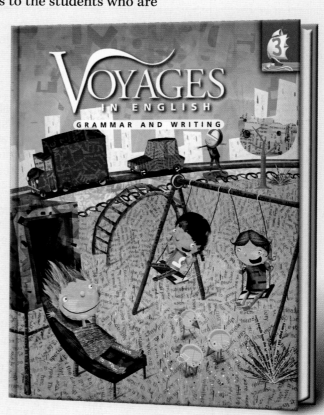

Extend

Have students study their book covers. Say: *We know that words are powerful. When words are used carefully and correctly, they can take us where we want to go in life. Look at your cover. Choose a person in it. Where do you think he or she is going in life? Take a few minutes to jot some ideas.*

Invite student volunteers to share their ideas. Close by saying: *Now we're going to go on a voyage together— to learn about words and writing so that we can go where we want to go. Let's get started!*

SECTION FOCUS
- Subjects and predicates
- Statements and questions
- Question words
- Commands
- Exclamations
- Kinds of sentences
- Subjects
- Predicates
- Combining subjects and predicates
- Combining sentences
- Run-on sentences

SUPPORT MATERIALS

Practice Book
Daily Maintenance, pages 1–4
Grammar, pages 5–16

Assessment Book
Section 1 Assessment, pages 1–4

Test Generator CD

Writing Chapter 1, Personal Narratives

Customizable Lesson Plans
www.voyagesinenglish.com

CONNECT WITH LITERATURE

Consider using the following titles throughout the section to illustrate the grammar concept:

Alexander and the Terrible, Horrible, No Good, Very Bad Day
by Judith Viorst
Leonardo, the Terrible Monster
by Mo Willems

Sentences

GRAMMAR FOR GROWN-UPS

Understanding Sentences

A sentence consists of several parts of speech organized into a meaningful pattern that expresses a complete thought. Every sentence has two basic parts: the subject, or the explicit or implicit person, place, or thing talked about, and the predicate, what the subject is, has, or does.

A **declarative sentence** makes a statement and ends with a period.

>*Sebastian walked.*

An **interrogative sentence** asks a question and ends with a question mark.

>*Did Sebastian walk?*

An **exclamatory sentence** expresses strong emotion and ends with an exclamation point.

>*I can't believe Sebastian walked!*

An **imperative sentence** gives a command and ends with a period.

>*Walk, Sebastian.*

In an imperative sentence the subject *you* is often implied and not stated explicitly.

>*Walk.*

Subjects can be combined.

>*Mary and Juana sit together.*

Predicates also can be combined.

>*Robert hopped and jumped.*

Occasionally, two complete sentences are combined incorrectly into a run-on sentence.

>*The sun came up it was a new day.*

A run-on sentence can be corrected by adding a comma and a coordinating conjunction.

>*The sun came up, and it was a new day.*

> ❝The words of the world
> want to make sentences.❞
>
> —Gaston Bachelard

COMMON ERRORS

Identifying Fragments

Some developing writers write sentence fragments rather than complete sentences. This error occurs because young writers often forget that all sentences must have a subject *and* a predicate.

> **ERROR:** Many children.
> **CORRECT:** Many children play soccer.

> **ERROR:** The frightened tiger.
> **CORRECT:** The frightened tiger is hiding.

As students revise their writing, remind them to check each sentence for a predicate, a word or phrase that tells what something is or does.

SENTENCE DIAGRAMMING

You may wish to teach sentences in the context of diagramming. Review these examples. Then refer to the Diagramming section or look for Diagram It! features in the Sentences section.

You ran.

You	ran
subject	verb

Did you run?

you	Did run
subject	verb

Run!

(you)	Run
implied subject	verb

ASK AN EXPERT

Real Situations, Real Solutions

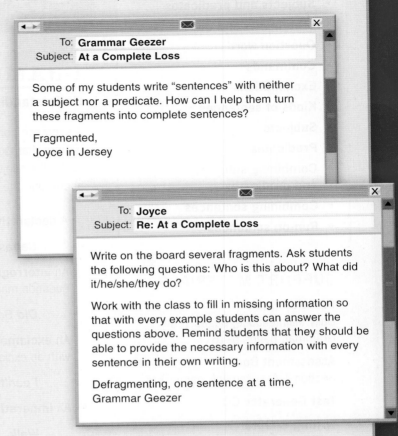

To: **Grammar Geezer**
Subject: **At a Complete Loss**

Some of my students write "sentences" with neither a subject nor a predicate. How can I help them turn these fragments into complete sentences?

Fragmented,
Joyce in Jersey

To: **Joyce**
Subject: **Re: At a Complete Loss**

Write on the board several fragments. Ask students the following questions: Who is this about? What did it/he/she/they do?

Work with the class to fill in missing information so that with every example students can answer the questions above. Remind students that they should be able to provide the necessary information with every sentence in their own writing.

Defragmenting, one sentence at a time,
Grammar Geezer

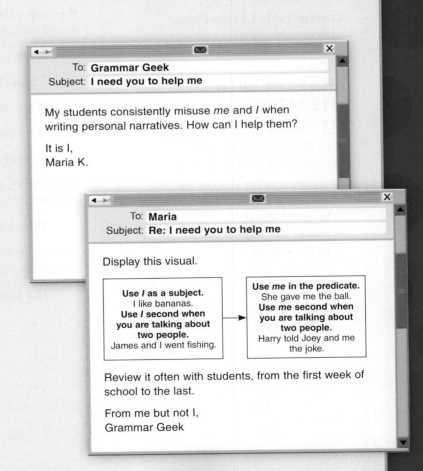

To: **Grammar Geek**
Subject: **I need you to help me**

My students consistently misuse *me* and *I* when writing personal narratives. How can I help them?

It is I,
Maria K.

To: **Maria**
Subject: **Re: I need you to help me**

Display this visual.

Use *I* as a subject. I like bananas. **Use *I* second when you are talking about two people.** James and I went fishing.	**Use *me* in the predicate.** She gave me the ball. **Use *me* second when you are talking about two people.** Harry told Joey and me the joke.

Review it often with students, from the first week of school to the last.

From me but not I,
Grammar Geek

SECTION ONE

Sentences

1.1 Sentences

1.2 Statements and Questions

1.3 Question Words

1.4 Commands

1.5 Exclamations

1.6 Kinds of Sentences

1.7 Subjects

1.8 Predicates

1.9 Combining Subjects and Predicates

1.10 Combining Sentences

1.11 Run-on Sentences

Sentence Review

Sentence Challenge

1.1 Sentences

OBJECTIVES
- To identify complete thoughts as sentences
- To construct complete sentences

 **Maintenance**

Assign **Practice Book** page 1, Section 1.1. After students finish,
1. Give immediate feedback.
2. Review concepts as needed.
3. Model the correct answer.

Pages 4–5 of the **Answer Key** contain tips for Daily Maintenance.

WARM-UP

Write the following subjects and predicates on note cards:

SUBJECTS	PREDICATES
Bill and José	has more boys than girls.
The girls	take turns cooking dinner.
Our class	are good friends.
Mom and Dad	plays soccer.
Jenny	like to swim.

Have partners make complete sentences and read aloud the sentences to each other.

📖 Read from a piece of writing that the class is currently reading. Emphasize that complete sentences provide complete thoughts.

TEACH

Display a photograph or poster. Ask volunteers to describe what they see and how they feel. Write on the board students' words, phrases, and sentences.

Have a volunteer read aloud about sentences. Tell students that a subject is a noun and a predicate tells what the noun is, has, or does.

Challenge students to identify which of their responses to the photograph or poster have a subject and a predicate and are sentences and which are not. Circle the complete sentences as students identify them.

PRACTICE

EXERCISE 1
Have volunteers read aloud each item, tell if it is a sentence, and explain why or why not.

EXERCISE 2
Explain that the phrases in Column A are subjects and those in Column B are predicates. Invite volunteers to read aloud each subject with several predicates, choose one predicate, and tell why it makes the most sense.

1.1 Sentences

A **sentence** is a group of words that expresses a complete thought.

Every sentence has a subject and a predicate. The **subject** names a person, a place, or a thing. The **predicate** tells what the subject is or does. It expresses an action or a state of being.

SUBJECT	PREDICATE
The pretzels	were hard and salty.
Sue	ate two pretzels.
My friends and I	liked the pretzels.
The bag of pretzels	is now empty.

To find the subject, ask yourself *who or what is doing something or being some way?* To find the predicate, ask *what is the subject doing or how is the subject being?* To find a sentence, make sure there is a subject and a predicate.

Which of these word groups are sentences?

A The tall apple trees
B The apple tastes good
C My sister picked apples
D Were left in the bowl

You are right if you said that B and C are sentences. Each one expresses a complete thought. Each has a subject and a predicate.

A and D are not sentences. They do not express complete thoughts. A doesn't have a predicate. D doesn't have a subject.

EXERCISE 1 Tell which of these word groups are sentences. Tell which are not sentences.

1. Our class enjoyed its visit to the zoo sentence
2. A huge gray elephant not a sentence
3. Eating food from a bucket not a sentence
4. A cub is a baby lion sentence

EXERCISE 3

Have partners complete the exercise. Invite students to read aloud their sentences.

APPLY

APPLY IT NOW

Remind students that each of their sentences must include a subject and a predicate. Have partners exchange sentences and check that each has a subject and a predicate. Students should demonstrate the ability to identify and construct complete sentences.

ASSESS

Note which students had difficulty identifying and constructing complete sentences. Assign **Practice Book** page 5 for further practice.

WRITING CONNECTION

Use pages 210–211 of the Writing portion of the book. Be sure to point out complete sentences in the literature excerpt and the student model.

Reteach

On a large poster board, copy a paragraph from a text that students have read. Cover parts of sentences with sticky notes so that only incomplete word groups remain. Slowly read the paragraph aloud. Ask students whether they had trouble understanding what you read. Have them explain their answers. Confirm that some of the sentences are incomplete and did not express complete thoughts. Remove the sticky notes and read the sentences aloud to illustrate that they are now sentences.

Meeting Individual Needs

Auditory Assign partners to describe their favorite games or sports to each other. Remind students to speak in complete sentences. Tell students to listen closely to each other's descriptions. If one partner expresses an incomplete thought, encourage the partners to discuss how to make the thought complete.

Meeting Individual Needs

Challenge Have students choose an article from an age-appropriate magazine. Ask students to copy five sentences from the article. Then have students draw a vertical line to separate the subject and predict in each sentence. Challenge students to use either the subject or predicate from each sentence to write a new sentence.

Diagram It!

To practice these concepts in the context of diagramming, turn to Section 8.1.

---

5. The lion was chewing a bone sentence
6. We couldn't count the leopard's spots sentence
7. The giraffe's long legs not a sentence
8. The keeper fed the seals sentence
9. Swimming under the water not a sentence
10. I liked the monkeys best sentence
11. We enjoyed the striped zebras sentence
12. Were swinging from branch to branch not a sentence

EXERCISE 2 Match each group of words in Column A with a group of words in Column B to make a sentence.

Column A		Column B
1. At the circus, clowns	b	a. galloped around the ring.
2. Eight brown horses	a	b. wore funny costumes.
3. Several acrobats	d	c. raised its trunk.
4. A baby elephant	c	d. walked on their hands.

Exercise 3
Answers will vary. Possible answers:
1. My class went to the zoo last week.
2. We saw a tall giraffe.
3. Some children watched the dolphin show.

EXERCISE 3 These groups of words are not sentences. Add subjects or predicates to make them sentences.

1. went to the zoo last week
2. saw a tall giraffe
3. some children
4. counted the penguins on the rocks
5. gave the seals food
6. dove into the water after the food
7. slept on a rock
8. workers at the zoo
9. roared and walked back and forth
10. the chimps
11. laughed at the monkeys
12. studied a map of the zoo

APPLY IT NOW

Imagine you are at the zoo. Choose three of these topics. Write a sentence about each.
A. dolphins   D. popcorn
B. tigers   E. monkeys
C. crowd

Sentences • 3

1.2 Statements and Questions

- **To identify and write statements**
- **To identify and write questions**
- **To distinguish between statements and questions**

DAILY Maintenance

Assign **Practice Book** page 1, Section 1.2. After students finish,
1. Give immediate feedback.
2. Review concepts as needed.
3. Model the correct answer.

Pages 4–5 of the **Answer Key** contain tips for Daily Maintenance.

WARM-UP

Have partners interview each other about a person, a hobby, or an event. At the end of the activity, ask students to describe the difference between questions and statements. Have volunteers write on the board their questions and responses. Encourage students to tell how the punctuation is different for each kind of sentence.

📖 Read from a piece of writing that the class is currently reading. Emphasize the difference between statements and questions.

TEACH

Explain that questions and statements are different types of sentences. Point out that whether a sentence makes a statement or asks a question, it still must have a subject and a predicate, and it must express a complete thought. Review the use of a capital letter at the beginning of both types of sentences.

Invite a volunteer to read aloud about statements and questions. Ask students to identify the subject and the predicate in each example sentence.

PRACTICE

EXERCISE 1
Have students read aloud their responses. Have the rest of the class tell which sentences end with a period and which end with a question mark.

EXERCISE 2
Ask students what clues in a sentence help to identify it as a question. Explain that a verb like *do* or *does* or a question word *(who, what, when, where, why,* or *how)* at the beginning of a sentence indicates that it is a question.

EXERCISE 3
Have students rewrite the sentence parts, adding the correct punctuation. As students read aloud their responses, have volunteers tell which sentences are statements and which are questions.

EXERCISE 4
Explain that students will use the words in parentheses to begin their sentences. Remind students to end each sentence with a period.

EXERCISE 5
Ask volunteers to read aloud their questions out of order. Have other students choose the best answer for each question.

1.2 Statements and Questions

A sentence begins with a capital letter and ends with a punctuation mark.

Some sentences tell things. A telling sentence is called a **statement.** A statement ends with a period (.).

> **There are many animals in the zoo.**
> **The lions are sleeping under a tree.**

Some sentences ask things. An asking sentence is called a **question.** A question ends with a question mark (?).

> **Do you like to go to the zoo?**
> **What do the lions eat?**

EXERCISE 1 Match each question in Column A with an answer in Column B. Then rewrite them. Add question marks at the end of questions. Add periods at the end of statements.

Column A	Column B
1. What is your favorite animal? b	a. I go there in the summer.
2. When do you go to the zoo? a	b. I like snakes the best.
3. Where do you see snakes? d	c. Only the zookeeper feeds them.
4. Who feeds the animals? c	d. I see them at the reptile house.

EXERCISE 2 Rewrite the sentences. Add periods at the end of statements. Add question marks at the end of questions.

1. Many people work at a zoo.
2. What does a zoo veterinarian do?
3. Veterinarians take care of sick animals.
4. Do zookeepers feed the animals?
5. They feed the animals and clean the cages.
6. How do volunteers help at a zoo?
7. Some volunteers lead tour groups through the zoo.
8. Would you like to be a zookeeper?

APPLY

APPLY IT NOW

Help students brainstorm topics for sentences. Check that students have correctly used beginning capital letters, periods, and question marks. Students should demonstrate the ability to distinguish between statements and questions.

Grammar in Action Ask volunteers to read aloud the first, second, and third questions. *(She wasn't sinking, so why would I?)*

ASSESS

Note which students had difficulty identifying or distinguishing between statements and questions. Assign **Practice Book** page 6 for further practice.

WRITING CONNECTION

Use pages 212–213 of the Writing portion of the book.

TEACHING OPTIONS

Reteach

Display a colorful poster or picture. Arrange the class in two groups— an Asking Group and a Telling Group. Have a student in the Asking Group ask a question about the picture. Then have a student in the Telling Group answer the question with a complete sentence. Have students in both groups tell what end punctuation to use. If time allows, switch the groups so students have a chance to form both types of sentences.

English-Language Learners

Place a large question mark in one corner of the room and a large period in another corner. Read aloud a series of statements and questions. Have students race to the appropriate corner to identify whether the sentence is a statement or a question.

Cooperative Learning

Have students work in small groups to choose a topic. Challenge each student to write a question about the topic. Have students review and correct all the questions. Then have groups exchange questions. Allow time for students to research answers to the questions. Have students write statements that answer the questions. Encourage students to present their research to the group that wrote the questions.

EXERCISE 3 Make statements or questions by matching the words in Column A with the words in Column B.

Column A		Column B
1. How many uses	c	a. can be used to make kitty litter.
2. Many people	b	b. enjoy peanut butter.
3. A lot of food	d	c. are there for peanuts?
4. Peanut shells	a	d. contains peanuts.

Exercise 4
Answers will vary.
Possible answers:
1. I am nine years old.
2. I have one brother and two sisters.
3. My favorite sport is basketball.
4. My favorite ice cream is chocolate.

EXERCISE 4 Write an answer for each question. Make sure your answer is a complete sentence. Begin with *My* or *I* as shown after each question. Put a period at the end of each sentence.

EXAMPLE **Do you like corn on the cob?** (I)
I like corn on the cob.

1. How old are you? (I)
2. Do you have any brothers or sisters? (I)
3. What is your favorite sport or activity? (My)
4. What is your favorite kind of ice cream? (My)
5. Do you like baseball? (I)
6. Do you have a pet? (I)
7. How do you get to school? (I)
8. What is your favorite holiday? (My)

Exercise 5
1. What do you eat for snacks?
2. What do you put in your backpack?
3. What do you have in your desk?
4. What do you do after school?

EXERCISE 5 Write a question for each answer. Make sure your question is a complete sentence. Begin each question with *What do you*. Put a question mark at the end.

1. I eat apples for snacks.
2. I put my books in my backpack.
3. I have pencils and paper in my desk.
4. I do my homework after school.

APPLY IT NOW

Write four sentences about yourself. Tell about these things. The sentences may be statements or questions.
1. your favorite TV show
2. a good book you've read
3. a food you like
4. a food you dislike

Grammar in Action Find the third question on page 211.

Sentences • 5

1.3 Question Words

 **Maintenance**

Assign **Practice Book** page 1, Section 1.3. After students finish,
1. Give immediate feedback.
2. Review concepts as needed.
3. Model the correct answer.

Pages 4–5 of the **Answer Key** contain tips for Daily Maintenance.

WARM-UP

Have students form a circle to play a game using the question words *who, what, when, where, why,* and *how.* Begin the game by asking a question using a question word. Have the student next to you answer the question and ask a question using a different question word. Continue around the circle until all students have had a chance to answer and ask a question, and all the question words have been used at least two times.

📖 Read from a piece of writing that the class is currently reading. Emphasize the question words.

TEACH

Read aloud about question words. Use the following questions to discuss a book or story the class recently read:

What was the name of the book?

Who are the main characters?

Where do the characters live?

When does the story take place?

Why did the main character do those things?

How does the story end?

Write the following on the board:

Who: asks about a person

What: asks about a thing

When: asks about a time

Where: asks about a place

Why: asks the reason

How: asks in what way

Have students ask questions using these words. Keep this information on the board for the remainder of the lesson.

PRACTICE

EXERCISES 1 & 2

Review the information on the board. Remind students to begin each question word with a capital letter. Discuss the answers with the class.

EXERCISE 3

When students have completed the exercise, invite volunteers to read aloud their questions and identify the question words.

1.3 Question Words

A question—a sentence that asks for information—often starts with a **question word.** Some question words are *who, what, when, where, why,* and *how.*

Who is the president of the United States?

What did the president say in the speech?

When was the president elected?

Where does the president live?

Why is a president elected for four years?

How do we elect a president?

EXERCISE 1 Read each statement. Complete the question after each statement. Use *who, what, when, where, why,* or *how.*

1. The president lives in the White House.
   <u>Who</u> lives in the White House?

2. The White House is located at 1600 Pennsylvania Avenue.
   <u>Where</u> is the White House located?

3. The first wedding at the White House was in 1812.
   <u>When</u> was the first wedding held in the White House?

4. Central heating was installed in the White House in 1835.
   <u>What</u> was installed in the White House in 1835?

5. The White House needed to be repaired because it was in bad condition.
   <u>Why</u> did the White House need to be repaired?

6. By fixing only the inside of the building, workmen around 1950 kept its original look.
   <u>How</u> did workmen keep its original look?

7. George Washington chose where the White House would be built.
   <u>Who</u> chose where the White House would be built?

8. The White House burned down in 1814.
   <u>When</u> did the White House burn down?

George Washington

APPLY

APPLY IT NOW

Brainstorm other well-known places that students might be curious about. List on the board these places and the question words *who, what, when, where, why,* and *how.*

When students have finished, have them share their questions. Check that students have applied each word to the correct type of question and information. Students should demonstrate the ability to use questions words.

Tech Tip Have students discuss the search terms they used to find answers to their four questions.

ASSESS

Note which students had difficulty identifying and using question words. Assign **Practice Book** page 7 for further practice.

> ### WRITING CONNECTION
> Use pages 214–215 of the Writing portion of the book.

TEACHING OPTIONS

Reteach

Write on sentence strips questions using the words *who, what, when, where, why,* and *how.* Cut the question words apart from the strips. Place the question words into six stacks, according to word. Distribute the other strips to the class. Have each student read aloud the partial question he or she received. Tell students to pair their questions with the correct question words. Ask volunteers to read aloud their completed questions.

English-Language Learners

Write on the board the question words *who, what, when, where, why,* and *how.* Ask simple questions for each word and have students answer them. Encourage students to identify the purpose of each question word—to ask about a person, a thing, a time, a place, a reason, or a way in which something happened.

Meeting Individual Needs

Interpersonal Share with students that news reporters use the question words *who, what, when, where, why,* and *how* to get information. Ask each student to write six questions, one for each question word, that students could ask their classmates. Have partners take turns asking and answering the questions.

EXERCISE 2 Complete the questions with question words. Then match the questions in Column A with the answers in Column B.

Column A	Column B
1. __What__ year was the White House named? d	a. Theodore Roosevelt named the White House.
2. __Who__ named the White House? a	b. You can write your member of Congress for tickets.
3. __Why__ is it called the White House? c	c. It is called the White House because of its color.
4. __How__ can you get tickets to visit the White House? b	d. It was named in 1901.

Theodore Roosevelt

Exercise 3

1. Where do the president and the Cabinet meet?
2. Who were the first residents of the White House?
3. What was the White House first called?
4. When did First Lady Abigail Fillmore start a library in the White House?
5. How do presidents entertain important guests?
6. What did Theodore Roosevelt hang in the State Dining Room?
7. Who built the West Wing?
8. When was the Oval Office built?
9. Who works in the West Wing?
10. What did President Franklin D. Roosevelt name his Scottish terrier?

EXERCISE 3 Write a question for each statement. Begin with the word or words given in parentheses. Put a question mark at the end of each question.

EXAMPLE **The Vice President lives at Number One Observatory Circle.** (Where does)
Where does the Vice President live?

1. The president and the Cabinet meet in the Cabinet Room. (Where do)
2. John Adams and Abigail Adams were the first residents of the White House. (Who)
3. The White House was first called the President's House. (What was)
4. First Lady Abigail Fillmore started a library in the White House in 1850. (When did)
5. Presidents entertain important guests by holding state dinners. (How do)
6. Theodore Roosevelt hung moose heads in the State Dining Room. (What did)
7. Theodore Roosevelt built the West Wing. (Who)
8. The Oval Office was built in 1909. (When was)
9. The president's staff works in the West Wing. (Who)
10. President Franklin D. Roosevelt named his Scottish terrier Fala, a Scottish word. (What did)

APPLY IT NOW

Think of a famous place, such as the George Washington Memorial, the Statue of Liberty, or the National Air and Space Museum. What would you like to know about that place? Write four questions. Use *who, what, where, when, why,* or *how.*

Tech Tip With an adult, research your famous place online.

Sentences • 7

1.4 Commands

OBJECTIVES

- **To identify and write sentences that give commands**
- **To use the correct punctuation with a command**

 **Maintenance**

Assign **Practice Book** page 2, Section 1.4. After students finish,
1. Give immediate feedback.
2. Review concepts as needed.
3. Model the correct answer.

Pages 4–5 of the **Answer Key** contain tips for Daily Maintenance.

WARM-UP

Invite students to play a quick game of Simon Says. Remind students that they must follow your commands only when you say "Simon says." Use commands such as these or make up some of your own: *Stand up. Sit down. Turn around. Clap your hands. Touch your toes.* At then end of the game, write some of the commands on the board. Ask students to tell what is similar about each sentence.

📖 Read from a piece of writing that the class is currently reading. Emphasize sentences that give commands.

TEACH

Have volunteers read aloud about commands. Then ask students to compare the examples in the text with the commands you used in Simon Says. Point out that the subject *you* is missing in all the sentences. Ask students to tell what else is similar. Tell students that each sentence begins with an action word such as *stand, sit,* or *turn.* Encourage students to think about commands that they hear throughout a school day. *(Open your books. Stand in a straight line. Raise your hand.)*

PRACTICE

EXERCISE 1
Complete this exercise as a class. Have volunteers read aloud each sentence and tell whether it is a command. Reread the sentences that are not commands. Encourage students to tell if those sentences are questions or statements.

EXERCISE 2
Remind students that in a command the subject *you* is generally not stated. After students have rewritten the sentences so that each sentence gives a command, have volunteers read their sentences aloud. Ask the rest of the class to check their answers. Discuss any sentences that differ.

EXERCISE 3
Before students begin the exercise, read and discuss each scene to be sure they understand it. Have students share their completed commands in small groups. Monitor the groups to make sure students have constructed their sentences correctly.

1.4 Commands

Some sentences tell people what to do. These sentences are called **commands.**

Directions for playing a game are examples of commands.

> **Take your turn.**
> **Select a card.**
> **Roll the number cube.**
> **Go to the next green square.**

The subject of a command is *you.* The subject is not stated in most commands. A command ends with a period (.).

When you give a command, it is polite to use a person's name and *please.*

> **Please do your homework, Katy.**
> **Open the window, please.**
> **Please have a seat right there.**
> **Follow me, please.**

Which of these sentences are commands?

> A **Have some juice, Gilly.**
> B **He finished the song.**
> C **Unwrap your gift.**
> D **Please blow out the candles.**
> E **Are we going to play games?**

You are right if you said that A, C, and D are commands. They tell someone what to do. Sentence B is a statement. Sentence E is a question.

EXERCISE 1 Tell which of these sentences are commands.

1. I want to make bananas on a stick. not a command
2. Do you have the recipe? not a command
3. Please hand it to me, Brad. command

APPLY

APPLY IT NOW

Tell students that the game can be a sport, a board game, a classroom game, or another game they enjoy. To add a little mystery, let students omit the name of the game. Ask volunteers to read aloud their directions. Have students guess the game. Students should demonstrate the ability to identify, write, and correctly punctuate commands.

Grammar in Action Guide students to the directions on this page. Point out that the subject of the commands is *you*, but is not stated.

ASSESS

Note which students had difficulty writing and correctly punctuating commands. Assign **Practice Book** page 8 for further practice.

> **WRITING CONNECTION**
> Use pages 216–217 of the Writing portion of the book.

TEACHING OPTIONS

Reteach

Have students sing and play the Hokey Pokey. Then write some of the commands on the board.

Put your right foot in.

Take your right foot out.

Put your right foot in and shake it all about.

Read aloud each sentence. Ask students to explain why the sentences are commands. Emphasize that each sentence tells someone what to do. Encourage students to write other commands for the Hokey Pokey. Write students' responses on the board.

Meeting Individual Needs

Extra Support Explain that students are already familiar with many types of commands, such as those in TV commercials and in everyday life. Point out, for example, that the word *stop* on a traffic sign is a command. Challenge students to supply other one-word commands, such as *go, turn, run,* and *help.* Write these on the board. Have students explain the command that is given or what is requested by each word.

Curriculum Connection

Connect to Art Remind students that art projects have instructions that appear in the form of commands. Encourage students to write instructions for an art project that they enjoy. Tell students to write their sentences as commands. Collect students' art instructions and combine them into a class book.

---

4. I need a banana, a flat stick, honey, and granola. not a command
5. First, peel the banana. command
6. Then cut it in half. command
7. Next, I need to put each half on a stick. not a command
8. Finally, roll the banana in honey and granola. command
9. Yum! It tastes good. not a command
10. Please give me a piece. command

Exercise 2
1. Get three apples, a balance scale, and some weights.
2. Leave one apple whole.
3. Peel one apple.
4. Cut the third apple into slices.
5. Leave the three apples out on the table.
6. Weigh the apples every day for a week.
7. Find out how much water evaporates.
8. Try the experiment with other kinds of fruit.

EXERCISE 2 Change each sentence into a command.

EXAMPLE **You can learn how fast water evaporates from a fruit.**
Learn how fast water evaporates from a fruit.

1. You need to get three apples, a balance scale, and some weights.
2. You have to leave one apple whole.
3. You should peel one apple.
4. You have to cut the third apple into slices.
5. You should leave the three apples out on the table.
6. You need to weigh the apples every day for a week.
7. You will find out how much water evaporates.
8. You can try the experiment with other kinds of fruit.

Exercise 3
Answers will vary.
Possible answers:
1. Feed your pet every day. Give your pet lots of love.
2. Draw a square. Draw a triangle on top of the square.
3. Walk, do not run, across the street. Wait for me to tell you when it is safe.

EXERCISE 3 Write two commands for each of these scenes. Remember to start each sentence with a capital letter and end it with a period.

1. You are the owner of a pet store. Tell a customer how to care for a pet.
2. You are an art teacher. Tell the class how to draw a house.
3. You are a crossing guard. Tell the younger children how to cross the street safely.

APPLY IT NOW

Think of a game you like to play. Write four directions for playing the game. Use commands.

Grammar in Action Find a command on this page.

Sentences • 9

1.5 Exclamations

OBJECTIVES

- **To identify and write sentences that are exclamations**
- **To use an exclamation point at the end of an exclamation**

 **Maintenance**

Assign **Practice Book** page 2, Section 1.5. After students finish,
1. Give immediate feedback.
2. Review concepts as needed.
3. Model the correct answer.

Pages 4–5 of the **Answer Key** contain tips for Daily Maintenance.

WARM-UP

Write several high-interest topics on note cards (*A Snow Day, A New Baby in the Family, A Surprise Party, Winning the Soccer Championship*). Have small groups choose a note card and discuss how they might feel in these situations. Ask students to share what they might say if they were to describe the event to a friend or family member. Encourage students to use sentences that express excitement, surprise, curiosity, and happiness.

📖 Read from a piece of writing that the class is currently reading. Emphasize the exclamations.

TEACH

Have volunteers read aloud the information about exclamations. Ask students to name clues that help to determine which sentences are exclamations. (*The sentences end with exclamation points. Sentences express sudden or strong emotions.*)

Point out that it is the emotion that determines the end punctuation because some exclamatory sentences may simply be statements if they are not expressed with special emotion.

PRACTICE

EXERCISE 1
Read aloud each sentence. Ask volunteers to tell what emotion is being expressed in each sentence. Point out that more than one emotion may be correct. Ask students to tell what is similar about each sentence. (*They all end with exclamation points.*)

EXERCISE 2
Read aloud each sentence. Ask students to think about the emotion that might be expressed in each sentence. Then have students write each sentence with the correct punctuation marks. Ask students to tell which sentences are exclamations. For sentences that are not exclamations, ask students what punctuation they chose and why.

EXERCISE 3
Read aloud the example statement and the two exclamations beginning with *How* and *What*. Explain that students need to write only one exclamation for each statement. Point out that students will need to rearrange the words in the sentences as in the example. Tell students to circle either *How* or *What* in each sentence.

1.5 Exclamations

Boa constrictor

Some sentences express strong or sudden emotion. These sentences are called **exclamations.**

Exclamations express feelings such as wonder, respect, surprise, happiness, worry, or fear.

What a lovely butterfly that is!
How noisy the parrots are!
Those tangled vines look like snakes!

An exclamation ends with an exclamation point (!).

Which of these sentences are exclamations?

A **What lives in the rain forest**
B **Mammals such as monkeys and jaguars live there**
C **How amazing this rain forest is**
D **Wow, I'd love to live there**
E **Name two animals that live in the rain forest**

You are right if you said that sentences C and D are exclamations. Each shows strong feeling. Sentence A is a question. Sentence B is a statement. Sentence E is a command.

EXERCISE 1 What emotions do these exclamations express? More than one answer may be correct.

1. Wow, many plants and animals live in rain forests!
2. How beautiful the butterflies are!
3. Oh no, rain forests are disappearing rapidly!
4. Yikes, every second we lose an area the size of two football fields!
5. Great, many groups are trying to save the rain forests!
6. What important work they do!
7. How strange some rain forest animals are!
8. Gosh, rain forests are really hot and humid places!

Exercise 1
1. surprise, wonder
2. surprise, wonder, happiness
3. worry, fear
4. worry, fear
5. happiness
6. respect
7. wonder, surprise
8. surprise

APPLY

APPLY IT NOW

Tell students to write sentences that clearly demonstrate an understanding of exclamations. As you review the original sentences, encourage students to explain the emotions expressed by their exclamations. Students should demonstrate the ability to write and punctuate exclamations correctly.

ASSESS

Note which students had difficulty identifying and writing exclamations. Assign **Practice Book** page 9 for further practice.

WRITING CONNECTION

Use pages 218–219 of the Writing portion of the book.

Reteach

Write the following exclamations on the board.

What a tall building that is!

We won!

The milk is spilling!

What a strange bug you caught!

I see lightning!

In a separate column, list these emotions: *fear, awe, curiosity, worry,* and *joy.* Discuss each sentence and the emotion that is expressed. Assign each sentence to a volunteer. Have each volunteer choose one of the emotions listed and read his or her sentence aloud, expressing the chosen emotion. If students are having difficulty matching the emotions with each sentence, take a few minutes to discuss each emotion.

Meeting Individual Needs

Extra Support Provide students with the following list of words that indicate feelings: *worried, happy, joyful, miserable, sad, fearful, disappointed, excited, relieved.* Ask students to act out or say sentences that convey each emotion. Write their sentences on the board, calling attention to the exclamation points.

Cooperative Learning

Provide students with copies of magazines and picture books. Have partners find photos or illustrations that show people expressing different emotions. Ask students to write an exclamation for each photo or illustration. Encourage partners to share their pictures and exclamations with the class. Ask the class to identify what emotion each sentence expresses.

Exercise 2

End punctuation may vary. Some students may use periods for sentences 2, 3, 11, 12, and 14 and question marks for 5, 7, and 10. Other students may use exclamation points for almost all the statements.

EXERCISE 2 Tell which sentences need exclamation points. Tell what punctuation marks the other sentences need.

1. What a magical place the rain forest is
2. Please stay on the path
3. Kapok trees can grow 150 feet tall
4. Oh, snakes really scare me
5. Did you see that butterfly flutter
6. How colorful the flowers are
7. Can you hear the chirping birds
8. We must save the rain forest
9. Hurry, it's starting to rain
10. Do you have an extra umbrella
11. Ouch, I tripped on a root
12. Please help me up
13. Wow, I don't ever want to leave the rain forest
14. We have to visit the rain forest again soon

Toucan

Exercise 3

Answers will vary. Possible answers:

1. How heavy these rocks are!
2. What a fierce lizard this is!
3. How quickly Sophia ran down the path!

EXERCISE 3 Change these statements to exclamations. Use the word *How* or *What* to begin each sentence. Use the correct punctuation mark at the end of each sentence.

EXAMPLE   **This bird is colorful.**

How colorful this bird is!

What a colorful bird this is!

1. These rocks are heavy.
2. The lizard is fierce.
3. Sophia quickly ran down the path.
4. It is very hot.
5. This is an old tree.
6. That monkey looks happy.
7. This part of the forest is dark.
8. These flowers have large petals.

APPLY IT NOW

Think of three things that caused you to have strong feelings. Write a statement describing the situation and an exclamation for your reaction.
Example:
I aced the math test.
I'm so happy!

Sentences • 11

OBJECTIVE

- **To identify the four types of sentences—statements, questions, commands, and exclamations**

 **Maintenance**

Assign **Practice Book** page 2, Section 1.6. After students finish,
1. Give immediate feedback.
2. Review concepts as needed.
3. Model the correct answer.

Pages 4–5 of the **Answer Key** contain tips for Daily Maintenance.

WARM-UP

Write statements, questions, commands, and exclamations on note cards. Have small groups play Sentence Swap. Give each group a stack of eight cards with a variety of sentence types. Have one student choose a card, read it aloud, tell what kind of sentence it is, and change the sentence into a different sentence type. Direct students to read aloud each sentence with the proper expression so that other students can tell which kind of sentence is being read.

📖 Read from a piece of writing that the class is currently reading. Emphasize the different kinds of sentences.

TEACH

Write on the board the following sentences:

We are going to the beach.

What fun it will be!

Watch out for the waves.

Where would you like to go?

Have students read aloud the sentences. Ask students to identify the different sentence types (*statement, exclamation, command,*

question). Encourage students to give reasons for their responses.

Read aloud the first paragraph and the chart. Point out that the chart shows the characteristics of each sentence type and which end mark goes with each type. Then ask a volunteer to read aloud the remaining text. Discuss each example sentence and ask students to give other examples for each type of sentence.

PRACTICE

EXERCISE 1

Read aloud each sentence. Ask students to tell if each sentence

is a statement, a question, a command, or an exclamation. Encourage students to tell what clues they used to decide.

EXERCISE 2

Tell students to refer to the chart on page 12 as they complete this exercise. Ask volunteers to share their responses with the class.

EXERCISE 3

Explain that students will write two types of sentences for each item. Remind students to use the correct punctuation mark for each sentence type and to begin each sentence with a capital letter. Have

---

1.6 Kinds of Sentences

What are the four kinds of sentences? A sentence can be a **statement,** a **question,** a **command,** or an **exclamation.** Let's review them.

KIND OF SENTENCE	WHAT IT DOES	END MARK
Statement	Tells something	Period (.)
Question	Asks something	Question mark (?)
Command	Gives a direction	Period (.)
Exclamation	Expresses a strong or a sudden feeling	Exclamation point (!)

Cocoa beans come from the fruit of the cacao tree.

Each of these four sentences is a different kind of sentence. Can you name what kind each is?

- A **Do you like cake**
- B **Chocolate comes from cocoa beans**
- C **Mix the batter**
- D **What a delicious cake you made**

You're right if you said sentence A is a question. It asks something. Sentence B is a statement. It tells about something (chocolate). Sentence C is a command. It tells what to do. Sentence D is an exclamation. It expresses a strong emotion (joy).

Cacao tree

EXERCISE 1 Tell what kind each of the following sentences is.

1. Do you like to cook? question
2. I sometimes help my parents in the kitchen. statement
3. What kinds of things do you do? question
4. Karen, help me mix the dough. command
5. How wonderful the bread tastes! exclamation
6. Wash the dishes, James. command
7. Don't eat all the bread. command
8. Mom's bread is better than store bread. statement

students complete the exercise independently. Then ask them to exchange papers with a partner to compare and correct their work.

APPLY

APPLY IT NOW

Suggest that students refer to the chart on page 12. Encourage them to consider what is special about each type of sentence as they write. As you review their sentences, check that students can explain or describe each type. Students should demonstrate the ability to write four kinds of sentences.

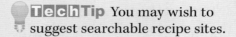 **TechTip** You may wish to suggest searchable recipe sites.

ASSESS

Note which students had difficulty identifying and writing the four types of sentences—statements, questions, commands, and exclamations. Assign **Practice Book** pages 10–11 for further practice.

WRITING CONNECTION

Use pages 220–221 of the Writing portion of the book.

TEACHING OPTIONS

Reteach

Create a large idea web on a sheet of poster board. In the center rectangle, write *Four Kinds of Sentences*. In the four outer rectangles, write *statement*, *question*, *command*, and *exclamation*. Have students look through classroom books to find examples of each sentence type. Add the sentences to the chart in the appropriate boxes. Ask students to tell how the sentences in each rectangle are similar.

Meeting Individual Needs

Intrapersonal Direct students to read through their journals to find examples of statements, questions, commands, and exclamations. Ask students to identify each sentence type by marking statements with an *S*, questions with a *Q*, commands with a *C*, and exclamations with an *E*.

Meeting Individual Needs

Interpersonal Tell students that when they talk to their family and friends, they should be polite by asking questions and expressing interest. Have students work with partners to practice these polite language habits as students exchange ideas or experiences.

Exercise 2
1. statement, period
2. question, question mark
3. statement, period
4. exclamation, exclamation point
5. command, period or exclamation, exclamation point
6. question, question mark
7. exclamation, exclamation point
8. command, period

EXERCISE 2 Tell what kind each of the following sentences is. Tell what punctuation mark is needed at the end of each sentence.

1. I like to make cookies
2. Do we have chocolate chips
3. We have all the ingredients
4. What hard work stirring the dough is
5. Don't touch the hot stove
6. When will the cookies be done
7. How good the cookies smell
8. Please share the cookies with your sister

Exercise 3
Answers will vary. Possible answers:
1. Question: Where is the banana bread? Command: Put the banana bread in the oven.
2. Statement: You should wash your hands. Question: Did you wash your hands?
3. Command: Eat that huge slice. Exclamation: What a huge slice you ate!

EXERCISE 3 Change each sentence to make it into a statement, a question, a command, or an exclamation.

1. The banana bread is in the oven.
   a. Question
   b. Command
2. Wash your hands.
   a. Statement
   b. Question
3. Can you eat that huge slice?
   a. Command
   b. Exclamation
4. Is it a delicious treat?
   a. Exclamation
   b. Statement
5. The dishes are in the dishwasher.
   a. Question
   b. Command

6. Put away the clean dishes.
   a. Question
   b. Statement
7. Can you set the table?
   a. Command
   b. Statement
8. Can you bake bread?
   a. Statement
   b. Command

APPLY IT NOW

You want to tell a friend how to make pancakes. Write four sentences, one of each type. Use the correct punctuation to end each sentence.

 Tech Tip With an adult, find a pancake recipe online.

Sentences • 13

1.7 Subjects

OBJECTIVE

- **To identify and use simple and complete subjects**

 **Maintenance**

Assign **Practice Book** page 3, Section 1.7. After students finish,
1. Give immediate feedback.
2. Review concepts as needed.
3. Model the correct answer.

Pages 4–5 of the **Answer Key** contain tips for Daily Maintenance.

WARM-UP

Write silly sentence starters and endings on separate sentence strips. Distribute the strips and explain that some students will have sentence starters, or subjects, and others will have endings, or predicates. Have students decide whether they have a starter or an ending strip. Then have students with starters find students with endings and combine their strips. Ask volunteers to share their silly sentences with the class.

📖 Read from a piece of writing that the class is currently reading. Emphasize simple and complete subjects.

TEACH

Write on the board some of the silly sentences from the Warm-Up. Circle the complete subjects.

Ask students to tell what the subjects have in common and tell what the subject does in a sentence. *(The subject names the person or thing doing the action.)*

Tell students that to determine the subject of a sentence, they can ask themselves questions such as *Who or what is this sentence about? Who or what is doing the action?*

Have a volunteer read aloud the first paragraph. Then ask students to tell the difference between simple and complete subjects. Ask where the subject of a sentence usually appears. *(The subject usually appears before the action word in a statement.)*

Ask volunteers to read the rest of the page. Then ask volunteers to underline the simple subjects in the silly sentences from the Warm-Up and circle the words that tell more about the simple subject.

PRACTICE

EXERCISE 1

Have students underline the complete subject. Challenge students to circle the simple subject in each sentence.

EXERCISE 2

Ask volunteers to read aloud a sentence and identify the simple subject and the words that tell more about the simple subject.

EXERCISE 3

Point out that students may have different answers. When students have finished, suggest that they share their work in small groups.

1.7 Subjects

A sentence has a subject and a predicate. The **subject** is who or what the sentence is about. The **simple subject** names the person, place, or thing that is talked about. The simple subject is usually a noun. A **complete subject** is the simple subject and words that describe it or give more information about it.

COMPLETE SUBJECT	COMPLETE PREDICATE
Mr. Liu	dived into the water.
The swim team	practices Tuesday.

In the first sentence, *Mr. Liu* is the simple subject and also the complete subject. In the second sentence, *team* is the simple subject. *The swim team* is the complete subject because *The* and *swim* tell more about *team*.

What is the complete subject in each of these sentences?

   A **The boy did the breaststroke.**
   B **Water splashed.**
   C **The excited students cheered loudly.**
   D **Our team's swimmers won the meet.**

If you said *The boy, Water, The excited students,* and *Our team's swimmers,* you are correct.

What is the simple subject of each of those sentences? If you said *boy, water, students,* and *swimmers,* you are correct. Each subject names a person or a thing.

EXERCISE 1 Tell what the complete subject is in each sentence.

  1. The swim team practiced every day.
  2. Sarub wanted to join the team.
  3. The coach watched Sarub in the pool.
  4. The determined boy finished his last lap.

APPLY

APPLY IT NOW

Brainstorm things that students might see at a swimming pool. Write their ideas on the board. Encourage students to use these ideas—or any others they come up with—to write their sentences. Remind students to underline the complete subject of each sentence. Students should demonstrate the ability to identify and use simple and complete subjects.

Grammar in Action. Guide students to find the simple subject *(Some)* and the complete subject *(Some of the best times of my life).*

ASSESS

Note which students had difficulty identifying and using simple and complete subjects. Assign **Practice Book** page 12 for further practice.

WRITING CONNECTION

Use pages 222–223 of the Writing portion of the book.

TEACHING OPTIONS

Reteach

Write on note cards words that can be used as subjects. Place the cards in a bag. You may wish to have students write subjects also. Make one card for each student in the class. Pass around the bag and have each student take a card. Direct each student to write a sentence that uses the word on his or her card as the subject. Have students write their sentences on the board and read them to the class. Ask the rest of the class to listen closely and identify the subjects as sentences are read.

Curriculum Connection

Direct students to choose a topic that they are studying in another subject and write four sentences about that topic. Encourage students to underline the complete subject of each sentence. You may wish to have students create information posters to go with the sentences. Display students' posters around the room.

Meeting Individual Needs

Extra Support Share with students that another way to identify the subject of a sentence is first to find the action word. Write the following sentence on the board:

Swimmers splashed in the shallow water.

Have students name the action word *(splashed).* Ask who or what splashed. *(Swimmers).* Point out that *Swimmers* is the subject of the sentence.

---

5. <u>Other swimmers</u> patted him on the back.

6. <u>The team members</u> welcomed him.

7. <u>Athletes</u> need to train for meets.

8. <u>The crowd</u> roared for our team.

9. <u>Our team</u> won!

10. <u>A win</u> always feels good.

Exercise 2
Complete subjects are underlined.
1. brother
2. Luke
3. coach
4. team
5. swimmers
6. Meets
7. swimmers
8. spectators
9. people
10. winners

EXERCISE 2 Tell what the complete subject is in each sentence. Then tell what the simple subject is.

1. <u>My brother</u> swims every day.

2. <u>Luke</u> belongs to the swim team.

3. <u>The coach</u> chose my brother for the team.

4. <u>The team</u> practices in the morning.

5. <u>The swimmers</u> can swim very fast.

6. <u>Meets</u> take place every month.

7. <u>The best swimmers</u> go to the meets.

8. <u>Many spectators</u> watch the meets.

9. <u>The people</u> cheer the swimmers along.

10. <u>All the winners</u> receive a lot of applause.

Exercise 3
Answers will vary.
Possible answers:
1. The coach, The cheerleaders, Our teacher
2. The team, The other school, We
3. The coach, The referee, The judge

EXERCISE 3 Finish each sentence with a complete subject.

EXAMPLE **My friend** clapped for the other team.

1. _____ led the cheer.

2. _____ finished in first place.

3. _____ blew a whistle.

4. _____ looked nervous.

5. _____ was too close to call.

6. _____ swam two laps of the pool.

APPLY IT NOW

Imagine that you are at a swimming pool. Write five sentences that describe what you see. Underline the complete subjects.
Example: <u>The children</u> paddle in the shallow pool.

Grammar in Action. Find the complete subject in the first sentence of the page 214 excerpt.

Sentences • 15

OBJECTIVE

- **To identify and use simple and complete predicates**

 **DAILY Maintenance**

Assign **Practice Book** page 3, Section 1.8. After students finish,
1. Give immediate feedback.
2. Review concepts as needed.
3. Model the correct answer.

Pages 4–5 of the **Answer Key** contain tips for Daily Maintenance.

WARM-UP

Help students brainstorm a list of sports, games, or other active things they like to do *(soccer, basketball, video games, running, playing tag)*. Write each suggestion on a note card and distribute them. Ask each student to write two sentences about the activity. Have volunteers read aloud their sentences and identify the action word and the words that tell more about the action word.

📖 Read from a piece of writing that the class is currently reading. Emphasize predicates.

TEACH

Write on the board the following sentences starters.

Our family

The school basketball team

The class hamster

Ask if the groups of words are complete sentences *(no)*. Ask what needs to be added to make them complete sentences *(an action word)*. Encourage students to complete each sentence with an action word and write their responses on the board.
    Read aloud the first paragraph. Then have students identify the subject and predicate of each sentence on the board. Have volunteers read aloud the rest of the page. Ask students to point out the simple predicate *(the verb)* and complete predicate *(the verb and the words that describe it)* for the sentences on the board.

PRACTICE

EXERCISE 1
Direct students to read each sentence and identify the complete predicate. Ask volunteers to identify the simple predicate in each sentence and to tell what words describe it.

EXERCISE 2
Have partners work together to identify the complete and simple predicate in each sentence. Remind students that they may find it helpful first to identify the subject of each sentence and then look for the predicate. Have volunteers read aloud their answers.

EXERCISE 3
Remind students that the predicate tells what the subject is or does. After students have completed the exercise, ask volunteers to share their answers with the class. Point out the variety of predicates possible for each subject.

1.8 Predicates

A sentence has a subject and a predicate. The **predicate** tells what the subject is or does. The **simple predicate** is a verb, which is the word or words that express an action or a state of being. A **complete predicate** is the simple predicate and any words that describe it.

COMPLETE SUBJECT	COMPLETE PREDICATE
The twins	cleaned their room.
Kate	folded all the laundry.

In the first sentence, *cleaned* is the simple predicate. In the second sentence, *folded* is the simple predicate.

What is the complete predicate in each of these sentences?

A **Mom dusted the shelves.**
B **Dad and Joseph washed the dishes.**
C **Maggie put her toys away.**
D **The house looked nice.**

If you said *dusted the shelves, washed the dishes, put her toys away,* and *looked nice,* you are correct.

What is the simple predicate of each of these sentences? You are correct if you said *dusted, washed, put,* and *looked.* These words tell what the subjects are or do.

EXERCISE 1 Tell what the complete predicate is in each sentence.
1. Luis helps at home.
2. His dad gives him a list of chores.
3. Luis's sister has jobs too.

APPLY

APPLY IT NOW

Suggest that students write about chores that they do in the classroom or at home. Remind students that each sentence must include a predicate to convey a complete thought. Students should demonstrate the ability to identify and use simple and complete predicates.

ASSESS

Note which students had difficulty identifying and using simple and complete predicates. Assign **Practice Book** page 13 for further practice.

WRITING CONNECTION

Use pages 224–225 of the Writing portion of the book.

Reteach

Write sentences on sentence strips. Cut the strips apart, separating the subjects and the predicates. Mix up the strips and place them in a bag. Then invite students to sort the strips into two piles—one for subjects and one for predicates. Have each student choose a strip, read it aloud, and tell whether it is a subject or a predicate. Encourage students to explain their responses. When students have identified all the subjects and predicates, have them make complete sentences by matching the subjects and predicates.

Meeting Individual Needs

Intrapersonal Ask students to identify predicates as they read newspapers, books, stories, or textbooks. Encourage students to write interesting and exciting action words in their journals. Explain that students should refer to their lists when they are writing to help make their writing more interesting.

English-Language Learners

Make a list of action verbs with students. You may wish to use words such as *run, eat, talk, write, jump,* and *sit.* Encourage students to act out each verb and say what they are doing. Then have students write complete sentences using all the action words.

---

4. She <u>makes the beds</u>.
5. The vacuum cleaner <u>broke</u>.
6. Mom <u>fixed it</u>.
7. Luis <u>dusts the furniture</u>.
8. He <u>finds coins under the couch sometimes</u>.
9. The house <u>smells of lemons</u>.
10. The family <u>cleans every week</u>.

Exercise 2
Complete predicates are underlined.
1. cleans
2. vacuums
3. sweeps
4. looks
5. wash
6. mows
7. work
8. talk
9. grow
10. picks

EXERCISE 2 Tell what the complete predicate is in each sentence. Then tell what the simple predicate is.

1. Luis's sister <u>cleans her room every week</u>.
2. Mom <u>vacuums the rugs</u>.
3. Luis <u>sweeps the floor</u>.
4. The house <u>looks wonderful</u>.
5. The children <u>wash the car with their dad on the weekend</u>.
6. Dad <u>mows the lawn</u>.
7. All the family members <u>work in the garden</u>.
8. The neighbors <u>talk to the family</u>.
9. Many vegetables <u>grow in the garden</u>.
10. The family <u>picks tomatoes in August</u>.

Exercise 3
Predicates will vary. Make sure each predicate includes an action or state of being that tells about the subject. Possible answers:
1. I help my mom wash the dinner dishes.
2. We have fun when we do the dishes together.
3. Grandmother dries the dishes.

EXERCISE 3 Finish each sentence with a complete predicate.

EXAMPLE **I <u>take out the trash</u>.**

1. I _____.
2. We _____.
3. Grandmother _____.
4. My friends _____.
5. The neighbors _____.
6. Our kitchen _____.

APPLY IT NOW

Do you help with chores? Write five sentences about what you do. Underline the complete predicates.
Example: I <u>wash windows</u>.

Sentences • 17

1.9 Combining Subjects and Predicates

OBJECTIVE

- To construct sentences by combining subjects or predicates

 **DAILY Maintenance**

Assign **Practice Book** page 3, Section 1.9. After students finish,
1. Give immediate feedback.
2. Review concepts as needed.
3. Model the correct answer.

Pages 4–5 of the **Answer Key** contain tips for Daily Maintenance.

WARM-UP

Write on the board the following sentences:

> I dance and sing.

> Jim and I dance.

Ask volunteers to say a sentence modeled after the first sentence on the board. (*I run and swim.*) Then ask if anyone in the class also enjoys one or more of the activities and have that person say a sentence modeled on the second sentence on the board. (*Jenny and I swim.*)

📖 Read from a piece of writing that the class is currently reading. Emphasize the compound subjects and predicates.

TEACH

Write on the board the following sentences:

> I like to read mystery stories.
> I like to write mystery stories.

> Matt went to the ball game.
> Kezia went to the ball game.

Ask volunteers to read aloud the sentences. Guide students to see how the sentences can be rewritten to be more interesting—both to read and to

hear. After students share ideas, invite volunteers to read aloud the information about combining subjects and predicates. Then have volunteers apply what they read to combine the sentences on the board.

> I like to read and write mystery stories.

> Matt and Kezia went to the ball game.

Challenge students to suggest sentences with compound subjects or compound predicates.

PRACTICE

EXERCISE 1

Have students complete the exercise independently. Then ask volunteers to write the sentences on the board. Discuss how the predicates were combined.

EXERCISE 2

Explain that sometimes when two single subjects are combined, the predicate may have to change. Write these sentences on the board and read them aloud: *The pot is hot. The pan is hot. The pot and pan are hot.* Have partners share their combined sentences with the class.

1.9 Combining Subjects and Predicates

Two or more sentences in a paragraph may give information about the same subject. When this happens, you can often use the subject once and combine the predicates to make a single, smoother sentence. Two predicates joined by *and, but,* or *or* are called a **compound predicate.**

> **My tabby cat sits in the sun. My tabby cat purrs softly.**

These sentences give information about the same subject—*My tabby cat.* The predicates, however, are different—*sits in the sun* and *purrs softly.* The two sentences can be made into one sentence by using the subject only once and combining the two predicates with the word *and.*

> **My tabby cat sits in the sun *and* purrs softly.**

You can also combine two sentences when they have different subjects but the same predicate.

> **My tabby cat plays with string. My kitten plays with string.**

These sentences have the same predicate—*plays with string.* They have different subjects, however—*My tabby cat* and *My kitten.* They can be combined by connecting the two subjects with *and* and by using the predicate only once. Two subjects joined by *and* or *or* are called a **compound subject.**

> **My tabby cat *and* my kitten play with string.**

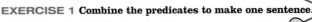

EXERCISE 1 Combine the predicates to make one sentence.

1. The dogs barked. The dogs howled.
2. The doctor petted Rex. The doctor spoke quietly.
3. Rex looked sick. Rex rested his head on his paws.
4. The dog looked out of its cage. The dog barked at the cat.
5. The vet examined Rex. The vet gave him a shot.
6. Rex barked. Rex put his head down.

Exercise 1

1. The dogs barked and howled.
2. The doctor petted Rex and spoke quietly.
3. Rex looked sick and rested his head on his paws.
4. The dog looked out of its cage and barked at the cat.
5. The vet examined Rex and gave him a shot.
6. Rex barked and put his head down.

EXERCISES 3 & 4

Have students complete the exercises independently. Invite students to share their completed sentences with the class.

APPLY

APPLY IT NOW

Read aloud the list of words. Help students realize that the subjects are things and the predicates are actions. Ask students which subjects and predicates listed have something in common. After students complete the exercise, ask them to share their

sentences with the class. Students should demonstrate the ability to construct sentences by combining subjects or predicates.

ASSESS

Note which students had difficulty constructing sentences by combining subjects or predicates. Assign **Practice Book** page 14 for further practice.

WRITING CONNECTION

Use pages 226–227 of the Writing portion of the book.

TEACHING OPTIONS

Reteach

Show students pairs of items that are similar such as a book and a notebook or a pencil and a marker. Ask students to make up sentences that have these items as their combined subjects. (*A book and a notebook fell on the floor.*) Write students' sentences on the board. Have students underline the combined subjects in the sentences. Then ask students to choose one object from each pair to write a sentence with a combined predicate. (*The book fell and hit Jen's foot.*) Write students' sentences on the board and have students underline the combined predicates.

Cooperative Learning

Have students work with partners. Tell one partner to write on a sheet of paper two related things, or subjects (*dog and cat, brother and sister*). Tell the other student to write on a sheet of paper two actions, or predicates (*tripped and fell, ate and drank*). Direct the partners to exchange papers and each write a sentence with the compound terms he or she received. Suggest that partners discuss their sentences and write additional sentences with those terms.

Meeting Individual Needs

Challenge Encourage students to use combined subjects and predicates to write a short personal narrative. Suggest topics such as *A Trip to the Zoo, My First Airplane Ride, My Favorite Grandparent,* or *The First Day of School.* Allow students to share their completed work with the class. Invite students to identify sentences with combined subjects and/or predicates.

Diagram It!

To practice these concepts in the context of diagramming, turn to Sections 8.6 and 8.7.

Exercise 2
1. Rex and Sparky were sick.
2. Mom and I took Rex to the vet.
3. Two dogs and two cats were in the waiting room.
4. A boy and a girl held a big cage.
5. Dr. Smith and I gave Rex a treat.
6. The vet and the vet's assistant looked at Rex.
7. The medicine and rest helped Rex.
8. The vet and I checked on Rex.
9. His treats and his new toy pleased Rex.
10. The vet and I felt happy about Rex.

Exercise 3
Answers will vary.
Possible answers:
1. Veterinarians and vets' assistants help sick animals.
2. Animal shelters and pet rescue groups save animals' lives.
3. Cats and dogs are common pets.

Exercise 4
Answers will vary.
Possible answers:
1. Veterinarians examine animals and give them medicine.
2. Volunteers feed the animals and clean their cages.
3. My brother and I walk and feed the dog every day.

EXERCISE 2 Combine the subjects to make one sentence.

1. Rex was sick. Sparky was sick.
2. Mom took Rex to the vet. I took Rex to the vet.
3. Two dogs were in the waiting room. Two cats were in the waiting room.
4. A boy held a big cage. A girl held a big cage.
5. Dr. Smith gave Rex a treat. I gave Rex a treat.
6. The vet looked at Rex. The vet's assistant looked at Rex.
7. The medicine helped Rex. Rest helped Rex.
8. The vet checked on Rex. I checked on Rex.
9. His treats pleased Rex. His new toy pleased Rex.
10. The vet felt happy about Rex. I felt happy about Rex.

EXERCISE 3 Write complete sentences with these compound subjects.

1. Veterinarians and vets' assistants _____.
2. Animal shelters and rescue groups _____.
3. Cats and dogs _____.
4. Food and water _____.
5. Gerbils and hamsters _____.
6. Canaries and parrots _____.

EXERCISE 4 Write complete sentences with these compound predicates.

1. _____ examine animals and give them medicine.
2. _____ feed the animals and clean their cages.
3. _____ walk and feed the dog every day.
4. _____ jumped onto the chair and fell asleep.
5. _____ flew to its perch and chirped.
6. _____ ran to the door and barked.

APPLY IT NOW

Use some of the words below to help you write two sentences. Each sentence should have two subjects or two predicates.

Subjects:

dog	cat
parrot	canary

Predicates:

growl	bark
purr	hiss
chew	sing
chatter	fly
perch	chirp
lick	sleep

Sentences • 19

1.10 Combining Sentences

OBJECTIVE
- **To combine sentences**

 **Maintenance**

Assign **Practice Book** page 4, Section 1.10. After students finish,
1. Give immediate feedback.
2. Review concepts as needed.
3. Model the correct answer.

Pages 4–5 of the **Answer Key** contain tips for Daily Maintenance.

WARM-UP

Write funny sentences on sentence strips. Put the strips in a bag. Have partners choose sentence strips and act out the sentences individually. *(Suzy stood on tippy toes. Tara tapped her nose.)* Ask a third student to combine the two sentences into one sentence and write it on the board. *(Suzy stood on tippy toes, and Tara tapped her nose.)* Have students act out the combined sentence. Ask the class what was added to the sentences to make one sentence. Continue as time allows.

📖 Read from a piece of writing that the class is currently reading. Emphasize the combined sentences.

TEACH

Review what students have learned about sentences. Remind students that sentences must be complete thoughts and must contain both a subject and a predicate. Reinforce that sentences can be combined to make writing more interesting. Write the following sentences on the board and read them aloud.

> Lightning flashed.
> Thunder boomed.
>
> The kicker scored.
> We lost the game.

Have volunteers read aloud about combining sentences. Then ask students to tell how they might combine the sentences on the board.

> Lightning flashed, and thunder boomed.
>
> The kicker scored, but we lost the game.

Ask students to tell the changes that were made to combine the sentences. *(A comma was added and the words* and *and* but *were added.)*

PRACTICE

EXERCISE 1
Tell students first to decide which sentences go together. Check students' sentences to make sure each sentence includes a comma.

EXERCISE 2
Ask volunteers to read aloud their sentences as you write them on the board. Have students identify the changes that were made to combine the sentences.

EXERCISE 3
Ask partners to share their completed sentences with another pair of students.

1.10 Combining Sentences

Several short sentences in a row can be boring to read. Putting short sentences together into longer sentences can make your writing more interesting.

To combine two short sentences into one longer sentence, add a comma followed by *and, but,* or *or.* Two short sentences joined this way form a **compound sentence.**

Two sentences:	Father read softly. The children listened.
Compound sentence:	Father read softly, *and* the children listened.
Two sentences:	Jim passes the library. Amy doesn't pass it.
Compound sentence:	Jim passes the library, *but* Amy doesn't pass it.

What two sentences were combined to make this compound sentence?

I'll study music, or maybe I'll play ball instead.

The first word in the second part of the compound sentence does not begin with a capital letter unless it is *I* or the name of a person or place. For example, in the compound sentence above, *maybe* does not start with a capital letter.

EXERCISE 1 **Match each sentence in Column A with a related sentence in Column B to make a compound sentence.**

Column A	Column B
1. Nonfiction books have facts, but b	a. people today still like to tell or read them.
2. Biographies are stories of people's lives, and c	b. fiction books are made up.
3. Adventure stories have lots of action, and d	c. they are nonfiction books.
4. Folktales are old, but a	d. the action is often scary.

20 • Section 1.10

APPLY

APPLY IT NOW

Have students name books that they have read recently. Write the book titles on the board. You might also ask students to provide brief summaries. Then have students write the sentences about their books. Have students read aloud their sentences and tell which sentences can be combined. Then have students read aloud their combined sentences and point out how the sentences were combined. Students should demonstrate the ability to combine sentences.

ASSESS

Note which students had difficulty understanding how to combine sentences. Assign **Practice Book** page 15 for further practice.

WRITING CONNECTION

Use pages 228-229 of the Writing portion of the book.

TEACHING OPTIONS

Reteach

Write on the board the following sentences:

We were walking down the quiet street.

Something strange happened during our science experiment.

The house was scary.

Read each sentence aloud and ask students how they would combine it with another sentence to continue telling a story. Have students tell exactly what they would add to the sentence, including punctuation and connecting words such as *and, but, and or.* Write on the board the combined sentences. Have volunteers read aloud the sentences.

Meeting Individual Needs

Auditory Provide partners with sentences that can be combined. Ask partners to take turns reading aloud their sentences. Then have students write a combined sentence. Have partners read aloud the combined sentences. Ask students to tell the differences between the separate sentences and the combined sentence.

Diagram It!

To practice these concepts in the context of diagramming, turn to Section 8.9.

Exercise 2

1. This book has many pages, but I read it in a week.
2. Alex read *Super Fudge,* and the funny story about two brothers made him laugh.
3. The mystery was exciting, and Jenny couldn't stop reading it.
4. Katie likes horses, and she would enjoy *The Black Stallion.*
5. Rosa likes reading mysteries, and Cam Jansen is one of her favorite characters.
6. *Charlotte's Web* is a classic, but I haven't read it yet.
7. The character Charlotte is a spider, and she helps a pig.
8. Beverly Cleary created the funny character Ramona, but I haven't read any books with Ramona.

Exercise 3

Answers will vary. Possible answers:

1. I might read a mystery, or I might read an adventure story.
2. The novel was long, but I finished it in one weekend.
3. The story was interesting, and it had wonderful illustrations.

EXERCISE 2 Combine each pair of short sentences with a comma and the word *and* or *but* to form a compound sentence.

1. This book has many pages. I read it in a week.
2. Alex read *Super Fudge.* The funny story about two brothers made him laugh.
3. The mystery was exciting. Jenny couldn't stop reading it.
4. Katie likes horses. She would enjoy *The Black Stallion.*
5. Rosa likes reading mysteries. Cam Jansen is one of her favorite characters.
6. *Charlotte's Web* is a classic. I haven't read it yet.
7. The character Charlotte is a spider. She helps a pig.
8. Beverly Cleary created the funny character Ramona. I haven't read any books with Ramona.
9. I saw a book with the funny title *How to Eat Fried Worms.* I wanted to read it.
10. In a series of novels, Pippi Longstocking lives with a horse and a monkey. She doesn't live with her parents.

9. I saw a book with the funny title *How to Eat Fried Worms,* and I want to read it.
10. In a series of novels, Pippi Longstocking lives with a horse and a monkey, but she doesn't live with her parents.

EXERCISE 3 Complete the following to make compound sentences. Remember to include *and, but,* or *or.*

1. I might read a mystery, _____.
2. The novel was long, _____.
3. The story was interesting, _____.
4. The biography was about Jackie Robinson, _____.
5. I saw a film of the story, _____.
6. I found an exciting adventure book, _____.
7. I have a book of folktales, _____.
8. The library has a section of fiction books, _____.
9. Writers come to the library, _____.
10. The library is my favorite place, _____.

APPLY IT NOW

Think about a book you have read. Write four short sentences about that book. Then combine two short sentences into one compound sentence.

Sentences • 21

OBJECTIVES
- **To identify run-on sentences**
- **To correct run-on sentences**

 **Maintenance**

Assign **Practice Book** page 4, Section 1.11. After students finish,
1. Give immediate feedback.
2. Review concepts as needed.
3. Model the correct answer.

Pages 4–5 of the **Answer Key** contain tips for Daily Maintenance.

WARM-UP

Have students tell a story about a bad day at school. Begin with this sentence: *I knew it was going to be a bad day when I woke up late.* Ask students to continue the story. Write students' sentences to continue the story, putting only commas between each addition. Keep adding their sentences until they notice what you are doing. Stop and discuss what is wrong with the way you are writing the story. Invite volunteers to make corrections so that the story is written with correct punctuation and capitalization.

📖 Read from a piece of writing that the class is currently reading. Emphasize that run-on sentences do not appear in good writing.

TEACH

Have volunteers read aloud the information about run-on sentences. Discuss how to identify run-on sentences and how to correct them.

Invite students to write some run-on sentences on the board. Have volunteers rewrite the sentences correctly.

PRACTICE

EXERCISE 1
Invite volunteers to read aloud each item and to determine whether it is a run-on. If it is, have them identify the two complete sentences in the run-on sentence.

EXERCISE 2
Ask volunteers to read aloud each sentence. Have students tell how to correctly combine the sentences. Encourage students to explain their responses.

EXERCISE 3
Have students read aloud the run-on sentences three times, inserting *and, but,* and *or.* Discuss which connector makes the most sense and why.

EXERCISE 4
Have students complete this exercise independently. Ask students to exchange papers with a partner and discuss their corrections. Remind students to check for correct punctuation and capitalization.

1.11 Run-on Sentences

A **run-on sentence** is one in which two or more sentences are put together without the proper connector.

Run-on sentences sometimes happen because two complete sentences are separated with only a comma.

A run-on is fixed easily by adding *and, but,* or *or* after the comma to make a compound sentence.

Run-on sentence:	It rained, I wanted to play outside.
Compound sentence:	It rained, *but* I wanted to play outside.

Which sentence is a run-on?

A The sun came out, and I went outside.
B I have a raincoat, it is yellow.
C My umbrella is large. It keeps me dry.

You are right if you said B. Sentence B has two complete sentences run together and joined by only a comma.

Sentence A is two sentences linked together with a comma followed by the word *and.* Sentence A is correct because both the comma and the word *and* are included.

C is correct because there are two separate sentences that have proper punctuation. Each sentence ends with a period.

EXERCISE 1 Tell whether each sentence is a run-on or a correctly combined sentence.

run-on **1.** Rain clouds rolled in, the sky turned dark.

run-on **2.** The teacher looked out the window, she frowned.

correct **3.** The children must stay inside for recess, and they are sad.

run-on **4.** There is more to do outside, it is more fun.

correct **5.** Most students play kickball, but some play basketball.

run-on **6.** It's not raining hard, we have raincoats.

Exercise 2
Answers will vary.
Possible answers:
1. The day was hot, and we decided to go to the beach.
2. The beach was crowded, and some people were sitting under umbrellas.
3. We wore hats, and we put on sunscreen.
4. The water was cold, but we still went swimming.

APPLY

APPLY IT NOW

Suggest that students first identify the four sentences. Then have students rewrite the sentences, adding the correct connectors and punctuation. Ask students to return the original sentences and the rewritten sentences to their partners and discuss their work. Students should demonstrate the ability to identify and correct run-on sentences.

ASSESS

Note which students had difficulty understanding how to identify and correct run-on sentences. Assign **Practice Book** page 16 for further practice.

WRITING CONNECTION

Use pages 230–231 of the Writing portion of the book.

Reteach

Write run-on sentences on sentence strips. Also, write commas and the words *and, but,* and *or* on strips as well. Ask students to determine whether each sentence is a run-on. Then ask students for suggestions to correct the run-ons. Have students cut apart the sentence strips where the connectors should go. Then have students add a connector to each sentence. Read aloud the sentences. Discuss how the sentences read more smoothly when the run-ons have been corrected.

Curriculum Connections

Display a poster, a photograph, or an illustration containing many details. Invite students to name the details they see and to express their ideas about the picture. Write students' ideas on the board as quickly as possible, creating run-on sentences as you write. Read students' ideas back to them and ask what they notice. Confirm that you have written run-on sentences. Ask the class to help you correct them.

Meeting Individual Needs

Intrapersonal Have students look through their journals or other writing for run-on sentences they may have written earlier. Tell any student who finds a run-on to write it on a sheet of paper and to write a corrected sentence below it. Check students' sentences to make sure they have rewritten the run-ons correctly.

---

run-on **7.** You will get wet, you might catch cold.

correct **8.** It will be sunny tomorrow, and we will go outside.

run-on **9.** I like sunny days best, Eric likes rainy days.

correct **10.** Eric likes cold days, and he doesn't like warm days.

Exercise 3

1. Rain clouds rolled in, and the sky turned dark.

2. The teacher looked out the window, and she frowned.

4. There is more to do outside, and it is more fun.

6. It's not raining hard, and we have raincoats.

7. You will get wet, and you might catch cold.

9. I like sunny days best, but Eric likes rainy days.

Exercise 4

Possible answers:

A. The thunder clapped loudly, and it shook the house. The little boy began to cry, and his mom said it was only a storm. He didn't like the dark, and she turned on a lamp. The boy fell asleep, but the light kept his brother awake.

B. There was a big storm, and the lights went out. Trees had fallen, and they had brought down the electrical wires. Dad made a fire in the living room, and we played cards near the fire. We expected the lights to come back soon, but they didn't come on until morning.

EXERCISE 2 Rewrite these run-on sentences. Add *and, but,* or *or* to make compound sentences.

1. The day was hot, we decided to go to the beach.

2. The beach was crowded, some people were sitting under umbrellas.

3. We wore hats, we put on sunscreen.

4. The water was cold, we still went swimming.

5. We played catch in the water, we played tag.

6. The lifeguard watched the swimmers, we felt safe.

7. We enjoyed the water, we had a great time at the beach.

8. We were tired, we were happy with our day.

EXERCISE 3 Rewrite the run-on sentences in Exercise 1 as compound sentences.

EXERCISE 4 Choose one group of run-on sentences. Then rewrite them as compound sentences.

A. The thunder clapped loudly, it shook the house, the little boy began to cry, his mom said it was only a storm, he didn't like the dark, she turned on a lamp, the boy fell asleep, the light kept his brother awake.

B. There was a big storm, the lights went out, trees had fallen, they had brought down the electrical wires, Dad made a fire in the fireplace, we played cards near the fire. We expected the lights to come on soon, they didn't come on until morning.

APPLY IT NOW

Think about what you did this morning. Write four sentences without any punctuation or connectors. Exchange papers with a partner. Then add correct punctuation and connectors to make the sentences complete.

Sentences • 23

Sentence Review

ASSESS

Use the Sentence Review as homework, as a practice test, or as an informal assessment. Following are some options for use.

Homework

You may wish to assign one group the odd items and another group the even items. When you next meet, review the correct answers as a group. Be sure to model how to arrive at the correct answer.

Practice Test

Use the Sentence Review as a diagnostic tool. Assign the entire review or only specific sections. After students have finished, identify which concepts require more attention. Reteach concepts as necessary.

Sentence Review

1.1
1. not a sentence
2. sentence
3. sentence
4. not a sentence
5. sentence

1.1 Tell which of these word groups are sentences. Tell which are not sentences.

1. Swimming with fins
2. A snorkel lets divers breathe
3. The snorkel sticks up out of the water
4. A cool way to see fish
5. Snorkeling is easy to learn

1.2 Rewrite the sentences. Add a period or a question mark to the end of each sentence.

6. Ana likes to dance.
7. Her parents are teaching her dances from Guatemala.
8. Do you know how to dance?
9. When did you learn to dance?
10. Square dancing is an American folk dance.

1.3 Find the question word in each sentence.

11. Who is going to the party?
12. What are you going to wear?
13. Where is Stuart's house?
14. Why is he having a party?
15. When does it start?

1.4 Tell whether each sentence is a statement, a question, or a command. Then rewrite each sentence. Add a period or a question mark to the end of each sentence.

16. Please go shopping with me.
17. I need juice and eggs.
18. Where did I put my wallet?
19. Bring me my keys.
20. Thanks for your help.

1.5 Rewrite the sentences. Add a question mark or an exclamation point to the end of each sentence.

21. Wow, I'm finally tall enough to ride the roller coaster!
22. Do you want to ride with me?
23. What an amazing view!
24. Hang on tight!
25. When does the park close?

1.6 Tell whether each sentence is a statement, a question, a command, or an exclamation. Then tell what punctuation mark is needed at the end of each sentence.

26. Where is the newspaper?
27. Please hand it to me.
28. Wow, what a terrific article!
29. My mom likes to read the city news first.
30. What a great photo!

1.4
16. command
17. statement
18. question
19. command
20. statement

1.6
26. question
27. command
28. exclamation
29. statement
30. exclamation

Informal Assessment

Use the review as preparation for the formal assessment. Count the review as a portion of the grade. Have students work to find the correct answers and use their corrected review as a study guide for the formal assessment.

WRITING CONNECTION

Use pages 232–233 of the Writing portion of the book.

1.7
Complete subjects are underlined.
31. aunt
32. vegetarian
33. Sara
34. food
35. diet

1.8
Complete predicates are underlined.
36. own
37. make
38. selects
39. creates
40. have

1.9
41. Shawn and Jo ride bikes.
42. We rode to the bike shop and looked at helmets.
43. The bike shop sells and repairs bikes.
44. My sister took a class and bought some tools.
45. We polish and decorate our bikes.

1.7 **Tell what the complete subject is in each sentence. Tell what the simple subject is.**

31. My aunt is a vegetarian.

32. A vegetarian is someone who doesn't eat meat.

33. Sara doesn't eat beef, poultry, or fish.

34. Good food is important for everyone.

35. Sara's diet includes vegetables and tofu.

1.8 **Tell what the complete predicate is in each sentence. Tell what the simple predicate is.**

36. My parents own a business.

37. They make cowboy boots.

38. My mom selects the leather.

39. My dad creates the designs for the boots.

40. I have several pairs of these beautiful boots.

1.9 **Combine the subjects or predicates to make one sentence.**

41. Shawn rides bikes. Jo rides bikes.

42. We rode to the bike shop. We looked at helmets.

43. The bike shop sells bikes. The bike shop repairs bikes.

44. My sister took a class. My sister bought some tools.

45. We polish our bikes. We decorate our bikes.

1.10 **Combine each pair of sentences with a comma and the word *and, but,* or *or* to form a compound sentence.**

46. My family went to Colorado. We tried skiing.

47. I took a lesson. My parents already knew how to ski.

48. I could take the chairlift up the hill. I could use the rope tow.

49. I was nervous. The instructor helped me feel better.

50. I finished the lesson. I skied down a hill by myself.

1.11 **Tell whether each sentence is a run-on or a correctly combined sentence. Rewrite the run-ons to make them correct.**

51. We bought apples, Grandma sliced them.

52. I walked to the park, I saw Grandpa.

53. I watched him play chess, and I asked if I could play.

54. We went home, Grandma had an apple pie ready.

1.10
46. My family went to Colorado, and we tried skiing.
47. I took a lesson, but my parents already knew how to ski.
48. I could take the chairlift up the hill, or I could use the rope tow.
49. I was nervous, but the instructor helped me feel better.
50. I finished the lesson, and I skied down a hill by myself.

1.11
51. run-on; We bought apples, and Grandma sliced them.
52. run-on; I walked to the park, and I saw Grandpa.
53. correct
54. run-on; We went home, and Grandma had an apple pie ready.

 Tech Tip Go to www.voyagesinenglish.com for more activities.

Sentences • 25

TEACHING OPTIONS

Reteach

Tell students they will be playing Sentence Scavenger Hunt. Have students reread a story or magazine article that they have previously read. Tell students you will give them 10 minutes to find as many different kinds of sentences as they can. Have students keep a tally of statements, questions, commands, exclamations, and combined sentences. Encourage students to share the sentences they found and to identify the kind of sentence.

Meeting Individual Needs

Challenge Give students a few days to be Sentence Sleuths. Have students compile lists of interesting sentences they find at home, at school, on signs, or any other places. Remind students to look for sentences that combine subjects and predicates and run-on sentences. At the end of the allotted time, have students share their sentences and tell what kind of sentences were found. If students found any incorrect sentences, ask how to correct them.

Tech Tip Encourage students to further review sentences, using the additional practice and games at www.voyagesinenglish.com.

Sentence Challenge

ASSESS

Encourage students to read the paragraph twice before answering the questions independently. If students have difficulty with any questions, remind them that they should refer to the section that teaches the skill. This activity can be completed by individuals, by small groups, or by the class as a whole.

After you have reviewed sentences, administer the Section 1 Assessment on pages 1–4 in the **Assessment Book,** or create a customized test with the optional **Test Generator CD.**

WRITING CONNECTION

Use pages 234–235 of the Writing portion of the book.

Students can complete a formal personal narrative using the Writer's Workshop on pages 236–247.

ANSWERS
1. question
2. statement
3. It gives information and ends with a period.
4. People
5. shoveled snow all day
6. exclamation
7. exclamation point
8. Everything froze. We all stayed inside.
9. What
10. The storm
11. exclamation
12. sentence 6
13. sentences 8 and 10
14. city
15. storm

Sentence Challenge

Read the paragraph and answer the questions.

1. Do you like snow? 2. All the kids in my building love snow. 3. Most of the adults hate snow. 4. Last year we had 24 inches of snow in one day! 5. People shoveled snow all day. 6. The city plowed the streets and salted the sidewalks. 7. Then it got really cold! 8. Everything froze, and we all stayed inside. 9. What do you think happened next? 10. In a few days, the sun came out, and most of the snow melted. 11. The storm was a real challenge. 12. What a big adventure we had!

1. What kind of sentence is sentence 1?
2. What kind of sentence is sentence 2?
3. Why is sentence 3 a statement?
4. What is the subject in sentence 5?
5. What is the complete predicate in sentence 5?
6. What kind of sentence is sentence 7?
7. What is the punctuation mark in sentence 7 called?
8. What two sentences were combined in sentence 8?
9. Which word is the question word in sentence 9?
10. What is the complete subject in sentence 11?
11. What kind of sentence is sentence 12?
12. What sentence has a compound predicate?
13. What sentences are compound sentences?
14. What is the simple subject in sentence 6?
15. What is the simple subject in sentence 11?

Nouns

SECTION FOCUS

- **Nouns**
- **Common and proper nouns**
- **Singular and plural nouns**
- **Irregular plural nouns**
- **Singular possessive nouns**
- **Plural possessive nouns**
- **Irregular plural possessive nouns**
- **Collective nouns**
- **Nouns as subjects**
- **Words used as nouns *and* as verbs**

SUPPORT MATERIALS

Practice Book
Daily Maintenance, pages 17–20
Grammar, pages 21–33

Assessment Book
Section 2 Assessment, pages 5–8

Test Generator CD

Writing Chapter 2,
  How-to Articles

Customizable Lesson Plans
www.voyagesinenglish.com

CONNECT WITH LITERATURE

Consider using the following titles throughout the section to illustrate the grammar concept:

A Cache of Jewels by Ruth Heller
If You Were a Noun by Michael Dahl
A Lime, a Mime, a Pool of Slime: More About Nouns by Brian P. Cleary

GRAMMAR FOR GROWN-UPS

Understanding Nouns

A **noun** is a word that names a person, a place, or a thing. Nouns can be categorized in several ways.

Common nouns name general, not specific, people, places, or things, such as *boy, garden,* and *van.*

Proper nouns name particular people, places, or things, such as *Marcus, Seattle,* or *Hubble Space Telescope.*

A **singular noun** names one person, place, or thing.

A **plural noun** names more than one person, place, or thing. Add *-s* to form the plural of most nouns, such as *cars, shoes, houses,* and *pencils.* Add *-es* to form the plural of nouns ending in *s, x, z, ch,* or *sh,* such as *buses, boxes, quizzes, inches,* and *brushes.* If a noun ends in a consonant and *y,* change *y* to *i* and add *-es* (*cities*). Some nouns have irregular plural forms (*women, geese*) or do not change form from singular to plural (sheep, moose).

Nouns can be made possessive to show ownership. A singular possessive noun is a singular noun that shows ownership (*pet's cage*). A plural possessive noun is a plural noun that shows ownership (*voters' ballots*).

Collective nouns name groups of people, places, things, or ideas that function as units (*jury, team, herd*).

Some words can be used as **nouns** and as **verbs**. These words are spelled the same but are used differently in sentences.

> *I have a wish.*
>
> *I wish I had a new bike.*

"Poetry is all nouns and verbs."

—Marianne Moore

COMMON ERRORS

Using Apostrophes Correctly

Some writers use an apostrophe in a plural noun, unintentionally making it possessive.

ERROR: Some girl's wore hats.
CORRECT: Some girls wore hats.

ERROR: The plant's needed water.
CORRECT: The plants needed water.

Remind students to check all words with apostrophes as they revise their writing. Students should be able to tell whether these words are meant to show ownership or are meant to show more than one person, place, or thing. Tell students that apostrophes are not used in plurals unless they are showing ownership.

SENTENCE DIAGRAMMING

You may wish to teach nouns in the context of diagramming. Review these examples. Then refer to the Diagramming section or look for Diagram It! features in the Nouns section.

Harriet spies.

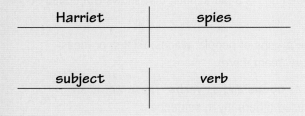

Harriet's partner spies.

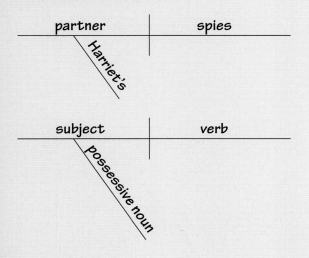

ASK AN EXPERT

Real Situations, Real Solutions

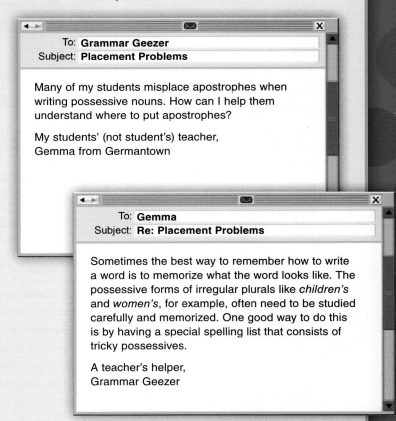

To: **Grammar Geezer**
Subject: **Placement Problems**

Many of my students misplace apostrophes when writing possessive nouns. How can I help them understand where to put apostrophes?

My students' (not student's) teacher,
Gemma from Germantown

To: **Gemma**
Subject: **Re: Placement Problems**

Sometimes the best way to remember how to write a word is to memorize what the word looks like. The possessive forms of irregular plurals like *children's* and *women's*, for example, often need to be studied carefully and memorized. One good way to do this is by having a special spelling list that consists of tricky possessives.

A teacher's helper,
Grammar Geezer

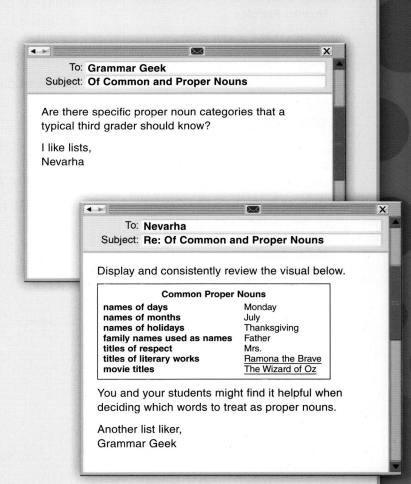

To: **Grammar Geek**
Subject: **Of Common and Proper Nouns**

Are there specific proper noun categories that a typical third grader should know?

I like lists,
Nevarha

To: **Nevarha**
Subject: **Re: Of Common and Proper Nouns**

Display and consistently review the visual below.

Common Proper Nouns	
names of days	Monday
names of months	July
names of holidays	Thanksgiving
family names used as names	Father
titles of respect	Mrs.
titles of literary works	Ramona the Brave
movie titles	The Wizard of Oz

You and your students might find it helpful when deciding which words to treat as proper nouns.

Another list liker,
Grammar Geek

2.1 Nouns

2.2 Common and Proper Nouns

2.3 Singular and Plural Nouns

2.4 More Plural Nouns

2.5 Irregular Plural Nouns

2.6 Singular Possessive Nouns

2.7 Plural Possessive Nouns

2.8 Irregular Plural Possessive Nouns

2.9 Collective Nouns

2.10 Nouns as Subjects

2.11 Words Used as Nouns *and* as Verbs

Noun Review

Noun Challenge

2.1   Nouns

OBJECTIVE

- **To identify nouns as words that name people, places, or things**

 **Maintenance**

Assign **Practice Book** page 17, Section 2.1. After students finish,
1. Give immediate feedback.
2. Review concepts as needed.
3. Model the correct answer.

Pages 4–5 of the **Answer Key** contain tips for Daily Maintenance.

WARM-UP

Write the following words on note cards:

cafeteria	gym
media center	art room
technology lab	front office
principal's office	auditorium

Give small groups a card, and give students two minutes to list people, places, and things that could be found in the room on their note card. Write on the board a three-column chart with the headings *People, Places,* and *Things.* Ask each group to name things from their list and write their words in the correct column on the board. Keep the chart on the board to use as you continue with the lesson.

📖 Read from a piece of writing that the class is currently reading. Emphasize the nouns.

TEACH

Invite a volunteer to read aloud the information about nouns. Then have students compare the chart in their books with the chart on the board. Have students name other nouns for each column.

Ask volunteers for sentences that contain a person, a place, and a thing. (*Mrs. Alvarez carried a suitcase to the train station.*) Ask

students to name the nouns in each sentence and to tell in which category each noun belongs.

PRACTICE

EXERCISE 1
Have students write the words on their own charts with the headings *People, Places,* and *Things.* When students are ready, have volunteers write each word in the correct column on the board. Review the words and their categories. Discuss any that prove confusing.

EXERCISE 2
While students work, have volunteers identify each noun as a person, place, or thing.

EXERCISE 3
Be sure students understand that the number in parentheses indicates the number of nouns to be identified. Have students exchange completed papers with partners to check the nouns that their classmates identified.

2.1   Nouns

A **noun** is a word that names a person, a place, or a thing.

If you were taking a trip, you might see many different people, places, and things.

PEOPLE	PLACES	THINGS
passengers	runway	airplane
pilot	shop	tickets
Mrs. Garcia	Idaho	baggage
ticket agent	cockpit	seat belt

Which of these words names a person?

A flight attendant
B suitcase
C East Coast

You are right if you said A. *Flight attendant* is a noun that names a person who works on an airplane.

Suitcase is a noun that names a thing. *East Coast* is a noun that names a place.

In the following sentence, can you tell whether each noun names a person, a place, or a thing?

Arnold bought a ticket to Los Angeles.

You are right if you said that *Arnold* names a person, *ticket* names a thing, and *Los Angeles* names a place.

Can you think of other people, places, and things? The words you think of are nouns.

EXERCISE 1 Tell whether each noun is a person, a place, or a thing.

1. propeller	**5.** Hawaii	**9.** bus driver
2. travel agent	**6.** zoo	**10.** statue
3. restaurant	**7.** map	**11.** city
4. guidebook	**8.** Janine	**12.** tourist

Exercise 1
1. thing
2. person
3. place
4. thing
5. place
6. place
7. thing
8. person
9. person
10. thing
11. place
12. person

APPLY

APPLY IT NOW

Point out that the nouns in the exercises are related to traveling. Tell students that they may use these words in their sentences but encourage them to use other nouns as well. Students should demonstrate the ability to identify nouns as words that name people, places, or things.

TechTip Have students use the underline function in a word-processing program to identify the nouns.

ASSESS

Note which students had difficulty identifying nouns as words that name people, places, or things. Assign **Practice Book** page 21 for further practice.

WRITING CONNECTION

Use pages 248–249 of the Writing portion of the book. Be sure to point out nouns in the literature excerpt and the student model.

Assign **Practice Book** page 21 for further practice.

TEACHING OPTIONS

Reteach

Invite students to help you draw a large, mural-sized map of the school, complete with labels. As volunteers suggest features of the school, have students draw and label the features on the map. Then review the words students wrote. Help students list the words on a chart.

People	Places	Things
principal	office	piano
music teacher	music room	bulletin board
cook	cafeteria	tables

Cooperative Learning

Arrange students into groups of three and instruct each group to create a noun collage. Tell students to assign these tasks: one student for people, one for places, and the last for things. Direct students to look through magazines for pictures of people, places, and things to cut out. Encourage students to work together to create their collages, sorting the pictures into categories and labeling each picture. Have the groups display their collages in the classroom.

Meeting Individual Needs

Intrapersonal Ask students to look through their journals or other writing for examples of nouns. Have each student create a chart and list the nouns in the appropriate column, according to person, place, and thing. Review students' charts to make sure the nouns are identified correctly.

EXERCISE 2 Use the nouns in the box to complete the sentences.

principal	children	Dallas	flowers
drum	camp	Jack	kitchen

1. The _children_ play at the park.
2. _Dallas_ is a large city.
3. We learned to swim at summer _camp_.
4. He plays a _drum_ in the school band.
5. _Jack_ is my younger brother.
6. The _flowers_ bloomed in the garden.
7. Dad cooked his famous chili in the _kitchen_.
8. The _principal_ read the announcements over the loudspeaker.

EXERCISE 3 Tell what the nouns are in these sentences. The number of nouns in each sentence is in parentheses.

1. Paolo visited New York City. (2)
2. The Empire State Building was once the tallest skyscraper. (2)
3. The buildings were tall. (1)
4. Mom saw a celebrity and got an autograph. (3)
5. A guidebook has sights to see. (2)
6. The guide knew cool facts about the city. (3)
7. My lunch was a hot dog from a stand. (3)
8. A boat moved up the river. (2)
9. Margarita found the museum on the map. (3)
10. The stores were packed with shoppers. (2)
11. There were big crowds on the streets. (2)
12. Times Square had many signs and lights. (3)

Statue of Liberty

APPLY IT NOW

Imagine you are going on a trip. Write one sentence for each of the following:
1. Name a person who would go with you.
2. Tell about a place you would visit.
3. Describe something you would take.

Underline all the nouns.

 Tech Tip Type your sentences, using a computer.

Nouns • 29

2.2 Common and Proper Nouns

OBJECTIVES

- **To distinguish between common and proper nouns**
- **To use a capital letter to begin most parts of a proper noun**

DAILY Maintenance

Assign **Practice Book** page 17, Section 2.2. After students finish,

1. Give immediate feedback.
2. Review concepts as needed.
3. Model the correct answer.

Pages 4–5 of the **Answer Key** contain tips for Daily Maintenance.

WARM-UP

Write on the board a chart such as the following:

JOB	NAME
teacher	Mrs. Gonzales
basketball player	Michael Jordan

Have students make their own two-column chart. Give students two minutes to list jobs and the people who perform the jobs. When time is up, have students count the number of jobs on their lists. Ask the student with the most responses to share some examples. Then have volunteers share their responses and list them on the board.

📖 Read from a piece of writing that the class is currently reading. Emphasize the common and proper nouns.

TEACH

Have students look at the chart of jobs and people from the Warm-Up. Challenge students to tell the differences between the words in each column. Point out that the words in the first column do not begin with capital letters and do not name specific people. Explain that the words in the second column begin with capital letters

and name specific people. Tell students that the words in the first column are called common nouns and the words in the second column are called proper nouns.

Invite volunteers to read aloud about common and proper nouns. Then ask students to name other nouns and to tell whether each one is a common or proper noun.

PRACTICE

EXERCISE 1

Have each student set up a two-column chart with the headings *Common* and *Proper*. Direct students to write each word from the exercise in the correct column. Ask volunteers to write their answers on a similar chart on the board. Have students check their answers against those of their classmates.

EXERCISE 2

Tell students that another way to talk about common and proper nouns is to think of them as general and specific. Have volunteers read aloud each common noun, or general category, and pause for students to suggest proper nouns, or specific people, places, or things.

2.2 Common and Proper Nouns

A **proper noun** names a particular person, place, or thing. A **common noun** names any one member of a group of people, places, or things.

In these two lists, which are common nouns and which are proper nouns?

COLUMN A	COLUMN B
teacher	Mrs. Filippo
student	Javier
day	Monday
holiday	Labor Day
book	*The Giving Tree*
city	Chicago
planet	Jupiter

The nouns in Column A name one member of a group of people, places, or things. They are common nouns.

The nouns in Column B name specific people, places, or things. They are proper nouns. Many proper nouns have more than one part, such as *Elm Street* and the *Poppy Popcorn Company*. Generally, every part of a proper noun begins with a capital letter.

EXERCISE 1 Tell whether each of the following nouns is a common noun or a proper noun.

1. Benjamin Franklin
2. president
3. Atlantic Ocean
4. athlete
5. Amelia Earhart
6. river
7. Ireland
8. state
9. continent
10. Mickey Mouse
11. Abraham Lincoln
12. TV show
13. *Sesame Street*
14. country
15. inventor
16. Indiana

Amelia Earhart, first woman to fly solo across the Atlantic Ocean

Exercise 1
1. proper
2. common
3. proper
4. common
5. proper
6. common
7. proper
8. common
9. common
10. proper
11. proper
12. common
13. proper
14. common
15. common
16. proper

30 • Section 2.2

EXERCISE 3

Remind students that some proper nouns consist of more than one word.

APPLY

APPLY IT NOW

Explain that students will be writing six sentences to answer the questions. Students should demonstrate the ability to distinguish between common and proper nouns.

ASSESS

Note which students had difficulty distinguishing between common and proper nouns. Assign **Practice Book** page 22 for further practice.

WRITING CONNECTION

Use pages 250–251 of the Writing portion of the book.

TEACHING OPTIONS

Reteach

Make several word webs. In the center rectangle of each web, write a common noun such as *athletes, national parks, book, states,* and *actors.* Set a time limit. Explain that students will add a proper noun to each web. When time is up, have volunteers read aloud the words from each word web. Discuss any incorrect words and ask students to offer additional suggestions for each web.

Curriculum Connection

Distribute to each student a passage from a biography. Review that a biography tells about a person's life. Ask volunteers to take turns reading aloud sentences from the passage. Encourage students to raise their hands if a sentence contains a proper noun. Call on a volunteer to identify the noun. You may wish to create a chart on the board to record the proper nouns and to list the common nouns to which they refer.

Exercise 2
Answers will vary. Be sure students capitalize each proper noun and that each proper noun relates correctly to the common noun.

EXERCISE 2 Name a proper noun for each common noun.

EXAMPLE
Common Noun	Proper Noun
neighbor	Mrs. Ahmed

1. friend
2. state
3. movie
4. grandmother
5. street
6. restaurant
7. song
8. country
9. singer
10. ocean
11. school
12. teacher
13. book
14. bicycle
15. store
16. mayor

Exercise 3
1. common, common
2. proper, proper
3. proper, common, proper
4. common, proper, common, common
5. common, common, common, common
6. common, common, common
7. proper, common, common
8. proper, common
9. common, proper, common
10. proper, common
11. proper, common, common
12. common, common, common

EXERCISE 3 Tell what the nouns are in each sentence. Then tell whether each is a common noun or a proper noun. The number of nouns in each sentence is in parentheses.

1. Many writers create interesting, young characters. (2)
2. Ramona Quimby was created by Beverly Cleary. (2)
3. Ramona has a sister called Beezus. (3)
4. In the book *Ramona Quimby, Age 8*, the main character is a third grader. (4)
5. The story tells about her life at school and at home. (4)
6. Readers enjoy the funny events in the book. (3)
7. In *Third Grade Baby*, a young student has a problem. (3)
8. Polly Peterson still has her baby teeth. (2)
9. A student teases Polly about her situation. (3)
10. But Polly has friends who help. (2)
11. Jenny Meyerhoff is the author of the novel. (3)
12. The library has many wonderful books and magazines. (3)

APPLY IT NOW

Write sentences with nouns to answer these questions:
1. Where do you live? Tell a fact about your city or town.
2. On what street do you live? Describe how it looks.
3. What is the name of a neighbor? Tell one interesting fact about that neighbor.

Nouns • 31

OBJECTIVES

- **To distinguish between singular and plural nouns**
- **To form plural nouns by adding -s or -es**

 **DAILY Maintenance**

Assign **Practice Book** page 17, Section 2.3. After students finish,
1. Give immediate feedback.
2. Review concepts as needed.
3. Model the correct answer.

Pages 4–5 of the **Answer Key** contain tips for Daily Maintenance.

WARM-UP

Write the following on the board:

one tree, two _____

one fox, two _____

one dish, two _____

one bus, two _____

one peach, two _____

Have students read each example and fill in the blank with the correct word. Then read aloud each example and ask students to name another word that rhymes with the noun in each example. Have students replace the singular noun with the new word and write it in the formula. For example, for one bag, two bags a student might say *one tree, two trees; one knee, two knees.* Continue as time allows.

📖 Read from a piece of writing that the class is currently reading. Emphasize the singular and plural nouns.

TEACH

Have volunteers read aloud about singular and plural nouns. Tell students that words like *fox, bus,* and *church* that end in *s, x, z, ch,* and *sh,* form plurals by adding *-es.*

Write on the board a two-column chart with the headings *s* and *es.* Have volunteers think of nouns and write their plurals in the correct columns.

PRACTICE

EXERCISE 1

Ask students how they can tell if a word is singular or plural. Have them complete the exercise independently. Suggest that students compare their answers with partners and discuss any answers that differ.

EXERCISE 2

Remind students that they will need to add *-s* to some words and *-es* to others. Review how to determine which ending is correct. After students finish, ask volunteers to add their answers to the chart on the board.

EXERCISE 3

Have volunteers read aloud each item. Discuss what other words in the sentences help determine if the noun should be singular or plural, such as the verb in item 1 or *a* in item 8. Have students read the sentences with both singular and plural nouns and decide which is correct.

2.3 Singular and Plural Nouns

A **singular noun** names one person, place, or thing.

A **plural noun** names more than one person, place, or thing.

I have one book. (singular)

Our library has many books. (plural)

The plural of most nouns is formed by adding *-s* to the singular.

SINGULAR	PLURAL
chapter	chapters
house	houses
Ford	Fords

The plural of a noun ending in *s, x, z, ch,* or *sh* is formed by adding *-es* to the singular.

SINGULAR	PLURAL	SINGULAR	PLURAL
glass	glasses	peach	peaches
box	boxes	wish	wishes
buzz	buzzes	stitch	stitches

Which of these nouns are plural nouns?

A bushes   **B** frogs   **C** bug

You are right if you said that *bushes* and *frogs* are plural nouns. *Bushes* means more than one bush. *Frogs* means more than one frog. *Bug* is singular and means one bug.

EXERCISE 1 Tell whether each underlined word is a singular or a plural noun.

1. The family went to the <u>ocean</u>. singular
2. They liked visiting <u>beaches</u>. plural
3. The <u>waves</u> were really big. plural
4. Mom read a <u>magazine</u>. singular
5. John built <u>castles</u> in the sand. plural

APPLY

APPLY IT NOW

Have students mention some ocean words to include in their sentences, such as *wave, beach, shell, gull, tide, crab, fish, sand,* and *coral.* Suggest that students use these and any other words they come up with. Students should demonstrate the ability to use singular and plural nouns and to form plurals by adding *-s* or *-es.*

Grammar in Action. Help students find the noun that names more than one person, place, or thing *(sandwiches).*

ASSESS

Note which students had difficulty distinguishing between singular and plural nouns and forming plural nouns by adding *-s* or *-es.* Assign **Practice Book** page 23 for further practice.

WRITING CONNECTION

Use pages 252–253 of the Writing portion of the book.

TEACHING OPTIONS

Reteach

Have students choose one of these nouns:

pen, pitch, guess, mix, patch, ax, peach, church, pan, box, chair, brush, glass, class, star

Ask students to write two sentences using their word. Explain that the first sentence should use their word in the singular form and the second should use their word in the plural form. Have each student read aloud his or her sentences, leaving out the noun in the second sentence. Ask volunteers to supply the missing plural noun. Check that students are forming plurals correctly and using each word properly in their sentences.

Meeting Individual Needs

Challenge Give each student 10 note cards. Instruct students to write a singular noun on one side of each card and the plural form of the noun on the other side. Check students' cards to make sure the plurals have been formed correctly. Have students work with partners. Tell one partner to show the singular form on one of his or her cards and ask the other partner to spell the plural form. Have the first partner turn over the card to reveal the correct form. Encourage partners to take turns showing their cards and spelling the plurals.

Meeting Individual Needs

Auditory Encourage students to notice when they and others use singular and plural nouns in everyday conversation. Suggest that students write the words they hear and use. At the end of the day, let students suggest sentences using both the singular and plural forms of the nouns that are listed.

---

6. A <u>gull</u> flew overhead. singular
7. <u>Shells</u> washed up on the shore. plural
8. Lily put them in a <u>box</u>. singular
9. She put the box in her <u>room</u>. singular
10. The box sits by her jar of <u>coins</u>. plural

EXERCISE 2 Write the plural for each singular noun.

1. pencil	pencils	6. mix	mixes	11. ring	rings
2. dish	dishes	7. race	races	12. pillow	pillows
3. grape	grapes	8. mitten	mittens	13. Friday	Fridays
4. ditch	ditches	9. match	matches	14. ax	axes
5. guess	guesses	10. patch	patches	15. watch	watches

EXERCISE 3 Complete each sentence with the singular or plural of the noun in parentheses.

1. The <u>beach</u> (beach) was filled with people on the weekend.
2. Many people were sitting under large <u>umbrellas</u> (umbrella).
3. There were many <u>boats</u> (boat) on the water.
4. My sister and I played on some <u>rocks</u> (rock) near the ocean.
5. Our <u>lunches</u> (lunch) were in our cooler.
6. We ate our <u>sandwiches</u> (sandwich) in the picnic area.
7. Dad bought me a <u>glass</u> (glass) of lemonade.
8. There was a <u>lifeguard</u> (lifeguard) near the water.
9. He was watching the <u>swimmers</u> (swimmer).
10. Some <u>teens</u> (teen) were playing volleyball.

APPLY IT NOW

Write four sentences about oceans. Underline all the nouns and tell if they are singular or plural. Write an *S* above each singular noun and a *P* above each plural noun.
Example:
   P   S
<u>Oceans</u> contain salty <u>water</u>.

Grammar in Action. Find the plural noun in the first sentence of the page 248 excerpt.

Nouns • 33

OBJECTIVE

- **To form the plural of nouns that end in *y***

 **Maintenance**

Assign **Practice Book** page 18, Section 2.4. After students finish,
1. Give immediate feedback.
2. Review concepts as needed.
3. Model the correct answer.

Pages 4–5 of the **Answer Key** contain tips for Daily Maintenance.

WARM-UP

Write these singular and plural nouns on individual note cards:

fly	flies	valley	valleys
ray	rays	story	stories
baby	babies	turkey	turkeys
pony	ponies	puppy	puppies
toy	toys	monkey	monkeys

Place the cards facedown on a table. Have students turn over two cards to match the singular and plural forms for each noun. If students cannot make a match, they turn the cards facedown and another student takes a turn. Continue playing until all the cards have been matched correctly.

📖 Read from a piece of writing that the class is currently reading. Emphasize the plurals of nouns ending in *y*.

TEACH

Write the following on the board:

lady   day   monkey   cherry   sky

Ask how these words are similar. *(They all end in* y. *They are all nouns.)* Write on the board the plural form of each word under its singular form. Point out that some words that end in *y* form plurals by adding *-s*, but other words that end in *y* form plurals differently.

Have volunteers read aloud the text. Summarize the ways to make plural nouns that end in *y*. *(If a noun ends in a consonant followed by* y, *change the* y *to* i *and add* -es. *If a noun ends in a vowel followed by* y, *add* -s.*)*

Encourage students to brainstorm examples of other nouns ending in *y* and list them on the board. Ask students to use the rules for forming the plurals for each word.

PRACTICE

EXERCISE 1

Explain that to answer each question, students must do two things—identify the nouns and determine whether each noun is singular or plural. Ask students to share their answers with the class.

EXERCISE 2

Have students complete the exercise with partners. Then have volunteers write their answers on the board and tell which rule for forming plurals applies.

2.4 More Plural Nouns

To make most nouns plural, you only need to add *-s* or *-es* to the singular form of the nouns. Some nouns that end in *y* are different. To form the plural of a noun ending in a consonant followed by *y*, change the *y* to *i* and add *-es*.

SINGULAR	PLURAL
baby	babies
country	countries
sky	skies
galaxy	galaxies

What is the correct plural form of the word *puppy*?

A **puppys**

B **puppies**

C **puppyes**

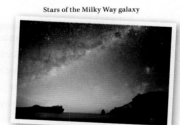

Stars of the Milky Way galaxy

If you said B, you are right. The word *puppy* ends in a consonant followed by *y*. To make *puppy* plural, change the *y* to *i* and add *-es*.

For nouns ending in a vowel and *y*, you just add *-s*, as with other nouns.

SINGULAR	PLURAL
monkey	monkeys
day	days
Kelley	Kelleys
boy	boys

EXERCISE 1 Find the nouns in each sentence. Tell whether each noun is singular or plural.

1. <u>Puppies</u> frequently try to catch their own <u>tails</u>.
2. My <u>kitten</u> likes to play with a <u>mouse</u>.
3. That <u>bunny</u> has a fluffy <u>tail</u>.

Exercise 1
Singular nouns are underlined once. Plural nouns are underlined twice.

EXERCISE 3

Have volunteers read aloud their completed sentences. Then have students make the nouns singular and say the sentences again. Ask what other words in the sentences had to change.

APPLY

APPLY IT NOW

Make sure students understand that they need to make the nouns plural. Ask volunteers to read aloud their sentences. Students should demonstrate the ability to form plurals of nouns ending in *y*.

Grammar in Action After students identify the five nouns (*cheese, bread, Mexicans, cheese, tortilla*), have them tell if they are common or proper and singular or plural.

ASSESS

Note which students had difficulty forming the plural of nouns that end in *y*. Assign **Practice Book** page 24 for further practice.

> ### WRITING CONNECTION
> Use pages 254–255 of the Writing portion of the book.

TEACHING OPTIONS

Reteach

Write on separate strips of paper a variety of nouns ending in *y* and nouns ending in a vowel and *y* (*valley, strawberry, turkey, story, alley, volley, study, duty, boy, chimney, turkey, city, play*). Place the strips in a box. Make a three-column chart on poster board with the headings *s*, *es*, and *ies*. Have each student choose a strip and explain how to make the word plural. Write the plural on the board as the student tells how to form it. Ask students to determine if the plural has been correctly formed. If it was, have the student tape the word in the correct column on the chart. If it was incorrect, put the strip back into the bag. Continue until all the strips have been chosen and the plurals have been formed correctly.

Curriculum Connection

Have students look through an animal encyclopedia to find animal names that require *-es* or *-ies* to make them plural. Also have students look for animal names that end with a vowel and *y*. Tell students to organize the names into a chart, such as the following:

-es	-ies	-s (after y)
walruses	canaries	bluejays
foxes	flies	monkeys
ostriches	huskies	stingrays

English-Language Learners

Ask partners to "tour" the classroom together. Have students identify objects in both singular and plural forms. Instruct students to work together to write the words. Encourage students to underline the letters used to form each plural.

book	book**s**
box	box**es**
copy	cop**ies**

---

4. <u>Guppies</u> swim in the <u>pond</u>.
5. Our <u>ferrets</u> like to sit on the <u>couch</u>.
6. The <u>bluebird</u> eats wild <u>blackberries</u>.
7. <u>Dad</u> told <u>stories</u> about his many <u>animals</u>.
8. <u>Jamie</u> called the <u>dog</u>.
9. <u>Gerbils</u> play on the <u>wheels</u> in their <u>cages</u>.
10. Those <u>canaries</u> sing constantly.
11. The <u>parrot</u> with red and blue <u>feathers</u> can talk.
12. <u>Toys</u> for the <u>cat</u> are in the <u>boxes</u>.

EXERCISE 2 Write the plural for each singular noun.

EXAMPLE	Singular	Plural
	army	armies

	Singular	Plural			Singular	Plural
1.	country	countries		9.	journey	journeys
2.	hobby	hobbies		10.	way	ways
3.	Frey	Freys		11.	duty	duties
4.	key	keys		12.	city	cities
5.	pantry	pantries		13.	chimney	chimneys
6.	play	plays		14.	turkey	turkeys
7.	daisy	daisies		15.	cry	cries
8.	melody	melodies		16.	valley	valleys

Exercise 3
Answers will vary.

EXERCISE 3 Write a sentence for each word.

1. donkeys
2. ponies
3. cities
4. parties

APPLY IT NOW

Write two sentences using the plural of these words.
pastry cherry bakery quality

Grammar in Action Tell the number of nouns in the second sentence of the page 248 excerpt.

Nouns • 35

OBJECTIVES

- **To recognize nouns that have irregular plurals**
- **To form irregular plural nouns correctly**

 **DAILY Maintenance**

Assign **Practice Book** page 18, Section 2.5. After students finish,
1. Give immediate feedback.
2. Review concepts as needed.
3. Model the correct answer.

Pages 4–5 of the **Answer Key** contain tips for Daily Maintenance.

WARM-UP

Make several plural puzzles. Choose nouns that have irregular plurals and write the singular and plural forms on a single sentence strip. Include some nouns that are the same in singular and plural form.

tooth	teeth	sheep	sheep
foot	feet	ox	oxen
mouse	mice	goose	geese
man	men	woman	women
child	children		

Cut the sentence strips apart between the singular and plural forms as if they were puzzle pieces. Have partners put the plural puzzles together and discuss the difference between the singular and plural nouns.

📖 Read from a piece of writing that the class is currently reading. Emphasize irregular plural nouns.

TEACH

Have volunteers read aloud the first two paragraphs of the text and the first chart. Suggest that students memorize these irregular plurals. Tell students that whenever they are unsure how to form a plural, they should look up the word in a dictionary.

Invite a volunteer to read aloud the rest of the page. Point out that some words use the same form in the singular and the plural. Encourage students to name other words they know with irregular plurals and other words that use the same form for singular and plural. List students' responses on the board.

PRACTICE

EXERCISE 1

Have students share their answers with the class. As a student answers a question, have him or her use the word in a sentence.

EXERCISE 2

Explain that some of the missing nouns in these sentences have irregular plurals. Have students complete the exercise in small groups. Ask volunteers to read aloud their sentences. If there are any discrepancies, have a volunteer look up the word in a dictionary.

EXERCISE 3

Have students tell which rule helps to form each plural. Tell students to refer to the charts in the lesson or use a dictionary to confirm their answers.

2.5 Irregular Plural Nouns

The plurals of some nouns look somewhat different from their singular forms. These **irregular plurals** are not formed by adding -s or -es to the singular forms.

You should memorize these irregular plurals. If you forget how to spell an irregular plural, you can look it up in a dictionary.

SINGULAR	PLURAL
ox	oxen
child	children
tooth	teeth
foot	feet
mouse	mice
woman	women
goose	geese

Some nouns that have irregular plurals have the same form in the plural as in the singular.

SINGULAR	PLURAL
sheep	sheep
deer	deer
moose	moose
Chinese	Chinese

EXERCISE 1 Tell whether each noun is singular or plural. Some nouns may be both singular and plural.

1. geese — plural
2. child — singular
3. mouse — singular
4. teeth — plural
5. oxen — plural
6. sheep — both singular and plural
7. deer — both singular and plural
8. women — plural

APPLY

APPLY IT NOW

Tell students that they may use other irregular plurals besides those listed. After students have finished writing their stories, have students circle the irregular plurals. Review students' work to make sure they have written and identified irregular plurals correctly. Students should demonstrate the ability to recognize and form irregular plural nouns.

ASSESS

Note which students had difficulty recognizing nouns that have irregular plurals and forming irregular plurals correctly. Assign **Practice Book** pages 25–26 for further practice.

WRITING CONNECTION

Use pages 256–257 of the Writing portion of the book.

TEACHING OPTIONS

Reteach

Write on the board a list of irregular plurals and words that use the same form in the singular and plural. Then write sentences using some of the words from the board, but leave a blank where the plural should go. Have a volunteer read aloud one sentence. Ask students to decide which word from the board best completes the sentence. Have a student come to the board and write the word to complete the sentence. Have volunteers read aloud the completed sentence and tell if the word makes sense. If it does, move on to the next sentence and repeat the same procedure. Continue until all the sentences are completed correctly. Then ask students to create additional sentences using any of the plurals from the list that have not been used.

Meeting Individual Needs

Extra Support On the board create a chart like the one below. Leave blanks for the words shown in parentheses. Have students complete the chart with the missing singular and plural nouns.

Singular	Plural
foot	(feet)
(tooth)	teeth
(goose)	geese
man	(men)
child	(children)
(mouse)	mice
sheep	(sheep)

Curriculum Connection

Have students choose an irregular plural and illustrate the singular and plural forms of the word. Have students write a caption for each drawing, including the noun in the correct form. Encourage students to discuss the plural and singular forms of each noun.

EXERCISE 2 Complete each sentence with the plural of the noun in parentheses.

1. The _children_ went to the nature center. (child)
2. They fed the _geese_. (goose)
3. Some animals had sharp _teeth_. (tooth)
4. The _oxen_ pulled a cart. (ox)
5. We saw _deer_ roaming in a field. (deer)
6. The _sheep_ were white and woolly. (sheep)
7. The center also had reptiles such as _turtles_. (turtle)
8. Black rat snakes are gray and six _feet_ long. (foot)
9. A dozen _mice_ shared a cage. (mouse)
10. Several _women_ fed the animals daily. (woman)
11. There is a lovely garden with _butterflies_. (butterfly)
12. The center doesn't have any _monkeys_. (monkey)
13. There are four nature _centers_ in our city. (center)
14. When I grow up, I want to take care of _animals_ in my job. (animal)

EXERCISE 3 Write the plural for each singular noun.

1. class — classes
2. moose — moose
3. berry — berries
4. brush — brushes
5. batch — batches
6. mouse — mice
7. wish — wishes
8. search — searches
9. dress — dresses
10. tax — taxes
11. crutch — crutches
12. sky — skies

APPLY IT NOW

Use these words to write a one-paragraph story about a make-believe situation.

mouse   mice
child   children

Nouns • 37

2.6 Singular Possessive Nouns

OBJECTIVES

- **To recognize the possessive form of singular nouns**
- **To create the possessive form of singular nouns**

 **Maintenance**

Assign **Practice Book** page 18, Section 2.6. After students finish,
1. Give immediate feedback.
2. Review concepts as needed.
3. Model the correct answer.

Pages 4–5 of the **Answer Key** contain tips for Daily Maintenance.

WARM-UP

Write on sentence strips phrases such as the following:

the notebook that belongs to Nan

the camera that belongs to Kendall

the ring that belongs to Lakshmi

Place the strips in a box. Tell students they will be playing In Other Words. Have students choose a card, read the phrase aloud, and say the phrase a different way *(Nan's notebook)*.

📖 Read from a piece of writing that the class is currently reading. Emphasize the singular possessive nouns.

TEACH

Have a volunteer read aloud the first paragraph, the examples sentences, and the second paragraph. Give examples of other sentences with possessives such as *Bob's shoes were under the table.* Ask students to tell which words are singular possessives.

Ask volunteers to read aloud the rest of the page. Write *the boss's pen* on the board. Circle the *'s*. Point out that words that end in *ss* are no different from any other singular noun and that *'s* is added to show ownership by a single person.

Point out that the word *possession* means "ownership." Stress that singular possessive nouns are nouns that show that a person, place, or thing belongs to just one person.

PRACTICE

EXERCISE 1
Remind students that the possessive form of a singular noun is formed by adding *-'s* to the noun. Ask volunteers to write their answers on the board and then say a sentence using the possessive form of the word.

EXERCISE 2
Make sure students understand that each answer is not a complete sentence but is the possessive noun and the item that is owned. Read the example. Then encourage students to complete the exercise independently. Invite volunteers to share their answers with the class.

EXERCISE 3
Suggest that students work with partners to rewrite each sentence, inserting the possessive noun and underlining the item possessed. Have volunteers write their sentences on the board for the class to discuss.

2.6 Singular Possessive Nouns

The **possessive form** of a noun shows possession, or ownership.

I walked to a *neighbor's* house.
Flowers grow in *Amy's* garden.

Neighbor's house means that the house belongs to a neighbor. *Amy's garden* means that the garden belongs to Amy.

To form the **singular possessive,** which is ownership by one person or thing, add an apostrophe and the letter *s (-'s)* to a singular noun.

SINGULAR	SINGULAR POSSESSIVE
friend	friend's
Pat	Pat's
bird	bird's
Mr. Storm	Mr. Storm's
Tess	Tess's

What is the correct way to show that the following things belong to Susan?

rake   **hose**   **seeds**

You are right if you said *Susan's rake, Susan's hose,* and *Susan's seeds.* By adding an apostrophe and *s (-'s)* to the noun *Susan,* you show that the rake, the hose, and the seeds belong to her.

EXERCISE 1 Write the possessive form of these singular nouns.

1. Nora — Nora's
2. fox — fox's
3. cousin — cousin's
4. Nicholas — Nicholas's
5. passenger — passenger's
6. student — student's
7. mouse — mouse's
8. book — book's

APPLY

APPLY IT NOW

Help students generate ideas by noting some possessives around the room (*the book's cover, Emma's backpack, the table's leg*). Encourage students to be creative as they use these and other possessives in their sentences. As you review their work, make sure students have formed possessive nouns correctly and that each possessive is followed by an object. Students should demonstrate the ability to create the possessive form of singular nouns.

ASSESS

Note which students had difficulty recognizing and creating the possessive form of singular nouns. Assign **Practice Book** page 27 for further practice.

WRITING CONNECTION

Use pages 258–259 of the Writing portion of the book.

TEACHING OPTIONS

Reteach

Invite students to play the Possessive Game. Ask one student to suggest a sentence that tells about an item that a classmate possesses. (*Anna's sweater is blue.*) Write the sentence on the board but omit the possessive noun. Have a volunteer fill in the possessive. Ask the student who is named in the sentence to suggest a new sentence, using another classmate's name. (*Bobby's pencil is broken.*) Write that sentence on the board and have a different volunteer fill in the possessive noun. Continue as time allows.

English-Language Learners

Students may need extra help understanding the possessive form of nouns because -'s is not used to form possessives in many languages. Have each student draw simple pictures showing objects that he or she owns. Help students write the names of the objects below each picture. Then show students how to write the possessive form of his or her name before each noun (*Kevin's shoes, Kim's hat, Madhuri's brother*).

Meeting Individual Needs

Encourage students to use possessive nouns in conversations throughout the day and to listen for them when other people speak. Have students write what they say and hear throughout the day, such as *Billy's jacket* or *Mom's car.* At the end of the day, have students share their lists.

Diagram It!

To practice these concepts in the context of diagramming, turn to Section 8.2.

Exercise 2

1. the gardener's flower
2. Mr. Shim's rake
3. the helper's watering can
4. the bee's sting
5. a butterfly's colors
6. the rabbit's carrot
7. the child's hoe
8. Gary's roses
9. Iris's eggplants
10. the girl's seeds

EXERCISE 2 Rewrite each of the following to show possession.

EXAMPLE **The farmer owns a field.**
the farmer's field

1. The gardener planted a flower.
2. Mr. Shim has a rake.
3. The helper found a watering can.
4. The bee has a sting.
5. A butterfly has colors.
6. The rabbit was given a carrot.
7. The child has a hoe.
8. Gary bought roses.
9. Iris grew eggplants.
10. The girl has some seeds.

Exercise 3

1. Peter's garden
2. grandmother's strawberries
3. Derek's vegetables
4. sun's rays
5. gardener's plants
6. uncle's tomatoes
7. brother's apples
8. James's beanstalks
9. Sarah's lettuce
10. aunt's yard
11. sister's flowers
12. Mr. Robinson's birdbath

EXERCISE 3 Complete each sentence with the possessive form of the noun in parentheses. Then tell what the owner possesses.

EXAMPLE **Rabbits ate _____ lettuce. (Mom)**
Mom's lettuce

1. We helped dig _____ garden. (Peter)
2. I picked my _____ strawberries. (grandmother)
3. _____ vegetables grew quickly. (Derek)
4. The _____ rays beat down. (sun)
5. The _____ plants grew tall. (gardener)
6. Our _____ tomatoes are turning red. (uncle)
7. My _____ apples are still green. (brother)
8. _____ beanstalks are the tallest. (James)
9. _____ lettuce was eaten by rabbits. (Sarah)
10. My _____ yard has only flowers. (aunt)
11. My _____ flowers are colorful. (sister)
12. I like _____ birdbath. (Mr. Robinson)

APPLY IT NOW

Look around you. What things do you see? Write five sentences telling who owns those things or what they belong to. Use singular possessive nouns in your sentences.

Nouns • 39

OBJECTIVES

- **To recognize the possessive form of plural nouns**
- **To create the possessive form of plural nouns**

 **DAILY Maintenance**

Assign **Practice Book** page 19, Section 2.7. After students finish,
1. Give immediate feedback.
2. Review concepts as needed.
3. Model the correct answer.

Pages 4–5 of the **Answer Key** contain tips for Daily Maintenance.

WARM-UP

Write on the board the beginning of several word equations, such as the following:

one boy + one bat =

two boys + two bats =

one plant + one leaf =

two plants + two leaves =

Write the answers on note cards *(boy's bat, boys' bats; plant's leaf, plants' leaves)*. Read aloud each equation and invite a student to choose a card from the pile and match it to the correct equation. Have students identify the words in each equation that show possession. Ask students to tell which words are singular and which are plural and to explain how they know.

Read from a piece of writing that the class is currently reading. Emphasize the plural possessives.

TEACH

Have a volunteer read aloud the first paragraph and the examples. Ask if one girl or more than one girl has a bicycle *(more than one)*. Ask students if one baby or more than one baby has toys *(more than one)*. Have volunteers read aloud the rest of the page.

Tell students that to make a plural noun possessive an apostrophe is added. Explain that if a plural noun does not end in an *s* as in words like *children* and *men*, an apostrophe and the letter *s* are added to form the plural possessive.

PRACTICE

EXERCISE 1
Point out that forming plural possessives starts with changing singular nouns to plural nouns. Have students work with partners to complete the chart. Encourage partners to help each other to form the correct plurals and plural possessives. Then discuss the answers with the class.

EXERCISE 2
Ask students what they notice about the words that are underlined. *(They end in* s.*)* Encourage students to explain how to make the possessive form of plural nouns. Have partners check each other's work.

EXERCISE 3
Ask volunteers to read aloud each item and the answer options. After each answer, have volunteers explain why it is or is not correct.

2.7 Plural Possessive Nouns

A **plural possessive** shows that more than one person owns something. To form the plural possessive of most nouns, first make the singular noun plural. Then add an apostrophe after the *s* of the plural form.

Mom washed the *girls' bicycles.*
Dad tripped over the *babies' toys.*

Girls' bicycles means that two or more girls own two or more bicycles. *Babies' toys* means that the toys belong to more than one baby.

SINGULAR	PLURAL	PLURAL POSSESSIVE
girl	girls	girls'
baby	babies	babies'
Smith	Smiths	Smiths'

Which is the plural possessive of *sister*?

My _____ bedroom is full of toys.

A sister

B sister's

C sisters'

You are right if you said that C is the plural possessive. When an apostrophe is added to the word *sisters*, it means the bedroom belongs to two or more sisters.

EXERCISE 1 Complete the chart with the plural form and the plural possessive form of each noun.

	Singular	Plural	Plural Possessive	
1.	boy	boys	boys'	pets
2.	Mann	Manns	Manns'	homes
3.	student	students	students'	books
4.	gerbil	gerbils	gerbils'	wheel
5.	puppy	puppies	puppies'	food
6.	fox	foxes	foxes'	cage

EXERCISE 4

Point out that the answers are not complete sentences. Have volunteers write their answers on the board. Ask students to explain why the answer is correct or how to correct it if it is not.

APPLY

APPLY IT NOW

Brainstorm ideas about each word to help students with their sentences. Check that each student has not only made each noun plural but has also used the apostrophe correctly to show the plural possessive form *(astronauts',* *bees', swimmers', ladies')*. Students should demonstrate the ability to create the possessive form of plural nouns.

ASSESS

Note which students had difficulty recognizing and creating the possessive form of plural nouns. Assign **Practice Book** page 28 for further practice.

WRITING CONNECTION
Use pages 260–261 of the Writing portion of the book.

Reteach
Create a display of classroom objects. Arrange the objects in groups of one and in groups of many *(one crayon, many crayons; one book, many books; one eraser, many erasers)*. Encourage students to create sentences that tell about each group, using a possessive noun in each sentence. Ask volunteers to write the possessive nouns on the board. Check that the singular and plural forms are written correctly.

desk's leg   desks' legs

Curriculum Connections
Display photographs depicting more than one subject, such as several animals, athletes, families, or cars. Have students name the plural subjects. Write the word for each subject on a card to post with the appropriate picture. Ask students to suggest possessives based on the images in the picture. Direct students to write the plural possessives *(the cars' big tires, the cars' bold colors)*.

Diagram It!
To practice these concepts in the context of diagramming, turn to Section 8.2.

Exercise 2
1. fans'
2. players'
3. runners'
4. vendors'
5. cheerleaders'
6. bands'
7. drummers'
8. singers'

EXERCISE 2 Write the possessive form of each underlined plural noun.

1. The <u>fans</u> applause was loud.
2. The <u>players</u> uniforms were blue and gold.
3. The <u>runners</u> top speeds were amazing.
4. The <u>vendors</u> hot dogs were very good.
5. The <u>cheerleaders</u> voices could be heard throughout the gym.
6. All the marching <u>bands</u> performances were great.
7. The <u>drummers</u> drums were really huge!
8. The <u>singers</u> voices rang out clear and strong.

EXERCISE 3 Choose the correct meaning of each possessive phrase.

1. the girl's CDs
   a. One girl has one CD.
   b. More than one girl has some CDs.
   c. One girl has some CDs.

2. the boys' bikes
   a. Two or more boys have two or more bikes.
   b. One boy has many bikes.
   c. Two boys have the same bike.

Exercise 4
1. George's cat
2. the sisters' dog
3. the parakeets' cage
4. the dogs' bones
5. Samantha's ferrets
6. the puppies' bed

EXERCISE 4 Rewrite each of the following to show possession.

EXAMPLE   The dogs have toys.
                    the dogs' toys

1. George has a cat.
2. The two sisters have a dog.
3. The parakeets have a big cage.
4. The dogs have bones.
5. Samantha has three ferrets.
6. The puppies have a bed.

APPLY IT NOW
Write the plural possessive forms of the following nouns. Then use each possessive in a sentence.
astronaut   bee
swimmer   lady

Nouns • 41

OBJECTIVE

- **To identify, form, and use irregular plural possessive nouns**

 **Maintenance**

Assign **Practice Book** page 19, Section 2.8. After students finish,
1. Give immediate feedback.
2. Review concepts as needed.
3. Model the correct answer.

Pages 4–5 of the **Answer Key** contain tips for Daily Maintenance.

WARM-UP

Write the following phrases on the board:

the toys that belong to the children

the nest that belongs to the geese

Have volunteers rewrite the phrases in a different way *(the children's toys, the geese's nest).* Ask students to explain why they rewrote the phrases the way they did. Ask what the *'s* means. *(It shows possession or ownership.)* Then ask students to suggest phrases like the ones on the board, using words with other irregular plurals. Have students trade phrases with a partner and rewrite the words that show possession.

📖 Read from a piece of writing that the class is currently reading. Emphasize the irregular plural possessive nouns.

TEACH

Have a volunteer read aloud the first two paragraphs and the chart. Refer students back to the chart and review each word and its different forms. Discuss what makes each word different in the plural form. Point out that the plural possessive of an irregular

noun is formed the same way that the singular possessive is formed in most words.

Invite a volunteer to read aloud the rest of the page. Write on the board additional sentences using irregular plurals and have students supply the plural possessive to complete each sentence.

PRACTICE

EXERCISE 1

Explain that students need to do two things to complete this exercise—form the plural of each noun and form the possessive of the plural.

EXERCISE 2

Point out that some words are regular plurals and some are irregular. Create on the board a chart with the headings *Regular Plurals* and *Irregular Plurals*. Have volunteers write their answers in the correct columns.

EXERCISE 3

Create on the board a chart with the headings *Singular, Singular Possessive,* and *Plural Possessive.* Ask volunteers to write their answers in the correct columns.

2.8 Irregular Plural Possessive Nouns

The plural forms of irregular nouns do not end in *s.* Words such as *men, women,* and *children* are irregular plurals.

To form the plural possessive of irregular nouns, add an apostrophe and the letter *s (-'s)* to the plural form of the word.

SINGULAR	PLURAL	PLURAL POSSESSIVE
ox	oxen	oxen's
mouse	mice	mice's
man	men	men's
goose	geese	geese's
woman	women	women's

In the sentence below, which is the correct way to show that the children have warm mittens?

The _____ mittens are warm.

A children

B childrens'

C children's

You are right if you said that C is the answer. When an *-'s* is added to the word *children,* the word means that the mittens belong to the children.

EXERCISE 1 Complete the chart with the plural form and the plural possessive form of each noun.

Singular	Plural	Plural Possessive
1. mouse	_____	_____ cheese
2. tooth	_____	_____ enamel
3. ox	_____	_____ tails
4. deer	_____	_____ tracks
5. policewoman	_____	_____ uniforms

Exercise 1
1. mice, mice's
2. teeth, teeth's
3. oxen, oxen's
4. deer, deer's
5. policewomen, policewomen's

APPLY

APPLY IT NOW

List various areas of a department store on the board. Point out that many of the terms are irregular possessive plurals, such as *women's, men's,* and *children's.* Encourage students to include these areas on their maps. Have partners trade maps to check for correct plural possessive nouns. Students should demonstrate the ability to identify, form, and use irregular plural possessive nouns.

TechTip Encourage students to use drawing tools and text boxes, as well as clip art to complete their maps.

ASSESS

Note which students had difficulty identifying, forming, and using irregular plural possessive nouns. Assign **Practice Book** page 29 for further practice.

WRITING CONNECTION

Use pages 262–263 of the Writing portion of the book.

TEACHING OPTIONS

Reteach

Create a grid with nine squares (three columns, three rows). Distribute a copy to each student. Have students suggest irregular plurals and their possessive forms for you to write on the board. Tell students to fill in each square on their grids with one of the words from the board, either an irregular plural or an irregular plural possessive. Explain that you will call out a singular word and also the term *plural* or *plural possessive.* Tell students to check their cards for that word in the form you called. If the word is on a grid, the student should cover it with a scrap of paper. Explain that the first person to cover three spaces in a row, either up, down, across, or diagonally, is the winner.

Meeting Individual Needs

Extra Support Create several word webs, each with a different irregular plural possessive in the center rectangle. Show things each could "own" in the outer circles. Invite students to use the irregular plural possessives and the ideas in the outer circles to make sentences.

Meeting Individual Needs

Interpersonal Explain that most examples using possessive nouns use concrete, material possessions. Point out that intangible things, such as kindness, caring, honesty, respect, and generosity, can also be possessed. Have students write sentences using plural possessives with good character traits. Ask volunteers to share their sentences with the class.

Diagram It!

To practice these concepts in the context of diagramming, turn to Section 8.2.

Exercise 2

1. women's purses
2. babies' diapers
3. children's backpacks
4. campers' tents
5. scarves from sheep's wool
6. men's suits
7. jackets filled with geese's feathers
8. boys' shoes
9. girls' hats
10. ladies' dresses
11. cooks' pots
12. hikers' boots

EXERCISE 2 Write each group of words. Insert missing apostrophes to show plural possession. Be careful! Some words are regular plurals, and some words are irregular plurals.

1. womens purses
2. babies diapers
3. childrens backpacks
4. campers tents
5. scarves from sheeps wool
6. mens suits
7. jackets filled with geeses feathers
8. boys shoes
9. girls hats
10. ladies dresses
11. cooks pots
12. hikers boots

Exercise 3

1. friend's, friends'
2. child's, children's
3. lady's, ladies'
4. sheep's, sheep's
5. skater's, skaters'
6. snowman's, snowmen's
7. country's, countries'
8. giraffe's, giraffes'
9. goose's, geese's
10. coach's, coaches'
11. rose's, roses'
12. fox's, foxes'
13. woman's, women's
14. lion's, lions'

EXERCISE 3 Write the singular possessive and plural possessive form of each noun.

| EXAMPLE | bunny | bunny's | bunnies' |

1. friend
2. child
3. lady
4. sheep
5. skater
6. snowman
7. country
8. giraffe
9. goose
10. coach
11. rose
12. fox
13. woman
14. lion

Giraffe

APPLY IT NOW

Draw a map of one floor of a department store. Put labels on the different sections. Use apostrophes in your labels. Use the phrases in Exercise 2 to help you.

Tech Tip Draw your map using an online drawing tool.

Nouns • 43

2.9 Collective Nouns

OBJECTIVE
- **To identify and use collective nouns**

 **DAILY Maintenance**

Assign **Practice Book** page 19, Section 2.9. After students finish,
1. Give immediate feedback.
2. Review concepts as needed.
3. Model the correct answer.

Pages 4–5 of the **Answer Key** contain tips for Daily Maintenance.

WARM-UP

Have students work in small groups to write a list of words that name groups of things *(a deck of cards, a bunch of grapes, a group of students, a flock of birds).* Give students three minutes to put together the list. When time is up, ask students to use two of the words to write complete sentences. Have groups share their lists and sentences with the class.

📖 Read from a piece of writing that the class is currently reading. Emphasize the singular nouns and plural nouns.

TEACH

Write the following sentence on the board:

The class is learning how to draw.

Ask students to identify the noun. Discuss the noun *class* and its definition. Write on the board the definition students give. Ask if the word *class* describes one person or more than one person *(more than one).* Reinforce that *class* describes a group students in a school. Have students give additional examples of similar words they listed in the Warm-Up and write them on the board.
Have a volunteer read aloud the first two paragraphs and the list

of collective nouns. Discuss how some of the words would be used in sentences. *(A swarm of bees buzzes around the tree. A crowd of people waits to get into the movie.)*
Explain that collective nouns are usually singular. Point out that although a collective noun may represent a group of things, it is treated as one thing or unit. Invite a volunteer to read aloud the rest of the page.

PRACTICE

EXERCISE 1
Tell students to look for words that name more than one person, place, or thing.

EXERCISE 2
Write the columns on the board and invite volunteers to draw lines from the collective nouns in Column A to the matching plural nouns in Column B.

EXERCISE 3
Explain that more than one collective noun can make sense in some sentences. Have students work with partners to complete the exercise, supplying the collective noun they think is best in each sentence. Invite volunteers to read aloud the sentences and explain their choices.

2.9 Collective Nouns

A noun that names a group of things or people is called a **collective noun.**

> A *flock* of geese is flying overhead.

The collective noun *flock* names a group of animals considered together as a unit.

Here are some common collective nouns.

audience	club	flock	pack
army	crew	group	pair
band	crowd	herd	swarm
class	family	litter	team

A collective noun usually uses an action word that ends in *s* in the present tense.

> The band *plays*.
> Our club *runs*.
> The class *takes* field trips.

Which sentences include collective nouns?

> A My family is large.
> B The judge spoke loudly.
> C The crowd rushed forward.

You are right if you said sentence A and sentence C. *Family* and *crowd* are collective nouns. Each names a group. *Judge* names one person.

EXERCISE 1 Find the collective noun or nouns in each sentence.
1. The <u>class</u> wrote a play.
2. The drama <u>club</u> made some scenery.
3. A <u>flock</u> of birds was painted on a curtain.
4. A small <u>band</u> performed music before the play started.
5. A <u>pair</u> of violinists played beautifully.

APPLY IT NOW

Have volunteers read aloud their sentences. Call attention to the verbs. Then have students change the collective noun to a matching plural noun and read the sentence again, changing the verb to match the plural noun. Students should demonstrate the ability to identify and use collective nouns.

💡 **TechTip** You may wish to direct students to specific Web sites, such as science sites or other sites about animals and their habitats.

ASSESS

Note which students had difficulty identifying and using collective nouns as words that name a group of things. Assign **Practice Book** pages 30–31 for further practice.

WRITING CONNECTION

Use pages 264–265 of the Writing portion of the book.

TEACHING OPTIONS

Reteach

Assign one collective noun to each student. Ask students to work silently to create a riddle for their collective nouns.

> **I am made of flowers. A pillow would crush me. What am I?** *(flower bed)*

Invite students to share their riddles. Invite the rest of the class to figure out the answers to the riddles.

Meeting Individual Needs

Challenge Have small groups write on separate note cards collective nouns, such as *team, flock, band, class, family, litter, swarm, herd, army,* and *pair*. Have students place the cards facedown in a pile. Direct one student to choose a card and say a sentence, omitting the collective noun. (*A _____ of cattle was in the pasture.*) Challenge the other group members to guess what the word is *(herd)*. Have the group to continue until each student has taken at least one turn.

Cooperative Learning

Have small groups brainstorm collective nouns, such as *a school of fish, an army of ants,* and *a team of horses.* Have each student choose one collective noun, write a sentence using it, and make an illustration for a book. Have students put the book together and plan and illustrate a book cover. You may wish to suggest they draw an army of ants with the ants in camouflage uniforms or a school of fish sitting behind desks in a classroom. Have students share their completed books with the class. Display the books in a classroom reading corner or on a bulletin board.

---

6. In the play the <u>family</u> was lost in the woods.
7. A <u>pack</u> of wolves howled in the distance.
8. The <u>crew</u> was playing a recording of howls.
9. At the end a <u>group</u> of scouts led the <u>family</u> to safety.
10. What a great job the <u>cast</u> did!
11. The <u>audience</u> stood and applauded.
12. A <u>crowd</u> gathered at the stage door entrance.

EXERCISE 2 Match each collective noun in Column A with a plural noun in Column B.

Column A		Column B
1. band	c	a. members
2. class	e	b. soldiers
3. club	a	c. musicians
4. army	b	d. athletes
5. team	d	e. students

EXERCISE 3 Complete each sentence with a collective noun. Use the list on page 44.

1. The _____ of elephants roamed on the African plain.
2. The _____ played my favorite songs at the concert.
3. Our soccer _____ won its first game.
4. The _____ of horses pulled the wagon across the prairie.
5. A _____ of birds was traveling south for the winter.
6. A _____ of children wrote about animals.
7. The fourth-grade _____ read the book it wrote.
8. The _____ of bees was protecting its hive.
9. The _____ of the boat rowed together.
10. We chose one kitten from the _____.
11. Our math _____ meets once a week
12. A _____ of raccoons is living under the porch.

Exercise 3
Answers will vary.
Possible answers:
1. herd, pack
2. band
3. team, club
4. pair, team
5. flock, family
6. group, pair, team
7. class
8. swarm
9. crew
10. litter
11. club, class
12. family, pack, group

APPLY IT NOW

Choose three collective nouns from page 44 and write a sentence for each.
Example: The team won the race.

 Tech Tip With an adult, find two more collective nouns online.

OBJECTIVE

- To recognize when a noun is used as the subject of a sentence

 **Maintenance**

Assign **Practice Book** page 20, Section 2.10. After students finish,
1. Give immediate feedback.
2. Review concepts as needed.
3. Model the correct answer.

Pages 4–5 of the **Answer Key** contain tips for Daily Maintenance.

WARM-UP

Write on note cards nouns that can be used as subjects, such as *Brianna, The bear, My doctor, My dad,* and *People.* Then write on strips sentence endings that can be combined with the subjects to make complete sentences, such as *is a great cook, checked my sore throat, plays baseball, lives in a cave, like to draw.* Place the nouns facedown on a table and the sentence endings faceup. Have students choose a card with a noun and find a sentence ending to form a complete sentence. Have volunteers read aloud the complete sentences. Discuss how students decided which sentence ending to use.

📖 Read from a piece of writing that the class is currently reading. Emphasize the nouns as subjects.

TEACH

Write on the board some of the sentences from the Warm-Up. Use the sentences to review subjects and predicates. Remind students that the subject of a sentence is the person, place, or thing that the sentence is about. Explain that the predicate tells what the subject is or does.

Invite a volunteer to read aloud the first two paragraphs. Ask students to suggest other nouns that might be used as subjects in each of the three example sentences.

Have volunteers read aloud the rest of the page. Ask volunteers to give examples of simple sentences and identify the subject of each sentence.

PRACTICE

EXERCISE 1

Have students read aloud their completed sentences and tell how they decided on the subject.

EXERCISE 2

Point out that students may find more than one noun in each sentence but that only one noun serves as the subject. Encourage students to explain how they identified the subjects.

2.10 Nouns as Subjects

A noun may be used as the **subject** of a sentence. The subject tells what the sentence is about. It tells who or what does something.

Artists **draw and paint pictures.**
Paints **can be messy.**
Zoe **is an artist.**

In the first sentence, *artists* is a noun that tells who draws and paints. In the second sentence, *paints* is a noun that tells what can be messy. In the third sentence, *Zoe* is a noun that tells who is an artist.

Which noun is the subject in this sentence?

Zack takes photos.

You are right if you said that *Zack* is the subject of the sentence. *Zack* tells who takes photos. *Photos* is a noun, but it is not the subject.

What noun is the subject in this sentence?

His photos include animals.

You are right if you said *photos. Photos* tells what includes animals. *Animals* is a noun, but it is not the subject of this sentence.

EXERCISE 1 Complete each sentence with a subject. Use these nouns.

activity	class	markers	Mrs. Jones	students

1. The ___class___ has art every week.
2. ___Mrs. Jones___ teaches art.
3. Some ___students___ are very good artists.
4. Our favorite ___activity___ is painting.
5. The ___markers___ come in many bright colors.

46 • Section 2.10

EXERCISES 3 & 4

Have students complete the exercise with a partner. Ask students to share their sentences.

APPLY

APPLY IT NOW

Create a chart on the board with four columns, one for each topic. Brainstorm specific nouns for each topic and list them on the chart. Suggest that students use these nouns or nouns of their own. Students should demonstrate the ability to recognize nouns as subjects.

ASSESS

Note which students had difficulty recognizing nouns used as subjects. Assign **Practice Book** page 32 for further practice.

WRITING CONNECTION

Use pages 266–267 of the Writing portion of the book.

TEACHING OPTIONS

Reteach

Read aloud a story that you have already read with the class. Then go back and reread some of the sentences one by one. Ask students to identify the nouns that are subjects in each sentence. Then write on the board a few additional sentences from the story. Ask volunteers to underline the nouns as subjects in each sentence. Have students tell whether each noun is singular, plural, or collective.

Meeting Individual Needs

Interpersonal Have partners choose a topic and write five sentences about it, using nouns as subjects. Have partners trade their sentences with another pair of students. Ask each pair to underline the nouns as subjects in each sentence. Allow time for students to discuss their responses.

Curriculum Connection

Invite students to write about a topic that interests them in another subject area, such as science or social studies. Tell them to write the main idea first and then to write sentences about the topic. Ask students to review their work and to circle the subject in each sentence. You may wish to have students create information posters to go with their writing. Display the posters and writing around the room for other students to enjoy.

Diagram It!

To practice these concepts in the context of diagramming, turn to Section 8.1.

EXERCISE 2 Find the subject in each sentence. Ask *who* or *what* is doing the action to help you.

1. The <u>teacher</u> announced the start of the art class.
2. <u>Sam</u> looked happy.
3. <u>Anita</u> traced shapes on paper.
4. Many <u>children</u> used easels to support their drawing pads.
5. One unsteady <u>easel</u> fell over.
6. <u>Paint</u> spilled on the floor.
7. <u>Towels</u> soaked up the mess.
8. <u>Clothespins</u> hung the paintings to dry.
9. The <u>children</u> later displayed the paintings on the bulletin board.

Exercise 3
Answers will vary. Each noun should match the content or idea of the sentence.

EXERCISE 3 Complete each sentence with a noun. You may use other words like *a* or *the*.

1. _____ took us to the art museum.
2. _____ hung on the walls.
3. _____ told us about some of the paintings.
4. _____ had a chance to draw pictures.
5. _____ gave us some notebooks and pencils.
6. _____ did a lovely drawing of a tree in pencil.
7. _____ helped us with our drawings.
8. _____ is a good artist.
9. _____ liked my drawing.
10. _____ is my favorite thing to draw.

Exercise 4
Answers will vary.

EXERCISE 4 Write sentences using each noun as the subject.

1. paints
2. brushes
3. friend

APPLY IT NOW

Write a sentence for each topic below. Use a noun as the subject of each sentence. Underline the subject.
1. a game to play
2. a movie to see
3. what to eat for lunch
4. a favorite color

Nouns • 47

OBJECTIVE

- To identify words that can be used as both nouns *and* verbs

 **Maintenance**

Assign **Practice Book** page 20, Section 2.11. After students finish,
1. Give immediate feedback.
2. Review concepts as needed.
3. Model the correct answer.

Pages 4–5 of the **Answer Key** contain tips for Daily Maintenance.

WARM-UP

Write on note cards sentences with words that can be used as both nouns *and* verbs. Underline in each sentence the word that can be used as a noun *and* a verb. Have partners choose a card and read it aloud and write another sentence using the underlined word in a different way. Use the following sentences as an example:

I like to <u>watch</u> sports.

I wear my <u>watch</u> on my right wrist.

📖 Read from a piece of writing that the class is currently reading. Emphasize the words that can be used as both nouns *and* as verbs.

TEACH

Write the following on the board:

I have a tomato plant.

I always plant a garden.

Ask if the word *plant* is used as a noun or as a verb *(It is a noun in the first sentence. It is the subject of the sentence. It is a verb in the second sentence. It tells the action done by the subject.)*
Have volunteers read aloud the text. Ask students to name other words that can be used as both nouns and verbs. List them on the board. Ask students to suggest

sentences using the words. Have volunteers tell if each word is being used as a noun or as a verb. If the word is being used as a noun, ask a volunteer to use the word as a verb. If the word is being used as a verb, have another student use it as a noun.

PRACTICE

EXERCISE 1
When students have completed the exercise, ask them to share their answers with the class. Discuss the clues that helped students identify each underlined word as a noun or as a verb.

EXERCISE 2
Tell students that they will use each word twice—once as a noun and once as a verb. Have students read aloud the sentences and tell how the word is used.

EXERCISE 3
Go over the example with the class. Suggest that students first write a sentence using each word as a verb and then as a noun.

2.11 Words Used as Nouns *and* as Verbs

Many words can be used both as nouns and as verbs. Check closely how a word is used in a specific sentence.

The word *walk,* for example, can be used as a noun or as an action word, a verb.

> **I *walk* to the store.**
> **Let's go for a *walk*.**

In the first sentence, *walk* is used as a verb. It shows action. In the second sentence, *walk* is used as a noun. It is a thing.

Tell how the word *talk* is used in these sentences. In which sentence is it a verb? In which sentence is it a noun?

> **A Can we have a talk?**
> **B We talk on the phone often.**

You are right if you said *talk* is used as a noun in sentence A and as a verb in sentence B. In the first sentence, *talk* is a thing. In the second sentence, *talk* is an action.

The word *sails* is another word that can be used as a noun or as a verb. Can you tell which it is in these sentences?

> **A My uncle sails in the navy.**
> **B The sails filled with air.**

You are right if you said *sails* is used as a verb in sentence A and as a noun in sentence B.

EXERCISE 1 Tell whether the underlined word in each sentence is used as a noun or as a verb.

verb **1.** Will you <u>watch</u> the baby?
noun **2.** The <u>watch</u> has a leather band.
verb **3.** Birds <u>fight</u> over a worm.
noun **4.** The children had a <u>fight</u> over the game.
verb **5.** Joggers <u>run</u> every day.

APPLY

APPLY IT NOW

Suggest that students look up the words in a dictionary to check their usage. Have students read aloud their sentences and identify the word and its usage. Students should demonstrate the ability to identify words that can be used as both nouns and verbs.

ASSESS

Note which students had difficulty distinguishing between the same word used as a noun and as a verb. Assign **Practice Book** page 33 for further practice.

> ### WRITING CONNECTION
> Use pages 268–269 of the Writing portion of the book.

---

noun **6.** He went for a <u>run</u>.

noun **7.** The class is putting on a <u>play</u>.

verb **8.** Some students <u>play</u> astronauts.

verb **9.** Please <u>ring</u> the doorbell.

noun **10.** Aunt Judy's <u>ring</u> has four rubies.

noun **11.** This letter needs a <u>stamp</u>.

verb **12.** Don't <u>stamp</u> your feet in the house.

EXERCISE 2 Complete each sentence with one of these words. Tell whether the word is used as a noun or as a verb.

blossoms	help	plant	practice	step

1. We <u>practice</u> volleyball after school. verb

2. Our soccer <u>practice</u> is on Tuesday. noun

3. I can <u>help</u> you with the math homework. verb

4. Thank your for your <u>help</u> yesterday. noun

5. That's a pretty <u>plant</u> in that pot. noun

6. Will you <u>plant</u> those seeds in the garden? verb

7. That plant <u>blossoms</u> once a year. verb

8. The plants have lovely red <u>blossoms</u>. noun

9. There is a toy on the <u>step</u>. noun

10. Don't <u>step</u> on the cat's tail. verb

Exercise 3

Sentences will vary. Make sure that each word has been used as both a noun and as a verb and that the usage is correct. Possible sentences:

1. Noun: I am going to be in the school play.
   Verb: I often play outside on a rainy day.

2. Noun: I got a cut on my finger.
   Verb: I cut my finger.

3. Noun: The teacher made a copy of the map.
   Verb: I can copy sentences from my textbook.

4. Noun: My family took a long drive in the country.
   Verb: My aunt will drive me to school.

EXERCISE 3 Write sentences using each word as a noun and as a verb. Tell how you used the word in each sentence.

EXAMPLE **A *fly* buzzed around my head.** (noun)
Airplanes *fly* at hundreds of miles per hour. (verb)

1. play

2. cut

3. copy

4. drive

APPLY IT NOW

Think of other words that can be used as nouns and as verbs. Choose a word that hasn't been used in Exercise 1, 2, or 3. Write two sentences, one using the word as a noun and one using it as a verb.

Nouns • 49

Noun Review

ASSESS

Use the Noun Review as homework, as a practice test, or as an informal assessment. Following are some options for use.

Homework

You may wish to assign one group the odd items and another group the even items. When you next meet, review the correct answers as a group. Be sure to model how to arrive at the correct answer.

Practice Test

Use the Noun Review as a diagnostic tool. Assign the entire review or just specific sections. After students have finished, identify which concepts require more attention. Reteach concepts as necessary.

Noun Review

2.1 Tell what the nouns are in each sentence. The number of nouns in each sentence is in parentheses.

1. Luke and his friends went to the big game at City Stadium. (4)
2. Crowds filled the stadium, and soon the two teams took the field. (4)
3. Luke sat next to his dad. (2)
4. Mike ate peanuts during the game. (3)
5. Our team won the game, and the fans cheered. (3)

2.2 Tell what the nouns are in each sentence. Then tell whether each is a common noun or a proper noun. The number of nouns in each sentence is in parentheses.

6. My older sister Amy lives in Philadelphia. (3)
7. My family sometimes goes to the city. (2)
8. My brother likes to visit the museum to see the dinosaurs. (3)
9. My mom likes to go to Independence Hall and other historic places. (3)
10. There is an old flag in the house where Betsy Ross lived. (3)

2.3 Write the plural for each singular noun.

11. dish
12. cave
13. song
14. class
15. speech

2.4 Complete each sentence with the plural of the noun in parentheses.

16. My grandmother has several _____. (hobby)
17. She volunteers at a school on _____. (Thursday)
18. She brings _____ to the food pantry. (grocery)
19. She also bakes pies with _____. (strawberry)

2.5 Complete each sentence with the singular or plural of the underlined noun.

20. Max caught one mouse, but Jenny caught six _____.
21. The man saw four other _____ waiting outside.
22. Yuan can balance on one foot as well as he can balance on both _____.
23. Mom said that geese can be mean, so I ran when I saw a _____.

2.2

Common nouns are underlined once. Proper nouns are underlined twice.

2.3
11. dishes
12. caves
13. songs
14. classes
15. speeches

2.4
16. hobbies
17. Thursdays
18. groceries
19. strawberries

2.5
20. mice
21. men
22. feet
23. goose

Informal Assessment

Use the review as preparation for the formal assessment. Count the review as a portion of the grade. Have students work to find the correct answers and use their corrected review as a study guide for the formal assessment.

WRITING CONNECTION

Use pages 270–271 of the Writing portion of the book.

TEACHING OPTIONS

Putting It All Together

Write the following on the board:

Common and Proper Nouns

Singular and Plural Nouns

Irregular Plural Nouns

Singular Possessive Nouns

Plural Possessive Nouns

Irregular Plural Possessive Nouns

Collective Nouns

Nouns as Subjects

Words Used as Nouns *and* as Verbs

Direct students to make a chart with the headings for each type of noun. Distribute to each student a copy of an age-appropriate magazine or newspaper. Have students read an article and then reread the article to search for the kinds of nouns listed on the board. Ask students to highlight each noun. Have students write under the correct heading on their charts each noun from the article. Discuss how students categorized each noun.

2.6
24. neighborhood's
25. friend's
26. Henry's
27. newpaper's

2.7
28. the girls' cleats
29. the players' mitts
30. the actors' scripts
31. the boys' CDs
32. the babies' bottles

2.8
33. men's
34. mice's
35. children's
36. sheep's
37. women's

2.11
48. verb
49. noun
50. noun
51. verb
52. verb
53. noun

2.6 Change the underlined noun to a singular possessive noun.

24. Henry helped organize his <u>neighborhood</u> annual party.
25. He borrowed his <u>friend</u> camera to take photos.
26. <u>Henry</u> sister Gloria painted faces all afternoon.
27. Henry got the photos published in the <u>newspaper</u>.

2.7 Rewrite each group of words to show plural possession.

28. the cleats of the girls
29. the mitts of the players
30. the scripts of the actors
31. the CDs of the boys
32. the bottles of the babies

2.8 Complete each of the following with the plural possessive form of the noun in parentheses.

33. _____ shorts (men)
34. _____ cage (mice)
35. _____ room (child)
36. _____ wool (sheep)
37. _____ blouses (women)

2.9 Find the collective noun in each sentence.

38. My <u>family</u> went to the circus.

39. A magician performed for the <u>crowd</u>.
40. A <u>band</u> played silly songs.
41. We laughed at a <u>pair</u> of jugglers.
42. Later, a <u>group</u> of acrobats performed.

2.10 Find the subject in each sentence.

43. My <u>cousin</u> rides a streetcar to work.
44. <u>Streetcars</u> were more common before World War II.
45. <u>San Francisco</u> has several old streetcars in use.
46. Many <u>tourists</u> ride them.
47. <u>Downtown</u> is a popular destination.

2.11 Tell whether the underlined word in each sentence is used as a noun or as a verb.

48. We <u>head</u> for the hills.
49. My <u>head</u> is too big for this hat.
50. Dion gave me funny <u>looks</u>.
51. The dog <u>looks</u> at his leash.
52. Why don't you <u>sketch</u> that apple?
53. Gina gave me a <u>sketch</u> of a boat.

 Tech Tip Go to www.voyagesinenglish.com for more activities.

Nouns • 51

Tech Tip Encourage students to further review nouns, using the additional practice and games at www.voyagesinenglish.com.

ASSESS

Encourage students to read the paragraph carefully before answering the questions. If they have difficulty with any question, have students refer to the section that teaches the skill. This activity can be completed individually, in small groups, or as a whole class.

After you have reviewed nouns, administer the Section 2

Assessment on pages 5–8 in the **Assessment Book,** or create a customized test with the optional **Test Generator CD.**

You may also wish to administer the Sections 1–2 Summative Assessment on pages 29–30 of the **Assessment Book.** This test is also available on the optional **Test Generator CD.**

WRITING CONNECTION

Use pages 272–273 of the Writing portion of the book.

Students can complete a formal how-to article using the Writer's Workshop on pages 274–285.

ANSWERS

1. aunt
2. common nouns: grandma, farm; proper nouns: Aunt Josie, Uncle Bueno
3. cows
4. collective noun
5. plural possessive; the eggs of the chickens
6. hives
7. herd, family
8. dairy
9. puppy
10. Dixie's, singular

Noun Challenge

Read the paragraph and answer the questions.

1. Our aunt owns a farm. 2. Aunt Josie, Uncle Bueno, and my grandma live and work on the farm. 3. The farm has many cows. 4. It also has a flock of chickens. 5. The chickens' eggs are big and brown. 6. Grandma has a hive of bees. 7. There's grass for the herd of cows, and there's a vegetable garden for the family. 8. Aunt Josie sells the cows' milk to dairies. 9. The milk is used to make butter and different kinds of cheeses. 10. On our last visit, Dixie, Aunt Josie's pet dog, was tending six fat puppies. 11. I played with Dixie's puppies all afternoon. 12. There's always something interesting for me to see and do on the farm.

1. In sentence 1 which noun is the subject?
2. In sentence 2 find two common nouns and two proper nouns.
3. In sentence 3 find the plural noun.
4. In sentence 4 what kind of noun is *flock*?
5. In sentence 5 what kind of plural is *chickens'*? What does *chickens' eggs* mean in the sentence?
6. In sentence 6 how do you form the plural of *hive*?
7. In sentence 7 what are the collective nouns?
8. In sentence 8 what is the singular form of *dairies*?
9. In sentence 10 what is the singular form of *puppies*?
10. In sentence 11 what is the possessive noun? Is it singular or plural?

Pronouns

SECTION FOCUS
- **Pronouns**
- **Subject pronouns**
- **Object pronouns**
- **Possessive pronouns**
- **Possessive adjectives**
- **Agreement of pronouns and verbs**
- **I** and **Me**
- **Compound subjects and objects**

SUPPORT MATERIALS

Practice Book
Daily Maintenance, pages 34–36
Grammar, pages 37–46

Assessment Book
Section 3 Assessment, pages 9–10

Test Generator CD

Writing Chapter 3, Descriptions

Customizable Lesson Plans
www.voyagesinenglish.com

CONNECT WITH LITERATURE

📖 Consider using the following titles throughout the section to illustrate the grammar concept:

Did I Ever Tell You How Lucky You Are? by Dr. Seuss
Mine, All Mine! by Ruth Heller
You and Me by Martine Kindermans

GRAMMAR FOR GROWN-UPS

Understanding Pronouns

Pronouns are words used in place of nouns. The word, phrase, or clause to which a personal pronoun refers is its **antecedent.** Some pronouns have the qualities of person, gender, and number.

First person pronouns identify the speaker.

> *I am alive. We are here.*

Second person pronouns identify the person spoken to.

> *You are there.*

Third person pronouns identify the person or thing spoken about. Third person singular pronouns reflect gender. These pronouns are masculine, feminine, or neuter. A pronoun agrees with its antecedent in person and number and, where applicable, in gender.

> *He is my favorite cousin.*

A **subject pronoun** must always agree with its verb.

> *She cries. They cry.*

Possessive pronouns stand alone.

> *This glove is mine.*

Possessive adjectives (*my, your, his, her, its, our, their*) modify nouns.

> *Your book is on the shelf.*

Pronouns can be part of **compound subjects.**

> *She and I went to the movies.*

Pronouns can also be part of **compound objects.**

> *Please call Esa and me.*

> ❝ **The frank yet graceful use of "I" distinguishes a good writer from a bad.** ❞
>
> —Ambrose Bierce

COMMON ERRORS

Distinguishing Between *It's* and *Its*

Many developing writers confuse the contraction *it's* with the possessive adjective *its*. The following examples show how the words are misused and used correctly.

> **ERROR:** Mexico and many of it's neighbors in Central America have beautiful beaches.
> **CORRECT:** Mexico and many of its neighbors in Central America have beautiful beaches.

> **ERROR:** Its not time for supper yet.
> **CORRECT:** It's not time for supper yet.

Point out *it's* and *its* in print—on posters and in textbooks, periodicals, and novels—and explain each word's meaning and purpose. Invite students to review their writing for the use of these words and correct the usage where necessary. Suggest that students substitute *it is* for *it's* to determine if the contraction is appropriate in context.

SENTENCE DIAGRAMMING

You may wish to teach pronouns in the context of diagramming. Review these examples. Then refer to the Diagramming section or look for Diagram It! features in the Pronouns section.

My sister and I play soccer.

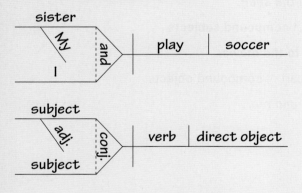

The spider bit me.

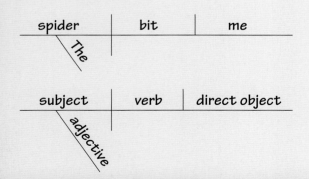

ASK AN EXPERT

Real Situations, Real Solutions

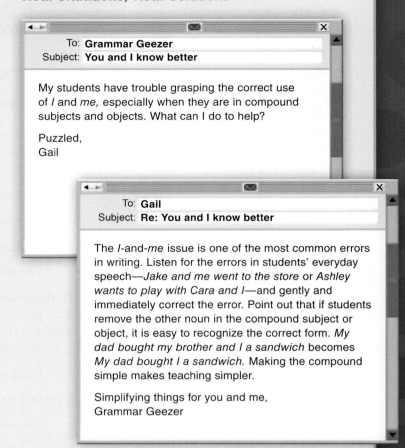

To: Grammar Geezer
Subject: You and I know better

My students have trouble grasping the correct use of *I* and *me*, especially when they are in compound subjects and objects. What can I do to help?

Puzzled,
Gail

To: Gail
Subject: Re: You and I know better

The *I*-and-*me* issue is one of the most common errors in writing. Listen for the errors in students' everyday speech—*Jake and me went to the store* or *Ashley wants to play with Cara and I*—and gently and immediately correct the error. Point out that if students remove the other noun in the compound subject or object, it is easy to recognize the correct form. *My dad bought my brother and I a sandwich* becomes *My dad bought I a sandwich.* Making the compound simple makes teaching simpler.

Simplifying things for you and me,
Grammar Geezer

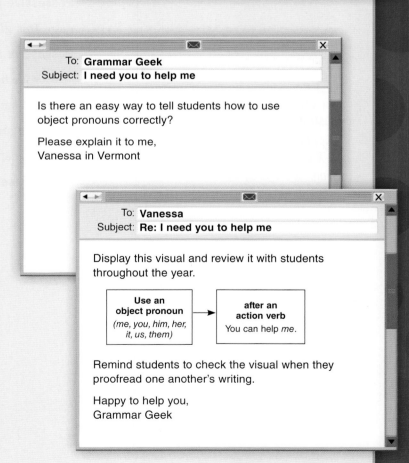

To: Grammar Geek
Subject: I need you to help me

Is there an easy way to tell students how to use object pronouns correctly?

Please explain it to me,
Vanessa in Vermont

To: Vanessa
Subject: Re: I need you to help me

Display this visual and review it with students throughout the year.

> **Use an object pronoun** (*me, you, him, her, it, us, them*) → **after an action verb** You can help *me*.

Remind students to check the visual when they proofread one another's writing.

Happy to help you,
Grammar Geek

Pronouns

3.1 Pronouns

3.2 Subject Pronouns

3.3 Object Pronouns

3.4 Possessive Pronouns

3.5 Possessive Adjectives

3.6 Agreement of Pronouns and Verbs

3.7 *I* and *Me*

3.8 Compound Subjects and Objects

Pronoun Review

Pronoun Challenge

3.1 Pronouns

OBJECTIVE

- **To identify pronouns as words that substitute for nouns**

 **Maintenance**

Assign **Practice Book** page 34, Section 3.1. After students finish,
1. Give immediate feedback.
2. Review concepts as needed.
3. Model the correct answer.

Pages 4–5 of the **Answer Key** contain tips for Daily Maintenance.

WARM-UP

Write on the board the following paragraph:

> Yesterday Dean and Dana went to the baseball game. Dean ate peanuts. Dana had a pretzel. Dean and Dana saw a fly ball coming toward Dean and Dana. Then Dana caught the ball.

Ask volunteers to change the underlined nouns in the paragraph to make it less repetitive.

📖 Read from a piece of writing that the class is currently reading. Emphasize the pronouns.

TEACH

Have a volunteer read aloud the first paragraph about pronouns. Ask students to tell why they think pronouns are used (*to make writing sound smoother, to avoid repetition*).

Have volunteers read aloud the rest of the page. Encourage students to suggest additional sentence pairs about black bears. Tell students to use nouns in the first sentence and then replace some of the nouns in the second sentence with pronouns.

PRACTICE

EXERCISE 1

Invite students to read the sentences aloud before the class completes the exercise. Remind students that pronouns generally can make sentences read more smoothly. Challenge students to work independently to find the pronouns in the sentences. Allow students to refer to the list of pronouns in the text to check their answers.

EXERCISE 2

Have students rewrite the sentences with pronouns. When students have finished, invite volunteers to write their sentences on the board. Ask students to compare their sentences. Discuss any discrepancies.

APPLY

APPLY IT NOW

List on the board some facts about bears. Encourage students to contribute what they know about bears. Suggest that students use the information for their

---

3.1 Pronouns

A **pronoun** is a word that takes the place of a noun. A **personal pronoun** refers to the person who is speaking or to the person or thing that is spoken to or about. Study the list of personal pronouns and read the sentences below them.

I	me	mine	we	us	ours
she	her	hers	they	them	theirs
he	him	his	you		yours
it		its			

Fred watches the bears.   **He watches the bears.**

In the second sentence, the pronoun *he* takes the place of the subject *Fred*.

Pronouns help avoid repeating nouns, and they make your writing sound smoother. Read this paragraph.

> **Black bears are one kind of bear. Black bears weigh about 300 pounds. The largest black bear ever sighted was in Wisconsin. The largest black bear weighed 802 pounds.**

Now read the paragraph with pronouns. What pronouns can you find? What word does each pronoun replace?

> **Black bears are one kind of bear. They weigh about 300 pounds. The largest black bear ever sighted was in Wisconsin. It weighed 802 pounds.**

Black bear cub

You are right if you said that *they* in the second sentence takes the place of *black bears* in the first sentence and that *it* in the fourth sentence takes the place of *black bear* in the third sentence.

Read the following pair of sentences. Which pronoun takes the place of the underlined word?

> **My <u>mother</u> was in Wisconsin. She saw a black bear.**

You are right if you said *she*. *She* takes the place of the noun *mother*.

sentences. Instruct students to reread their sentences, listening for the nouns and pronouns. Encourage students to determine whether the pronouns make the sentences read more smoothly. Ask volunteers to read aloud their sentences and identify each pronoun. Students should demonstrate the ability to use pronouns in sentences.

Grammar in Action. Suggest that students work with partners to find and list the pronouns in the excerpt (*his, he, it, its, him*).

ASSESS

Note which students had difficulty identifying pronouns as words that substitute for nouns. Assign **Practice Book** page 37 for further practice.

WRITING CONNECTION

Use pages 286–287 of the Writing portion of the book. Be sure to point out pronouns in the literature excerpt and the student model.

TEACHING OPTIONS

Reteach

Write on note cards sentences with nouns that can be replaced with pronouns, such as the following:

> **The boat** sailed across the water.
>
> **The boys** saw a shrimp boat.
>
> Jeffrey saw **Bill and Mike** at the beach.
>
> Kaleigh and Kenna were with **the boys**.
>
> We built a sandcastle but the waves washed **the sandcastle** away.

Have students choose a note card and replace the underlined word or words with the appropriate pronoun.

Meeting Individual Needs

Extra Support Write on the board the list of personal pronouns from page 54. Walk around the room and pick up items that belong to different people, such as books, pencils, and jackets (*Sara's book, Kenny's pencil, Bill's and Tim's jackets*). Have students replace the nouns with appropriate pronouns from the list on the board (*her book, his pencil, their jackets*). Have volunteers point out other items in the room and have the rest of the class replace the nouns with pronouns.

Meeting Individual Needs

Intrapersonal Encourage students to review their writing for pronouns they have used in the past. Ask students to copy the sentences with pronouns onto note cards and to underline the pronouns. Review students' sentences with them to make sure they have correctly identified the pronouns.

EXERCISE 1 Find all the personal pronouns in these sentences. Some sentences have more than one pronoun.

1. You can see bears at Yellowstone National Park.
2. They are called grizzly bears.
3. I saw one grizzly bear when I was hiking.
4. I was with my friends.
5. We watched it from far away.
6. The park ranger told me that the bears could be dangerous.
7. He said to avoid them.
8. I listened to him.
9. A bear's strength is much greater than ours.
10. I told my teacher about the bear I saw.
11. I told her the bear actually wasn't near me.
12. We were all fascinated by it.

EXERCISE 2 Use personal pronouns to take the place of the underlined word or words.

1. Polar bears live in the Arctic. They
2. My friends and I learned some facts about polar bears. them
3. A polar bear can weigh more than 1,000 pounds. It
4. Their fur is very thick and covers their feet. It
5. Jessica, Juan, and Jeff saw polar bears at the zoo. They
6. The zookeeper, Eva, gave a fish to the biggest bear. it
7. Eva gave another fish to a baby bear. She
8. Juan asked how much fish the polar bears ate daily. He
9. The zookeepers give the polar bear four pounds of fish daily. They
10. The bear also eats five pounds of meat and two pounds of apples. It
11. Did you know that bears eat apples? them
12. Jess and Juan did not know that either. They

Grammar in Action. Find the five different pronouns in the page 286 excerpt.

APPLY IT NOW

Tell about bears you have seen at a zoo, on TV, or in a movie. Write four sentences. Use a pronoun in each sentence.

Pronouns • 55

3.2 Subject Pronouns

OBJECTIVE

- **To identify and use the pronouns that serve as the subjects of sentences**

 **Maintenance**

Assign **Practice Book** page 34, Section 3.2. After students finish,
1. Give immediate feedback.
2. Review concepts as needed.
3. Model the correct answer.

Pages 4–5 of the **Answer Key** contain tips for Daily Maintenance.

WARM-UP

Write on the board this nursery rhyme:

> Jack and Jill went up the hill,
> to fetch a pail of water.
> Jack fell down, and broke his crown,
> and Jill came tumbling after.

Have students replace the underlined nouns with pronouns. Ask students to recall other nursery rhymes that use names, such as Humpty-Dumpty and Jack Sprat. Challenge students to replace some of the nouns with pronouns.

📖 Read from a piece of writing that the class is currently reading. Emphasize the subject pronouns.

TEACH

Ask volunteers to read aloud about subject pronouns. Have students locate in the lists in the text the pronouns from the Warm-Up. Stress that *they*, *he*, and *she* are subject pronouns and that each replaces a subject noun in a sentence. Let students suggest other sentences with pronouns for subjects. Write the sentences on the board and discuss them.

PRACTICE

EXERCISE 1
Review the list of subject pronouns. Explain that these pronouns are the ones students should find in the sentences. Tell students to list each subject pronoun they find. Have students exchange papers with partners to check their answers. Discuss pronouns that differ on students' lists.

EXERCISE 2
After students have finished the exercise, have them rewrite the sentences, replacing the nouns with pronouns and the pronouns with nouns. Ask volunteers to read aloud their rewritten sentences.

EXERCISE 3
Ask students to explain how they will determine which pronoun to choose for each subject. Point out, for example, some questions they can ask themselves: *Does this sentence tell about a female or a male? Does it tell about one person or more than one person?*

Encourage students to work with partners to choose the correct subject pronouns. Have partners share their answers with the class.

3.2 Subject Pronouns

Some personal pronouns may be used as the subject of a sentence. These are called **subject pronouns.**

> *I* dance.
> *He* dances.
> *We* dance.

In these sentences *I, he,* and *we* are subject pronouns. The subject tells what the sentence is about. It tells who or what does something.

Here is a list of the subject pronouns.

SINGULAR	PLURAL
I	we
you	you
he, she, it	they

Which of these sentences uses a pronoun as a subject?

   A Jane is doing a square dance with Joe.
   B She likes to square-dance.
   C Wade watches them dance.

You are right if you said sentence B. *She* is a subject pronoun.

Tell which pronoun can take the place of the underlined words in this sentence.

   Jane and Joe learned how to square-dance.

You are right if you said *they.*

EXERCISE 1 **Find the subject pronoun in each sentence.**

  1. Greta and I take jazz dance lessons together.
  2. She dances on her toes.
  3. We danced the Hokey Pokey.
  4. It is a fun dance.

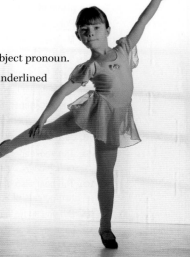

APPLY

APPLY IT NOW

Help students brainstorm a list of dance moves they have seen or done. Record on the board keywords that students may use in their writing. Suggest that students first write sentences with subject nouns and then rewrite the sentences, replacing the subject nouns with subject pronouns. Review students' work to make sure they used the correct words. Students should demonstrate the ability to identify and use subject pronouns.

ASSESS

Note which students had difficulty identifying and using subject pronouns. Assign **Practice Book** page 38 for further practice.

WRITING CONNECTION

Use pages 288–289 of the Writing portion of the book.

TEACHING OPTIONS

Reteach

Have partners write sentence pairs with subject nouns and subject pronouns. Direct one student to write a sentence with a noun as the subject and a partner to rewrite the sentence, replacing the noun with a subject pronoun. Then have students reverse roles. Ask students to write sentence pairs that use each subject pronoun (*I, you, he, she, it, we, you, they*).

English-Language Learners

Write on the board a chart like the one on page 56. Next to *he* and *she*, place a picture of a boy and a girl, respectively. Review each subject pronoun by physically indicating the meaning of *I, we, you, he, she*, and *it*. Read aloud sentences with subject pronouns. Point to the correct person or thing (*I, we, you, he, she, it*) or the incorrect person or thing. (*Say* I, *but point to another person, or say* she *and point to a boy.*) Have students use a thumbs up or thumbs down to indicate whether or not you are using the correct subject pronoun.

Meeting Individual Needs

Auditory Encourage students to listen for subject pronouns used in everyday speech. Have students record sentences with subject pronouns they recall hearing throughout the day. Ask students to identify the subject noun that each subject pronoun replaces. Point out that sentences in which pronouns follow nouns, such as *Carla she went to the game* are not correct.

Diagram It!

To practice these concepts in the context of diagramming, turn to Section 8.1.

5. <u>He</u> taps his feet.
6. <u>They</u> clap to the music.
7. Does <u>he</u> dance well?
8. <u>I</u> like dancing.
9. Do <u>you</u> know this dance?
10. <u>We</u> can dance it together.

EXERCISE 2 Tell whether the underlined subject in each sentence is a noun or a pronoun.

1. <u>Dogs</u> are wonderful pets. noun
2. <u>They</u> are fun and loving. pronoun
3. The <u>Jacksons</u> bought a rescue dog from the animal shelter. noun
4. <u>Danny Jackson</u> picked out a cute brown and white puppy. noun
5. <u>He</u> named the dog Princess. pronoun
6. <u>She</u> followed Danny everywhere he went. pronoun
7. One day <u>Princess</u> followed Danny to the river near his house. noun
8. <u>We</u> laughed when Princess jumped into the water after Danny. pronoun

Exercise 3
1. She
2. He
3. They
4. We
5. He
6. She
7. They
8. It
9. She

EXERCISE 3 Use a subject pronoun to take the place of the underlined word or words.

1. <u>Mrs. Kim</u> planned a dances-from-around-the-world day.
2. <u>Max</u> danced the csárdás, a Hungarian folk dance.
3. <u>The students</u> know many dances.
4. <u>Margarita and I</u> did the macarena for the class.
5. <u>Christopher</u> can do the polka.
6. <u>Hannah</u> showed an Indian dance called kathak.
7. <u>Eileen and Patrick</u> did a jig.
8. <u>The jig</u> was very well done.
9. <u>Greta</u> waltzed to pretty Viennese music.

APPLY IT NOW

Think about a time when you danced or saw people dancing. Write four sentences about dancing. Use subject pronouns in one or more sentences. Underline the pronouns.

Pronouns • 57

OBJECTIVE

• **To identify and use object pronouns**

 **Maintenance**

Assign **Practice Book** page 34, Section 3.3. After students finish,
1. Give immediate feedback.
2. Review concepts as needed.
3. Model the correct answer.

Pages 4–5 of the **Answer Key** contain tips for Daily Maintenance.

WARM-UP

Write on the board all the object pronouns. Write on sentence strips simple subjects and verbs and on separate strips nouns used as objects. Have students choose subject and verb strips from a facedown pile. Place the object strips on a table so students can choose one to complete their sentences. Ask students to read aloud their completed sentences. Then have students choose a word from the board to replace the noun on their second strip and read aloud the new sentences.

📖 Read from a piece of writing that the class is currently reading. Emphasize the object pronouns.

TEACH

Review that a subject noun usually appears before the verb, the word that tells the action in a sentence. Tell students that sometimes a noun can appear after an action verb. Explain that a noun used in this way is often the object of a sentence—it receives the action of the verb.
    Have volunteers read aloud about object pronouns.

PRACTICE

EXERCISE 1
Have volunteers read the sentences aloud. After each sentence has been read, invite a volunteer to identify the object pronoun. Remind students that an object pronoun not only follows an action verb but also receives the action of the verb.

EXERCISE 2
Have students refer to the object pronouns chart in the text. Have students complete this exercise independently. Ask partners to compare their answers.

EXERCISE 3
Ask students to point out where the underlined word appears in each sentence. Have students note that it appears after the verb and that this word is therefore the object of the sentence. Have students refer to the list of object pronouns in the text. Ask students to read aloud their sentences.

3.3 Object Pronouns

Some personal pronouns may be used after an action verb in a sentence. They are called **object pronouns.**

> **The teacher asked** David **a question.**
> **The teacher asked** him **a question.**

The noun *David* comes after the action verb. It is an object in the sentence. It can be replaced with the object pronoun *him.*

Here is a list of the object pronouns.

SINGULAR	PLURAL
me	us
you	you
him, her, it	them

Ursa Major

Which of these sentences uses an object pronoun?

   A He is interested in the stars.
   B They are interesting.
   C The stars interest me.

You are right if you said sentence C. *Me* is the object of the sentence. It comes after the action verb, *interest. Me* is an object pronoun.

Which pronouns can take the place of the underlined words in these sentences?

   A The guide told <u>Jane</u> about the star map.
   B She hung the <u>map</u> on the wall.

You are right if you said *her* in sentence A and *it* in sentence B.

EXERCISE 1 Find the object pronoun in each sentence.
  1. Mr. Kovach taught <u>us</u> about the features of the moon.
  2. I lent <u>you</u> a telescope.
  3. You borrowed <u>it</u> for the lunar eclipse.

APPLY

APPLY IT NOW

Ask students to name places that might be fun to explore. Guide students in deciding where they should use object pronouns. Check that students choose the correct object pronouns for their sentences. Students should demonstrate the ability to use object pronouns.

💡 **TechTip** You may wish to direct students to specific, child-appropriate Web sites.

ASSESS

Note which students had difficulty using object pronouns. Assign **Practice Book** pages 39–40 for further practice.

WRITING CONNECTION

Use pages 290–291 of the Writing portion of the book.

Reteach

Say a sentence, such as one of the following, and have two students act it out.

> **Toni and Blair sing a song.**

> **Corey and Leon help Tanya and Walter.**

As students act out a sentence, encourage the class to say the sentence, replacing the object noun with an object pronoun.

> **Toni and Blair sing it.**

> **Corey and Leon help them.**

Continue with additional sentences.

English-Language Learners

Explain that the word *you* is both singular and plural in English. Write on the board several sentences using *you* as both a singular and plural object pronoun. Have students raise one hand if *you* is used as a singular object pronoun and both hands if it is used as a plural object pronoun.

Meeting Individual Needs

Extra Support Write on the board a two-column chart with the headings *Subject Pronouns* and *Object Pronouns*. Have volunteers fill in the chart. Then ask students to write sentences for each pronoun on the chart. Have students copy the chart into their notebooks to use for reference.

---

4. Tell <u>us</u> about the eclipse.

5. The eclipse amazed <u>him</u>.

6. Jenna gave <u>them</u> a report on the eclipse.

7. The class liked <u>it</u>.

8. They told <u>her</u> about the nature of a lunar eclipse.

EXERCISE 2 Choose the correct pronoun or pronouns to complete each sentence.

1. Lunar eclipses are rare, and ancient people feared (they <u>them</u>).

2. Mr. Lin told (<u>us</u> we) that ancient Chinese people believed there was a dragon in the moon.

3. Eclipses fascinate (I <u>me</u>).

4. Mr. Lin showed (she <u>her</u>) a book with old Chinese legends.

5. The colorful pictures interested (she <u>her</u>) and (<u>him</u> he).

6. Fiona wants (I <u>me</u>) to teach (she <u>her</u>) about eclipses.

Exercise 3
1. us
2. it
3. them
4. it
5. him
6. them

EXERCISE 3 Use an object pronoun to take the place of the underlined words in each sentence.

1. Tell <u>Jonah and me</u> about the moon landing.

2. Neil Armstrong reached <u>the moon's surface</u>.

3. A small ship took <u>Neil Armstrong and Buzz Aldrin</u> to the moon.

4. People watched <u>the moon landing</u> on TV.

5. People saw <u>Neil Armstrong</u> on the moon.

6. The astronauts' bravery amazed <u>Maria and Jon</u>.

Michael Collins, Neil Armstrong, and Buzz Aldrin

APPLY IT NOW

Write four sentences about a place you would like to explore. Use object pronouns in some of your sentences. Underline the object pronouns you used.

Tech Tip With an adult, do research on a science Web site.

Pronouns • 59

3.4 Possessive Pronouns

OBJECTIVE
- **To identify and use possessive pronouns**

 **DAILY Maintenance**

Assign **Practice Book** page 35, Section 3.4. After students finish,
1. Give immediate feedback.
2. Review concepts as needed.
3. Model the correct answer.

Pages 4–5 of the **Answer Key** contain tips for Daily Maintenance.

WARM-UP

Write on the board these sentences:

This desk is <u>mine</u>.

This is <u>my</u> desk.

Have students replace the words *desk* with other objects in the room and then change the underlined word to identify to whom each object belongs. *(This coat is <u>Jared's</u>. This is <u>his</u> coat.)* Challenge students to use singular and plurals nouns and pronouns.

📖 Read from a piece of writing that the class is currently reading. Emphasize the possessive pronouns.

TEACH

Write on the board the following sentences:

My basketball is here.

Mine is here.

Have a volunteer read aloud the sentences. Ask which words are replaced by *mine* in the second sentence (*My basketball*).

Have volunteers read aloud about possessive pronouns. Reinforce that possessive pronouns can take the place of the person who owns the object and the object that is owned.

Have students name all the possessive pronouns. Write them on the board. Ask students to tell which are singular and which are plural. Point out that *yours* is both singular and plural, depending upon the noun it replaces.

Ask students to suggest sentences with possessive pronouns. Write their sentences on the board and have students replace the nouns and the person, or persons, that owns each noun with the appropriate possessive pronoun. Write the new sentences on the board under the original sentence.

PRACTICE

EXERCISE 1
Review the list of possessive pronouns in the text. Have students write the possessive pronoun from each sentence. Read the sentences aloud and ask students to raise their hands when you say each possessive pronoun.

EXERCISE 2
Have students refer to the chart in the text. Ask students to find the noun phrase that most closely resembles each item and find its corresponding possessive pronoun.

3.4 Possessive Pronouns

A **possessive pronoun** shows who or what owns something. A possessive pronoun takes the place of a noun. It takes the place of both the person who owns the thing and the object that is owned.

Mine, yours, his, hers, its, ours, and *theirs* are possessive pronouns.

NOUN PHRASES	POSSESSIVE PRONOUNS
My bicycle is here.	*Mine* is here.
Our bicycle is here.	*Ours* is here.
Your bicycle is here.	*Yours* is here.
Brandon's bicycle is here.	*His* is here.
Nina's bicycle is here.	*Hers* is here.
Mom's and Dad's bicycles are here.	*Theirs* are here.
That is Leon's bicycle.	That is *his*.

In each sentence above, the noun and the person or thing that possesses it are replaced by a possessive pronoun. Possessive pronouns can be used as subjects, and they can be used in other parts of a sentence.

Mona admired *Lisa's bicycle.*   **Mona admired** *hers.*

Which of these sentences uses a possessive pronoun?

   A I ride my bicycle.

   B Sam rides his.

   C Stacy rides a bicycle.

You are right if you said sentence B. *His* means that the bicycle belongs to Sam.

EXERCISE 1 Find the possessive pronoun or pronouns in each sentence.

  1. <u>Hers</u> is the red one.

  2. What color is <u>yours</u>?

  3. <u>Mine</u> has a bell.

  4. <u>Yours</u> is bigger than my bicycle.

EXERCISE 3

Point out how the sentences are similar to the example sentence. Have students complete the exercise independently. Then ask volunteers to write their new sentences on the board.

APPLY

APPLY IT NOW

Suggest that students make a list of items they can write about. Allow time for students to work on their lists and their sentences. Invite students to share their sentences with the class. Students should demonstrate the ability to use possessive pronouns.

ASSESS

Note which students had difficulty using possessive pronouns. Assign **Practice Book** page 41 for further practice.

WRITING CONNECTION

Use pages 292–293 of the Writing portion of the book.

TEACHING OPTIONS

Reteach

Distribute newspapers and magazines. Have students choose a picture that shows a person with something that belongs to him or to her. Direct students to write two sentences about their picture to describe the person and the object he or she owns. Use the following sentences as examples:

The girl's coat is green.
Hers is green.

Jacob's puppy is cute.
His is cute.

Have students cut out their pictures and make a poster with the pictures and sentences.

Meeting Individual Needs

Extra Support Students may find the use of *his* as a possessive pronoun confusing because it is also a possessive adjective. Write on the board these sentences:

Manuel's book is funny.

His is funny.

Ask students to tell what words *his* replaces (*Manuel's book*). Point out that the word *his* only makes sense because the thing Manuel owns is mentioned in the first sentence. Explain that *his* could not be used without identifying the words to which it refers. Have students suggest other sentence pairs using other possessive pronouns.

5. We keep <u>ours</u> at the bicycle rack during school.
6. <u>Theirs</u> are ten-speeds.
7. <u>His</u> is a mountain bike.
8. They rode <u>theirs</u> on the path.
9. That water bottle is <u>hers</u>.
10. <u>Mine</u> is the pink one next to <u>yours</u>.

Exercise 2
1. c
2. e
3. b
4. a
5. f
6. d

EXERCISE 2 Match the object owned in Column A with the correct possessive pronoun in Column B.

Column A	Column B
1. my bike lock	a. his
2. her bike pump	b. theirs
3. Josh's and Min's flags	c. mine
4. Tom's handlebars	d. yours
5. our helmets	e. hers
6. your compass	f. ours

Exercise 3
1. Mine has a basket.
2. The tandem is theirs.
3. Where is yours?
4. Ours have flags.
5. His is the fastest.
6. Is that hers?
7. Did they ring theirs?
8. Yours has a flat tire.
9. Hers has streamers.
10. Mine is yellow, and yours is green.

EXERCISE 3 Change the sentences so that they have possessive pronouns. Use the pronoun in place of the underlined words.

EXAMPLE **<u>Malia's bicycle</u> is missing.**
Hers is missing.

1. <u>My bicycle</u> has a basket.
2. The tandem is <u>Mickey and Mary's bicycle</u>.
3. Where is <u>your lock</u>?
4. <u>My bicycle and my sister's bicycle</u> have flags.
5. <u>Jacob's bicycle</u> is the fastest.
6. Is that <u>Ana's helmet</u>?
7. Did they ring <u>their bells</u>?
8. <u>Your bike</u> has a flat tire.
9. <u>Keesha's bicycle</u> has streamers.
10. <u>My bike</u> is yellow, and <u>your bike</u> is green.

APPLY IT NOW

Choose three different objects found either at school or at home. Write a sentence with possessive pronouns for each object. Underline the possessive pronouns.
Example:
My sister and I have raincoats.
<u>Mine</u> is red. <u>Hers</u> is blue.

Pronouns • 61

OBJECTIVE
- **To identify and use possessive adjectives**

 **Maintenance**

Assign **Practice Book** page 35, Section 3.5. After students finish,
1. Give immediate feedback.
2. Review concepts as needed.
3. Model the correct answer.

Pages 4–5 of the **Answer Key** contain tips for Daily Maintenance.

WARM-UP

Write on the board the possessive adjectives *(my, our, your, his, her, its, their)* and the following sentences. Ask students to fill in the blanks.

> That cat belongs to me, so it is _____ cat.

> That dog belongs to Sally, so it is _____ dog.

Encourage students to generate similar sentences using the words on the board.

📖 Read from a piece of writing that the class is currently reading. Emphasize the possessive adjectives.

TEACH

Write on the board the following sentences:

> I have a green lizard.

> Her dog is jumping on me.

> The cat licked its paws.

Tell students that adjectives describe nouns. Explain that adjectives answer questions such as *Which one? What kind? How much? How many?* and *Whose?* Ask volunteers to underline the adjective in each sentence *(green, her, its)*. Point out that some pronouns are adjectives that show possession like *her* and *its*.

Have volunteers read aloud about possessive adjectives. Write on the board a two-column chart with the headings *Possessive Pronouns* and *Possessive Adjectives*. Ask students to name the possessive pronouns and possessive adjectives as you write them on the board. Have students point out the similarities and differences in each column.

PRACTICE

EXERCISE 1
Review the list of possessive adjectives. Explain that students will find one of these possessive adjectives in each item. Lead students to understand *your* in item 4 refers to one person and *your* in item 8 refers to more than one person.

EXERCISE 2
Have volunteers read aloud each sentence, identify the subjects, and tell whether the possessive adjective should be singular or plural. Have students explain the reasons for their choices.

EXERCISE 3
Have students refer to the chart on the board. Ask volunteers to read aloud each sentence, provide the answer, and tell whether each pronoun is singular or plural.

3.5 Possessive Adjectives

An adjective is a word that describes a noun. Some adjectives show who owns something. *My, our, your, his, her, its,* and *their* are adjectives that go before nouns to show ownership. They are called **possessive adjectives.**

> *Our* **wagon has a broken wheel.**
> *Her* **wagon is in the garage.**

The words *our* and *her* are adjectives. They are used before the noun *wagon* to show who owns each wagon.

These are the possessive adjectives.

SINGULAR	PLURAL
my	our
your	your
his, her, its	their

Which of these sentences uses a possessive adjective?

> A Her wagon is red.
> B A wagon has four wheels.
> C Hers is red.

You are right if you said sentence A. The word *her* shows that the wagon belongs to the girl. It comes before the noun *wagon*. In sentence C the possessive is a pronoun—it stands by itself and it points out both the owner and the thing that is owned.

Do not confuse possessive pronouns and possessive adjectives. Remember that possessive adjectives always come before nouns.

EXERCISE 1 Find the possessive adjective in each sentence.

1. Laura wants to play <u>her</u> new game.
2. Please be on <u>my</u> team.
3. Mark wants to make <u>his</u> own rules.
4. Take <u>your</u> turn, Phil.

APPLY

APPLY IT NOW

Suggest that students list a few nouns to include in their sentences, such as the names of people and items. As students write their sentences, remind them to include possessive adjectives. Invite volunteers to read their sentences aloud. Challenge the rest of the class to identify the possessive adjectives that were used. Students should demonstrate the ability to use possessive adjectives.

Grammar in Action. After students have identified the possessive adjectives *(their, their)*, ask them to identify the noun that goes after each pronoun *(knees, mouths)*.

ASSESS

Note which students had difficulty identifying and using possessive adjectives. Assign **Practice Book** page 42 for further practice.

WRITING CONNECTION

Use pages 294–295 of the Writing portion of the book.

TEACHING OPTIONS

Reteach

Have students play Possessive Adjective Bingo. Make blank bingo cards with three rows of three squares each. Have students put an X in the center square as a free square. Then have students write a different possessive adjective in each blank square. Direct students to make two squares with the word *your* and to mark one *singular* and one *plural*.

Read aloud sentences to be completed using possessive adjectives, such as *The dog chased _____ tail*. Tell students to place a scrap of paper over the word *its* on their card. Explain that the first student to cover one complete row wins the game. Continue playing until all the possessive adjectives have been used at least once.

Cooperative Learning

Have students work in small groups. Distribute two note cards to each student. Instruct students to write the name of a person or a group of people on one card and the name of an object on the second card. Have groups mix up the cards and place them in two separate piles. Ask students to choose a card from each pile and use the words to make up two different possessive phrases *(Billy's baseball and his baseball)*.

Curriculum Connection

Display an illustration of a famous piece of art. Have students use possessive adjectives to write what they see *(his bright smile, her colorful dress, their silly faces)*. Ask students to identify the possessive adjectives and use them in complete sentences.

Diagram It!

To practice these concepts in the context of diagramming, turn to Section 8.2.

5. May we play <u>their</u> game next?
6. <u>Its</u> rules are easy to follow.
7. <u>Our</u> game pieces are missing.
8. Ana and Kim, <u>your</u> pieces are mixed up.

Exercise 2
Answers will vary.

EXERCISE 2 Complete each sentence with a possessive adjective.

1. The children played with _____their_____ action figures.
2. Emily found _____her_____ missing puzzle piece.
3. Brendan set up _____his_____ game.
4. I said that this is _____my_____ best sticker.
5. We played with _____our_____ toy bricks.
6. Ed, are those _____your_____ crayons?
7. Mom asked us to put away _____our_____ games.
8. Christa and Brendan cleaned _____their_____ play area.

Exercise 3
1. possessive pronoun
2. possessive pronoun
3. possessive adjective
4. possessive pronoun
5. possessive adjective
6. possessive pronoun
7. possessive pronoun
8. possessive adjective
9. possessive adjective
10. possessive adjective

EXERCISE 3 Find the possessive pronoun or possessive adjective in each sentence. Then tell whether it is a possessive pronoun or a possessive adjective.

EXAMPLE **Our** crayons are in the box. (possessive adjective)
The crayons in the box are **ours**. (possessive pronoun)

1. Those paints are <u>mine</u>.
2. Are these green beads <u>hers</u>?
3. <u>My</u> scissors are on the table.
4. The glue stick is <u>his</u>, isn't it?
5. Is that <u>his</u> construction paper?
6. The blue marker isn't <u>yours</u>.
7. The red clay sculpture is <u>ours</u>.
8. Where are <u>their</u> watercolors?
9. <u>Your</u> paintbrush has a blue handle.
10. <u>Its</u> bristles are thick and black.

APPLY IT NOW

Write four sentences about things, such as toys or sports equipment, that you and your friends like to play with. Use possessive adjectives before nouns.

Grammar in Action. Find the possessive adjective in the page 298 excerpt.

Pronouns • 63

OBJECTIVE

- **To identify and use subject pronoun and verb agreement**

 **Maintenance**

Assign **Practice Book** page 35, Section 3.6. After students finish,
1. Give immediate feedback.
2. Review concepts as needed.
3. Model the correct answer.

Pages 4–5 of the **Answer Key** contain tips for Daily Maintenance.

WARM-UP

Write on the board the following tongue twister:

> She sells seashells by the seashore.

Invite students to read it aloud with you. Then replace *she* with *I* and write the new sentence.

> I sell seashells by the seashore.

Have students read aloud the second sentence. Ask students what else changed when you replaced the word *she* with *I*. (*Sells* became *sell*.) Repeat using other subject pronouns.

📖 Read from a piece of writing that the class is currently reading. Emphasize agreement of pronouns and verbs.

TEACH

Have volunteers read aloud the first paragraph and the chart with singular and plural subjects. Have students suggest sentences using all the subject pronouns and several different verbs such as *call*, *send*, *tell*, and *make*. Point out that the subjects *I, you, we,* and *they* all use the same verb form in the present tense. Emphasize that with *he, she,* and *it,* an *-s* is added to the verb.

Have volunteers read aloud the rest of the page. Reinforce that *I, you, he, she,* and *it* are singular subject pronouns and that *we, you,* and *they* are plural. Point out that since *you* can be both singular and plural, students will have to read the sentence to figure out which number is being used.

PRACTICE

EXERCISE 1
Have students complete this exercise independently. Ask volunteers to write their completed sentences on the board.

EXERCISE 2
Review which pronouns require that the verb end in an *s* and which pronouns require no special ending for verb agreement. Point out that most items have more than one correct answer. Encourage students to choose the pronoun that they feel fits the sentence best. Have students read their sentences aloud.

EXERCISE 3
Have students refer to the chart in the text and work with partners to complete this activity. Challenge students to change the subject

---

3.6 Agreement of Pronouns and Verbs

A subject and its verb must agree. A verb that shows an action is often in the present tense. Most subjects take the same form of the verb in the present tense. An *-s* is added to the verb only after *he, she,* or *it*—or the noun that each replaces.

SINGULAR SUBJECT	PLURAL SUBJECT
I sit.	We sit.
You sit.	You sit.
He sits.	They sit.
She sits.	
It sits.	

When a noun is used as a subject, *-s* is added to the verb form, just as it is for *he, she,* or *it.*

PRONOUN SUBJECT	NOUN SUBJECT
He sits.	Paul sits.
She sits.	Amy sits.
It sits.	The cat sits.

Which sentence shows correct agreement of subject and verb?

- A It growl.
- B It growls.
- C They growls.

You are right if you said sentence B. The pronoun *It* is singular. It needs the verb *growls.*

EXERCISE 1 Choose the verb that agrees with the subject pronoun to complete each sentence.

1. She (work <u>works</u>) with animals.
2. We (<u>walk</u> walks) the dogs.

pronoun to singular or plural and to rewrite the sentence with the correct verb form.

TechTip You may wish to direct students to specific Web sites to find images of animals.

APPLY

APPLY IT NOW

Brainstorm with students stories or songs with animal characters. Write on the board a list of the characters and have students choose the correct pronoun for each. Have them suggest verbs that agree with each pronoun. Students should demonstrate correct pronoun and verb agreement.

ASSESS

Note which students had difficulty with pronoun and verb agreement. Assign **Practice Book** pages 43–44 for further practice.

WRITING CONNECTION

Use pages 296–297 of the Writing portion of the book.

TEACHING OPTIONS

Reteach

Write on the board the following paragraph:

> I love my cat. Her name is Boots. She _____ (sit sits) on my lap all the time. She _____ (purr purrs) softly until she falls asleep. I _____ (take takes) Boots outside to play with my friends. We _____ (laugh laughs) as she runs through the bushes. My friends wish they had a cat like Boots. They _____ (hope hopes) she has kittens one day.

Have students complete each sentence. Then help them underline the subject pronouns and the verbs.

Meeting Individual Needs

Extra Support Because students generally learn subject-verb agreement through auditory experience, reinforce this learning through a visual exercise. Write each subject pronoun on a separate note card. Write a verb card to agree with each pronoun card. Have students take turns choosing a pronoun card and then selecting the correct verb card. Confirm that each subject pronoun agrees with the verb selected. Ask students to use the subject pronoun and the verb in a sentence.

English-Language Learners

Some students may have difficulty with agreement of pronouns and verbs. Have students brainstorm a list of action verbs (*play, run, jump, throw, walk, chase, draw,* and *read*). Then have students write sentences using each subject pronoun and the action verbs. Ask volunteers to identify the subject pronouns and the verbs in each sentence.

3. I (train trains) dogs.
4. It (jump jumps) on things.
5. They (chew chews) the furniture.
6. He (play plays) with the cats.
7. You (feeds feed) the cat.
8. It (chase chases) the ball.
9. She (make makes) the dog stay.
10. They (like likes) bones.
11. I (give gives) the dog commands.
12. It (obey obeys) me.

Exercise 2
Answers will vary.
Possible answers:
1. I, You, We, They
2. It, She, He
3. It, She, He
4. They

EXERCISE 2 Complete each sentence by adding a subject pronoun. Make sure the subject pronoun and verb agree.

1. _____ bring my dog to school.
2. _____ knows how to sit.
3. _____ does many tricks.
4. _____ speak by barking.
5. _____ teaches him to obey.
6. _____ watch the dog with interest.
7. _____ believes the dog is trying to speak.
8. _____ think that too.

EXERCISE 3 Complete each sentence with the correct form of the verb in parentheses.

1. He __plays__ with his dog after school. (play)
2. She __likes__ to teach her dog tricks. (like)
3. It __takes__ a lot of patience. (take)
4. We __hear__ them talking to their dogs. (hear)
5. You __want__ your dog to behave. (want)
6. They __laugh__ a lot when playing with the dogs. (laugh)

APPLY IT NOW

Write four sentences about an animal. Use subject nouns and subject pronouns. Make sure each subject agrees with its verb.
Example:
Max does tricks.
He gives a high five with his right paw.

 Tech Tip Illustrate your sentences in a PowerPoint slideshow.

Pronouns • 65

3.7   *I and Me*

OBJECTIVE

- **To use the pronouns *I* and *me* correctly**

 **Maintenance**

Assign **Practice Book** page 36, Section 3.7. After students finish,
1. Give immediate feedback.
2. Review concepts as needed.
3. Model the correct answer.

Pages 4–5 of the **Answer Key** contain tips for Daily Maintenance.

WARM-UP

Write on the board the following sentences:

_____ went to the store with my parents.

Mom bought _____ bananas.

_____ like to help Dad shop.

Sometimes he buys _____ something special.

Have volunteers use the word *I* or *me* to complete each sentence.

📖 Read from a piece of writing that the class is currently reading. Emphasize the pronouns *I* and *me*.

TEACH

Draw on the board a Venn diagram. In one circle write the word *I*. In the other write the word *me*. In the area where the circles overlap write *both*. Explain that you will be comparing the words *I* and *me*.

Have volunteers read aloud about *I* and *me*. Then review the information on the page and add the similarities and differences of the words to the Venn diagram. Review the sentences from the Warm-Up to show the similarities and differences. *(Similarities: They are both pronouns. Differences: I is used as a subject. Me is used as an object. I comes before the verb. Me comes after the verb.)*

Encourage students to suggest sentences that demonstrate the correct usage of *I* and *me*.

PRACTICE

EXERCISE 1

Before students begin the exercise, have them explain when they should use the pronoun *I* and when they should use the pronoun *me*. Direct partners to complete the exercise. Encourage partners to read and explain their answers to the class.

EXERCISE 2

Have students complete the exercise independently. Ask volunteers to write their sentences on the board. Discuss students' pronoun choices. Have students tell why they made their choices.

EXERCISE 3

Have partners complete the exercise. Tell students first to identify the subject of each sentence and then to determine which pronoun to use. Ask volunteers to read aloud their corrected sentences.

3.7   *I and Me*

I and *me* are used when you talk about yourself. *I* is used as the subject of a sentence.

> **I like fruit.**
> **For a snack I prefer grapes.**

In both sentences *I* is the subject. *I* tells who does something.

Me is used as an object. It usually comes after an action verb.

> **Tell me about your favorite food.**
> **Mom gave me a new video game.**

Which sentence uses *I* or *me* correctly?

> A **Me slice the potato.**
> B **I eat the celery.**

You are right if you chose sentence B. The pronoun *I* is used before the verb.

Which pronoun, *I* or *me*, is correct in each of these sentences?

> A **Jasmine e-mailed (I me).**
> B **Can you send (I me) the message?**

Me is correct in both sentences because it is an object in both.

EXERCISE 1 Choose the correct pronoun or pronouns to complete each sentence.

1. Mom gave (I me) some vegetables for lunch.
2. (I Me) eat five pieces of fruit every day.
3. (I Me) usually have an apple for lunch.
4. My mother sometimes makes (I me) a salad for dinner.
5. Yesterday (I me) traded vegetables with Ty.
6. He gave (I me) some carrots.

APPLY

APPLY IT NOW

Encourage students to consider fruits they enjoy. Have volunteers read aloud their sentences. Ask students to raise their hands when they hear *I* and *me* and tell whether the pronoun is an object or a subject. Students should demonstrate the ability to use the pronouns *I* and *me* correctly.

ASSESS

Note which students had difficulty understanding how to use the pronouns *I* and *me* correctly. Assign **Practice Book** page 45 for further practice.

WRITING CONNECTION

Use pages 298–299 of the Writing portion of the book.

TEACHING OPTIONS

Reteach

Write on the board sentences that can be completed using the words *I* or *me*. Write on separate note cards the words *I* and *me*. Have volunteers read aloud the sentences and choose the card with the correct word to complete the sentence. Encourage each student to explain how he or she decided which word to choose. Reinforce that *I* is used as a subject before the verb and *me* is used as an object after the verb.

Curriculum Connection

Select a high-interest, age-appropriate autobiography to read aloud to the class. Tell students that an autobiography is the true story of a person's life written by that person. As you read aloud passages from the book, have students raise their hands when they hear the words *I* or *me*. Write on the board the sentences. Have students read aloud the sentences, identify the pronouns *I* and *me,* and discuss how each is being used.

Meeting Individual Needs

Intrapersonal Point out that when students write in their journals, they are usually writing about themselves. Have students look back through some journal entries to find six sentences using the pronouns *I* or *me*. Have students write the sentences and decide if the words were used correctly. If not, have students correct the incorrect sentences.

---

7. (**I** Me) like blueberries and grapes.

8. She offered (I **me**) oranges, but (I **me**) prefer pears.

EXERCISE 2 Use *I* or *me* to complete each sentence correctly.

1. ____I____ picked apples from a tree.

2. My friend helped ____me____.

3. ____I____ climbed the ladder.

4. Grandma baked ____me____ a pie with fresh fruit.

5. ____I____ sprinkled sugar on the apples.

6. Then ____I____ waited for the pie to bake.

7. She cut ____me____ a huge piece.

8. ____I____ told Grandma that it tasted great.

9. ____I____ ate two pieces of apple pie.

10. She hugged ____me____ and said ____I____ am great!

11. ____I____ thanked her and smiled.

12. Grandma gave ____me____ some pie to take home.

EXERCISE 3 Choose the correct pronoun to complete each sentence. Tell whether each pronoun is a subject pronoun or an object pronoun.

1. Helen and (I me) are sisters. subject pronoun

2. She gave (I **me**) the best birthday present. object pronoun

3. (**I** Me) like to skateboard. subject pronoun

4. The skateboard Helen gave (I **me**) is green with black stripes. object pronoun

5. (**I** Me) fell the first time I rode it. subject pronoun

6. My friends want (I **me**) to compete in a skateboarding contest. object pronoun

7. They think (I **me**) can do tricks better than other skateboarders. subject pronoun

8. (**I** Me) am excited about the contest next Saturday. subject pronoun

APPLY IT NOW

Use *I* and *me* to write four sentences about your favorite fruit. Choose from the following list or choose a fruit of your own.

blueberries   strawberries
pineapple   peaches

Pronouns • 67

OBJECTIVE

- **To use pronouns as compound subjects and objects**

 **Maintenance**

Assign **Practice Book** page 36, Section 3.8. After students finish,
1. Give immediate feedback.
2. Review concepts as needed.
3. Model the correct answer.

Pages 4–5 of the **Answer Key** contain tips for Daily Maintenance.

WARM-UP

List on the board all the subject and object pronouns. Ask students to suggest a sentence that tells about something that happened to two people. Tell students that they can be one of the people. Model the following examples:

_____ and I won the doubles tournament.

Cal gave _____ and _____ birthday cards.

📖 Read from a piece of writing that the class is currently reading. Emphasize the compound subjects and objects.

TEACH

Write on the board the following groups of sentences:

I went to the game.
She went to the game.
She and I went to the game.

Coach gave him a ball.
Coach gave me a ball.
Coach gave him and me a ball.

Ask volunteers to read aloud about compound subjects and objects. Encourage students to suggest sentences using pronouns as compound subjects. Write the sentences on the board. Then ask students to write on the board sentences using compound objects.

PRACTICE

EXERCISE 1
Ask volunteers to write the sentences on the board, using the correct pronouns. Have students explain why they chose each pronoun.

EXERCISE 2
Review all the object pronouns. You may wish to suggest that students review Section 3.3 if they are unsure which pronouns are object pronouns. Have students read aloud their completed sentences and tell the reason for their choice of pronoun.

EXERCISE 3
Review subject and object pronouns. Have partners work together to complete the exercise. Encourage students to use the chart in the text to decide the correct pronoun for each sentence.

3.8 Compound Subjects and Objects

Pronouns can be used in compound subjects and compound objects.

SUBJECT PRONOUNS

I went to the park.
She went to the park.
She and I went to the park. (compound subject)

OBJECT PRONOUNS

Al told *me* about the team.
Al told *him* about the team.
Al told *him and me* about the team. (compound object)

Pronouns can be used with nouns in compound subjects and compound objects.

Jennie and I went to the park. (compound subject)

Sherry told *Larry and me* about them. (compound object)

In speaking and writing, it is polite to put *I* and *me* after words that refer to other people.

Which sentences use pronouns in compounds correctly?

A I want to play tag.
B You and I will play tag.
C Ben plays with Sherry and me.

You are right if you said sentences B and C. Sentence B includes compound subject pronouns. Sentence C includes a pronoun in the compound object.

EXERCISE 1 Choose the correct subject pronoun or pronouns to complete each sentence.

1. Pat and (I me) walked to the park.
2. Karen and (he him) swung from the monkey bars.
3. Martina and (her she) climbed the ladder.
4. Jim and (them they) played kickball.

APPLY IT NOW

List on the board students' suggestions for how they might help others. Suggest that students choose from these ideas or use others of their own. Ask students to underline the pronouns in their sentences. Students should demonstrate the ability to use pronouns as compound subjects and objects.

ASSESS

Note which students had difficulty using pronouns as compound subjects and objects. Assign **Practice Book** page 46 for further practice.

WRITING CONNECTION

Use pages 300–301 of the Writing portion of the book.

TEACHING OPTIONS

Reteach

Write pairs of similar sentences on the board. Help students combine the subjects or the objects.

> **Charles went to the beach.**
> **I went to the beach.**
>
> **Charles and I went to the beach.**
> **He and I went to the beach.**
>
> **Mr. Han gave me an A.**
> **Mr. Han gave Sheila an A.**
>
> **Mr. Han gave Sheila and me an A.**
> **He gave Sheila and me an A.**

Meeting Individual Needs

Interpersonal Tell students that it is polite to name the other person first in a compound subject or object.

> **Mary and I play a game.**
> **Ken called Jim and me.**

Have partners discuss things they do together, using compound subjects with *I* and compound objects with *me*. (*Bill and I went to the movies. Dad bought Brianna and me some popcorn.*)

Meeting Individual Needs

Auditory Explain that the words *I* and *me* are often used incorrectly, especially in compound subjects and objects. Have students listen for a day for sentences using *I* and *me* in compound subjects and objects. Direct students to write the sentences they hear. If the words are used incorrectly, have students rewrite the sentences correctly. Have volunteers share their sentences with the class.

Diagram It!

To practice these concepts in the context of diagramming, turn to Section 8.7.

---

5. (Her <u>She</u>) and I ran through the grass.
6. John and (<u>they</u> them) sat on the swings.
7. (<u>He</u> Him) and (me <u>I</u>) stayed until dark.
8. (Her <u>She</u>) and (them <u>they</u>) went home together.

EXERCISE 2 **Choose the correct object pronoun or pronouns to complete each sentence.**

1. Nancy invited Kevin and (we <u>us</u>) for a game of tag.
2. The team captains picked (she <u>her</u>) and (I <u>me</u>).
3. Kurt wants Jerry and (he <u>him</u>) on his team.
4. The fastest runners caught Carl and (<u>me</u> I).
5. Jess tagged Kathy and (I <u>me</u>).
6. The girls chased (they <u>them</u>) and (<u>us</u> we).
7. Derek tried to get Lily and (he <u>him</u>).
8. Nadia caught (she <u>her</u>) and (I <u>me</u>).

EXERCISE 3 **Choose the correct subject or object pronoun to complete each sentence.**

1. My friends and (<u>I</u> me) played statue tag.
2. Some classmates taught Jessica and (he <u>him</u>) the rules.
3. Jeff and (<u>she</u> her) explained that a tagged player stays frozen.
4. Jeff was it, and he tagged Ty and (I <u>me</u>).
5. Amy and (<u>he</u> him) were the last tagged.
6. Jeff then twirled my friends and (I <u>me</u>) around.
7. My friends and (<u>I</u> me) stayed in that position as statues.
8. Liz and (her <u>she</u>) were lying on the ground.
9. Jeff and (<u>he</u> him) chose the best statues.
10. The funniest statues were made by Luke and (she <u>her</u>).

APPLY IT NOW

Write four sentences about how you and your friends help other people at school, at home, or in your community. Write two sentences with compound subject pronouns and two sentences with compound object pronouns.

Pronouns • 69

Pronoun Review

ASSESS

Use the Pronoun Review as homework, as a practice test, or as an informal assessment. Following are some options for use.

Homework

You may wish to assign one group the odd items and another group the even items. When you next meet, review the correct answers as a group. Be sure to model how to arrive at the correct answer.

Practice Test

Use the Pronoun Review as a diagnostic tool. Assign the entire review or just specific sections. After students have finished, identify which concepts require more attention. Reteach concepts as necessary.

Pronoun Review

3.1 Find the personal pronoun in each sentence.

1. Did <u>you</u> snorkel in the ocean?
2. <u>I</u> saw many fish near the reef.
3. <u>It</u> is the best place to see fish.
4. The blue fish were not afraid of <u>me</u>.
5. <u>We</u> were amazed at the colorful creatures.
6. What are <u>they</u> called?
7. <u>She</u> told everyone about coral reefs.

3.2 Use a subject noun to take the place of the underlined word or words.

3.2
8. They
9. He
10. We
11. It
12. She
13. They

8. <u>Coconuts</u> grow on trees.
9. <u>Tom</u> found a ripe coconut.
10. <u>Dad and I</u> cracked the coconut open.
11. <u>The coconut</u> was tasty.
12. <u>Mom</u> drank some coconut milk.
13. <u>Sherry and Georgia</u> made a coconut cream pie.

3.3 Find the object pronoun in each sentence.

14. Mrs. Blair invited <u>us</u> to tea.
15. The guests helped <u>her</u> with the tea.
16. Mrs. Blair passed <u>them</u> the sandwiches.
17. Kara gave <u>me</u> a cup of tea.
18. Edward brought <u>him</u> a cucumber sandwich.
19. Many people enjoy <u>it</u>.
20. Mary and Isabel had never tasted <u>them</u> before.

3.4 Find the possessive pronoun in each sentence.

21. <u>Mine</u> has a tall sail.
22. <u>Hers</u> has a motor made from rubber bands.
23. Let's race <u>ours</u> across the pond.
24. <u>Yours</u> is sinking quickly.
25. <u>His</u> won the race by a yard.
26. <u>Theirs</u> finished second.

Informal Assessment

Use the review as preparation for the formal assessment. Count the review as a portion of the grade. Have students work to find the correct answers and use their corrected review as a study guide for the formal assessment.

WRITING CONNECTION

Use pages 302–303 of the Writing portion of the book.

3.5 Find the possessive adjective in each sentence.

27. Our yard is full of leaves.
28. My chore is to rake the leaves.
29. Tabitha wants to jump in their piles of leaves.
30. Your tree is beautiful.
31. Linda wants to press her favorite leaf in a book.
32. There are some funny photos in his album.

3.6 Choose the verb that agrees with the subject pronoun to complete each sentence.

33. She (pick picks) the apples from the tree.
34. He (reach reaches) the high branches.
35. They (peel peels) apples for the pie.
36. You (make makes) the crust.
37. We (eat eats) the pie after dinner.
38. It (taste tastes) delicious.

3.7 Choose the correct pronoun to complete each sentence.

39. (I Me) like watching squirrels in the backyard.
40. (I Me) saw the squirrels bury acorns.
41. Squirrels interest (I me).
42. (I Me) laughed when a squirrel ran across the yard.
43. The squirrel surprised (I me) by digging in a flowerpot.
44. The squirrel saw (I me) and ran away.

3.8 Find the compound subject or the compound object in each sentence. Then choose the correct pronoun or pronouns to complete each sentence.

45. The other students and (I me) looked at the map.
46. The teacher asked (he him) and (I me) to find China.
47. I asked my partner and (she her) for help.
48. Kelly and (them they) are good at geography.
49. (He Him) and Javier located Antarctica.
50. I showed (he him) and (she her) where Australia is.

3.8
Compound subjects and compound objects are underlined.
45. I
46. him, me
47. her
48. they
49. He
50. him, her

Tech Tip Go to www.voyagesinenglish.com for more activities.

Pronouns • 71

TEACHING OPTIONS

Reteach

Distribute newspapers or age-appropriate magazines. Have students read an article. Then have them reread the article to search for pronouns, subject pronouns, object pronouns, possessive pronouns, possessive adjectives, sentences with *I* and *me*, and pronouns used in compound subjects and compound objects.

Ask students to highlight each pronoun. Direct students to make a chart with the headings for each category of pronoun. Have students write in the correct category on their charts each pronoun from the article. Discuss how students categorized each pronoun.

Meeting Individual Needs

Challenge Give students a few days to be Pronoun Sleuths. Have students compile lists of pronouns they find at home, at school, on television, on signs, or any other places. Remind students to look for a variety of pronouns and pronouns used in different ways. At the end of the allotted time, have students share their lists and discuss pronouns and their uses in everyday writing.

Tech Tip Encourage students to further review pronouns, using the additional practice and games at www.voyagesinenglish.com.

Pronoun Challenge

ASSESS

Encourage students to read the paragraph twice before answering the questions. If students have difficulty with any questions, suggest that they refer to the section that teaches the skill. This activity can be completed by individuals, small groups, or the class as a whole.

After you have reviewed pronouns, administer the Section 3 Assessment on pages 9–10 in the **Assessment Book,** or create a customized test with the optional **Test Generator CD.**

WRITING CONNECTION
Use pages 304–305 of the Writing portion of the book.

EXERCISE 1 (Answers)

1. possessive pronoun
2. It
3. possessive adjective
4. My friends and I
5. him
6. She and he
7. her; object
8. They are both possessive adjectives.
9. Theirs; possessive pronoun

Pronoun Challenge

EXERCISE 1 Read the paragraph and answer the questions.

1. Schools are different sizes. 2. Ours is rather big. 3. It has about 1,000 students. 4. The middle school in my town is even bigger. 5. It has 1,500 students. 6. My friends and I like our big school. 7. We all have lots of friends.

8. My dad went to a really small school. 9. The third-grade teacher taught him and only five other children. 10. She and he still see each other at school reunions. 11. My mom did not go to a regular school. 12. Mom's dad taught her at home. 13. She and her four brothers had class in their kitchen. 14. Theirs was a home school.

1. In sentence 2 what kind of pronoun is *ours*?
2. In sentence 3 what is the subject pronoun?
3. In sentence 4 is *my* a pronoun or an adjective?
4. In sentence 6 what is the compound subject?
5. In sentence 9 what is the object pronoun?
6. In sentence 10 what are the subjects?
7. In sentence 12 what is the pronoun? How is it used?
8. In sentence 13 how are *her* and *their* alike?
9. In sentence 14 find the pronoun. What kind of pronoun is it?

EXERCISE 2 Write a six-sentence paragraph about your school. Use at least three different kinds of pronouns and circle them.

SECTION FOCUS

- Action verbs
- Being verbs
- Helping verbs
- Principal parts of verbs
- Regular and irregular verbs
- *Bring, Buy, Come,* and *Sit*
- *Eat, Go,* and *See*
- *Take, Tear,* and *Write*
- Simple present tense
- Simple past tense
- Future tense with *Will*
- Future tense with *Going To*
- Present progressive tense
- Past progressive tense
- *Is* and *Are, Was* and *Were*
- Contractions with *Not*

SUPPORT MATERIALS

Practice Book
Daily Maintenance, pages 47–52
Grammar, pages 53–72

Assessment Book
Section 4 Assessment,
    pages 11–14

Test Generator CD

Writing Chapter 3,
    Descriptions

Writing Chapter 4,
    Personal Letters

Customizable Lesson Plans
www.voyagesinenglish.com

CONNECT WITH LITERATURE

Consider using the following titles throughout the section to illustrate the grammar concept:

If You Were a Verb by Michael Dahl
Kites Sail High by Ruth Heller

Verbs

GRAMMAR FOR GROWN-UPS

Understanding Verbs

A **verb** is a word that tells what a subject is or does. Every sentence must have a verb. A verb gives a sentence meaning and movement; without a verb the words form an incomplete thought.

An **action verb** describes what a subject does.

> *John jumps.*

A **being verb** tells what a subject is. Some common being verbs are *am, is, are, was, were, has been, had been, have been,* and *will be.*

> *John is awake.*

The **main verb** in a sentence tells what the subject does or is.

> *I am alone.*

> *I eat an apple every day.*

A **helping verb** helps the main verb show an action or make a statement. Some common helping verbs are *have, am, was, has, is, were, had, are,* and *will.*

> *The boy has cut the grass.*

A **verb** has four principal parts—present (*run*), present participle (*running*), past (*ran*), and past participle (*run*).

Verbs have tenses, including simple present (*send*), past (*sent*), and future, (*will send* or *going to send*); present, past, and future progressive (*am planning, was planning, will be planning*); and present, past, and future perfect (*have played, had played, will have played*).

Regular verbs form the past and the past participle by adding *-d* or *-ed* (*boil, boiled, boiled*). The past and the past participle of irregular verbs do not follow any standard rules (*do, did, done*).

In a sentence the verb and the subject must agree. In the present tense, *-s* or *-es* is added to the verb when the subject is a singular noun or pronoun. (*The girl talks. The girls talk.*)

> " The noun of self becomes a verb. This flashpoint of creation in the present moment is where work and play merge. "

—Stephen Nachmanovitch

COMMON ERRORS

Using the Past Tense of *Bring*

When speaking and writing, some students make the common error of using *brang* or *brung*, two words that really aren't words, instead of past tense *brought*.

> **ERROR:** Grace brang her tap shoes to class.
> **CORRECT:** Grace brought her tap shoes to class.

> **ERROR:** Marco brung me some flowers.
> **CORRECT:** Marco brought me some flowers.

Listen for *brang* and *brung* in students' everyday speech and guide them to correct the mistake each time you hear it. From time to time, have students check for the error during the revision stage in writing. Help students change *brang* and *brung* to *brought*. With consistent oral and written practice, students will begin to use the correct form of the verb.

SENTENCE DIAGRAMMING

You may wish to teach verbs in the context of diagramming. Review these examples. Then refer to the Diagramming section or look for Diagram It! features in the Verbs section.

Gordon cooks.

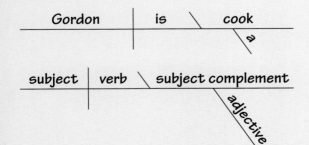

Gordon has cooked.

Gordon is a cook.

ASK AN EXPERT

Real Situations, Real Solutions

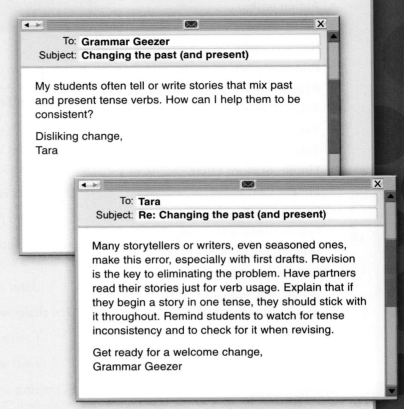

To: **Grammar Geezer**
Subject: **Changing the past (and present)**

My students often tell or write stories that mix past and present tense verbs. How can I help them to be consistent?

Disliking change,
Tara

To: **Tara**
Subject: **Re: Changing the past (and present)**

Many storytellers or writers, even seasoned ones, make this error, especially with first drafts. Revision is the key to eliminating the problem. Have partners read their stories just for verb usage. Explain that if they begin a story in one tense, they should stick with it throughout. Remind students to watch for tense inconsistency and to check for it when revising.

Get ready for a welcome change,
Grammar Geezer

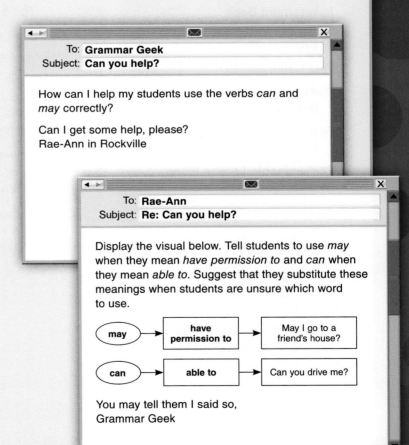

To: **Grammar Geek**
Subject: **Can you help?**

How can I help my students use the verbs *can* and *may* correctly?

Can I get some help, please?
Rae-Ann in Rockville

To: **Rae-Ann**
Subject: **Re: Can you help?**

Display the visual below. Tell students to use *may* when they mean *have permission to* and *can* when they mean *able to*. Suggest that they substitute these meanings when students are unsure which word to use.

You may tell them I said so,
Grammar Geek

4.1 Action Verbs

4.2 Being Verbs

4.3 Helping Verbs

4.4 Principal Parts of Verbs

4.5 Regular and Irregular Verbs

4.6 *Bring, Buy, Come,* and *Sit*

4.7 *Eat, Go,* and *See*

4.8 *Take, Tear,* and *Write*

4.9 Simple Present Tense

4.10 Simple Past Tense

4.11 Future Tense with *Will*

4.12 Future Tense with *Going To*

4.13 Present Progressive Tense

4.14 Past Progressive Tense

4.15 *Is* and *Are, Was* and *Were*

4.16 Contractions with *Not*

Verb Review

Verb Challenge

OBJECTIVE

- **To identify certain verbs as words that express action**

 **Maintenance**

Assign **Practice Book** page 47, Section 4.1. After students finish,
1. Give immediate feedback.
2. Review concepts as needed.
3. Model the correct answer.

Pages 4–5 of the **Answer Key** contain tips for Daily Maintenance.

WARM-UP

Write on the board several sentences with action verbs for which students can perform the actions. Start with the following:

I jump in place.

I raise my arms.

I clap my hands.

Have students stand and perform the actions after you read aloud the sentences. Ask volunteers to circle the words that name an action. Encourage students to name other action words and list them on the board.

📖 Read from a piece of writing that the class is currently reading. Emphasize the action verbs.

TEACH

Point out the action words on the board. Tell students these words are called *verbs*. Explain that some verbs show actions. Ask students to tell where in each sentence the verb appears *(after the subject)*. Then have students name other action verbs. List the action verbs on the board.

Have a volunteer read aloud the first three paragraphs and example sentences about action verbs. Encourage students to make up sentences using the action verbs on the board.

Ask volunteers to read aloud the rest of the page. For each action verb in the example sentences, have students identify who or what is doing the action.

PRACTICE

EXERCISE 1

Review subjects *(the person, place, or thing that the sentence is about)*. Invite volunteers to read aloud the sentences. Tell students to first identify the subject and then the verb *(what the subject does)*.

EXERCISE 2

Ask volunteers to read the sentences aloud. Make sure students realize that the action verbs are missing. Tell students to choose the best verb from word box to complete each sentence. Discuss whether their chosen verbs make sense.

EXERCISE 3

Have students choose a subject for each verb and add details to write a complete sentence. Ask volunteers to share their sentences with the class.

4.1 Action Verbs

Many verbs express action. An **action verb** tells what someone or something does.

These action verbs tell what a child does.

    A child *plays.*
    A child *runs.*
    A child *laughs.*

These action verbs tell what water does.

    Water *spills.*
    Water *freezes.*
    Water *bubbles.*

Which word is the action verb in the following sentence?

    Arun jumps rope.

You are right if you said *jumps. Arun* is the subject. The verb *jumps* tells what Arun does.

Which word is the action verb in this sentence?

    We studied about the rain forest.

You are right if you said *studied*. The verb *studied* tells what we did.

Which word is the action verb in this sentence?

    The rain dripped down the window.

You are right if you said *dripped*. The verb *dripped* tells what the rain did.

New Zealand rain forest

EXERCISE 1 **Find the action verb in each sentence.**

1. Kurt and Elena joined the school science club.
2. They learn about the rain forest.
3. The world's largest rain forest grows in South America.
4. Many animals live in the rain forest.

74 • Section 4.1

APPLY

APPLY IT NOW

Challenge students to use a different action verb in each of their sentences. Advise students to reread their sentences and to underline the action verbs. Students should demonstrate the ability to use action verbs.

ASSESS

Note which students had difficulty identifying action verbs as words that express action. Assign **Practice Book** page 53 for further practice.

WRITING CONNECTION

Use pages 306–307 of the Writing portion of the book.

Reteach

Help students brainstorm a list of action verbs. Write on the board the heading *Things We Do*. Model action verbs by offering personal examples, such as the following: *I teach. I exercise every day. I read books. I cook dinner.* List on the board the verbs from your examples. Then encourage students to name verbs and list them on the board. Have students write the list in their notebooks to use as a reference when they write.

Curriculum Connections

Display a poster or an illustration of a scene that shows action. Have students make up sentences using action verbs to describe the picture, such as the following:

The children jump rope.

The dog catches a Frisbee.

Write on the board students' responses and ask volunteers to circle the action verbs.

Meeting Individual Needs

Kinesthetic Write action verbs (*run, shout, jump, tag, dance, twist, turn, shake, sing, write, read*) on slips of paper and place the slips in a bag. Have a student choose a slip and act out the verb. Ask a volunteer to name the action verb. Tell the student who guesses correctly to choose the next verb to act out. Have students continue playing until all verbs have been acted out.

Diagram It!

To practice these concepts in the context of diagramming, turn to Section 8.1.

---

5. Jaguars <u>hunt</u> for food.
6. Toucans <u>pick</u> fruit with their beaks.
7. The basilisk lizard <u>walks</u> on water.
8. Sloths <u>move</u> very slowly.
9. The trees <u>grow</u> tall and leafy.
10. More than 100 inches of rain <u>fall</u> in some rain forests each year.

Emerald basilisk

EXERCISE 2 Use an action verb to complete each sentence. Use an action word from the word box.

| calls | dribbles | drinks | shoots | play |
| shake | wears | wins | trips | block |

1. Some students ___play___ on basketball teams.
2. Our school's team ___wears___ red uniforms.
3. Kate ___dribbles___ the basketball.
4. Avery ___drinks___ lots of water.
5. Eddie ___trips___ running down the court.
6. The coach ___calls___ time-out.
7. A player ___shoots___ the ball through the hoop.
8. Simon and Trevor ___block___ a shot.
9. The other team ___wins___ the game.
10. The players ___shake___ hands.

EXERCISE 3 Write a sentence using each action verb.

Exercise 3
Answers will vary.

1. jump
2. run
3. talk
4. play
5. climb
6. throw

APPLY IT NOW

What do you do after school? Do you play sports, take lessons, practice band, or belong to any clubs? Write four sentences about activities you do. Use an action verb in each sentence.

Verbs • 75

OBJECTIVES

- **To identify being verbs as words that tell what someone or something is**
- **To distinguish between being verbs and action verbs**

DAILY Maintenance

Assign **Practice Book** page 47, Section 4.2. After students finish,
1. Give immediate feedback.
2. Review concepts as needed.
3. Model the correct answer.

Pages 4–5 of the **Answer Key** contain tips for Daily Maintenance.

WARM-UP

Write on the board sentence starters using being verbs, such as the following:

I am _____.

Frogs are _____.

The water was _____.

We were _____.

Have volunteers write words to complete the sentences.

📖 Read from a piece of writing that the class is currently reading. Emphasize the being verbs.

TEACH

Ask students to identify in the sentences from the Warm-Up the words that describe what someone or something is or was *(am, are, was, were)*. Tell students that these verbs are called being verbs. Explain that being verbs show what someone or something is.

Have a volunteer read aloud the first paragraph about being verbs and the being verbs chart. Write on the board the being verbs. Ask students to make up sentences with the being verbs. Write the sentences on the board.

Have volunteers read aloud the rest of the page. Encourage students to make up sentences with being verbs and action verbs. Have students tell which kind of verb is used in each sentence.

PRACTICE

EXERCISE 1
Have students refer to the list of being verbs on the board as they complete the exercise.

EXERCISE 2
Review the difference between action verbs and being verbs. As

students work, create on the board a two-column chart of action verbs and being verbs. Ask volunteers to write the verbs in the correct column of the chart. Help students understand why each verb is either a being verb or an action verb.

EXERCISE 3
Explain that the missing words in the sentences are being verbs and that more than one verb could be used in some sentences. Invite students to share their sentences with the class. Have students notice which sentences could have more than one correct verb.

4.2 Being Verbs

A **being verb** shows what someone or something is. Being verbs do not express action.

Here is a list of some being verbs.

BEING VERBS

am	is	are	was	were
has been	had been	have been	will be	

Sentences That Show Action

Cindy *sings*.
The plants *grow*.
The bird *pecks*.

Sentences That Show Being

Cindy *is* **happy**.
The plants *are* **green**.
The bird *was* **hungry**.

The action verbs tell what Cindy, the plants, and the bird do. The being verbs do not express action.

Which one of these sentences has a being verb?

A **Pedro is ready for school.**
B **Angie ate a peach.**
C **Kevin laughed at the movie.**

You are right if you said that sentence A uses a being verb. The word *is* is a being verb. In sentences B and C, *ate* and *laughed* are action verbs.

EXERCISE 1 Find the being verb in each sentence.

1. Many students <u>are</u> at home this week.
2. They <u>have been</u> sick with colds.
3. I <u>was</u> sick last week.
4. I <u>am</u> fine now.

APPLY

APPLY IT NOW

Tell students to underline the being verbs they use. Have volunteers read aloud their sentences. Students should demonstrate the ability to use being verbs.

Grammar in Action Have a volunteer read aloud the sentence. Ask students to point out the being verbs *(is, are)*.

ASSESS

Note which students had difficulty identifying being verbs as words that tell what someone or something is, as well as distinguishing between being verbs and action verbs. Assign **Practice Book** pages 54–55 for further practice.

WRITING CONNECTION

Use pages 308–309 of the Writing portion of the book.

TEACHING OPTIONS

Reteach

Write each being verb on a note card. Distribute a note card and a sentence strip to each student. Ask students to use the being verb to write a sentence on their sentence strip. Display students' sentence strips. Encourage students to read aloud their sentences and to identify the being verbs in each sentence.

Meeting Individual Needs

Extra Support Write on the board a two-column chart with the headings *Action Verb* and *Being Verb*. Write on individual note cards all the being verbs and a variety of action verbs. Shuffle the cards and place them facedown in a pile. Have a student choose a card, read the word aloud, and write it in the correct column. Continue until all the cards have been used. If students have difficulty tell them to decide whether the verb can be acted out. Explain that if it can, the verb is an action verb.

Meeting Individual Needs

Challenge Encourage students to use being verbs as they role-play telephone conversations. Remind students to listen for the being verbs in one another's speech. You might start this activity with the following play prompt:

Student 1: Where have you been?

Student 2: I was at school.

Student 1: Where will you be later?

Student 2: I will be at the soccer practice.

EXERCISE 2 Find the verb in each sentence. Tell whether it is an action verb or a being verb.

being   **1.** Louie <u>was</u> sick.

being   **2.** He <u>had</u> a cold.

being   **3.** He <u>will be</u> home from school today.

action   **4.** Mom <u>took</u> Louie to the doctor.

being   **5.** They <u>had been</u> in the waiting room one hour.

being   **6.** Finally, the doctor <u>was</u> ready for them.

action   **7.** Dr. McGrath <u>listened</u> to Louie's cough.

action   **8.** The doctor <u>gave</u> Louie some medicine.

being   **9.** Louie <u>is</u> better.

action   **10.** Mom <u>sent</u> him to school.

Exercise 3
Answers will vary.
Possible answers:
1. is
2. was
3. were, had been
4. am
5. are, were
6. is, will be
7. is
8. has been
9. is
10. am, will be

EXERCISE 3 Complete each sentence with a verb from the list on page 76. More than one verb may fit.

1. Chicken pox _____ a virus.

2. I _____ four years old when I had it.

3. My brother and sister _____ sick then too.

4. I _____ glad I had it when I was little.

5. You _____ hot and tired.

6. Your skin _____ itchy.

7. Molly _____ ill now.

8. She _____ scratching her skin.

9. She _____ in bed.

10. I _____ sure Molly _____ better soon.

APPLY IT NOW

Tell about a time when you were not feeling well. Write four sentences about how you were feeling. Use being verbs.

Grammar in Action Find the two being verbs in the third sentence of the letter on page 330.

Verbs • 77

OBJECTIVES

- **To identify and use helping verbs**
- **To distinguish between main verbs and helping verbs in sentences**

DAILY Maintenance

Assign **Practice Book** page 47, Section 4.3. After students finish,
1. Give immediate feedback.
2. Review concepts as needed.
3. Model the correct answer.

Pages 4–5 of the **Answer Key** contain tips for Daily Maintenance.

WARM-UP

Create two sets of note cards on which you have written all the helping verbs from the chart on this page. Place the cards facedown in two stacks. Arrange the class into two teams to have a relay race. When you say "go," have one student from each team choose a note card, write a sentence on the board using the word, underline the word from the note card, and hand the chalk to the next person on their team. The team that uses all the helping verbs first wins.

📖 Read from a piece of writing that the class is currently reading. Emphasize the helping verbs.

TEACH

Circle the main verbs in the sentences on the board from the Warm-Up. Ask students what they notice about the verbs you have circled. Confirm that these verbs are made up of two separate verbs—a helping verb followed by a main verb.

Invite volunteers to read aloud about helping verbs. Pause after the first set of example sentences and have students explain how the helping verbs change the meaning of the sentences. Reinforce that helping verbs always come before the main verbs in a sentence.

PRACTICE

EXERCISES 1 & 2

Remind students that helping verbs work with main verbs. Point out that in each of these sentences, students will see two verbs next to each other and they must decide which verb is the helping verb. Have students exchange papers with partners and compare their answers.

EXERCISE 3

Explain that more than one helping verb could be correct in these sentences. Encourage volunteers to read aloud their completed sentences. Invite students who chose different helping verbs to read aloud their sentences. Discuss how the choice of a helping verb changes the meaning of a sentence.

4.3 Helping Verbs

A verb can have more than one word. A **helping verb** is a verb added before a main verb to make the meaning clear.

WITHOUT A HELPING VERB

We *sleep* in a tent.

WITH A HELPING VERB

We *will sleep* in a tent.
We *might sleep* in a tent.

Here are some helping verbs.

HELPING VERBS

am	was	have	can	do
is	were	had	might	does
are		has	will	did

A helping verb always comes before the main verb of the sentence.

Which sentences have a helping verb?

- A **The family plans a trip.**
- B **The family planned a trip.**
- C **The family is planning a trip.**
- D **The family has planned a trip.**

You are right if you said sentences C and D. In sentence C, *is* is a helping verb that is added before *planning*. In sentence D, *has* is a helping verb that is added before *planned*.

Can you find the helping verb and main verb in these sentences?

- A **We have decided on Colorado for our vacation.**
- B **We are thinking about a camping trip.**

In sentence A, *have* is the helping verb, and *decided* is the main verb. In sentence B, *are* is the helping verb, and *thinking* is the main verb.

APPLY

APPLY IT NOW

Help students brainstorm what they imagine a camping trip to be like. Have any students who have been camping to tell about their experiences. Discuss what students need to bring with them *(a backpack, a tent, bug spray, a flashlight, a sleeping bag, food, water)*. Ask volunteers to read aloud their sentences and identify each helping verb. Students should demonstrate the ability to use helping verbs.

ASSESS

Note which students had difficulty identifying and using helping verbs and distinguishing between main verbs and helping verbs. Assign **Practice Book** pages 56–57 for further practice.

WRITING CONNECTION

Use pages 310–311 of the Writing portion of the book.

TEACHING OPTIONS

Reteach

Remind students that the predicate of a sentence is the part that tells about the subject of the sentence. Explain that the predicate includes all the verbs, the helping verb as well as the main verb. Write several sentences on the board and have students identify each helping verb and each main verb. Write the verbs in a two-column chart like the one below. As you review the chart, have students generate new sentences for the helping verbs and the main verbs listed.

Helping Verb	Main Verb
are	helping
was	going
will	cook
is	playing

Meeting Individual Needs

Musical Have small groups make a list of helping verbs. Then have students use the list to make up rhymes, raps, chants, or jingles to help memorize helping verbs. Encourage students to make up their own rhythms or to use the melodies of popular children's rhymes or songs. Have students perform their works.

English-Language Learners

Write simple sentences on sentence strips, omitting the helping verbs. Write the helping verbs on separate note cards. Have students place helping verbs into the sentences. Help students decide which helping verb works best in each sentence.

Diagram It!

To practice these concepts in the context of diagramming, turn to Section 8.1.

EXERCISE 1 Find the helping verb in each sentence.

1. My family is going to Yellowstone National Park.
2. We might leave next week.
3. I had hoped to go tomorrow.
4. Mom will buy a tent.
5. Dad has planned the route.
6. I am hoping to see moose and bear.
7. We can see the geyser called Old Faithful.
8. It will shoot water high into the air.

Old Faithful

Exercise 2
Helping verbs are underlined once. Main verbs are underlined twice.

EXERCISE 2 Find the helping verb and the main verb in each sentence.

1. Yellowstone has been a national park since 1872.
2. Many people have visited it.
3. You can camp in some areas of the park.
4. You might make reservations for a camping spot.
5. Some parts of the park will close in the winter.
6. We are going there this summer.

Exercise 3
Answers will vary. Possible answers:
1. might, can, will
2. are, were
3. has, had
4. are, were
5. might, can, will, did

EXERCISE 3 Complete each sentence with a helping verb from the list on page 78. More than one verb may fit.

1. It _____ turn cooler tonight.
2. We _____ sitting around the campfire.
3. Dad _____ gone to get wood for the fire.
4. They _____ telling camp stories.
5. We _____ sing silly songs.
6. She _____ roast marshmallows.
7. I _____ sleeping in a tent.
8. The mosquitoes _____ biting me.
9. I _____ put on bug spray.
10. I _____ be awake all night.

APPLY IT NOW

Imagine you are packing for a camping trip. What do you think you might need? Write five sentences. Use helping verbs. Underline them.
Example:
I might need some warm clothes tonight.
I will take a sweater.

Verbs • 79

4.4 Principal Parts of Verbs

- **To identify and use the present, past, present participle, and past participle parts of verbs**

 **Maintenance**

Assign **Practice Book** page 48, Section 4.4. After students finish,
1. Give immediate feedback.
2. Review concepts as needed.
3. Model the correct answer.

Pages 4–5 of the **Answer Key** contain tips for Daily Maintenance.

WARM-UP

Write on the board the following sentence starters:

Everyday, I _____.

Yesterday I _____.

Right now I am _____.

I have _____.

Ask students to complete each sentences with a verb *(walk, walked, walking, walked)*. Have volunteers fill in the blanks with their verbs.

📖 Read from a piece of writing that the class is currently reading. Emphasize the principal parts of verbs.

TEACH

Review the definition of a helping verb *(verb added before a main verb to make the meaning clear)*. Ask students to identify the helping verbs in the sentences from the Warm-Up *(am, have)*.
    Have a volunteer read aloud the first half of the page about principal parts of verbs. Then ask students to identify the main verb in each sentence on the board and name each part *(1. present, 2. past, 3. present participle, 4. past participle)*.

Ask volunteers to read aloud the rest of the page. Encourage students to name the four principal parts of the verbs *watch* and *jump*.

PRACTICE

EXERCISE 1
Tell students to refer to the chart of principal parts of verbs for this exercise. Point out which parts need helping verbs *(present participle and past participle)*. Remind students to look for helping verbs and to pay close attention to verb endings when making their choices.

EXERCISE 2
Make sure students understand that they must complete each sentence with the verb and verb part in parentheses. Complete the first item as a class. Then have partners complete the rest of the exercise. Encourage volunteers to write their sentences on the board. Discuss why the chosen verb works or does not work in a sentence.

Invite students to share their answers with the class. Discuss the function of the verb in each sentence.

4.4 Principal Parts of Verbs

A verb has four principal parts: **present, present participle, past,** and **past participle.**

PRESENT	PRESENT PARTICIPLE	PAST	PAST PARTICIPLE
learn	learning	learned	learned
walk	walking	walked	walked

The present participle is formed by adding *-ing* to the present. The past and the past participle of a verb are usually formed by adding *-ed* to the present.

My friends *play* **the drums.** (present)
My friends *are playing* **a march.** (present participle)
The band *played* **works by John Philip Sousa.** (past)
The band *had played* **a song before my arrival.** (past participle)

Note these points:

- With a singular noun subject (and with *he, she,* or *it*), an *-s* is added to the present part of the verb: Kim *plays* in the band.
- The present participle is often used with forms of the helping verb *be* (*am, is, are, was,* and *were*).
- The past participle is often used with *has, have,* or *had.*

In this sentence what principal part is the underlined verb?

I never had <u>played</u> in a band before.

You are right if you said past participle. The verb *played* ends in *ed,* and it is used with *had.*

EXERCISE 1 **Tell whether each underlined verb is in the present, present participle, past, or past participle. Look for *be* verbs before present participles and for *have, has,* or *had* before past participles.**

1. I <u>like</u> classical music.
2. I was <u>listening</u> to a Mozart symphony last night.

APPLY

APPLY IT NOW

Help students brainstorm a list of games and write them on the board. Review the four principal parts of verbs *(present, present participle, past, past participle)*. Have students read aloud their sentences. Students should demonstrate the ability to use principal parts of verbs.

ASSESS

Note which students had difficulty identifying and using principal parts of verbs. Assign **Practice Book** pages 58–59 for further practice.

WRITING CONNECTION

Students can complete a formal description using the Writer's Workshop on pages 312–323.

Reteach

Have two teams play Verb-Part Trivia. Have one student from each team stand. Say a sentence. Tell students to listen closely for the verb and to raise their hands when they can identify the principal part of the verb. Ask the first student to raise his or her hand to tell the verb's principal part. For example, for the sentence *Joe is talking,* the answer is *The present participle of talk.* Give teams one point for each correct response. Have another pair of students stand to respond to the next sentence. If a student responds incorrectly, the team loses a point. The team with the most points wins.

Meeting Individual Needs

Extra Support Write on the board a four-column chart with the headings *Present, Present Participle, Past,* and *Past Participle.* Say a verb and ask volunteers to write each of the four parts of that verb. Be sure to use only regular verbs, such as *call, talk, help, ask,* and *cook.* Encourage students to use the four principal parts of each verb in complete sentences.

Cooperative Learning

Have partners search magazines, newspapers, and classroom books for sentences with each of the principal parts of verbs. Ask students to make a chart with the headings *Present, Present Participle, Past,* and *Past Participle.* Encourage students write their sentences in the appropriate columns and underline the verbs.

Exercise 1
1. present
2. present participle
3. past
4. past participle
5. past
6. past
7. past
8. present
9. past participle
10. past participle
11. present
12. present participle

3. Mozart <u>learned</u> to play piano when he was four years old.
4. He had <u>composed</u> his first symphony by the age of nine.
5. Mozart <u>produced</u> several other symphonies during his lifetime.
6. He <u>earned</u> little money from his music.
7. He <u>created</u> several famous operas too.
8. My collection <u>contains</u> a CD with songs from *The Magic Flute.*
9. I have <u>listened</u> to his music many times.
10. Mozart's popularity has <u>lasted</u> for hundreds of years.
11. People still <u>enjoy</u> his music today.
12. Leigh is <u>downloading</u> some music onto his MP3 player.

Wolfgang Amadeus Mozart, 1756–1791

EXERCISE 2 Complete each sentence with the form of the verb in parentheses.
1. The band <u>plays</u> every Friday. (play—present).
2. The students are <u>listening</u>. (listen—present participle)
3. The band <u>practiced</u> many hours. (practice—past).
4. I am <u>learning</u> to play the flute. (learn—present participle)
5. I have <u>studied</u> the flute for six months. (study—past participle)
6. The band teacher has <u>helped</u> me. (help—past participle)
7. My best friend also <u>takes</u> flute lessons. (take—present)
8. I had never <u>performed</u> onstage before. (perform—past participle).
9. People <u>applauded</u> us. (applaud—past)
10. Our teacher was <u>cheering</u>. (cheer—present participle)

APPLY IT NOW

Write four sentences about a game you like. Write one sentence using each of the principal parts of a verb.

Verbs • 81

4.5 Regular and Irregular Verbs

OBJECTIVE

• **To define, use, and distinguish between regular and irregular verbs**

 **Maintenance**

Assign **Practice Book** page 48, Section 4.5. After students finish,
1. Give immediate feedback.
2. Review concepts as needed.
3. Model the correct answer.

Pages 4–5 of the **Answer Key** contain tips for Daily Maintenance.

WARM-UP

Ask students questions using irregular verbs, such as the following:

Did you sing in music class yesterday?

Did you write anything yesterday?

Did you send a thank-you note for your birthday gift?

Have students respond in complete sentences. Write students' responses on the board. Have volunteers underline the verbs.

📖 Read from a piece of writing that the class is currently reading. Emphasize the regular and irregular verbs.

TEACH

Review the principal parts of several regular verbs. Discuss how the past and the past participle are formed *(by adding* -d *or* -ed *to the present part).* Write several examples on the board *(cooked, learned, cleaned, walked).*

Have a volunteer read aloud about regular and irregular verbs. Read aloud each present tense verb in the chart. Encourage volunteers to name the past and past participle of each verb without looking at the chart.

Write on the board the present tense of the verbs from the questions in the Warm-Up *(sing, write, send).* Direct students to read aloud the responses to the questions and to identify the past tense of each verb *(sang, wrote, sent).* Point out that these irregular verbs do not have a *d* or an *ed* ending in the past or the past participle.

PRACTICE

EXERCISE 1
Write on the board the chart from the exercise and ask volunteers to fill it in. Ask students to make up sentences using the past participle of the words in the chart. Remind students to use *has, have,* or *had* with the past participle.

EXERCISE 2
Remind students that the past of regular verbs is formed by adding *-d* or *-ed* but that the past of irregular verbs is not formed the same way. Have students write their answers in a two-column chart.

4.5 Regular and Irregular Verbs

The past and the past participle of **regular verbs** usually end in *d* or *ed.*

PRESENT	PAST	PAST PARTICIPLE
jump	jumped	jumped
wave	waved	waved

The past and the past participle of **irregular verbs** are not formed by adding *-d* or *-ed* to the present.

Here are some common irregular verbs.

PRESENT	PAST	PAST PARTICIPLE
begin	began	begun
do	did	done
feel	felt	felt
fly	flew	flown
give	gave	given
put	put	put
send	sent	sent
sing	sang	sung

Which sentence has an irregular verb?

A Paul Revere lived about 250 years ago.

B Paul Revere rode a horse.

C Paul Revere worked many jobs.

You are right if you said sentence B. The past of *ride* is not formed with the ending *d* or *ed.* That makes it an irregular verb.

Statue of Paul Revere

EXERCISE 3

Have students complete the exercise independently. Ask volunteers to write their sentences on the board. Direct students to underline each verb and to write above each verb *R* for *regular* or *I* for *irregular*.

APPLY

APPLY IT NOW

Help students brainstorm a list of family activities. Encourage students to use the verbs from the list of irregular verbs in the lesson. Have volunteers read aloud

their sentences. Students should demonstrate the ability to use regular and irregular verbs.

ASSESS

Note which students had difficulty using regular and irregular verbs. Assign **Practice Book** page 60 for further practice.

WRITING CONNECTION

Use pages 324–325 of the Writing portion of the book. Be sure to point out verbs in the literature excerpt and student model.

Reteach

Have students use regular and irregular verbs (*sing, fly, send, talk, grow, help, give, feel, call*) in the sentences, such as the following:

I play today.

I played yesterday.

I have played many times.

Ask volunteers to reread the sentences, replacing the verb with a different verb. Have students tell if the verb is regular or irregular.

Meeting Individual Needs

Challenge Have students make a four-column chart with the headings *Present, Present Participle, Past,* and *Past Participle*. Ask students to close their books. Read aloud one part of each irregular verb from the chart in the lesson. Have students write each part of the verbs in the correct column. Point out that only the present participle of the irregular verbs is formed the same as in regular verbs (*by adding* -ing). Emphasize that it is important to memorize the other forms of irregular verbs.

English-Language Learners

Display a calendar and point out today's date. Write on the board the following sentence starters:

Today, I _____.

Yesterday, I _____.

Many times in the past, I have _____.

Point to today's date, yesterday's date, and all of last week as you have students fill in the blanks, using the verb lists on page 82.

EXERCISE 1 Complete the chart with the correct parts of the verbs.

PRESENT	PRESENT PARTICIPLE	PAST	PAST PARTICIPLE
make	making	made	made
forget	forgetting	forgot	forgotten
tell	telling	told	told
ride	riding	rode	ridden

Exercise 2
1. regular
2. irregular
3. irregular
4. irregular
5. regular
6. regular
7. irregular
8. irregular
9. irregular

EXERCISE 2 Tell whether each underlined verb is regular or irregular.

1. Paul Revere <u>lived</u> from 1735 to 1818 in Boston, Massachusetts.
2. He <u>became</u> a silversmith.
3. He <u>made</u> eating utensils and tea sets.
4. People <u>bought</u> his silver pieces.
5. He <u>joined</u> a secret group named the Sons of Liberty.
6. The members <u>opposed</u> British authority in the colonies.
7. The British <u>sent</u> soldiers against the colonists in Concord.
8. Revere <u>spread</u> that news to colonists on his famous ride.
9. The first battle <u>began</u> at Lexington and Concord.

Exercise 3
1. irregular
2. regular
3. irregular
4. regular

EXERCISE 3 Complete each sentence, using one of the past tense verbs in the word box. Tell whether the verb is regular or irregular.

called	hated	put	threw

1. The British government __put__ a tax on tea.
2. The colonists __hated__ the tax.
3. They __threw__ the tea into Boston Harbor.
4. People __called__ this event the Boston Tea Party.

APPLY IT NOW

Think about things that you do with your family. Write four sentences, using regular and irregular verbs. Underline the verbs and label them.
Example:
I <u>built</u> a tree house with my dad. (irregular)
I <u>hammered</u> the nails. (regular)

Verbs • 83

OBJECTIVE
* **To use the parts of the irregular verbs *bring*, *buy*, *come*, and *sit* correctly**

 **Maintenance**

Assign **Practice Book** page 48, Section 4.6. After students finish,
1. Give immediate feedback.
2. Review concepts as needed.
3. Model the correct answer.

Pages 4–5 of the **Answer Key** contain tips for Daily Maintenance.

WARM-UP

Write on the board the following sentences:

I _____ my lunch to school.

I am _____ my lunch today.

I _____ my lunch yesterday.

I have _____ my lunch all week.

Have students complete each sentence with the correct form of the verb *bring (bring, bringing, brought, brought)*.

📖 Read from a piece of writing that the class is currently reading. Emphasize the principal parts of *bring*, *buy*, *come*, and *sit*.

TEACH

Have students read aloud the completed sentences from the Warm-Up. Ask if *bring* is a regular or an irregular verb *(irregular)* and why *(because the past is not formed by adding -d or -ed)*.

Tell students that *buy*, *come* and *sit* are also irregular verbs. Have volunteers read aloud the first half of the pages, including the example sentences. Encourage students to suggest sentences with the various forms of the verbs in the chart.

Have a volunteer read aloud the rest of the page. Have volunteers write one sentence using each of the different irregular verb forms.

PRACTICE

EXERCISE 1
Point out that this chart resembles the chart on page 83. Have students copy the chart and then close their books. Challenge students to complete the chart. Then have students share their answers as they use each word in a sentence. Allow students to compare their completed charts with the chart in the lesson to confirm their answers.

EXERCISE 2
Have partners complete this exercise. Remind students that the past participle requires a helping verb. Ask volunteers to read aloud their answers.

EXERCISE 3
Be sure students understand that they should use the verb in parentheses to complete each sentence. Have partners complete the sentences and write them on the board. Review the sentences with the class, encouraging students to express any confusion.

4.6 *Bring, Buy, Come, and Sit*

Bring, buy, come, and *sit* are irregular verbs. The chart shows the principal parts of each. Remember that the present participle and the past participle are often used with helping verbs.

PRESENT	PRESENT PARTICIPLE	PAST	PAST PARTICIPLE
bring	bringing	brought	brought
buy	buying	bought	bought
come	coming	came	come
sit	sitting	sat	sat

I *buy* pens at the office-supply store. (present)

I *am buying* a purple pen now.
(present participle, with the helping verb *am*)

I *bought* a red pen yesterday. (past)

I *have bought* a green pen already.
(past participle, with the helping verb *have*)

Which choice correctly completes the sentence?

Marie (buy buys) pens at the stationery store.

You're right if you chose *buys*. Singular noun subjects in the present tense use the present verb with -s added. The subject is the singular noun *Marie*. Note that -s is also added to present verbs for the pronoun subjects *he, she*, and *it*.

EXERCISE 1 Complete the chart with the correct parts of the verbs.

PRESENT	PRESENT PARTICIPLE	PAST	PAST PARTICIPLE
bring	bringing	brought	brought
buy	buying	bought	bought
come	coming	came	come
sit	sitting	sat	sat

APPLY

APPLY IT NOW

Suggest that students try to use as many parts of the four verbs as possible. Tell students to underline each part of the verb with a different pencil color; for example:

   red: present

   blue: past

   green: present participle

   yellow: past participle

Students should demonstrate the ability to use the parts of the irregular verbs *bring, buy, come,* and *sit.*

Tech Tip Explain that e-mails should be well written and grammatically correct, as well as polite. Have students hightlight the verbs.

ASSESS

Note which students had difficulty using the irregular parts of the verbs *bring, buy, come,* and *sit.* Assign **Practice Book** page 61 for further practice.

WRITING CONNECTION

Use pages 326–327 of the Writing portion of the book.

Reteach

Distribute copies of a Bingo grid with four rows of four boxes. Have students fill in the squares with verbs from the chart in the lesson. Direct students to include the helping verb *have* with the past participles. Tell students you will say a verb and its part. Instruct them to cover the correct verb form with a scrap of paper. Explain that the first student with four squares in a row wins the game.

Meeting Individual Needs

Auditory Have small groups practice role-playing buying, selling, giving, and taking items at a school fair or bake sale. Have groups present their role-plays to the class. Encourage students who are listening to make a list of all the forms of irregular verbs they hear in each role-playing presentation.

Curriculum Connection

Have students write math problems using *buy, bought, bring,* and *brought.* Write the following model on the board:

I want to buy 20 cards. I bought 10 cards. How many more should I buy?

Tell students to write their problems on note cards and the answers on the back of the cards. Have students exchange problems for other students to solve.

Exercise 2
1. present participle
2. past
3. past participle
4. past participle
5. present
6. past
7. past
8. past participle
9. present participle
10. present participle

EXERCISE 2 Find the part of *bring, buy, come,* or *sit* in each sentence. Then tell whether the part is present, present participle, past, or past participle.

1. I was <u>sitting</u> outside on the stairs.
2. My grandmother <u>came</u> up the walk.
3. She had <u>brought</u> us some tomatoes from her garden.
4. She has <u>come</u> to take us to the antique store.
5. She often <u>buys</u> things there.
6. At the store my grandmother <u>sat</u> in an old rocking chair.
7. She liked the chair, and she <u>bought</u> it.
8. My dad has <u>brought</u> the chair to her home.
9. Grandma is <u>sitting</u> in the chair and talking to me on the phone.
10. She is <u>coming</u> to visit again next week.

Exercise 3
1. present
2. present participle
3. past
4. past participle
5. present
6. past
7. past participle
8. present
9. past
10. past participle
11. past
12. present participle

EXERCISE 3 Complete each sentence with the correct part of *bring, buy, come,* or *sit.* Identify each verb as present, present participle, past, or past participle.

1. The mail carrier ___brings___ the mail every day. (bring)
2. He is ___bringing___ a package today. (bring)
3. I ___brought___ in the mail a few minutes ago. (bring)
4. I have ___brought___ the package inside. (bring)
5. We ___buy___ stamps at the post office. (buy)
6. Gail ___bought___ some flag stamps yesterday. (buy)
7. Elliot has ___bought___ envelopes at the store. (buy)
8. The mail carrier always ___comes___, even in rain. (come)
9. The letter ___came___ from Max last week. (come)
10. A letter has ___come___ for you today. (come)
11. Josie ___sat___ down and wrote a letter. (sit)
12. The mail carrier is ___sitting___ after walking all day. (sit)

APPLY IT NOW

Write a short letter to a friend. Include the verbs *bring, buy, come,* and *sit* in your letter.

 Tech Tip Type your letter and highlight the verbs.

Verbs • 85

- **To identify and use the principal parts of the irregular verbs *eat*, *go*, and *see***

 **Maintenance**

Assign **Practice Book** page 49, Section 4.7. After students finish,
1. Give immediate feedback.
2. Review concepts as needed.
3. Model the correct answer.

Pages 4–5 of the **Answer Key** contain tips for Daily Maintenance.

WARM-UP

Write on the board the following:

| eat | go | see |

| always | yesterday |

Have partners write 30-second dialogues about a favorite food, using the words on the board. Have them include where they eat it and what they see there. As volunteers perform their dialogues, have a student put a tally mark on the board next to each form of *eat*, *go*, or *see* that is used.

📖 Read from a piece of writing that the class is currently reading. Emphasize the principal parts of *eat*, *go*, and *see*.

TEACH

Write on the board the following sentences and read them aloud:

I ate a peanut butter sandwich.

I went to the baseball game.

I saw the best movie.

Have volunteers identify the verb in each sentence (*ate*, *went*, *saw*). Ask students to tell the present form of the verbs (*eat*, *go*, *see*). Ask if they are regular or irregular verbs and how students know (*irregular because they do not have an* ed *ending*). Have students find the verbs *ate*, *went*, and *saw* on the chart in the lesson. Ask students to identify the form of the verb (*past*).

Invite volunteers to read aloud about these irregular verbs. Encourage students to make up sentences using all the parts of these verbs. Have students tell which part is being used in each sentence.

PRACTICE

EXERCISE 1
Have students close their books. Write the chart on the board. Invite volunteers to fill in the missing words. Encourage students to make up sentences with the verbs to help reinforce the answers.

EXERCISE 2
Have partners complete the exercise. Point out that the correct part of the verb in parentheses is the one students should use to complete each sentence. Encourage students to use the chart in the lesson to help them identify the principal part of each verb.

4.7 *Eat, Go, and See*

Eat, go, and *see* are irregular verbs. The chart shows the principal parts of each verb. Remember that the present and past participles are often used with helping verbs.

PRESENT	PRESENT PARTICIPLE	PAST	PAST PARTICIPLE
eat	eating	ate	eaten
go	going	went	gone
see	seeing	saw	seen

We *eat* potato pancakes every Friday. (present)
We *are eating* potato pancakes today. (present participle, with the helping verb *are*)
We *ate* potato pancakes last Friday. (past)
We *have eaten* all the potato pancakes on the platter. (past participle, with the helping verb *have*)

Which form of the verb correctly completes the sentence?

Have you ever (went gone go) to a deli?

You're right if you chose *gone.* The past participle is needed when the helping verb *have* is used.

Which form correctly completes the sentence?

My sister (go goes) to the deli after school.

You are correct if you chose *goes.* It is the present of *go.*

Note that to make *go* agree with a singular subject, you must add *-es* instead of *-s.*

APPLY

APPLY IT NOW

Suggest that students choose a single topic for their sentences. Have students write ideas pertaining to the topic. Encourage them to include those ideas in their sentences.

Tell students to underline the verb in each sentence and to note which part of *eat* is used. Students should demonstrate the ability to use the principal parts of the irregular verb *eat*.

ASSESS

Note which students had difficulty using principal parts of the irregular verbs *eat, go,* and *see.* Assign **Practice Book** page 62 for further practice.

> ### WRITING CONNECTION
> Use pages 328–329 of the Writing portion of the book.

TEACHING OPTIONS

Reteach

Work with students to pantomime actions that represent the words *eat, go,* and *see.* Model some suggestions for students. Read aloud sentences that contain these verbs, but pantomime the action where the verb should be. Have students complete the sentence with the correct form of the verb. Then ask students to suggest sentences of their own, using pantomime. Have volunteers complete the sentences with the correct form of the verb.

Cooperative Learning

Have small groups make posters to advertise the opening of a restaurant. Challenge students to include on the poster phrases or sentences using as many parts as possible of the verbs *eat, go,* and *see.* As groups present their posters to the class, have students find the forms of the verbs *eat, go,* and *see* and tell which form is being used in each phrase or sentence. Display the posters in the classroom.

EXERCISE 1 Complete the chart with the correct parts of the verbs.

PRESENT	PRESENT PARTICIPLE	PAST	PAST PARTICIPLE
eat	eating	ate	eaten
go	going	went	gone
see	seeing	saw	seen

Exercise 2
1. present
2. present
3. present
4. past participle
5. present participle
6. past
7. past participle
8. past participle
9. present
10. past
11. past
12. present participle
13. past
14. past participle
15. past
16. present participle

EXERCISE 2 Complete each sentence with the correct part of *eat, go,* or *see.* Identify each verb as present, present participle, past, or past participle.

1. I often ___go___ to the deli on Saturday. (go)
2. I usually ___eat___ a club sandwich there. (eat)
3. My father ___goes___ there all the time. (go)
4. Sammy has ___eaten___ a bowl of noodle soup. (eat)
5. They are ___eating___ all the pickles. (eat)
6. Jill ___went___ there yesterday. (go)
7. She has ___gone___ there before. (go)
8. We have ___seen___ our teacher at the deli. (see)
9. I sometimes ___see___ friends there. (see)
10. I ___saw___ Louisa there last week. (see)
11. She ___ate___ a corned beef sandwich for lunch. (eat)
12. I was ___eating___ a bowl of chili. (eat)
13. Louisa ___saw___ my father there last Friday. (see)
14. I have ___seen___ her there too. (see)
15. She often ___went___ to the deli after school. (go)
16. I am ___going___ there with my father next week. (go)

APPLY IT NOW
Write four sentences, one each with the present, present participle, past, and past participle of *eat.*

Verbs • 87

OBJECTIVE

- **To identify and use the principal parts of the irregular verbs *take*, *tear*, and *write***

 Maintenance

Assign **Practice Book** page 49, Section 4.8. After students finish,
1. Give immediate feedback.
2. Review concepts as needed.
3. Model the correct answer.

Pages 4–5 of the **Answer Key** contain tips for Daily Maintenance.

WARM-UP

Perform a series of actions and have students say what you are doing. First, tear a sheet of paper in half. As you do it, ask students what you are doing *(tearing a sheet of paper)*. Then ask what you did *(tore a sheet of paper)*. Ask the same questions while writing on the board and taking an item, such as a pencil or a book, from a student.

📖 Read from a piece of writing that the class is currently reading. Emphasize the principal parts of *take*, *tear*, and *write*.

TEACH

Ask students to identify verbs from the Warm-Up *(write, tear, take)*. Ask if they are regular or irregular verbs and how they know *(irregular because the past is not formed by adding –ed)*.

Have volunteers read aloud about these irregular verbs. Emphasize the second and fourth example sentences with the helping verbs *(are, have)*. Point out that the present participle and past participle are always used with helping verbs. Encourage students to make up sentences using the principal parts of these verbs.

PRACTICE

EXERCISE 1
Have students close their books. Copy the chart on the board and ask volunteers to fill it in with the correct forms of the verbs. Discuss the past and past participle and have students make up sentences using those parts. Point out the helping verb in each sentence.

EXERCISE 2
Have students use the chart to complete this exercise independently. Point out that students need to both find the verb and identify the correct part of the verb.

EXERCISE 3
Make sure students understand that they are to complete each sentence with the correct form of the verb in parentheses and to identify the correct part of the verb. Encourage students to suggest strategies for recognizing the correct verb part *(looking for helping verbs such as* are *and* have*)*. Ask partners to complete the sentences. Read aloud the correct sentences for students to check their work.

4.8 *Take, Tear and Write*

Take, tear, and *write* are irregular verbs. The chart shows the principal parts of each verb. Remember that the present and the past participles are often used with helping verbs.

PRESENT	PRESENT PARTICIPLE	PAST	PAST PARTICIPLE
take	taking	took	taken
tear	tearing	tore	torn
write	writing	wrote	written

We *take* math. (present)

We *are taking* math. (present participle, with the helping verb *are*)

We *took* math. (past)

We *have taken* math. (past participle, with the helping verb *have*)

Which form of the verb correctly completes the sentence?

Sally has (took taken) the math test.

You're right if you chose *taken*. The past participle is needed when the helping verb *has* is used.

EXERCISE 1 Complete the chart with the correct forms of the verbs.

PRESENT	PRESENT PARTICIPLE	PAST	PAST PARTICIPLE
take	taking	took	taken
tear	tearing	tore	torn
write	writing	wrote	written

APPLY

APPLY IT NOW

Help students brainstorm writing situations that students might use for their sentences (*taking a test, writing a letter or a story*). Have students label the verb part in each sentence. Students should demonstrate the ability to identify and use the principal parts of the irregular verb *write*.

ASSESS

Note which students had difficulty using the principal parts of the irregular verbs *take*, *tear*, and *write*. Assign **Practice Book** page 63 for further practice.

WRITING CONNECTION

Use pages 330–331 of the Writing portion of the book.

Reteach

Write the principal parts of the verbs *take*, *tear*, and *write* on separate note cards. Write 12 sentences on strips, using the verbs in each principal part, but omitting the verbs. Display the verb cards. Read aloud the sentences. Ask volunteers to find the card with the correct word to complete each sentence. Have students read aloud the completed sentences.

Meeting Individual Needs

Visual Demonstrate how to make a torn-paper picture without verbalizing the procedure. Then have students give directions for this activity as you write their sentences on the board. Encourage students to use the verb *tear* in sentences such as the following:

1. **<u>Tear</u> two sheets of different-colored paper into pieces.**

2. **If you <u>tore</u> big pieces, tear some small pieces too.**

3. **After you <u>have torn</u> the paper, place the pieces on white paper in a way that forms an interesting design.**

Sharing and Caring

Point out that the verbs *write* and *take* can be used when talking about ways to share or to care for people. Begin with some example sentences, like the ones below. Then invite students to supply additional sentences that use the verbs *write* or *take*. Suggest that students make a collage of their sentences for a Sharing and Caring poster.

I <u>wrote</u> a card for someone in the hospital.

I <u>am taking</u> my little sister to the park on Saturday.

Exercise 2
1. past participle
2. past
3. present participle
4. past
5. past participle
6. past participle
7. past
8. past
9. present
10. present participle

EXERCISE 2 Find the part of *take, tear,* or *write* in each sentence. Then tell whether the part is present, present participle, past, or past participle.

1. We had <u>written</u> to the national park before our trip.
2. The park ranger <u>wrote</u> back with information.
3. We are <u>taking</u> the easier trail up the mountain.
4. We <u>took</u> backpacks with lunches and water bottles.
5. My bag was so heavy that the bottom has <u>torn</u>.
6. Jake had never <u>taken</u> a boat tour on a lake.
7. My net <u>tore</u> when I was catching fish at the pond.
8. We <u>took</u> photos of birds, including bald eagles.
9. I always <u>take</u> a lot of photos.
10. We are <u>writing</u> a thank-you letter to the park rangers.

Exercise 3
1. present
2. past
3. present participle
4. past participle
5. past participle
6. past
7. present participle
8. present
9. present participle
10. past participle

EXERCISE 3 Complete each sentence with the correct part of *take, tear,* or *write.* Identify each verb as present, present participle, past, or past participle.

1. Our class __takes__ a field trip every spring and fall. (take)
2. Last year we __took__ a trip to the planetarium. (take)
3. This year we are __taking__ a trip to a forest. (take)
4. The strap of my backpack has __torn__. (tear)
5. Many students have __taken__ cameras with them. (take)
6. I __tore__ my jacket sleeve in the forest. (tear)
7. We each are __writing__ a letter to thank our guide on the trip. (write)
8. The teacher always __writes__ some ideas on the board. (write)
9. Mary is __tearing__ a sheet of paper out of her notebook for me. (tear)
10. Sanjay has __written__ a report on ants. (write)

APPLY IT NOW

Write four sentences, one each with the principal parts of *write*: present, present participle, past, and past participle.

Verbs • 89

OBJECTIVES

- **To identify, form, and use the simple present tense of verbs**
- **To recognize that the present tense describes action that is always true or that happens again and again**

DAILY Maintenance

Assign **Practice Book** page 49, Section 4.9. After students finish,
1. Give immediate feedback.
2. Review concepts as needed.
3. Model the correct answer.

Pages 4–5 of the **Answer Key** contain tips for Daily Maintenance.

WARM-UP

Describe your morning routine for students. *(I wake up. I brush my teeth. I walk the dog. I eat breakfast. I read the newspaper. I drive to school.)* Ask students to share their morning routines. Write on the board students' sentences. Ask students to identify the verb in each sentence. Discuss when the action of each verb is taking place. *(The action always happens again and again or every morning. The verb is in the present tense.)*

Read from a piece of writing that the class is currently reading. Emphasize verbs in the simple present tense.

TEACH

Write on the board these sentences:

We ride the bus to school.

Jenna lives in New York City.

Have students identify the verb in each sentence *(ride, lives)*. Ask if these sentences describe actions that are always true or that happen again and again *(yes)*. Tell students that these verbs are in the simple present tense.

Have a volunteer read aloud the first paragraph, the example sentences, and the second paragraph about simple present tense. Ask students to look at the verb chart from Section 4.7 to 4.8. Ask students to tell into which column the verbs in the example sentences would go *(the first column)*.

Have volunteers read aloud the rest of the page. Discuss when *-s* or *-es* is added to a verb in the simple present tense. Point out that this only happens when the subject is a singular noun or pronoun.

PRACTICE

EXERCISES 1 & 2

Review the rules for changing some verbs to go with their subjects. Have partners complete the exercises and share the answers with the class. Encourage students to discuss any differing answers.

EXERCISE 3

Ask students to compare the subject in the sentence with the subject in parentheses. Have students notice that one subject is singular and one is plural. Emphasize that when the subject is changed, the spelling of the verb also changes.

4.9 Simple Present Tense

The tense of a verb shows when the action takes place. A verb in the **simple present tense** tells about something that is always true or about an action that happens again and again.

Frogs *live* in or near water.
A frog *catches* flies.
Flies *stick* to a frog's tongue.

The verbs *live, catches,* and *stick* are in the simple present tense. The verbs tell things that are true about frogs. They tell about actions that happen again and again.

Use the present part of a verb for the present tense. In simple present tense, *-s* (or *-es*) is added to the verb when the subject is a singular noun or *he, she,* or *it.*

Crickets *make* a good meal for my frog. (plural subject)
It *lives* in a tank. (a singular noun subject, *frog,* so the present tense verb ends in *s*)

For verbs ending in *y* following a consonant, change the *y* to *i* and add *-es: fly—flies.* For verbs ending in *s, z, ch,* or *sh,* add *-es: buzz—buzzes.*

Which present tense verb form is correct in this sentence?

Bullfrog

My friend (want wants) a pet frog.

The correct answer is *wants.* The subject *friend* is a singular noun, so the present tense verb should end in *s.*

EXERCISE 1 Choose the correct verb to complete each sentence.

1. Frogs (<u>belong</u> belongs) to a group called amphibians.
2. An amphibian (live <u>lives</u>) in water and on land.
3. Frogs (<u>like</u> likes) warm weather.

APPLY

APPLY IT NOW

Suggest that students write their animal's name at the top of their papers and list a few things about the animal. Challenge students to compose their sentences using the animal's name and these facts. Remind students to use the present tense of the verb and to make sure the verb goes with the subject. Students should demonstrate the ability to use the simple present tense.

ASSESS

Note which students had difficulty using the simple present tense. Assign **Practice Book** page 64 for further practice.

WRITING CONNECTION

Use pages 332–333 of the Writing portion of the book.

TEACHING OPTIONS

Reteach

Write on the board a three-column chart with the headings below. Ask students to suggest verbs for the first column. Direct students to make up simple sentences using each verb with both a singular subject and a plural subject. Emphasize that verbs for singular subjects must have an -s or -es added in the simple present tense, but that all the verbs for plural nouns do not.

Verb	Singular	Plural
laugh	My friend laughs.	My friends laugh.
play	The team plays.	Two teams play.
call	She calls him.	They call you.

Cooperative Learning

Have small groups work together. Ask one student at a time to describe actions for the other students to perform, by giving directions in complete sentences, such as the following:

One student hops.

Two students jump.

Mario claps.

Mario and Julie sing.

Tell students to be sure that the verbs in their sentences go with their subjects.

Meeting Individual Needs

Extra Support Display a picture of something from nature (tree, grasshopper). Have students write simple sentences about the picture. (The tree grows. The grasshopper jumps.) Then ask students to rewrite the sentences by using the plural form of the nouns. (Trees grow. Grasshoppers jump.)

Red-eyed tree frog

4. Their sticky tongues (<u>trap</u> traps) insects.

5. Their skin (protect <u>protects</u>) frogs from enemies.

6. A frog's color (match <u>matches</u>) the surroundings.

7. Frogs (<u>burrow</u> burrows) in mud if they are cold.

8. A tree frog (hide <u>hides</u>) from its enemies.

9. Leopard frogs (plays <u>play</u>) dead.

10. Poison dart frogs (tastes <u>taste</u>) bad to other animals.

Poison dart frog

Exercise 2
1. singular
2. singular
3. singular
4. plural
5. singular
6. plural
7. plural
8. plural

EXERCISE 2 The subject in each sentence is underlined. Tell if it is singular or plural. Then choose the verb that correctly completes each sentence.

1. A <u>frog</u> (lay <u>lays</u>) eggs in water.

2. Each <u>egg</u> (hatch <u>hatches</u>) into a tadpole.

3. The <u>tadpole</u> (swim <u>swims</u>) underwater.

4. <u>People</u> also (<u>call</u> calls) tadpoles pollywogs.

5. A <u>tadpole</u> (develop <u>develops</u>) legs and lungs.

6. <u>Lungs</u> (<u>help</u> helps) frogs breathe on land.

7. Frogs' hind <u>legs</u> (<u>make</u> makes) them good jumpers.

8. Some <u>frogs</u> (<u>leap</u> leaps) 20 times their body length.

Exercise 3
1. A tadpole lives in water.
2. A pollywog eats plants.
3. It seems more like a fish.
4. A tadpole grows hind legs and short arms.
5. The tail goes away.
6. The young frog hops out of the pond.
7. A frog communicates by croaking.
8. A croak sometimes signals danger.

EXERCISE 3 Rewrite each sentence with the singular subject shown. Be sure the verb goes with the subject.

1. Tadpoles live in water. (a tadpole)

2. Pollywogs eat plants. (a pollywog)

3. They seem more like a fish. (It)

4. Tadpoles grow hind legs and short arms. (a tadpole)

5. The tails go away. (the tail)

6. The young frogs hop out of the pond. (the young frog)

7. Frogs communicate by croaking. (a frog)

8. Croaks sometimes signal danger. (a croak)

Tadpoles

APPLY IT NOW

Write four sentences about the habits of frogs or another type of animal. Use the simple present tense.

Verbs • 91

OBJECTIVES

- **To identify, form, and use the simple past tense of verbs**
- **To recognize that the past tense describes action that has already happened**

DAILY Maintenance

Assign **Practice Book** page 50, Section 4.10. After students finish,
1. Give immediate feedback.
2. Review concepts as needed.
3. Model the correct answer.

Pages 4–5 of the **Answer Key** contain tips for Daily Maintenance.

WARM-UP

Toss a beanbag to a student and say a time period in the past, such as *yesterday, last weekend,* or *last month*. Direct the student to say a sentence about something he or she did at that time. *(Last weekend I visited my grandparents.)* After the student has given his or her sentence, tell the student to toss the beanbag to another student and say a time period. Have the student who catches the bean bag make up a sentence to go along with the given time period.

📖 Read from a piece of writing that the class is currently reading. Emphasize simple past tense.

TEACH

Write on the board the following sentence pairs:

Today I listen in class.
Yesterday I listened in class.

Today Paul helps the teacher.
Yesterday he helped the teacher.

Have volunteers circle the verb in each sentence *(listen, listened, helps, helped)*. Ask when the action takes place in each sentence *(today, yesterday)*.

Have a volunteer read aloud the first paragraph and the example sentences about the simple past tense. Ask students to tell how the past tense is formed *(by adding -ed)*. Reinforce that if the verb already ends in *e*, only *-d* should be added. Have a volunteer read aloud the rest of the page.

PRACTICE

EXERCISE 1

Remind students that some verbs are irregular *(items 4, 6, and 10)*. Ask partners to complete the exercise.

EXERCISE 2

Copy the exercise as a paragraph on a large sheet of poster board, omitting the verbs. Invite volunteers to fill in the missing verbs. Read the entire paragraph to the class and discuss any verbs that have been formed incorrectly.

4.10 Simple Past Tense

A verb in the **simple past tense** tells about something that happened in the past.

Our class *studied* history.
We *learned* about colonial America.
Everyone *wrote* a report.
Maria *drew* a map.
Our teacher *talked* about the American Revolution.
I *asked* a question about the Boston Tea Party.

The verbs *studied, learned, wrote, drew, talked,* and *asked* are in the simple past tense.

Most past tense verbs end in *ed*. Remember that irregular verbs do not end in *ed*.

We *discussed* colonial life. (regular verb)
I *read* a book on colonial life. (irregular verb)

If a regular verb ends in *e*, just add *-d*. If a verb ends in *y* following a consonant, change the *y* to *i* and add *-ed*.

name + -d = named   try + -ed = tried

Which sentence shows simple past tense?

A We learn about Thomas Jefferson.
B We are learning about Thomas Jefferson.
C We learned about Thomas Jefferson.

You are right if you said that sentence C shows simple past tense. The *ed* ending on *learned* signals the past tense.

Thomas Jefferson

Monticello

APPLY

APPLY IT NOW

Help students brainstorm a list of well-known people from the past about whom students can write. Explain that when students write about someone's life, they will use the past tense because the events and actions happened in the past. Students should demonstrate the ability to use the simple past tense of verbs.

TechTip Help students find facts about their historical figure. You may wish to suggest specific, age-appropriate history Web sites.

ASSESS

Note which students had difficulty forming and using the simple past tense of verbs. Assign **Practice Book** page 65 for further practice.

WRITING CONNECTION

Use pages 334–335 of the Writing portion of the book.

EXERCISE 1 Write the simple past tense of each verb. Be careful! Some verbs are irregular.

Verb	Simple Past		Verb	Simple Past
1. help	helped		6. win	won
2. talk	talked		7. try	tried
3. raise	raised		8. listen	listened
4. take	took		9. offer	offered
5. serve	served		10. grow	grew

EXERCISE 2 Complete each sentence with the verb in parentheses. Use the simple past tense.

1. Thomas Jefferson __lived__ in Charlottesville, Virginia. (live)
2. He __owned__ a plantation. (own)
3. Jefferson __studied__ the law. (study)
4. He __built__ a home called Monticello. (build)
5. Martha Wayles Skelton __married__ Thomas Jefferson. (marry)
6. Jefferson __wrote__ the Declaration of Independence. (write)
7. He __wanted__ freedom for the colonies. (want)
8. He __knew__ Ben Franklin and George Washington. (know)
9. Jefferson __supported__ liberty and people's rights. (support)
10. He __went__ to France as an ambassador. (go)
11. He __got__ help from France to fight the war against Britain. (get)
12. He __served__ in President Washington's first Cabinet. (serve)
13. Jefferson __ran__ for president of the United States. (run)
14. He __became__ the third president of the United States. (become)
15. The United States __purchased__ the Louisiana Territory while Jefferson was president. (purchase)

The signing of the Declaration of Independence

APPLY IT NOW

Write four sentences about a historical figure you have been studying. Use the simple past tense in your sentences.

 Tech Tip With an adult, research a historical figure online.

Verbs • 93

TEACHING OPTIONS

Reteach

Write on the board some sentences that reflect actions that students have recently completed, such as the following:

We learn about fractions

We go to lunch.

We complete a science experiment.

Ask students to identify the verbs and to tell how to make each verb past tense. Include time words to show that these actions happened in the past as in the following sentences:

We learned about fractions yesterday.

An hour ago we went to lunch.

Last week we completed a science experiment.

Curriculum Connection

Have available a selection of age-appropriate biographies. Discuss why biographies most likely have many examples of past tense verbs. Explain that biographies are written about things that happened to people in the past. Direct students to choose a biography and read from it. Ask students to choose one paragraph from which to list all the past tense verbs. Have students share their lists with a partner.

Meeting Individual Needs

Auditory Have partners tell each other interesting or funny stories about things that happened when students were younger. Remind students to use past tense verbs. Monitor students to check that they are using the simple past tense correctly. Encourage volunteers to share their stories with the class.

OBJECTIVES
- **To identify and use the future tense of verbs with *will***
- **To recognize that the future tense of a verb describes an action that has not yet happened**

DAILY Maintenance

Assign **Practice Book** page 50, Section 4.11. After students finish,
1. Give immediate feedback.
2. Review concepts as needed.
3. Model the correct answer.

Pages 4–5 of the **Answer Key** contain tips for Daily Maintenance.

WARM-UP

Tell students about activities you have planned for the weekend. (*I will go for a walk in the park. I will watch my daughter play baseball.*) Write your sentences on the board. Ask volunteers to circle the word that shows that the action has not yet happened (*will*). Then have students discuss their own plans for the weekend. Tell students to include the word *will* in their sentences. Write their sentences on the board.

📖 Read from a piece of writing that the class is currently reading. Emphasize the future tense with *will*.

TEACH

Read aloud the sentences on the board from the Warm-Up. Ask what word appears in all the sentences (*will*). Explain that the helping verb *will* is used with the present part of a verb to express an action that has not yet taken place.

Have volunteers read aloud about the future tense with *will*. Reinforce that *will* is used with the present part of a verb to form a future tense. Encourage students

to find the present part of the verb in each sentence on the board. Challenge students to make up sentences telling about things your class might do later in the day, using the future tense with *will*.

PRACTICE

EXERCISE 1
Complete this exercise as a class. Have students read aloud each item and insert the verb in parentheses in the future tense with *will*.

EXERCISE 2
Tell students that they must first identify the verb in each sentence. Point out how a verb changes when the subject is singular (*items 4, 7, and 8*). Explain that the verb ending *-s* is dropped when the future tense is formed.

EXERCISE 3
Remind students that the main verb includes the helping verb if there is one. Have students share their answers with partners.

4.11 Future Tense with *Will*

The word *will* is one way to express something that will take place in the future. The helping verb *will* is used with the present part of a verb to form a future tense. For example, *will + help = will help.*

> I *will help* on the project.

The sentence tells what you will do in the future.

What do these sentences tell?

> **Our youth group** *will organize* **an activity.**
> **The activity** *will raise* **money for charity.**
> **Our advisor** *will help* **us in our decision.**
> **We** *will decide* **on a project soon.**

Will organize, will raise, will help, and *will decide* are in the future tense.

Which sentence expresses the future?

A **I worked on the fund-raising project.**
B **Marti worked on the fund-raising project.**
C **Patrick will work on the fund-raising project.**

You are right if you said sentence C expresses the future. *Will* means that Patrick has agreed to work on the project at a later time.

EXERCISE 1 Complete each sentence with the verb in parentheses. Use the future tense with *will*.

1. Our class _____ our fund-raising project. (discuss) will discuss
2. Our teachers _____ the discussion. (lead) will lead
3. Some students _____ presentations. (make) will make
4. I _____ a clothing drive. (suggest) will suggest
5. Lily _____ a car wash. (recommend) will recommend
6. We all _____ on the best project. (vote) will vote
7. The winning project hopefully _____ a lot of money. (raise) will raise

APPLY

APPLY IT NOW

To help students get started, you might recall moments when the class or school has worked to assist the community or to raise money. Invite students to consider ways that they could help people. Have students write their sentences as a pledge to help. (*I will collect canned foods for the food drive. I will recycle.*) Students should demonstrate the ability to use the future tense of verbs with *will*.

ASSESS

Note which students had difficulty identifying and using the future tense of verbs with *will*. Assign **Practice Book** page 66 for further practice.

> ### WRITING CONNECTION
>
> Use pages 336–337 of the Writing portion of the book.

TEACHING OPTIONS

Reteach

List on the board activities in which the class will participate later this week.

> **Tuesday: music**
> **Wednesday: special guest speaker**
> **Thursday: field day**
> **Friday: clean the classroom**

Have students write on the board sentences for the activities, using the future tense with *will*. (*Tomorrow we will sing in music. Wednesday we will listen to a special guest speaker.*) Have students circle each future tense verb.

Meeting Individual Needs

Kinesthetic Tell students they will be following other students' commands. Give the first command to one student. (*Nicole will shake hands with Natalie.*) Then have that student (*Nicole*) give the next command. (*Pedro will open and close the door.*) Emphasize that each command must use a student's name and the future tense with *will*. Remind students to make the commands fun, but to keep safety in mind.

Meeting Individual Needs

Intrapersonal Invite students to write in their journals five sentences that tell about things they would like to do in the future. Challenge students to use a different main verb in each sentence.

Exercise 2

1. We will help with the clothing drive.
2. They will collect more clothes than usual.
3. You will put the items on tables.
4. Monica will get the tables.
5. The teachers will decide the prices.
6. I will write the price tags.
7. Darnell will hand out flyers.
8. Jasmine will make signs.
9. We will take turns working at the clothing drive.
10. People will buy the items.
11. We will give the money to charity.
12. They will appreciate our donation.

Exercise 3

1. simple present
2. simple past
3. future
4. simple past
5. future
6. future
7. future
8. future
9. simple past
10. simple present

EXERCISE 2 Change each sentence to the future tense by using *will*.

1. We help with the clothing drive.
2. They collect more clothes than usual.
3. You put the items on tables.
4. Monica gets the tables.
5. The teachers decide the prices.
6. I write the price tags.
7. Darnell hands out flyers.
8. Jasmine makes signs.
9. We take turns working at the clothing drive.
10. People buy the items.
11. We give the money to charity.
12. They appreciate our donation.

EXERCISE 3 Find the verb in each sentence and tell its tense: future, simple present, or simple past.

1. Marcie helps with the project.
2. Kevin collected old clothes.
3. I will take the clothes to school.
4. I asked my family for old items.
5. My brother will give me some old CDs.
6. My mom will find some old clothes.
7. Dad will donate a winter coat.
8. We will put the clothes in the school basement.
9. The teachers put some tables there.
10. Our fund-raisers are very successful.

APPLY IT NOW

How would you like to help other people? Write five sentences about what you would like to do. Use the future tense with *will*.

Verbs • 95

OBJECTIVES

- **To identify and use the future tense of verbs with *going to***
- **To recognize that the future tense of a verb describes an action that has not yet happened**

 **Maintenance**

Assign **Practice Book** page 50, Section 4.12. After students finish,
1. Give immediate feedback.
2. Review concepts as needed.
3. Model the correct answer.

Pages 4–5 of the **Answer Key** contain tips for Daily Maintenance.

WARM-UP

Tell students something you plan to do in the future. (*I am going to take my family to Italy. I am going to buy a new computer.*) Encourage students to think about something they plan to do in the future. Have students make up sentences to describe what they are going to do. (*I am going to walk on the moon. I am going to be an architect.*) Write of their responses on the board. Have volunteers circle the verbs in each sentence (*going to walk, going to be*).

📖 Read from a piece of writing that the class is currently reading. Emphasize the future tense with *going to*.

TEACH

Read aloud the sentences you wrote on the board in the Warm-Up. Point out that a form of the verb *be* appears before the words *going to* in each sentence. Remind students that *am, is,* and *are* are forms of the verb *be*.

Have volunteers read aloud about the future tense with *going to*. Reinforce that the present part of a verb appears after *going to* in a sentence. Have students identify the form of the verb *be* and the present part of each verb in the sentences on the board.

Explain that *going to* is used in the future tense when the future event is planned or predicted. (*We are going to compete for the championship on Saturday.*) Encourage students to suggest additional sentences using the future tense with *going to*.

PRACTICE

EXERCISE 1
Remind students that the future tense with *going to* includes a form of the verb *be* + *going to* + the present part of a verb. Have partners complete this exercise.

EXERCISE 2
Explain that students will have to change the verb to the present tense. Have partners complete this activity. Ask volunteers to share their sentences with the class.

4.12 Future Tense with *Going To*

Like *will,* the phrase *going to* is used to express future tense. A form of the helping verb *be* must go in front of *going to.*

Use *am going to, is going to,* or *are going to* followed by the present part of the verb. For example, *is going to + make = is going to make.*

Nina *is going to make* **breakfast.**

This sentence tells what Nina is going to do at some time in the future.

What does each of these sentences tell?

I *am going to cook.*
You *are going to cook.*
We *are going to cook.*
They *are going to cook.*

Each sentence describes something that will happen in the future.

Which sentence uses the future tense with *going to*?

A **Nick made pancakes.**
B **Nisha is going to make scrambled eggs.**
C **Nellie makes French toast.**

You are right if you said sentence B uses the future tense with *going to.* Sentence A uses the past tense. Sentence C uses the simple present tense.

EXERCISE 1 **Find the verb in the future tense in each sentence.**

1. What <u>are</u> you <u>going to eat</u> for breakfast?
2. Mary Jo <u>is going to eat</u> oatmeal.
3. She <u>is going to toast</u> a bagel.
4. I <u>am going to have</u> an omelet.
5. Idalia <u>is going to drink</u> a smoothie.

96 • Section 4.12

EXERCISE 3

Have partners complete this exercise. Remind students that the form of *be* should go with the subject in parentheses. Ask volunteers to read aloud their sentences.

APPLY

APPLY IT NOW

So that students' sentences don't all include *going to have*, brainstorm with students other words they can use to talk about future meals, such as *eat, munch, enjoy, taste,* and *try.*

Students should demonstrate the ability to use the future tense of verbs with *going to.*

ASSESS

Note which students had difficulty forming the future tense with *going to.* Assign **Practice Book** page 67 for further practice.

> **WRITING CONNECTION**
>
> Use pages 338–339 of the Writing portion of the book.

TEACHING OPTIONS

Reteach

Discuss things you have planned for the rest of the day such as recess, lunch, music, physical education, art, reading, or computer lab. Write on the board the following formula and example sentence:

Subject + form of *be* + *going to* + present part of verb

We are going to sing.

Have students use the formula to write sentences that tell about things they will be doing later in the day. Have volunteers their sentences.

Meeting Individual Needs

Extra Support To clarify that *going to* acts as a helping verb in the future tense and is not the main verb expressing the action, have students act out future tense phrases as you pair the statements with commands. Direct students to perform the actions when you give the commands.

We are going to clap. Clap!

We are going to stomp. Stomp!

We are going to stand. Stand!

We are going to sit. Sit!

English-Language Learners

Students may have difficulty recognizing that the written form of the future tense plus *going to* is the same as people saying, "I am gonna go to the movies this weekend." You may wish to point out that *gonna* is not correct in speaking or in writing.

---

6. We all <u>are going to go</u> to a restaurant.
7. Roberto <u>is going to order</u> pancakes.
8. They <u>are going to make</u> grits.
9. He <u>is going to try</u> something new.
10. It <u>is going to cook</u> quickly.

EXERCISE 2 **Change each sentence to use the future tense with *going to.***

1. We made brunch.
2. I was squeezing the oranges.
3. Freddy toasts the bread.
4. Mom is scrambling the eggs.
5. Santiago set the table.
6. You had poured the juice.
7. Brody is flipping the pancakes.
8. I put blueberries on my cereal.
9. Michael cut some melon.
10. They did the dishes.

EXERCISE 3 **Write a sentence in the future tense with *going to* for each verb. Use the subject in parentheses.**

1. grill (he)
2. chop (they)
3. bake (she)
4. boil (it)
5. wait (we)
6. taste (you)
7. clean (they)
8. sweep (I)

Exercise 2
1. We are going to make brunch.
2. I am going to squeeze the oranges.
3. Freddy is going to toast the bread.
4. Mom is going to scramble the eggs.
5. Santiago is going to set the table.
6. You are going to pour the juice.
7. Brody is going to flip the pancakes.
8. I am going to put blueberries on my cereal.
9. Michael is going to cut some melon.
10. They are going to do the dishes.

Exercise 3
1. He is going to grill.
2. They are going to chop.
3. She is going to bake.
4. It is going to boil.
5. We are going to wait.
6. You are going to taste.
7. They are going to clean.
8. I am going to sweep.

> ### APPLY IT NOW
>
> Tell what you are going to have for breakfast, lunch, or dinner tomorrow. Write three sentences. Use the future tense with *going to.*

Verbs • 97

OBJECTIVES

- To identify, form, and use the present progressive tense, using the helping verbs *am*, *is*, and *are*
- To recognize that the present progressive tense of a verb describes something that is happening now

DAILY Maintenance

Assign **Practice Book** page 51, Section 4.13. After students finish,
1. Give immediate feedback.
2. Review concepts as needed.
3. Model the correct answer.

Pages 4–5 of the **Answer Key** contain tips for Daily Maintenance.

WARM-UP

Write on note cards actions for several students to perform (*running, jumping, dancing, singing, juggling*). Have a volunteer choose a cart to act out. Ask students to tell what the volunteer is doing. Write on the board sentences that tell about the action. (*Alex is running. Amy is jumping. Kyra is singing.*) Discuss the similarities between the sentences. (*They all have helping verbs, and the main verbs end in* ing.)

📖 Read from a piece of writing that the class is currently reading. Emphasize verbs in the present progressive tense.

TEACH

Have a volunteer read aloud the sentences from the Warm-Up. Ask students to identify the verbs in each sentence (*is running, is jumping, is singing*). Ask when the action is taking place (*now, in the present*). Have students determine what is similar about each main verb. (*They end in* ing.) Point out

that each verb is made up of a helping verb plus a verb that ends in *ing*.

Have a volunteer read aloud the first two paragraphs about the present progressive tense and the example sentences. Ask students to identify the helping verbs in each example sentence. Remind students that the verbs *am, is,* and *are* are all forms of the verb *be*.

Ask a volunteer to read aloud the rest of the page. Reinforce that the present progressive tense describes something that is happening now. Ask students to suggest additional sentences using the present progressive tense.

PRACTICE

EXERCISE 1
Write on the board these subjects and verbs:

I am	we are
you are	you are
she, he, it is	they are

Have students refer to the lists while completing the exercise.

EXERCISE 2
Suggest that students start by identifying the verb in each sentence. After students have completed the exercise, have them read aloud their answers.

4.13 Present Progressive Tense

A verb in the **present progressive tense** tells what is happening now. This tense is formed with *am, is,* or *are* and the present participle. For example, *is + fishing = is fishing*.

	PRESENT FORM OF *BE*	PRESENT PARTICIPLE OF *FISH*
Bob	is	fishing.

The sentence tells what Bob is doing right now. What does each of these sentences tell?

I *am fishing*.
You *are fishing*.
She *is fishing*.
We *are fishing*.
They *are fishing*.

Which sentence uses the present progressive tense?

A I am using worms for bait.
B I will use bread for bait.

You are right if you said sentence A. Sentence A tells about an action that is happening now. It has the verb *am* and the present participle of a verb: *am using*. Sentence B tells something about the future and is in the future tense.

To form the present participle, for verbs ending in *e*, drop the *e* and add *-ing*: *use + ing = using*. For many verbs ending with a consonant following a vowel, double the consonant before adding *-ing*: *grab + ing = grabbing*.

EXERCISE 3

Remind students that the present progressive tense is formed with *am, is,* or *are* and the present participle. After students have completed the exercise, have them read aloud their answers.

APPLY

APPLY IT NOW

Suggest that students use a variety of subjects in their sentences. Remind students to use a form of *be* with a verb ending in *ing.* Students should demonstrate the ability to use the present progressive tense, using the helping verb *am, is,* and *are.*

ASSESS

Note which students had difficulty forming verbs in the present progressive tense, using the helping verbs *am, is,* and *are.* Assign **Practice Book** page 68 for further practice.

WRITING CONNECTION

Use pages 340–341 of the Writing portion of the book.

Exercise 1
1. You are trying.
2. We are looking.
3. He is steering.
4. They are diving.
5. It is bubbling.
6. They are swimming.
7. It is sinking.
8. I am paddling.

EXERCISE 1 Write the present progressive tense of each verb. Use the subject in parentheses.

EXAMPLE   **take (I)   I am taking**

1. try (you)
2. look (we)
3. steer (he)
4. dive (they)
5. bubble (it)
6. swim (they)
7. sink (it)
8. paddle (I)

Exercise 2
1. is rowing
2. is hoping
3. is shining
4. is helping
5. are dropping
6. is tugging
7. is hooking
8. is taking
9. is getting
10. are laughing

EXERCISE 2 Change the verb in each sentence to the present progressive tense.

1. Bob rows the boat.
2. He hopes to catch a big fish.
3. The sun shines.
4. Lynn helps him row.
5. They drop the anchor.
6. Something tugs the line.
7. Bob hooks a big fish.
8. Lynn takes a picture.
9. The fish gets away.
10. People laugh at Bob's fish story.

Exercise 3
Answers will vary.
Possible answers:
1. is putting
2. are sitting
3. is opening
4. are eating
5. am having
6. are drinking

EXERCISE 3 Complete each sentence with a verb in the present progressive tense.

1. Jessica _____ a blanket on the grass.
2. We _____ on the blanket.
3. Mom _____ the picnic basket.
4. They _____ chicken salad.
5. I _____ an apple.
6. You _____ a glass of water.

APPLY IT NOW

Imagine you are at a lake. Write five sentences that tell the things you are doing. Use the present progressive tense. Try to use some of these verbs: *row, swim, dive, build, run, float.*

Verbs • 99

OBJECTIVES

- **To identify, form, and use the past progressive tense, using the helping verbs *was* and *were***
- **To recognize that the past progressive tense of a verb describes something that was happening in the past**

 **Maintenance**

Assign **Practice Book** page 51, Section 4.14. After students finish,
1. Give immediate feedback.
2. Review concepts as needed.
3. Model the correct answer.

Pages 4–5 of the **Answer Key** contain tips for Daily Maintenance.

WARM-UP

Describe some things you and your family were doing yesterday evening. *(I was working on lesson plans. My son was practicing piano.)* Ask students to make up similar sentences telling what they were doing yesterday evening, beginning with *I was*. Write their sentences on the board. Encourage students to tell how the sentences are similar.

📖 Read from a piece of writing that the class is currently reading. Emphasize verbs in the past progressive tense.

TEACH

Have volunteers identify the verbs in the sentences from the Warm-Up. Ask how the verbs are similar. *(They all have a being verb plus a verb that ends in* ing.*)* Point out that the action took place in the past in all the sentences. Tell students this verb tense is called the past progressive.

Have volunteers read aloud about the past progressive tense. Then write on the board the past tense of the verb *be*.

I was	we were
you were	you were
he, she, it was	they were

Have students suggest additional sentences about what they and their family were doing last night, using the past progressive tense. Tell students to use the lists on the board for help.

PRACTICE

EXERCISE 1
Remind students that in the past progressive tense, the past tense forms of *be*, which are the helping verbs, must go with the subject and that the present participle remains the same throughout. Have partners complete the exercise.

EXERCISE 2
Remind students to check that the subjects and helping verbs agree. Have volunteers write their sentences on the board. Discuss sentences that proved confusing.

4.14 Past Progressive Tense

A verb in the **past progressive tense** tells what was happening in the past. This tense is formed with *was* or *were* and the present participle. For example, *was + clapping = was clapping*.

	PAST FORM OF *BE*	PRESENT PARTICIPLE OF *CLAP*
The clown	was	clapping.

The sentence tells what the clown was doing in the past. What does each of these sentences tell?

I *was clapping.*
It *was clapping.*
You *were clapping.*
We *were clapping.*
They *were clapping.*

Which of the following sentences uses the past progressive tense?

A **We are petting the seal.**
B **We could pet the seal.**
C **We were petting the seal.**

You are right if you said sentence C. *Were petting* is in the past progressive tense. It tells about something that was going on in the past.

EXERCISE 1 Write the past progressive tense of each verb below. Use the subject in parentheses.

EXAMPLE **think (I)** **I was thinking.**

1. climb (you)
2. stand (we)
3. swing (he)
4. throw (they)
5. hang (it)
6. play (they)
7. sing (we)
8. cheer (I)
9. step (she)

Exercise 1
1. You were climbing.
2. We were standing.
3. He was swinging.
4. They were throwing.
5. It was hanging.
6. They were playing.
7. We were singing.
8. I was cheering.
9. She was stepping.

EXERCISE 3

Remind students that each verb should consist of a helping verb, a form of *be*, and the participle, which ends in *ing*. Have students determine if the action already happened or is happening now.

APPLY

APPLY IT NOW

Write on the board a list of additional verbs that students can use for their sentences. Tell students to use the words on the board as well as the verbs in their books. Students should demonstrate the ability to identify and use verbs in the past progressive tense.

ASSESS

Note which students had difficulty identifying and using verbs in the past progressive tense. Assign **Practice Book** page 69 for further practice.

WRITING CONNECTION

Use pages 342–343 of the Writing portion of the book.

Reteach

Write on the board sentences using the present progressive tense. Point out that the forms of the verb *be* in the present progressive tense are *am*, *is*, and *are* and that in the past progressive tense, the forms of the verb *be* are *was* and *were*. Have students rewrite the sentences on the board from the present progressive tense to the past progressive tense. Ask students to read aloud the rewritten sentences.

Meeting Individual Needs

Extra Support Ask students to write about an interesting place they have visited. Have students use past progressive tense to write a paragraph describing what they saw and did. Use the following as a model:

> **We were visiting my grandparents in Santa Fe. One day we were exploring the Bandelier National Monument. I was crawling through a cave room, and my brother was making echo noises.**

Cooperative Learning

Tell students that the past progressive tense often shows that an action is interrupted by another action. Have small groups write paragraphs using story starters, such as the following:

> **They were exploring a cave, when . . .**

> **The ship was rocking gently, when . . .**

Encourage each student to write at least one sentence in the paragraph. Have students share their completed paragraphs with the class.

Exercise 2
1. were waiting
2. were sitting
3. was selling
4. were flying
5. were jumping
6. were roaring
7. was juggling
8. was twisting
9. were eating
10. were applauding
11. were trotting
12. was watching

EXERCISE 2 Find the verb in each sentence. Change the verb to the past progressive tense.

1. We waited for the show to start.
2. We sat in the bleachers.
3. The man sold peanuts.
4. Acrobats flew through the air.
5. Penguins jumped out of a tiny car.
6. Lions roared.
7. A man juggled.
8. A woman twisted balloons into animal shapes.
9. We ate popcorn.
10. People applauded.
11. Horses trotted around the ring.
12. I watched three things at once.

Exercise 3
1. present progressive
2. present progressive
3. past progressive
4. past progressive
5. present progressive
6. present progressive
7. past progressive
8. present progressive

EXERCISE 3 Find the verb in each sentence. Tell whether the verb is in the present progressive tense or the past progressive tense.

1. The children are attending a summer circus camp.
2. Eliza is twirling a plate on a stick.
3. Mike was walking on a low tightrope.
4. The instructors were teaching different tricks.
5. Performers are demonstrating the tricks.
6. I am swinging on a trapeze.
7. Everyone was having fun.
8. We are returning next year.

APPLY IT NOW

Imagine that you have just come home from a circus. Write five sentences that tell about the things that were happening and what you were seeing and doing. Use the past progressive tense. Try using some of these words: *eating, swinging, falling, jumping, dancing, juggling.*

Verbs • 101

OBJECTIVE

- **To use the verbs *is*, *are*, *was*, and *were* correctly**

 **Maintenance**

Assign **Practice Book** page 51, Section 4.15. After students finish,

1. Give immediate feedback.
2. Review concepts as needed.
3. Model the correct answer.

Pages 4–5 of the **Answer Key** contain tips for Daily Maintenance.

WARM-UP

Write on the board *is, are, was,* and *were*. Have a volunteer use the name of one or more students with a verb from the board to make a complete sentence. Write students' sentences on the board. Discuss which verbs describe things that are happening in the present and which describe things that happened in the past.

Read from a piece of writing that the class is currently reading. Emphasize the verbs *is, are, was* and *were*.

TEACH

Write on the board the following sentences:

Your science book is in your backpack today.

Your math book was in your backpack yesterday.

Have students identify the subject and verb in each sentence, tell whether the subject is singular or plural, and tell if the sentence is about something that is happening in the past or the present (*book, is, singular, present; book, was, singular, past*). Then repeat, using the following sentences:

Ken and Jen are hungry now.

Ken and Jen were really hungry after practice.

Have volunteers read aloud about *is* and *are,* and *was* and *were.* Emphasize that *is* and *are* are present forms and *was* and *were* are past forms of the verb *be.* Have volunteers suggest sentences using each verb.

PRACTICE

EXERCISE 1

Suggest that students first look for the subject in each sentence and determine whether it is singular or plural. Allow students to exchange papers with partners to compare answers. Have students explain their answers as you create on the board a two-column chart with the headings singular and plural. Challenge students to write the subjects in the correct columns.

EXERCISE 2

Explain that for this exercise students must first determine whether the subject is singular or plural and then use the correct tense shown in parentheses. Invite volunteers to write their sentences on the board. Ask students which sentences have singular subjects (*items 2, 3, and 5*).

4.15 *Is and Are, Was and Were*

Is, are, was, and *were* are being verbs. These words do not express actions.

- *Is* and *was* are always used with singular subjects.
- *Are* and *were* are always used with plural subjects.

SINGULAR SUBJECT	VERB
A *tiger*	*is* a cat.

PLURAL SUBJECT	VERB
Tigers	*are* the biggest cats in the world.

Which verb correctly completes the sentence?

This tiger (was were) the biggest in the zoo.

You are right if you said *was.* The subject *tiger* is singular. The past tense verb *was* is used with a singular subject.

Which verb correctly completes the sentence?

The Siberian tiger (is are) endangered.

You are right if you said *is.* The subject *Siberian tiger* is singular, so the verb form *is* is needed.

Which verb correctly completes the sentence?

Tigers' claws (is are) sharp.

You are right if you said *are.* The subject *claws* is plural, so the verb form *are* is needed.

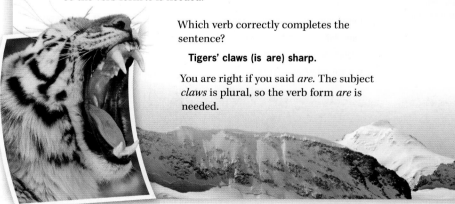

102 • Section 4.15

APPLY

APPLY IT NOW

Help students brainstorm a list of animals and facts about the animals. When students have finished, ask volunteers to share their sentences with the class. Students should demonstrate the ability to use *is, are, was,* and *were.*

ASSESS

Note which students had difficulty using the verbs *is, are, was,* and *were* correctly. Assign **Practice Book** pages 70–71 for further practice.

WRITING CONNECTION

Use pages 344–345 of the Writing portion of the book.

Reteach

Allow time for students to look through books for examples of sentences with *is, are, was, and were.* Have volunteers write the sentences on the board. Ask students to tell whether each subject is singular or plural and whether it is in the present or past tense. Then have students suggest sentences of their own for each verb.

Meeting Individual Needs

Extra Support Encourage partners to use *is, are, was,* and *were* in related sentences. Model an example for students such as the following:

> **Kendall is my name. Brianna and Cole are my friends. Dani was my best friend last year. Dani and Devon were friends in first grade. We are all best friends now.**

Have volunteers share their sentences with the class.

Meeting Individual Needs

Challenge Ask students to invent jingles or rhymes to help remember when to use *is, are, was,* and *were.* Model these examples for students:

> Use *is* with *he, she,* or *it.*
> If it's happening now, *is* is it.

> Use *are* with *we, you,* or *they.*
> If it's plural, *are* is the way.

Point out that rhymes and jingles are fun ways to help remember when to use each verb form.

EXERCISE 1 Choose the verb that correctly completes each sentence.

1. Tropical jungles (is <u>are</u>) the home of some tigers.
2. The cold forest (<u>is</u> are) the home of other tigers.
3. Asia (<u>is</u> are) the native home of all tigers.
4. Tigers (was <u>were</u>) once widespread in Asia.
5. A tiger's coat (<u>is</u> are) striped.
6. The stripes (is <u>are</u>) different for each tiger, just as fingerprints are for humans.
7. A tiger's teeth (is <u>are</u>) between two and three inches long.
8. The ancient saber-toothed tiger (<u>was</u> were) not a direct ancestor of the modern-day tiger.
9. The bite of the saber-toothed tiger (<u>was</u> were) deadly.
10. A tiger (<u>is</u> are) a solitary hunter.
11. Tigers (is <u>are</u>) nocturnal, which means they move around at night.
12. At a year old, a tiger cub (<u>is</u> are) already a good hunter.

Siberian tiger

EXERCISE 2 Complete each sentence with *is, are, was,* or *were.* Use the tense shown in parentheses.

1. Hunters ___are___ a danger to tigers. (present)
2. Tiger fur ___is___ a valuable product. (present)
3. The sale of tiger fur ___is___ illegal. (present)
4. Tiger bones ___are___ sometimes used in Asian folk medicine. (present)
5. Iran ___was___ once home to tigers. (past)
6. At one time tigers ___were___ plentiful there.
7. Now tigers ___are___ gone from the area. (present)
8. Protected parks ___are___ important to help save tigers.

APPLY IT NOW

Write four sentences about an animal. Use *is, are, was,* and *were* in your sentences.
Example:
My cat is white and brown.
My cat was the tiniest in the shelter.

Verbs • 103

OBJECTIVE
• **To identify and use contractions using the word *not***

 **Maintenance**

Assign **Practice Book** page 52, Section 4.16. After students finish,
1. Give immediate feedback.
2. Review concepts as needed.
3. Model the correct answer.

Pages 4–5 of the **Answer Key** contain tips for Daily Maintenance.

WARM-UP

Have students play a game of Concentration. Write on individual note cards contractions with *not*. Write on other note cards, the two words that make up each contraction. Mix up the cards and place them facedown on a table. Have students take turns turning over two cards and trying to match contractions with the words that make up the contractions. Have students keep the cards when they make another match and continue their turn until they cannot make a match. Have students continue until all the cards have been matched. The student with the most matches wins.

📖 Read from a piece of writing that the class is currently reading. Emphasize contractions with *not*.

TEACH

Ask students to read aloud each contraction on their cards from the Warm-Up. Encourage students to make up sentences first using the word *not* and then using the contraction, such as the following:

Mike was not happy yesterday.

Make wasn't happy yesterday.

Have volunteers read aloud about contractions with *not*. Discuss how each contraction is formed. Write on the board *can't = cannot* and *won't = will not*. Ask students which two letters the apostrophe replaces in *can't (n, o)*. Explain that *won't* does not follow any pattern.

PRACTICE

EXERCISE 1
Read aloud the list of words. Point out that each pair contains the word *not*, including the compound word *cannot*. Invite volunteers to explain how to form each contraction. Write the contractions on the board. Ask students to check their contractions against your work.

EXERCISE 2
Have partners complete this exercise. Point out the more difficult contraction *won't* from *will* and *not*. Be sure students understand this irregular form.

EXERCISE 3
Remind students that the verb form will have to be changed in some sentences (*items 3, 4, 8, and 11*). Have small groups complete this exercise.

4.16 Contractions with *Not*

A **contraction** is a short way to write some words. An apostrophe (') marks the place where one or more letters have been left out of the words.

The word *not* is often part of a contraction. The letter *o* in *not* is left out, and an apostrophe is used in its place.

> **Caroline *is not* going to the movie.**
> **Caroline *isn't* going to the movie.** (contraction with *not*)

Here are some other contractions with *not*.

aren't = are not	don't = do not
wasn't = was not	doesn't = does not
weren't = were not	didn't = did not

The following contractions with *not* are different in form.

can't = cannot	won't = will not

Which of these sentences does not use a correct contraction with *not*?

A The movie wasn't really funny.
B The theater does'nt sell popcorn.
C The children didn't like the movie.

You are correct if you chose sentence B. The correct form is *doesn't*.

EXERCISE 1 Make a contraction from each word group.

1. were not	weren't	5. do not	don't
2. did not	didn't	6. are not	aren't
3. is not	isn't	7. does not	doesn't
4. will not	won't	8. cannot	can't

APPLY

APPLY IT NOW

Ask students to write the following contractions across the top of their papers: *wasn't, aren't, didn't, can't, isn't, doesn't, don't, weren't, won't.* Encourage students to to underline the contraction they use in each sentence and circle that contraction at the top of their papers. Challenge students to write an additional sentence using one of the uncircled words. Students should demonstrate the ability to use contractions using the word *not.*

Grammar in Action — Point out that *can* is a helping verb, even when in a contraction with *not* as in *can't.* Ask what is the main verb in the sentence *(wait).*

ASSESS

Note which students had difficulty forming contractions using the word *not.* Assign **Practice Book** page 72 for further practice.

> ### WRITING CONNECTION
> Use pages 346–347 of the Writing portion of the book.

Exercise 2
1. wasn't
2. didn't
3. don't
4. isn't
5. can't
6. aren't
7. weren't
8. doesn't
9. wasn't
10. doesn't, didn't
11. won't
12. don't

Exercise 3
1. I don't like scary movies.
2. I won't go see scary movies.
3. I didn't see a scary movie last Friday.
4. My sister doesn't like scary movies.
5. We don't sit in the back of the theater.
6. You can't bring in your bottled water.
7. The ticket line wasn't long.
8. We didn't buy popcorn.
9. The theater wasn't filled.
10. The actors in the movie weren't very good.
11. My friends didn't stay for the whole movie.
12. We weren't surprised by the ending.

EXERCISE 2 Rewrite each sentence with a contraction for the underlined words.

1. Henry was not in front of the theater when I arrived.
2. The movie did not start on time.
3. I do not want to sit in the front row.
4. Lynn is not sitting with her friends.
5. I cannot see the screen because of the tall person in front of me.
6. The children are not laughing much.
7. We were not talking during the movie.
8. The movie does not have a happy ending.
9. It was not my favorite movie.
10. Sydney does not understand why I did not like the movie.
11. I will not recommend the movie to my friends.
12. Most of my friends do not plan to see it.

EXERCISE 3 Change each sentence using a contraction with *not.*

1. I like scary movies.
2. I will go see scary movies.
3. I saw a scary movie last Friday.
4. My sister likes scary movies.
5. We sit in the back of the theater.
6. You can bring in your bottled water.
7. The ticket line was long.
8. We bought popcorn.
9. The theater was filled.
10. The actors in the movie were very good.
11. My friends stayed for the whole movie.
12. We were surprised by the ending.

APPLY IT NOW

Tell about a time you could not do something or go somewhere. Write four sentences that tell what you missed. Use a contraction with *not* in each sentence.
Example:
I didn't go to the beach last weekend because the weather wasn't good.

Grammar in Action — Find the contraction with *not* on page 325.

Verbs • 105

TEACHING OPTIONS

Reteach

To play Contraction Bingo, distribute to each student a grid with three rows of three boxes. Direct students to write in random order the following contractions in the boxes: *can't, doesn't, weren't, didn't, isn't, won't, don't, wasn't, aren't.*

Say two words that form a contraction. Have students find the appropriate contraction on their grid and draw an X through it. The first student to get three Xs horizontally, vertically, or diagonally wins the game.

English-Language Learners

Because contractions are not used in most languages, students sometimes avoid using them. Have students make up equations for contractions, leaving the solution blank. Direct students to trade equations and to solve them. Then ask students to use each contraction in a sentence.

$$\text{is} + \text{not} =$$

$$\text{are} + \text{not} =$$

$$\text{do} + \text{not} =$$

Cooperative Learning

Have partners create contraction flash cards by writing a contraction on one side of each note card and the two words that are used to form the contraction on the opposite side. Have students use their flash cards to quiz each other. Have one student read aloud each contraction and have the other student tell the two words that form it. Then have partners switch roles. Point out that students may quiz each other beginning with the contractions or beginning with the words used to make up the contractions.

Verb Review

ASSESS

Use the Verb Review as homework, as a practice test, or as an informal assessment. Following are some options for use.

Homework

You may wish to assign one group the odd items and another group the even items. When you next meet, review the correct answers as a group. Be sure to model how to arrive at the correct answer.

Practice Test

Use the Verb Review as a diagnostic tool. Assign the entire review or just specific sections. After students have finished, identify which concepts require more attention. Reteach concepts as necessary.

Verb Review

4.1 Find the action verb in each sentence.

1. The girls often <u>drink</u> hot chocolate.
2. Shelly <u>likes</u> whipped cream.
3. Erin <u>adds</u> marshmallows.
4. The marshmallows <u>melt</u> in the hot chocolate.

4.2 Find the being verb in each sentence.

5. I <u>was</u> hungry at breakfast.
6. The cartons of orange juice <u>were</u> empty.
7. Mom and Dad <u>are</u> tired in the morning.

4.3 Find the helping verb and the main verb in each sentence.

8. The family <u>is</u> <u>eating</u> dinner.
9. The roast <u>has</u> <u>cooled</u> enough to eat.
10. We <u>will</u> <u>clear</u> the table.

4.4 Tell if the underlined verb part is present, present participle, past, or past participle.

11. The farmer <u>grew</u> pumpkins.
12. He has <u>stacked</u> them.
13. We <u>pick</u> pumpkins every fall.
14. Gail is <u>choosing</u> her pumpkin.

4.5 Tell whether each underlined verb is regular or irregular.

15. We <u>planned</u> a toy drive.
16. Trina <u>colored</u> posters.
17. I <u>brought</u> blocks to donate.
18. Justin <u>donated</u> puzzles.

4.6 Complete each sentence with the correct part of the verb in parentheses.

19. I am <u>sitting</u> in the park. (sit)
20. My friends <u>came</u> late. (come)
21. They have <u>brought</u> the kites. (bring)
22. I <u>bought</u> some ice cream, and I ate it. (buy)

4.7 Complete each sentence with the correct part of the verb in parentheses.

23. Joy and her mom always <u>go</u> grocery shopping. (go)
24. They are <u>eating</u> samples from the trays. (eat)
25. Now Joy <u>sees</u> cake, shrimp, and fruit. (see)
26. She had <u>gone</u> home with a stomachache. (go)

4.3
The helping verbs are underlined once. Main verbs are underlined twice.

4.4
11. past
12. past participle
13. present
14. present participle

4.5
15. irregular
16. regular
17. irregular
18. regular

Informal Assessment

Use the review as preparation for the formal assessment. Count the review as a portion of the grade. Have students work to find the correct answers and use their corrected review as a study guide for the formal assessment.

WRITING CONNECTION

Use pages 348–349 of the Writing portion of the book.

TEACHING OPTIONS

Putting It All Together

Have students choose an article from an age-appropriate magazine or newspaper. Write the following directions on the board:

- **Use a highlighter to mark all the verbs.**
- **Draw a box around all the action verbs.**
- **Circle all the helping verbs.**
- **Write *I* above all the irregular verbs.**
- **Write *P* above all the past tense verbs.**
- **Write *F* above all the future tense verbs.**

Have students read the article and follow the directions. Then have partners exchange articles and discuss their answers.

Meeting Individual Needs

Challenge Give students a few days to be Verb Sleuths. Have students compile lists of verbs they hear or see at home, at school, on television, on signs, or any other places. Remind students to look for a variety of verbs and verbs used in the present, past, and future tenses. At the end of the allotted time, have students share their lists and discuss verbs and their uses in everyday writing.

4.10

33. Clouds drifted in the sky.
34. The forecast called for rain.
35. We buttoned our raincoats.

4.11

36. Our group will plan the party.
37. Jean will make the decorations.
38. Bill will bring some food.

4.12

39. My grandma is going to make lasagna.
40. She is going to boil the noodles.
41. I am going to help Grandma.

4.13

42. A sidewalk artist is sketching.
43. Her customer is sitting still.
44. I am waiting in line for my portrait.

4.14

45. My friends were playing tennis.
46. Connie was serving the ball.
47. Tanner was returning the ball.
48. Lin and I were watching the game.

4.8 **Complete each sentence with the correct part of the verb in parentheses.**

27. Max __takes__ his clothes to the cleaners every week. (take)
28. The cleaners __tore__ his shirt. (tear)
29. Yesterday Max __wrote__ a letter of complaint. (write)

4.9 **Choose the correct verb to complete each sentence.**

30. Birds (build builds) nests.
31. They (gather gathers) twigs.
32. Maya (watch watches) them.

4.10 **Change each sentence to the simple past tense.**

33. Clouds drift in the sky.
34. The forecast calls for rain.
35. We button our raincoats.

4.11 **Change each sentence to the future tense using *will*.**

36. Our group plans the party.
37. Jean made the decorations.
38. Bill is bringing some food.

4.12 **Change each sentence to use the future tense using *going to*.**

39. My grandma made lasagna.
40. She boils the noodles.
41. I helped Grandma.

4.13 **Change each sentence to use the present progressive tense.**

42. A sidewalk artist sketches.
43. Her customer sits still.
44. I wait in line for my portrait.

4.14 **Change each sentence to use the past progressive tense.**

45. My friends played tennis.
46. Connie served the ball.
47. Tanner returned the ball.
48. Lin and I watched the game.

4.15 **Choose the verb that correctly completes each sentence.**

49. A quilt (is are) pretty.
50. Quilt makers (is are) patient.
51. The quilt's squares (was were) colorful.
52. The quilt (was were) warm.

4.16 **Write a contraction for the underlined words in each sentence.**

53. I did not want to eat corn.
54. Corn was not my favorite vegetable.
55. Kai is not eating corn either.
56. The dog will not eat the corn.

4.16

53. didn't
54. wasn't
55. isn't
56. won't

Tech Tip Go to www.voyagesinenglish.com for more activities.

Verbs • 107

TechTip Encourage students to further review verbs, using the additional practice and games at www.voyagesinenglish.com.

ASSESS

Encourage students to read the paragraph twice before answering the questions independently. If students have difficulty with any of the questions, suggest that they refer to the section that teaches the skill. This activity can be completed by individuals, small groups, or the class working as a whole.

After you have reviewed verbs, administer the Section 4 Assessment on pages 11–14 in the **Assessment Book,** or create a customized test with the optional **Test Generator CD.**

You may also wish to administer the Sections 3–4 Summative Assessment on pages 31–32 of the **Assessment Book.** This test is also available on the optional **Test Generator CD.**

WRITING CONNECTION

Students can complete a formal personal letter using the Writer's Workshop on pages 350–361.

ANSWERS

1. a being verb; does not tell about an action
2. past; present: bring; present participle: bringing; past participle: brought; irregular
3. past
4. past progressive
5. present
6. past; regular
7. might
8. had; past participle
9. present progressive; regular; learn, learning, learned, learned
10. will provide; future

Verb Challenge

Read the paragraph and answer the questions.

1. Tim and Tina were excited about the field trip to the dinosaur museum. 2. Each student brought lunch and wore old clothes. 3. A bus took the class to the site of the museum. 4. Everyone was talking about the dinosaur pit there. 5. In the pit children sift through soil. 6. They look for dinosaur bones. 7. Tina hoped she might find something. 8. She had dug in the pit last year. 9. Scientists are learning more and more about dinosaurs all the time. 10. The museum will provide a great experience to any student with an interest in dinosaurs.

1. In sentence 1 is the verb *were* an action verb or a being verb? How do you know?
2. In sentence 2 what form is the verb *brought*? Name its other principal parts. Is it a regular or an irregular verb?
3. In sentence 3 what tense is the verb?
4. In sentence 4 what tense is the verb?
5. In sentence 6 what tense is the verb?
6. In sentence 7 what tense is the verb *hoped*? Is it a regular or an irregular verb?
7. In sentence 7 what is the helping verb?
8. In sentence 8 what is the helping verb? What part of the main verb follows the helping verb?
9. In sentence 9 what tense is the verb? Is it a regular or an irregular verb? Give its principal parts.
10. In sentence 10 what is the verb? What is its tense?

SECTION FOCUS

- **Identifying adjectives**
- **Adjectives before nouns**
- **Subject complements**
- **Compound subject complements**
- **Adjectives that compare**
- **Irregular adjectives that compare**
- **Adjectives that tell how many**
- **Articles**
- **Demonstrative adjectives**
- **Proper adjectives**
- **Nouns used as adjectives**

SUPPORT MATERIALS

Practice Book
Daily Maintenance, pages 73–76
Grammar, pages 77–87

Assessment Book
Section 5 Assessment,
   pages 15–18

Test Generator CD

**Writing Chapter 5,
   Book Reports**

Customizable Lesson Plans
www.voyagesinenglish.com

CONNECT WITH LITERATURE

📖 Consider using the following titles throughout the section to illustrate the grammar concept:

*A Is for Angry: An Animal
   and Adjective Alphabet*
   by Sandra Boynton
*Alexander and the Terrible, Horrible,
   No Good, Very Bad Day*
   by Judith Viorst
One Fish Two Fish Red Fish Blue Fish
   by Dr. Seuss

Adjectives

GRAMMAR FOR GROWN-UPS

Understanding Adjectives

Adjectives are used to modify nouns or pronouns by describing, identifying, or quantifying words. Adjectives answer the questions *which*, *what kind*, and *how many*.

Articles are adjectives that point out nouns. The articles are *a*, *an*, and *the*.

> *Eleanor ate **a** banana and **an** apple on **the** bus.*

Demonstrative adjectives answer the question *which*. The demonstrative adjectives are *this*, *that*, *these*, and *those*.

> ***This** scooter is faster than **those** scooters.*

Proper adjectives and **adjectives that tell how many** come before the words they describe.

> *The **Spanish** team is in **first** place.*

Descriptive adjectives tell what kind.

> *We wear **white** shirts, **black** pants, and **dress** shoes for our **band** performance.*

Adjectives used as subject complements come after linking verbs.

> *Wen is **smart**. Casey seems **tired**.*

Most adjectives have three degrees of comparison—positive, comparative, and superlative.

The **comparative degree** is used to compare two people, places, things, or ideas. It is regularly formed either by adding *-er* to the positive (*faster*) or by using *more* or *less* before the positive.

> *Our garden is **healthier** and **more beautiful** than last year.*

The **superlative degree** is used to compare three or more people, places, things, or ideas. It is regularly formed either by adding *-est* to the positive (*fastest*) or by using *most* or *least* before the positive (*least beautiful*). Some adjectives have irregular comparative and superlative forms (*good, better, best*).

> *Our school has the **brightest** and **most talented** students in the spelling bee.*

> ❝**A man's character
> may be learned from the adjectives
> which he habitually uses in conversation.**❞
>
> —Mark Twain

COMMON ERRORS

Knowing When to Use *More*

Some young speakers and writers make the common error of using both -er or -est with *more* or *most* when trying to use comparative or superlative adjectives.

ERROR: His house is more bigger than mine is.
CORRECT: His house is bigger than mine is.

ERROR: The baby is most happiest in the morning.
CORRECT: The baby is happiest in the morning.

To help students avoid this common error, remind them that for one adjective, the ending -er or -est is never used with *more* or *most*. Have partners look for these mistakes during the proofreading stage. Gently correct this error when students use it in their speech.

SENTENCE DIAGRAMMING

You may wish to teach adjectives in the context of diagramming. Review these examples. Then refer to the Diagramming section or look for Diagram It! features in the Adjectives section.

A blue ribbon means first place.

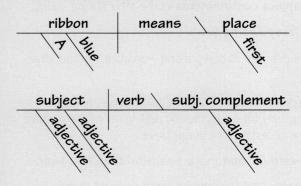

The scooter is red.

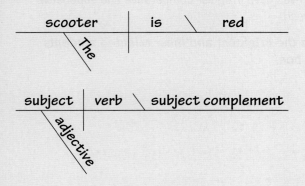

ASK AN EXPERT

Real Situations, Real Solutions

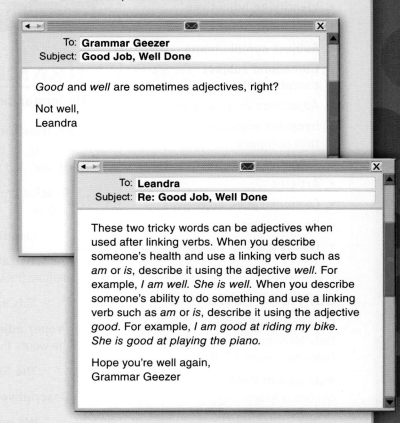

> **To:** Grammar Geezer
> **Subject:** Good Job, Well Done
>
> *Good* and *well* are sometimes adjectives, right?
>
> Not well,
> Leandra

> **To:** Leandra
> **Subject:** Re: Good Job, Well Done
>
> These two tricky words can be adjectives when used after linking verbs. When you describe someone's health and use a linking verb such as *am* or *is*, describe it using the adjective *well*. For example, *I am well. She is well.* When you describe someone's ability to do something and use a linking verb such as *am* or *is*, describe it using the adjective *good*. For example, *I am good at riding my bike. She is good at playing the piano.*
>
> Hope you're well again,
> Grammar Geezer

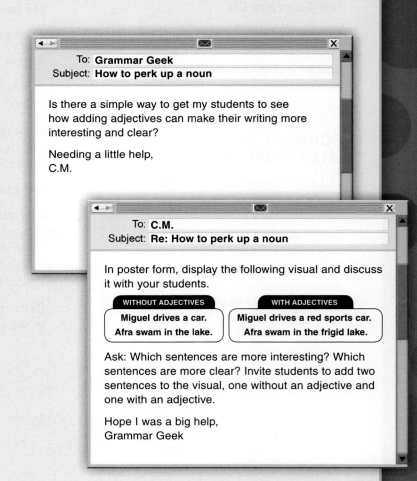

> **To:** Grammar Geek
> **Subject:** How to perk up a noun
>
> Is there a simple way to get my students to see how adding adjectives can make their writing more interesting and clear?
>
> Needing a little help,
> C.M.

> **To:** C.M.
> **Subject:** Re: How to perk up a noun
>
> In poster form, display the following visual and discuss it with your students.
>
> | WITHOUT ADJECTIVES | WITH ADJECTIVES |
> | --- | --- |
> | Miguel drives a car. Afra swam in the lake. | Miguel drives a red sports car. Afra swam in the frigid lake. |
>
> Ask: Which sentences are more interesting? Which sentences are more clear? Invite students to add two sentences to the visual, one without an adjective and one with an adjective.
>
> Hope I was a big help,
> Grammar Geek

5.1 Identifying Adjectives

5.2 Adjectives Before Nouns

5.3 Subject Complements

5.4 Compound Subject Complements

5.5 Adjectives That Compare

5.6 Irregular Adjectives That Compare

5.7 Adjectives That Tell How Many

5.8 Articles

5.9 Demonstrative Adjectives

5.10 Proper Adjectives

5.11 Nouns Used as Adjectives

Adjective Review

Adjective Challenge

OBJECTIVE
• **To identify and use adjectives**

 **DAILY Maintenance**

Assign **Practice Book** page 73, Section 5.1. After students finish,
1. Give immediate feedback.
2. Review concepts as needed.
3. Model the correct answer.

Pages 4–5 of the **Answer Key** contain tips for Daily Maintenance.

WARM-UP

Write on the board a five-column chart with the headings *1, 2, 3, 4,* and *5.* Place five different objects in separate bags and number the bags. Choose items that have different textures and shapes *(sandpaper, an apple, a cotton ball, chalk, a shell).* Have students take turns feeling the item in each bag without looking at it. Ask students to write words in the appropriate column, describing the object without naming it. Open the bags to reveal their contents.

📖 Read from a piece of writing that the class is currently reading. Emphasize the adjectives.

TEACH

Have a volunteer read aloud the first paragraph about identifying adjectives and the chart. Reinforce that adjectives are words that tell more about nouns. Point out that students can think about all five senses when they try to identify adjectives to describe nouns.

Explain that adjectives can tell about size, shape, color, texture, sound, and smell. Tell students that the names of the items in the bags from the Warm-Up are nouns and that the words to describe the nouns are adjectives. Ask students to add to the appropriate columns from the Warm-Up adjectives that tell how each object looks. Have volunteers read aloud the rest of the page. Encourage students to suggest other adjectives that tell how something might look, taste, sound, feel, or smell.

PRACTICE

EXERCISE 1
Write on the board each adjective-noun pair and ask students what they notice. Confirm that in each of these sentences, the adjective appears before the noun.

EXERCISE 2
Point out that there is more than one possible answer for each noun but that every adjective choice should make sense with the noun.

EXERCISE 3
Have students identify the nouns in each sentence. Then have students look for words that describe nouns.

EXERCISE 4
Have partners complete the exercise. Challenge students to think of adjectives that are not on the chart. Have volunteers read aloud their answers.

5.1 Identifying Adjectives

An **adjective** tells more about a noun. Adjectives describe nouns. They can tell how something looks, tastes, sounds, feels, or smells.

LOOKS	TASTES	SOUNDS	FEELS	SMELLS
tired	sour	loud	rough	smoky
huge	sweet	quiet	hard	fragrant
pink	tasty	silent	oily	stinky
happy	bitter	musical	smooth	fresh

Adjectives tell such things as size, number, color, shape, and weight.

   That cactus has *red* flowers.

In this sentence *red* is an adjective. It tells more about the noun *flowers.* Red tells what color the flowers are. Here are some other adjectives you could use to describe a flower: *small, beautiful, round, fragrant, delicate,* and *fresh.*

What is the adjective in this sentence?

   The cactus was in a large pot.

   A was

   B large

   C pot

You are right if you said B. The word *large* describes the noun *pot. Large* tells about the size of the pot.

EXERCISE 1 Find the adjective that describes the underlined noun in each sentence.

1. Deserts are dry <u>areas</u>.
2. Deserts usually have hot <u>days</u>.
3. Cold <u>nights</u>, however, follow them.
4. Deserts are difficult <u>places</u> to live because of the lack of water.
5. Animals in the deserts are usually small <u>creatures</u>.
6. Colorful <u>flowers</u> bloom quickly after rains.

APPLY

APPLY IT NOW

Discuss plants and animals with which students are familiar. Write their ideas on the board. Challenge students to use a variety of adjectives in their sentences. Students should demonstrate the ability to use adjectives in sentences.

Grammar in Action. Tell students to identify the nouns and then the adjectives *(church, familiar, mysterious)*. Tell students that *church* is an adjective here because it describes *steeple*.

ASSESS

Note which students had difficulty identifying and using adjectives in sentences. Assign **Practice Book** page 77 for further practice.

WRITING CONNECTION

Use pages 362–363 of the Writing portion of the book. Be sure to point out adjectives in the literature excerpt and the student model.

TEACHING OPTIONS

Reteach

Work with students to choose eight different objects from the classroom. Display the objects. Tell students to look at each object and write as many adjectives as possible to describe the object. Encourage students not to repeat adjectives. Allow time for students to add adjectives to each list. Then have students write at least one sentence about each object, using adjectives.

Meeting Individual Needs

Extra Support Discuss the five senses. Explain that students can use their senses to help describe things, using adjectives. *(An orange is a round fruit. It has bumpy skin. It tastes sweet and juicy. It smells fresh and clean.)* Ask students to name the senses you used to describe the orange *(sight, touch, smell, taste)*. Then have students choose a noun to describe, using as many senses as possible.

Meeting Individual Needs

Challenge Have students play I Spy, using adjectives. Ask one student to describe something he or she sees using as many adjectives as possible. Encourage students to use words that tell how the item looks, feels, smells, sounds, and tastes. Have the rest of the class try to guess the item that is being described. Ask the student who correctly identifies the item to be the next to use adjectives to give a description. Continue as time allows.

Diagram It!

To practice these concepts in the context of diagramming, turn to Section 8.3.

Exercise 2
Answers will vary. Accept all reasonable answers.

EXERCISE 2 Add an adjective to describe each noun. Choose a word from the word box.

| broken | funny | good | happy | heavy | loud |
| pretty | sad | soft | spicy | tired | warm |

1. the _____ girl
2. a _____ joke
3. a _____ backpack
4. the _____ window
5. a _____ blanket
6. a _____ coat
7. the _____ music
8. the _____ food

Exercise 3
Adjectives are underlined once. The nouns they describe are underlined twice.

EXERCISE 3 Find the adjective in each sentence. Tell the noun it describes.

1. The cactus is an <u>unusual</u> <u>plant</u>.
2. Cactuses have <u>sharp</u> <u>spikes</u>.
3. The spikes are <u>good</u> <u>protection</u> against animals.
4. Cactuses can survive for <u>long</u> <u>periods</u> without water.
5. <u>Waxy</u> <u>stems</u> help them hold in water.
6. Cactuses can produce <u>sweet</u> <u>fruit</u>.

Exercise 4
Answers will vary.

EXERCISE 4 Add an adjective before each noun. Use the kind of adjective in parentheses. Use the chart on page 110 for help.

1. _____ baby (looks)
2. _____ sandpaper (feels)
3. _____ flower (smells)
4. _____ horn (sounds)
5. _____ peach (tastes)

Prickly pear and dragon fruit

Grammar in Action. Find three adjectives in the first sentence of the page 367 excerpt.

APPLY IT NOW

Write five sentences about plants and animals that you are familiar with. Use an adjective before a noun in each sentence.
Example:
Robins are <u>common</u> birds in my area.
<u>Pink</u> roses are my favorite flowers.

Adjectives • 111

5.2 Adjectives Before Nouns

OBJECTIVE

* **To identify and use adjectives before nouns**

 **Maintenance**

Assign **Practice Book** page 73, Section 5.2. After students finish,
1. Give immediate feedback.
2. Review concepts as needed.
3. Model the correct answer.

Pages 4–5 of the **Answer Key** contain tips for Daily Maintenance.

WARM-UP

Write on the board the following sentences:

I had a _____ apple in my lunch.

Daniel brought _____ carrots.

Mary had a _____ sandwich.

Owen ate _____ pretzels.

Kate had _____ yogurt.

Ask students to fill in the blanks. Then ask volunteers to generate similar sentences about what they had for breakfast or lunch. If a student does not use an adjective, ask him or her to add one.

📖 Read from a piece of writing that the class is currently reading. Emphasize adjectives before nouns.

TEACH

Remind students that adjectives are words that describe nouns. Ask students what they notice about the position of the adjectives in the Warm-Up. Confirm that in each sentence the adjective comes before the noun.

Ask volunteers to read aloud about adjectives before nouns. Encourage students to substitute other adjectives for those in the example sentences.

PRACTICE

EXERCISES 1 & 2

Tell students first to identify the nouns in each sentence and then to find the word before the noun that describes it. Ask volunteers to share their answers with the class.

EXERCISE 3

Explain that more than one adjective may be correct in each sentence. After students have finished the exercise, ask volunteers to read aloud their sentences. Discuss how different adjective choices changed the sentences' meanings.

5.2 Adjectives Before Nouns

Most adjectives describe various features of nouns. They are called **descriptive adjectives.** Descriptive adjectives generally come before the nouns they describe.

> **The town has a *shady* park.**
> **There are *old* statues in the park.**

Shady and *old* are adjectives. In the first sentence, *shady* describes the noun *park*. In the second sentence, *old* describes the noun *statues*. In both sentences the adjectives come before the nouns they describe.

What are the adjectives in this sentence? What are the nouns they describe?

> **A large statue shows a man with a long beard.**

You are right if you said *large* and *long*. *Large* tells about the size of the *statue*. *Long* describes the noun *beard*. Both adjectives come before the nouns they describe.

EXERCISE 1 **Find the descriptive adjectives in each sentence. The number of adjectives is in parentheses.**

1. Benjamin Franklin was an extraordinary leader. (1)
2. Franklin was a talented writer who wrote a popular book. (2)
3. The famous book contains clever sayings. (2)
4. Franklin also produced useful inventions and did scientific experiments. (2)
5. His tireless work helped build an early library in Philadelphia. (2)
6. He was an able statesman who supported independence. (1)
7. His political ideas contributed to the Declaration of Independence. (1)

Benjamin Franklin

112 • Section 5.2

APPLY

APPLY IT NOW

Invite students to discuss places they have been or places that would be interesting to visit. Encourage students to think about the features that make these places interesting. Challenge students to use a variety of adjectives—adjectives other than *big, small, nice, bad,* and *good.* Students should demonstrate the ability to use adjectives before nouns.

💡 **TechTip** You may wish to suggest specific, age-appropriate travel sites or assist students in using a search engine. Remind students that using Web sites for ideas and information is encouraged, but copying directly from them is not.

ASSESS

Note which students had difficulty identifying and using adjectives before nouns. Assign **Practice Book** page 78 for further practice.

WRITING CONNECTION

Use pages 364–365 of the Writing portion of the book.

Exercise 2
Adjectives are underlined once. The nouns the adjectives describe are underlined twice.

EXERCISE 2 Find the descriptive adjective in each sentence. Tell the noun the adjective describes.

1. Philadelphia has <u>interesting</u> <u>sights</u>.
2. An <u>old</u> <u>building</u> is Independence Hall.
3. The <u>famous</u> <u>hall</u> was built in 1732.
4. Leaders held <u>long</u> <u>meetings</u> there in 1787.
5. It was where they wrote an <u>important</u> <u>document</u>—the U.S. Constitution.
6. One <u>great</u> <u>leader</u> there was George Washington.
7. He had a reputation as an <u>honest</u> <u>man</u>.
8. Washington was a <u>brave</u> <u>leader</u> during the Revolutionary War.
9. His troops survived a <u>difficult</u> <u>winter</u> at Valley Forge.
10. George Washington lived on a <u>beautiful</u> <u>estate</u> in Virginia called Mount Vernon.

Exercise 3
Answers will vary. Accept all reasonable answers. The nouns the adjectives describe are underlined.

EXERCISE 3 Complete each sentence with a descriptive adjective. Tell the noun the adjective describes. Choose from the adjectives in the word box.

important	cracked	curious	helpful
historic	blue	interested	large

1. In Philadelphia Julie saw the _____ <u>Liberty Bell</u>.
2. The _____ <u>visitors</u> asked questions about the bell.
3. She learned about the bell's history from the _____ <u>guide</u>.
4. Independence Hall is where the _____ <u>bell</u> once hung.
5. The _____ <u>bell</u> no longer rings.

Replica of the Liberty Bell

APPLY IT NOW

Write three sentences about a place you have visited or would like to visit. Use a descriptive adjective in each sentence.

Example:
San Francisco has a <u>pleasant</u> climate. I couldn't wait to see the <u>famous</u> Golden Gate Bridge. A <u>noisy</u> bus stopped at the corner near our hotel.

Tech Tip With an adult, research the place you chose online.

Adjectives • 113

Reteach

Write on the board sentences about a class project, a field trip, or other activity the class has recently enjoyed. Leave a space before each noun. Read aloud the sentences and ask students to supply adjectives that describe each noun. Write the adjectives under the space before each noun. Have volunteers read aloud each sentence several times, substituting a different adjective each time.

Curriculum Connection

Challenge students to write sentences with adjectives to describe the main characters, setting, and plot of a book or story the class is currently reading. Model some examples for students.

The brave heroine saves the day.

No one lives in the spooky, old house.

Display students' sentences along with copies of the book or story in the classroom reading center.

Cooperative Learning

Have small groups make adjective mobiles. Give each group magazines and newspapers, a hanger, and string. Direct each group to find a picture of an interesting noun to describe. Tell students that the noun will be used as the centerpiece for their mobile. Have students glue the picture to the center of a hanger. Then encourage students to write on separate note cards adjectives to describe the noun. Have students use different lengths of string to attach the cards to the mobile. If possible, hang the completed mobiles from the ceiling. Challenge students to write a paragraph describing the noun, using all the adjectives from the mobile.

OBJECTIVE

- **To identify and use adjectives as subject complements**

 **Maintenance**

Assign **Practice Book** page 73, Section 5.3. After students finish,
1. Give immediate feedback.
2. Review concepts as needed.
3. Model the correct answer.

Pages 4–5 of the **Answer Key** contain tips for Daily Maintenance.

WARM-UP

Write on the board the following sentence starters:

I am _____.

A tree is _____.

Snakes are _____.

Have students suggest adjectives to complete each sentence. Discuss the placement of the adjective in each sentence.

📖 Read from a piece of writing that the class is currently reading. Emphasize adjectives used as subject complements.

TEACH

Point out that the adjective in each sentence in the Warm-Up does not come before the noun. Explain that the adjectives describe the subject and come after the being verb.

Have volunteers read aloud about subject complements. List on the board *is, are, was,* and *were.* Model sentences such as the following:

The snake was long.

Tina is happy to have the day off.

Ask students to suggest sentences using being verbs and adjectives as subject complements.

PRACTICE

EXERCISE 1
Point out that although the construction is not as simple as that of the example sentences, each sentence does include a being verb and an adjective used as a subject complement. Have partners complete the exercise. Ask volunteers to tell the adjective used as a subject complement and the being verb in each sentence.

EXERCISE 2
Write on the board a two-column chart with the headings *Noun* and *Subject Complement.* Have volunteers complete the chart for each sentence.

EXERCISE 3
Point out that students may need to make the nouns in Group A plural. Ask volunteers to read aloud their sentences.

5.3 Subject Complements

Some descriptive adjectives come after a being verb. They are called **subject complements.** An adjective used as a subject complement tells more about the subject of the sentence. Some being verbs are *is, are, was,* and *were.*

> **The ocean is** *salty.*
> **Fish are** *scaly.*

In the first sentence, *salty* is the subject complement. It follows the being verb *is. Salty* tells about the subject, *ocean.* In the second sentence, *scaly* is the subject complement. It follows the being verb *are. Scaly* tells more about the subject, *fish.*

Which sentence has a subject complement?

A Brown trout live in lakes.
B The sunfish were colorful.
C Guppies eat plants.

You are right if you said sentence B. *Colorful* is a subject complement. It describes *sunfish,* and it comes after *were,* a being verb.

EXERCISE 1 **Find the adjective used as a subject complement in each sentence.**

1. The aquarium in my city is big.
2. A visit to the aquarium is enjoyable.
3. The area near the shark tank is always quiet.
4. The sand tiger sharks are really scary.
5. Their teeth are sharp.
6. Their skin is brown.
7. They are not dangerous to humans, however.
8. To me, the divers feeding the sharks are extremely brave.

APPLY

APPLY IT NOW

Provide interesting photos of fish and other sea creatures. Allow students to refer to the photos as needed to come up with appropriate nouns and adjectives. Students should demonstrate the ability to use adjectives as subject complements.

Grammar in Action Guide students to find the subject and subject complement *(character, likeable)*. Point out that the next sentence has two subject complements *(long, satisfying)*.

ASSESS

Note which students had difficulty identifying and using adjectives as subject complements. Assign **Practice Book** page 79 for further practice.

WRITING CONNECTION
Use pages 366–367 of the Writing portion of the book.

Reteach

Explain that adjectives used as subject complements come after being verbs in sentences. Help students brainstorm nouns that could be described and list them on the board. Write one of the nouns in the center of a word web. Have students suggest adjectives to describe the noun and write them in the connecting ovals. Ask students to write sentences using the noun and adjectives from the web.

Meeting Individual Needs

Challenge Prepare two sets of 10 note cards. Write nouns on one set and adjectives on the other set. Mix up all the cards. Challenge students to sort the cards into two piles—one for nouns and one for adjectives. Have volunteers match nouns and adjectives to write sentences using the adjectives as subject complements.

Meeting Individual Needs

Auditory Encourage students to listen throughout the day for sentences in which adjectives are used as subject complements. Tell students to listen to their classmates, teachers, family, and friends. Have students write the sentences they hear. Ask volunteers to share their sentences with the class.

Diagram It!

To practice these concepts in the context of diagramming, turn to Section 8.5.

Exercise 2
Subject complements are underlined once. The nouns the subject complements describe are underlined twice.

EXERCISE 2 Find the adjective used as a subject complement in each sentence. Tell the noun the subject complement describes.

1. The tank in the center of the aquarium is large.
2. The view from the staircase is great.
3. The seahorses in the tank are tiny.
4. The stingray's fins are wide.
5. The sea turtle is gigantic.
6. The eel's skin is green.
7. Eels are really ugly.
8. Our visit to the aquarium was wonderful.
9. The guide was helpful.
10. Her information was interesting.

Exercise 3
Answers will vary.

EXERCISE 3 Write five sentences with adjectives used as subject complements. Use a noun from Group A and an adjective from Group B in each sentence.

EXAMPLE **The fish was colorful.**

Group A	Group B	
aquarium	cloudy	dirty
fish	quick	brave
scuba diver	colorful	big
shark	beautiful	scary
tank	new	shiny

Stingray

APPLY IT NOW

Imagine you are looking into a fish tank. Write four sentences describing what you see. Use an adjective as a subject complement in each sentence.
Example:
Some fish are yellow.

Grammar in Action Find the subject complement in the second sentence of the third paragraph on page 362.

Adjectives • 115

5.4 Compound Subject Complements

OBJECTIVE

- **To identify and use adjectives as compound subject complements**

 **Maintenance**

Assign **Practice Book** page 74, Section 5.4. After students finish,
1. Give immediate feedback.
2. Review concepts as needed.
3. Model the correct answer.

Pages 4–5 of the **Answer Key** contain tips for Daily Maintenance.

WARM-UP

Write on the board the following sentences:

My brother is _____ and _____.

Basketball players are _____ and _____.

My teacher is _____ and _____.

Read aloud the sentences. Have students suggest adjectives to complete each sentence.

📖 Read from a piece of writing that the class is currently reading. Emphasize the adjectives used as compound subject complements.

TEACH

Ask students to identify the adjectives in each sentence in the Warm-Up (*funny, athletic; tall, fast; friendly, organized*). Ask what word appears between the adjectives in each sentence (*and*). Point out that the adjectives describe the subjects of the sentences.

Have a volunteer read aloud the first paragraph about compound subject complements. Reinforce that two adjectives joined by *and* or *or* after a being verb form a compound subject complement.

Have volunteers read aloud the rest of the page. Encourage students to suggest sentences with compound subject complements.

PRACTICE

EXERCISE 1
Explain that only some of the sentences contain compound subject complements. Challenge students to identify all the adjectives used as subject complements and to tell whether each subject complement is compound.

EXERCISE 2
Explain that although no one adjective is correct, certain adjectives may make more sense than others in a sentence. Encourage students not to use an adjective more than once. Point out that they will not use all the adjectives in the word box. Invite volunteers to write their sentences on the board.

EXERCISE 3
Have partners complete the exercise. Suggest that students include more than just a subject and verb. Have volunteers read aloud their sentences.

5.4 Compound Subject Complements

Some sentences have more than one adjective used as a subject complement. Two adjectives joined by *and* or *or* after a being verb form a **compound subject complement.** Both adjectives tell more about the subject.

> **Some dinosaurs were *big* and *scary*.**

The adjectives *big* and *scary* come after the being verb *were*. Both *big* and *scary* tell more about the subject, *dinosaurs*. *Big* and *scary* form a compound subject complement joined by *and*.

> **Dinosaurs might be *large* or *small*.**

In this sentence the adjectives *large* and *small* come after the being verb *be*. *Large* and *small* form a compound subject complement joined by *or*.

Which sentence has a compound subject complement?

A **Dinosaurs are extinct.**
B **Some dinosaurs were small and fast.**
C **Dinosaurs ate plants or meat.**

You are right if you said sentence B. *Small* and *fast* are adjectives used as subject complements. They describe the subject *dinosaurs* and come after the being verb *were*. Sentence A also has a subject complement, but the complement is not compound. Sentence C does not have a being verb.

EXERCISE 1 Find all the adjectives used as subject complements in these sentences. Tell which are compound subject complements.

1. T. rex was <u>big</u> and <u>fierce</u>.
2. Many plant-eating dinosaurs were <u>huge</u> and <u>heavy</u>.
3. Their necks were <u>long</u>.
4. Their back legs were <u>strong</u> and <u>thick</u>.

Exercise 1
Adjective subject complements are underlined. The following sentences have compound subject complements:
1, 2, 4, 5, 7, 8, 9, 10.

APPLY

APPLY IT NOW

Encourage students to create a list of adjectives they could use to describe dinosaurs. Challenge students to write as many adjectives as possible. Instruct students to use those adjectives in sentences as compound subject complements. Have students underline the adjectives. Students should demonstrate the ability to use adjectives as compound subject complements.

TechTip Have partners compile their sentences about dinosaurs and create a video or podcast with visual aids or sound effects.

ASSESS

Note which students had difficulty identifying and using adjectives as compound subject complements. Assign **Practice Book** page 80 for further practice.

> ### WRITING CONNECTION
> Use pages 368–369 of the Writing portion of the book.

---

5. The teeth of meat-eating dinosaurs were <u>long</u> and <u>sharp</u>.
6. The teeth of plant-eating dinosaurs were <u>flat</u>.
7. Some predator dinosaurs were <u>intelligent</u> and <u>quick</u>.
8. A few dinosaurs' skin was <u>hairy</u> or <u>feathery</u>.
9. Dinosaurs are <u>unusual</u> and <u>fascinating</u>.
10. The disappearance of dinosaurs is <u>mysterious</u> and <u>puzzling</u>.

Exercise 2
Answers will vary.
Possible answers:
1. crowded, huge
2. complete, ancient

EXERCISE 2 Complete each sentence with a compound subject complement. Choose from the adjectives in the word box.

amazing	ancient	complete	crowded	excited
happy	huge	interested	interesting	tall

1. The dinosaur exhibit is _____ and _____.
2. The dinosaur skeleton was _____ and _____.
3. The children are _____ and _____.
4. The visit was _____ and _____.

Exercise 3
Answers will vary.
Possible answers:
1. I was hungry and tired after the race.
2. Mary was pleased and delighted to win second place.

EXERCISE 3 Use these adjective pairs to write four sentences with compound subject complements.

1. hungry and tired
2. pleased and delighted
3. tall and skinny
4. slow or fast

APPLY IT NOW

Write four sentences about dinosaurs. The sentences can be about a particular dinosaur, a TV program, a book, or a museum exhibit. Use a compound subject complement in each sentence.
Example:
T. rex was <u>mean</u> and <u>scary</u>.

Tech Tip Videotape or podcast a dinosaur fun-facts program.

Adjectives • 117

TEACHING OPTIONS

Reteach

Write 10 sentences with spaces for compound subject complements, such as the following:

Cara is _____ and _____.

Police officers are _____ and _____.

Dogs can be _____ and _____.

Display the sentences and have volunteers write appropriate adjectives to form compound subject complements. Have students read aloud the complete sentences and identify the compound subject complements.

Meeting Individual Needs

Intrapersonal Have students write in their journals about activities that occurred throughout the day, using compound subject complements. Model the following examples:

Math was quick and easy.

Lunch was tasty and hot.

Our story was exciting and funny.

Meeting Individual Needs

Interpersonal Have partners write descriptions about each other, using sentences with compound subject complements. Model an example for students, describing another teacher or student:

Mrs. Li is hardworking and kind. She is always cheerful and helpful. Mrs. Li is reliable and prepared all the time.

Have partners exchange their descriptions and identify the adjectives used as compound subject complements.

Diagram It!

To practice these concepts in the context of diagramming, turn to Section 8.8.

5.5 Adjectives That Compare

- **To identify, form, and use adjectives that compare two or more things**

 **Maintenance**

Assign **Practice Book** page 74, Section 5.5. After students finish,
1. Give immediate feedback.
2. Review concepts as needed.
3. Model the correct answer.

Pages 4–5 of the **Answer Key** contain tips for Daily Maintenance.

WARM-UP

Have three volunteers stand in front of the class in height order. Ask students to suggest sentences comparing the height of the volunteers. Then write on the board the following sentences, adding students' names in the blanks:

_____ is tall.

_____ is taller than _____.

_____ is the tallest of all.

Ask students to circle the words that compare.

📖 Read from a piece of writing that the class is currently reading. Emphasize adjectives that compare.

TEACH

Have students identify the adjectives in each sentence from the Warm-Up *(tall, taller, tallest)*. Ask how many people are being compared in the second sentence *(two)* and how many people are being compared in the last sentence *(three)*. Reinforce that *-er* is added to adjectives when comparing two people and *-est* is added when comparing more than two people.

Have a volunteer read aloud the first paragraph, the example sentences, and the second

paragraph about adjectives that compare. Ask students to suggest other sentences that include words used to compare two things or more than two things.

Have volunteers read aloud the rest of the page. Review the spelling changes. Write on the board the words *large* and *happy*. Have students add *-er* and *-est* to each word and use them in sentences.

PRACTICE

EXERCISE 1

Review the rules for adding *-er* and *-est* to adjectives. On the board, re-create the chart and have

volunteers say the correct forms for each word. Write the words in the chart. Discuss the spelling rule that pertains to each word *(no change: short, small; drop the final e: wide; change the y to i: windy, scary; double the final consonant: hot)*.

EXERCISE 2

Invite students to share strategies for finding adjectives that compare. *(Look for words that end with -er or -est.)* Suggest that students write their answers in a two-column chart with the headings *End in* -er and *End in* -est. Have volunteers read aloud their answers.

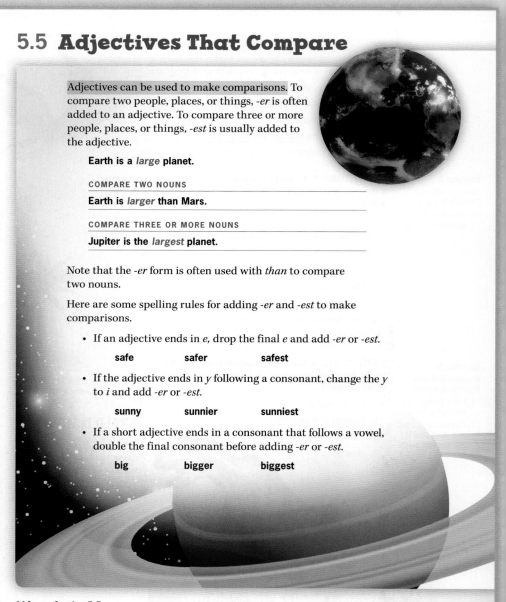

5.5 Adjectives That Compare

Adjectives can be used to make comparisons. To compare two people, places, or things, *-er* is often added to an adjective. To compare three or more people, places, or things, *-est* is usually added to the adjective.

Earth is a *large* planet.

COMPARE TWO NOUNS

Earth is *larger* than Mars.

COMPARE THREE OR MORE NOUNS

Jupiter is the *largest* planet.

Note that the *-er* form is often used with *than* to compare two nouns.

Here are some spelling rules for adding *-er* and *-est* to make comparisons.

- If an adjective ends in *e*, drop the final *e* and add *-er* or *-est*.

  safe   safer   safest

- If the adjective ends in *y* following a consonant, change the *y* to *i* and add *-er* or *-est*.

  sunny   sunnier   sunniest

- If a short adjective ends in a consonant that follows a vowel, double the final consonant before adding *-er* or *-est*.

  big   bigger   biggest

APPLY

APPLY IT NOW

Help students brainstorm a list of places around the community or state—natural sites as well as monuments, stores, malls, and skateboard parks. Challenge students to choose places to compare, using comparative adjectives in their sentences. Suggest that students underline the places being compared and circle the adjective used to compare them. Students should demonstrate the ability to use adjectives that compare.

> **Grammar in Action** Guide students to find the adjective that compares *(older)* and the nouns that are compared *(world, time)*.

ASSESS

Note which students had difficulty identifying, forming, and using adjectives that compare two or more things. Assign **Practice Book** page 81 for further practice.

> ### WRITING CONNECTION
> Use pages 370–371 of the Writing portion of the book.

EXERCISE 1 Complete the chart.

ADJECTIVE	COMPARE TWO NOUNS	COMPARE THREE OR MORE NOUNS
short	shorter	shortest
hot	hotter	hottest
wide	wider	widest
windy	windier	windiest
small	smaller	smallest
scary	scarier	scariest
brave	braver	bravest
tiny	tinier	tiniest
sad	sadder	saddest

EXERCISE 2 Find the adjective that compares in each sentence.

1. Mercury is the <u>closest</u> planet to the sun.
2. The planet Venus has <u>longer</u> days than any other planet.
3. Do you know what the <u>hottest</u> planet is?
4. The <u>sandiest</u> desert is the Arabian Desert in Africa.
5. Australia is a <u>smaller</u> continent than Antarctica.
6. The <u>warmest</u> continent is Africa.
7. Antarctica is the <u>emptiest</u> continent.
8. The Pacific Ocean is <u>deeper</u> than the Atlantic Ocean.
9. The Amazon River is <u>shorter</u> than the Nile River.
10. The Amazon is called the <u>mightiest</u> river because of the amount of water it carries.
11. Mount Everest is <u>higher</u> than Mount McKinley.
12. The <u>deepest</u> lake in the world is Lake Baikal.

> **Grammar in Action** Find the adjective that compares in the excerpt on page 367.

APPLY IT NOW

Write four sentences about places you know. Use an adjective that compares in each sentence.
Example:
The park near school is the <u>largest</u> park in town.

Adjectives • 119

OBJECTIVE

- **To identify and use the comparative and superlative forms of the adjectives *good* and *bad***

**DAILY Maintenance**

Assign **Practice Book** page 74, Section 5.6. After students finish,
1. Give immediate feedback.
2. Review concepts as needed.
3. Model the correct answer.

Pages 4–5 of the **Answer Key** contain tips for Daily Maintenance.

WARM-UP

Write on the board the following sentences:

Last week our team had the _____ (better best) game ever!

I don't think we will ever play any _____ (better best).

The weather today is much _____ (worse worst) than yesterday.

Tomorrow may be the _____ (worse worst) day of the week.

Have students choose the word that best completes each sentence. Ask students to explain their choices.

📖 Read from a piece of writing that the class is currently reading. Emphasize the comparative and superlative forms of *good* and *bad*.

TEACH

Write on the board the following sentences:

Rich is a better soccer player than José.

Jorge is the best player on the team.

Ask students to identify the adjectives that show a comparison in each sentence (*better, best*).

Ask students to tell how many players are being compared in each sentence (*two, more than two*). Point out that *better* and *best* are irregular adjectives because they are not formed by simply adding *-er* and *-est*. Explain that adjectives that have irregular forms when used to compare have to be memorized.

Have volunteers read aloud about irregular adjectives that compare. Ask volunteers to suggest sentences using *better, best, worse* and *worst*. Ask volunteers to tell how many things are being compared in each sentence.

PRACTICE

EXERCISE 1

Have volunteers read aloud the sentences and tell how many things are being compared. Then have them refer to the chart on page 120 to decide which adjective is correct.

EXERCISE 2

Ask volunteers to read aloud the sentences with the correct adjective and tell why they chose that word for each item.

EXERCISE 3

Point out that Exercise 2 focused on the forms of *good* and that this

---

5.6 Irregular Adjectives That Compare

Some adjectives that compare are irregular. They are not formed by adding *-er* or *-est*. Two common irregular adjectives are *good* and *bad*.

	COMPARE TWO NOUNS	COMPARE THREE OR MORE NOUNS
good	better	best
bad	worse	worst

A *good* snack is a cookie.
Cheese is a *better* snack than candy. (compares two nouns)
The *best* snack of all is fruit. (compares three or more nouns)

Which sentence uses an irregular adjective that compares?

A A tasty fruit for a snack is an apple.
B My favorite fruit is grapes.
C The best fruit for lunch is a pear.

You are right if you said sentence C. *Best* is part of the irregular adjective *good*.

Which choice correctly completes the sentence?

The purple jelly bean tastes even (worse worst) than the yellow jelly bean.

The correct answer is *worse*. It is used to compare two things. Note that *better* and *worse* are often used with *than*.

exercise focuses on forms of *bad*. Have students read aloud their answers and point out the things being compared.

APPLY

APPLY IT NOW

Discuss students' regular activities *(playing or watching sports, reading books, helping at home).* Direct students to compare the experiences, using the words *good, better, best, bad, worse,* and *worst.* Students should demonstrate the ability to identify and use the comparative and superlative forms of the adjectives *good* and *bad*.

ASSESS

Note which students had difficulty using the comparative and superlative forms of the adjectives *good* and *bad*. Assign **Practice Book** page 82 for further practice.

WRITING CONNECTION

Use pages 372–373 of the Writing portion of the book.

TEACHING OPTIONS

Reteach

Help students brainstorm subjects that make good comparisons, such as sports, types of music, games, and TV shows. Then have students write sentences about one of the topics comparing two or more things, using *good, better, best, bad, worse,* and *worst.* Encourage students to write sentences using all the words. Have students share their sentences with a partner.

English-Language Learners

Read aloud several sentences using irregular adjectives that compare. Have students raise two fingers if the sentence compares two things and a fist if the sentence compares more than two things.

Curriculum Connection

Play several pieces of different types of music. Invite students to compare the music styles, using the words *good, better, best, bad, worse,* and *worst.* Write students' sentences on the board. Help students recognize how the adjectives are used.

Pop music sounds <u>good</u>.

Classical music sounds <u>better</u> than pop music.

Show tunes are the <u>worst</u>.

EXERCISE 1 Choose the correct adjective to complete each sentence.

1. Water is a (good <u>better</u>) drink than lemonade.
2. Fruit smoothies are (good <u>better</u>) for you than soda.
3. Potato chips are a (<u>worse</u> worst) snack than carrots.
4. Apples are the (better <u>best</u>) snack of all.
5. A (<u>good</u> best) snack is raisins and celery.
6. This is the (bad <u>worst</u>) pizza I've ever eaten.
7. Candy is (<u>bad</u> worst) for your teeth.
8. Fried foods are (<u>worse</u> worst) for your health than grilled foods.

EXERCISE 2 Use *good, better,* or *best* to complete each sentence.

1. <u>Good</u> food contributes to a person's health.
2. Strawberry is the <u>best</u> ice cream flavor.
3. Chocolate pudding is <u>better</u> than vanilla.
4. The runner gave his <u>best</u> effort.
5. We had a <u>good</u> time at the fair.
6. Fairs are <u>better</u> than zoos.
7. Dogs are <u>better</u> than cats.

EXERCISE 3 Use *bad, worse,* or *worst* to complete each sentence.

1. I have the <u>worst</u> cold I've ever had.
2. I am <u>worse</u> today than yesterday.
3. She has the <u>worst</u> luck of all.
4. Ken was in trouble for his <u>bad</u> behavior.
5. His project was <u>worse</u> than mine.
6. The weather today is <u>worse</u> than yesterday.
7. The pool was closed during <u>bad</u> weather.

APPLY IT NOW

Think about something you do regularly. Write three sentences about it. Use an adjective that compares in each sentence. Choose from *good, better, best, bad, worse,* and *worst.*
Example:
The <u>best</u> sport at school is soccer.
I am a <u>worse</u> player than Myra.

Adjectives • 121

5.7 Adjectives That Tell How Many

OBJECTIVE

- **To identify and use adjectives that tell how many or about how many**

 **Maintenance**

Assign **Practice Book** page 75, Section 5.7. After students finish,
1. Give immediate feedback.
2. Review concepts as needed.
3. Model the correct answer.

Pages 4–5 of the **Answer Key** contain tips for Daily Maintenance.

WARM-UP

Display pictures of paintings of several people doing different actions (*Sunday Afternoon on the Island of La Grande Jatte* by George Seurat or *The Dance Foyer at the Opera on the Rue Le Peletier* by Edgar Degas). Ask volunteers to tell what they see (*two men wearing top hats, one dancer stretching*). Ask students to identify words that tell how many in each sentences.

Read from a piece of writing that the class is currently reading. Emphasize adjectives that tell how many or about how many.

TEACH

Display a group of similar objects (*six crayons, three chairs, five books*). Ask students to describe the group of objects. When students use a sentence with an adjective that tells how many or about how many, write that sentence on the board. Then ask students to tell if the sentences have adjectives and to identify them. Underline the adjectives that tell how many or about how many.

Have volunteers read aloud about adjectives that tell how many. Write on the board the following sentence:

Four students are coming over to study.

Encourage volunteers to replace the adjective that tells how many with an adjective that tells about how many. Have students brainstorm a list of adjectives that tell about how many. Write students' responses on the board and ask volunteers to use the words in sentences.

PRACTICE

EXERCISE 1

Have students read the items and tell what is the same about them. Confirm that each contains an adjective that tells how many, followed by a noun. Suggest that students record their answers in a two-column chart with the headings *Exactly How Many* and *About How Many*.

EXERCISE 2

Have partners complete this exercise. Suggest that students add the adjectives to the appropriate columns of the chart they started for Exercise 1.

EXERCISE 3

After students have completed the exercise, have small groups compare their answers.

5.7 Adjectives That Tell How Many

Adjectives can tell how many or about how many.

Adjectives that tell how many include numbers, such as *one, two, five, ninety*.

> Derek has *two* brothers and *one* sister.
> I'm taking *four* classes this semester.
> *Sixteen* people are coming to the party.

Adjectives also include words that tell numerical order; for example, *first, second, fifth, ninetieth*.

> Her house is the *third* one on the right.
> The alarm sounded for the *second* time.
> That was my *fourth* trip to California.

Some adjectives tell about how many; for example, *few, several, many, some*. They do not tell exact numbers.

> **Exactly how many** *Six* hikers went down into the canyon today.
> **About how many** *Several* people went to the visitor's center to see the film.

Which sentence has an adjective that tells about how many?

- A The Grand Canyon is in Arizona.
- B Some trails are quite steep.
- C The canyon is a natural wonder.

You are right if you said sentence B. The adjective *Some* tells about how many trails. *Some* is not an exact amount.

EXERCISE 1 Find the adjectives. Tell whether each tells about how many or exactly how many.

1. many tourists
2. ten mules
3. third trail
4. some rocks
5. few people
6. twenty miles
7. several schools
8. two guides

Exercise 1
1. about how many
2. exactly how many
3. exactly how many
4. about how many
5. about how many
6. exactly how many
7. about how many
8. exactly how many

APPLY

APPLY IT NOW

Invite students to think about adventures they have had or adventures they imagine having in the future. Encourage students to write sentences that tell exactly how many in two sentences and adjectives that tell about how many in two sentences. Ask students to underline each adjective. Students should demonstrate the ability to use adjectives that tell how many and about how many.

ASSESS

Note which students had difficulty identifying and using adjectives that tell how many or about how many. Assign **Practice Book** page 83 for further practice.

WRITING CONNECTION

Use pages 374–375 of the Writing portion of the book.

Reteach

Have students find classroom objects that can be described by using adjectives that tell how many or about how many. Ask partners to write sentences for the objects. Have students identify the adjectives that tell how many or about how many in each sentence. Model these sentences for students: *Three plants sit on the windowsill. There are several board games on the shelf.*

English-Language Learners

To help students become familiar with written number words, create a chart of numerals and number words. Ask students to use several number words as adjectives in sentences.

Curriculum Connection

Encourage students to use classroom items to put together a make-believe classroom store. Tell students to gather the following items: books, folders, erasers, pencils, pens, markers, and paper. Invite small groups to visit the store and gather items they would like to buy. Have students working in the store write sentences that describe the items, using adjectives that tell how many or about how many. Ask students who are shopping to identify the adjectives that tell how many or about how many in each sentence.

Exercise 2

1. exactly how many
2. exactly how many
3. about how many
4. about how many
5. exactly how many
6. about how many
7. about how many
8. about how many
9. about how many
10. exactly how many
11. exactly how many
12. exactly how many
13. exactly how many
14. about how many

EXERCISE 2 Find the adjective that tells how many in each sentence. Tell whether the adjective tells about how many or exactly how many.

1. <u>Ten</u> people were in our tour group to the Grand Canyon.
2. I became friendly with <u>two</u> students from Mexico.
3. <u>Many</u> visitors to the canyon make the hike.
4. <u>Some</u> visitors prefer to ride on mules.
5. The <u>first</u> settlers in the area were the Pueblo.
6. <u>Some</u> Native Americans still live in the area.
7. My family has made a <u>few</u> trips to the Grand Canyon.
8. <u>Many</u> friends of mine have also visited there.
9. It took us <u>several</u> hours to make the hike.
10. We spent <u>three</u> nights camping in the Grand Canyon.
11. My cousin's trip through the Grand Canyon lasted <u>four</u> days.
12. <u>Millions</u> of people see the Grand Canyon every year.
13. The Grand Canyon is <u>one</u> mile deep in places.
14. There are <u>some</u> mountain lions in the park.

Grand Canyon

Exercise 3

Answers will vary. Possible answers:

1. Twenty students have visited the Grand Canyon.
2. We spent four days at the canyon.

EXERCISE 3 Complete each sentence with an adjective that tells how many. Use the directions in parentheses.

1. _____ students have visited the Grand Canyon. (exactly how many)
2. We spent _____ days at the canyon. (exactly how many)
3. We saw _____ sunrises over the Grand Canyon. (exactly how many)
4. Our family took _____ photos. (about how many)
5. There were _____ tourists in the canyon. (about how many)

APPLY IT NOW

Write four sentences to tell about an adventure you have had or would like to have. Use adjectives that tell how many in each sentence.
Example:
I swam in a lake that was twenty feet deep.

Adjectives • 123

5.8 Articles

124 • Section 5.8

OBJECTIVE
- **To identify and use articles**

 **Maintenance**

Assign **Practice Book** page 75, Section 5.8. After students finish,
1. Give immediate feedback.
2. Review concepts as needed.
3. Model the correct answer.

Pages 4–5 of the **Answer Key** contain tips for Daily Maintenance.

WARM-UP

Write on the board the articles *the, an,* and *a* and the following sentences:

There is _____ squirrel under the tree.

_____ squirrel is eating an acorn.

The test will start in _____ minute.

You have _____ hour to finish it.

Have volunteers use the words on the board to complete each sentence.

📖 Read from a piece of writing that the class is currently reading. Emphasize the articles.

TEACH

Explain that *a, an,* and *the* are special adjectives called articles. Ask students to identify the nouns in the sentences on the board. Point out that articles, like many other adjectives, appear before nouns.

Have volunteers read aloud about articles. Point out that *a* is used before nouns that begin with a consonant sound. Explain that *an* is used before nouns that begin with a vowel sound. Tell students that *the* is used to point out specific people, places, and things. Encourage students to suggest sentences using *a, an,* and *the.*

PRACTICE

EXERCISE 1
Tell students that some sentences have more than one article. Have partners complete the exercise. Then read aloud the sentences and invite students to follow along. Have students raise their hands when you come to a word that is an article. Discuss any articles that students miss or identify incorrectly.

EXERCISE 2
Invite students to explain when to use *a* and when to use *an.* Have them complete the exercise independently.

EXERCISE 3
Remind students that *the* points out a specific person, place, or thing and that *a* and *an* point out any one of a class of people, places, or things. Review that *a* is used before a word that begins with a consonant sound and that *an* is used before a word that begins with a vowel sound. Have partners compare their answers.

5.8 Articles

The, an, and *a* point out nouns. They are called **articles.**

> I saw **an** airplane in **a** museum.
> There were many old airplanes in **the** museum.

- *A* and *an* point out any one of a class of people, places, or things. This sentence tells about one of several guides.

  > **A** guide took us around and told us interesting facts.

- Use *a* before a word that begins with a consonant sound.

  > **a** glider   **a** plane   **a** uniform

- Use *an* before a word that begins with a vowel sound.

  > **an** airplane   **an** inspection   **an** hour

- *The* points out a specific person, place, or thing. This sentence tells about one specific museum.

  > **The** aircraft museum was interesting.

Which one of these sentences uses an article?

A **My family flew to Orlando.**
B **Our flight was on time.**
C **An attendant showed us to our seats.**

You are right if you said sentence C. *An* is an article. Because *attendant* begins with a vowel sound, the article *an* is used.

EXERCISE 1 Find all the articles in each sentence.

1. Orville and Wilbur Wright were the first inventors to make a successful flight in an airplane.
2. First they tested a glider at Kitty Hawk, North Carolina.
3. The early test flights failed.
4. They finally flew a glider they could control.
5. The Wright brothers were in a race to build a powered aircraft.

APPLY

APPLY IT NOW

Write the word *airplane* on the board and ask students which article should come before it— *a* or *an*. Encourage students to name other machines that fly, such as helicopters, jets, rockets, and remote-control planes. Direct students to write five sentences about airplanes or other flying machines. Have students underline each article. Students should demonstrate the ability to use articles.

ASSESS

Note which students had difficulty identifying and using articles. Assign **Practice Book** page 84 for further practice.

WRITING CONNECTION

Use pages 376–377 of the Writing portion of the book.

Reteach

Write on the board a two-column chart with the headings *Article* and *Noun*. Brainstorm with students a list of at least 10 nouns. Be sure that students include nouns that begin with both vowel and consonant sounds. Have students supply the articles that can be used with each noun. Then direct students to choose three nouns and to use them along with articles to write sentences.

Meeting Individual Needs

Extra Support Encourage students to look in newspapers and magazines for sentences with the articles *a, an,* and *the.* Ask volunteers to read aloud the sentences as you write them on the board. Challenge students to identify the articles and the nouns they point out in each sentence. Ask students to explain why each article was used.

English-Language Learners

In some languages, such as French, Italian, and Spanish, articles agree in number and gender with the nouns they point out. Tell students that articles in English have no gender or number. Explain that *a, an,* and *the* are the only articles in English. Review the uses of each article. Provide students with sentences in which articles are omitted. Have students work with partners to complete the sentences.

6. In 1903 the Wright brothers successfully flew an aircraft that had an engine.

7. Someone took a picture of the first flight, but it received little attention.

8. Eventually, someone wrote an article about the flight.

EXERCISE 2 Add *a* or *an* before each noun.

1. an event
2. a pilot
3. an adventure
4. a wing
5. a runway
6. a hangar
7. an aisle
8. a passenger
9. a helicopter
10. an instrument

EXERCISE 3 Choose the correct articles to complete the sentences.

1. Working with machines was (a an) interest of (a the) Wright brothers.
2. Orville and Wilbur worked to build (an a) airplane with (a an) engine.
3. They spent much time studying (a the) flight of birds.
4. They built (a an) wind tunnel to test different designs of wings.
5. (The A) first flight of the Wright brothers lasted only 12 seconds.
6. But it was (a an) amazing moment in history.
7. After (a the) first flight, the Wright brothers kept experimenting.
8. (An The) plane the Wright brothers used in their first flight is at (an the) National Air and Space Museum in Washington, D.C.

APPLY IT NOW

Have you flown on a plane, been to an airport, or seen a plane in the sky? Write five sentences about airplanes. Underline each article you use.
Example:
I saw an airplane with a propeller.

Adjectives • 125

5.9 Demonstrative Adjectives

OBJECTIVE

- **To identify and use the demonstrative adjectives *this, that, these,* and *those***

**Maintenance**

Assign **Practice Book** page 75, Section 5.9. After students finish,
1. Give immediate feedback.
2. Review concepts as needed.
3. Model the correct answer.

Pages 4–5 of the **Answer Key** contain tips for Daily Maintenance.

WARM-UP

Write on the board the words *this, that, these,* and *those.* Say sentences about classroom objects as you point to them. *(This book belongs to you. That book is mine. These backpacks are very heavy. Those look very light.)* Ask students to use the words on the board in sentences pointing out nouns in the classroom. Discuss how students chose which word to use in each sentence.

📖 Read from a piece of writing that the class is currently reading. Emphasize demonstrative adjectives.

TEACH

Write on the board the following sentences and read them aloud:

Please hand me that pencil.

Which of these books is mine?

Is this book yours?

May I please have those folders?

Ask students to identify the nouns in each sentence and underline them. Then ask students to circle the words that come before each noun. Tell students that the words *that, these, this,* and *those* are adjectives that point out nouns in each sentence.

Have volunteers read aloud about demonstrative adjectives. Summarize when to use each demonstrative adjective.

PRACTICE

EXERCISE 1

Ask students to explain the difference between *this* and *these.* Have students read aloud their answers and tell why they chose *this* or *these* for each item.

EXERCISE 2

Encourage students to explain the difference between *that* and *those.* Have students complete the exercise independently. Invite volunteers to read aloud and explain their answers.

EXERCISE 3

After students identify each demonstrative adjective, discuss the sentence in which it is used and the noun it describes.

EXERCISE 4

Ask students what clue will help them choose the correct adjective *(the singular or plural noun).* Have students read aloud and explain their answers.

5.9 Demonstrative Adjectives

This, that, these, and *those* are called **demonstrative adjectives.** They point out or tell about a specific person, place, or thing.

SINGULAR

Near:	*This* swim mask fits me.
Far away:	*That* swim mask is too big.

PLURAL

Near:	*These* swim masks are on sale.
Far away:	*Those* swim masks are too costly.

This and *these* point out something that is near. *That* and *those* point out something that is farther away.

Which sentence has a demonstrative adjective?

A **The locker room is to the left of the pool.**
B **My swimming gear is in this bag.**
C **I have a new swim mask.**

You are right if you said sentence B. *This* tells about a bag that is nearby.

EXERCISE 1 Add *this* or *these* to show that the things are near.

1. __this__ pool
2. __these__ backpacks
3. __these__ keys
4. __this__ sweater
5. __these__ chairs
6. __this__ air mattress

EXERCISE 2 Add *that* or *those* to show that the things are far away.

1. __that__ swimsuit
2. __that__ kickboard
3. __those__ lanes
4. __those__ sunglasses
5. __that__ diving board
6. __those__ goggles

APPLY

APPLY IT NOW

Help students brainstorm things people see at a beach or swimming pool. Encourage students to decide on a topic before writing their sentences. Invite volunteers to read aloud their sentences and explain the use of each demonstrative adjective. Students should demonstrate the ability to use demonstrative adjectives.

ASSESS

Note which students had difficulty identifying and using the demonstrative adjectives *this, that, these,* and *those.* Assign **Practice Book** page 85 for further practice.

WRITING CONNECTION

Use pages 378–379 of the Writing portion of the book.

Use pages 378–379 of the Writing portion of the book.

TEACHING OPTIONS

Reteach

Have students look outside the classroom window and use demonstrative adjectives to describe objects they see. Write on the board their descriptions. Ask students to decide whether the objects are near or far and also whether they are singular or plural. Model the following sentences:

> **These** leaves are changing colors.

> **Those** birds are loud.

Meeting Individual Needs

Challenge Have students play a guessing game. Ask a volunteer with eyes closed to put his or her head down on a desk. Have another student choose an object and point it out. Have the volunteer lift up his or head and open his or her eyes. Then tell the volunteer to ask questions using demonstrative adjectives to try to identify the object. Have the rest of the class respond to the questions, using demonstrative adjectives. Continue until the student is able to identify the object.

> **Volunteer:** "Is it on **this** side of Amy's desk?"

> **Other students:** "No, it is on **that** side of Amy's desk."

Continue until the object is located.

Meeting Individual Needs

Kinesthetic Have partners give each other commands using demonstrative adjectives. *(Put this book on the shelf. Clean off that table.)* Tell students to use hand motions to distinguish between *this* and *that* and *these* and *those.*

EXERCISE 3 Find the demonstrative adjective in each sentence. Tell whether the adjective tells about something that is near or far away.

1. This swimming pool is deep. near
2. Those children are having fun. far away
3. These flippers are mine. near
4. Is that towel yours? far away
5. Those flip-flops are Sarah's. far away
6. Mike is playing with that pool float. far away
7. Give me that swim vest. far away
8. I like these mermaid swim fins. near
9. Come and sit down under this umbrella. near
10. Don't slip on that puddle of water. far away

EXERCISE 4 Complete each sentence with a demonstrative adjective. Use the directions in parentheses to tell whether the thing is near or far away.

1. __This__ part of the pool is fairly deep. (near)
2. __Those__ children are great swimmers. (far)
3. __That__ man is my swimming teacher. (far)
4. __These__ shoes are mine. (near)
5. Use __this__ red towel. (near)
6. __That__ beach ball is Jackie's. (far)
7. Please hand me __those__ swim goggles. (far)
8. Is __this__ diving ring yours? (near)
9. __These__ bottles of sunscreen are full. (near)
10. __That__ sun hat is for my baby sister. (near)

APPLY IT NOW

Write five sentences describing the people and things at a beach or swimming pool. Use a demonstrative adjective in each sentence.
Example:
That woman is the lifeguard.
These shells are orange.

Adjectives • 127

OBJECTIVE

- **To identify, form, and use proper adjectives**

 **Maintenance**

Assign **Practice Book** page 76, Section 5.10. After students finish,
1. Give immediate feedback.
2. Review concepts as needed.
3. Model the correct answer.

Pages 4–5 of the **Answer Key** contain tips for Daily Maintenance.

WARM-UP

Discuss foods from different countries. Ask students to tell which kind of food they like best. Write on the board their responses (*Indian food, Mexican food, Chinese food*). Ask students to tell the country from which each type of food comes. Write the country names on the board. Discuss the similarities and differences between the adjectives and the nouns that name the countries.

📖 Read from a piece of writing that the class is currently reading. Emphasize proper adjectives.

TEACH

Write on the board the following:

(Cuba) _____ sandwiches

(Mexico) _____ flag

(China) _____ lanterns

Encourage students change each word in parentheses to a word that can be used to fill in the blank. Model an example, such as *Italian shoes*. Write on the board students' responses. Point out that the words in parentheses are proper nouns and the words that were used to complete the items are proper adjectives.

Have volunteers read aloud about proper adjectives. Point out that proper adjectives are formed from proper nouns and are always capitalized. Ask students to look at the list of proper adjectives and to identify common endings for proper adjectives (*-an, -ian, -ish, -ese*). Encourage students to suggest additional proper adjectives.

PRACTICE

EXERCISES 1 & 2

Encourage students to explain what clues identify a proper adjective. Confirm that a proper adjective always begins with a capital letter. Have students share their answers with the class.

EXERCISE 3

Point out that the words in parentheses are all names of places. Have small groups complete the exercise. Tell students that most of the proper adjectives end in *-ian (Russian, Indian, Siberian, Italian, Asian, Brazilian)*, two end in *-ish (Irish, Swedish)*, one ends in *-ic (Icelandic)*, and one ends in *-k (Greek)*.

5.10 Proper Adjectives

A proper noun names a particular person, place, or thing. Some adjectives are formed from proper nouns. These adjectives are called **proper adjectives.** A proper adjective always begins with a capital letter.

> **The world's largest country is** *China.* (proper noun)
> **I like to eat** *Chinese* **food.** (proper adjective)

Here are some proper nouns and their proper adjectives.

PROPER NOUN	PROPER ADJECTIVE
Mexico	Mexican
Canada	Canadian
Spain	Spanish
Japan	Japanese

Which of these word groups include a proper adjective?

A the trip to Japan
B a Polish dish
C a Vietnamese doll

You're right if you said B and C. *Polish* and *Vietnamese* are proper adjectives. They are formed from the proper nouns *Poland* and *Vietnam.*

EXERCISE 1 **Choose the proper adjective from each pair of words.**

1. America — American
2. Romania — Romanian
3. Chilean — Chile
4. Jamaica — Jamaican
5. Texan — Texas
6. Korean — Korea

Moai statues on Easter Island (Chile)

APPLY

APPLY IT NOW

Help students brainstorm a list of countries and write them on the board. Work with students to change the proper nouns to proper adjectives. Encourage students to choose four proper adjectives to include in their sentences. Remind students that proper adjectives should be capitalized. Students should demonstrate the ability to use proper adjectives.

TechTip You may wish to suggest a specific online atlas or geography Web site.

ASSESS

Note which students had difficulty identifying, using, and forming proper adjectives. Assign **Practice Book** page 86 for further practice.

> ### WRITING CONNECTION
> Use pages 380–381 of the Writing portion of the book.

TEACHING OPTIONS

Reteach

Display a map of the world. Have volunteers point to different places. Write the city or country names students identify. Then work with students to change the proper nouns into proper adjectives. Encourage students to suggest sentences for each adjective. Write on the board the sentences and have students identify the proper adjectives and the nouns they describe.

Meeting Individual Needs

Extra Support Write on the board a five-column chart with the headings *-an, -ian, -ese, -ish,* and *other.* Help students brainstorm a list of proper nouns. Have students change each proper noun into a proper adjective. Ask volunteers to write each proper adjective in the correct column of the chart. Point out that there are many different ways to form proper adjectives, so students will have to memorize them or check a dictionary. Encourage students to use the proper adjectives in sentences.

Curriculum Connection

Have students choose a country to research. Tell students to write a short paragraph describing the country, its history, traditions, and foods. Direct students to include at least two proper adjectives in their paragraphs. Allow time for students to illustrate their paragraphs. Have volunteers share their work with the class.

Exercise 2

Proper adjectives are underlined once. The nouns the adjectives describe are underlined twice.

EXERCISE 2 Find the proper adjective in each sentence. Then tell the noun the adjective describes.

1. My mom has a Swiss watch.
2. Have you ever had French cheese?
3. That Italian car is fast!
4. Diego Rivera was a famous Mexican artist.
5. My grandparents went on a trip to see the Alaskan coast.
6. The Egyptian pyramids are amazing.
7. Russian winters are very cold.
8. Portuguese beaches are very beautiful.
9. The handmade Peruvian sweaters were colorful.
10. Shish kebab is a Turkish food.
11. Laila is a Moroccan name.
12. A kangaroo is an Australian animal.

EXERCISE 3 Complete each sentence with the proper adjective for the proper noun in parentheses. Use a dictionary if you need help.

1. I have a __Russian__ e-mail pal. (Russia)
2. The __Indian__ subcontinent is huge. (India)
3. How rare is a __Siberian__ tiger? (Siberia)
4. He reads about __Icelandic__ history. (Iceland)
5. An __Irish__ sweater makes a nice gift. (Ireland)
6. I like __Italian__ food. (Italy)
7. She is fascinated by __Greek__ culture. (Greece)
8. Tigers are __Asian__ animals. (Asia)
9. We ate __Swedish__ meatballs. (Sweden)
10. Trevor visited a __Brazilian__ rain forest. (Brazil)

Vases from Greece

APPLY IT NOW

Write four sentences about special things from other countries.

Example:
Pierogi are a kind of Polish dumpling.
Tomie dePaola's book retells an Italian tale.

Tech Tip With an adult, find facts about countries online.

Adjectives • 129

5.11 Nouns Used as Adjectives

OBJECTIVE

- **To recognize nouns that can be used as adjectives**

 **Maintenance**

Assign **Practice Book** page 76, Section 5.11. After students finish,
1. Give immediate feedback.
2. Review concepts as needed.
3. Model the correct answer.

Pages 4–5 of the **Answer Key** contain tips for Daily Maintenance.

WARM-UP

Write on the board the following nouns: *towels, apple, game, food, store, juice, paper, cat, computer,* and *book*. Point out that these words are nouns. Have students put two words from the list together to make up a word pair.

📖 Read from a piece of writing that the class is currently reading. Emphasize nouns used as adjectives.

TEACH

Write on the board sentences using word pairs from the Warm-Up, such as the following:

The apple juice is on the top shelf.

That is my favorite computer game.

Ask volunteers to circle the adjective and underline the noun in each sentence. Point out that all the adjectives can also be used as nouns. Write these sentences under the ones on the board:

An apple is a good snack.

My dad has a laptop computer.

Have volunteers read aloud about nouns used as adjectives. Remind students that adjectives describe nouns. Point out that when two nouns are used together, the

first noun describes or tells more about the second noun. Challenge students to write sentences using the remaining word pairs they suggested in the Warm-Up plus additional word pairs.

PRACTICE

EXERCISES 1 & 2

Stress that nouns used as adjectives appear before the nouns that they describe. Have partners find the nouns in each sentence and then discuss which nouns function as adjectives. Invite students to share their answers with the class. Encourage students

to explain the information each noun-adjective pair provides about the noun it describes.

EXERCISE 3

Point out that the words in both groups are nouns. Explain that the nouns in Group A can also be used as adjectives. Be sure students understand that a phrase is a group of words.

EXERCISE 4

Ask students to trade sentences with a partner to check that each noun and adjective is identified correctly.

5.11 Nouns Used as Adjectives

Sometimes a noun can be used as an adjective. When two nouns are used together, the first noun often acts as an adjective. It tells more about the second noun.

> **All the** *strawberry* **jam is gone.**
> **Put it on our** *grocery* **list.**

In these sentences the nouns *strawberry* and *grocery* act as adjectives. *Strawberry* tells more about *jam*. *Grocery* tells more about *list*.

What are the two nouns in this sentence? Which noun acts as an adjective?

> **I often go to the hobby shop.**

You are right if you said *hobby* and *shop* are nouns. *Hobby* acts as an adjective. It tells more about *shop*.

Which sentence has a noun that acts as an adjective?

> A **It has hundreds of model planes.**
> B **I like to build miniature airplanes.**
> C **My dad bought me a new kit.**

You are right if you said sentence A. *Model* tells more about the noun *planes*.

EXERCISE 1 Tell if the underlined word is used as a noun or as an adjective.

1. We go on a <u>class</u> trip every year.
2. This year our <u>class</u> is going to a farm.
3. The farm has an <u>apple</u> orchard.
4. I picked an <u>apple</u> from a tree and ate it.
5. We went to a <u>pumpkin</u> patch.
6. We each got a <u>pumpkin</u> to take home.
7. A <u>bus</u> took us back to school.
8. We sang during the <u>bus</u> trip.

Exercise 1
1. adjective
2. noun
3. adjective
4. noun
5. adjective
6. noun
7. noun
8. adjective

APPLY

APPLY IT NOW

Have students work with partners to help each other choose objects and adjectives. Invite students to share their word pairs with the class. Ask if students agree that the first word in each pair is a noun that acts as an adjective. Students should demonstrate the ability to use nouns as adjectives.

ASSESS

Note which students had difficulty recognizing nouns used as adjectives. Assign **Practice Book** page 87 for further practice.

WRITING CONNECTION

Use pages 382–383 of the Writing portion of the book.

Reteach

Write on individual note cards the following words:

teacher	game	paper
television	bag	star
football	beach	soccer
window	math	field
shopping	ball	

Place the cards faceup on a table. Have students choose two cards to make an adjective-noun pair. Then ask students to write on the board a sentence using the word pairs.

Cooperative Learning

Have small groups brainstorm a list of adjective-noun pairs that describe items found around their homes (*floor lamp, kitchen sink, desk chair, salad fork, butter knife*). Challenge students to come up with as many pairs as possible. Then ask each student to write a sentence for one word pair and illustrate it. Have groups combine their pages to make a book. Encourage students to make a book cover with a title and an illustration. Display the books in the classroom.

Curriculum Connection

Invite students to help you write directions for planting some simple seeds, such as radish seeds. If possible, have planting supplies on hand for small groups to follow along and suggest ideas. Encourage students to use nouns as adjectives in their directions.

- **Get some *radish* seeds.**
- **Fill a *paper* cup with soil.**
- **Put the seeds in the soil.**
- **Water the seeds.**
- **Put the cup on a *window* ledge.**

Exercise 2
Nouns are underlined once. The nouns used as adjectives are underlined twice.

EXERCISE 2 Find all the nouns in each sentence. Tell which noun acts as an adjective.

1. Our school has many student activities.
2. There is a computer lab.
3. My math teacher runs it.
4. I take music lessons after school.
5. We have an art fair in the spring.
6. We also have a science fair.
7. In the fall we go on a class trip.
8. Once we went to the city aquarium.
9. Our history teacher gives us a lot of homework.
10. He wants to try out for the baseball team.

Exercise 3
movie star
movie theater
apple pie
apple tree
pencil holder
pencil sharpener

EXERCISE 3 Write six phrases by using the nouns in Group A as adjectives before the nouns in Group B.

EXAMPLE   **movie star**

Group A	Group B	
movie	holder	star
apple	pie	theater
pencil	sharpener	tree

Exercise 4
Answers will vary.

EXERCISE 4 Write two sentences with each word. Use it once as a noun and once as an adjective. Tell how you used the word in each sentence.

1. spring
2. library
3. garden
4. orange
5. mud

APPLY IT NOW

Look around your classroom. What do you see? Make a list of noun pairs in which the first noun acts as an adjective.
Example: trash can
   chalkboard eraser
   math book

Adjectives • 131

Adjective Review

ASSESS

Use the Adjective Review as homework, as a practice test, or as an informal assessment. Following are some options for use.

Homework

You may wish to assign one group the odd items and another group the even items. When you next meet, review the correct answers as a group. Be sure to model how to arrive at the correct answer.

Practice Test

Use the Adjective Review as a diagnostic tool. Assign the entire review or only specific sections. After students have finished, identify which concepts require more attention. Reteach concepts as necessary.

Adjective Review

5.1 Find the adjective that describes a noun in each sentence.

1. Poodles are <u>fluffy</u> dogs.
2. The <u>white</u> dog was the color of a cloud.
3. She wore a <u>sparkly</u> collar.
4. The <u>black</u> poodle is barking.
5. My dog sleeps near the <u>sunny</u> window.

5.2 In each sentence, find the descriptive adjective. Tell the noun it describes.

6. A <u>rusty</u> <u>plow</u> sat in the field.
7. The <u>old</u> <u>rooster</u> crowed.
8. The farmer planted an <u>early</u> <u>crop</u>.
9. <u>Sweet</u> <u>corn</u> grows in rows.
10. Cows grazed by the <u>red</u> <u>barn</u>.

5.3 In each sentence, find the adjective used as a subject complement. Tell the noun it describes.

11. <u>Geodes</u> are <u>interesting</u>.
12. These <u>rocks</u> are <u>hollow</u>, with crystals inside.
13. <u>Geodes</u> are <u>dull</u> on the outside.
14. The <u>inside</u> of a <u>geode</u> is glittery.
15. <u>Tanya</u> is <u>careful</u> with her geode collection.

5.4 In each sentence, find the adjectives used as compound subject complements.

16. Many <u>ladybugs</u> are <u>red</u> or <u>orange</u>.
17. Their <u>backs</u> are <u>spotted</u> or <u>unspotted</u>.
18. The <u>spots</u> are usually <u>black</u> and <u>round</u>.
19. A <u>ladybug</u> is <u>useful</u> and <u>valuable</u> in gardens.
20. A <u>gardener</u> is <u>lucky</u> and <u>thankful</u> for ladybugs.

5.5 Find the adjective that compares in each sentence.

21. Wear the <u>warmest</u> coat you have.
22. The temperatures will be <u>colder</u> today than yesterday.
23. That is the <u>longest</u> scarf I have ever seen.
24. It is the <u>windiest</u> day of the year.
25. Her hat is <u>cuter</u> than mine.

5.6 Use *good, better,* or *best* to complete each sentence.

26. Chris and I had a <u>good</u> time at the park.
27. He thinks the slides are <u>better</u> than the swings.
28. The monkey bars are <u>best</u> of all.

5.2
Adjectives are underlined once. The nouns the adjectives describe are underlined twice.

5.3
Subject complements are underlined once. The nouns the subject complements describe are underlined twice.

Informal Assessment

Use the review as preparation for the formal assessment. Count the review as a portion of the grade. Have students work to find the correct answers and use their corrected review as a study guide for the formal assessment.

WRITING CONNECTION

Use pages 384–385 of the Writing portion of the book.

Putting It All Together

Distribute magazines or newspapers. Have students read an article. Then write the following directions on the board:

- **Use a highlighter to mark all the adjectives.**
- **Draw a box around all the proper adjectives.**
- **Write *SC* above all the adjectives used as subject complements.**
- **Write a *C* above all the adjectives that compare.**
- **Write a number sign *(#)* above the adjectives that tell how many.**
- **Write a *D* above all the demonstrative adjectives.**

Have partners exchange papers and explain their labels.

Meeting Individual Needs

Challenge Give students a few days to be Adjective Sleuths. Have students compile lists of adjectives they find at home, at school, on television, on signs, or any other places. Remind students to look for a variety of adjectives and adjectives used in different ways. At the end of the allotted time, have students share their lists and discuss adjectives and their uses in everyday writing.

5.7
31. about how many
32. exactly how many
33. about how many
34. exactly how many
35. about how many

5.10
Proper adjectives are underlined once. The nouns the adjectives describe are underlined twice.

Use *bad*, *worse*, or *worst* to complete each sentence.

29. There was a ___bad___ storm last night.

30. The storm last April was the ___worst___ our state has ever had.

5.7 Find the adjectives that tell how many in each sentence. Tell if the adjective tells exactly how many or about how many.

31. <u>Many</u> people were waiting for the bus.

32. <u>Two</u> buses arrived.

33. <u>Most</u> seats were taken.

34. The bus drove <u>twenty</u> blocks to the train station.

35. <u>Some</u> passengers got off the bus there.

5.8 Find all the articles in each sentence.

36. <u>The</u> rainy days kept <u>the</u> children inside.

37. Let's find <u>a</u> project we can work on.

38. We used <u>the</u> magazines and <u>a</u> glue stick to make <u>a</u> collage.

39. Gilda learned how to make collages in <u>an</u> art class.

40. Mom hung <u>the</u> collages on <u>the</u> refrigerator.

5.9 Find the demonstrative adjective in each sentence.

41. <u>This</u> truck is full of boxes.

42. <u>Those</u> movers must be tired from the heavy lifting.

43. Take <u>these</u> boxes upstairs.

44. The dishes are in <u>that</u> box.

45. <u>Those</u> plates are broken.

5.10 Find the proper adjective in each sentence. Name the noun the adjective describes.

46. My family took a <u>European</u> <u>vacation</u>.

47. We ate <u>German</u> <u>sausages</u>.

48. We drove through the <u>French</u> <u>countryside</u>.

49. We visited many <u>Italian</u> <u>towns</u>.

50. We saw old <u>Roman</u> <u>ruins</u>.

5.11 Find the noun that acts as an adjective in each sentence.

51. Dad made <u>beef</u> stew.

52. What kind of <u>salad</u> dressing do you like?

53. Use the <u>can</u> opener to open the soup.

54. I put <u>apple</u> butter on bread.

55. Please hand me the <u>pepper</u> mill.

Tech Tip Go to www.voyagesinenglish.com for more activities.

Adjectives • 133

Tech Tip Encourage students to further review adjectives, using the additional practice and games at www.voyagesinenglish.com.

Adjective Challenge

ASSESS

Encourage students to read the paragraph twice before answering the questions. If students have difficulty with any question, suggest that they refer to the section that teaches that skill. This activity can be done individually, in small groups, or as a whole class.

Then have students complete the second exercise. Be sure to check that their paragraphs contain the different kinds of adjectives.

After you have reviewed adjectives, administer the Section 5 Assessment on pages 15–18 in the **Assessment Book,** or create a customized test with the optional **Test Generator CD.**

WRITING CONNECTION
Use pages 386–387 of the Writing portion of the book Students can complete a formal book report using the Writer's Workshop on pages 388–399.

EXERCISE 1 (Answers)

1. Some, some
2. cold, hot
3. coldest
4. one place
5. many, green, colorful; green, colorful
6. the
7. colder
8. icy
9. Antarctic

EXERCISE 2

Answers will vary.

Adjective Challenge

EXERCISE 1 Read the paragraph and answer the questions.

1. Some places on Earth are cold, and some places are hot. 2. The North Pole is one of the coldest spots on Earth. 3. This frozen place is home to polar bears, not people. 4. As you move south toward the equator, the climate becomes warmer. 5. You begin to see many trees, green grass, and colorful flowers. 6. As you travel south from the equator, temperatures get cooler again. 7. Finally, you get to the South Pole in Antarctica. 8. The South Pole is even colder than the North Pole. 9. Antarctic temperatures are icy. 10. They go down to 129 degrees below zero!

1. In sentence 1 find the adjectives that tell about how many.
2. In sentence 1 what are the two descriptive adjectives?
3. In sentence 2 find an adjective that compares.
4. In sentence 3 does the adjective *this* refer to one place or more than one place?
5. In sentence 5 find three adjectives. Which two are descriptive adjectives?
6. In sentence 7 find an article.
7. In sentence 8 find the adjective that compares.
8. In sentence 9 find the subject complement.
9. Find the proper adjective in the paragraph.

EXERCISE 2 Write a five-sentence paragraph about one of the hottest places on Earth, such as the equator or a desert. Use at least four different kinds of adjectives.

SECTION FOCUS

- **Adverbs**
- **Adverbs that tell when or how often**
- **Adverbs that tell where**
- **Adverbs that tell how**
- **Negative words**
- *Good* and *Well*
- *To, Too,* and *Two*
- *Their* and *There*
- **Coordinating conjunctions**

SUPPORT MATERIALS

Practice Book
Daily Maintenance, pages 88–90
Grammar, pages 91–100

Assessment Book
Section 6 Assessment,
     pages 19–20

Test Generator CD

Writing Chapter 6,
     Persuasive Writing

Customizable Lesson Plans
www.voyagesinenglish.com

CONNECT WITH LITERATURE

📖 Consider using the following titles throughout the section to illustrate the grammar concept:

If You Were a Conjunction
     by Nancy Loewen
Never Smile at a Monkey
     by Steve Jenkins
Up, Up and Away by Ruth Heller

Adverbs and Conjunctions

GRAMMAR FOR GROWN-UPS

Understanding Adverbs and Conjunctions

Adverbs modify verbs, adjectives, or other adverbs. Adverbs answer the questions *when, how often, where,* and *how.*

Adverbs of time tell when or how often (*again, weekly, late, tomorrow, soon, then, today, always*).

> *Lucy **always** arrives **late.***

Adverbs of place tell where (*away, down, far, here, inside, there, up*).

> *We play **inside** on rainy days.*

Adverbs of manner tell how or in what manner (*dangerously, purposely, quickly*).

> *Gloria sang **softly** to herself.*

Adverbs of negation express a negative condition or refusal (*no, not, never*).

> *We **never** write letters.*

Writers may sometimes confuse **homophones**, words that sound alike but have different meanings.

The word *too,* an **adverb of degree,** is often confused with the word *two,* an adjective, a noun, or a pronoun, or *to,* a preposition or an adverb.

The **adverb of place** *there* is often confused with *their,* an adjective, and *they're,* a contraction formed from *they* and *are.* Writers sometimes misuse *well,* an adverb, and the adjective *good.*

Coordinating conjunctions (*and, but, or*) join two similar words or groups of words.

> *Karen had to choose to play soccer **or** tennis.*

> *Karen **and** Ricky are doubles partners.*

> 66 *Always and never are two words you should always remember never to use.* 99
>
> —Wendell Johnson

COMMON ERRORS

Using Adverbs Correctly

Some developing writers use an adjective when they should use an adverb, even when speaking.

ERROR: The boy ran quick across the field.
CORRECT: The boy ran quickly across the field.

ERROR: Tracy sat silent.
CORRECT: Tracy sat silently.

To help students avoid this common error, ask them to think about what they are describing and to ask themselves, *Am I describing a person, a place, or a thing, or am I describing an action?* Guide students to see that if they are describing an action, they need an adverb not an adjective. Help students change each incorrect word to its correct form. Work one-on-one with students as you check their writing until they begin to understand when to use adverbs and when to use adjectives.

SENTENCE DIAGRAMMING

You may wish to teach adverbs and conjunctions in the context of diagramming. Review these examples. Then refer to the Diagramming section or look for Diagram It! features in the Adverbs section.

Mateo always walks slowly.

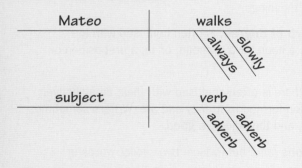

Sylvia and Piper will not attend today.

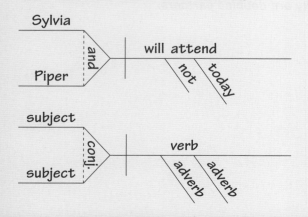

ASK AN EXPERT

Real Situations, Real Solutions

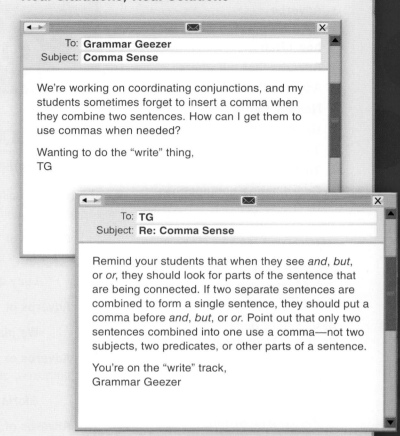

To: **Grammar Geezer**
Subject: **Comma Sense**

We're working on coordinating conjunctions, and my students sometimes forget to insert a comma when they combine two sentences. How can I get them to use commas when needed?

Wanting to do the "write" thing,
TG

To: **TG**
Subject: **Re: Comma Sense**

Remind your students that when they see *and*, *but*, or *or*, they should look for parts of the sentence that are being connected. If two separate sentences are combined to form a single sentence, they should put a comma before *and*, *but*, or *or*. Point out that only two sentences combined into one use a comma—not two subjects, two predicates, or other parts of a sentence.

You're on the "write" track,
Grammar Geezer

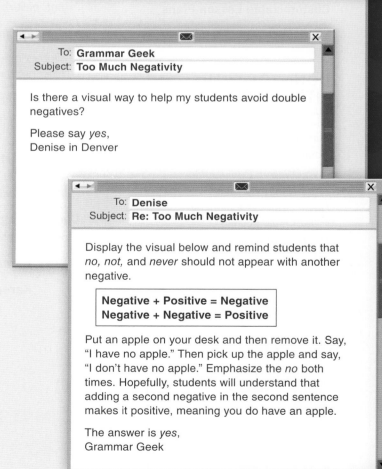

To: **Grammar Geek**
Subject: **Too Much Negativity**

Is there a visual way to help my students avoid double negatives?

Please say *yes*,
Denise in Denver

To: **Denise**
Subject: **Re: Too Much Negativity**

Display the visual below and remind students that *no, not,* and *never* should not appear with another negative.

> **Negative + Positive = Negative**
> **Negative + Negative = Positive**

Put an apple on your desk and then remove it. Say, "I have no apple." Then pick up the apple and say, "I don't have no apple." Emphasize the *no* both times. Hopefully, students will understand that adding a second negative in the second sentence makes it positive, meaning you do have an apple.

The answer is *yes*,
Grammar Geek

Adverbs and Conjunctions

6.1 Adverbs

6.2 Adverbs That Tell When or How Often

6.3 Adverbs That Tell Where

6.4 Adverbs That Tell How

6.5 Negative Words

6.6 *Good* and *Well*

6.7 *To, Too,* and *Two*

6.8 *Their* and *There*

6.9 Coordinating Conjunctions

Adverb and Conjunction Review

Adverb and Conjunction Challenge

6.1 Adverbs

OBJECTIVES

- **To identify adverbs as words that describe verbs**
- **To identify adverbs that tell when, where, and how**

 **DAILY** **Maintenance**

Assign **Practice Book** page 88, Section 6.1. After students finish,

1. Give immediate feedback.
2. Review concepts as needed.
3. Model the correct answer.

Pages 4–5 of the **Answer Key** contain tips for Daily Maintenance.

WARM-UP

Invite volunteers to stand by their desks and to follow your directions.

Walk slowly.   Walk quickly.

Walk loudly.   Walk quietly.

Ask students to explain which word told them how to walk. Write the words *slowly, quickly, loudly,* and *quietly* on the board.

📖 Read from a piece of writing that the class is currently reading. Emphasize the adverbs.

TEACH

Write on the board the following sentences:

I had soccer practice yesterday.

I brought my backpack downstairs.

Anil wrote his answer easily.

Have volunteers read aloud each sentence. Ask students to identify the words that tell when, where, or how the action in each sentence is taking place. Underline *yesterday, downstairs,* and *easily.* Explain that these words are adverbs, or words that tell more about verbs.

Have volunteers read aloud about adverbs. Suggest that students ask themselves when, where, and how actions are taking place in sentences to help find the adverbs. Challenge students to make up one sentence for each different type of adverb.

Ask students to point out the adverbs on the board from the Warm-Up.

PRACTICE

EXERCISE 1

Have partners complete the exercise. Suggest that they ask the questions *where, when,* and *how* to find the adverbs. Ask volunteers to share their answers with the class.

EXERCISE 2

Make sure students realize that only one word choice is correct for each sentence. Suggest that students first read all the sentences to get the general topic. Have volunteers write their sentences on the board. Discuss what each adverb tells about the verb.

EXERCISE 3

Have partners choose appropriate adverbs. Tell students to refer to the chart on page 136 if they need help.

6.1 Adverbs

An **adverb** tells more about a verb. Some adverbs tell when, where, or how something happens. Many adverbs end in *ly*.

When:	I walked in the park *today*.
Where:	The leaves were colorful *there*.
How:	I *happily* gathered some red leaves.

In the first sentence, *today* tells when about the verb *walked*. In the second sentence, *there* tells where about the verb *were*. In the third sentence, *happily* tells how about the verb *gathered*.

Each of these sentences has an adverb. Can you find it?

A We listen for the weather report daily.

B We go outside in warm clothes.

C We all listen carefully.

You're right if you said *daily, outside,* and *carefully*. *Daily* tells when. *Outside* tells where, and *carefully* tells how.

Study this list of common adverbs.

WHEN	WHERE	HOW
yesterday	far	quickly
always	nearby	noisily
soon	upstairs	easily
first	up	nervously
last	beneath	slowly
never	there	anxiously
sometimes	inside	colorfully

EXERCISE 1 Find the adverb in each sentence.

1. In the fall the weather <u>suddenly</u> gets cool.
2. Colorful fall leaves appear <u>everywhere</u>.
3. They glow <u>brilliantly</u> in the warm sun.
4. We are studying plants <u>now</u> in class.

APPLY

APPLY IT NOW

Help students brainstorm projects or field trips. Suggest that students ask themselves how, when, and where they did the activity or project. Students should demonstrate the ability to use adverbs in sentences.

ASSESS

Note which students had difficulty identifying and using adverbs that tell when, where, or how. Assign **Practice Book** page 91 for further practice.

WRITING CONNECTION

Use pages 400–401 of the Writing portion of the book. Be sure to point out adverbs in the literature excerpt and the student model.

TEACHING OPTIONS

Reteach

Write on the board a three-column chart with the headings *When, Where,* and *How*. Ask students to name as many adverbs as possible and to decide in which column to write each one. Have volunteers use the adverbs from the chart in sentences.

Meeting Individual Needs

Kinesthetic Write on a note card one verb and three adverbs (*write, slowly, quickly, carefully*). Give the card to a student and challenge him or her to act out the verb along with each of the different adverbs. Have the rest of the class guess what the student is doing and write the actions on the board. Repeat the activity with a different verb and a different group of adverbs.

Cooperative Learning

Have partners look through books, newspapers, or magazines to find adverbs. Ask students to copy five sentences with adverbs. Have students underline each adverb and tell whether the adverbs tell how, when, or where. Challenge partners to replace the adverbs with others of their choosing and discuss how the sentences' meanings change.

Diagram It!

To practice these concepts in the context of diagramming, turn to Section 8.4.

Chlorophyll

5. In the fall, trees <u>slowly</u> stop making chlorophyll.
6. <u>Then</u> the green color disappears from their leaves.
7. The colors yellow and orange were <u>always</u> in the leaves.
8. Without the green, we see the other colors <u>clearly</u>.

EXERCISE 2 Complete each sentence with an adverb from the word box.

carefully	inside	later	outside	yesterday

1. We did an experiment on leaf color <u>yesterday</u> in class.
2. We went <u>outside</u> and got some green leaves and crushed them.
3. We put the leaves and some rubbing alcohol <u>inside</u> a jar.
4. We <u>carefully</u> put a piece of special filter paper into the jar.
5. <u>Later</u> we looked at the strip and saw the colors green, yellow, and orange.

Exercise 3
Answers will vary.
Possible answers:
1. yesterday
2. first
3. carefully
4. outside
5. slowly
6. There
7. quickly
8. easily

EXERCISE 3 Complete each sentence with an adverb. Have the adverb tell what is in parentheses.

1. Our class was assigned a science project _____. (when)
2. Mr. Gonzalez _____ showed us pictures of trees common in our area. (when)
3. We studied them _____. (how)
4. Today our class went _____. (where)
5. We _____ walked to the park. (how)
6. _____ we looked for trees. (where)
7. We _____ found four common types of trees. (how)
8. We _____ recognized the trees by their leaves. (how)

APPLY IT NOW

Write five sentences about a recent class project or field trip. Use at least one adverb in each sentence. Then underline all the adverbs.

Adverbs • 137

OBJECTIVE
- **To identify and use adverbs that tell when or how often**

 **Maintenance**

Assign **Practice Book** page 88, Section 6.2. After students finish,
1. Give immediate feedback.
2. Review concepts as needed.
3. Model the correct answer.

Pages 4–5 of the **Answer Key** contain tips for Daily Maintenance.

WARM-UP

Discuss how often or when students participate in different activities. Ask questions that can be answered using adverbs that tell when or how often. *(When do you go to dance class? How often do you read? When did you visit your grandparents?)* Write on the board students' responses.

📖 Read from a piece of writing that the class is currently reading. Emphasize the adverbs that tell when or how often.

TEACH

Write on the board sentences suggested in the Warm-Up or use the following sentences:

I go to dance class weekly.

I read daily.

We visited my grandparents yesterday.

Have a volunteer read aloud about adverbs that tell when or how often. Have students choose adverbs from the list to use in sentences. Ask volunteers if the adverbs tell when or how often.

PRACTICE

EXERCISE 1
Have students review the list of adverbs on page 138. Challenge students to read each sentence carefully and to refer to the lists as necessary to check their ideas. Read each sentence aloud and ask students to raise their hands when you say an adverb.

EXERCISE 2
Explain that one adverb from the word box works better than the other three in each sentence. Ask students which words in each sentence tell them which adverb fits best. Have students rewrite each sentence, inserting the adverb that makes the most sense. Have volunteers write their sentences on the board. Underline the adverbs.

EXERCISES 3 & 4
Have partners complete the exercises. Suggest that students refer to the list of adverbs on page 138 for help. Point out that there is more than one correct answer for each sentence. Have volunteers read aloud their sentences.

6.2 Adverbs That Tell When or How Often

An adverb tells more about a verb. Some adverbs tell when or how often something happens.

When: Our teacher read a great story *yesterday*.
How often: He *always* reads after lunch.

Here are some adverbs that tell when or how often.

always	ever	never	then
again	first	now	today
after	forever	often	tomorrow
before	frequently	sometimes	weekly
early	later	soon	yesterday

Which of these sentences have adverbs that tell when?

A Mr. Marsh read us a story about Harriet Tubman.
B Before I did not know much about her.
C Now I know some facts about her life.

You are right if you said sentence B and sentence C. *Before* and *now* are adverbs that tell when.

EXERCISE 1 Find the adverb or adverbs that tells when or how often in each sentence.

1. I have <u>often</u> heard stories about Harriet Tubman.
2. <u>First</u>, she was a slave.
3. <u>Then</u> she escaped to the North.
4. She was <u>soon</u> traveling to the South and leading slaves to freedom in the North.
5. She went to the South <u>again</u> and <u>again</u>.
6. She <u>never</u> lost any of the hundreds of slaves she guided.
7. <u>Later</u> she campaigned for women's rights.
8. We <u>now</u> consider her a great hero.

Harriet Tubman

APPLY

APPLY IT NOW

Help students brainstorm topics to write about that could include the adverbs they choose, such as plans for the weekend, a community event, or a class field trip. Students should demonstrate the ability to identify and use adverbs that tell when or how often.

Grammar in Action. Help students first identify the verb *(have worked)*. Then have students identify the adverb *(ever)* and decide if it tells when or how often *(how often)*.

ASSESS

Note which students had difficulty identifying and using adverbs that tell when or how often. Assign **Practice Book** page 92 for further practice.

WRITING CONNECTION

Use pages 402–403 of the Writing portion of the book.

TEACHING OPTIONS

Reteach

Write on sentence strips sentences with blanks where adverbs should be. Ask students to choose a strip and find an adverb from the list on page 138 that can be used to complete the sentence. Have students read aloud the completed sentences. Have students tell if the adverb tells when or how often. Ask students to suggest other adverbs from the list that may also be appropriate.

Meeting Individual Needs

Auditory Have small groups make up imaginary weather forecasts using adverbs that tell when or how often. Challenge students to use as many adverbs as possible in their forecasts. Model a forecast, such as the following:

Today will be sunny. We will have sunny weather tomorrow morning. The weather will be cooler later in the day. Then we might get some frost.

Invite a volunteer from each group to read aloud their forecast. Have the rest of the class identify the adverbs that tell when or how often.

Meeting Individual Needs

Extra Support Have students hunt for adverbs in magazines and newspapers. Give students 10 minutes to find as many adverbs as possible that tell when or how often. Instruct students to list the adverbs. Have students share their lists with a partner. Encourage partners to choose three adverbs from their list and write sentences using the adverbs.

EXERCISE 2 Complete each sentence with an adverb from the word box that tells when.

| later | now | today | yesterday | tomorrow |

1. <u>Yesterday</u> I looked for a book on Harriet Tubman at the library.
2. I read the book <u>today</u>.
3. I <u>now</u> know a lot about Harriet Tubman.
4. <u>Later</u> I will write a report on what I learned.
5. I will present my report to class <u>tomorrow</u>.

Exercise 3
Answers will vary.

EXERCISE 3 Complete each sentence with an adverb that tells when or how often.

1. Sojourner Truth was <u>first</u> a slave, and her original name was Isabella.
2. <u>After</u> escaping to freedom, Isabella moved to New York City.
3. She <u>soon</u> changed her name to Sojourner Truth.
4. Sojourner <u>often</u> spoke at antislavery meetings.
5. People <u>frequently</u> came to hear her powerful words.
6. Sojourner <u>then</u> decided to be a traveling preacher.
7. We <u>forever</u> remember her as a strong voice against slavery and for women's rights.

Exercise 4
Answers will vary.
Possible answers:
1. often
2. sometimes
3. never
4. frequently

EXERCISE 4 Complete each sentence with an adverb that tells how often.

1. I _____ read biographies.
2. I _____ go to the library.
3. I _____ watch history programs on TV.
4. I _____ read fiction books.

APPLY IT NOW

Look at the list of adverbs on page 138 that tell when or how often. Choose five adverbs and write a sentence using each one. Underline the adverbs you use.

Grammar in Action. Find the adverb in the first sentence on page 401. Does it tell when or how often?

Adverbs • 139

6.3 Adverbs That Tell Where

OBJECTIVE

- **To identify and use adverbs that tell where**

 **Maintenance**

Assign **Practice Book** page 88, Section 6.3. After students finish,
1. Give immediate feedback.
2. Review concepts as needed.
3. Model the correct answer.

Pages 4–5 of the **Answer Key** contain tips for Daily Maintenance.

WARM-UP

Have students follow a set of directions, such as the following:

Stand up.	Turn around.
Sit down.	Come here.
Move backward.	Step forward.

Write the sentences on the board. Then repeat the directions and ask students to identify the verb in each command and cross it out.

📖 Read from a piece of writing that the class is currently reading. Emphasize the adverbs that tell where.

TEACH

Have students look at the list of words on the board. Ask what the words have in common. *(They answer the question* where.*)* Point out that these words are adverbs that tell where something takes place.

Have a volunteer read aloud the first paragraph about adverbs that tell where and the list of adverbs. Write on the board the following paragraph:

My puppy was running away. I yelled, "Come here!" He kept moving forward. I yelled louder, "Come here!" He turned around. He stopped. "Sit down!" I said.

Ask students to identify the adverbs that tell where *(away, here, forward, here, around, down)*. Have a volunteer read aloud the rest of the page. Ask students to use the adverbs in sentences.

PRACTICE

EXERCISE 1

Suggest that students read each sentence and then find the action and where it happened. Tell students that the word that tells where is the adverb.

EXERCISE 2

Explain that the missing words are the adverbs listed in the word box. Tell students to use each word only once. Invite students to compare answers.

EXERCISE 3

Suggest that students refer to the list on page 140. Point out that more than one answer is correct for each sentence. Ask volunteers to read aloud their answers.

6.3 Adverbs That Tell Where

Some adverbs tell where something takes place. These adverbs answer the question *where.*

Where: The bear scampered *inside.*
        We stayed *there* and watched it go *in* and *out.*

Here are some adverbs that tell where.

above	downstairs	inside
alongside	everywhere	nearby
away	far	nowhere
back	farther	out
backward	forward	outside
below	here	there
down	in	up

These sentences include adverbs. Which adverbs tell where?

The leaves fell swiftly down after the storm.
The hawk came back to the nest yesterday.

Did you choose *down* and *back*? You are right. *Down* and *back* are adverbs that tell where. *Swiftly* is an adverb that tells how, and *yesterday* is an adverb that tells when.

EXERCISE 1 Find the adverb that tells where in each sentence.

1. We rode <u>everywhere</u> in the zoo on a tram.
2. The guide told us to look <u>up</u>.
3. We moved <u>forward</u> to get a closer look at the great apes.
4. A mother panda with a baby slept <u>nearby</u>.
5. Then we heard a noise <u>above</u>.
6. A flock of noisy geese flew <u>away</u>.
7. Did they live <u>here</u> at the zoo?
8. No, the geese just come <u>here</u> to get food.

APPLY

APPLY IT NOW

Encourage students to think about objects or areas at each place listed *(a reference desk at a library, a food court at a mall)*. Explain that including these places in their sentences will help students use adverbs that tell where. *(You will find the reference desk above the fiction section. We can eat upstairs at the food court.)* Students should demonstrate the ability to use adverbs that tell where.

> **Grammar in Action** Guide students to identify the subject *(They)* and verb *(come)*. Then tell them to refer to the list on page 140 to help identify the adverb that tells where *(here)*.

ASSESS

Note which students had difficulty identifying and using adverbs that tell where. Assign **Practice Book** page 93 for further practice.

> **WRITING CONNECTION**
> Use pages 404–405 of the Writing portion of the book.

9. If you look <u>down</u>, you can see two bear cubs.
10. The bear stayed <u>inside</u>.
11. I think the elephants are <u>there</u>.
12. The tigers were walking <u>outside</u>.
13. We jumped <u>back</u> when the lion roared.
14. The park attendant was pointing <u>backward</u>.

EXERCISE 2 Complete each sentence with an adverb from the word box that tells where.

above	back	below	far	outside

1. We stayed __outside__ all day.
2. We hiked __far__.
3. We could see the mountaintop __above__.
4. __Below__ we could view the green valley and the rivers.
5. We didn't want to come __back__ home.

Exercise 3
Answers will vary.

EXERCISE 3 Complete each sentence with an adverb that tells where.

1. My family and I often go to the zoo __nearby__.
2. We always have a good time __there__.
3. Sometimes we watch the monkeys __outside__.
4. We took a chairlift __above__ the African area.
5. Our chairlift went __up__.
6. __Below__ we saw lions, zebras, and wildebeest.
7. Dad rented a canoe, and we all got __in__.
8. Soon the canoe went __down__ the river.
9. We saw dingoes __alongside__ the river bank.
10. The river took us __everywhere__ in the zoo.

> **Grammar in Action** Find the adverb that tells where in the second sentence of the second paragraph on page 401.

APPLY IT NOW
Choose one of these places: amusement park, mall, or library. Then write four sentences about it, using adverbs from the list on page 140.

Adverbs • 141

TEACHING OPTIONS

Reteach

Choose an object in the classroom for students to locate. *(I'm thinking of an object. It sits nearby.)* Continue giving directions until students identify the object. Use sentences with adverbs that tell where, such as the following:

Look at the shelves.

Look a little farther.

Check the closet. The object is inside.

Look closer.

Ask students to identify the adverbs as you give clues. After students have located the object, ask them to name the adverbs that helped find the object. Repeat the activity. Encourage volunteers to choose an object and give clues.

Meeting Individual Needs

Challenge Point out that many adverbs that tell where are opposites. Have partners make a list of adverbs that are opposites. Direct students to make up sentences using the adverb pairs, such as the following: *up/down, in/out, backward/forward, inside/outside, here/there, above/below,* and *upstairs/downstairs.*

English-Language Learners

Have partners work together to find objects that are in places that can be described using adverbs that tell where *(inside, outside, up, down, here, there, nearby)*. Encourage students to use the words in sentences.

6.4 Adverbs That Tell How

OBJECTIVE
- **To identify and use adverbs that tell how**

 **Maintenance**

Assign **Practice Book** page 89, Section 6.4. After students finish,
1. Give immediate feedback.
2. Review concepts as needed.
3. Model the correct answer.

Pages 4–5 of the **Answer Key** contain tips for Daily Maintenance.

WARM-UP

Write on the board the following sentence:

Some adverbs tell how.

Have students read it aloud with you. Tell students to reread the sentence as described in these directions:

Read the sentence slowly.

Read the sentence quickly.

Read the sentence loudly.

Read the sentence softly.

📖 Read from a piece of writing that the class is currently reading. Emphasize the adverbs that tell how.

TEACH

Reread the directions you gave students in the Warm-Up. Ask them to identify the adverbs in the directions. Write the adverbs on the board (*slowly, quickly, loudly, softly*). Ask what the adverbs tell about the verb. Emphasize that these adverbs tell how to read the sentence. Ask what the words have in common. (*They end in* ly.)

Have volunteers read aloud about adverbs that tell *how*. Ask which adverb in the list is different from all the others (*hard*) and why. (*It does not end in* ly). Point out that *fast* in the first example

sentence is another adverb that does not end in *ly*.

Ask students to choose an adverb from the list to pair with a verb and pantomime the action. Have the class guess the verb and adverb each student pantomimes.

PRACTICE

EXERCISE 1
Review that many adverbs that tell how end in *ly*. Tell students that many adverbs in the sentences are not in the list. Have students complete the exercise independently. Ask volunteers to read aloud each sentence and identify the adverb that tells how.

EXERCISE 2
Read aloud the example and then complete item 1 with the class. Explain that because *carefully* was used for item 1, students cannot use that adverb for the remaining sentences. Have partners complete the rest of the exercise.

EXERCISE 3
Have partners complete the exercise. Tell students to use the adverbs in the word box only once. Then ask students to read aloud their answers and tell what words in each sentence helped to choose an appropriate adverb.

6.4 Adverbs That Tell How

Some adverbs tell how an action takes place. These adverbs answer the question *how*.

How: My pizza maker rolls out the dough *fast*.
My mother makes pancakes *expertly*.

Here are some other adverbs that tell how.

carefully	gently	kindly	sadly
cleverly	gingerly	lightly	safely
clumsily	gracefully	loudly	slyly
coolly	happily	quickly	softly
frivolously	hard	quietly	sweetly

These sentences include adverbs. Which adverbs tell how?

The waiter always carries the dishes carefully.
The dishwasher here operates noisily.

Did you choose *carefully* and *noisily*? You are right. *Always* is an adverb that tells when, and *here* is an adverb that tells where.

EXERCISE 1 Find the adverb that tells how in each sentence.
1. The day started <u>perfectly</u>.
2. Both mom and dad were sleeping <u>peacefully</u>.
3. I crept <u>noiselessly</u> into the kitchen.
4. The sun was rising <u>slowly</u>.
5. I <u>carefully</u> stirred the batter for the pancakes.
6. My sister and I worked <u>quietly</u>.
7. We <u>eagerly</u> went upstairs to wake our parents.
8. Our parents ate their surprise breakfast <u>happily</u>.
9. We spoke <u>softly</u> so as not to wake up our younger brother.
10. We <u>quickly</u> ate all the pancakes.

APPLY

APPLY IT NOW

Help students brainstorm activities and hobbies. Encourage students to write sentences that tell how about a single activity. Remind students that most adverbs that tell how have an *ly* ending and often follow the verb. Ask students to underline the adverbs in each sentence. Students should demonstrate the ability to use adverbs that tell how.

TechTip Help students create a new document and find appropriate clip art or royalty-free pictures online. Suggest that students use the copy and paste functions as well as inserting clip art from the menu.

ASSESS

Note which students had difficulty identifying and using adverbs that tell how. Assign **Practice Book** page 94 for further practice.

WRITING CONNECTION

Use pages 406–407 of the Writing portion of the book.

Reteach

Brainstorm with students a list of actions the class can perform while seated at their desks or standing beside their desks (*clapping, singing, tapping, stomping, waving, cheering, marching, jumping*). Ask students to name adverbs that tell how they might perform these actions. Have volunteers take turns directing the class to perform three different actions. Then discuss the actions the class performed. Have volunteers write on the board the actions they followed. Ask students to identify the adverbs that tell how.

Meeting Individual Needs

Kinesthetic Write on separate note cards action verbs and adverbs that tell *how*. Make half the cards adverbs and the other half action verbs. Make enough cards so that each student can choose one card. Place the cards faceup on a table and have each student choose a card. Then have students with verb cards find a partner with an adverb card. Have each pair act out the phrase. Have the class guess what they are doing and identify the adverb that tells how.

Curriculum Connection

Display a poster or photograph of a professional sporting event or a theater production that shows a lot of action. Encourage students to describe the poster or photograph using adverbs that tell how. Write students' sentences on a sheet of paper next to the photo or poster. Challenge students to identify the adverbs that tell how in each sentence.

Exercise 2
1. A tightrope walker walks carefully.
2. A ballerina dances gracefully.
3. A jet plane flies fast.
4. A turtle walks slowly.
5. A band plays loudly.

EXERCISE 2 Find the adverb in Column B that best answers the question in Column A. Write your answer as a sentence.

EXAMPLE **How does a baby sleep?**
A baby sleeps peacefully.

Column A	Column B
1. How does a tightrope walker walk?	loudly
2. How does a ballerina dance?	fast
3. How does a jet plane fly?	gracefully
4. How do turtles walk?	carefully
5. How does a band play?	slowly

In 1876 Maria Spelterini crossed the gorge below Niagara Falls on a tightrope, blindfolded, and with weights attached to her feet.

EXERCISE 3 Complete each sentence with an adverb from the word box that tells how.

softly	safely	gently	fast	sadly
quickly	loudly	frivolously	sweetly	cleverly

1. I __gently__ placed the locket in the jewelry box.
2. Jamie called __loudly__ to wake up the campers.
3. Martine __frivolously__ spent her entire allowance on baseball cards.
4. The pilot __safely__ landed the damaged plane in a nearby field.
5. When the fire drill started, everyone __quickly__ left the classroom.
6. Joanie __sadly__ waved good-bye to her friends and got on the bus.
7. The yellow bird sang __sweetly__.
8. My brother and I cleaned the room __fast__.
9. The fox __cleverly__ outwitted the crow.
10. The rain fell __softly__ on the spring flowers.

APPLY IT NOW

Make a list of things you like to do. Think of one or more adverbs that tell how you do each thing. Write four sentences with those adverbs.
Example:
I play the piano.
I play loudly, fast, and happily.

Tech Tip Make a PowerPoint slide with art for each sentence.

Adverbs • 143

6.5 Negative Words

OBJECTIVES

- **To identify the negative words *not* and *never* as adverbs**
- **To use negative adverbs in sentences**

Maintenance

Assign **Practice Book** page 89, Section 6.5. After students finish,
1. Give immediate feedback.
2. Review concepts as needed.
3. Model the correct answer.

Pages 4–5 of the **Answer Key** contain tips for Daily Maintenance.

WARM-UP

Write on the board the following sentences:

I like broccoli.

I always eat green beans.

My favorite food is eggplant.

I always read the newspaper.

Have students change each sentence into a negative statement. *(I do not like broccoli. I never eat green beans. My favorite food is not eggplant. I never read the newspaper.)* Ask students to identify the words that show that each statement is negative *(not, never).*

📖 Read from a piece of writing that the class is currently reading. Emphasize the negative words.

TEACH

Review the class schedule for the day. Write on the board two sentences that tell about something the class is not going to do. Ask students to suggest similar sentences.

We will not go on a field trip.

Our class never has art on Tuesdays.

Ask students to tell what word *not* and *never* describe. Point out that *not* and *never* describe the verbs *go* and *has*. Explain that *not* and *never* are adverbs.

Have volunteers read aloud about negative words. Reinforce that using more than one negative word in a sentence is incorrect. Explain that two negative words cancel each other out and make a positive sentence.

PRACTICE

EXERCISE 1
Remind students that sometimes the negative word *not* is part of a contraction. Tell students to look for contractions formed with the word *not*.

EXERCISE 2
Ask students to explain when negative words are used incorrectly *(when there is more than one negative word in a sentence)*. Invite volunteers to write their corrected sentences on the board.

EXERCISE 3
Ask volunteers to explain how to make sentences have negative meanings. Emphasize that the negative word should tell more about the verbs in each sentence.

6.5 Negative Words

A negative idea is formed in several ways.

- Add *not* to the verb.
- Add *not* as part of a contraction: *didn't, can't, won't.*
- Add *never* before the verb.

Because these words tell more about verbs, they are adverbs. Study these negative sentences.

The cage *was not* clean.
She *didn't* feed the canary.
She *never* feeds the class pet.

Which of these sentences expresses a negative idea?

A I never let my cat outside.
B She is always in the house.

If you chose sentence A, you are right. Sentence A uses *never.*

Be careful to use only one negative word in a sentence. Is this sentence correct? Why or why not?

I don't never forget to walk my dog.

The sentence is incorrect because it has two negative words: *don't* and *never.* To correct it, remove one of the negative words: *I don't forget to walk my dog* or *I never forget to walk my dog.*

EXERCISE 1 Find the negative word in each sentence.
1. Wild animals <u>never</u> make good pets.
2. People <u>can't</u> provide a good home for a tiger.
3. A yard <u>isn't</u> big enough for animals that like to roam.
4. Even a gentle wild animal should <u>not</u> be kept as a pet.
5. Parents <u>shouldn't</u> let young children play with wild animals.

APPLY

APPLY IT NOW

Help students generate a list of animals that should never be kept as pets *(sharks, giraffes, Komodo dragons)*. Ask each student to choose one animal to write about. Allow students to transfer their sentences onto posters, complete with illustrations. Students should demonstrate the ability to use negative adverbs in sentences.

Grammar in Action Remind students that contractions with *not* are negative words. As a volunteer reads aloud the excerpt, have the class raise their hands when they hear the negative words *(doesn't, shouldn't)*.

ASSESS

Note which students had difficulty recognizing the negative words *not* and *never* as adverbs, as well as using negative adverbs in sentences. Assign **Practice Book** page 95 for further practice.

WRITING CONNECTION

Use pages 408–409 of the Writing portion of the book.

Reteach

Write several sentences on the board. Read them with the class. You might use sentences from a text the class is currently reading, inviting students to read along in their books. Ask students to help you rewrite the sentences to make them negative. Have students dictate what to write as you follow their directions. Read the sentences aloud and ask students whether the negative words have been formed correctly.

English-Language Learners

Because some English-language learners may have difficulty with negative words, review the contractions formed with *not*, such as *can't, don't, won't, didn't, doesn't,* and *couldn't*. Tell students that the apostrophe takes the place of a missing letter, in this case an *o*. Have students underline *n't* in each contraction to help them recognize the word *not*. Show students sentences with negative words and help them find the negative adverbs.

Social Studies Connection

Invite students to compare the weather in their community or state with weather in an area with more extreme weather. Challenge students to write sentences that tell about the differences in weather, using negative adverbs.

We get a lot of rain.

It <u>never</u> rains in the desert.

In the winter we get some snow.

Rain forests do <u>not</u> have snow.

Exercise 2

1. My parents won't let me have a pet. *or* My parents never let me have a pet.
2. Correct
3. They don't want to walk a dog. *or* They never want to walk a dog.
4. Correct
5. Correct
6. It isn't any trouble to care for a bird. *or* It is no trouble to care for a bird.
7. My sister doesn't want a dog.
8. We don't have any room in our house. *or* We have no room in our house.
9. Correct
10. My mother didn't have pets as a child.
11. Correct
12. Correct
13. I didn't see any black cats in the pet shop.
14. Correct

Exercise 3

Answers will vary. Possible answers:

1. Snakes are not my favorite animals.
2. I don't like the way they move.
3. For my parents a boa is not a good choice for a pet.
4. Mom really doesn't like most reptiles.
5. My sister isn't scared of snakes.

EXERCISE 2 Rewrite each sentence that incorrectly expresses a negative idea. Not all sentences have errors.

1. My parents won't never let me have a pet.
2. They don't like cats.
3. They don't never want to walk a dog.
4. I can't even get a bird.
5. I don't want a goldfish.
6. It isn't no trouble to care for a bird.
7. My sister doesn't want no dog.
8. We don't have no room in our house.
9. We have no garden or yard.
10. My mother didn't have no pets as a child.
11. My father never had pets either.
12. I never pass a pet shop without looking at the dogs.
13. I didn't see no black cats in the pet shop.
14. I haven't given up on my wish for a pet.

EXERCISE 3 Rewrite each sentence so that it expresses a negative idea.

1. Snakes are my favorite animals.
2. I like the way they move.
3. For my parents a boa is a good choice for a pet.
4. Mom really does like most reptiles.
5. My sister is scared of snakes.
6. Some snakes are poisonous.
7. I have seen a boa at the zoo.
8. Many people fear snakes.
9. Some owners feed frogs to their snakes.
10. Snakes get sick often.

APPLY IT NOW

Write five negative sentences about animals that should not be kept as pets.

Grammar in Action Find the two negative words in the page 408 excerpt.

Adverbs • 145

6.6 *Good* and *Well*

OBJECTIVE

- **To understand when to use the adjective *good* and the adverb *well***

 **Maintenance**

Assign **Practice Book** page 89, Section 6.6. After students finish,
1. Give immediate feedback.
2. Review concepts as needed.
3. Model the correct answer.

Pages 4–5 of the **Answer Key** contain tips for Daily Maintenance.

WARM-UP

Tell students to think about their talents as you write on the board the following sentences:

I am good at _____ (skating).

I _____ (skate) well.

Have students say aloud each sentence and complete it with their special talents.

📖 Read from a piece of writing that the class is currently reading. Emphasize *good* and *well*.

TEACH

Write on the board the following sentences:

Brianna is a good student.

She does very well in math.

Ask students which word the word *good* describes in the first sentence *(student)*. Ask students which word *well* tells about in the second sentence *(does)*.

Have volunteers read aloud about *good* and *well*. Review the sentences on the board and point out that in the first sentence, *good* is an adjective that describes the word *student*, and in the second sentence, *well* is an adverb that tells about the verb *does*.

Have students suggest sentences using *good* and *well*. Write the sentences on the board. Have students point out the nouns and verbs that *good* and *well* describe or tell about in each sentence.

PRACTICE

EXERCISE 1

Ask students to explain the difference between *good* and *well*. Make sure they recognize that *good* describes a noun and *well* tells about a verb.

EXERCISE 2

Have students ask and then answer a question about each sentence to decide whether to use *good* or *well*. (*What kind of catcher is she? She is quite good.*) Have volunteers read aloud their sentences and identify whether *good* or *well* describe a noun or a verb.

EXERCISE 3

Have students complete the exercise independently. Ask partners to compare their sentences.

6.6 *Good and Well*

Good is an adjective that describes a noun. It tells what kind. *Well* is an adverb that tells about a verb. It tells how. Be careful to use *good* and *well* correctly.

Adjective: We saw a *good* game last night.
Our family had *good* seats in the front row.

Adverb: Ryan hit the ball *well*.
The home team played *well*.

Tell why *good* and *well* are used correctly in these sentences.

A The new coach is good.

B He works well with young players.

In sentence A *good* is an adjective. It is a subject complement that tells more about the noun *coach*. In sentence B *well* is an adverb that tells how he works.

Which word completes the sentence correctly?

We could see (good well) from our seats.

You are correct if you chose *well*. *Well* is an adverb that describes the verb *see*.

EXERCISE 1 Add *good* or *well* to each group of words.

EXAMPLE   **can spell *well***
               ***good* grades**

1. swimming teachers
2. swimmers
3. can swim
4. does dive
5. basketball players
6. can dribble
7. plays basketball
8. point guards

Exercise 1
1. good swimming teachers
2. good swimmers
3. can swim well
4. does dive well
5. good basketball players
6. can dribble well
7. plays basketball well
8. good point guards

APPLY

APPLY IT NOW

Review schoolwork students have recently completed, such as a mural, a science project, or a book. Ask students to choose an activity and to write their sentences about that activity. Students should demonstrate the ability to use *good* and *well.*

ASSESS

Note which students had difficulty understanding when to use the adjective *good* and the adverb *well.* Assign **Practice Book** page 95 for further practice.

WRITING CONNECTION

Use pages 410–411 of the Writing portion of the book.

Reteach

Write on the board simple sentences for students to complete with either *good* or *well.*

> **Jason eats _____.** *(well)*
>
> **He eats _____ food.** *(good)*
>
> **Kelli draws _____.** *(well)*
>
> **She draws _____ pictures.** *(good)*

Ask students first to identify what is being described—a noun *(food, pictures)* or a verb *(eats, draws).* Have students read aloud each complete sentence. Invite students to suggest sentences for their classmates to complete.

Meeting Individual Needs

Extra Support Write on separate note cards 20 words. Make 10 cards with nouns and 10 cards with verbs. Mix up the cards. Have students sort the cards into two piles—one pile for nouns and the other for verbs. Review when to use the words *good* and *well.* Ask students to make up sentences using *good* or *well.*

Meeting Individual Needs

Auditory Ask students to practice using *good* and *well* in conversations at home for several days. Challenge students to keep a list of the sentences in which they use each word. At the end of the week, have volunteers share their sentences with the class. Have the class confirm that *good* and *well* were used correctly in each sentence.

EXERCISE 2 Complete each sentence with *good* or *well*.

1. a. The new catcher is quite __good__.
   b. She has been playing __well__ all season.

2. a. Brad doesn't bat very __well__.
   b. That's OK because he's a __good__ pitcher.

3. a. Your field has __good__ seats.
   b. Everyone has a __good__ view of home plate.
   c. Yes, everyone speaks __well__ of it.

4. a. Baseball is a __good__ game.
   b. You need to throw, catch, bat, and run to play it __well__.

5. a. The shortstop is a __good__ fielder.
   b. Does she bat __well__?
   c. She was hitting __well__ until she hurt her shoulder.

6. a. The center fielder made a __good__ catch.
   b. Then he made a __good__ throw to home plate.
   c. It's fun to see someone play __well__.

7. a. The team doesn't play __well__ on the road.
   b. They played __well__ last week, however.

8. a. Mark throws the ball __well__.
   b. I think that he would be a __good__ pitcher.

Exercise 3
Answers will vary.

EXERCISE 3 Use each word in a sentence with *good* or *well*.

1. sing	**3.** plays	**5.** draw
2. dancer	**4.** reader	**6.** musician

APPLY IT NOW

Write four sentences about your schoolwork. Use *good* in two sentences and *well* in two sentences.

Adverbs • 147

6.7 To, Too, and Two

OBJECTIVES

- **To distinguish between *to*, *too*, and *two***
- **To use *to*, *too*, and *two* correctly**

DAILY ⬡ Maintenance

Assign **Practice Book** page 90, Section 6.7. After students finish,
1. Give immediate feedback.
2. Review concepts as needed.
3. Model the correct answer.

Pages 4–5 of the **Answer Key** contain tips for Daily Maintenance.

WARM-UP

Read aloud the following sentences for the class:

We are going *to* the park.

You can come *too*.

Two people ride this bike.

Ask them to listen carefully for a word that sounds the same in each sentence.

📖 Read from a piece of writing that the class is currently reading. Emphasize *to*, *too*, and *two*.

TEACH

After students identify the word that sounds the same in the Warm-Up, repeat each sentence. Ask students to spell the word (*to, too, two*) for that sentence. Explain that these words sound the same but have different spellings and different meanings.

Have students read aloud about *to*, *too*, and *two*. Explain that learning the definitions of *to*, *too*, and *two* will help students remember how these words are used in sentences. Review the

meaning of each word. After reading aloud each definition, suggest that students use the phrase in each item in a sentence.

Encourage students to make up additional sentences with *to*, *too*, and *two*.

PRACTICE

EXERCISE 1

Have students refer to the definitions on the page as you complete this exercise as a class. Have volunteers read aloud each definition and spell the correct word.

EXERCISES 2 & 3

Discuss strategies for choosing the correct word.

Two—usually appears before a noun or an adjective

To—often appears before a word that names a place or a time

Too—often appears at the end of a sentence or before the words *many* or *much*

Have students work with partners to choose the correct word for each sentence. As you discuss the sentences, ask students which clues helped students choose the correct word.

6.7 *To, Too, and Two*

To, *too*, and *two* sound alike. Each word means something different, however. Be careful to use the words correctly.

- *To* means "in the direction of" or "until."
- *Too* means "also" or "more than enough."
- *Two* means "the number 2."

To: Chickadees come *to* the bird feeder from dawn *to* dusk.

Too: Squirrels come *too*. They eat way *too* much seed.

Two: Yesterday I saw *two* blue jays.

Can the same word complete each of these sentences? Why or why not?

A Bees fly _____ the hive.

B There are _____ kinds of bees—social bees and solitary bees.

C Sometimes a hive has _____ many bees.

Each sentence needs a different word to make sense. Sentence A needs *to*, sentence B needs *two*, and sentence C needs *too*.

EXERCISE 1 Choose the word from the word box for each definition.

to	too	two

1. in the direction of   to
2. more than enough   too
3. also   too
4. toward a place   to
5. more than one   two
6. until   to

APPLY

APPLY IT NOW

Encourage students to explain the difference between *to, too,* and *two*. Have students underline *to, two,* and *too* in their sentences. Ask volunteers to read aloud their sentences. If students write sentences such as *I like to play video games,* explain that *to* is part of the verb. Students should demonstrate the ability to use *to, too,* and *two* in sentences.

ASSESS

Note which students had difficulty using *to, too,* and *two* correctly. Assign **Practice Book** page 97 for further practice.

WRITING CONNECTION

Use pages 412–413 of the Writing portion of the book.

TEACHING OPTIONS

Reteach

Have students play Beat the Clock. Write on note cards the words *to, too,* and *two*. Make enough cards so that there is one card for each set of partners. Have students choose a card and give them two minutes to make up as many sentences as possible using their word. Ask volunteers to tell which word is being used in each group of sentences.

Meeting Individual Needs

Extra Support Have students work in groups of three to find sentences with *to, too,* and *two* in newspapers, magazines, or classroom books. Assign one word to each student. Then have students share the sentences they find.

Meeting Individual Needs

Challenge Have students make up riddles, rhymes, or jingles to help remember the meanings and uses for *to, too,* and *two*. Tell students they can make up individual rhymes, riddles, or jingles for each word or one for all three words. Have students share their work with the class.

EXERCISE 2 **Choose the word that correctly completes each sentence.**

1. Chris and I went (<u>to</u> two) the park.
2. We saw butterflies, and we saw bees (to <u>too</u>).
3. The bees flew (<u>to</u> two) the pretty spring flowers.
4. The gardener spoke to the (too <u>two</u>) of us.
5. She gave interesting information about bees (<u>to</u> two) us.
6. She told us about the flowers (to <u>too</u>).
7. It got (to <u>too</u>) cold for us to stay in the park very long.

Honeybees carry pollen on their back legs.

EXERCISE 3 **Complete each sentence with *to, too,* or *two*.**

1. There are ___two___ groups of honey bees in a hive—worker bees and drones—as well as a queen.
2. Worker bees leave the hive and fly ___to___ flowers.
3. They gather nectar and carry it back ___to___ the hive.
4. If there are ___too___ many bees, the queen stops laying eggs.
5. The queen and some workers move ___to___ a new place.
6. Bees can sting one another ___to___ death.
7. Some people can die from bee stings ___too___.
8. Bees make ___two___ important products—honey and beeswax.
9. Bees collect nectar from morning ___to___ night.
10. Nectar from ___two___ million flowers makes one pound of honey.
11. Bees are important in pollination ___too___.
12. They carry pollen from one flower ___to___ another.
13. The queen may live three ___to___ five years.
14. Settlers from Europe brought bees ___to___ North America in the 17th century.

APPLY IT NOW

Choose a subject from the list below. Write three sentences about it, using *to, too,* and *two*.

school	fishing
video games	reading
horses	skateboards
a mall	reptiles

Adverbs • 149

 **Maintenance**

Assign **Practice Book** page 90, Section 6.8. After students finish,
1. Give immediate feedback.
2. Review concepts as needed.
3. Model the correct answer.

Pages 4–5 of the **Answer Key** contain tips for Daily Maintenance.

WARM-UP

Give each student a note card on which you have written *their* or *there*. Have students write a sentence using the word on their card. Invite several volunteers to write their sentences on the board and underline *their* or *there*.

📖 Read from a piece of writing that the class is currently reading. Emphasize *their* and *there*.

TEACH

Write on the board the words *their* and *there*. Ask students to tell how the words are alike and how they are different. *(The words sound alike but are spelled differently and have different meanings.)*

Have volunteers read aloud about *their* and *there*. Then have students reread the sentences on the board from the Warm-Up. Ask if *their* and *there* were used correctly in the sentences. Have volunteers correct any mistakes. Ask students to make up additional sentences with *their* and *there*.

PRACTICE

EXERCISE 1
Discuss strategies to help students recognize when to use *their* and *there*. Point out that because *their* is an adjective, it usually comes before a noun or another adjective and that because *there* is usually an adverb, it follows a verb or another adverb. Encourage students to consider whether the word that is needed in each item is an adjective or an adverb. Have partners compare their answers.

EXERCISE 2
Complete this exercise as a class. Have students read aloud each sentence and spell the word or words that correctly complete the sentence.

EXERCISE 3
Have students complete the sentences with *their* or *there*. To emphasize that *their* tells about a noun and that *there* tells about a verb, you may wish to have students tell which nouns *their* refers to *(projects, skills, clothes, faces, messes, paintings, work, creativity)* and which verbs *there* refers to *(put, will make, hanging, remained, hang)*.

6.8 *Their* and *There*

Their and *there* sound alike. Each word means something different, however. Be careful to use the two words correctly.

- *Their* tells who owns something. *Their* is an adjective.
- *There* usually means "in that place." *There* is an adverb.

Their: The children let go of *their* balloons.
(*Their* tells that the children own the balloons.)

There: We went *there* to watch the many balloons.
(*There* tells where we went.)

Can the same word complete each sentence? Why or why not?

A _____ paintings are hanging in the library.

B Mine is _____, near the door.

Each sentence needs a different word to make sense. Sentence A needs *their* to show whose paintings are hanging. Sentence B needs *there* to show where the speaker's painting is.

EXERCISE 1 Add *their* or *there* to complete a word group that makes sense.

1. crayons	5. scrap paper	9. drawings
2. over	6. standing	10. go
3. scissors and tape	7. art projects	11. mural
4. up	8. stay	12. sit

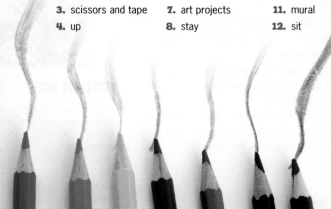

Exercise 1
1. their crayons
2. over there
3. their scissors and tape
4. up there
5. their scrap paper
6. standing there
7. their art projects
8. stay there
9. their drawings
10. go there
11. their mural
12. sit there

APPLY

APPLY IT NOW

Allow students to write about another school, another school team, another school mascot, or another community if they choose to do so. Ask volunteers to write their sentences on the board and to explain why *their* or *there* is correct in each sentence. Students should demonstrate the ability to use *their* and *there* correctly.

ASSESS

Note which students had difficulty distinguishing between *their* and *there,* as well as using *their* and *there* correctly. Assign **Practice Book** page 98 for further practice.

WRITING CONNECTION

Use pages 414–415 of the Writing portion of the book.

Reteach

Display pictures of various animals. Tell students to figure out which animal you are describing as you read aloud sentences with *their* and *there.*

Their stripes help them blend in.

They hang there by their tails.

Ask students to identify each animal. Reread the sentences and have students tell if they can be completed using *their* or *there.*

Curriculum Connection

Invite students to write sentences about characters and settings from books students enjoy. Encourage them to use the words *their* and *there* in their sentences. You might have students create book-cover illustrations for their books. Suggest that students use their sentences as captions or book summaries to place in the classroom reading center.

Their bravery saved the day.

It was hot sailing there.

They reached their destination in a week.

No one was there to meet them.

Meeting Individual Needs

Challenge You may wish to present the contraction *they're* as another word that sounds like *their* and *there.* Remind students that the apostrophe in *they're* replaces the letter *a* in *are.* Have students say the words *they are* and *they're* to help become familiar with this contraction. Also have students use the contraction in sentences, such as the following:

They're late every morning.

Do you know if they're coming?

EXERCISE 2 Choose the correct word or words to complete each sentence.

1. The children's art area is (their <u>there</u>).
2. The art supplies are kept (their <u>there</u>).
3. (<u>Their</u> There) art supplies include paints and markers.
4. You can see (<u>their</u> there) artwork on the walls.
5. Look (their <u>there</u>) on the walls.
6. Those are (<u>their</u> there) watercolor pictures of flowers.
7. Do you see that big blossom (their <u>there</u>)?
8. (<u>Their</u> There) pictures are very colorful.
9. Which of (<u>their</u> there) drawings do you like best?
10. I like (<u>their</u> there) artwork over (their <u>there</u>).

EXERCISE 3 Complete each sentence with *their* or *there*.

1. The art teacher put the paint jars __there__.
2. The young children will work on __their__ projects.
3. They will make a big mess __there__.
4. __Their__ painting skills aren't too good.
5. They will get paint on __their__ clothes.
6. They can use the smocks hanging __there__.
7. They can wash the paint off __their__ faces.
8. Some paint remained on the wall __there__.
9. I don't really mind __their__ messes.
10. __Their__ paintings are such fun to look at.
11. We can hang the paintings over __there__.
12. Put the paintbrushes __there__.
13. The children are proud of __their__ work.
14. __Their__ creativity is amazing.

APPLY IT NOW

Write four sentences about another grade or class in your school. Use *their* in two sentences and *there* in two sentences.

Adverbs • 151

 **Maintenance**

Assign **Practice Book** page 90, Section 6.9. After students finish,
1. Give immediate feedback.
2. Review concepts as needed.
3. Model the correct answer.

Pages 4–5 of the **Answer Key** contain tips for Daily Maintenance.

WARM-UP

Write the following sentence starters on the board:

    I like to _____.

    I like to _____.

Ask students to combine the sentences into a single sentence. Write their sentences on the board.

    I like to _____ and _____.

📖 Read from a piece of writing that the class is currently reading. Emphasize the coordinating conjunctions, *and*, *but*, and *or*.

TEACH

Have students note which word helped them combine the sentences from the Warm-Up. Ask what type of words these are. Explain that *and* joins two similar words to make one sentence. Discuss whether *and* could combine other words or groups of words.

    Have volunteers read aloud about coordinating conjunctions. Guide students to notice how the underlined words in the example sentences are similar. *(Canaries and* parakeets *are nouns. Sings and* does talk *are verbs. Near a window and* on a shelf *are word groups that tell where.)*

PRACTICE

EXERCISE 1
Have students complete the exercise independently. Challenge students to write three additional sentences using *and, but,* and *or*.

EXERCISE 2
Complete this exercise as a class. Read aloud each sentence. Have a volunteer identify the coordinating conjunction and the words or word groups that the conjunction joins. Ask the class to confirm each answer.

EXERCISE 3
Suggest that students preview these sentences to get the general idea of the topic. Explain that they must insert a conjunction to join the words or phrases on both sides of each blank. Point out that more than one conjunction can make sense in some sentences. Encourage volunteers to read their sentences aloud.

6.9 Coordinating Conjunctions

A **coordinating conjunction** joins two words or groups of words. The words *and, but,* and *or* are coordinating conjunctions. Use them when you want to join words or groups of words that are similar.

And:	Canaries and parakeets are good pets.
But:	My parakeet sings but does not talk.
Or:	Put the cage near a window or on a shelf.

In these sentences the conjunctions join similar words or groups of words: *canaries* and *parakeets, sings* but *does talk, near a window* or *on a shelf.*

These sentences have coordinating conjunctions. What do the conjunctions join?

  A Give your pet fresh food and clean water.
  B My dog often jumps and licks my face.
  C Our cat is usually sleeping in the yard or on the porch.
  D Our cat is independent but cute.
  E My dog likes to sleep in my bed or on the sofa.
  F Our cat sometimes scratches but rarely bites.

In sentence A *and* connects *fresh food* and *clean water.*
In sentence B *and* connects *jumps* and *licks.*
In sentence C *or* connects *in the yard* and *on the porch.*
In sentence D *but* connects *independent* and *cute.*
In sentence E *or* connects *in my bed* and *on the sofa.*
In sentence F *but* connects *sometimes scratches* and *rarely bites.*

EXERCISE 1 Find the coordinating conjunction in each sentence.

1. Baby otters are called cubs or pups.
2. Otters can live in fresh water or in the ocean.
3. Otters are good swimmers and divers.
4. They hold and toss small objects.

Sea otter pup with mother

APPLY

APPLY IT NOW

Help students brainstorm a list of animals that live in their area, including birds, small mammals, reptiles, fish, and insects. Suggest that students choose one of the animals on the list or another animal that interests them. Provide time for students to research their animals. Students should demonstrate the ability to use coordinating conjunctions.

TechTip You may wish to direct students to a specific, child-friendly wildlife Web site.

ASSESS

Note which students had difficulty using the coordinating conjunctions *and, but,* and *or* to join similar groups of words. Assign **Practice Book** pages 99–100 for further practice.

WRITING CONNECTION

Use pages 416–417 of the Writing portion of the book.

Use pages 416–417 of the Writing portion of the book.

TEACHING OPTIONS

TEACHING OPTIONS

Reteach

Write on sentence strips several words or word groups that can be connected using the coordinating conjunctions *and, but,* and *or.* Have students read aloud the strips. Ask students to tell which coordinating conjunction should be used to join the word or word group. Then have a volunteer add a conjunction to join the word or word group and make up a sentence using the strips. Continue with the remaining sentence strips.

Meeting Individual Needs

Intrapersonal Direct students to write in their journals three sentences telling about activities students plan to take part in during the weekend. Tell students to use a coordinating conjunction in each sentence. Model some sentences for students:

> **This weekend I will visit my grandparents and play with their new puppy.**
>
> **We will go to the park but not to the lake.**
>
> **We will barbecue hamburgers or chicken.**

Curriculum Connection

Display a picture of a piece of fine art, such as modern art or an impressionist painting. Challenge students to make up sentences using coordinating conjunctions about the style of the artwork and the use of color in the piece. Encourage students to give their reactions to the artwork, using coordinating conjunctions.

---

5. Otters eat fish <u>or</u> shellfish.
6. They also sometimes eat frogs <u>or</u> snakes.
7. Otters often play <u>and</u> romp.
8. They slide down muddy slopes <u>and</u> icy riverbanks.
9. I think otters are funny-looking <u>but</u> cute.

Sea otter

Exercise 2
Coordinating conjunctions are underlined once. The words or groups of words that the conjunctions join are underlined twice.

EXERCISE 2 **Find the coordinating conjunction in each sentence. Name the words or groups of words that the conjunction joins.**

1. Otters have <u>thick fur</u> <u>but</u> <u>no layer of fat</u>.
2. <u>Otters</u> <u>and</u> <u>birds</u> are among the few animals that use tools.
3. Otters use <u>rocks</u> <u>or</u> <u>other small objects</u> as tools.
4. They <u>get</u> <u>and</u> <u>open</u> shellfish with the tools.
5. <u>Oil spills</u> <u>and</u> <u>pollution</u> are dangers to otters.
6. All otters have <u>slim bodies</u> <u>and</u> <u>webbed claws</u>.
7. You can see otters in <u>zoos</u> <u>or</u> <u>nature centers</u>.

EXERCISE 3 **Complete each sentence with a coordinating conjunction from the word box that makes sense.**

and	but	or

1. Beavers have long front teeth <u>and</u> a flat tail.
2. Beavers build dams <u>and, or</u> lodges to store food.
3. Beavers live in water <u>but, and</u> don't eat fish.
4. Beavers cut down <u>and</u> eat trees.
5. Otters are not found in Australia <u>and, or</u> Antarctica.
6. Otters usually eat fish <u>but, and</u> will also eat crayfish and crabs.

Beavers

APPLY IT NOW

Choose an animal common to your area. Write three sentences telling about the animal. Write one sentence with *and,* one with *but,* and one with *or.*

Tech Tip With an adult, find facts about your animal online.

Conjunctions • 153

Adverb and Conjunction Review

ASSESS

Use the Adverb and Conjunction Review as homework, as a practice test, or as an informal assessment. Following are some options for use.

Homework

You may wish to assign one group the odd items and another group the even items. When you next meet, review the correct answers as a group. Be sure to model how to arrive at the correct answer.

Practice Test

Use the Adverb and Conjunction Review as a diagnostic tool. Assign the entire review or only specific sections. After students have finished, identify which concepts require more attention. Reteach concepts as necessary.

Adverb and Conjunction Review

6.1 Find the adverb in each sentence.

1. To play a song, hum loudly into the kazoo.
2. We practiced yesterday and learned the songs.
3. The group gathered quickly to play their kazoos.
4. We happily played the new songs.
5. Mr. Bell asked us to play quietly.
6. We moved away from the window.

6.2 Find the adverb that tells when or how often in each sentence.

7. I see an opossum in the backyard frequently.
8. The animal was on the deck today.
9. Then I saw it in the yard.
10. The opossum never comes out before dark.
11. I did not know before that opossums have trouble seeing in the day.
12. I now know that it is a nocturnal animal.

6.3 Find the adverb that tells where in each sentence.

13. We climbed inside to see the hot-air balloon basket.
14. Other hot-air balloons floated above.
15. Our balloon went up.
16. We could see far into the distance.
17. We headed back, returning to the launch pad.
18. A red and blue balloon landed nearby.

6.4 Find the adverb that tells how in each sentence.

19. Sheila acted perfectly at the dinner table.
20. Her baby brother chewed noisily.
21. He clumsily shoved peas into his mouth.
22. Then he laughed loudly as the mushy peas ran down his chin.
23. His mother quickly wiped his face with a napkin.

6.5 Rewrite each sentence to express a negative idea.

24. Riding a bike at night is a good idea.
25. Drivers can see bike riders in the dark.

6.5
24. Riding a bike at night is not a good idea.
25. Drivers can't [or cannot] see bike riders in the dark.
26. She never rides [or doesn't ride] her bike without a helmet.
27. Some bike riders don't [or do not] follow the rules of the road.
28. Never [or Don't] ride your bike into oncoming traffic.

Informal Assessment

Use the review as preparation for the formal assessment. Count the review as a portion of the grade. Have students work to find the correct answers and use their corrected review as a study guide for the formal assessment.

WRITING CONNECTION

Use pages 418–419 of the Writing portion of the book.

26. She rides her bike without a helmet.

27. Some bike riders follow the rules of the road.

28. Ride your bike into oncoming traffic.

6.6 **Complete each sentence with *good* or *well*.**

29. Storytelling is a ___good___ skill to have.

30. The storyteller told the story ___well___.

31. The audience listened ___well___ to the story.

32. We had a ___good___ time.

33. The story had a ___good___ ending.

6.7 **Complete each sentence with *to, too,* or *two*.**

34. The mail carrier brings us ___two___ packages.

35. He rings the doorbell if a package is ___too___ big for the mailbox.

36. Mail delivery is easier than going ___to___ the post office for mail.

37. The mail carrier brings us letters and cards ___too___.

38. Some packages need ___two___ stamps.

6.8 **Complete each sentence with *their* or *there*.**

39. ___Their___ favorite hobby is stargazing.

40. Did the group members bring ___their___ telescopes?

41. The Big Dipper is ___there___, to the left.

42. Thick fog makes it difficult to see the stars ___there___.

43. The planetarium is where people can learn about space, so we often go ___there___.

44. ___Their___ tour is fun and educational.

6.9 **Find the coordinating conjunction in each sentence.**

45. Sunflowers <u>and</u> daisies are pretty flowers.

46. The houseplant has leaves <u>but</u> no blossoms.

47. Put the vase of flowers on the table <u>or</u> on the desk.

48. The petals wilted <u>and</u> fell off.

49. Those flowers are beautiful <u>but</u> don't last long.

50. I will pick more flowers from the yard <u>or</u> from the garden.

Tech Tip Go to www.voyagesinenglish.com for more activities.

Adverb and Conjunction Challenge

ASSESS

Encourage students to read the paragraph twice before answering the questions. If students have difficulty with any of the questions, remind them that they should refer to the section that teaches the skill. This activity can be completed by individuals, small groups, or the class working as a whole.

After you have reviewed adverbs and conjunctions, administer the Section 6 Assessment on pages 19–20 in the **Assessment Book,** or create a customized test with the **Test Generator CD.**

You may also wish to administer the Sections 5–6 Summative Assessment on pages 33–34 of the **Assessment Book.** This test is also available on the optional **Test Generator CD.**

WRITING CONNECTION

Use pages 420–421 of the Writing portion of the book. Students can complete a formal persuasive article using the Writer's Workshop on pages 426–437.

ANSWERS

1. eagerly
2. always
3. First; an adverb that tells when
4. and, *designed* and *sold*
5. well
6. then
7. and; *DVDs* and *CDs*
8. Yesterday, eagerly
9. there
10. Now, again; adverbs that tell when

Adverb and Conjunction Challenge

Read the paragraph and answer the questions.

1. Our class eagerly planned a special field trip. 2. The third-grade class always goes on a field trip. 3. We decided to go to a children's hospital and to take gifts. 4. First, we planned a fund-raising project for the gifts—making T-shirts. 5. Next, students designed and sold T-shirts. 6. The fund-raising went well. 7. We raised $500 for gifts. 8. We then bought DVDs and CDs for the children. 9. Yesterday we eagerly took our gifts to the hospital. 10. We were warmly welcomed there. 11. We played games with the children. 12. Now we plan to go again in the spring.

1. In sentence 1 find the adverb that tells how.
2. In sentence 2 find the adverb that tells how often.
3. In sentence 4 what is the adverb? What kind of adverb is it?
4. In sentence 5 what is the coordinating conjunction? What words does it connect?
5. In sentence 6 what is the adverb?
6. In sentence 8 what is the adverb?
7. In sentence 8 what is the coordinating conjunction? What words does it connect?
8. In sentence 9 what are the two adverbs?
9. In sentence 10 what adverb tells where?
10. In sentence 12 what are the two adverbs? What kind of adverbs are they?

SECTION FOCUS

- End punctuation
- Capitalization
- Abbreviations
- Personal titles and initials
- Titles of books and poems
- Commas in a series
- Commas in direct address
- Commas in compound sentences
- Apostrophes
- Addresses
- Direct quotations

SUPPORT MATERIALS

Practice Book
Daily Maintenance, pages 101–104
Grammar, pages 105–116

Assessment Book
Section 7 Assessment,
    pages 21–24

Test Generator CD

Writing Chapter 7,
    Creative Writing

Customizable Lesson Plans
www.voyagesinenglish.com

CONNECT WITH LITERATURE

Consider using the following titles throughout the section to illustrate the grammar concept:

The Perfect Pop-Up Punctuation Book by Kate Petty
Punctuation Takes a Vacation by Robin Pulver
Twenty-Odd Ducks: Why, Every Punctuation Mark Counts! by Lynne Truss

Punctuation and Capitalization

GRAMMAR FOR GROWN-UPS

Understanding Punctuation and Capitalization

While capitalization and punctuation are not the only important elements of writing, correct mechanics are critical if a reader is to understand a writer's intended message. Written material with incorrect punctuation and capitalization can be confusing; written material with correct mechanics is clearer and more fluent.

Common punctuation marks include periods, question marks, exclamation points, commas, apostrophes, and quotation marks. There are many rules and exceptions that apply to the use of these marks, each determined by context and purpose.

Periods, question marks, and **exclamation points** are used to indicate the kind of sentence. Periods end sentences that tell something. Question marks end sentences that ask a question. Exclamation points end sentences that express strong or sudden feeling.

> *Running is good exercise. Do you run? Let's race!*

Commas are used to separate words in a series, to indicate direct address, and, along with conjunctions, to create compound sentences.

> *I am going to walk home, do my homework, and help with dinner. You can come along, Jason, and you can bring your brother.*

Just as there are many rules and exceptions for punctuation, so there are also for capitalization. Some of the things that determine the capitalization of a word are its position in a sentence, whether it is part of a title, or whether it is part of a proper name.

Guides such as *The Chicago Manual of Style* can provide a comprehensive list of standardized rules and examples for the mechanics of writing. Having good sources at hand helps writers sift through the vast array of writing guidelines and procedures.

> **"The writer who neglects punctuation, or mispunctuates, is liable to be misunderstood for the want of merely a comma . . ."**
>
> —Edgar Allan Poe

COMMON ERRORS

Using Apostrophes Correctly

Young writers often forget to use apostrophes in contractions and to show possession.

ERROR: Jim wasnt home.
CORRECT: Jim wasn't home.

ERROR: I borrowed Pablos book.
CORRECT: I borrowed Pablo's book.

A missing apostrophe is an error that does not show up in speech but only in writing; therefore, it is important to take a little extra time to help students avoid this error. Have partners trade any piece of writing on which they are currently working. Ask partners to skim each other's work for contractions and possessive nouns. Invite students to suggest where to insert any needed apostrophes. Then invite students to write on the board a correct version of one of the words. Remind students that an apostrophe replaces a missing letter in a contraction and shows possession.

ASK AN EXPERT

Real Situations, Real Solutions

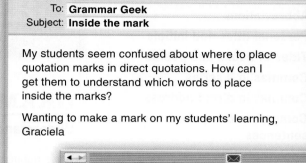

To: **Grammar Geek**
Subject: **Inside the mark**

My students seem confused about where to place quotation marks in direct quotations. How can I get them to understand which words to place inside the marks?

Wanting to make a mark on my students' learning,
Graciela

To: **Graciela**
Subject: **Re: Inside the mark**

A fun way to help students understand this concept is to tell students that the quotation marks can be seen as a drawing that represents a person's mouth (" "). Only the words that come out of the person's mouth go inside the marks. All the other words in the sentence stay outside of the mouth. With reinforcement of this image, students will soon understand where to place the marks in direct quotations.

You can quote me on that,
Grammar Geek

SENTENCE DIAGRAMMING

You may wish to teach punctuation and capitalization in the context of diagramming. Review these examples. Then refer to the Diagramming section or look for Diagram It! features in the Punctuation and Capitalization section.

I don't sleep late.

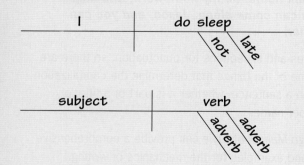

I've never been to Italy.

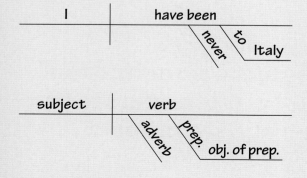

I like pop music, but my sister prefers country music.

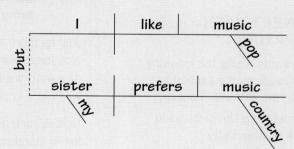

Punctuation and Capitalization

7.1 End Punctuation

7.2 Capitalization

7.3 Abbreviations

7.4 Personal Titles and Initials

7.5 Titles of Books and Poems

7.6 Commas in a Series

7.7 Commas in Direct Address

7.8 Commas in Compound Sentences

7.9 Apostrophes

7.10 Addresses

7.11 Direct Quotations

Punctuation and Capitalization Review

Punctuation and Capitalization Challenge

OBJECTIVES

- **To identify three types of sentences—statements, questions, exclamations**
- **To use the correct end punctuation for each type of sentence**

 **Maintenance**

Assign **Practice Book** page 101, Section 7.1. After students finish,
1. Give immediate feedback.
2. Review concepts as needed.
3. Model the correct answer.

Pages 4–5 of the **Answer Key** contain tips for Daily Maintenance.

WARM-UP

Write on large sentence strips statements, questions, and exclamations. Then make up two sets of three note cards, each with one period, one question mark, and one exclamation point. Place the sets of marks on two desks at the front of the room. Arrange the class into two teams. Hold up a sentence strip. Have one student from each team choose the correct end punctuation and stand at the end of the sentence. The student who gets there first with the correct punctuation wins the round.

📖 Read from a piece of writing that the class is currently reading. Emphasize end punctuation.

TEACH

Write on the board the following sentences:

Little League baseball is fun to watch

Have you ever seen the national championships on TV

The players are just amazing

Read aloud the sentences. Ask volunteers to write the correct

end marks *(period, question mark, exclamation point)*.

Have volunteers read aloud about end punctuation. Ask why sentences need end punctuation. *(It helps you see where one sentence ends and another begins. It tells what type of sentence you are reading or writing.)* Have a volunteer read aloud each sentence on the board and tell which type of sentence it is. Point out that the type of sentence determines the correct end punctuation.

Have volunteers suggest examples of each sentence type and identify the correct end punctuation.

PRACTICE

EXERCISE 1

Encourage students to explain the difference among sentences that end with periods, question marks, and exclamation points. Have students identify the end punctuation in each sentence.

EXERCISE 2

Have partners complete the exercise. Invite volunteers to write on the board their sentences with end punctuation. Have the rest of the class compare their work with that of their classmates. Discuss any sentences and end punctuation that prove confusing.

7.1 End Punctuation

End punctuation makes your sentences clear. It lets readers know where one sentence ends and the next one begins, and it signals the kind of sentence you are writing.

- A sentence that tells something ends with a **period.**

    Baseball is a sport.
    A baseball team has nine players.
    The two leagues in baseball are the American League and the National League.

- A sentence that asks a question ends with a **question mark.**

    Do you like baseball?
    Have you ever been to a major league baseball game?
    Do you play baseball?

- A sentence that expresses strong or sudden feeling ends with an **exclamation point.**

    I love baseball!
    My team won the championship!
    I hit a home run!

Which punctuation mark goes at the end of this sentence?

Who was Jackie Robinson

A a period (.)
B a question mark (?)
C an exclamation point (!)

You are right if you said B. The sentence uses a question word *(Who)* and asks a question. It needs to end with a question mark.

APPLY

APPLY IT NOW

Help students brainstorm a list of people they consider brave. Then have them write their sentences. Provide the following examples:

Neil Armstrong was the first man to set foot on the moon.

What year did he do that?

How cool it must be to walk on the moon!

Students should demonstrate the ability to use end punctuation.

TechTip Have students write questions they have about their brave person and then research the answers online.

ASSESS

Note which students had difficulty identifying three types of sentences and using the correct end punctuation. Assign **Practice Book** page 105 for further practice.

WRITING CONNECTION

Use pages 438–439 of the Writing portion of the book. Be sure to point out punctuation and capitalization in the literature excerpt and the student model.

Reteach

Provide students with the following sentences:

> **How many players are on a baseball team**
>
> **There are nine players on a team**
>
> **What is your favorite position**
>
> **I like to play first base**
>
> **Did you get any hits in the game**
>
> **I hit a home run and we won**

Have students use a red marker to add the end punctuation to each sentence. Tell students that using red is a reminder that end punctuation signals the end of a sentence just like a stop sign signals drivers to stop.

English-Language Learners

Explain that the punctuation rules for some foreign languages differ from those of English. For example, point out that in Spanish, sentences that end with a question mark or an exclamation point also begin with these punctuation marks printed upside down. Reinforce the rules for punctuating sentences in English by reading aloud short sentences that use the various end punctuation marks.

> **What is your name?**   **It's Elena.**
>
> **How are you?**   **I feel great!**

Ask students to write the correct end punctuation on a note card and hold it up.

Cooperative Learning

Provide small groups worksheets of sentences without end punctuation. Be sure to include statements, questions, and exclamations. Have students add the end punctuation as a group, or have each group member take a few sentences. Then have students make up 10 sentences without end punctuation. Have groups exchange sentences and add the correct end punctuation.

Exercise 1

1. tells something
2. asks a question
3. tells something
4. expresses a strong feeling
5. asks a question
6. tells something
7. tells something
8. asks a question
9. asks a question
10. tells something

EXERCISE 1 Tell whether each sentence tells something, asks a question, or expresses a strong feeling.

1. Jackie Robinson was a baseball player.
2. Why is he famous?
3. He was the first African American in major league baseball.
4. What an amazing athlete he was!
5. When did he join the major leagues?
6. He helped his team win the World Series.
7. He was voted the National League Most Valuable Player in 1949.
8. What position did he play?
9. Is he in the Baseball Hall of Fame?
10. Robinson is also famous for his commitment to civil rights.

Jackie Robinson

EXERCISE 2 Rewrite the sentences, adding the correct punctuation at the end of each sentence.

1. In 1947 Robinson played his first major league game.
2. What team did he play for?
3. He played for the Brooklyn Dodgers.
4. Robinson's talent and pride won him respect.
5. He was really awesome!
6. Robinson became the first African American in the Baseball Hall of Fame in 1962.
7. When did he get a postage stamp in his honor?
8. The Post Office honored him with a postage stamp in 1982.

APPLY IT NOW

Think about a famous person who is brave. Write three sentences about that person. Use all three kinds of end punctuation.

 Tech Tip With an adult, research your famous person online.

Punctuation • 159

7.2 Capitalization

 **Maintenance**

Assign **Practice Book** page 101, Section 7.2. After students finish,
1. Give immediate feedback.
2. Review concepts as needed.
3. Model the correct answer.

Pages 4–5 of the **Answer Key** contain tips for Daily Maintenance.

WARM-UP

Write on the board four lists of five words each with people's names, days of the week, months of the year, street names, holidays, cities, and countries. Do not capitalize the words. Include in each list two nouns or pronouns that do not need to be capitalized. Arrange students into four teams. Have each team stand in a line in front of a list. Challenge teams to come to the board, one student at a time, and capitalize a word or write *no* next to a word that does not need to be capitalized. The team that correctly completes their list first wins.

📖 Read from a piece of writing that the class is currently reading. Emphasize the capital letters.

TEACH

Ask students to name words they think should begin with capital letters. Then ask students to explain what types of words should be capitalized *(proper nouns—names, cities, countries, states, and days of the week).* Have volunteers read aloud about capitalization.

Invite students to dictate sentences as you write them on the board without any capital letters. Have volunteers come to the board and add the correct capitalization.

PRACTICE

EXERCISE 1
Complete the exercise as a class. Ask what the words have in common. *(Most begin with capital letters.)* Have volunteers tell why each item is capitalized. Then help students group the words according to category.

EXERCISE 2
Have students skim the sentences. Ask what students notice and confirm that the sentences do not have capital letters. Have small groups complete this exercise. Invite volunteers to write their corrected sentences on the board. Read aloud each sentence, pausing at the words that have been capitalized. Discuss the rule for capitalizing each word.

EXERCISE 3
When students have finished, have them write their answers on the board and tell why each word is capitalized.

7.2 Capitalization

Certain words always begin with a capital letter.

- The first word in a sentence
- Names of people and pets

Jennifer	Luis	Lucky
Min	Tom	Rover

- Names of streets, cities, states, and countries

Elm Avenue	Chicago	Ohio
First Street	New Orleans	Canada

- Names of days, months, and holidays

Monday	September	Labor Day
Friday	June	Memorial Day

- The personal pronoun *I* is a capital letter.

Which word group needs capital letters?

A last weekend with my sister
B holiday shopping in town
C valentine's day party on february 12

You are right if you said C. Both *Valentine's Day* and *February* need capital letters. *Valentine's Day* names a holiday, and *February* names a month.

Which word groups need capital letters?

A my sister holly
B houston, texas
C my birthday

You are right if you said A and B. *Holly* is a person's name. *Houston* is a city, and *Texas* is a state.

APPLY

APPLY IT NOW

Help students recall that capital letters should be used when naming holidays, months, and days. Suggest that students also include the names of people or places in their sentences. Students should demonstrate the ability to use capital letters.

ASSESS

Note which students had difficulty understanding which words begin with capital letters. Assign **Practice Book** page 106 for further practice.

WRITING CONNECTION

Use pages 440–441 of the Writing portion of the book.

TEACHING OPTIONS

Reteach

Write on the board a paragraph with no capital letters. Tell students the number of capital letters that should be used in the paragraph. Ask students to copy the paragraph, inserting capital letters as appropriate. Instruct students to count the number of capital letters they used to be sure that all were found. Then have volunteers read aloud the words that are capitalized in the paragraph and tell why each word is capitalized.

Meeting Individual Needs

Extra Support Write on note cards 20 words—half common nouns (*boy, girl, dog, city, street, date, school*) and half proper nouns without capital letters (*joseph, marisa, fido, chicago, park street, friday, august*). Mix up the cards and have students sort the cards into two piles—one for common nouns and one for proper nouns. Then ask students to rewrite the proper nouns with correct capitalization.

Curriculum Connection

Have available a variety of books about famous people, places, or historical events. Ask students to find and write on separate note cards words that begin with capital letters. Then direct students to sort the words into the following categories: first word in a sentence, place names, names of people, names of months, and names of days of the week. Have students share the words they found. As an alternative activity, you may wish to have students mix up their cards and exchange them with a partner who sorts the cards into categories.

Exercise 1
1. name of a person
2. name of a country
3. name of a street
4. name of a holiday
5. name of a state
6. name of a person
7. name of a day
8. name of a holiday
9. name of a month
10. name of a pet

Exercise 2
1. The last day of school is Thursday, May 28.
2. Sam and his family leave for Denver the next day.
3. There are high mountains in Colorado.
4. My family and I are going to New York on vacation.
5. We are going to visit Karen, my mother's sister.
6. She lives near Central Park in Manhattan.
7. Her address is on Fifth Avenue.
8. We'll be back home for Independence Day on July 4.
9. In August we are going camping.
10. We camp at a state park in northern Wisconsin.
11. My cousin Lorenzo is coming with us.
12. My favorite part of camping is sitting around the campfire.

EXERCISE 1 Tell why each word or word group uses a capital letter.

1. Matthew
2. England
3. Maple Lane
4. New Year's Day
5. Florida
6. Rachel
7. Monday
8. Thanksgiving
9. October
10. our dog, Whiskers

EXERCISE 2 Rewrite each sentence, adding capital letters where they are needed.

1. the last day of school is thursday, may 28.
2. sam and his family leave for denver the next day.
3. there are high mountains in colorado.
4. my family and i are going to new york on vacation.
5. we are going to visit karen, my mother's sister.
6. she lives near central park in manhattan.
7. her address is on fifth avenue.
8. we'll be back home for independence day on july 4.
9. in august we are going camping.
10. we camp at a state park in northern wisconsin.
11. my cousin lorenzo is coming with us.
12. my favorite part of camping is sitting around the campfire.

EXERCISE 3 Complete each sentence. Use capital letters correctly.

1. _____ is a place I would like to visit.
2. If I had a snake, I'd name it _____.
3. _____ is the capital of my state.
4. The Golden Gate Bridge is in _____.
5. _____ is my favorite day of the week.
6. We celebrate Presidents' Day in _____.

Exercise 3
Answers will vary.

APPLY IT NOW

Write three sentences about your favorite holiday. Use capital letters correctly.
Example:
My favorite holiday is Thanksgiving.

Capitalization • 161

OBJECTIVE

- **To correctly abbreviate days, months, places, directions, and measurements**

DAILY Maintenance

Assign **Practice Book** page 101, Section 7.3. After students finish,
1. Give immediate feedback.
2. Review concepts as needed.
3. Model the correct answer.

Pages 4–5 of the **Answer Key** contain tips for Daily Maintenance.

WARM-UP

Write on the board *Days of the Week, Months of the Year, Addresses,* and *Units of Measure.* Toss a beanbag to a student and ask that student to name a word from one of the categories on the board *(Saturday, Avenue, March, inches).* Then have that student toss the beanbag to another student. Tell students that whoever catches the beanbag must spell the abbreviation for the word, name a different word from one of the categories on the board, and then toss the beanbag to another student.

📖 Read from a piece of writing that the class is currently reading. Emphasize the abbreviations.

TEACH

Write on the board the following:

April	St.
Wednesday	Apr.
Street	Blvd.
quart	Sat.
Saturday	Wed.
Boulevard	qt.

Ask students what the letters in the second column stand for. *(They are abbreviations for the* words in the first column.) Have students match the words and abbreviations.

Have volunteers read aloud about abbreviations. Tell students to look at the lists of abbreviations for days of the week and months of the year. Point out that *May, June,* and *July* are not abbreviated.

Ask students what is different about abbreviations for units of measure. *(They do not begin with capital letters.)* Point out that abbreviations are always in singular form and do not end in *s.*

PRACTICE

EXERCISE 1 & 2

Have small groups complete the exercises. Challenge students to write their answers without looking at the lesson. Then check their answers against the lists in the lesson.

EXERCISE 3

Have partners complete the exercise. Challenge them to add an additional sentence to each item, using abbreviations.

7.3 Abbreviations

A short form of a word is called an **abbreviation.** Abbreviations often end with periods.

DAYS OF THE WEEK

Sunday—Sun.	Thursday—Thurs.
Monday—Mon.	Friday—Fri.
Tuesday—Tues.	Saturday—Sat.
Wednesday—Wed.	

MONTHS OF THE YEAR

January—Jan.	September—Sept.
February—Feb.	October—Oct.
March—Mar.	November—Nov.
April—Apr.	December—Dec.
August—Aug.	

May, June, and *July* are not abbreviated.

ADDRESSES

Street—St.	Avenue—Ave.	Road—Rd.	Boulevard—Blvd.
North—N.	South—S.	East—E.	West—W.

UNITS OF MEASURE

inch—in.	foot—ft.	yard—yd.
pint—pt.	quart—qt.	gallon—gal.

Abbreviations for units of measure do not begin with capital letters.

APPLY

APPLY IT NOW

Review abbreviations for the days of the week, names of the months, and addresses. Have volunteers write their abbreviations on the board. Discuss how each abbreviation has been formed. Students should demonstrate the ability to correctly abbreviate days, months, places, directions, and measurements.

ASSESS

Note which students had difficulty correctly abbreviating days, months, places, directions, and measurements. Assign **Practice Book** page 107 for further practice.

WRITING CONNECTION

Use pages 442–443 of the Writing portion of the book.

TEACHING OPTIONS

Reteach

Have students play Abbreviation Bingo. Distribute grids with four columns of four squares each for a total of 16 squares with column headings *Days, Months, Addresses,* and *Units of Measure.*

Have students fill in the squares under each column with appropriate abbreviations. After students have completely filled in their grids, explain that you will say a category and a word. Tell students that if they have the abbreviation for that word on their grid, they should draw an X through it. Explain that the first person who has a complete row of Xs horizontally, vertically, or diagonally, and calls Bingo! is the winner.

Meeting Individual Needs

Extra Support Have students make abbreviation books. Explain that the abbreviations for words will be hidden inside the word. Have students list on the board months, days, addresses, and measurements. Ask volunteers to point out the letters that are used in the words' abbreviations. Then challenge students to make a book of abbreviations with the word, draw an illustration, and the abbreviation hidden somewhere in the illustration. Have volunteers share their completed books with the class.

Curriculum Connection

Have students use a yardstick to measure objects in the classroom. Ask students to make a chart that lists the items and their measurements.

	Width	Length	Depth
shelf	10 in.	3 yd.	1 in.
chair	2 ft.	1 ft. 10 in.	2 ft. 4 in.
book	8 in.	10 in.	1½ in.

EXERCISE 1 Rewrite each word group, using the abbreviation for each underlined word.

1. Logan <u>Boulevard</u> Logan Blvd.
2. <u>West</u> 57th <u>Street</u> W. 57th St.
3. one <u>quart</u> of paint one qt. of paint
4. Mulberry <u>Street</u> Mulberry St.
5. one <u>foot</u> of rope one ft. of rope
6. one <u>gallon</u> of gasoline one gal. of gasoline
7. one <u>yard</u> of fabric one yd. of fabric
8. North Oak <u>Road</u> North Oak Rd.
9. Prairie <u>Avenue</u> Prairie Ave.
10. <u>Tuesday, October</u> 10 Tues., Oct. 10
11. one <u>inch</u> of rain one in. of rain
12. <u>Sunday, March</u> 21 Sun., Mar. 21

EXERCISE 2 Write the word for each abbreviation.

1. Sun. Sunday
2. qt. quart
3. W. West
4. in. inch
5. Sept. September
6. yd. yard
7. S. South
8. Thurs. Thursday
9. gal. gallon
10. Wed. Wednesday

Exercise 3

1. Mon., Dec. 22 Buy mom a yd. of ribbon at Edwards Fabric Store on E. 25th St. Buy a pt. of strawberries at the supermarket.
2. Tues., Dec. 23 Remind dad to buy a gal. of milk. Go to Gina's house. Her address is 781 W. Jefferson Ave.

EXERCISE 3 Rewrite each of the following. Use abbreviations where you can.

1. Monday, December 22
Buy mom a yard of ribbon at Edwards Fabric Store on East 25th Street. Buy a pint of strawberries at the supermarket.

2. Tuesday, December 23
Remind Dad to buy a gallon of milk. Go to Gina's house. Her address is 781 West Jefferson Avenue.

APPLY IT NOW

Write today's day and date, your birthday, and your address. Rewrite them, using abbreviations where you can.
Example: Monday, January 19
Mon., Jan. 19

Capitalization • 163

7.4 Personal Titles and Initials

 **DAILY Maintenance**

Assign **Practice Book** page 102, Section 7.4. After students finish,
1. Give immediate feedback.
2. Review concepts as needed.
3. Model the correct answer.

Pages 4–5 of the **Answer Key** contain tips for Daily Maintenance.

WARM-UP

Write on the board the following names with titles:

Capt. Tom Roth

Dr. Chin

Mr. Sam Smith

Gov. Reese Martinez

Read aloud the names with titles. Ask students to tell if the words you are saying sound like the words on the board. Ask what is different. Then ask volunteers to spell out the titles on the board.

📖 Read from a piece of writing that the class is currently reading. Emphasize personal titles and initials.

TEACH

Help students brainstorm names of people in their town or state. Suggest doctors, government officials, and military people. Write on the board the names with titles.

Circle the titles and ask students what the letters stand for. Point out that titles are abbreviations and begin with capital letters and end with periods.

Have volunteers read aloud about personal titles and initials. Then ask students to share their full names, including their middle names. Write on the board their names replacing the middle name with an initial. Point out that initials are always capitalized and are always followed by a period.

PRACTICE

EXERCISE 1

Have partners correct the titles and names. Ask volunteers to write the names on the board and to explain their choices for letters to capitalize and the placement of periods.

EXERCISE 2

Have small groups complete this exercise. Point out that the sentences do not have end punctuation and that no words are capitalized. Explain that students must add periods to titles and initials and find titles that could be abbreviated.

7.4 Personal Titles and Initials

The titles *Mr., Mrs., Ms., Dr., Gov.,* and *Capt.* are abbreviations. Each one begins with a capital letter and ends with a period.

TITLE	USE FOR	EXAMPLE
Mr.	a man	Mr. Sam Doherty
Mrs.	a married woman	Mrs. Mai Nguyen
Ms.	an unmarried or a married woman	Ms. Cathy Whalen
Dr.	a doctor	Dr. Ramon Ramirez
Gov.	governor, a state's leader	Gov. Anton Jones
Capt.	captain, a group leader	Capt. Joy Sears

A person may use an initial instead of his or her first or middle name. An initial is a capital letter followed by a period.

Martha Alice Russo   Martha A. Russo

M. Alice Russo   M. A. Russo

Which name is written correctly?

A dr Marc Wood

B Mrs Kris Chow

C Mr. A. P. Smith

You are right if you said C. Both A and B have mistakes. In A *dr* should be capitalized and followed by a period. In B *Mrs* needs a period.

EXERCISE 1 Rewrite these names, using periods and capital letters.

1. dr richard p dean   Dr. Richard P. Dean
2. ms elizabeth a young   Ms. Elizabeth A. Young
3. mrs nisha n barimi   Mrs. Nisha N. Barimi

APPLY

APPLY IT NOW

Review the names of people students identified earlier and help them brainstorm a list of other people. Have students circle the titles and initials in their sentences. Students should demonstrate the ability to correctly capitalize and punctuate personal titles and initials.

ASSESS

Note which students had difficulty recognizing personal titles, as well as correctly capitalizing and punctuating personal titles and initials. Assign **Practice Book** page 108 for further practice.

WRITING CONNECTION

Use pages 444–445 of the Writing portion of the book.

Reteach

Write on the board the initials of familiar people (*an adult in school, a well-known athlete, a historical figure, an author the class is reading*). As you write the initials, say the letters and the punctuation, as well as the title. (*For Mr. G. W., say, G, period, W, period.*) Give clues to help students identify the person. When students correctly identify the person, have them tell you how to write the first initial and last name (*Mr. G. Washington*). Continue with other names or have students suggest initials.

Meeting Individual Needs

Challenge Have students look through magazines and newspapers to find 10 personal titles and names with initials. For the names with titles, challenge students to write the names as they appear and then write the full title each abbreviation stands for. Have partners share their lists.

Teacher Tip

Many abbreviated titles come from ranks within the military or the police force. Invite students who have parents who are serving in the military or who are police officers to share titles. List the abbreviations for these titles.

Private: Pvt.	Lieutenant: Lt.
Colonel: Col.	Corporal: Cpl.
Sergeant: Sgt.	Commander: Comdr.

---

4. mr patrick r monocelli Mr. Patrick R. Monocelli
5. ms mary m reilly Ms. Mary M. Reilly
6. a n fiorito A. N. Fiorito
7. gov thomas willner Gov. Thomas Willner
8. capt barbara laboure Capt. Barbara Laboure
9. mrs emily d maggio Mrs. Emily D. Maggio
10. mr michael e lewis Mr. Michael E. Lewis

Exercise 2
1. Dr. Kerry Murphy is our family dentist.
2. Mr. N. Patel is a pharmacist.
3. Mrs. Lee Balbo runs the local flower shop.
4. Ms. Kathy Heedum is an artist.
5. Gov. J. P. Weinstein is visiting our school.
6. Ms. Nadiah Alizadeh is in college.
7. Mrs. A. R. Taylor works at the bank.
8. Capt. C. J. Smith is a police officer.
9. Ms. Sandra Rasche is a lawyer.
10. Mrs. Susan P. Taylor works in the school library.
11. Ms. Janet Jefferies is a science teacher.
12. The leader of the state is Gov. James W. Quinn.
13. The city council is led by Mr. Michael M. Olson.
14. Mr. Richard J. Martinez is the mayor of our town.

EXERCISE 2 Rewrite these sentences. Use periods and capital letters where they are needed. Use abbreviations where you can.

1. doctor kerry murphy is our family dentist
2. mr n patel is a pharmacist
3. mrs lee balbo runs the local flower shop
4. ms kathy heedum is an artist
5. governor j p weinstein is visiting our school
6. ms nadiah alizadeh is in college
7. mrs a r taylor works at the bank
8. captain c j smith is a police officer
9. ms sandra rasche is a lawyer
10. mrs susan p taylor works in the school library
11. ms janet jefferies is a science teacher
12. the leader of the state is gov james w quinn
13. the city council is led by mr michael m olson
14. mr richard j martinez is the mayor of our town

APPLY IT NOW

Write five sentences with names of people from your neighborhood or people who help you, such as doctors, teachers, or firefighters. Use abbreviations where you can.

Capitalization • 165

OBJECTIVE

- To write the titles of books and poems correctly

 **Maintenance**

Assign **Practice Book** page 102, Section 7.5. After students finish,
1. Give immediate feedback.
2. Review concepts as needed.
3. Model the correct answer.

Pages 4–5 of the **Answer Key** contain tips for Daily Maintenance.

WARM-UP

Distribute to each student a note card with the title of a book or poem. Underline the book title and put the poems within quotation marks. Ask volunteers to write on the board their title as it is written on the note card. Have students tell if they know whether their title is a book or a poem.

📖 Read from a piece of writing that the class is currently reading. Emphasize titles of books and poems.

TEACH

Have volunteers name the titles of some of their favorite books, or use the titles students wrote in the Warm-Up. Write on the board the titles. Ask what the titles all have in common. Use students' responses to formulate rules for capitalizing book titles.

Have volunteers read aloud about titles of books and poems. Challenge students to compare the rules the class put together with the rules in the lesson. Ask students how titles of books and poems should be written in book reports or journals.

PRACTICE

EXERCISE 1

Encourage students to recall how the titles for books and poems are written differently. Then invite students to identify each title as belonging to a book or a poem. Discuss words for which capitalizing may be problematic, such as *than* in item 5. Be sure students see the difference between not capitalizing short words such as *of* or *the* and capitalizing the short word *go* in item 6. Explain that verbs are always capitalized in titles. Sort the titles into a two-column chart to reinforce that poem titles are placed within quotation marks and that book titles are underlined.

EXERCISE 2

Suggest that students skim the titles. Ask how they know which titles belong to books and which belong to poems (*by the word in parentheses*).

Ask small groups to complete the exercise. Point out the verb *was* in item 13, which needs to be capitalized. Have volunteers write on the board each title under the heading *book* or *poem*. Review each category and circle each capital letter.

7.5 Titles of Books and Poems

There are special rules for writing the titles of books and poems.

- Each important word in a title begins with a capital letter. The first word and the last word of a title always begin with a capital letter. Short words such as *of, to, for, a, an,* and *the* are not capitalized unless they are the first or last word in the title.
- Underline the title of a book.
- Put quotation marks around the title of a poem.

Book: The Chocolate Touch by Patrick Skene Catling
The Little House on the Prairie by Laura Ingalls Wilder

Poem: "Nine Mice" by Jack Prelutsky
"The Pork" by James S. Tippett

Which of the following is a poem? How do you know?

A The Giving Tree by Shel Silverstein
B "The Barefoot Boy" by John Greenleaf Whittier
C Babe, the Gallant Pig by Dick King-Smith

You are right if you said B. "The Barefoot Boy" has quotation marks around it. It is the title of a poem. The Giving Tree and Babe, the Gallant Pig are books. They are underlined.

EXERCISE 1 Rewrite the titles. Use capital letters where they are needed. Tell whether each is a book or a poem.

1. "by myself" by Eloise Greenfield
2. where the sidewalk ends by Shel Silverstein
3. the cat in the hat by Dr. Seuss
4. ramona's world by Beverly Cleary
5. "louder than a clap of thunder" by Jack Prelutsky
6. the watsons go to birmingham by Christopher Paul Curtis
7. mr. popper's penguins by Richard Atwater and Florence Atwater

Exercise 1
1. "By Myself" by Eloise Greenfield, poem
2. Where the Sidewalk Ends by Shel Silverstein, book
3. The Cat in the Hat by Dr. Seuss, book
4. Ramona's World by Beverly Cleary, book
5. "Louder Than a Clap of Thunder" by Jack Prelutsky, poem
6. The Watsons Go to Birmingham by Christopher Paul Curtis, book
7. Mr. Popper's Penguins by Richard Atwater and Florence Atwater, book

APPLY

APPLY IT NOW

Help students brainstorm books and poems they have read recently. Suggest that students first write the words of each title as they remember it. Direct students to determine which words should begin with capital letters and to either underline or put quotation marks around the title, depending on what kind of work it is. Students should demonstrate the ability to write the titles of books and poems correctly.

Grammar in Action Have students tell what the title is *(Fly Away Home)* and then write it.

Ask students whether they underlined the title or placed it within quotation marks and why.

ASSESS

Note which students had difficulty writing correctly the titles of books and poems. Assign **Practice Book** page 109 for further practice.

> **WRITING CONNECTION**
>
> Use pages 446–447 of the Writing portion of the book.

TEACHING OPTIONS

Reteach

Use a Venn diagram to help students recall the rules for writing the titles of books and poems. Point out that the outer parts of the diagram show how the titles are handled differently and that the middle, overlapping part shows the rules that are common to both types of titles. Show students book titles and poem titles to confirm the rules in the diagram.

Book Title   Both   Poem Title

underline | Capitalize the first and last words. Capitalize important words. Do not capitalize short words such as *of, for, to, an, and,* and *the.* | quotation marks

Meeting Individual Needs

Challenge Write on note cards words that might appear in imaginary book titles, such as animal names, places, and people, as well as short words such as *the, to, but, or, a,* and *an.* Place the cards faceup on a table and have students choose cards to make up an imaginary book title. Then ask students to tell which words should be capitalized in their titles. Challenge students to write a story or poem with one of the imaginary titles.

Curriculum Connection

Invite students to review a poem or a book. Encourage students to write the title several times in the review. Emphasize the need to check that students have not only capitalized the title correctly but that they have also underlined it or placed it within quotation marks as necessary.

8. The Hundred Dresses by Eleanor Estes and Louis Slobodkin, book
9. "Evangeline" by Henry Wadsworth Longfellow, poem
10. Chasing Vermeer by Blue Balliett, book
11. Little House in the Big Woods by Laura Ingalls Wilder, book
12. "My Hippo Has the Hiccups" by Kenn Nesbitt, poem

Exercise 2
1. Kate and the Beanstalk
2. Sarah, Plain and Tall
3. There's an Owl in the Shower
4. "You've No Need to Light a Nightlight"
5. Horrible Harry and the Purple People
6. "A Fly and a Flea in a Flue"
7. Commander Toad and the Planet of the Grapes
8. "Keep a Poem in Your Pocket"
9. The Bears on Hemlock Island
10. "Until I Saw the Sea"
11. "Sing a Song of People"
12. The Lion, the Witch and the Wardrobe
13. "I Dreamed I Was Riding a Zebra"
14. "My Robot's Misbehaving"
15. Abel's Island
16. Stuart Little

8. the hundred dresses by Eleanor Estes and Louis Slobodkin
9. "evangeline" by Henry Wadsworth Longfellow
10. chasing vermeer by Blue Balliett
11. little house in the big woods by Laura Ingalls Wilder
12. "my hippo has the hiccups" by kenn nesbitt

EXERCISE 2 Write the titles correctly. Underline book titles. Put quotation marks around poem titles. Use capital letters where they are needed.

1. kate and the beanstalk (book)
2. sarah, plain and tall (book)
3. there's an owl in the shower (book)
4. you've no need to light a nightlight (poem)
5. horrible harry and the purple people (book)
6. a fly and a flea in a flue (poem)
7. commander toad and the planet of the grapes (book)
8. keep a poem in your pocket (poem)
9. the bears on hemlock island (book)
10. until i saw the sea (poem)
11. sing a song of people (poem)
12. the lion, the witch and the wardrobe (book)
13. i dreamed i was riding a zebra (poem)
14. my robot's misbehaving (poem)
15. abel's island (book)
16. stuart little (book)

APPLY IT NOW

Write the titles of five books or poems that you have read. Remember to underline book titles and to put quotation marks around poem titles.

Grammar in Action Write the title of the book from the excerpt on page 438.

Capitalization • 167

7.6 Commas in a Series

OBJECTIVE

- **To use commas to separate words or groups of words in a series**

 **DAILY Maintenance**

Assign **Practice Book** page 102, Section 7.6. After students finish,
1. Give immediate feedback.
2. Review concepts as needed.
3. Model the correct answer.

Pages 4–5 of the **Answer Key** contain tips for Daily Maintenance.

WARM-UP

Write on the board the following sentences:

Kerry took a _____ a _____ and a _____ out of her backpack.

Tia had _____ _____ and _____ for lunch.

Mike's favorite sports are _____ _____ and _____.

Write commas on six note cards and put tape on the backs. Invite students to fill in the blanks and then place the commas in each sentence.

📖 Read from a piece of writing that the class is currently reading. Emphasize commas in a series.

TEACH

Display sets of three items *(a piece of chalk, a pencil, and a marker)*. Ask students to suggest sentences using the items. Write on the board students' sentences omitting the commas. *(You can write with chalk a pencil or a marker.)* Ask students to tell what is missing in the sentences. Have students determine where the commas should go in each sentence.

Ask volunteers to read aloud about commas in a series. Write on the board some sentences that need commas in a series but to omit the commas. Have volunteers place the commas correctly.

PRACTICE

EXERCISE 1

Have partners complete the exercise. Remind students to insert commas before the words *and* and *or*.

EXERCISE 2

Tell students first to identify the series within each sentence before inserting commas. Point out that the words in each group have something in common. Have students identify how the words are similar.

EXERCISE 3

Have volunteers read aloud their sentences and say the word *comma* when there is a comma.

7.6 Commas in a Series

Commas separate words and groups of words so that they are easier to read. Three or more words or groups of words of the same kind written one after another are called a **series**. Often part of the series is connected by the coordinate conjunction *and* or *or*. Commas are used to separate words in a series.

I play football, soccer, and baseball.
I hit, pitch, and catch for my baseball team.
Ping, Ana, or Carl will bring a soccer ball.
I will play midfielder, forward, or goalie.

Which sentence uses commas in a series correctly?

A We need helmets, footballs, and uniforms.
B We need helmets footballs and uniforms.
C We need helmets, footballs and uniforms.

You are right if you said sentence A. There are commas between the words in the series.

Which sentences use commas in a series correctly?

A I am bringing balloons candles and streamers to the party.
B We still need to buy cake, ice cream, and milk.
C Don't forget the wrapping paper, bows, and ribbons.

You are right if you said sentences B and C. There are commas separating the words in the series.

EXERCISE 1 Rewrite the word groups. Use commas to separate the words in a series.

1. quarterbacks mascots and fans
2. referees coaches and players
3. socks shoes and shoulder pads
4. popcorn peanuts or pretzels
5. balls jerseys and helmets

Exercise 1

1. quarterbacks, mascots, and fans
2. referees, coaches, and players
3. socks, shoes, and shoulder pads
4. popcorn, peanuts, or pretzels
5. balls, jerseys, and helmets
6. Monday, Wednesday, and Thursday
7. run, catch, and throw
8. first place, second place, or third place
9. touchdown, field goal, or safety
10. black, red, and white stripes

168 • Section 7.6

APPLY

APPLY IT NOW

Ask how the words in each series are related. Point out that a series can come at the beginning of the sentence or after the verb. When students have finished, ask volunteers to read aloud their sentences and tell where commas are used. Students should demonstrate the ability to use commas to separate words or groups of words in a series.

ASSESS

Note which students had difficulty using commas to separate words or groups of words in a series. Assign **Practice Book** page 110 for further practice.

WRITING CONNECTION

Use pages 448–449 of the Writing portion of the book.

TEACHING OPTIONS

Reteach

Make and display several word webs on poster board. Write simple topics or themes such as sports, pets, games, or clothing in the center rectangles.

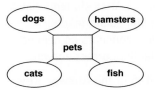

Have students write items for the outer ovals on each web. Then ask students to write sentences that use the words from the web in a series. Remind students to include commas in the correct places.

Meeting Individual Needs

Intrapersonal Have students list in their journals sentences that tell about their favorite foods, their favorite things to do, or their favorite family activities. Challenge students to write sentences using the words from their lists in a series, inserting commas in the appropriate places.

Cooperative Learning

Have small groups list three different Olympic sports. Tell students to list at least three things that describe each different sport or the athletes that participate in each sport. For example, students might choose volleyball and list *height, quickness,* and *teamwork.* Then have groups choose one sport about which to make a poster. Tell students that the poster should include a sentence using commas in a series, some of the words students listed, and an illustration. Have groups present their posters to the class.

Exercise 2
1. Olympic Games were held in Beijing, Athens, and Sydney.
2. We watched swimming, track, and gymnastics.
3. We saw gymnasts from China, Russia, Sweden, and Romania.
4. The gymnasts jumped, tumbled, and leaped.
5. The audience watched, waited, and applauded.
6. Winter Olympics sports include skiing, snowboarding, and ice-skating.
7. The ice-skater jumped, twirled in the air, and landed.
8. Cycling, gymnastics, and running have been sports at all the modern Olympic Games.
9. The three Olympic medals are gold, silver, and bronze.
10. Running, biking, and swimming are part of the triathlon.
11. Swimming, diving, and water polo take place at a pool.
12. Water polo players swim, throw, and score goals.

Exercise 3
Answers will vary.

6. Monday Wednesday and Thursday
7. run catch and throw
8. first place second place or third place
9. touchdown field goal or safety
10. black red and white stripes

EXERCISE 2 Rewrite the sentences. Put commas in each sentence to separate the words in a series.

1. Olympic Games were held in Beijing Athens and Sydney.
2. We watched swimming track and gymnastics.
3. We saw gymnasts from China Russia Sweden and Romania.
4. The gymnasts jumped tumbled and leaped.
5. The audience watched waited and applauded.
6. Winter Olympics sports include skiing snowboarding and ice-skating.
7. The ice-skater jumped twirled and landed.
8. Cycling gymnastics and running have been sports at all the modern Olympic Games.
9. The three Olympic medals are gold silver and bronze.
10. Running biking and swimming are part of the triathlon.
11. Swimming diving and water polo take place at a pool.
12. Water polo players swim throw and score goals.

EXERCISE 3 Complete each sentence with at least three words. Put commas in each sentence to separate the words in a series.

1. My favorite sports are _____.
2. Some famous athletes are _____.
3. I like to play _____.
4. At recess we _____.

APPLY IT NOW

Use the two groups of words below to write two sentences. Each sentence should contain a series.
1. soccer baseball tennis
2. shorts shirts sneakers

Punctuation • 169

 **Maintenance**

Assign **Practice Book** page 103, Section 7.7. After students finish,
1. Give immediate feedback.
2. Review concepts as needed.
3. Model the correct answer.

Pages 4–5 of the **Answer Key** contain tips for Daily Maintenance.

WARM-UP

Ask students to perform some simple tasks. Each time you assign a task, address the student by name at the beginning or the end of your sentence. *(Kelly, please erase the board. Please get me a marker, Brianna.)*
   Write on the board your instructions, omitting the commas. Have students decide if each sentence has correct punctuation.

📖 Read from a piece of writing that the class is currently reading. Emphasize commas in direct address.

TEACH

Have volunteers read aloud the first paragraph and the examples about commas in direct address. Ask students to tell what *direct address* means. Encourage students to suggest sentences with direct address, using names of their classmates.
   Have volunteers read aloud the rest of the page. Refer students to the sentences on the board from the Warm-Up. Ask students to add commas where they belong.

PRACTICE

EXERCISE 1
Tell students that a sentence with direct address names the person being spoken to. Read aloud the example sentences to demonstrate the pauses that occur when saying sentences with direct address. After students have completed the exercise, ask volunteers to read aloud their sentences, pausing after each name.

EXERCISE 2
Explain that the commas have been put in the wrong places. Have partners complete the exercise. Tell students to identify which words are the direct address. Ask volunteers to read aloud the sentences with you, pausing at the commas.

7.7 Commas in Direct Address

Speaking directly to a person and using that person's name is called **direct address.** Commas are used to set off the name of the person spoken to from the rest of the sentence. Use one comma to separate the name if it is at the beginning or the end of a sentence. Use two commas to separate the name if it is in the middle of a sentence.

> *Ben,* let's build a playhouse.
> We'll put it behind the garage, *Ben.*
> Do you think, *Callie,* we can build it in a day?

Which sentences are correct?

A I think we can Ben.
B I think we can, Ben.
C Ben, I think we can.

You are right if you said sentences B and C. The name *Ben* is in direct address. It comes at the beginning or the end of a sentence and is separated from the rest of the sentence by a comma.

Which sentence is correct?

A Please, Bernie, draw a plan.
B Please Bernie, draw a plan.
C Please, Bernie draw a plan.

You are right if you said sentence A. The name *Bernie* is in direct address. It comes in the middle of a sentence. Two commas separate it from the rest of the sentence.

EXERCISE 1 Find the name in direct address in each sentence. Rewrite the sentences, using commas where they are needed.

1. Paula, tell us where to build the playhouse.
2. I think, Mark, it should go near the fence.

APPLY

APPLY IT NOW

Discuss foods that students have cooked or things students have built. On the board list the projects, such as eggs, oatmeal, models, or toy structures. Encourage each student to choose one of the activities to write about. Remind students to use the names of friends in the sentences. Students should demonstrate the ability to use commas in direct address.

ASSESS

Note which students had difficulty understanding direct address and using commas in direct address. Assign **Practice Book** page 111 for further practice.

WRITING CONNECTION

Use pages 450–451 of the Writing portion of the book.

Reteach

Direct students to write on sentence strips a sentence that uses direct address, leaving out the commas. Display the sentences, one at a time, and read them aloud, pausing where the comma should be. Ask students to listen closely to the sound of the sentences and then to tell where to insert the commas. Ask volunteers to write on the board sentences with direct address. Have volunteers underline the names and insert commas in the correct places.

Meeting Individual Needs

Auditory Give small groups a ball and tell students to pass it around. Each time a student passes the ball to another student, tell him or her to say a sentence that uses direct address. *(Darren, I am giving the ball to you. Here, Tasha, is the ball.)* After students have gone around the circle once, invite student to address the same person as before but with a different sentence. *(Darren, I really like your shoes. You were great, Tasha, in kickball.)*

Curriculum Connection

Discuss famous people from history. Ask students to imagine they are having a conversation with one of the people. Have students write sentences about that person, using direct address. *(George Washington, you were the first president. Martin Luther King Jr., you gave a speech about having a dream.)* Have students share their sentences with the class.

---

3. Give me the plans, Ellen.

4. Help us with this hammering, Mr. Ashton.

5. Felix, let's paint the playhouse red.

6. Be careful, kids, the paint is wet.

7. We are almost done, Jamie.

8. Dad, will you help us clean up?

9. It seems to me, Ken, that the kids will really like it.

10. Put the sign up over there, Jackie.

11. Olivia, put the chair inside the playhouse.

12. Leigh, have you chosen a name for your playhouse?

13. I want to hang some of my paintings on the wall, Mom.

14. The inside of the playhouse, Jake, is tiny.

15. Come over, David, and see our playhouse.

Exercise 2

1. Mom, will you make us some sandwiches?

2. Tell me, Bob and Claire, what kind would you like?

3. Kevin, here is your ham and cheese sandwich.

4. Please pass the mustard, Evan.

5. Hand me a napkin, Maddie.

6. Pam, clear the table.

7. I'd like some potato salad, Mom.

8. I want some lemonade, Diane, and some pickles too.

9. Is there any more milk, Kate?

10. Oh, Mom, I dropped my fork.

11. Give me another fork, Mom, please.

12. Here is a plastic fork, Luke.

13. This lemonade, Dad, tastes great!

14. Sam, help us clean up.

EXERCISE 2 Rewrite the sentences, using commas correctly.

1. Mom will, you, make us some sandwiches?

2. Tell me Bob and Claire, what kind would you like?

3. Kevin here is, your ham and cheese sandwich.

4. Please pass, the mustard Evan.

5. Hand, me, a napkin Maddie.

6. Pam clear the table.

7. I'd like, some potato salad Mom.

8. I want some lemonade Diane, and some pickles too.

9. Is there, any more milk Kate?

10. Oh, Mom I dropped my fork.

11. Give, me, another fork Mom please.

12. Here is a plastic, fork, Luke.

13. This lemonade, Dad tastes great!

14. Sam help us clean up.

APPLY IT NOW

Imagine that you are cooking or building something with friends. Write three sentences that ask or tell your friends to do things. Use their names in direct address.

Punctuation • 171

7.8 Commas in Compound Sentences

OBJECTIVE
- To form compound sentences using commas and *and, but,* or *or*

 **DAILY Maintenance**

Assign **Practice Book** page 103, Section 7.8. After students finish,
1. Give immediate feedback.
2. Review concepts as needed.
3. Model the correct answer.

Pages 4–5 of the **Answer Key** contain tips for Daily Maintenance.

WARM-UP

Write on the board the words *and, or,* and *but* and a list of topics *(baseball, thunder, movies, homework, field trips).* Ask partners to choose a topic and each say aloud a sentence about it. Then ask them to combine their sentences, using *and, or,* or *but.*

📖 Read from a piece of writing that the class is currently reading. Emphasize the compound sentences.

TEACH

Write on the board the following sentences:

John reads all the time.

John likes to play outside too.

Have a volunteer combine the two sentences into one sentence. Write on the board two different ways to combine the sentences.

John reads all the time, but he likes to play outside too.

John reads all the time, and he likes to play outside too.

Explain that the combined sentences are called compound sentences. Point out that sometimes there is more than one way to make a compound sentence.

Have volunteers read aloud about commas in compound sentences. Reinforce that *and, but, or or* and a comma are used to make compound sentences.

PRACTICE

EXERCISE 1

Have students tell where the comma in each compound sentence should go and why. Ask which clue tells where one short sentence ends and the other begins *(and, but,* or *or).*

EXERCISE 2

Be sure students understand that they should use the sentence in Column B that is directly across from the sentence in Column A to form the compound sentences. Ask volunteers to write their sentences on the board. Help students determine whether the compound sentences have been formed correctly.

EXERCISE 3

Have partners complete the exercise. Ask volunteers to read aloud their sentences and tell where and why they used commas.

7.8 Commas in Compound Sentences

A comma is used when two short sentences are combined into one longer sentence. This longer sentence is called a **compound sentence.** Compound sentences can make writing easier to understand and more enjoyable to read.

> ***Wagon Wheels* by Barbara Brenner is set in the Old West,** *and* **it tells the story of three brothers.**
>
> **The brothers faced a hard winter,** *but* **they survived.**
>
> **Ryan and Tim may read this story in class,** *or* **they may borrow it from the library.**

To make a compound sentence, use a comma followed by *and, but,* or *or* to join two sentences.

Which of these choices makes a compound sentence from the two short sentences?

> **The brothers faced dangers.**
> **They survived in the wilderness.**
>
> **A** **The brothers faced dangers in the wilderness.**
>
> **B** **The brothers faced dangers, but they survived in the wilderness.**
>
> **C** **The brothers faced dangers and the wilderness.**

You are right if you said sentence B. This sentence joins two shorter sentences with a comma and the word *but* to make one longer compound sentence.

EXERCISE 1 Rewrite the sentences, adding commas where they are needed.

1. Laura Ingalls Wilder was born in Wisconsin in 1867, but she grew up mostly in the prairie states.

2. Her family traveled west in a covered wagon, and they lived in several different places.

3. Her father tried to earn a living by farming, but the family faced many problems.

Exercise 2

Students may choose either *and* or *but* to join their sentences. Make sure the placement of the comma and the conjunction is correct.

1. Tomie de Paola writes books, and he draws the pictures too.

2. I looked for *Baseball Saved Us,* but it was checked out of the library.

3. Alma Flor Ada writes in English, and she writes in Spanish too.

APPLY

APPLY IT NOW

Help students brainstorm a list of books and recall their main characters, settings, and plots. Have each student choose a book from the list to write about. Ask students to underline the complete sentences within the compound sentences and to circle the commas and words that join the sentences. Students should demonstrate the ability to form compound sentences using commas and *and, but,* or *or.*

TechTip You may wish to suggest appropriate book review Web sites. Challenge students to find compound sentences in the book reviews.

ASSESS

Note which students had difficulty forming compound sentences using commas and *and, but,* or *or.* Assign **Practice Book** pages 112–113 for further practice.

> **WRITING CONNECTION**
>
> Use pages 452–453 of the Writing portion of the book.

Reteach

On sentence strips write short sentences for students to combine. On separate note cards, write a comma and the words *and, but,* and *or.* Read aloud two sentences from the sentence strips, inviting students to read along with you. Ask students which word they would use to join the sentences. Then have a volunteer place the card with the comma and a card with one of the words in the proper places to form a compound sentence. Continue until all the sentence strips have been used.

Meeting Individual Needs

Kinesthetic Reinforce forming compound sentences by encouraging students to act out two motions, for example, clapping their hands and stomping their feet or marching across the room and then returning to their seats. After each set of motions, invite students to help you write two sentences that explain what students did. Ask students to explain how to join the sentences into one compound sentence.

Meeting Individual Needs

Interpersonal Have partners make up three different sets of sentence pairs that describe things they like to do. Ask students to combine the sentence pairs into compound sentences by using *and, but,* and *or.* (*Jin likes to play computer games. Ashley likes to draw. Jin likes to play computer games, but Ashley likes to draw.*)

Diagram It!

To practice these concepts in the context of diagramming, turn to Section 8.9.

---

4. *Stone Fox* tells about dogsled racing, and it has a lot of action.

Exercise 3

1. Alice, please tell about me about your favorite books.
2. My favorite authors are Louis Sachar, Ann Cameron, and E. B. White.
3. I like detective stories, and Encyclopedia Brown is my favorite detective.
4. Do you read detective stories, Robin?
5. I like mysteries, tall tales, and nature books.
6. Aliki's books include *Feelings, Dinosaur Bones,* and *Mummies Made in Egypt.*
7. Rick, Elaine, and Pat like books about science.
8. I have read the book, but I haven't written my report yet, Mr. Jones.

4. Wilder later wrote about her childhood experiences, and people enjoyed her *Little House* books.
5. You may have read Wilder's stories, or you may have seen some of them on TV.

EXERCISE 2 Join the sentence from Column A with the one in Column B to make a compound sentence. Add a comma and the word *and* or *but* when joining the sentences.

Column A	Column B
1. Tomie de Paola writes books.	He draws the pictures too.
2. I looked for *Baseball Saved Us.*	It was checked out of the library.
3. Alma Flor Ada writes in English.	She writes in Spanish too.
4. *Stone Fox* tells about dogsled racing.	It has a lot of action.

EXERCISE 3 Rewrite the sentences. Add commas for a series, names in direct address, and compound sentences.

1. Alice please tell about me about your favorite books.
2. My favorite authors are Louis Sachar Ann Cameron and E. B. White.
3. I like detective stories and Encyclopedia Brown is my favorite detective.
4. Do you read detective stories Robin?
5. I like mysteries tall tales and nature books.
6. Aliki's books include *Feelings Dinosaur Bones* and *Mummies Made in Egypt.*
7. Rick Elaine and Pat like books about science.
8. I have read the book but I haven't written my report yet Mr. Jones.

King Tut's burial mask

APPLY IT NOW

Write three compound sentences about books that you have read.

Punctuation • 173

Tech Tip With an adult, read an online book review.

7.9 Apostrophes

OBJECTIVE
- To use apostrophes to show possession and to form contractions

 **Maintenance**

Assign **Practice Book** page 103, Section 7.9. After students finish,
1. Give immediate feedback.
2. Review concepts as needed.
3. Model the correct answer.

Pages 4–5 of the **Answer Key** contain tips for Daily Maintenance.

WARM-UP

Write on the board these contractions: *can't, won't, isn't, aren't, wasn't, weren't, don't, doesn't, haven't.* Point out objects belonging to students *(Ben's book, Amy's pen)* and model sentences using the object and a contraction. *(This is Amy's pen. It isn't mine. I haven't read Ben's book.)* Ask students to say similar sentences using the words on the board and including an object belonging to a student.

📖 Read from a piece of writing that the class is currently reading. Emphasize the apostrophes.

TEACH

Write on the board the following words:

can't	don't
Maria's	aren't
weren't	Tony's

Ask students what the words have in common *(apostrophes)*. Have students tell how the apostrophe is used in each word *(to form a contraction, to show possession)*.

Have volunteers read aloud about apostrophes. Ask students to sort the words from the list on the board according to types—contractions and possessive.

CONTRACTIONS	POSSESSIVES
can't	Maria's
don't	Tony's
aren't	
weren't	

Then ask volunteers to write additional words in both columns.

PRACTICE

EXERCISE 1

Encourage students to read each sentence, locate the word with the apostrophe, and decide whether the word shows possession or is a contraction. Ask students to explain how they can tell the difference.

EXERCISE 2

Have partners complete the exercise. Ask volunteers to write their sentences on the board and underline the words with apostrophes. Ask volunteers to add the words to the two-column chart on the board.

7.9 Apostrophes

The **apostrophe** is a punctuation mark used in several ways.

- An apostrophe is used to form the possessive of a noun.

    The lunch box belongs to Jason.
    It is *Jason's* **lunch box.** (possessive noun)

- An apostrophe can replace letters left out in a contraction. Common contractions are *isn't, aren't, wasn't, weren't, don't, doesn't, didn't, can't, won't,* and *shouldn't.*

    Jason cannot find his lunch box.
    Jason *can't* **find his lunch box.**

Which sentence uses an apostrophe to show possession?

    A Kathy's lunch is missing.
    B I didn't eat her lunch.
    C She doesn't know where her lunch is.

You are right if you said sentence A. The apostrophe and *s* added to the name *Kathy* show that the lunch belongs to her. Sentences B and C use apostrophes to form contractions.

Which sentences use an apostrophe to replace letters left out in a contraction?

    A I didn't eat breakfast today.
    B Paul's bag is on the counter.
    C I can't stay after class today.

You are right if you said sentences A and C. Sentence B uses an apostrophe to show possession.

APPLY

APPLY IT NOW

Discuss when an apostrophe might appear in a word—to form a contraction and to show possession. Suggest that students underline the words with apostrophes in each sentence. Students should demonstrate the ability to use apostrophes to show possession and to form contractions.

Grammar in Action Have students identify how the apostrophe in *Keenan's* is used *(to show possession)*, who is in possession of something *(Keenan)*, and what he possesses

(dad). Challenge students to identify additional apostrophes in the story.

ASSESS

Note which students had difficulty using apostrophes to show possession and to form contractions. Assign **Practice Book** page 114 for further practice.

WRITING CONNECTION

Use pages 454–455 of the Writing portion of the book.

Exercise 1
1. contraction
2. contraction
3. possession
4. contraction
5. contraction
6. contraction
7. possession
8. possession
9. possession
10. possession
11. contraction
12. possession

EXERCISE 1 Tell whether the apostrophe in each sentence shows possession or forms a contraction.

1. Jane wasn't in the cafeteria line.
2. Matt can't save that seat for you.
3. That is Brian's seat.
4. We aren't able to sit together.
5. There aren't any seats at that table.
6. Erin won't be able to sit with us.
7. George's coat is on the back of that chair.
8. Karin's tray is at the end of the table.
9. Macaroni and cheese is Carrie's favorite food.
10. Tamara's choice was soup.
11. I don't like carrot soup.
12. Stacy's snack was a kiwi.

Exercise 2
1. Isn't
2. can't
3. Alicia's
4. doesn't
5. Patty's
6. won't
7. Valerie's
8. don't
9. doesn't
10. won't
11. wasn't
12. Mark's, doesn't

EXERCISE 2 Rewrite the sentences, adding apostrophes where they are needed.

1. Isnt it the day for pizza in the cafeteria?
2. Jimmy cant decide what kind of pizza to have.
3. Pepperoni is Alicias favorite.
4. She doesnt like mushrooms.
5. Pattys pizza slice has sausage.
6. Malcolm wont eat green peppers.
7. That is Valeries second slice.
8. I dont like pizza with just cheese.
9. Pete doesnt like some toppings.
10. He wont eat pizza with onions.
11. Pizza wasnt on the menu last week.
12. Marks sandwich looks good, doesnt it?

APPLY IT NOW

Write three sentences about your lunch and your friends' lunches at the cafeteria or in the lunchroom yesterday. Use a word with an apostrophe in each sentence.

Grammar in Action How is an apostrophe used in the first sentence on page 439?

Reteach

Arrange the class into two teams for an Apostrophe Spelling Bee. Say possessives, such as *Al's*, *Li's*, and *Etta's*, and contractions. Use the words in sentences. Invite players to spell each contraction or possessive, including the placement of the apostrophe. Explain that students should say "apostrophe" to tell where it goes. The team with more points wins.

Meeting Individual Needs

Extra Support Create three sets of note cards: 10 cards with contractions, 10 cards with possessives, and 10 cards with words that don't have apostrophes. Mix up the cards. Work with students to sort the cards into two piles: words with apostrophes and words without apostrophes. Then have students sort the apostrophe cards into contractions and possessives. Say a sentence that uses each word to help students determine whether it is a contraction or a possessive.

Cooperative Learning

Have students find examples of contractions and possessives. Ask students to write each complete sentence they find. Challenge them to find at least two examples of each. Have students trade sentences with partners. Direct partners to read each other's sentences and to circle each word with an apostrophe and to label it *C* for contraction or *P* for possessive. If students find contractions such as *I'll* or *we're* that do not contain *not*, be sure they understand what the full forms are.

Diagram It!

To practice these concepts in the context of diagramming, turn to Section 8.2.

7.10 Addresses

OBJECTIVE

- **To use capital letters and commas in addresses**

DAILY  Maintenance

Assign **Practice Book** page 104, Section 7.10. After students finish,
1. Give immediate feedback.
2. Review concepts as needed.
3. Model the correct answer.

Pages 4–5 of the **Answer Key** contain tips for Daily Maintenance.

WARM-UP

Write on the board the name, address, city, state, and zip code of your school. Ask a volunteer to circle the capital letters and comma.

📖 Read from a piece of writing. Emphasize capital letters and commas in addresses.

TEACH

Ask students to look at the address on the board from the Warm-Up and tell why each word or abbreviation is capitalized. Point out that the proper nouns—the school name, the street name, the city, and the state abbreviations are all capitalized. Ask what purpose commas serve in the address. Explain that the comma separates the name of the city and the state.

Have volunteers read aloud about addresses. Have students compare the addresses in the text with the address on the board. Encourage students to practice writing their own addresses. If students live in apartments, review how to add an apartment number to an address.

PRACTICE

EXERCISE 1
Review the three main parts of an address.

Line 1: The name of the person or place

Line 2: The building number, the street name, and any apartment number

Line 3: The city, state, and Zip Code

Ask students whether the addresses in this exercise have all three parts. Discuss the errors in each address—none of the words begin with capital letters. Have volunteers write on the board the corrected addresses. Discuss each part of the address and what each state abbreviation stands for.

EXERCISE 2
Point out that not only are capital letters missing in the sentences but also that the commas are missing. Review where commas are used in addresses. Have volunteers write the addresses on the board for other students to check against. Ask volunteers to identify any state abbreviations that are familiar. Identify those that are not.

7.10 Addresses

Capital letters and commas are used in writing addresses. An address is written like this.

> **Name**
> **Street Address, Apartment Number**
> **City, State Abbreviation Zip Code**

In an address capitalize the first letter of every word and abbreviation. Capitalize both letters of a state abbreviation.

> **Ms. Kathleen Connor**
> **313 N. Melrose St., Apt. 3**
> **Chicago, IL 60657**

A comma always separates the city and the state, but there is no comma between the state abbreviation and the zip code. If there is an apartment or a floor number, it is separated from the rest of the address by a comma.

Is this address written correctly?

> **James Jones**
> **215 Broadway, 15th Floor**
> **Minneapolis, MN 55413**

You are right if you said yes. The first letter of each word is capitalized. Commas are used between the street address and floor number and between the city and state.

176 • Section 7.10

APPLY

APPLY IT NOW

Distribute envelopes or ask students to bring envelopes from home. Because students may already be familiar with their addresses and the school address, invite them to address envelopes to other schools or to businesses in the area, such as a local restaurant or bookstore. Write the addresses on the board without capital letters or commas for students to copy and fix. Students should demonstrate the ability to use capital letters and commas in addresses.

ASSESS

Note which students had difficulty using capital letters and commas in addresses. Assign **Practice Book** page 115 for further practice.

WRITING CONNECTION

Use pages 456–457 of the Writing portion of the book.

Reteach

Turn a large sheet of poster board on its side to resemble the shape of an envelope. In large letters write the name of the school and its address. Then ask students to help you label the parts of the address. Display the poster in the classroom.

Curriculum Connection

Have small groups use the Internet to find addresses of three different famous buildings, such as the White House, the Empire State Building, or the Lincoln Memorial. Ask students to choose one address and to write it on poster board to resemble an envelope. Have students use the school address as the return address. Then have students use the Internet to find the location of their building on a map. Have groups present their envelopes to the class. If you have the ability to show a computer screen to the whole class, encourage groups to show the map they found for their addresses.

Exercise 1

1. Ms. Carolyn Walters
   2232 S. Main St., Apt. 334
   Ann Arbor, MI 48103
2. Mr. Ron Harty
   44 Hillvale Rd.
   Westport, CT 06880
3. Mrs. Sarah Jemielity
   418 Benton Court
   South Bend, IN 46615
4. Ms. Taylor Thomas
   35 Queens Blvd.
   New York, NY 10001

Exercise 2

1. Mr. Hector Perez
   1220 Oak Ave., Apt. 3
   Salem, OR 97302
2. Mrs. Jackie Kim
   115 W. 101st St., Apt. 4D
   Jefferson, MO 50025
3. Dr. Charles Mattes
   341 E. Irving Park Rd.
   Las Vegas, NV 80503
4. Ms. Rose Whitelaw
   2110 W. Orchard Avenue
   Philadelphia, PA 19129
5. Mrs. Jennon Bodini
   600 19th St., Apt. 301
   Denver, CO 80202
6. The City Company
   1209 Market Parkway,
   9th Floor
   St. Louis, MO 63103
7. Mr. Peter Sabarsky
   5990 W. Loomis Rd.,
   Apt. 10
   Greendale, WI 53129
8. Mrs. Michelle McCarthy
   870 W. Beach Blvd.
   Jacksonville, FL 32246

EXERCISE 1 Rewrite each address, using capital letters where they are needed.

1. ms. carolyn walters
   2232 s. main st., apt. 334
   ann arbor, mi 48103

2. mr. ron harty
   44 hillvale rd.
   westport, ct 06880

3. mrs. sarah jemielity
   418 benton court
   south bend, in 46615

4. ms taylor thomas
   35 queens blvd.
   new york, ny 10001

EXERCISE 2 Rewrite each address, using commas and capital letters where they are needed.

1. mr. hector perez
   1220 oak ave. apt 3
   salem or 97302

2. mrs. jackie kim
   115 w. 101st st. apt. 4D
   jefferson mo 50025

3. dr. charles mattes
   341 e. irving park rd.
   las vegas nv 80503

4. ms rose whitelaw
   2110 w. orchard avenue
   philadelphia pa 19129

5. mrs jennon bodini
   600 19th st. apt. 301
   denver co 80202

6. the city company
   1209 market parkway 9th floor
   st. louis mo 63103

7. mr. peter sabarsky
   5990 w. loomis rd. apt. 10
   greendale wi 53129

8. mrs. michelle mccarthy
   870 w beach blvd.
   jacksonville fl 32246

APPLY IT NOW

Address an envelope. Use your name and address in the upper left corner for the return address. Use your teacher's name and the school address for the mailing address.

Punctuation • 177

OBJECTIVE

- To use quotation marks to indicate the words a person says

DAILY Maintenance

Assign **Practice Book** page 104, Section 7.11. After students finish,
1. Give immediate feedback.
2. Review concepts as needed.
3. Model the correct answer.

Pages 4–5 of the **Answer Key** contain tips for Daily Maintenance.

WARM-UP

Distribute copies of an age-appropriate cartoon that contains dialogue in balloons. Instruct students to write on the board the dialogue from each balloon.

📖 Read from a piece of writing that the class is currently reading. Emphasize direct quotations.

TEACH

Have volunteers read aloud about direct quotations. Point out the comma and quotation marks in each example sentence. Then refer back to the dialogue students wrote on the board in the Warm-Up. Have volunteers add the character's name who said each sentence and write commas and quotation marks where they belong.

   Ask students why quotation marks are needed in the sentences in the lesson but were not needed in the cartoons (*because the balloons showed which person was talking*).

PRACTICE

EXERCISE 1
Point out that the sentences contain quotation marks and periods. Explain that the commas are missing. Write the sentences on the board. Have volunteers insert and circle the commas.

EXERCISE 2
Tell students that they first need to identify the person's exact words in each sentence. Encourage students to share strategies to help locate the direct quotations. Have partners decide where to place the quotation marks. Write the sentences on the board. Ask volunteers to add the quotation marks in the correct places.

EXERCISE 3
Discuss how to locate direct quotations and where to place commas. Have students read aloud the sentences and tell where to place the quotation marks and commas.

7.11 Direct Quotations

A **direct quotation** contains the exact words a person says. Use quotation marks before and after the words of a speaker. Use a comma to set off what is said from the rest of the sentence.

Cargo ships entering the Gatun Locks

> Javier said, "I know a lot about the Panama Canal."
> "You are smart," replied Lucy.

Which sentence tells Mrs. Becker's exact words?

   A Mrs. Becker said, "We will learn about the canal."
   B Mrs. Becker said that the canal is important.
   C Mrs. Becker said that ships sail on the canal.

You are right if you said sentence A. This sentence tells Mrs. Becker's exact words. Her exact words are inside the quotation marks. A comma sets off what she said from the rest of the sentence.

EXERCISE 1 Rewrite each sentence. Use a comma to separate what is being said from the rest of the sentence.

1. Mrs. Becker said, "Tell me about the Panama Canal."
2. Rick replied, "The Panama Canal joins the Atlantic Ocean and the Pacific Ocean."
3. Casey exclaimed, "That's a long canal!"
4. Suzanne added, "It is more than 50 miles long."
5. Miguel said, "The canal was opened in 1914."
6. Mrs. Becker asked, "Who was president when the Panama Canal was built?"
7. "It was Theodore Roosevelt," answered Iris.
8. "The Panama Canal has been called the eighth wonder of the world," said Ana.

Gatun Lake

178 • Section 7.11

APPLY

APPLY IT NOW

Have small groups discuss their weekend's activities to help generate ideas. Remind students to include themselves in their dialogues by using the pronoun *I*. Have students write dialogue to express their recollections. Students should demonstrate the ability to use quotation marks to indicate the words a person says.

Grammar in Action. Have volunteers read aloud the story on page 439 to find the direct quotations. Have students read the second direct quotation *("It's only seven o'clock!")* with the expression indicated by the punctuation.

ASSESS

Note which students had difficulty using quotation marks to indicate the words a person says. Assign **Practice Book** page 116 for further practice.

WRITING CONNECTION

Use pages 458–459 of the Writing portion of the book.

TEACHING OPTIONS

Reteach

Distribute a page from a play. Have students read aloud the parts. Then have each student write on the board a line of dialogue with a dialogue tag, a comma, and quotation marks. Model the first line of dialogue.

Meeting Individual Needs

Auditory Have small groups find in books passages that contain direct quotations. Ask students to take the roles of the characters in their passages. Have students read the words in quotation marks that pertain to their roles. Ask students how they know who is speaking. Have them explain the function of quotation marks in the sentences.

Cooperative Learning

Have small groups make up the dialogue for a comic strip. Tell students to use characters from popular comic strips or make up characters of their own. Point out that students are writing the dialogue only, so they need to write the dialogue using quotation marks and identifying the speaker for each sentence. Have groups share their work with the class.

Exercise 3

1. "We found some interesting facts about the canal," said Louis.
2. Anita said, "The canal has three sets of locks."
3. "Thirty ships go through the canal every day," reported Edward.
4. "A man once swam across the canal," began Jake.
5. Jake continued, "He had to pay a toll for using the canal!"
6. I said, "A hydrofoil ship went through it in under three hours."
7. Mrs. Ricci asked, "Do you know the nickname for the canal?"
8. "It's called the Big Ditch," replied Emma.
9. Mrs. Ricci continued, "By how many miles did the canal shorten the trip?"
10. Inez quickly responded, "A boat cuts about 8,000 miles off the trip from east to west."

EXERCISE 2 Rewrite each sentence. Put quotation marks around each person's exact words.

1. "It takes my ship eight to ten hours to travel through the canal," said the ship's captain.
2. He said, "Without the canal we would have to travel around South America to go from New York to California."
3. "The canal's locks are like giant stairs," the teacher said.
4. She explained, "Locks let water in and out to raise and lower ships."
5. "I read that a new canal may be needed," said Mr. Michaels.
6. Yolanda asked, "Why do people want a new canal?"
7. "Modern ships are much larger," answered Robin.
8. Robin continued, "They cannot fit through this canal."
9. "There may be a new canal in Mexico," reported Fernando.
10. "We can research the topic of a new canal," suggested Madison.

EXERCISE 3 Rewrite each sentence. Use a comma to separate what is being said from the rest of the sentence. Put quotation marks around each person's exact words.

1. We found some interesting facts about the canal said Louis.
2. Anita said The canal has three sets of locks.
3. Thirty ships go through the canal every day reported Edward.
4. A man once swam across the canal began Jake.
5. Jake continued He had to pay a toll for using the canal!
6. I said A hydrofoil ship went through it in under three hours.
7. Mrs. Ricci asked Do you know the nickname for the canal?
8. It's called the Big Ditch replied Emma.
9. Mrs. Ricci continued By how many miles did the canal shorten the trip?
10. Inez quickly responded A boat cuts about 8,000 miles off the trip from east to west.

APPLY IT NOW

Imagine you are talking with a few friends about what you did last weekend. Write four sentences that contain your friends' exact words.

Grammar in Action. Find the second direct quotation on page 439.

Punctuation • 179

Punctuation and Capitalization Review

ASSESS

Use the Punctuation and Capitalization Review as homework, as a practice test, or as an informal assessment. Following are some options for use.

Homework

You may wish to assign one group the odd items and another group the even items. When you next meet, review the correct answers as a group. Be sure to model how to arrive at the correct answer.

Practice Test

Use the Punctuation and Capitalization Review as a diagnostic tool. Assign the entire review or just specific sections. After students have finished, identify which concepts require more attention. Reteach concepts as necessary.

Punctuation and Capitalization Review

7.2
6. Thanksgiving is always on a Thursday in November.
7. Pilgrims held the first celebration in Massachusetts.
8. My family travels to Denver, Colorado, for the holiday.
9. We drive through Pueblo, Fairplay, and Littleton.
10. We will return on Sunday.

7.3
11. one qt. of oil
12. Mon., Aug. 7
13. 1 yd. of rope
14. N. Waterford St.
15. Feb. 14, 20–

7.4
16. Mrs. Hilbert hurt her knee.
17. Dr. Kerry suggested surgery.
18. Mr. Hilbert came to visit.
19. Gov. Jim F. Tan was also there.
20. Capt. Hidalgo had the flu.

7.1 **Rewrite the sentences. Put the correct punctuation at the end of each sentence.**
1. How do we get to the park?
2. We will take the subway.
3. What fun the subway is!
4. Why is it called the subway?
5. The train runs underground.

7.2 **Rewrite the sentences, adding capital letters where they are needed.**
6. thanksgiving is always on a thursday in november.
7. pilgrims held the first celebration in massachusetts.
8. my family travels to denver, colorado, for the holiday.
9. we drive through pueblo, fairplay, and littleton.
10. we will return on sunday.

7.3 **Rewrite each word group, using an abbreviation for each underlined word.**
11. one quart of oil
12. Monday, August 7
13. 1 yard of rope
14. North Waterford Street
15. February 14, 20–

7.4 **Rewrite the sentences, using capital letters and periods where they are needed.**
16. mrs hilbert hurt her knee.
17. dr kerry suggested surgery.
18. mr hilbert came to visit.
19. gov jim f tan was also there.
20. capt hidalgo had the flu.

7.5 **Rewrite the titles correctly.**
21. it's a fair day, amber brown by Paula Danziger (book)
22. big anthony by Tomie de Paola (book)
23. the purple cow by gelett burgess (poem)
24. holes by Louis Sachar (book)
25. fireflies in the garden by Robert Frost (poem)

7.6 **Rewrite the sentences, using commas to separate the words in a series.**
26. Please set the table with forks spoons and knives.
27. Do you want milk water or juice?
28. We ate turkey potatoes and peas for dinner.
29. The family talked laughed and ate at the table.

7.5
21. It's a Fair Day, Amber Brown
22. Big Anthony
23. "The Purple Cow"
24. Holes
25. "Fireflies in the Garden"

7.6
26. Please set the table with forks, spoons, and knives.
27. Do you want milk, water, or juice?
28. We ate turkey, potatoes, and peas for dinner.
29. The family talked, laughed, and ate at the table.

7.7
30. Daren, please walk on the pool deck.
31. I think, Shauna, that the water is too deep.
32. It's your turn, Kevin, to go down the water slide.
33. Be careful on the stairs, Liz.
34. Watch your sister, Jo.

7.8
35. Kate ate spaghetti, and she spilled some on her shirt.
36. She wiped the shirt with a napkin, but it made the mess worse.
37. Her dad quickly washed the shirt, or the stain would never have come out.

Informal Assessment

Use the review as preparation for the formal assessment. Count the review as a portion of the grade. Have students work to find the correct answers and use their corrected review as a study guide for the formal assessment.

WRITING CONNECTION

Use pages 460–461 of the Writing portion of the book.

Answer Key

38. Kate went shopping, and she bought a new shirt anyway.
39. Kate still eats spaghetti, but she's more careful now.

7.9
40. People aren't the only ones who get sick. contraction
41. My pet bunny wasn't well. contraction
42. Ty's dog had a broken leg. possession
43. The vet's office was open. possession
44. The doctor didn't turn any animal away. contraction

7.10
45. Mr. Stan Moore
    123 Boxcar St., Apt. 3B
    Wysox, PA 18854
46. Mrs. Georgia Molder
    500 Flat River Lane
    Pickering, OH 43147
47. Ms. Maria E. Garcee
    34 W. Oak Ave.
    Ann Arbor, MI 48103

7.11
48. Mr. Davis said, "I grew up on a farm."
49. "We grew corn," he continued.
50. "Tell me if you have a story to share about a farm," the teacher continued.
51. "My grandparents have a farm in Iowa," Lena said.
52. She exclaimed, "They wake me up at 4 a.m. to milk the cows!"

7.7 Rewrite the sentences, using commas for direct address where they are needed.

30. Daren please walk on the pool deck.
31. I think Shauna that the water is too deep.
32. It's your turn Kevin to go down the water slide.
33. Be careful on the stairs Liz.
34. Watch your sister Jo.

7.8 Rewrite the compound sentences, adding commas where they are needed.

35. Kate ate spaghetti and she spilled some on her shirt.
36. She wiped the shirt with a napkin but it made the mess worse.
37. Her dad quickly washed the shirt or the stain would never have come out.
38. Kate went shopping and she bought a new shirt anyway.
39. Kate still eats spaghetti but she's more careful now.

7.9 Rewrite the sentences, adding apostrophes where they are needed. Then tell whether each apostrophe is used to show possession or forms a contraction.

40. People arent the only ones who get sick.

41. My pet bunny wasnt well.
42. Tys dog had a broken leg.
43. The vets office was open.
44. The doctor didnt turn any animal away.

7.10 Rewrite each address, using commas and capital letters where they are needed.

45. mr stan moore
    123 boxcar st apt 3B
    wysox pa 18854
46. mrs georgia molder
    500 flat river lane
    pickering oh 43147
47. ms maria e garcee
    34 w oak ave
    ann arbor mi 48103

7.11 Rewrite each sentence, adding quotation marks and commas where they are needed.

48. Mr. Davis said I grew up on a farm.
49. We grew corn he continued.
50. Tell me if you have a story to share about a farm the teacher said.
51. My grandparents have a farm in Iowa Lena said.
52. She exclaimed They wake me up at 4 a.m. to milk the cows!

Tech Tip · Go to www.voyagesinenglish.com for more activities.

Punctuation and Capitalization • 181

TEACHING OPTIONS

Putting It All Together

Have students copy a section from their favorite book, or choose an article from a magazine or newspaper. Ask students to use double-spacing if they are typing on a computer, or to write on every other line if using pen and paper. Write on the board the following directions:

- **Circle all the end punctuation—periods, question marks, and exclamation points.**
- **Underline all the capital letters.**
- **Write an *A* above all the abbreviations.**
- **Write *DQ* above all the direct quotations.**
- **Write a *C* above commas in compound sentences.**
- **Highlight commas.**

Have students exchange papers with a partner and discuss their choices.

TechTip Encourage students to further review punctuation and capitalization, using the additional practice and games at www.voyagesinenglish.com.

ASSESS

Encourage students to read the paragraph twice before answering the questions independently. If students have difficulty with any questions, suggest that they refer to the lesson in the chapter that teaches the skill. This activity can be completed by individuals, small groups, or the class working as a whole.

After you have reviewed punctuation and capitalization, administer the Section 7 Assessment on pages 21–24 in the **Assessment Book,** or create a customized test with the **Test Generator CD.**

You may also wish to administer the Section 7 Summative Assessment on pages 35–36 of the **Assessment Book.** This test is also available on the optional **Test Generator CD.**

WRITING CONNECTION

Use pages 462–463 of the Writing portion of the book.

Students can complete a formal realistic-fiction story using the Writer's Workshop on pages 464–475.

ANSWERS

1. Thursday is the name of a day of the week.
2. Thurs.
3. to separate words in a series
4. A sentence that expresses emotion; it ends with an exclamation point.
5. Miami is the name of a city.
6. Nov.
7. The words inside the quotation marks are words that someone is saying.
8. *Ms.* is a title. *Talbot* is the name of a person.
9. question mark
10. *And* connects two sentences to form a compound sentence. The two sentences are *She told the class to draw his or her hand on the paper* and *then she said to cut it out.*
11. Kelly

Punctuation and Capitalization Challenge

Read the paragraph and answer the questions.

1. On Thursday the third graders were going to make Thanksgiving turkey decorations. 2. They needed feathers, paper, and a school picture. 3. Kelly was so excited! 4. She thought she would send the turkey to her grandparents in Miami. 5. If she mailed it by Wednesday, November 8, the turkey would arrive in time for Thanksgiving. 6. The day finally came to make the turkeys. 7. "Does everyone have materials?" asked Ms. Talbot. 8. She told the class to draw his or her hand on the paper, and then she said to cut it out. 9. Each student glued a feather to the finger of each hand. 10. "Kelly, can you guess where you will put your picture?" asked Ms. Talbot.

1. In sentence 1 why does *Thursday* begin with a capital letter?
2. What is the abbreviation for *Thursday* in sentence 1?
3. In sentence 2 why is a comma used after *feathers* and after *paper*?
4. What kind of sentence is sentence 3? How do you know?
5. In sentence 4 why is the first letter in *Miami* capitalized?
6. What is the abbreviation for *November* in sentence 5?
7. In sentence 7 why are quotation marks used before *Does* and after *materials*?
8. In sentence 7 why do *Ms.* and *Talbot* begin with capital letters?
9. What is the punctuation after the direct quotation in sentence 7?
10. In sentence 8 what does *and* connect?
11. In sentence 10 what name is in direct address?

SECTION FOCUS
- **Subjects and predicates**
- **Possessives**
- **Adjectives**
- **Adverbs**
- **Adjectives as subject complements**
- **Compound subjects**
- **Compound predicates**
- **Compound subject complements**
- **Compound sentences**

SUPPORT MATERIALS

Practice Book
Daily Maintenance, pages 117–120
Grammar, pages 121–131

Assessment Book
Section 8 Assessment,
   pages 25–28

Test Generator CD

Writing Chapter 8,
   Research Reports

Customizable Lesson Plans
www.voyagesinenglish.com

CONNECT WITH LITERATURE

📖 Consider using the following titles throughout the section to illustrate the grammar concept:

Fritz and the Beautiful Horses
   by Jan Brett
Harriet the Spy
   by Louise Fitzhugh
When I Was Young in the Mountains
   by Cynthia Rylant

Diagramming

GRAMMAR FOR GROWN-UPS

Understanding Diagramming

A diagram is a picture of a sentence. Diagramming can be especially beneficial for visual learners and English-language learners. To diagram a sentence, grammar learners break it into its individual parts—words, phrases, and clauses—based on their function.

Diagrams demonstrate that the subject and the predicate are the bedrock of every sentence and that the remainder of a sentence is built upon those two required structural parts. In a diagram the subject and predicate belong on one horizontal line divided by a vertical line.

Joaquín reads.

In a diagram **adjectives** and **adverbs** are physically connected, using a diagonal line, to the words they modify.

Asian elephants communicate well.

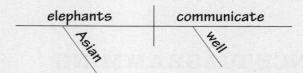

Compound sentence parts function equally within a sentence and are connected by a dotted line in a diagram.

Joaquín reads fast and walks slowly.

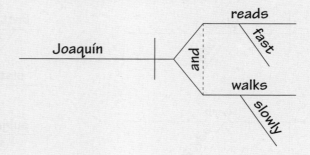

> **"Good writing is clear thinking made visible."**
>
> —Bill Wheeler

COMMON ERRORS

Diagramming Adjectives and Adverbs

Tell students that adjectives and adverbs are diagrammed in a similar way. Help students identify adjectives and adverbs by asking what questions the words answer in a sentence. (*Adjectives answer what kind or how many about a noun. Adverbs answer when, where, or how about a verb.*) Help students diagram the following sentence:

Careful students write well.

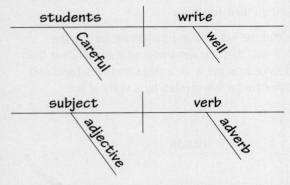

Have students answer *what kind* about the noun *students*. (*The answer is* careful, *so* careful *is an adjective.*) Then have them answer *how do students write?* (*Students write well. Well is an adverb*).

ASK AN EXPERT

Real Situations, Real Solutions

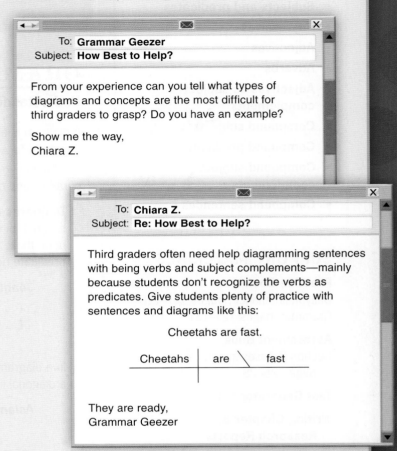

To: **Grammar Geezer**
Subject: **How Best to Help?**

From your experience can you tell what types of diagrams and concepts are the most difficult for third graders to grasp? Do you have an example?

Show me the way,
Chiara Z.

To: **Chiara Z.**
Subject: **Re: How Best to Help?**

Third graders often need help diagramming sentences with being verbs and subject complements—mainly because students don't recognize the verbs as predicates. Give students plenty of practice with sentences and diagrams like this:

Cheetahs are fast.

| Cheetahs | are \ fast |

They are ready,
Grammar Geezer

SENTENCE DIAGRAMMING

Below are diagramming examples of different types of sentences. The first is a simple sentence. The second is a sentence with a compound subject and a subject complement.

I sleep late.

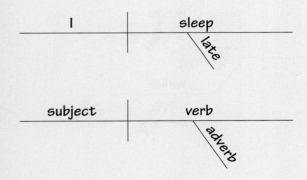

My brother and sister are twins.

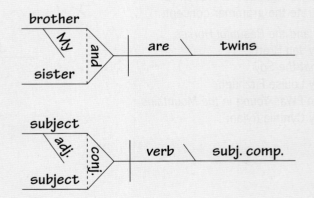

Diagramming

8.1 Subjects and Predicates

8.2 Possessives

8.3 Adjectives

8.4 Adverbs

8.5 Adjectives as Subject Complements

8.6 Compound Subjects

8.7 Compound Predicates

8.8 Compound Subject Complements

8.9 Compound Sentences

8.10 Diagramming Practice

8.11 More Diagramming Practice

Diagramming Review

Diagramming Challenge

8.1 Subjects and Predicates

OBJECTIVE

- **To diagram sentences with simple subjects and simple predicates**

DAILY  Maintenance

Assign **Practice Book** page 117, Section 8.1. After students finish,
1. Give immediate feedback.
2. Review concepts as needed.
3. Model the correct answer.

Pages 4–5 of the **Answer Key** contain tips for Daily Maintenance.

WARM-UP

Display a T-chart, a Venn diagram, and a map. Discuss what the examples have in common. *(They are used to organize and display information.)* Have groups brainstorm and draw other visuals, such as road maps, blueprints, and story webs, that help people understand rules, ideas, and connections. Tell students that each visual is worth one point. When time is up, tally the number of points for each group.

TEACH

Write on the board the sentence *Kaley runs.* Ask students to identify the subject *(Kaley)* and predicate *(runs).* Explain that a sentence diagram, like the examples they gave in the Warm-Up, gives a picture of a sentence and its parts.

Have volunteers read about diagramming subjects and predicates. Review the sample diagram. Point out that the subject is shown on the left side of the vertical line and the predicate is shown on the right side of the line.

Explain that sentence punctuation is not added to the diagram. Point out that any capitalized words in the sentence are also capitalized in the diagram.

PRACTICE

EXERCISE 1

Remind students that subjects are nouns in a sentence and that the predicates are action words, or verbs. Have volunteers write on the board their completed sentences.

EXERCISE 2

Draw on the board a horizontal line and vertical line for the sentence diagram. Point out that the vertical line cuts through the horizontal line. Remind students that the subject can be a noun or a pronoun. Suggest that students first draw the lines and then write each part of the sentence in the correct position. Ask volunteers to write their sentences on the board. Challenge students to identify each subject as a noun or a pronoun.

APPLY

APPLY IT NOW

Encourage students to write the names of three people and to think of a simple activity for each person. Students should demonstrate the ability to diagram sentences with simple subjects and simple predicates.

8.1 Subjects and Predicates

A **sentence diagram** is a drawing that shows how the parts of a sentence go together.

The most important parts of a sentence are the subject and the predicate. The **simple subject** of a sentence is usually a noun, a word that names a person, a place, or a thing. It may also be a subject pronoun, a word that takes the place of a noun. The **simple predicate** of a sentence is a verb.

In a sentence diagram, the simple subject and the simple predicate go on a horizontal line (a line that goes across). The subject is at the left, and the predicate is at the right. A vertical line (a line that goes up and down) separates them.

subject (noun or pronoun)	predicate (verb)

Let's do an example: **Birds fly.**
1. Draw a horizontal line.
2. The verb in the sentence is *fly.* Write it on the line at the right.

	fly

3. Think: *What can fly?* The answer is *Birds. Birds* is the simple subject. Write it to the left. Draw a vertical line to separate the subject and the predicate.

Birds	fly

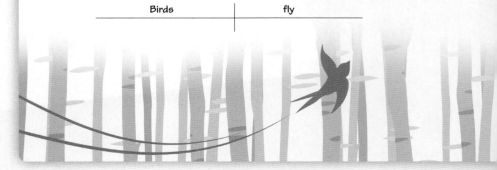

ASSESS

Note which students had difficulty diagramming sentences with simple subjects and simple predicates. Assign **Practice Book** page 121 for further practice.

WRITING CONNECTION

Use pages 476–477 of the Writing portion of the book. Be sure to point out subjects and predicates in the literature excerpt and the student model.

EXERCISE 1 Copy each diagram. Finish it by adding a subject or a predicate. Choose a word from the word box.

bees   cats   talk   bark

1. Cats | meow   3. Bees | buzz

2. Dogs | bark   4. People | talk

EXERCISE 2 Diagram each sentence.

1. Eva cooks.
2. Globes spin.
3. Bees sting.
4. Len swims.
5. Wolves howl.
6. Keith writes.
7. Lions roar.
8. I sew.
9. He reads.
10. We hike.
11. Balls bounce.
12. She swims.
13. They dance.
14. Lightning strikes.
15. Popcorn pops.

Wolf pup

APPLY IT NOW

Write three sentences about people you know and something that each person does. Use only a simple subject and a simple predicate. Diagram each sentence.
Examples: Mom works.
Sarah skates.

Diagramming • 185

EXERCISE 2 (Answers)

1. Eva | cooks

2. Globes | spin

3. Bees | sting

4. Len | swims

5. Wolves | howl

6. Keith | writes

7. Lions | roar

8. I | sew

9. He | reads

10. We | hike

11. Balls | bounce

12. She | swims

13. They | dance

14. Lightning | strikes

15. Popcorn | pops

8.2 Possessives

- **To diagram sentences with possessives**

 **Maintenance**

Assign **Practice Book** page 117, Section 8.2. After students finish,
1. Give immediate feedback.
2. Review concepts as needed.
3. Model the correct answer.

Pages 4–5 of the **Answer Key** contain tips for Daily Maintenance.

WARM-UP

Ask each student to choose one thing to place on top of his or her desk. Then invite volunteers to look around the room, choose an item, and write on the board a phrase that tells to whom the item belongs *(Carla's crayon)*. Challenge students to find items that more than one student has and write a phrase that shows that more than one student possesses the same item *(the students' pencils, the boys' books)*.

TEACH

Ask a volunteer to read aloud the first paragraph about diagramming possessives. Have students point out the *'s* or *s'* that shows possession in the phrases on the board from the Warm–Up. Ask which words are plural possessives and which are singular possessives.

Write on the board a sentence with a possessive noun. *(Carly's dog barks.)* Ask students to identify whose dog barks *(Carly's)*.

Invite volunteers to read aloud the rest of the page. Ask a volunteer to diagram the sentence on the board. Point out that the possessive describes the word *dog*, so it is written on a slanted line under the word. Have students suggest sentences with possessives and practice diagramming them.

PRACTICE

EXERCISE 1
Ask how the possessive nouns in each item are different. Be sure students understand that *Dogs'* is a plural possessive and *Dad's* is a singular possessive.

EXERCISE 2
Remind students that possessives and possessive adjectives *(my, your, his, her, its, our, their)* should be connected to the noun they go with.

APPLY

APPLY IT NOW
Work with students to write sentences that include objects at home to which students can apply possessives. Students should demonstrate the ability to diagram sentences with possessives.

Grammar in Action Remind students that things, as well as people, can be possessives as in the excerpt *(earth's)*.

8.2 Possessives

The **possessive form** of a noun shows who possesses or owns something. Possessive nouns end in *'s* or just in an apostrophe: the *cat's* food, the *cats'* food. The noun that follows a possessive noun names what is owned.

In a sentence diagram, a possessive noun is written on a slanted line under the noun it goes with. The possessive adjectives *my, your, his, her, its, our,* and *their* are diagrammed the same way.

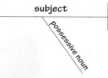

subject	predicate

possessive noun

Let's do an example: **Jeff's bird sings.**

1. Write the simple subject and the simple predicate on the horizontal line.

bird	sings

2. Think: *Who owns the bird?* Jeff owns the bird. It is *Jeff's* bird. Write *Jeff's* on a slanted line under *bird.*

bird	sings

Jeff's

Here's another example: **Mom's vase broke.**

1. Write the simple subject and the simple predicate on the horizontal line.
2. Think: *Who owns the vase?* Mom owns the vase. It is *Mom's* vase. Write *Mom's* on a slanted line under *vase.*

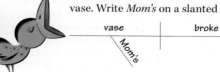

vase	broke

Mom's

ASSESS

Note which students had difficulty diagramming sentences with possessives. Assign **Practice Book** page 122 for further practice.

WRITING CONNECTION

Use pages 478–479 of the Writing portion of the book.

EXERCISE 2 (Answers)

1 sister | skis — Mark's

2 plane | landed — Our

3 bodies | glow — Fireflies'

4 coach | disappeared — Cinderella's

5 phone | rang — Your

6 brother | runs — His

7 watch | stopped — Kate's

8 robot | talks — Their

9 beanstalk | grew — Jack's

10 mother | teaches — Amy's

11 backpack | tore — Her

12 ears | flap — Elephants'

13 pocket | ripped — Its

14 kite | flew — Chris's

15 seeds | sprouted — My

EXERCISE 1 Copy each diagram. Finish it by adding the possessive noun.

1. Dogs'

   tails | wag — Dogs'

2. Dad's

   computer | froze — Dad's

EXERCISE 2 Diagram each sentence.

1. Mark's sister skis.
2. Our plane landed.
3. Fireflies' bodies glow.
4. Cinderella's coach disappeared.
5. Your phone rang.
6. His brother runs.
7. Kate's watch stopped.
8. Their robot talks.
9. Jack's beanstalk grew.
10. Amy's mother teaches.
11. Her backpack tore.
12. Elephants' ears flap.
13. Its pocket ripped.
14. Chris's kite flew.
15. My seeds sprouted.

APPLY IT NOW

Write two sentences about people you know and things they own. Use a possessive in each sentence. Then diagram each sentence.
Examples:
Grandma's rocker squeaks.
Wally's hamsters play.

Grammar in Action Find a possessive in the page 476 excerpt.

Diagramming • 187

OBJECTIVE

- **To identify and diagram sentences with adjectives, including the articles *a*, *an*, and *the***

Assign **Practice Book** page 117, Section 8.3. After students finish,
1. Give immediate feedback.
2. Review concepts as needed.
3. Model the correct answer.

Pages 4–5 of the **Answer Key** contain tips for Daily Maintenance.

WARM-UP

Write on the board the following:

_____ babies play.

Give small groups three minutes to list as many adjectives as they can to complete the sentence (*Small, Little, Tiny, Cute, Newborn, Cuddly, Funny*). Have students share their lists with the class.

TEACH

Write on the board a sentence students made up in the Warm-Up. (*Cute babies play.*)

Invite a volunteer to diagram the sentence on the board. Ask students where they think the word *cute* should go on the diagram. Point out that *cute* is an adjective that describes the word *babies* and that it should go on a slanted line below the word *babies*. Remind students that possessives also go on a slanted line because possessives also describe nouns.

Have volunteers read aloud about diagramming sentences with adjectives. Explain that the articles *a, an,* and *the* are

all diagrammed the same way because they are all adjectives. Have students suggest other sentences with adjectives to diagram.

PRACTICE

EXERCISES 1 & 2

Point out that each sentence begins with an adjective, followed by a noun and a verb. Ask volunteers to write on the board their completed diagrams. Remind students that words that are capitalized in sentences should be capitalized in diagrams.

APPLY

APPLY IT NOW

Help students generate a list of objects that could be described (*a ball, a class pet, the school bell, a computer, a flag*). Then have students diagram their sentences. Students should demonstrate the ability to diagram sentences with adjectives.

Grammar in Action. Have students first find the nouns (*monkeys, creatures, groups, omnivores*), then find the words that tell more about the nouns (*these, small, lovable, fascinating*).

8.3 Adjectives

An **adjective** tells more about a noun. An adjective tells how something looks, tastes, sounds, or smells. Adjectives can also tell how many. The articles *a, an,* and *the* are adjectives; they point out nouns.

Add an adjective to a sentence diagram by writing it on a slanted line under the noun it tells more about.

Let's do an example: **Colorful flags flew.**

1. Write the simple subject and the simple predicate on the horizontal line.

flags	flew

2. Think: *What kind of flags flew?* The answer is *colorful*. *Colorful* is an adjective that tells more about the noun *flags*. Write *colorful* on a slanted line under *flags*.

What does the adjective tell more about in this sentence diagram?

You are right if you said *drums*.

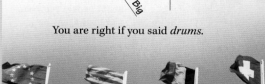

ASSESS

Note which students had difficulty diagramming sentences with adjectives. Assign **Practice Book** page 123 for further practice.

WRITING CONNECTION

Use pages 480–481 of the Writing portion of the book.

EXERCISE 2 (Answers)

1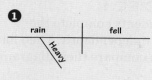

2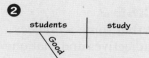

3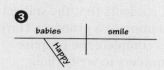

4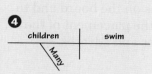

5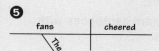

6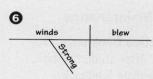

7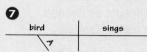

8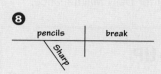

9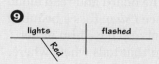

10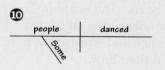

11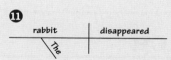

12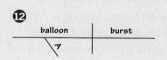

13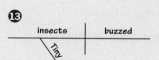

14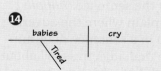

15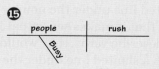

EXERCISE 1 Copy each diagram. Finish it by adding the adjective under the subject.

1. Dark

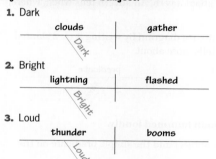

2. Bright

3. Loud

EXERCISE 2 Diagram each sentence.

1. Heavy rain fell.
2. Good students study.
3. Happy babies smile.
4. Many children swim.
5. The fans cheered.
6. Strong winds blew.
7. A bird sings.
8. Sharp pencils break.
9. Red lights flashed.
10. Some people danced.
11. The rabbit disappeared.
12. A balloon burst.
13. Tiny insects buzzed.
14. Tired babies cry.
15. Busy people rush.

APPLY IT NOW

Write two sentences to describe things around you. Use an adjective that tells about the simple subject in each sentence. Then diagram each sentence.
Examples:
Beautiful flowers bloom.
Busy students write.
Fluffy clouds float.

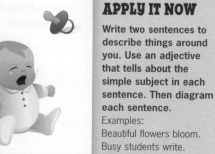

Grammar in Action. Name the adjectives in the fourth sentence on page 477.

Diagramming • 189

8.4 Adverbs

OBJECTIVE
* **To diagram sentences with adverbs**

 **Maintenance**

Assign **Practice Book** page 118, Section 8.4. After students finish,
1. Give immediate feedback.
2. Review concepts as needed.
3. Model the correct answer.

Pages 4–5 of the **Answer Key** contain tips for Daily Maintenance.

WARM-UP

Write on the board and read aloud the sentence *I sing*. Toss a beanbag to a student and have him or her add a word that tells when, where, or how. *(I sing often.)* Then have the student toss the beanbag to another student. Repeat with a new sentence and words that tell where and then how.

TEACH

Ask what is the purpose of an adverb *(to tell more about a verb).* Point out that adverbs answer the questions *when, where,* or *how* about a verb. Write on the board the following sentence:

The crowd cheered happily.

Ask a volunteer to identify the adverb in the sentence *(happily)* and to explain where the adverb should go in a sentence diagram. Reinforce that adjectives tell about nouns and that adjectives appear on a slanted line under the noun. Point out that it makes sense that if adverbs describe verbs, they would appear on a slanted line under the verb. Have a volunteer diagram the sentence on the board.

Invite volunteers to read aloud about diagramming sentences with adverbs. Challenge students to make up sentences with adverbs and to diagram them on the board.

PRACTICE

EXERCISE 1
Have students complete the exercise independently. Then have partners compare their diagrams.

EXERCISE 2
Point out that some sentences contain adjectives and that one sentence contains a possessive. Remind students that the subject can be a noun or a pronoun. Have partners complete the exercise. Ask volunteers to write their diagrams on the board and to explain the placement of the adjectives and adverbs.

APPLY

APPLY IT NOW
Suggest that students list activities they do in the morning *(wake, dress, eat, brush, talk)*. Encourage students to think of an adverb that describes each activity, write three sentences, and then diagram them. Students should demonstrate the ability to diagram sentences with adverbs.

TechTip Have students choose a sentence from the Apply It Now to diagram. You may wish to suggest the drawing tool in a word-processing program and have students use text boxes to place the words in the diagrams.

8.4 Adverbs

An **adverb** tells more about a verb. An adverb tells when, where, or how about a verb.

Add an adverb to a sentence diagram by writing it on a slanted line under the verb it tells more about.

Let's do an example: **Juan hummed loudly.**

1. Write the simple subject and the simple predicate on the horizontal line.

   | Juan | hummed |

2. Think: *How did Juan hum?* The answer is *loudly. Loudly* is an adverb that tells how about the verb *hummed.* Write *loudly* on a slanted line under *hummed.*

   | Juan | hummed |
   (loudly on slanted line)

EXERCISE 1 Copy each diagram. Finish it by adding the adverb under the verb.

1. beautifully

   | Clara | paints |
   (beautifully on slanted line)

2. fast

   | Neil | runs |
   (fast on slanted line)

ASSESS

Note which students had difficulty diagramming sentences with adverbs. Assign **Practice Book** page 124 for further practice.

WRITING CONNECTION

Use pages 482–483 of the Writing portion of the book.

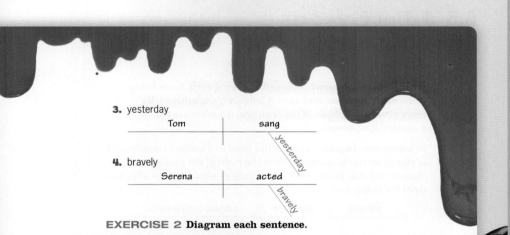

3. yesterday

Tom | sang
  — yesterday

4. bravely

Serena | acted
  — bravely

EXERCISE 2 Diagram each sentence.

1. Ballerinas dance gracefully.
2. Toddlers walk clumsily.
3. Careful students write neatly.
4. Safe drivers drive attentively.
5. The monkey chattered nearby.
6. Carol's bird sang loudly.
7. The librarian spoke quietly.
8. The doctor operated yesterday.
9. Wet paint dries slowly.
10. Good teachers explain patiently.
11. The boys laughed upstairs.
12. She tripped accidentally.
13. The bell rang suddenly.
14. We arrived late.
15. Jennifer answered confidently.

EXERCISE 2 (Answers)

1
Ballerinas | dance
  — gracefully

2
Toddlers | walk
  — clumsily

3
students | write
  — Careful — neatly

4
drivers | drive
  — Safe — attentively

5
monkey | chattered
  — The — nearby

6
bird | sang
  — Carol's — loudly

7
librarian | spoke
  — The — quietly

8
doctor | operated
  — The — yesterday

9
paint | dries
  — Wet — slowly

10
teachers | explain
  — Good — patiently

11
boys | laughed
  — The — upstairs

12
She | tripped
  — accidentally

13
bell | rang
  — The — suddenly

14
We | arrived
  — late

15
Jennifer | answered
  — confidently

APPLY IT NOW

Write three sentences about getting ready for school. Use an adverb to tell when, where, or how in each. Diagram your sentences.
Examples:
I wake early.
I dress quickly.
I eat downstairs.

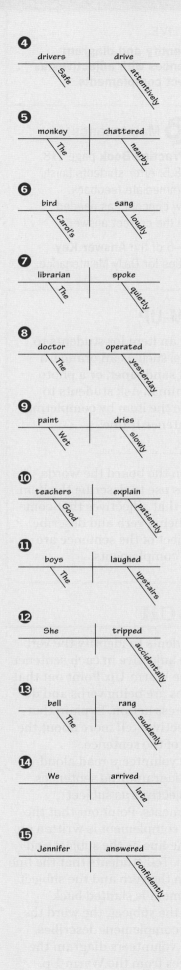

Tech Tip — Use a computer program to create a sentence diagram.

Diagramming • 191

8.5 Adjectives as Subject Complements

OBJECTIVE

- **To identify and diagram sentences with adjectives as subject complements**

 **Maintenance**

Assign **Practice Book** page 118, Section 8.5. After students finish,
1. Give immediate feedback.
2. Review concepts as needed.
3. Model the correct answer.

Pages 4–5 of the **Answer Key** contain tips for Daily Maintenance.

WARM-UP

Display an item for students to describe, such as an orange, a piece of sandpaper, or a photo of an animal. Ask students to describe the item by completing this sentence frame:

The _____ is _____.

Write on the board the words students use to describe the item. Review that adjectives that come after a being verb and describe the subject of the sentence are subject complements.

TEACH

Ask students to identify the verb and the adjective in each sentence from the Warm-Up. Point out that the verbs are being verbs and do not express action. Explain that the adjectives tell more about the subject of the sentence.

Have volunteers read aloud about diagramming sentences with adjectives as subject complements. Point out that the subject complement is written on the same line as the subject and the verb. Tell students that the line between the verb and the subject complement is slanted back toward the subject, the word the subject complement describes.

Have volunteers diagram the sentences from the Warm-Up.

PRACTICE

EXERCISE 1

Remind students that the line between the being verb and the subject complement points back to the subject. Challenge students to complete each sentence with another adjective. Have volunteers write on the board their completed sentences.

EXERCISE 2

Have partners complete the exercise. Explain that many sentences require diagramming of possessives and articles as well as of subject complements.

APPLY

APPLY IT NOW

Help students brainstorm places they could describe *(a park, a museum, a store).* Students should demonstrate the ability to diagram sentences with adjectives as subject complements.

Grammar in Action. Help students identify the subject *(Callimicos),* the verb *(are),* and the subject complement in the sentence *(omnivorous)* before they diagram the sentence. Have a volunteer write the diagram on the board.

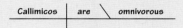

8.5 Adjectives as Subject Complements

A **subject complement** comes after a being verb. Some being verbs are *is, are, was,* and *were.* A subject complement tells more about the subject of the sentence. An adjective can be a subject complement.

In a sentence diagram, an adjective used as a subject complement is placed on the horizontal line to the right of the predicate. A slanted line that points back to the subject separates the adjective from the being verb.

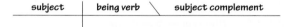

Let's do an example: **Giraffes are tall.**

1. Write the subject and the being verb on the horizontal line.

Giraffes	are

2. Think: *What are giraffes?* Giraffes are *tall. Tall* is a subject complement. It is an adjective that tells more about the subject, *giraffes.* Draw a slanted line after the being verb that points back to *giraffes.* Write *tall* after the verb.

Giraffes	are	\ tall

ASSESS

Note which students had difficulty diagramming sentences with adjectives as subject complements. Assign **Practice Book** page 125 for further practice.

WRITING CONNECTION

Use pages 484–485 of the Writing portion of the book.

EXERCISE 2 (Answers)

1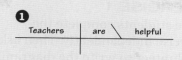

Teachers | are \ helpful

2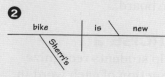

bike | is \ new — Sherri's

3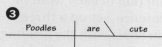

Poodles | are \ cute

4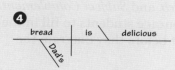

bread | is \ delicious — Dad's

5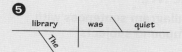

library | was \ quiet — The

6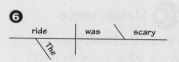

ride | was \ scary — The

7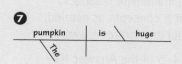

pumpkin | is \ huge — The

8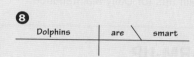

Dolphins | are \ smart

9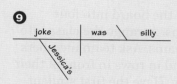

joke | was \ silly — Jessica's

10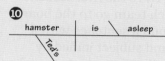

hamster | is \ asleep — Ted's

11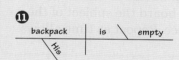

backpack | is \ empty — His

12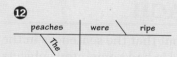

peaches | were \ ripe — The

13

cat | is \ black — Ida's

14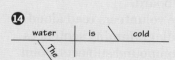

water | is \ cold — The

15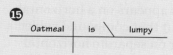

Oatmeal | is \ lumpy

EXERCISE 1 Copy each diagram. Finish it by adding the adjective as a subject complement.

1. sweet

Sugar | is \ sweet

2. dark

Caves | are \ dark

3. funny

Monkeys | are \ funny

EXERCISE 2 Diagram each sentence.

1. Teachers are helpful.
2. Sherri's bike is new.
3. Poodles are cute.
4. Dad's bread is delicious.
5. The library was quiet.
6. The ride was scary.
7. The pumpkin is huge.
8. Dolphins are smart.
9. Jessica's joke was silly.
10. Ted's hamster is asleep.
11. His backpack is empty.
12. The peaches were ripe.
13. Ida's cat is black.
14. The water is cold.
15. Oatmeal is lumpy.

APPLY IT NOW

Write two sentences about places you know. Use adjectives as subject complements in your sentences. Then diagram the sentences.
Examples:
The beach is noisy.
The sand is hot.

Grammar in Action — Diagram the third sentence in the fourth paragraph on page 477.

Diagramming • 193

OBJECTIVE

- **To diagram sentences with compound subjects**

 **Maintenance**

Assign **Practice Book** page 118, Section 8.6. After students finish,
1. Give immediate feedback.
2. Review concepts as needed.
3. Model the correct answer.

Pages 4–5 of the **Answer Key** contain tips for Daily Maintenance.

WARM-UP

Divide the board into four sections. Arrange the class into four teams. Ask team members to stand in rows in front of their section. Have the first student from each team go to the board. Read aloud a sentence with a compound subject joined by *and*. Challenge students to write on the board the subject of the sentence. Repeat as time allows.

TEACH

Point out that the sentences in the Warm-Up had compound subjects joined together by the word *and*. Ask students to give additional examples of sentences with compound subjects. Write them on the board.

Have volunteers read aloud about diagramming sentences with compound subjects. Point out that the subject of a sentence always appears on a horizontal line, but that compound subjects appear on separate horizontal lines connected by a dashed line with the conjunction. Encourage students to diagram some the sentences you wrote on the board.

PRACTICE

EXERCISE 1

Have students complete the exercise independently. Then ask a volunteer to write the diagram on the board.

EXERCISE 2

To help students recognize the function of each word in the sentence, set up a three-column chart with the headings *Subjects, Conjunction, Verb, Adverb,* and *Subject Complement.* Encourage students to fill in the chart before they diagram the sentences. Point out that most of the items do not have adverbs or subject complements.

APPLY

APPLY IT NOW

Help students brainstorm a list of friends and things they do together. Explain that students' sentences should have a simple, one-word predicate as in the example sentence. Students should demonstrate the ability to diagram sentences with compound subjects.

8.6 Compound Subjects

A sentence may have more than one subject.

SIMPLE SUBJECT	CONJUNCTION	SIMPLE SUBJECT	SIMPLE PREDICATE
Eagles	**and**	**hawks**	**soar.**

In a sentence diagram, each subject goes on a separate line. The conjunction that connects the subjects goes on a dashed line.

Bald eagle

Let's do an example: **Eagles and hawks soar.**

1. Draw two short horizontal lines. Write a subject on each line. Connect the subjects as shown. Write *and* on the dashed vertical line.

2. What do eagles and hawks do? They *soar. Soar* is the predicate. Write *soar* on a horizontal line after the subjects. Draw a vertical line to separate the verb from the subjects.

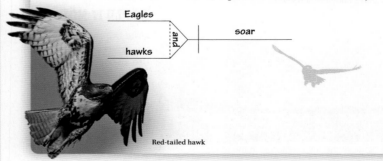

Red-tailed hawk

ASSESS

Note which students had difficulty diagramming sentences with compound subjects. Assign **Practice Book** page 126 for further practice.

WRITING CONNECTION

Use pages 486–487 of the Writing portion of the book.

EXERCISE 2 (Answers)

❶ Lions **and** tigers | growl

❷ Lily **and** Hope | sail

❸ Flowers **and** trees | grow

❹ Carrots **and** celery | crunch

❺ Fingers **and** toes | wiggle

❻ Nurses **and** doctors | help

❼ Sarah **and** Ben | write \ neatly

❽ Airplanes **and** helicopters | fly

❾ Horses **and** zebras | run \ swiftly

❿ Mom **and** Dad | clean \ carefully

⓫ Apples **and** cherries | taste \ sweet

⓬ Diamonds **and** emeralds | sparkle

⓭ Rabbits **and** kangaroos | hop

⓮ Whales **and** porpoises | swim

⓯ Molly **and** Alicia | laughed

EXERCISE 1 Copy the diagram. Finish it by adding the compound subject.

Bats and bees

Bats **and** bees | fly

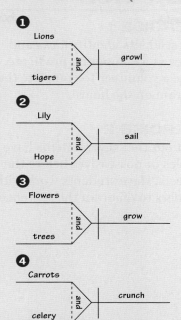

EXERCISE 2 Diagram each sentence.

1. Lions and tigers growl.
2. Lily and Hope sail.
3. Flowers and trees grow.
4. Carrots and celery crunch.
5. Fingers and toes wiggle.
6. Nurses and doctors help.
7. Sarah and Ben write neatly.
8. Airplanes and helicopters fly.
9. Horses and zebras run swiftly.
10. Mom and Dad clean carefully.
11. Apples and cherries taste sweet.
12. Diamonds and emeralds sparkle.
13. Rabbits and kangaroos hop.
14. Whales and porpoises swim.
15. Molly and Alicia laughed.

APPLY IT NOW

Write two sentences with compound subjects. You might use the names of friends as the subjects of your sentences. Diagram your sentences.
Example:
Don and Marco race.

Diagramming • 195

OBJECTIVE

- **To diagram sentences with compound predicates**

DAILY Maintenance

Assign **Practice Book** page 119, Section 8.7. After students finish,
1. Give immediate feedback.
2. Review concepts as needed.
3. Model the correct answer.

Pages 4–5 of the **Answer Key** contain tips for Daily Maintenance.

WARM-UP

Write the following on the board:

I _____ and _____.

Tell students to think of two things they do every day. Ask several volunteers to complete the sentence on the board.

TEACH

Ask students to tell what a compound subject is *(a sentence that has more than one subject joined by the word* and*)*. Review how sentences with compound subjects are diagrammed. Ask a volunteer to write on the board a diagram of a sentence with a compound subject.

Have volunteers read aloud about diagramming sentences with compound predicates. Ask students to tell how diagramming sentences with compound predicates is similar to diagramming sentences with compound subjects. *(The subjects and predicates both appear on horizontal lines connected by a dashed line and the word* and.*)* Ask students to diagram the sentences on the board from the Warm-Up.

PRACTICE

EXERCISE 1

Help students identify *kicks* and *passes* as a compound predicate. Invite a volunteer to complete the diagram on the board.

EXERCISE 2

Point out that several items have articles or possessives before the subjects. Have students work with partners to diagram the sentences.

APPLY

APPLY IT NOW

Help students brainstorm sports and list the verbs on the board. Suggest that students choose four verbs for their sentences. Students should demonstrate the ability to diagram sentences with compound predicates.

8.7 Compound Predicates

A sentence may have more than one predicate.

SIMPLE SUBJECT	SIMPLE PREDICATE	CONJUNCTION	SIMPLE PREDICATE
Jason	bats	and	catches.

In a sentence diagram, each verb goes on a separate line. The verbs are connected by a dashed line for the conjunction.

Let's do an example: **Jason bats and catches.**

1. Write the subject on the horizontal line. Draw a vertical line after the subject.
2. What does Jason do? Jason *bats* and *catches.* Draw two horizontal lines, one for each verb. Write a verb on each line. Connect the horizontal lines with a dashed vertical line. Write *and* on the dashed line.

196 • Section 8.7

ASSESS

Note which students had difficulty diagramming sentences with compound predicates. Assign **Practice Book** page 127 for further practice.

WRITING CONNECTION

Use pages 488–489 of the Writing portion of the book.

EXERCISE 2 (Answers)

1 horses | Bob's | and — trot / gallop

2 Farmers | and — plant / harvest

3 kite | The | and — rose / fell

4 Sean | and — dusts / irons

5 audience | The | and — stood / applauded

6 teachers | Our | and — instruct / explain

7 Monkeys | and — climb / swing

8 George | and — reads / writes

9 Artists | and — imagine / create

10 students | The | and — listened / discussed

11 flowers | The | and — bloomed / faded

12 Cats | and — purr / meow

13 Stars | and — twinkle / glow

14 hearts | Our | and — beat / pump

15 friends | Good | and — call / e-mail

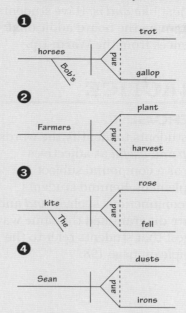

EXERCISE 1 Copy the diagram. Finish it by adding the compound predicate.

kicks and passes

Kate | and — kicks / passes

EXERCISE 2 Diagram each sentence.

1. Bob's horses trot and gallop.
2. Farmers plant and harvest.
3. The kite rose and fell.
4. Sean dusts and irons.
5. The audience stood and applauded.
6. Our teachers instruct and explain.
7. Monkeys climb and swing.
8. George reads and writes.
9. Artists imagine and create.
10. The students listened and discussed.
11. The flowers bloomed and faded.
12. Cats purr and meow.
13. Stars twinkle and glow.
14. Our hearts beat and pump.
15. Good friends call and e-mail.

APPLY IT NOW

Write two sentences with compound predicates about playing a sport. **Diagram your sentences.**
Examples:
I swim and dive.
The player shoots and scores.

Diagramming • 197

OBJECTIVE

- **To diagram sentences that have adjectives as compound subject complements**

 **Maintenance**

Assign **Practice Book** page 119, Section 8.8. After students finish,
1. Give immediate feedback.
2. Review concepts as needed.
3. Model the correct answer.

Pages 4–5 of the **Answer Key** contain tips for Daily Maintenance.

WARM-UP

Write on the board a topic that can be described with many adjectives *(koalas)*. Ask students to brainstorm a list of adjectives to describe the topic *(cute, cuddly, slow)*. Arrange the class into two teams and give students five minutes to write as many sentences as possible that have two subject complements that describe koalas. The team with the most correct sentences wins.

TEACH

Write on the board a diagram of a sentence with a subject complement.

Koalas are cuddly.

Ask students to describe how they think a sentence with two subject complements might be diagrammed.

Have volunteers read aloud about diagramming sentences with adjectives as compound subject complements. Point out that diagramming sentences with compound subject complements is similar to diagramming sentences with compound subjects and compound predicates. Point out that *but* is also a conjunction and

is written on the dashed vertical line, just like *and* is. Have students diagram on the board additional sentences from the Warm-Up.

PRACTICE

EXERCISE 1

Ask students to identify the words *sharp* and *useful* as adjectives used as a compound subject complement. Remind students that conjunctions such as *and* and *but* are diagrammed the same way. Suggest that students refer to the example on page 198.

EXERCISE 2

Suggest that students copy each sentence, circle the adjectives used as subject complements, and underline the conjunction before diagramming.

APPLY

APPLY IT NOW

As a class, match each season with the appropriate adjectives from the list. Students should demonstrate the ability to diagram sentences with adjectives as compound subject complements.

8.8 Compound Subject Complements

Some sentences have more than one adjective used as a subject complement.

SIMPLE SUBJECT	BEING VERB	TWO ADJECTIVES AS SUBJECT COMPLEMENTS
Bats	**are**	**scary but helpful.**

To diagram a compound subject complement, you will need a line for each adjective and a place to write the conjunction.

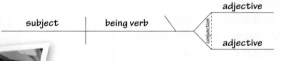

Let's do an example:

Bats are scary but helpful.

1. Diagram the subject and the being verb.
2. *Scary* and *helpful* are adjectives used as subject complements that tell more about bats. Draw a slanted line that points back to the subject. Then draw a horizontal line for each adjective. Use a dashed vertical line to connect these horizontal lines. Write *but* on the dashed line.

The Indian flying fox is one of the world's largest bats.

Grey long-eared bat

ASSESS

Note which students had difficulty diagramming sentences with adjectives as compound subject complements. Assign **Practice Book** page 128 for further practice.

WRITING CONNECTION

Use pages 490–491 of the Writing portion of the book.

EXERCISE 2 (Answers)

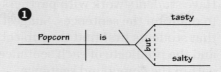

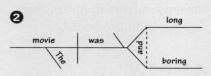

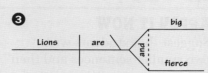

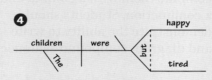

❺ street / was / and — dark / quiet (The)

❻ marathon / was / and — long / tiring (The)

❼ doctor / is / but — concerned / hopeful (The)

❽ blanket / is / and — warm / cozy (Judy's)

❾ soup / is / but — hot / bland (The)

❿ vase / is / and — beautiful / expensive (Her)

⓫ cat / is / and — black / white (The)

⓬ Michael / was / but — exhausted / happy

⓭ roses / were / and — large / fragrant (The)

⓮ story / was / and — weird / scary (Jaime's)

⓯ sneakers / are / but — old / comfortable (My)

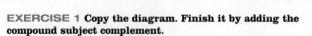

EXERCISE 1 Copy the diagram. Finish it by adding the compound subject complement.

sharp but useful

Scissors / are / but — sharp / useful

EXERCISE 2 Diagram each sentence.

1. Popcorn is tasty but salty.
2. The movie was long and boring.
3. Lions are big and fierce.
4. The children were happy but tired.
5. The street was dark and quiet.
6. The marathon was long and tiring.
7. The doctor is concerned but hopeful.
8. Judy's blanket is warm and cozy.
9. The soup is hot but bland.
10. Her vase is beautiful and expensive.
11. The cat is black and white.
12. Michael was exhausted but happy.
13. The roses were large and fragrant.
14. Jaime's story was weird and scary.
15. My sneakers are old but comfortable.

APPLY IT NOW

Write a sentence about summer, winter, spring, or fall. Use a compound subject complement. Choose from the list below. Diagram your sentence.

cool but sunny
hot and humid
crisp and colorful
cold and snowy

Diagramming • 199

OBJECTIVE

- **To diagram compound sentences**

 **Maintenance**

Assign **Practice Book** page 119, Section 8.9. After students finish,
1. Give immediate feedback.
2. Review concepts as needed.
3. Model the correct answer.

Pages 4–5 of the **Answer Key** contain tips for Daily Maintenance.

WARM-UP

Invite two volunteers at a time to come to the front of the room. Have students suggest two actions for the volunteers to act out. Then have students use one sentence to describe what the two students did. Write on the board the sentences students suggest.

TEACH

Have volunteers read aloud about diagramming compound sentences. Discuss how diagramming compound sentences is similar to diagramming sentences with compound subjects and compound predicates.

Tell students to identify both subjects and predicates in the example diagram. Then remind students to diagram the individual sentences within the compound sentence. Explain that the two sentences are connected with a dashed line and a conjunction. Invite volunteers to diagram the sentences from the Warm-Up.

PRACTICE

EXERCISE 1

Have volunteers diagram their sentences on the board. Ask students to identify each sentence in the compound sentence.

EXERCISE 2

Have students work with partners to diagram the sentences. Suggest that students first find the subject and the predicate of each sentence within the compound sentence. Have volunteers diagram their sentences on the board.

APPLY

APPLY IT NOW

Suggest that students write two smaller sentences and then combine them with a comma and a conjunction. Students should demonstrate the ability to write and diagram compound sentences.

TechTip Have students download a royalty-free MP3 file or find the lyrics to a popular song online.

ASSESS

Note which students had difficulty diagramming compound sentences. Assign **Practice Book** page 129 for further practice.

WRITING CONNECTION

Use pages 492–493 of the Writing portion of the book.

8.9 Compound Sentences

Compound sentences—sentences that are made up of two smaller sentences—can also be diagrammed.

SIMPLE SUBJECT	SIMPLE PREDICATE	CONJUNCTION	SIMPLE SUBJECT	SIMPLE PREDICATE
Jane	watered,	and	Joe	weeded.

To diagram this sentence, put two sentence diagrams together. Connect the sentences with a dashed vertical line. Write the conjunction on the dashed line.

```
          subject    |    predicate
conjunction
          subject    |    predicate
```

Let's do an example: **Jane watered, and Joe weeded.**

1. Diagram each smaller sentence. Put one above the other.
2. Draw a dashed vertical line to connect the sentences. Write the conjunction on the dashed line.

```
       Jane    |    watered
and
       Joe     |    weeded
```

EXERCISE 2 (Answers)

1

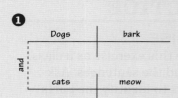

2

3

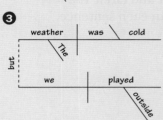

4

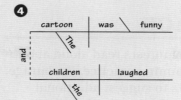

5

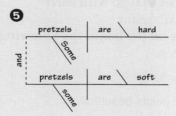

6

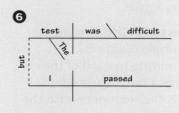

7

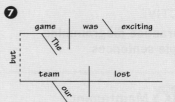

8

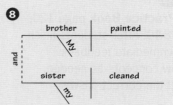

9

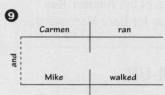

10

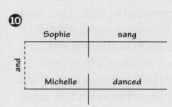

11

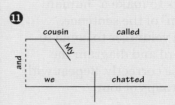

12

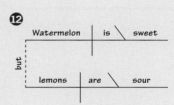

13

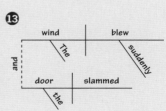

14

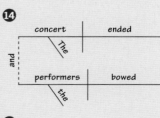

15

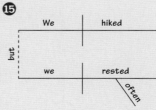

EXERCISE 1 Copy each diagram. Finish it by adding the second sentence.

1. Bart sings.

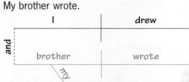

2. My brother wrote.

EXERCISE 2 Diagram each sentence.

1. Dogs bark, and cats meow.
2. The wind howled, and the lightning flashed.
3. The weather was cold, but we played outside.
4. The cartoon was funny, and the children laughed.
5. Some pretzels are hard, and some pretzels are soft.
6. The test was difficult, but I passed.
7. The game was exciting, but our team lost.
8. My brother painted, and my sister cleaned.
9. Carmen ran, and Mike walked.
10. Sophie sang, and Michelle danced.
11. My cousin called, and we chatted.
12. Watermelon is sweet, but lemons are sour.
13. The wind blew suddenly, and the door slammed.
14. The concert ended, and the performers bowed.
15. We hiked, but we rested often.

APPLY IT NOW

Write two compound sentences. Trade your sentences with a partner. Diagram each other's sentences.

Tech Tip Diagram a compound sentence from a popular song.

Diagramming • 201

8.10 Diagramming Practice

OBJECTIVE
• **To practice diagramming simple sentences**

 **Maintenance**

Assign **Practice Book** page 120, Section 8.10. After students finish,
1. Give immediate feedback.
2. Review concepts as needed.
3. Model the correct answer.

Pages 4–5 of the **Answer Key** contain tips for Daily Maintenance.

WARM-UP

Write on separate note cards *subject, predicate, adjective,* and *adverb*. Choose four students and give each student a card. Challenge students to give a word for their sentence part and to stand together with the other students to make a "human diagram" of the sentence. Invite a volunteer to come to the board and diagram the sentence correctly. Repeat with more groups of four.

TEACH

Have volunteers read aloud about diagramming practice. Encourage students to suggest additional sentences that go with each sample diagram.

Write on the board the following sentences:

Turner sang.

Jenna paints beautifully.

The sky is blue.

Write on the board in random order sample diagrams corresponding to each of the sentences. Challenge students to match the sentences with the correct diagrams.

PRACTICE

EXERCISE 1
Complete this exercise as a class. Read aloud the sentences. Ask volunteers to identify the parts of each sentence before they identify the correct diagram for each sentence.

EXERCISE 2
Suggest that students underline the subject and circle the predicate in each sentence.

8.10 Diagramming Practice

You have learned to diagram different kinds of sentences. Can you match the correct diagram with each of these sentences?

1. Jake snowboards fast.
2. We skated.
3. The lake is beautiful.

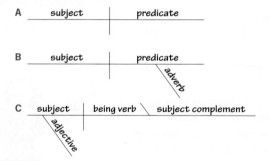

You are right if you matched sentence 1 with B, sentence 2 with A, and sentence 3 with C. Notice that in sentence 3, the article *the* goes with the noun *lake*.

EXERCISE 1 Match each sentence with one of the diagrams above—A, B, or C.

1. The milk is cold. C
2. Parades move slowly. B
3. Bands played. A
4. Drummers drummed loudly. B
5. People cheered. A
6. The dogs are hungry. C
7. Corinna answered last. B
8. The car is old. C
9. Musicians practice. A
10. Authors write. A

202 • Section 8.10

APPLY

APPLY IT NOW

Suggest that students copy the diagram and insert words into the diagram. Then have students write the sentence that the diagram illustrates. Students should demonstrate the ability to write and diagram simple sentences.

ASSESS

Note which students had difficulty diagramming simple sentences. Assign **Practice Book** page 130 for further practice.

WRITING CONNECTION

Use pages 494–495 of the Writing portion of the book.

EXERCISE 2 **Write out the sentences.**

1. Roses | smell
2. Mom | works / late
3. snakes | slither / Shiny / swiftly
4. grapes | are \ sour / The
5. eggs | are \ brown / Some
6. Flowers | wilt
7. Ice | melts / slowly
8. Julie | practices / often
9. Tara | paints / well
10. Antelopes | run / fast
11. peanuts | are \ salty / The
12. Fire | burns / rapidly

APPLY IT NOW

Write one sentence for each diagram pattern on page 202. Then diagram the sentences.

Diagramming • 203

EXERCISE 2 (Answers)

1. Roses smell.
2. Mom works late.
3. Shiny snakes slither swiftly.
4. The grapes are sour.
5. Some eggs are brown.
6. Flowers wilt.
7. Ice melts slowly.
8. Julie practices often.
9. Tara paints well.
10. Antelopes run fast.
11. The peanuts are salty.
12. Fire burns rapidly.

OBJECTIVE

- **To practice diagramming sentences with compound parts**

DAILY Maintenance

Assign **Practice Book** page 120, Section 8.11. After students finish,
1. Give immediate feedback.
2. Review concepts as needed.
3. Model the correct answer.

Pages 4–5 of the **Answer Key** contain tips for Daily Maintenance.

WARM-UP

Have each student write a sentence describing his or her favorite activity. Then have small groups combine two sentences at a time to make compound sentences. Ask groups to write the words from each sentence on separate note cards. Ask students to put the cards together on the floor in the correct places to make a large diagram for each sentence.

TEACH

Write on the board one sentence with each of the following: compound subject, compound predicate, adjective as compound subject complement, compound sentence. Ask volunteers to identify the compound part of each sentence.

Have a volunteer read aloud about more diagramming practice. Ask students to identify the compound parts of each example sentence. Have students match the sentences to the diagrams. Ask students which diagram they would use for each sentence on the board. Invite volunteers to come to the board and to diagram each sentence you wrote there.

PRACTICE

EXERCISE 1

Suggest that students first identify the compound part in each sentence. Review how each compound part is shown in a diagram. Ask volunteers to match each sentence with the appropriate diagram.

EXERCISE 2

Suggest that students identify the subject and predicate before diagramming. Remind them that the first word of the sentence is capitalized in the diagram. Remind students that compound sentences have a comma before the conjunction.

8.11 More Diagramming Practice

You have learned to diagram sentences that have compound parts. Can you match the correct diagram with each of these sentences?

1. Mom shops and cooks.
2. Jim and Chloe bake.
3. Papayas are orange, and strawberries are red.

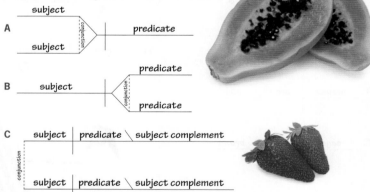

You are right if you matched sentence 1 with B, sentence 2 with A, and sentence 3 with C.

EXERCISE 1 Match each sentence with one of the diagrams above—A, B, or C.

1. Planes land and depart. B
2. Bands and choirs practice. A
3. Cherries are sweet, and lemons are sour. C
4. Mom is busy, and Dad is tired. C
5. Scientists study and discover. B
6. Tops and pinwheels spin. A
7. Class was hard, but I was successful. C
8. Diamonds shine and sparkle. B

APPLY

APPLY IT NOW

Suggest that students write three sentences on a single topic, such as a movie, a sport, or a hobby. Suggest that students draw the blank diagrams and write a sentence that matches each diagram. Ask students to write their diagrams on the board and point out the compound parts. Students should demonstrate the ability to write and diagram sentences with compound parts.

ASSESS

Note which students had difficulty practicing diagramming sentences with compound parts. Assign **Practice Book** page 131 for further practice.

WRITING CONNECTION

Use pages 496–497 of the Writing portion of the book.

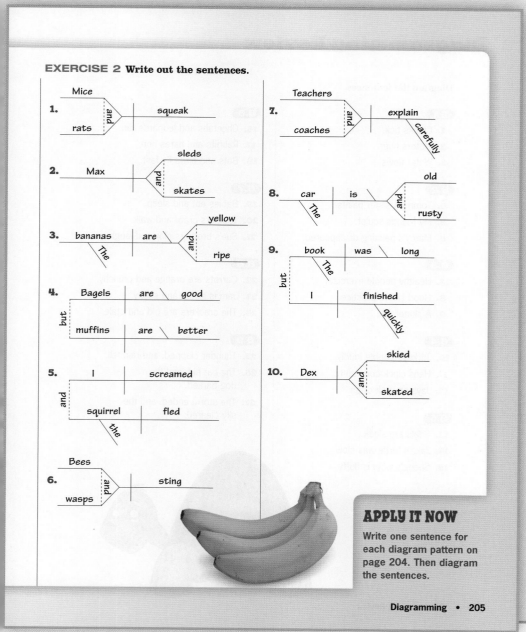

EXERCISE 2 Write out the sentences.

APPLY IT NOW

Write one sentence for each diagram pattern on page 204. Then diagram the sentences.

EXERCISE 2 (Answers)

1. Mice and rats squeak.
2. Max sleds and skates.
3. The bananas are yellow and ripe.
4. Bagels are good, but muffins are better.
5. I screamed, and the squirrel fled.
6. Bees and wasps sting.
7. Teachers and coaches explain carefully.
8. The car is old and rusty.
9. The book was long, but I finished quickly.
10. Dex skied and skated.

Diagramming Review

ASSESS

Use the Diagramming Review as homework, as a practice test, or as an informal assessment. Following are some options for use.

ANSWERS

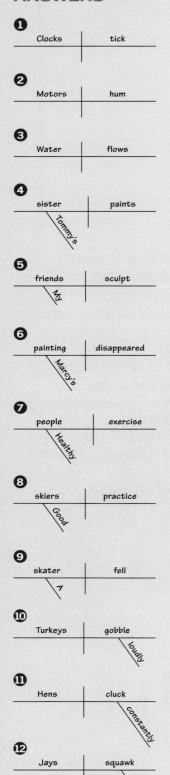

1
| Clocks | tick |

2
| Motors | hum |

3
| Water | flows |

4
| sister | paints |
Tommy's

5
| friends | sculpt |
My

6
| painting | disappeared |
Marcy's

7
| people | exercise |
Healthy

8
| skiers | practice |
Good

9
| skater | fell |
A

10
| Turkeys | gobble |
loudly

11
| Hens | cluck |
constantly

12
| Jays | squawk |
often

Homework

You may wish to assign one group the odd items and another group the even items. When you next meet, review the correct answers as a group. Be sure to model how to arrive at the correct answer.

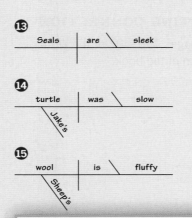

13
| Seals | are | sleek |

14
| turtle | was | slow |
Jake's

15
| wool | is | fluffy |
Sheep's

Practice Test

Use the Diagramming Review as a diagnostic tool. Assign the entire review or just specific sections. After students have finished, identify which concepts require more attention. Reteach concepts as necessary.

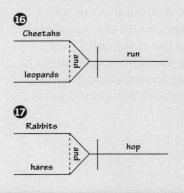

16
Cheetahs
and / leopards — run

17
Rabbits
and / hares — hop

Diagramming Review

Diagram the sentences.

8.1
1. Clocks tick.
2. Motors hum.
3. Water flows.

8.2
4. Tommy's sister paints.
5. My friends sculpt.
6. Marcy's painting disappeared.

8.3
7. Healthy people exercise.
8. Good skiers practice.
9. A skater fell.

8.4
10. Turkeys gobble loudly.
11. Hens cluck constantly.
12. Jays squawk often.

8.5
13. Seals are sleek.
14. Jake's turtle was slow.
15. Sheep's wool is fluffy.

8.6
16. Cheetahs and leopards run.
17. Rabbits and hares hop.
18. Bats and birds fly fast.

8.7
19. Babies eat and sleep.
20. Toddlers crawl and walk.
21. Sue's brothers play and laugh.

8.8
22. Carrots are orange and crunchy.
23. Jam is sweet and sticky.
24. The crackers are old and stale.

8.9
25. Thunder clapped, and rain fell.
26. The cat hid, and the dog barked.
27. The storm ended, and the sky cleared.

Informal Assessment

Use the review as preparation for the formal assessment. Count the review as a portion of the grade. Have students work to find the correct answers and use their corrected review as a study guide for the formal assessment.

WRITING CONNECTION

Use pages 498–499 of the Writing portion of the book.

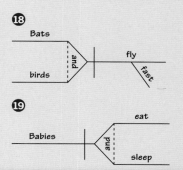

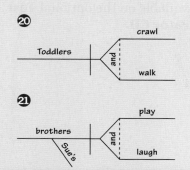

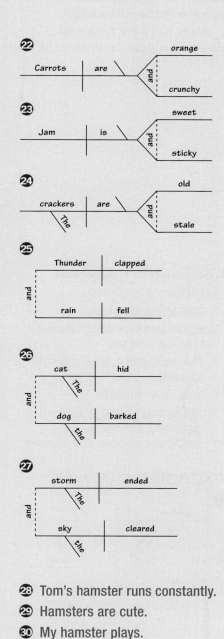

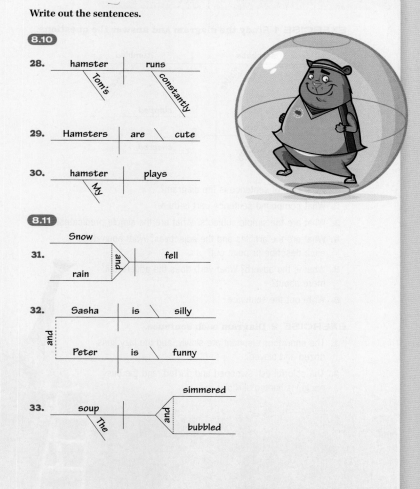

Write out the sentences.

28. Tom's hamster runs constantly.

29. Hamsters are cute.

30. My hamster plays.

31. Snow and rain fell.

32. Sasha is silly, and Peter is funny.

33. The soup simmered and bubbled.

Diagramming • 207

Diagramming Challenge

ASSESS

Allow students time to study the diagram carefully. If students have difficulty with any questions or the diagrams, suggest that they refer to the section that teaches that skill. These exercises can be completed by individuals, small groups, or the entire class.

After you have reviewed diagramming, administer the Section 8 Assessment on pages 25–28 in the **Assessment Book,** or create a customized test with the optional **Test Generator CD.**

You may also wish to administer the Section 8 Summative Assessment on pages 37–38 of the **Assessment Book.** This test is also available on the optional **Test Generator CD.**

WRITING CONNECTION

Use pages 500–501 of the Writing portion of the book.

Students can complete a formal research report using the Writer's Workshop on pages 502–513.

EXERCISE 1 (Answers)

1. compound sentence
2. compound predicate
3. acrobats, spectators; tumbled, clapped, cheered
4. The, nimble, the, happy; acrobats, spectators
5. gracefully; tumbled
6. The nimble acrobats tumbled gracefully, and the happy spectators clapped and cheered.

EXERCISE 2 (Answers)

❶

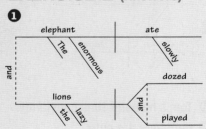

❷

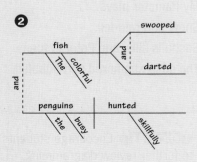

Diagramming Challenge

EXERCISE 1 Study the diagram and answer the questions.

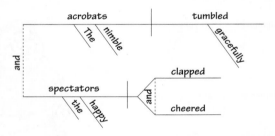

1. What kind of sentence is the diagram?
2. What compound sentence part is there?
3. What are the simple subjects? What are the simple predicates?
4. What are the articles and the adjectives? What noun does each describe or point out?
5. What is the adverb? What verb does the adverb tell more about?
6. Write out the sentence.

EXERCISE 2 Diagram each sentence.

1. The enormous elephant ate slowly, and the lazy lions dozed and played.
2. The colorful fish swooped and darted, and the busy penguins hunted skillfully.

WRITTEN AND ORAL COMMUNICATION

Chapters

1 Personal Narratives

2 How-to Articles

3 Descriptions

4 Personal Letters

5 Book Reports

6 Persuasive Writing

7 Creative Writing: Realistic Fiction

8 Research Reports

CHAPTER FOCUS

LESSON 1: What Makes a Good Personal Narrative?

LESSON 2: Beginning, Middle, and Ending

- **GRAMMAR:** Sentences
- **WRITING SKILLS:** Strong Verbs
- **WORD STUDY:** Colorful Adjectives
- **STUDY SKILLS:** Dictionary
- **SPEAKING AND LISTENING SKILLS:** Oral Personal Narratives
- **WRITER'S WORKSHOP:** Personal Narratives

SUPPORT MATERIALS

Practice Book
Writing, pages 132–136

Assessment Book
Chapter 1 Writing Skills, pages 39–40
Personal Narrative Writing Prompt, pages 41–42

Rubrics
Student, page 247y
Teacher, page 247z

Test Generator CD

Grammar
Section 1, pages 1–26

Customizable Lesson Plans
www.voyagesinenglish.com

Personal Narratives

WHAT IS A PERSONAL NARRATIVE?

Personal narratives are about significant events in writers' lives. The writer of a good personal narrative knows how to let his or her personality shine through by the use of humor, phrasing, dialogue, or a combination of these. Good personal narratives use natural language that does not seem stiff or contrived.

A good personal narrative includes the following:

- ☐ A topic relating to a real event in the writer's life
- ☐ A first-person point of view
- ☐ A structure that includes an engaging introduction, a cohesive body, and a satisfying conclusion
- ☐ A coherent organization that uses chronological order, flows logically, and excludes unnecessary details
- ☐ Strong verbs and colorful adjectives
- ☐ A voice that allows the narrator's personality to come through

LiNK Use the following titles to offer your students examples of well-crafted personal narratives:

Cal Ripken, Jr.: Play Ball!
by Gail Herman, Cal Ripken, and Mike Bryan

Uncle Andy's by James Warhola

Water Buffalo Days by Huynh Quang Nhuong

When Everybody Wore a Hat by William Steig

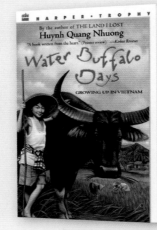

> **"Sometimes you can tell a large story with a tiny subject."**
>
> —Eliot Porter

WRITER'S WORKSHOP TIPS

Follow these ideas and tips to help you and your class get the most out of the Writer's Workshop:

- Review the traits of good writing. Use the chart on the inside back cover of the student and teacher editions.
- Encourage students to keep a journal to record important or interesting personal experiences.
- Invite students to bring in family photos or drawings of favorite family events.
- Fill your classroom library with autobiographies and novels written in the first person.
- Bring in songs that tell a first-person narrative.
- Bring in podcasts or recordings of personal narratives from public radio programs, the library, or the Internet.
- Have partners interview each other about significant life events. Tell students that the questions can prompt ideas for developing their personal narratives.
- Show documentaries of children or adults telling their own stories.
- Have students create time lines of their personal narratives.
- Invite columnists or memoirists to speak to the class about why and how they publish their own stories.

CONNECT WITH GRAMMAR

Throughout the Writer's Workshop, look for opportunities to integrate sentences with writing personal narratives.

- ☐ During the drafting stage, encourage students to use statements, questions, commands, and exclamations in their personal narratives.
- ☐ During the copyediting stage, have students read aloud and combine sentences to improve sentence fluency.
- ☐ During the proofreading stage, have students make sure each sentence has a subject and a predicate.
- ☐ Have students identify and correct run-on sentences.

SCORING RUBRIC

Personal Narrative

Point Values
0 = not evident
1 = minimal evidence of mastery
2 = evidence of development toward mastery
3 = strong evidence of mastery
4 = outstanding evidence of mastery

Ideas	POINTS
topic relating to a real event	
events in time order	
Organization	
a beginning	
a middle	
an ending	
Voice	
the writer's point of view, using *I, me, we,* and *us*	
Word Choice	
colorful adjectives	
time words	
Sentence Fluency	
strong verbs	
Conventions	
correct grammar and usage	
correct spelling	
correct punctuation and capitalization	
Presentation	
neatness	
consistent margins and spacing	
photos or illustrations	
Additional Items	
Total	

Full-sized, reproducible rubrics can be found at the end of this chapter.

Personal Narratives

INTRODUCING THE GENRE

Tell students they will learn about personal narratives in this chapter. Write the following sentence on the board:

> Each student will have a personal copy of the book.

Ask the following question: *What do you think the word* personal *means? (It means "individual," or "belonging to someone.")* Then tell students that *narrative* means "story." Explain that if you asked the question *What did you do last weekend?* their answer would be a personal narrative.

Introduce the following characteristics of a personal narrative:

- A personal narrative is a true story about the writer.
- A personal narrative is told from the writer's point of view.
- A personal narrative has a beginning, a middle, and an ending.
- The events are described in the order in which they happened.

Reading the Literature Excerpt

Have a student read aloud the excerpt. Ask volunteers to point out reasons that this piece is a personal narrative. Ask students to name similar pieces they have read or heard.

Personal Narratives

LiNK Water Buffalo Days

The excerpts in Chapter 1 introduce students to relevant examples of personal narratives. *Water Buffalo Days* is a strong example of a personal narrative because it does the following:

- Tells a true story about the writer
- Is told from the writer's point of view
- Has a clear beginning—the writer's birth

As students encounter the different examples throughout the chapter, be sure to point out characteristics of personal narratives. You may wish to have students identify kinds of sentences, subjects and predicates, and combined sentences in the literature excerpts.

LiNK Water Buffalo Days
Growing Up in Vietnam
by Huynh Quang Nhuong

I was born in the central highlands of Vietnam in a small hamlet on a riverbank that had a deep jungle on one side and a chain of high mountains on the other. . . . Like all farmers' children in the hamlet, I started working at the age of six. I helped look after the family herd of water buffaloes. Someone always had to be with the herd, because no matter how carefully water buffaloes were trained, they were always ready to nibble young rice plants when no one was looking.

> In *Water Buffalo Days*, a man recounts his childhood in Vietnam, a country in Southeast Asia. *Water Buffalo Days* has many characteristics of a personal narrative. It is a true story, told from the writer's point of view, and it tells about events in the order they happen.

210

Reading the Student Model

Explain that the story on page 211 is about Melissa and Charlotte. Write the names on the board. Have a volunteer read aloud the model. Ask who is telling the story (*Charlotte*). Ask what words in the story helped to know that Charlotte is telling the story (*I, me*). Ask a volunteer to read what he or she thinks is the beginning of the story (*It all started when . . .*). Remind students that the topic is what the story is about. Ask students to tell what the topic of this story is (*how Charlotte got stuck in and rescued from the mud*).

Read aloud the entire personal narrative. Ask students to tell the order of events in the story. As students identify the events, list them on the board.

Ask students what might happen if the events were told out of order. (*The story would not make sense.*) Emphasize the importance of putting events in the order they happened.

TEACHING OPTIONS

○ Scavenger Hunt

Have small groups search the classroom and the library for examples of personal narratives. Remind students to look for stories about events that really happened to the writers. Suggest that students look for the words *I, me,* and *my* to be sure the story is about the person who wrote it.

For Tomorrow

Have students find an example of a personal narrative. Explain that personal narratives can be stories, letters, and newspaper or magazine articles. Point out that an e-mail can even be a personal narrative if it has the right characteristics. Tell students they should be prepared to share what they have found during the next class. Bring in your own example of a personal narrative to share.

CHAPTER 1

Bad, Bad Mud
by Charlotte Eaton

I come to you today with some good advice: DON'T WALK IN MUD! It all started when Melissa and I were walking outside, with umbrellas, rainboots, rain jackets, and no fear of the rain. We were set for anything. At least that's what we thought.

Then Melissa asked, "Can we go into the cow pasture?" "Sure," I said. We ran to the edge of the barn and came to a halt. There before us was a pasture full of mud. Melissa said, "What are you stopping for?" I said, "MUD!" She said, "Look, just follow me. You won't get stuck. I promise." Before I could say yes or no, she was off. My heart was pounding. A little voice in my head kept saying, "Don't do it" over and over again.

Melissa was going deeper and deeper into the cow pasture. She wasn't sinking, so why would I? It's just a bunch of dirt, I said to myself. So I took one step, then another, and there I was in the middle of the pasture, actually, standing there in mud. "Melissa," I said. "This isn't so bad."

Wait, what am I feeling? Thick, cold, gooey, watery, mud. I was sinking as fast as a lightbulb burns out. I felt like someone was pushing and pulling me under. My fear was coming true! I started yelling for help.

Melissa heard me and came running over to see what my problem was. I told Melissa, "The ground is sucking me under!" "Quick, pull me out!" She tugged and tugged at my boots, but the mud was winning. We both started screaming for help.

Finally, my sister Jennie and my cousin Natasha came to the rescue. They grabbed ahold of me and all pulled. Out I popped, but my boots remained. I stepped on my umbrella and then pulled my boots out. My feet were now black and freezing. I put my boots back on and made a mad dash, barely touching the ground, and I was out of the gate. I said, "Melissa, score one for mud and I'm out!"

211

OBJECTIVE

- **To recognize the characteristics of a personal narrative**

WARM-UP

Read, Listen, Speak

Read aloud the personal narrative you brought in for yesterday's For Tomorrow homework. Point out the characteristics of a personal narrative in your example. Have small groups share their personal narratives. Challenge students to explain how they know their examples are personal narratives.

GRAMMAR CONNECTION

Take this opportunity to talk about sentences and statements and questions. You may wish to have students point out sentences and statements and questions in their Read, Listen, Speak examples.

TEACH

Invite a volunteer to read aloud the opening paragraph. Then have volunteers read aloud the second paragraph and the section Topic. Challenge students to name topics for personal narratives they might write.

Read aloud the first paragraph of the section Point of View. Have students turn to page 211 and count the occurrences of the word *I*. Ask students why they think the writer uses the word *I* instead of her name *(because the writer is writing about herself)*. Then read aloud the second paragraph. Ask students to say sentences using the words listed. Tell students to remember to use these words when they write personal narratives.

Have a volunteer read aloud the section Time Order. Ask students to suggest sentences using each time word. Emphasize that telling a story in the order it happened makes the story easier to understand.

PRACTICE

ACTIVITY A

Have partners complete the activity. Encourage students to share their answers with the class. Compare the interesting details students mentioned in their answers.

ACTIVITY B

Ask students to tell the events of the student model. Write them on the board. Then have small groups complete the activity. Invite volunteers to present and explain their comic strips.

ACTIVITY C

Have a volunteer read aloud the personal narrative. Then ask volunteers to read aloud and to answer each question.

LESSON **1** PERSONAL NARRATIVES

What Makes a Good Personal Narrative?

The story on page 211 is about Melissa and Charlotte's muddy adventure. Because Charlotte tells this true story about herself, it is a personal narrative. The interesting details of the events, people, and things make this personal narrative fun to read.

A well-written personal narrative has the following things.

Topic

What is the topic of a personal narrative? The topic of a personal narrative is you, the writer. A personal narrative might be about something that you did or something that happened to you. It might also tell how you feel about something.

A personal narrative can be about almost anything, but it should be a true story. When you write a personal narrative, you should tell what happened just as you remember it.

Point of View

Personal narratives are always told from the writer's point of view. Did you notice how Charlotte is always part of the story? Go back and count the number of times you see the word *I*.

The words *I, we, me, us, my,* and *our* signal that you might be reading a personal narrative. When the audience reads these words, they know the story is told from the writer's point of view.

Time Order

When you write a personal narrative, tell about the events in the order that they happened. Use time words such as *first, next, after that, then, finally,* and *last* to show how one event comes after another.

APPLY

WRITER'S CORNER

Explain that students will be choosing topics to write their own personal narratives. Help students brainstorm possible topics such as *A Scary Night, My First Day of School, The Best Birthday Ever.* Challenge students to draw three pictures that show the beginning, middle, and ending of their stories. Invite volunteers to share their work. Students should demonstrate the ability to recognize the characteristics of a personal narrative.

ASSESS

Note which students had difficulty understanding the characteristics of a personal narrative. Use the Reteach option with those students who need additional reinforcement.

TEACHING OPTIONS

Reteach

Have students develop a checklist of the characteristics of a personal narrative. Ask students to find words and phrases on pages 212–213 to use in their checklist. Some examples are *topic, point of view, beginning, middle, ending,* and *time order.* Then give students a personal narrative to read. Ask them to check off each item on their checklist as they find it in the personal narrative.

Getting Ready for School

Have students draw comic strips showing what they do to get ready for school each morning. Remind students to make sure all the frames are in the correct order. Challenge students to write under each frame one sentence that describes the picture. Display students' work in the classroom.

For Tomorrow

Have students ask an adult family member to share a personal narrative from his or her life. Tell students to write the events of the story in order. Remind students to bring their notes to the next class. Obtain a narrative from a friend or family member and bring in your list of events to share.

Activity A

1. why you shouldn't walk in mud
2. Answers will vary.
3. *I, me, my,* and *we*
4. *when, then,* and *finally;* accept other appropriate answers

ACTIVITY A Read the personal narrative "Bad, Bad Mud" on page 211. Work with a partner to answer the following questions.

1. What is the topic?
2. What interesting details are included?
3. What words in the story tell you that it is a personal narrative?
4. What words in the story show the order that the events happened?

ACTIVITY B Work in groups to draw a comic strip of "Bad, Bad Mud." The pictures in the comic strip should follow the order of the story. Then write a sentence about what is happening in each picture.

ACTIVITY C Read this excerpt from a personal narrative. Then answer the questions.

Clubhouse Surprise

My friends and I thought it would be fun to build a clubhouse. First, we chose a secret spot in the back of my yard. We put boards on the ground under a big, old pine tree. We were sure no one could see us hidden under the branches. But then we were surprised when a little skunk waddled into the clubhouse.

Activity C

1. *my, I, we*
2. building a clubhouse
3. Answers will vary.
4. *first, then*

1. What words show the point of view?
2. What is the topic?
3. What interesting details are there in the story?
4. What words show the order of the story?

WRITER'S CORNER

Think about a personal narrative that you would like to write. Then write a sentence that tells the topic.

Personal Narratives • 213

WARM-UP

Read, Listen, Speak

Read aloud the personal narrative from yesterday's For Tomorrow homework. Discuss how your story reflects the characteristics of a personal narrative. Have small groups share their personal narratives. Ask students to listen for the topic, point of view, and order of events in the story. Discuss how each story exemplifies the personal narrative genre.

GRAMMAR CONNECTION

Take this opportunity to talk about question words. You may wish to have students point out any question words in their Read, Listen, Speak examples.

TEACH

Review topic, point of view, and time order. Ask a volunteer to explain what a topic is. Invite students to give examples of topics for personal narratives. List their suggestions on the board. Ask volunteers to name words that signal to the reader that the story is told from the writer's point of view *(I, me, my, our, we)*. Invite volunteers to use each word in a sentence that they might find in a personal narrative about one of the topics listed on the board. Ask a volunteer to explain why time order is important in a personal narrative.

LiNK Ask a volunteer to read aloud the excerpt from *Water Buffalo Days*. Ask students to tell what characteristics identify this excerpt as a personal narrative.

PRACTICE

ACTIVITY D

Ask volunteers to name words that might be clues to which topics would make good personal narratives. Then complete the activity as a class.

ACTIVITY E

Have students complete the activity independently. Then have students work with partners to share and discuss their answers.

ACTIVITY F

Have students complete the activity independently. Then ask volunteers to read aloud their completed narratives. Allow several students to read aloud so that the class can hear that different answers might make the story a little different, but they are still correct. Have students tell why they chose each time word.

ACTIVITY G

Have students complete the activity with partners. Encourage students to copy the sentences onto separate slips of paper and then to put the sentences in the correct order. Invite volunteers to write on the board the sentences in the correct order.

LiNK

Water Buffalo Days

Some of the best times of my life were spent roaming the rice field, riding on the young buffalo's back.... The calf's time was not yet in demand, so we were free to explore all the nooks and corners of the field or leisurely catch all kinds of living creatures for food or for fun.

Huynh Quang Nhuong

ACTIVITY D Read the following topics. Which ones are good topics for personal narratives? Why?

1. teaching your dog to wave
2. the day I got lost at the mall
3. grandma and I go skating
4. what I want to be when I grow up
5. our winter camping trip
6. how to ride a horse
7. my favorite character in a book
8. the life of a famous person
9. the day I met my best friend
10. how I learned to ride a bike

Activity D
Accept any answers students can justify.

ACTIVITY E Each sentence comes from a personal narrative, but the time words are missing. Complete each sentence with a time word from the word box to show when things happened. More than one answer may be correct.

Activity E
Answers will vary.
Possible answers:
1. After
2. when
3. Before
4. Today
5. during

after	before	during	finally	first
then	today	until	when	while

1. _____ I cleaned my room, I went to the park.
2. I could smell breakfast cooking _____ I woke up.
3. _____ I played my soccer game, I put on my shin guards.
4. _____ will be the first day of my summer vacation.
5. Those people would not stop talking _____ the movie.
6. _____ we ate dinner, we went outside.
7. I never went fishing _____ one day last June.
8. Tommy says he can snap his fingers _____ singing "Row, Row, Row Your Boat."
9. I worked and worked, and I _____ finished the jigsaw puzzle.
10. We bought our tickets for the movie, _____ we bought popcorn.

APPLY

WRITER'S CORNER

Remind students to state the topic at the beginning of their narrative. Point out that they should tell the story from their own point of view and put the events in the correct order. Have students share their narratives in small groups. Allow time for groups to discuss each story. Students should demonstrate the ability to use time order in constructing a personal narrative.

ASSESS

Note which students had difficulty with topics, point of view, and time order in personal narratives. Use the Reteach option with those students who need additional reinforcement.

Practice Book page 132 provides additional work with personal narratives.

TEACHING OPTIONS

Reteach

Recall the Read, Listen, Speak activity at the beginning of the lesson. Work with students to develop a list of the things you did during that activity. Write the list on the board. Then invite students to put each step in the correct order. (*1. We sat in groups. 2. We shared the stories we found. 3. We talked about topics and time order.*)

What If This Happened?

Challenge small groups to rewrite the events of the model on page 211. Ask students to keep the same characters but to change the setting, dialogue, and events. Ask students to role-play the events of their new stories.

Activity F

1. First
2. Next
3. Then
4. After that, Then
5. Finally

ACTIVITY F Complete the personal narrative with the time words from the word box. More than one answer may be correct.

after that	finally	first	next	then

An Easy Choice

It was going to be a special day. My parents and I had decided to adopt a cat from a local animal shelter.

At the shelter we told the volunteers that we were looking for a cat. (1)_____, they gave us a form to fill out. (2)_____, the volunteers took us to a room with several cats. Some were playing in the center of the room, and some were sleeping on shelves in the wall.

I just stood and looked around. (3)_____, I took a piece of string out of my pocket and begin to twirl it. A little calico cat came up to me. She batted the string with her paw. I knelt down. She kept hitting the string. Slowly I petted the back of her head. She started to purr loudly. (4)_____ she rubbed her body against my leg.

(5)_____, I knew that this was the cat for me. Cali (short for calico), has become a member of the family. She is sitting on my lap as I write this.

ACTIVITY G Here is a personal narrative. The order of the sentences is mixed up. Put the sentences in the correct order.

7 **1.** He picked me up.
2 **2.** I was having fun until I reached the top of a hill.
4 **3.** I tried to steer, but I was going too fast.
8 **4.** I never went near that hill again.
3 **5.** Zoom, I flew down the hill!
6 **6.** A man ran to help me.
1 **7.** One Saturday I went for a ride on my new bike.
5 **8.** I hit the curb and tumbled over the handlebars.

WRITER'S CORNER

Tell a personal narrative about a pet or other animal to a partner. Use time words. Be sure you tell the narrative in the correct order. Have your partner write the time words you used.

For Tomorrow

Tell students to list in order three things they will do after school today. Bring in your own list to share.

Personal Narratives • 215

OBJECTIVES
- **To identify the beginning, the middle, and the ending of a personal narrative**
- **To understand the function of a title**

WARM-UP
Read, Listen, Speak
Share your list of after-school activities from yesterday's For Tomorrow homework. Ask small groups to share their lists. Invite students to tell stories using the events from their lists in the correct time order.

GRAMMAR CONNECTION
Take this opportunity to talk about commands. You may wish to have students write commands from some of the sentences in their Read, Listen, Speak examples.

TEACH
Read aloud the opening paragraph. Then invite volunteers to read aloud the section Beginning. Ask students what it means that a good beginning grabs your attention. Have students turn to page 211. Ask a volunteer to identify the beginning of the student model and to explain how the beginning gives readers a hint of what the story will be about.

Invite volunteers to read the first two paragraphs of the section Middle. Explain that in the model on page 211, the middle of the story is the part where the narrator sinks and gets stuck in the mud. Then have volunteers read aloud the rest of the section.

Discuss the importance of including enough details in the middle so that the reader gets a clear picture of the events. Explain that missing details can make the middle confusing.

Ask volunteers to read aloud the section Ending. Remind students that at the end of "Bad, Bad Mud," the narrator is rescued by Jennie and Natasha. Explain that a strong ending wraps up the details of the story and emphasizes the importance of the story.

PRACTICE
ACTIVITY A
Invite partners to complete the activity. When students have finished, ask volunteers to share their answers.

ACTIVITY B
Have students reread the personal narrative "An Easy Choice" on page 215. Then have them write the answers to the questions. Invite volunteers to share their answers with the class.

Beginning, Middle, and Ending

A personal narrative is a story. Because it is a story, it should have a beginning, a middle, and an ending.

Beginning
The beginning of a personal narrative tells the reader what the story is about. A good beginning grabs the reader's attention and makes the reader want to read more.

The beginning of the story is also where you let the reader know why you're telling the story. For example, the beginning of a narrative might say, "Let me tell you the funny story about how I learned to ride a bike." The reader will be interested because everyone wants to read a funny story.

Middle
The middle of a narrative is important because this is where you tell the story. The middle is usually the longest part of a narrative.

The middle tells the events in the order they happened. It also has details that help the reader paint a picture in his or her mind about what happens.

You need to think carefully about all the parts of the story. Be sure the middle includes everything important to your story so that the reader doesn't get mixed up.

Suppose you were telling a story about learning to ride a bike. While you were learning, the bike tipped over and you scraped

APPLY

WRITER'S CORNER

Tell students they will write a beginning for a personal narrative of their own. Encourage students to write a strong beginning that grabs the reader's attention and makes the reader want to continue reading their story. Then have students complete the activity independently. Invite volunteers to share their story beginnings with the class. Students should demonstrate the ability to write a beginning for a personal narrative.

> **Grammar in Action.** Remind students that the subject is what or who the sentence is about.

ASSESS

Note which students had difficulty writing beginnings for personal narratives. Use the Reteach option with those students who need additional reinforcement.

your knee. The reader would want to know what you were doing before and after your bike tipped over. The reader would also want to know why the bike tipped over. Did it hit a big rock, or did it slide in a puddle of water?

Ending

The ending tells how the story comes out. A good ending might leave readers with a smile or a new idea to think about. The ending can tell something you learned or how you felt about what happened.

The ending is where you tell the reader what the story means to you and why the story is important. Suppose you are telling about a time that your baseball team won a game. The middle of the narrative might tell about all the time you spent practicing. The ending might tell how proud you were that your hard work helped win the game.

Activity A
1. paragraph 1
2. paragraphs 2, 3, 4, 5
3. Answers will vary.
4. paragraph 6

ACTIVITY A Answer the questions about the personal narrative "Bad, Bad Mud" on page 211.

1. Which paragraph is the beginning?
2. Which paragraphs are the middle?
3. What are some details in the personal narrative?
4. Which paragraph is the ending?

Activity B
1. The first paragraph is the beginning. It tells about how the writer wanted a cat and was going to get one.
2. The middle paragraphs tell how the writer chose a cat.
3. Answers will vary.

ACTIVITY B Answer the questions about the personal narrative "An Easy Choice" on page 215.

1. Which paragraph is the beginning? What information is in that paragraph?
2. What information is in the middle paragraphs?
3. Do you think that the ending is interesting? Why or why not?

WRITER'S CORNER

Write two sentences that begin a personal narrative about a family trip, a school field trip, or a vacation. Save your work.

> **Grammar in Action.** Circle the subject in both sentences.

Personal Narratives • 217

Read, Listen, Speak

Read the beginning sentences of your personal narrative from yesterday's For Tomorrow homework. Then have students in small groups share their story beginnings. Encourage students to tell what grabs their attention from each beginning. Have them discuss what might be included in the middle of each story.

GRAMMAR CONNECTION

Take this opportunity to talk about exclamations. You may wish to have students point out any exclamations in their Read, Listen, Speak examples.

TEACH

Write on the board as column headings *Beginning, Middle,* and *Ending*. Review each of these parts of a personal narrative. Then ask the following questions:

* What does a beginning do?
* What might be an example of a beginning?
* Why is the middle important?
* What does a writer include in the middle?
* What does an ending do?
* What might be an example of an ending?

Write students' responses on the board in the appropriate column. Invite a volunteer to read aloud the section Title. Then ask volunteers to make up titles for narratives and have the class describe what each story could be about.

LiNK Discuss the title *Water Buffalo Days*. Ask students what the title tells about the story and how it is reflected in the excerpt.

PRACTICE

ACTIVITY C

Have partners complete the activity. When students have finished, encourage volunteers to share their answers with the class. Discuss whether all the information is correctly placed on the chart.

ACTIVITY D

Have students complete this activity independently. Tell students to write at least one sentence explaining each of their choices. When students have finished, invite volunteers to share their answers with the class.

ACTIVITY E

Suggest that students write a list of interesting details and then write sentences using the details. Encourage students who chose the same part to compare their sentences.

Title

The title should give readers a hint about what the story is about. A funny or an interesting title can make people want to read your narrative.

LiNK

Water Buffalo Days

It was very tiring to walk in the mud, so I rode on the calf's back when I wanted to catch land lobsters. When I spotted a nest, I poured salt water into it, and the land lobsters jumped out like crazy.

Huynh Quang Nhuong

ACTIVITY C Read this personal narrative. Copy the chart below. Then use your own words to fill in the chart. Use the information in the chart to think of a title for the narrative.

What a horrible morning! My pet snake, Snerdly, was missing. Where could he be?

First, I looked in the living room. I checked under the couch and behind the cushions. I thought I heard soft, shooshing noises, but I couldn't find my little snake.

After that, I looked in the hall closet. I saw something long and slithery behind the coats. Was it Snerdly? No, it was just some ribbon.

Then I went to the laundry room. There was Snerdly, fast asleep on top of the warm dryer. I've never been so happy to see him!

Title	
Topic	
Beginning	
Middle	
Ending	

APPLY

WRITER'S CORNER

Review the answers to the questions about the middle of a personal narrative from Teach. Give students time to write three sentences to include in the middle of their personal narratives. Have students share their sentences in small groups. Students should demonstrate the ability to write a middle for a personal narrative.

ASSESS

Note which students had difficulty identifying beginnings, middles, endings, and titles. Use the Reteach option with those students who need additional reinforcement.

Practice Book page 133 provides additional work with the beginning, middle, ending, and title of a personal narrative.

TEACHING OPTIONS

◯ Reteach

Help students recall the first day of school. Have students write the headings *Beginning, Middle,* and *Ending* on a sheet of paper. Ask students to write details that describe each part of their day. Then have students write a title they might use if they were to write this narrative. Have students discuss the details from their charts and the titles. Ask students to explain why they chose the details and the title.

◯ My Life as an Animal

Encourage students to name their favorite animals. Write a list on the board as students suggest the animals. Challenge students to pretend they are one of the animals and to write at least one sentence each for the beginning, the middle, and the ending of a brief narrative about their daily life as that animal. Then ask students to write an appropriate title for the narrative. Invite volunteers to share what they wrote with the class.

Activity D
1. middle
2. beginning
3. ending
4. middle
5. beginning
6. ending

ACTIVITY D Below are parts of personal narratives. Which parts are they? Tell which part of a personal narrative they come from: the beginning, the middle, or the ending. Explain your answers.

1. Just then the roaring of the wind stopped. Was the tornado over? Dad crept up the stairs. He looked out the back door. He saw something and ran back down into the basement really fast.

2. Everyone asks how I got such a strange first name. The story of my name began a long time ago when my mom was a little girl.

3. It was such a hard way to learn that words can really hurt a person's feelings. After what happened to me, I'll never again say mean things about someone just to get a laugh.

4. Things were going fine. I was walking in time to the music. I was holding my basket of flowers and smiling. But when I heard our dog barking outside, I forgot everything I had practiced

5. I want to tell you about the first time I rode a roller coaster. It was not a good idea to have a lunch of three chili dogs before climbing aboard.

6. I enjoyed all the applause. I can't believe I was ever nervous about going on the stage. Now I'm planning to try out for the lead in the next school play.

ACTIVITY E Work with a partner. Choose one of the parts from a personal narrative in Activity D. Think of ideas for the two missing parts. Make up interesting details. Share your ideas for the personal narrative with the class.

WRITER'S CORNER

Look at the sentences you wrote for the previous Writer's Corner. Then write three sentences for the middle of your personal narrative. Save your work.

For Tomorrow

Have students choose three personal narrative parts from Activity D. Ask them to write titles for each part. Tell students to be prepared to share their work during the next class. Bring in three titles to share.

Personal Narratives • 219

OBJECTIVE
- **To identify and use strong verbs**

WARM-UP

Read, Listen, Speak

Read aloud the items you chose and the titles you wrote for yesterday's For Tomorrow homework. Have students read aloud their personal narrative parts and share their titles. Challenge students to decide whether the titles are appropriate.

GRAMMAR CONNECTION

Take this opportunity to talk about kinds of sentences. You may wish to have students point out kinds of sentences in the personal narratives they chose for their Read, Listen, Speak examples.

TEACH

Read aloud the first paragraph and the example sentence, and write the sentence on the board. Invite a volunteer to circle the verb in the sentence and to demonstrate the action.

Have volunteers read aloud the next two paragraphs and the two example sentences. Ask a volunteer to answer the question. Then have a volunteer read aloud the paragraph following the example sentences. Tell students that the mouse might move in other ways.

Write on the board the word *went*. Invite volunteers to name stronger verbs for *went (crept, darted)*. List their suggestions on the board. Read the sentence aloud several times, using the suggested words. Ask students to picture the mouse's actions as each sentence is being read.

Ask volunteers to read aloud the rest of the page. Invite volunteers to describe the picture they have in their minds when they read the second sentence of each example. Ask volunteers to demonstrate the action of each strong verb. Explain that using strong verbs helps a reader see something the way that the writer pictures it.

PRACTICE

ACTIVITY A

Have students work in small groups. Encourage them to describe the pictures each verb creates and tell which verb is stronger. Invite volunteers to share their answers with the class.

LiNK Invite volunteers to read aloud the excerpt from *Water Buffalo Days*. Ask students to point out the verbs in the excerpt. Then have students tell which are strong verbs *(stretch, gazed)* and why they are strong.

Strong Verbs

A verb is often the action word in a sentence. It tells what the subject does. In this sentence *Jan* is the subject. The verb *jumped* tells what Jan did.

Jan *jumped* off the diving board.

Some action verbs are stronger than others. They can tell the reader more clearly what the subject does. Use strong verbs when you write. Strong verbs make clear pictures in the reader's mind.

Which of these sentences creates a clearer picture in your mind?

The mouse *went* into its hole.
The mouse *ran* into its hole.

Ran is a stronger verb than *went* because it tells how the mouse moved. *Went* is a weaker verb because it tells only that the mouse did move. *Ran* makes a clearer picture in the reader's mind than *went* does.

Read the following pairs of sentences. In each pair the second sentence uses a stronger verb or verbs than the first sentence does.

I *asked* my brother to teach me.
I *begged* my brother to teach me.

I *went* off the skateboard as soon as I *got* on.
I *tumbled* off the skateboard as soon as I *stepped* on.

With a little practice, your writing will soon be full of strong, clear verbs.

APPLY

WRITER'S CORNER

Remind students what a good ending should do for a personal narrative. *(It should tell how the story comes out and tell the reader what the story means to the writer.)* Suggest that students use strong verbs throughout their personal narratives. Students should demonstrate an understanding of the importance of endings in personal narratives.

ASSESS

Note which students had difficulty using strong verbs. Use the Reteach option with those students who need additional reinforcement.

ACTIVITY A Which sentence in each pair has the stronger verb or verbs? Explain why.

1. a. The dog <u>walked</u> down the street.
   b. The dog <u>trotted</u> down the street.
2. a. Celia <u>cleaned</u> her dog before the show.
   b. Celia <u>bathed</u> her dog before the show.
3. a. Jason was late, so he <u>hurried</u> to the bus stop.
   b. Jason was late, so he <u>went</u> to the bus stop.
4. a. People <u>come</u> to the beach to <u>see</u> the sunset.
   b. People <u>drive</u> to the beach to <u>gaze</u> at the sunset.
5. a. Suze <u>whispered</u> softly into her dog's ear.
   b. Suze <u>talked</u> softly into her dog's ear.
6. a. Shawn <u>made</u> a model ship out of toothpicks.
   b. Shawn <u>built</u> a model ship out of toothpicks.
7. a. The snake <u>slithered</u> away from the campfire.
   b. The snake <u>moved</u> away from the campfire.
8. a. A kangaroo <u>hopped</u> behind the hill.
   b. A kangaroo <u>went</u> behind the hill.
9. a. The class <u>did</u> the school project on time.
   b. The class <u>finished</u> the school project on time.
10. a. Is it too cold to <u>go</u> across the river?
    b. Is it too cold to <u>wade</u> across the river?

LiNK

Water Buffalo Days

Sometimes . . . I would just stretch myself on the calf's back and let him carry me where he liked. I gazed at the sky and forgot everything around me. I felt as if the sky moved, but not the calf and I.

Huynh Quang Nhuong

WRITER'S CORNER

Look at the beginning and middle that you wrote in previous Writer's Corners. Then write a two-sentence ending. Tell the reader what the story means to you.

Personal Narratives • 221

TEACHING OPTIONS

Reteach

Make two columns on the board. Label one column *Verbs* and the other *Strong Verbs*. Ask students to work together to identify a verb in the model on page 211. Have students place the verb in one of the two categories. Accept any answer students can justify. Repeat the activity with other verbs from the model.

Strong Verbs Charades

Write on separate slips of paper simple action verbs that students can role-play.

run

jump

walk

Invite each student to choose a slip of paper. Have students in small groups take turns role-playing their action, using detailed or exaggerated physical movements. As each student role-plays his or her action, tell the group to list strong verbs for that action. Encourage students to use a thesaurus to find strong verbs.

For Tomorrow

Ask students to choose three verbs from this lesson. Have students list two strong verbs for each verb that they choose. Tell students to be prepared to share their work. Bring in your own strong verbs to share.

WARM-UP

Read, Listen, Speak

Read aloud your list of verbs from yesterday's For Tomorrow homework. Explain why you chose those particular verbs and how you chose stronger verbs. Then have small groups share their verbs. Challenge students to choose one strong verb from another student's list and use it in a sentence.

GRAMMAR CONNECTION

Take this opportunity to talk about subjects. You may wish to have students point out subjects in their Read, Listen, Speak sentences.

TEACH

Discuss why students should use strong verbs when they write. *(Strong verbs create clear pictures in readers' minds.)* Then write on the board the following verbs:

went   asked   go

Ask students to give examples of stronger verbs that might be used to replace the verbs on the board. Have students write their responses on the board. Then ask volunteers to use each word in a sentence.

PRACTICE

ACTIVITY B

Complete this activity as a class. Ask volunteers to brainstorm strong verbs for each answer and write them on the board.

ACTIVITY C

Discuss what students know about the animals in the activity. Then have students complete the activity independently. When students have finished, have them discuss the differences in the meaning of each sentence as the verb changes.

ACTIVITY D

Have partners complete this activity. When students have finished, ask volunteers to share their answers with the class. Ask students to justify their word choices. Then ask students to suggest alternative strong verbs for each sentence.

ACTIVITY E

Have students complete the activity independently. Then ask volunteers to read aloud their completed paragraphs. Have volunteers identify the strong verbs in each paragraph and write them on the board.

ACTIVITY B Read the following sentences. Replace each underlined verb with a stronger verb.

1. I <u>went</u> down the hill on my new sled.
2. I <u>go</u> to school on the bus every day.
3. The penguin <u>walked</u> toward me.
4. I <u>looked</u> at the rows of colorful sneakers in the window.
5. Our cat <u>likes</u> his cat food.
6. My little brother <u>looked</u> everywhere for his shoe.
7. We <u>put</u> one block on top of the other.
8. Leandro <u>put</u> his sister into the crib.
9. We <u>go</u> the same way to the gym every time.
10. The dish <u>broke</u> into tiny pieces.

ACTIVITY C Read each set of sentences. How does the verb in each sentence create a different picture? Add two more sentences to each set. Use strong verbs to show other actions the animals might do.

1. The dragon snorts.
   The dragon breathes.
   The dragon sneezes.
2. The eagle flies.
   The eagle soars.
   The eagle swoops.
3. The rabbit hopped.
   The rabbit leaped.
   The rabbit jumped.
4. The horse strutted.
   The horse galloped.
   The horse ran.
5. The cat meows.
   The cat hisses.
   The cat purrs.

Short

APPLY

WRITER'S CORNER

Ask volunteers to read aloud sentences from their personal narratives and point out the strong verbs. Challenge students to suggest other strong verbs for each sentence. Students should demonstrate the ability to use strong verbs in a personal narrative.

ASSESS

Note which students had difficulty using strong verbs. Use the Reteach option with those students who need additional reinforcement.

Practice Book page 134 provides additional work using strong verbs.

TEACHING OPTIONS

Reteach

Describe an exciting event that has happened to you. When you have finished, ask students if they could visualize the experience that you described based on the words you used. Invite students to draw pictures of the event and list strong verbs that describe each picture. Then ask students to retell the event, using the strong verbs and the pictures.

I Can See It All Now

Play a radio sportscast for students. Explain that it is important for radio announcers to use strong verbs when describing a game because the audience cannot see the action. Have students list verbs that the announcers use. Then ask students to role-play each action being described.

ACTIVITY D Choose a verb from the word box to complete each sentence. Use each verb only once.

dialed	roamed	sprayed	leaped
limped	swim	peered	sold
spun	barked	drives	flew

1. The volleyball ___flew___ through the air.
2. Some alligators ___peered___ above the water's surface.
3. The dogs ___barked___ at the mail carrier.
4. Dad ___drives___ to his office every day.
5. Spiders ___spun___ webs under the eaves.
6. Dean ___sold___ four subscriptions last week.
7. Wild buffalo once ___roamed___ across the Great Plains.
8. I ___dialed___ Toby on my cell phone.
9. The skunk ___sprayed___ its startled enemies.
10. She ___leaped___ from the barge.
11. With a twisted ankle, Tad ___limped___ away from the field.
12. The tigers ___swim___ on hot days.

ACTIVITY E Write strong verbs for each blank to complete the paragraph.

The fans _____ as the players _____ onto the field. The cheerleaders _____ as they _____ up and down. Music _____ through the stadium. Everyone _____ when the game ended.

WRITER'S CORNER

Look at the beginning, middle, and ending that you wrote in previous Writer's Corners. Replace the verbs with strong verbs to help paint a picture in the reader's mind.

For Tomorrow

Ask students to search a fiction book for strong verbs. Tell students to list five strong verbs. Remind students to bring their lists to class tomorrow. Bring in your own list of strong verbs to share.

Personal Narratives • 223

OBJECTIVE

- **To understand and use colorful adjectives**

WARM-UP

Read, Listen, Speak

Read aloud the verb list you brought in and discuss why you thought the words were good examples of strong verbs. Model using the words to tell a brief story. Have students share their student lists in small groups. Direct students to use five verbs to write a story. Have groups share their stories with the class.

GRAMMAR CONNECTION

Take this opportunity to talk about predicates. You may wish to have students point out predicates in their Read, Listen, Speak stories.

TEACH

Ask a volunteer to read aloud the title of the lesson. Tell students that an adjective is a word that describes a noun and that a noun is the name of a person, place, or thing. Explain that *colorful* means "full of color." Tell students that *colorful* can also mean "interesting" or "descriptive." Then read aloud the first paragraph and the example sentences.

Have students role-play what an oak grove might look like if a gentle wind was blowing. Then have them role-play what the grove would look like if there was a fierce wind. Point out that the colorful adjectives in the example sentences change a reader's picture of the oak grove.

Read aloud the second paragraph. Ask volunteers to answer the questions. Have volunteers read aloud the rest of the page. Invite students to brainstorm a list of other colorful adjectives to replace those in the example sentences.

PRACTICE

ACTIVITY A

Have volunteers read aloud each set of adjectives. Then have students determine which items contain more colorful adjectives. Ask them to explain why their choices are more colorful.

ACTIVITY B

Have students complete the activity independently. Suggest that students picture each sentence in their minds before deciding which adjective is more colorful. When students have finished, invite them to explain why they chose each adjective.

ACTIVITY C

As a class, brainstorm a list of adjectives that describe a park. Invite students to write on the board their suggestions for each item. Then have students complete the second part of the activity with a partner. Ask volunteers to share their most colorful adjectives with the class and to use those adjectives in sentences.

LiNK Have a volunteer read aloud the excerpt from *Water Buffalo Days*. Ask students to point out the colorful adjectives (*monotonous, prostrate*). Have students substitute other words for *monotonous* and *prostrate* as they read aloud the sentences.

LESSON **4** WORD STUDY

Colorful Adjectives

Adjectives are words that tell something about nouns. Colorful adjectives are like strong verbs. They can paint clear pictures in the reader's mind.

> A *gentle* wind blew through the oak grove.
> A *fierce* wind blew through the oak grove.

The adjectives *gentle* and *fierce* both tell something about the wind. Which kind of wind blows harder—a gentle wind or a fierce one? How is the picture that *gentle* makes in your mind different from the picture that *fierce* makes?

Colorful adjectives make clearer pictures.

> a *nice*, *cute* puppy
> a *wrinkled*, *black* puppy

Which set of adjectives makes a clearer picture—*nice* and *cute* or *wrinkled* and *black*? Adjectives like *nice* and *cute* are not exact. Many people have different ideas about what is nice or cute. *Wrinkled* and *black* are colorful, exact adjectives. Good writers put just one idea in the reader's mind. That idea is the one they are writing about.

ACTIVITY A **Which set of adjectives makes a clearer picture? Explain why.**

1. a sweet, little kitten   a tiny, playful kitten
2. a steep, winding road   a long, narrow road
3. slender, golden stalks   thin, yellow stalks
4. a large, bright fire   a gigantic, glowing, orange fire
5. a tall, steel skyscraper   a towering, glass skyscraper

APPLY

WRITER'S CORNER

Before students begin, ask these questions:

- What does the object look like?
- What does it feel like?
- Does it make a noise?
- Does it have a smell?

Encourage students to use their responses to describe the object. Have volunteers share their descriptions with the class without naming the object. Have students guess what classroom object is being described. Students should demonstrate the ability to use colorful adjectives.

ASSESS

Note which students had difficulty identifying and using colorful adjectives. Use the Reteach option with those students who need additional reinforcement.

TEACHING OPTIONS

Reteach

Have students choose an adjective such as *little*, *good*, or *pretty*. Assign partners a letter from the alphabet. Ask partners to identify three colorful adjectives that begin with their assigned letter to replace the original adjective. Suggest that students use a children's dictionary or thesaurus to search for words. Help students understand that there are many alternatives to common adjectives.

Picture Words

Give students copies of a simple children's poem that describes nature. Read aloud the poem. Ask students to identify the colorful adjectives in the poem. Allow students time to draw pictures that the poem communicates. Encourage students to focus on one word or image from the poem. When students have finished drawing, invite volunteers to share their pictures and to name the words that inspired their pictures.

ACTIVITY B Which sentence in each pair has a more colorful adjective? Give reasons for your answer.

1. a. The big boat sailed on the lake.
   b. The huge boat sailed on the lake.
2. a. I bit into a good apple.
   b. I bit into a crispy apple.
3. a. Will you wear your worn jeans?
   b. Will you wear your old jeans?
4. a. That dog has stinky breath.
   b. That dog has bad breath.
5. a. Ryan had a great time yesterday.
   b. Ryan had a thrilling time yesterday.
6. a. Aunt Jane gave me a yummy treat.
   b. Aunt Jane gave me a nice treat.

ACTIVITY C Describe a park. Write two adjectives for each noun.

1. _____ _____ trees
2. _____ _____ pond
3. _____ _____ picnic tables
4. _____ _____ flowers
5. _____ _____ squirrels

Describe your classroom. Write two adjectives for each noun.

6. _____ _____ room
7. _____ _____ desks
8. _____ _____ windows
9. _____ _____ floor
10. _____ _____ lights

LiNK

Water Buffalo Days

Often on the way home, I would lean forward, hold the calf's shoulders in my arms, and close my eyes to rest. And often the monotonous movements of the calf would lull me to sleep. One evening I did not wake up even when the calf crossed the gate to our house. My parents panicked when they saw me in this prostrate state, and were quite relieved when they found out there was nothing wrong with me.

Huynh Quang Nhuong

Water buffalo working in rice paddies in Vietnam

WRITER'S CORNER

Write three sentences to describe an object in your classroom. Use three colorful adjectives.

For Tomorrow

Ask students to write two sentences describing an object in their home. Have students include two or more colorful adjectives in each sentence. Tell students to bring their work to the next class. Bring in your own sentences using colorful adjectives to describe something in your home.

Personal Narratives • 225

WARM-UP

Read, Listen, Speak

Read aloud your sentences using colorful adjectives from yesterday's For Tomorrow homework. Ask students if they were able to see a picture of the object in their minds. Identify the colorful adjectives that helped to picture the object. Then ask students to share their sentences in small groups. Have groups discuss how these adjectives make the writing more interesting. Ask students to suggest additional words that might be used in all their sentences.

GRAMMAR CONNECTION

Take this opportunity to talk about combining subjects and predicates. You may wish to have students use compound subjects and predicates in their Read, Listen, Speak examples.

TEACH

Ask students what a colorful adjective is *(an adjective that brings a clear picture to the reader's mind)*. Write on the board the following sentence pairs:

> Casey built a bright fire.
> Casey built a crackling fire.

> We had good tacos for dinner.
> We had tasty tacos for dinner.

> Look at that gigantic elephant!
> Look at that big elephant!

Ask volunteers to circle the adjective in each sentence pair that is more colorful. Discuss how the circled words change the meaning of the less colorful sentences. Remind students that writers use colorful adjectives to put a clear idea in the reader's mind.

PRACTICE

ACTIVITY D

Direct students to rewrite each sentence with colorful adjectives. Have students share their sentences with the class. Ask students to tell how the colorful adjectives change the sentence.

ACTIVITY E

Complete the first sentence as a class. Then have students complete the activity with partners. When students have finished, invite volunteers to share with the class their most descriptive sentences.

ACTIVITY F

Clarify that students should choose one adjective for each blank from those in the lists below. When students have finished their paragraphs, invite volunteers to share their work. Then discuss how each adjective creates for the reader a picture of the room.

ACTIVITY G

Have volunteers tell about the kind of day they wish to describe. Some suggestions might be windy and cold, sunny and warm, or cloudy and cool. Have students complete the

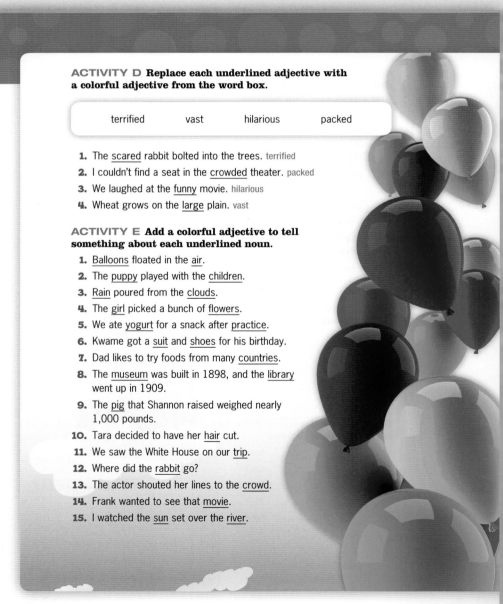

ACTIVITY D Replace each underlined adjective with a colorful adjective from the word box.

terrified	vast	hilarious	packed

1. The <u>scared</u> rabbit bolted into the trees. terrified
2. I couldn't find a seat in the <u>crowded</u> theater. packed
3. We laughed at the <u>funny</u> movie. hilarious
4. Wheat grows on the <u>large</u> plain. vast

ACTIVITY E Add a colorful adjective to tell something about each underlined noun.

1. <u>Balloons</u> floated in the <u>air</u>.
2. The <u>puppy</u> played with the <u>children</u>.
3. <u>Rain</u> poured from the <u>clouds</u>.
4. The <u>girl</u> picked a bunch of <u>flowers</u>.
5. We ate <u>yogurt</u> for a snack after <u>practice</u>.
6. Kwame got a <u>suit</u> and <u>shoes</u> for his birthday.
7. Dad likes to try foods from many <u>countries</u>.
8. The <u>museum</u> was built in 1898, and the <u>library</u> went up in 1909.
9. The <u>pig</u> that Shannon raised weighed nearly 1,000 pounds.
10. Tara decided to have her <u>hair</u> cut.
11. We saw the White House on our <u>trip</u>.
12. Where did the <u>rabbit</u> go?
13. The actor shouted her lines to the <u>crowd</u>.
14. Frank wanted to see that <u>movie</u>.
15. I watched the <u>sun</u> set over the <u>river</u>.

activity independently. Then ask volunteers to share their completed paragraphs with the class.

APPLY

WRITER'S CORNER

Work with one group to model the process for students. Then allow time for each group to write adjectives and use them in a story. Have groups share their stories with one another. Students should demonstrate the ability to use colorful adjectives.

ASSESS

Note which students had difficulty using colorful adjectives. Use the Reteach option with those students who need additional reinforcement.

Practice Book page 135 provides additional work with colorful adjectives.

TEACHING OPTIONS

Reteach

Have students review the student model on page 211. Ask students to find and list the adjectives from the narrative. Then ask students to decide where a more colorful adjective might be used. Have students share their new versions of the narrative. Remind students to consider whether each adjective provides a clear picture for the reader.

Writing Together

Ask students to suggest animals that people could see in a zoo. Write their suggestions on the board. Then have small groups each choose an animal. Tell students to work together to write a short narrative about what might happen if the animal escaped from the zoo. Remind students to use colorful adjectives. When students have finished, invite volunteers to read aloud or role-play their narratives.

ACTIVITY F **Add colorful adjectives to the paragraph about a room. Use the list after the paragraph to help you. The way the room you describe looks, feels, and even smells will depend on which adjective you choose.**

I walked slowly into the (1)________ room. (2)________ flowers rested on the (3)________, (4)________ table in the corner. Next to the table was a (5)________ chair. A (6)________ book was lying by the chair on the (7)________ floor. (8)________ light streamed through the (9)________ window. I shut the (10)________ curtains and strolled out of the room.

1.	stuffy	dark	small
2.	Colorful	Drooping	Fake
3.	old	shaky	polished
4.	broken	dusty	white
5.	velvet	wooden	soft
6.	torn	new	thick
7.	spotless	tile	sticky
8.	Golden	Bright	Dim
9.	cracked	large	open
10.	dirty	heavy	red

ACTIVITY G **Write colorful adjectives to complete the paragraph.**

It was a ________ day. ________ clouds moved across the ________ sky. The ________ trees swayed in the ________ wind. Then a ________ rain began to fall on the ________ grass. I got on my ________ bicycle and rode home.

WRITER'S CORNER

Work in groups to use adjectives to tell a story. Write an adjective on a slip of paper. Place the slips in a box. Each person chooses a slip and uses the adjective on it in a sentence. When your group has used all the adjectives, the story is done.

For Tomorrow

Ask students to copy three sentences from a fiction book. Have students add colorful adjectives to their sentences. Bring in your own sentences to share.

OBJECTIVE

- **To use alphabetical order and guide words to find words in a dictionary**

WARM-UP

Read, Listen, Speak

Read aloud the sentences that you chose for yesterday's For Tomorrow homework. Model the activity by writing on the board one of the sentences. Explain how you thought you could improve the sentence by using a more colorful adjective. Write your edited sentence on the board. Have small groups share their sentence pairs. Allow time for students to discuss how the colorful adjectives helped to create pictures in their minds.

GRAMMAR CONNECTION

Take this opportunity to talk about combining sentences. You may wish to have students combine sentences in their Read, Listen, Speak examples.

TEACH

Read aloud the first paragraph. Ask students if they know what an English horn and a joist are. Have a volunteer read aloud the second paragraph and bulleted list. Then read aloud the sample dictionary entry. Challenge students to match each part of the sample entry to one of the bulleted items.

Read aloud the next paragraph. Ask students to name the three parts of a dictionary entry and to read aloud the entry word, pronunciation, and definitions.

Invite a volunteer to explain the meaning of alphabetical order. Then invite a volunteer to read aloud the section Alphabetical Order. Write on the board the words *account, absolute,* and *accept.*

Ask students to alphabetize the words. Explain that each letter of the alphabet has a section in the dictionary. Emphasize that the entries within that section are listed in alphabetical order, using the letters that come second, third, and so on.

PRACTICE

ACTIVITY A

Complete the first item with the class. Then allow students to complete the activity independently. Invite volunteers to write their answers on the board.

ACTIVITY B

Allow students to work with partners to complete the activity. Have volunteers write their alphabetical lists on the board.

ACTIVITY C

Allow partners to complete the activity. Ask volunteers to share the words they unscrambled. Challenge students to name other words that might be listed in the dictionary near each unscrambled word.

Dictionary

Do you know what an English horn is? What about a joist? Every day we read words that we may not know. A dictionary is a book we use to look up these kinds of words.

A dictionary is a book of words and their meanings. In a dictionary you can find these things:

- how words are spelled
- the way words are pronounced
- what words mean

> **A** **B** **C**
> **quest** (kwest) **1.** A hunt or search [a quest for gold] **2.** A journey in search of adventure [the quests of medieval knights]
>
> **A.** Entry word
> **B.** Pronunciation
> **C.** Word definition(s)

Each word listed in a dictionary is called an entry word. The entry word is followed by the pronunciation and the definition of the word. The pronunciation is the way to say the word correctly. The definition is what the word means. Many words have more than one definition.

Alphabetical Order

Entry words are listed in alphabetical order. When more than one word begins with the same letter, the words are alphabetized by the second letter. When more than one word begins with the same two letters, the words are alphabetized by the third letter. What order would the words *account, absolute,* and *accept* be in?

APPLY

WRITER'S CORNER

Have a volunteer read aloud the sentence containing the word *monotonous*. Have students guess at the meaning of the word. Then have them look up the word and copy the definition. Ask students to compare the definition with their guess. Point out that *monotonous* is a colorful adjective. Students should demonstrate the ability to locate words in a dictionary.

💡 **TechTip** Provide a link to an online student dictionary. Tell students that online dictionaries have a search function so that finding a word doesn't require using guide words. Point out that some online dictionaries have audio of a word's pronunciation and that some have a column for browsing nearby entries.

ASSESS

Note which students had difficulty alphabetizing words. Use the Reteach option with those students who need additional reinforcement.

TEACHING OPTIONS

Reteach

Write on the board a list of 20 words from a recent reading or spelling lesson. Have students write the letters of the alphabet on a sheet of paper in a vertical list. Tell students to look at the first letter of each word and to write each word next to that letter on the list. Explain that if two or more words begin with the same letter, then students should look at the second letters to put those words in the correct order. Have students write their alphabetized lists on another sheet of paper. Review the correctly alphabetized list.

A Name Game

Ask students to write their first names on the board. Have students determine whose name is first alphabetically. Then erase that student's name from the board and have that student stand in front of the classroom. Have students determine the next name that comes alphabetically. Ask that student to stand next to the first student. Continue until all students are standing in line in alphabetical order, from left to right, according to their names.

ACTIVITY A Put each group of letters in alphabetical order.

1. s, v, y, t	s, t, v, y	**5.** f, k, d, b	b, d, f, k
2. k, h, i, j	h, i, j, k	**6.** m, c, h, i	c, h, i, m
3. r, t, e, o	e, o, r, t	**7.** w, m, q, r	m, q, r, w
4. n, l, g, q	g, l, n, q	**8.** j, t, h, k	h, j, k, t

ACTIVITY B Put each list of words in alphabetical order.

1. space	moon		**3.** Earth	Earth
planet	planet		enormous	encounter
rocket	rocket		explore	enormous
moon	space		encounter	explore
2. Saturn	Jupiter		**4.** astronaut	adventure
Jupiter	Mars		asteroid	asteroid
Mars	Pluto		adventure	astronaut
Pluto	Saturn		atmosphere	atmosphere

Activity C
1. cane, cat, copy, cost
2. film, flag, flew, four
3. test, the, tie, toad
4. poem, porch, port, pour

ACTIVITY C Rewrite the scrambled letters to make a word. Then put the words in each list in alphabetical order.

1. yocp	**2.** mfil	**3.** tset	**4.** roup
tac	rofu	het	trpo
tosc	wlfe	doat	moep
enac	aflg	ite	cophr

Tech Tip With an adult, explore an online dictionary.

WRITER'S CORNER

Reread the excerpt from *Water Buffalo Days* on page 225. Then look up *monotonous* in a dictionary. Write the definition. How does the meaning of the word change your understanding of the story?

Personal Narratives • 229

For Tomorrow

Ask students to make a list of 10 toys, games, or books they have at home. Challenge students to alphabetize their lists. Bring in your own list to share.

WARM-UP

Read, Listen, Speak

Write on the board your list of toys, books, or games from yesterday's For Tomorrow homework. Model for students how you alphabetized the first five items on the list. Ask students to alphabetize the rest of your list. Then have volunteers share their lists. Ask students to check one another's lists for correct alphabetical order.

GRAMMAR CONNECTION

Take this opportunity to talk about run-on sentences. You may wish to have students check for and revise run-on sentences in classroom books.

TEACH

Help students find the first page of the section in a dictionary that lists words that begin with the letter *t*. Tell students to find the word *tabby* on that page and to read the entry. Ask a volunteer to explain what *tabby* means.

Read aloud the first paragraph of the section Guide Words. Help students find the entry for the word *tiger* in their dictionaries. Invite a volunteer to read aloud the entry. Ask volunteers to name the first and last entries on the page on which the word *tiger* appears. Then have students read aloud the guide words at the top of the page.

Read aloud the rest of the section. Then write the word *calico* on the board. Have a volunteer read aloud the first step. Have students complete that step as they search for the word *calico*. Repeat this process with the remaining steps until all students have found the entry. Ask a volunteer to tell what *calico* means.

PRACTICE

ACTIVITY D

Have students use a dictionary to complete the activity in small groups. Encourage groups to share their answers with the class.

ACTIVITY E

Have students complete this activity with partners. Write the guide words on the board and invite volunteers to write their answers below the guide words.

ACTIVITY F

Have students work with partners to complete this activity. Invite students to share their answers with the class.

ACTIVITY G

Have partners complete this activity. When students have finished, have them look up their answers in a dictionary and check that each answer appears alphabetically between the two guide words in each item. Ask a volunteer to explain why the guide words in the activity are different from the guide words in students' dictionaries.

Guide Words

To save time when you're looking up a word in a dictionary, you can use guide words. Guide words tell the first and last words found on a dictionary page. The guide words are located at the top corner of the page.

When you look for a word in a dictionary, you should follow these steps.

1. Decide whether the word can be found at the beginning, middle, or end of the dictionary. (Think of where the first letter of the word comes in the alphabet.)
2. Look at the guide words at the top of the pages.
3. Decide whether you can find the word between the two guide words.
4. If so, look for the word on that page.

Fawn-colored lark

ACTIVITY D Where in the dictionary would you find the following words—toward the beginning, the middle, or the end?

1.	batter	beginning	7.	vine	end
2.	staff	end	8.	jump	middle
3.	maiden	middle	9.	exile	beginning
4.	dowel	beginning	10.	undo	end
5.	afghan	beginning	11.	rural	end
6.	lark	middle	12.	cinder	beginning

ACTIVITY E Below are three sets of guide words with a page number for each. Tell the page number where you would find each word.

linger—list 430	listen—liven 431	liver—loan 432

1.	liter	431	4.	lisp	430	7.	lint	430
2.	load	432	5.	little	431	8.	lizard	432
3.	livery	432	6.	lipstick	430	9.	lip	430

APPLY

WRITER'S CORNER

Ask students to complete this activity independently. Then have volunteers share their answers. Challenge students to choose an unfamiliar word on the page and to read aloud the definitions. Students should demonstrate the ability to use guide words in a dictionary.

Grammar in Action. Have students look up the word *hamlet* in a classroom or an online dictionary.

ASSESS

Note which students had difficulty using guide words in dictionaries. Use the Reteach option with those students who need additional reinforcement.

Practice Book page 136 provides additional work with using dictionaries.

TEACHING OPTIONS

Reteach

Have students write pairs of dictionary guide words on note cards, one pair per card. Then ask students to write on separate note cards individual words that can be found on pages with those guide words. Have students lay out on a table the note cards with guide words. Ask students first to alphabetize the word cards and then to place those words under the correct pair of guide words. Ask students to check their work by using a dictionary.

Learning While Reading

Encourage students to look up words they don't know as they read. Provide books that are two or three levels above students' reading level. Tell students to find a difficult word in the book. Have them look up the word in a dictionary, using guide words. Have students record the definition. Invite students to share with the class the word they chose and what it means. Then have them read aloud the original sentence that uses the word.

For Tomorrow

Tell students to ask a family member to list for them three difficult words. Ask students to look up the words in a dictionary and write each word and its definition. Bring in your own three words and definitions to share.

ACTIVITY F Tell if each word comes before, after, or between each pair of guide words.

		Word	Guide Words
between	**1.**	double	door—dove
between	**2.**	rug	ruby—rule
between	**3.**	gravel	grasp—gull
between	**4.**	spruce	sponge—square
before	**5.**	power	practice—praise
after	**6.**	watch	wallet—warmth
before	**7.**	kitchen	knife—koala
after	**8.**	normal	nomad—noon
before	**9.**	movie	multiply—mumps
between	**10.**	electric	elbow—empty
between	**11.**	shave	sharpen—sheepdog
after	**12.**	latitude	larva—lateral
after	**13.**	bowl	bought—bow
after	**14.**	profile	probe—produce
between	**15.**	certain	ceremony—chairperson

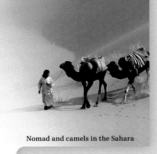

Nomad and camels in the Sahara

ACTIVITY G Write a word that comes between each of the following pairs of guide words.

1. land—life
2. shallow—sky
3. background—balance
4. crawl—crusade
5. pack—penny
6. train—trout

WRITER'S CORNER

Use a dictionary to find where your first name would appear if it were an entry word. Write the entry word just before and just after where your name would appear. Then write the guide words for that page of the dictionary.

Grammar in Action. What does *hamlet* mean in the page 210 excerpt?

Personal Narratives • 231

OBJECTIVES

- To identify the characteristics of an oral personal narrative
- To write and practice an oral personal narrative
- To practice speaking and listening skills

WARM-UP

Read, Listen, Speak

Write on the board the three difficult words you chose for yesterday's For Tomorrow homework. Tell students how you found the words in the dictionary and read aloud the definition for each word. You may wish to write on the board the definitions and guide words for one of the words as you model.

Have students share their homework with a partner and check each other's work, using a dictionary. Invite volunteers to share their words with the class.

GRAMMAR CONNECTION

Take this opportunity to review sentences. You may wish to have students write sentences using the words from their Read, Listen, Speak examples.

TEACH

Invite a volunteer to read aloud the first paragraph. Discuss brief personal narratives students have told to a friend or family member recently *(something that happened on the playground, a friend's birthday party students attended).*

Have volunteers read aloud the section Get Ready. Encourage students to mention topics for personal narratives that they might enjoy telling. Review the characteristics of a personal narrative. *(It is a true story of something that happened to the writer. It is told from the writer's point of view. It has a beginning, a middle, an ending, and a title. Events are told in the order that they happened.)*

Invite volunteers to read aloud the section Plan Your Story. Challenge students to talk about the characteristics of each part of an oral personal narrative.

PRACTICE

ACTIVITY A

Have students write their sentences independently. Encourage students to write beginning sentences that tell the audience what their chosen topic is. Then have students read their sentences to a partner. Ask students to suggest other ways their partners could say the same thing.

ACTIVITY B

Have students form small groups and take turns reading the sentences, using the appropriate feelings.

Oral Personal Narratives

An oral personal narrative is a story about you. You tell personal narratives every day. Have you ever told your family about your day? Have you ever told a friend about learning to ride a bike? These are personal narratives.

Get Ready

Telling a story to the class can be like telling a story to your friends. Try to choose a story that your classmates would like. It can be about almost anything, but it should be true.

Just like stories that you write, oral personal narratives use time words to show the order that things happened. Personal narratives are told from your point of view.

A good personal narrative should also include something that you learned or how you felt. You should share what you learned or how you felt with your audience.

Plan Your Story

Just like a personal narrative that you write, a personal narrative that you tell has a title, a beginning, a middle, and an ending. A good beginning opens the story and gives the audience a clue about what they will find out.

The middle is the main part of your story. It tells what happened in the order the events took place.

The ending finishes your story. It tells what you learned or how you felt. Many endings give listeners something extra to think about. An ending might show a new way to think about something.

APPLY

SPEAKER'S CORNER

Have students meet with partners to share their ideas. Encourage students to summarize the story they want to tell. Ask students to discuss engaging ways to begin their oral personal narratives. Students should demonstrate the ability to choose an appropriate topic for an oral personal narrative.

ASSESS

Note which students had difficulty understanding the characteristics of an oral personal narrative. Use the Reteach option with those students who need additional reinforcement.

Reteach

Tell students an engaging story about yourself. Be sure to incorporate the points given in the sections Get Ready and Plan Your Story. When you have finished, discuss the story. Work with students to develop a checklist of characteristics of an oral personal narrative by referring to the story you told and the information in the lesson.

Ask a Friend

Ask students to write a topic for an oral personal narrative by using the ideas in Activity A or by coming up with topics of their own. Then have students summarize for partners the story they want to tell. When students have finished, tell them to ask their partners one question about the story they heard. Explain that the question can be about something that confused them or about some part of the story they are curious to know more about. Explain that listener feedback can help a speaker tell the story more clearly or focus on the most interesting parts of the story.

ACTIVITY A Choose two of these ideas and write a beginning sentence for each. Read aloud the sentences to a partner.

1. Saturday fun
2. My first time to . . .
3. A special trip
4. An accident
5. A pet gets into trouble
6. My last birthday
7. A big success
8. A dream I've had
9. A scary experience

ACTIVITY B Read aloud the following sentences from personal narratives. Use the feelings given in parentheses.

1. I had never had an experience as scary as this before, or ever again. (frightened)
2. My aunt Sarah was coming to stay with us for a visit. (happy)
3. The day our dog Max was lost was a day I won't forget. (sad)
4. It was another rainy day—the third in a row. (disappointment)
5. So I learned the hard way that I should always lock my bike. (sad)
6. My dad announced one Saturday morning that we were going ice-skating, which we had never done before. (surprise)
7. I always put away my homework in a special folder after I finish it. I never want to repeat the experience I had last fall. (determination)
8. Harry is my best friend, and we do lots of things together. (happy)

SPEAKER'S CORNER

Think of an idea for an oral personal narrative. You can use an idea you had during this chapter or a new idea. Write your idea and save it.

For Tomorrow

Have students practice their speaking skills by telling their families a story of something that happened to them at school or after school. Practice telling a story of your own.

Personal Narratives • 233

WARM-UP
Read, Listen, Speak

Tell students you are going to tell a story about something that happened yesterday at school. Model telling an oral personal narrative as students were asked to do in yesterday's For Tomorrow homework. Ask students to listen for the beginning, middle, and ending of your story.

Have students share their own stories in small groups. Encourage students to discuss how telling the story to their family first may have changed the way they told their story in class.

TEACH

Invite a volunteer to read aloud the first paragraph of the section Write and Practice. Help students understand that even though students may know their story by heart, they might want to use note cards to help remember all the parts and to keep the parts in order.

Read the second paragraph aloud. Ask students to name skills that they can improve through practice *(playing the piano, hitting a baseball, working math problems)*. Tell students that the more times they practice telling an oral personal narrative, the better they will remember the story. Point out that a partner can help by telling a speaker whether he or she is talking clearly, loudly, and slowly enough and if anything is hard to understand.

Have volunteers read aloud the section Present. Tell students that using their voices or acting out parts of the story can make it more exciting, scary, or funny. Provide an example of a gesture added to a story, such as a karate chop for a story about the first day at karate class.

Invite volunteers to read aloud the section Listen. Ask volunteers to tell ways to be good listeners.

Point out that if students do not listen carefully, they might miss part of the story and not understand what happens in the ending.

PRACTICE

ACTIVITY C
Have students draw their pictures independently. Invite partners to share their pictures and describe what is happening in each picture.

ACTIVITY D
Have students complete this activity independently. When students have finished, have partners share their pictures. Tell students to cover the sentences they wrote for each picture and to describe to their partner what is happening. Direct students to describe all three pictures and then share the sentences they wrote.

ACTIVITY E
Have students practice their oral personal narratives with a partner. Encourage students to give feedback that is positive and shows interest in the story. Invite volunteers to present their oral personal narratives to the class.

Write and Practice

Write your personal narrative on note cards. Write the beginning on the first card. Write the middle on two or three cards. Write the ending on the last card.

Practice your personal narrative by telling it aloud. First, tell it aloud to yourself in front of a mirror. Then tell it to a partner. Ask your partner to tell you any parts of your story that were confusing or too long. Fix those parts. Ask your partner for help on how to tell your story better. For example, should you speak louder or slower?

Present

Here are some tips for presenting your story.

- Look at the audience as much as you can. Move your eyes from person to person.
- Speak up so everyone can hear you, but do not shout.
- Use your voice, your face, and your body movements to share the feelings the people in your story were showing.
- Be sure to breathe when you tell your story.

Listen

Listening to a speaker is almost as important as telling the story. Here are some tips for listening to your classmates when they tell their stories.

- Look at the speaker. Try not to move your arms or legs or tap your feet.
- Picture in your mind what the speaker is talking about. Think about how the story will end.
- Save your questions until the speaker has finished.

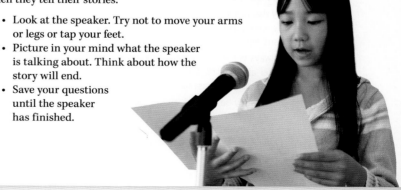

APPLY

SPEAKER'S CORNER

Have students complete this activity with a partner. Remind students to offer encouragement to their partners. Emphasize that their comments should be constructive and positive. Students should demonstrate the ability to present an oral personal narrative and practice listening skills.

TechTip Invite students to post their podcasts to a classroom Web page or blog. You may wish to send the link to other students or to parents.

ASSESS

Note which students had difficulty presenting an oral personal narrative. Use the Reteach option with those students who need additional reinforcement.

After you have reviewed Lessons 3–5, administer the Writing Skills Assessment on pages 39–40 in the **Assessment Book.** This test is also available on the optional **Test Generator CD.**

ACTIVITY C Use the idea for a personal narrative that you wrote in the Speaker's Corner on page 233. Ask yourself what happened.

Think about the order that things happened. Then draw a set of pictures. Draw one picture for each thing that happened.

Think about what the people in your story said. Write what they said in "word balloons" above each person. Leave some space to write about your pictures at the top of your paper. Save your work.

ACTIVITY D Take the set of pictures you drew for Activity C. Write a sentence that tells what happens in each picture.

ACTIVITY E Practice your oral personal narrative. Ask a family member or a classmate to give you ideas to help make your story better. Tell your story to the class.

SPEAKER'S CORNER

Listen to a classmate's oral personal narrative. Write anything that you like or that you think is funny. Think about ways the speaker could make the story better. Share your notes with the speaker. Remember to make positive suggestions for improvement.

 Record a podcast of your personal narrative for review.

OBJECTIVES

- **To choose a topic for a personal narrative**
- **To use pictures to storyboard events in a personal narrative**

PREWRITING AND DRAFTING

Explain that students will begin writing a personal narrative. Tell students that they will follow a writing process that has seven steps. Have students turn to the inside back cover of their books. Review the traits of good writing. Refer to this chart as needed. The chart is also printed on the inside back cover of your edition.

Invite volunteers to read aloud the opening paragraph. Encourage volunteers to answer the questions. Then review the following about personal narratives:

- A personal narrative tells a true story of something that happened to the writer.
- It is told from the point of view of the writer, using words such as *I, me, my,* and *we.*
- It tells events in the order that they happened, using time words such as *first, next, then,* and *finally.*
- It includes a beginning, a middle, an ending, and a title.

Prewriting

Tell students that the first step in the writing process is prewriting. Explain that prewriting is the time when they will choose a topic, explore their ideas, and make a plan for their writing.

Have a volunteer read aloud this section. Ask students to name ways that Ivan might find an idea for a personal narrative topic *(browsing a scrapbook or family photo album, talking to family members about memories).*

👀 Encourage students to articulate their ideas clearly. Explain that their topic should be focused, not vague *(My first piano lesson, as opposed to Learning to play the piano).*

Choosing a Topic
Ask students why it might be a good idea for Ivan to come up with more than one topic. *(If he makes a list of topics, Ivan can choose the best one.)*

Invite volunteers to read aloud the first paragraph. Then have volunteers read aloud the topics on Ivan's list. Ask students which topic they would most like to read about.

Encourage students to explain what interests them about the topic. Invite a volunteer to read aloud the last paragraph. Ask students what might be interesting about the topic Ivan chose. Guide students to understand that most people are afraid of something and that they often like to know about how another person overcame a fear.

Your Turn
Read aloud this section and the list of topic ideas. Explain that writers often write best when writing about important experiences. Encourage students to write all the topics that come to mind while reading the list.

Writer's Workshop
Personal Narratives

Prewriting and Drafting

The story you tell in a personal narrative can be about anything that happened to you, as long as it is true. Has something funny happened to you? Do you remember a time when you learned an important lesson? These things can be topics for personal narratives.

Prewriting

Ivan was assigned to write a personal narrative for class. Before he could start writing, he needed an idea. He took time to do some prewriting. Ivan knew that this was the time when he could plan out the ideas that would go into his narrative.

👀 Ideas

Choosing a Topic
Ivan remembered that the topic of his personal narrative should be something that happened to him. He sat in a quiet place and began to think about a topic. However, Ivan didn't know where to begin. So he made a list to help him choose a topic. Here is part of Ivan's list.

> *Possible Topics*
> *a trip I'll never forget—the time I visited Uncle Max in Florida*
> *I've never laughed so hard—when my older sister Isabel and I pretended to be monkeys*
> *an experience with an animal—when I was scared of dogs but became friends with Britney's dog, Shadow*
> *my proudest moment—when my painting won the district art contest*

Ivan decided to write about becoming friends with the dog, Shadow. He thought this would be a good topic because it was about how he overcame a fear.

Allow students time to generate a list of topics. Have students circle the topic they are most excited to write about. Invite volunteers to share their topics with the class.

Storyboarding

Have volunteers read aloud this section. Ask students how storyboarding might help Ivan plan his personal narrative. *(Storyboarding helps him see the story, remember details, determine the major events, and order the events.)* Challenge students to guess what might happen in Ivan's story based on the pictures he drew.

👀 Remind students to relay the events in the order in which they happened and to take their time in explaining each event.

Your Turn

Read aloud this section. Encourage students to close their eyes and recall the story they have decided to write about. Tell students to decide on three events that show what happened in their story. Then have students draw a picture of each event. When students have finished, ask volunteers to share their work with the class.

TEACHING OPTIONS

Teaching Tip
Some students may benefit from rereading the personal narrative on page 211. Others might enjoy retelling the story or performing it as a skit. Use the model to review the characteristics of a personal narrative.

Writer's Road Map
To reinforce the seven steps of the writing process in the Writer's Workshop, make a poster with each of the seven steps listed.

1. **Prewriting**
2. **Drafting**
3. **Content Editing**
4. **Revising**
5. **Copyediting**
6. **Proofreading**
7. **Publishing**

Cut out paper in the shape of an arrow and attach tape to the back. Use the poster and arrow to track which step of the writing process students are working on.

Your Turn

Use the following list to help you think of ideas for your personal narrative. After you finish the list, circle the topic that you are the most excited to write about. Remember that the topics have to be about something that really happened to you.
- a trip I'll never forget
- I've never laughed so hard
- an experience with an animal
- my proudest moment
- an event I'll never forget
- my biggest surprise
- the hardest thing I ever did
- the most excited I've ever been

Storyboarding
Now that Ivan had a topic, he started to plan for his first draft. Ivan drew pictures of three

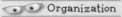 **Organization**

major events from his topic.
After he drew each picture, he wrote a sentence about what was happening in each one.

In Ivan's first picture, he drew himself sitting in his desk next to the dog and its owner. The second picture showed Ivan watching Shadow kick his legs while dreaming. The third picture showed Shadow using Ivan's foot as a pillow.

Ivan knew that personal narratives were written in time order. He drew the pictures and wrote the sentences in the order they happened.

Your Turn

Think about the three most important events that happened during the story you have chosen to tell. Draw each event on its own sheet of paper. Write a sentence about the picture at the bottom of the sheet. Then put the pictures in the order that the story happened.

Writer's Workshop   Personal Narratives

OBJECTIVE
- **To draft a personal narrative**

Drafting

Explain that drafting is the time when writers first put their ideas into sentences and paragraphs. Tell students that a draft is a writer's first try at writing a personal narrative. Explain that writers use the rest of the steps in the writing process to make their first drafts better.

Invite a volunteer to read aloud the first paragraph. Ask a volunteer to explain what a draft is *(a piece of writing that the writer is still improving)*.

Have volunteers read aloud Ivan's draft. Turn back to page 237 and review what Ivan drew for each of his pictures when he was storyboarding. Challenge students to tell which sentences in Ivan's draft go with each picture. *(Shadow slept under Britney's desk. He was on his side, and he kicked his legs. Shadow was using my foot as a pillow!)*

Discuss Ivan's draft by asking the following questions:

- **What part is the beginning, the middle, and the ending?**
- **How does the beginning grab your attention?**
- **What did Ivan learn at the end of the story?**
- **How can you tell the events were put in the order they happened?**

Invite volunteers to read aloud the last paragraph of the section. Ask students to name words in Ivan's draft that show it is a story that happened to him *(I, me, my)*. Ask

Drafting

It was now time for Ivan to write a draft. First, he wrote the beginning. It told what his narrative was going to be about. Then Ivan used his pictures to help him write the middle. He finished with an ending that told how his story turned out. Here is Ivan's draft.

When I was three years old, I was bitten by a German shepherd. The bite made me scared of big dogs, but I'm not anymore. It all changed last year when Britney was in my class. She is blind. Brings her helper dog. His name is Shadow, and he is a German Shepherd. When I saw him, I was so scared!

One day Ivan sat next to Britney and Shadow. It was the day everybody had to give a speech about the state they studied. Mine was Iowa. Shadow slept under Britney's desk. I looked at him. He was on his side, and he kicked his legs. He must have been dreaming. he didn't look as scary when he was asleep. I felt something on my foot. I looked under my desk. Shadow was using my foot as a pillow! He must have liked me and trusted me. I am still a little nervous when I meet new dogs, but I am not as scared as before.

Thanks, Shadow

students why Ivan left extra space between the lines of his draft *(to make room to write changes later)*. Point out that as Ivan wrote his draft, he concentrated on telling the whole story in time order.

Your Turn

Read aloud the first paragraph. Remind students that as they write their beginnings, they should be sure to tell what the narrative is about.

Read aloud the bulleted items. Suggest that students put the pictures they drew during prewriting in time order and use the pictures to help write the middle of their drafts. Review time words and remind students that using time words will help to keep events in order.

Allow time for students to write their drafts. As students work, encourage them to use strong verbs and colorful adjectives. Remind students to think of an interesting title for their personal narrative.

TEACHING OPTIONS

Title Partner

Have partners share their topics and pictures. Encourage students to use their pictures to summarize for their partners the story they want to write. Then challenge students to write three possible titles for their partners' narratives.

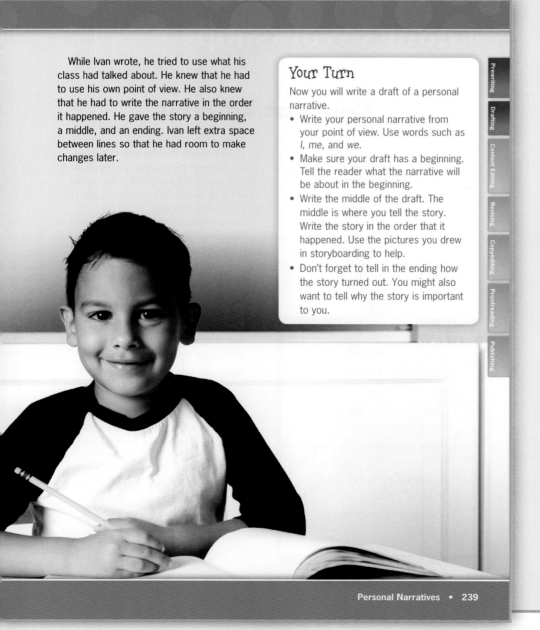

While Ivan wrote, he tried to use what his class had talked about. He knew that he had to use his own point of view. He also knew that he had to write the narrative in the order it happened. He gave the story a beginning, a middle, and an ending. Ivan left extra space between lines so that he had room to make changes later.

Your Turn

Now you will write a draft of a personal narrative.

- Write your personal narrative from your point of view. Use words such as *I, me,* and *we.*
- Make sure your draft has a beginning. Tell the reader what the narrative will be about in the beginning.
- Write the middle of the draft. The middle is where you tell the story. Write the story in the order that it happened. Use the pictures you drew in storyboarding to help.
- Don't forget to tell in the ending how the story turned out. You might also want to tell why the story is important to you.

Prewriting

Drafting

Content Editing

Revising

Copyediting

Proofreading

Publishing

Personal Narratives • 239

OBJECTIVE
- **To edit a first draft for content**

CONTENT EDITING

Invite volunteers to read aloud the first two paragraphs. Tell students that they are going to work with partners to complete the next step of the writing process, which is content editing. Explain that content editing is making sure the ideas in their story make sense.

Discuss why students think writers might ask another person to read their drafts. *(A new reader can tell whether the story is confusing and whether information is missing.)*

Have volunteers read aloud the Content Editor's Checklist. Ask students to explain what each question asks. Point out that a checklist like this helps a writer look for mistakes that are often made when writing a personal narrative.

Read aloud the two paragraphs that follow the checklist. Discuss how to give positive feedback. Encourage volunteers to role-play comments they might make about a partner's work. Remind students to think about their partners' feelings when talking about one another's work.

Read aloud Sal's comments one by one and discuss them with students. Point out that Sal's comments are helpful ideas for how to make the writing better, but they are said in a kind way. Have students compare Sal's comments with the questions on the Content Editor's Checklist. Challenge students to use the checklist to find something that Sal missed. *(Ivan's narrative does not have a title.)* Ask students to imagine that Ivan asked for their comments. Encourage volunteers to suggest what they might say to Ivan.

Have a volunteer read aloud the last paragraph of this section. Explain that Sal made good comments but that Ivan will decide what changes to make.

Editor's Workshop

Content Editing

Now that Ivan had a draft, he wanted to make it better. He knew that he could if he edited the content. Content editors make sure the writing and the ideas make sense. They also check that the writing stays on the topic.

Ivan thought it would be a good idea to ask a friend to content edit his personal narrative. He asked Sal. Sal was in the class with Ivan and Britney. He knew about Shadow. Sal used the Content Editor's Checklist below.

Content Editor's Checklist

- ☐ Does the writing stay on the topic?
- ☐ Is the story told from the writer's point of view?
- ☐ Are the events described in time order?
- ☐ Are time words used to explain the order?
- ☐ Does the story have a title, a beginning, a middle, and an ending?

Sal read Ivan's personal narrative a few times. He used the Content Editor's Checklist to help him. Sal wrote his ideas for making Ivan's draft better. When he was finished, he had a meeting with Ivan.

Sal first told Ivan what he liked about the personal narrative. Sal liked how the narrative was told in time order. Nothing happened out of place. He also liked how Ivan was honest with his feelings. Then Sal told Ivan these ideas:

- The writing gets off the topic when you talk about the state reports.
- You used your name instead of the word *I* at the start of the second paragraph.
- Maybe you could use some time words to show the order. The second paragraph doesn't tell how much time took place between the different things that happened.
- I had trouble understanding where the middle stopped and the ending started.

Your Turn

Read aloud the first bulleted item. Tell students to read one question at a time from the checklist and then to check their drafts to answer the question. Have them continue until they have checked their drafts against all the questions.

When students have finished, read aloud the other bulleted items. Choose a volunteer and demonstrate how to have a peer conference with a classmate. Start your comments by saying positive things about the writing. Talk about how to state comments so that they are positive and polite. Then have partners read and edit each other's work. Encourage students to listen to their partners' ideas because they are reading the narrative the way other readers will. Tell students to think about which of their partners' suggestions they might use.

Writer's Tip As students work, remind them to use considerate language. Tell them to think about how they would want comments to be phrased and to use a tone that they would appreciate.

TEACHING OPTIONS

English-Language Learners

Some English-language learners may feel more comfortable with their speaking ability than with their writing ability. Invite students who share the same language or the same English-language level to work together. Encourage them to provide one another help and support during the prewriting, drafting, and content editing stages.

Ivan thanked Sal for his help. Ivan wasn't sure if he was going to use all of Sal's ideas. He wanted to take time to think about how to use the ideas to make his narrative better.

Your Turn

- Read your first draft. Use the Content Editor's Checklist to help you improve the draft.
- Work with a partner and read each other's narratives. Pay attention to only one question from the checklist at a time. Take notes about your partner's draft. Then take turns talking about each other's drafts.
- Write your partner's ideas about your draft. Think about each one. The personal narrative is made up of your own ideas. Make the changes that seem right to you.

Writer's Tip When meeting with your partner about his or her draft, remember to start with something you liked.

Prewriting

Drafting

Content Editing

Revising

Copyediting

Proofreading

Publishing

Personal Narratives • 241

REVISING

Tell students that when writers revise their writing, they change it to make it better. Explain that some changes are the writer's own ideas and some changes come from suggestions that other readers have made.

Ask students to look over Ivan's revised draft. Point out that Ivan left extra space and used a different pencil color to mark his changes so that they would be easy to see. Tell students that Ivan used proofreading marks to write his changes. Explain that proofreading marks are a kind of code and that each mark means something. Ask students to look at the chart of proofreading marks on page 245.

Help students understand the purpose of each proofreading mark by writing on the board examples of usage. Challenge students to name ways that they could remember what each symbol means. *(The symbol for delete looks like the words might be thrown away. The symbol for a capital letter looks like it is making the letter taller.)*

Encourage students to use proofreading marks when they are making changes to their work. Ask students to tell what changes Ivan made with his proofreading marks.

Read aloud the sentences following Ivan's draft and the bulleted list.

- The information on state speeches is not necessary to telling the story.
- Personal narratives are told from the narrator's point of view.
- He added *A little later.*
- He made two paragraphs out of the second paragraph.
- It told that Shadow and he became friends.

Writer's Workshop   Personal Narratives

Revising

This is how Ivan revised his draft.

> ^Scared of Shadow
>
> When I was three years old, I was biten by a German shepherd. The bite made me scared of big dogs, but I'm not anymore. It all changed last year when Britney was in my class. She is blind. Brings her helper dog. His name is Shadow, and he is a German Shepherd. When I ^first saw him, I was so scared!
>
> One day ~~Ivan~~ sat next to Britney and Shadow. ~~It was the day everybody had to give a speech about the state they studied. Mine was Iowa.~~ Shadow slept under Britney's desk. I looked at him. He was on his side, and he kicked his legs. He must have been dreaming. he didn't look as scary when he was asleep. ^A little later, I felt something on my foot. ^Then I looked under my desk. Shadow was using my foot as a pillow! ¶ That's how Shadow and I became friends. He must have liked me and trusted me. I am still a little nervous when I meet new dogs, but I am not as scared as before.
>
> Thanks, Shadow

Ask a volunteer to read aloud the last paragraph. Point out that even after Ivan used Sal's ideas, Ivan kept looking for ways to improve his draft and that Ivan discovered on his own that he needed to write a title. Ask students why they think Sal didn't notice the missing title.

👓 Tell students that in a personal narrative, it is important to let their personality come through their writing. Ask them to identify where in Ivan's personal narrative they hear his voice coming through.

Your Turn

Have a volunteer read aloud this section. Encourage students to use proofreading marks to help make changes on their draft. Remind students to consider the comments from their partner and to use the Content Editor's Checklist to help make their changes.

Grammar in Action. Have volunteers read aloud each sentence in the first paragraph and identify the incomplete sentence *(Brings her helper dog)*. Remind students that a complete sentence has a subject and predicate. Ask what is missing from the incomplete sentence *(a subject)*.

TEACHING OPTIONS

What Does It All Mean?

Remind students that the ending of a personal narrative might tell what a writer learned or how he or she felt. Help students check their endings to see whether they are sharing a lesson. Suggest that students write a sentence about what they learned if they think that one would improve their personal narrative.

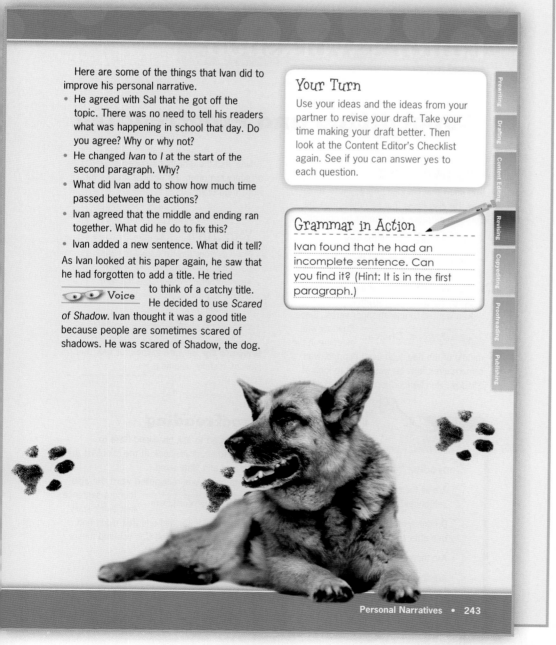

Here are some of the things that Ivan did to improve his personal narrative.

- He agreed with Sal that he got off the topic. There was no need to tell his readers what was happening in school that day. Do you agree? Why or why not?
- He changed *Ivan* to *I* at the start of the second paragraph. Why?
- What did Ivan add to show how much time passed between the actions?
- Ivan agreed that the middle and ending ran together. What did he do to fix this?
- Ivan added a new sentence. What did it tell?

As Ivan looked at his paper again, he saw that he had forgotten to add a title. He tried 👓 Voice to think of a catchy title. He decided to use *Scared of Shadow*. Ivan thought it was a good title because people are sometimes scared of shadows. He was scared of Shadow, the dog.

Your Turn

Use your ideas and the ideas from your partner to revise your draft. Take your time making your draft better. Then look at the Content Editor's Checklist again. See if you can answer yes to each question.

Grammar in Action

Ivan found that he had an incomplete sentence. Can you find it? (Hint: It is in the first paragraph.)

Preediting | Drafting | Content Editing | Revising | Copyediting | Proofreading | Publishing

Personal Narratives • 243

OBJECTIVE
- **To copyedit and proofread a personal narrative**

COPYEDITING AND PROOFREADING

Ask students to explain what content editing is *(making the ideas in a piece of writing clearer and better)*. Explain that the next step in the writing process is called copyediting. Tell students that in copyediting, writers and editors make sure the words and sentences are strong and correct.

Copyediting

Invite a volunteer to read aloud the first paragraph. Discuss how a checklist might help Ivan when copyediting. *(It can help him identify mistakes often made when writing a personal narrative.)*

Tell students that sentence fluency is how the writing sounds. To improve sentence fluency, tell students that it is helpful to read aloud as they copyedit.

Ask volunteers to read aloud the Copyeditor's Checklist and tell what it means to use strong verbs and colorful adjectives. Ask for examples of sentences that use strong verbs and colorful adjectives. Guide students to understand that the first two questions on the Copyeditor's Checklist are about sentences. Point out that the last two questions are about words.

Tell students that word choice brings their writing to life by using sensory language to create a vivid picture for readers.

Invite a volunteer to read aloud the rest of this section. Ask students to explain why *napped* and *peeked* are more

effective than *was sleeping* and *looked*. Ask students why Ivan might change one use of the word *scary* to *frightening*.

Have students match these three revisions to the items on the Copyeditor's Checklist. Ask students whether they think Ivan's revisions made his draft better.

Your Turn

Read aloud this section. Ask students to think about the verbs and adjectives they choose and whether their choices help the reader better understand the story.

Review the checklist and tell students to answer each question about their drafts. Allow time for students to copyedit and make changes to their drafts.

Writer's Tip Explain the importance of checking for one type of mistake at a time to avoid missing something students might want to change.

Proofreading

Point out the proofreading marks that appear on page 245. Explain that students should use these marks while proofreading their drafts.

Invite volunteers to read aloud the first paragraph. Point out that Ivan asked Nate to read his

---

Editor's Workshop   Personal Narratives

Copyediting and Proofreading

Copyediting

Ivan knew that his ideas made more sense now. He also knew that he could make his personal narrative even better by copyediting it. When you **Sentence Fluency** you copyedit you check that all the sentences work. You also check if you used all the words correctly. Ivan used this checklist to copyedit his personal narrative.

Ivan wanted to use stronger verbs. Since Shadow was sleeping in the **Word Choice** middle of the day, Ivan used *napped*. Ivan remembered how he was afraid to look at Shadow. He changed *looked* to *peeked*.

Ivan also thought that he used *scared* or *scary* too often. He decided to use the word *frightening*.

Your Turn

Now it's your turn to copyedit your personal narrative. You might add stronger verbs. Make sure the new words you use don't change the meaning of the sentence.

Writer's Tip Be sure to look for only one type of mistake at a time.

Proofreading

Ivan decided to ask his friend Nate to proofread his draft. Look at the checklist that both Ivan and Nate used.

Nate found one misspelled word. He also **Conventions** found a sentence that didn't start with a capital letter and one that didn't end with a punctuation mark. Can you find these three errors in Ivan's draft?

Copyeditor's Checklist

- [ ] Are all the sentences complete sentences?
- [ ] Do the sentences make sense one after the other?
- [ ] Are there strong verbs?
- [ ] Are there colorful adjectives?

244 • Chapter 1

---

draft because Nate had not read the draft before. Tell students that a new reader often catches additional mistakes because he or she is reading the story for the first time. Explain that sometimes when writers are fixing their writing, they accidentally make new mistakes.

Tell students that writing conventions include spelling, punctuation, capitalization, and grammar.

Read aloud the Proofreader's Checklist. Then invite a volunteer to read aloud the last two paragraphs. Have students locate the misspelled word *(biten)*. Ask a volunteer to use a dictionary to find the correct spelling *(bitten)*. Guide students to find the mistakes. *(The missing capitalization is in the second paragraph, and the last sentence has no punctuation mark.)*

Your Turn

Read aloud this section. Remind students to check for one kind of mistake at a time. When students have finished, have them give their drafts to a partner. Invite partners to proofread one another's drafts. Remind students to use a different pencil color as they work.

TEACHING OPTIONS

Getting Advice

As students copyedit, they may have questions about when to use strong verbs or colorful adjectives. Work individually with students to determine whether the word substitutions they have in mind make the writing stronger and to check whether the substitutions unnecessarily change the meaning of the sentence.

Spell-Check Backward

Explain that one way to check writing for misspelled words is to read backward from right to left, one word at a time. Help students begin by pointing at and checking the last word in a personal narrative. Tell students that they should point at and check each word, moving backward through the narrative.

Proofreader's Checklist

- ☐ Are the paragraphs indented?
- ☐ Are all the words spelled correctly?
- ☐ Is the first word of each sentence capitalized?
- ☐ Are proper nouns capitalized?
- ☐ Does each sentence end with the correct punctuation mark?
- ☐ Have you checked to be sure that no new mistakes were made?

Ivan found a capitalization problem too. He saw that he capitalized *shepherd* one of two times he used the word. Ivan looked in the dictionary and found that *German shepherd* was correct.

Your Turn

Use the Proofreader's Checklist to proofread your draft. Then ask a partner to use the checklist to check your work.

Common Proofreading Marks

Symbol	Meaning	Example
¶	begin new paragraph	over. Begin a new
⌒	close up space	close u p space
∧	insert	students think *should*
ℒ	delete, omit	that the the book
/	make lowercase	Mathematics
∿	reverse letters	reverse letters
≡	capitalize	washington
⌄" ⌄"	add quotation marks	I am, I said.
⊙	add period	Marta drank tea

OBJECTIVE
- **To publish a personal narrative**

PUBLISHING

Tell students that publishing happens when writers decide to share their work with an audience. Explain that for students, publishing could be sharing work by handing it in to a teacher or by reading it aloud to the class.

Invite a volunteer to read aloud the opening paragraph. Then have students read aloud Ivan's finished personal narrative. Encourage volunteers to comment on Ivan's story. Ask students why Ivan might have chosen to draw Shadow sleeping on Ivan's foot as the picture to share with his story.

Tell students that no matter how they decide to publish their writing, presentation matters. Explain that presentation is the look of a piece of writing. Point out that it includes neatness as well as consistent margins and spacing. Explain that it also includes visuals, such as photos or illustrations.

Have volunteers read aloud the many ways students might publish their personal narratives. Then ask students to name other ways they could publish their work (*letting their parents read it, putting it in a scrapbook, posting the work on a bulletin board*).

Your Turn

Read aloud this section. Suggest that students use the Proofreader's Checklist again when they have finished just to make sure they did not make any mistakes.

Writer's Workshop   Personal Narratives

Publishing

Presentation Ivan carefully typed the final draft of his personal narrative. He slowly added the proofreading changes. Ivan knew that publishing is sharing work with an audience. Ivan drew a picture and shared the picture and narrative with the class. The picture was of Shadow sleeping on Ivan's foot.

Scared of Shadow

When I was three years old, I was bitten by a German shepherd. The bite made me scared of big dogs, but I'm not anymore. It all changed last year when Britney was in my class. She is blind and brings her helper dog. His name is Shadow, and he is a German shepherd. When I first saw him, I was so scared!

One day I sat next to Britney and Shadow. Shadow napped under Britney's desk. I peeked at him. He was on his side, and he kicked his legs. He must have been dreaming. He didn't look as frightening when he was asleep. A little later I felt something on my foot. Then I looked under my desk. Shadow was using my foot as a pillow!

That's how Shadow and I became friends. He must have liked me and trusted me. I am still a little nervous when I meet new dogs, but I am not as scared as before.

Thanks, Shadow!

Have students make a final copy of their personal narratives. As students work, encourage them to write or type carefully and to reread each sentence to make sure they do not make any new mistakes.

Allow time for students to draw pictures to accompany their personal narratives. When students have finished, encourage volunteers to share their narratives and drawings with the class. Remind students of the speaking and listening tips in Lesson 6.

ASSESS

Have students assess their finished personal narrative using the reproducible Student Self-Assessment on page 247y. A separate Personal Narrative Scoring Rubric can be found on page 247z for you to use to evaluate their work.

Plan to spend tomorrow doing a formal assessment. Administer the Personal Narrative Writing Prompt on **Assessment Book** pages 41–42.

Eventually, a professional writer submits his or her personal narrative to a magazine or book publisher. Whenever you publish your work, your goal is to share your thoughts and experiences with other people. There are many ways you can publish your personal narrative.

 Create a classroom book. Include classmates' photos, drawings, or other souvenirs of their experience.

 Have your class book on hand for Parents' Night. You might wish to present it as a PowerPoint presentation or a video.

 Make a classroom newsletter. Use a digital camera to add photos of your classmates.

 Post it to a Web site that publishes student writing. Work with an adult to find an appropriate site.

 Draw one part of your story on a separate sheet of paper. Then play a guessing game. Put all the narratives on one bulletin board and all the pictures on another board. Have everyone read the narratives and try to match each picture to its story.

Your Turn

- Make a final copy of your personal narrative. You can use a pencil and paper or a computer. Include the proofreading corrections.
- Take plenty of time finishing your work. You are going to share it with your audience. Be careful not to make any new mistakes while writing or typing.

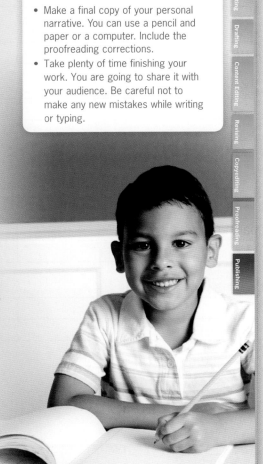

Prewriting | Drafting | Content Editing | Revising | Copyediting | Proofreading | Publishing

Personal Narratives • 247

TEACHING OPTIONS

Journal Jottings

Encourage students to keep notes in a writing journal about ideas for further personal narratives. Explain that many professional writers keep journals to jot down ideas, stories, and things that happen. Tell students that if they write about something that happens to them, such as an exciting family trip or a funny moment, right after it happens, they can remember more about the story. Explain that a journal is also a personal space for writings that no one else will read, so students don't have to worry about writing perfectly.

Portfolio Opportunity

Have students begin keeping a portfolio of their finished drafts from the Writer's Workshops throughout the year. Distribute folders or have students use their own. Ask them to decorate their folders any way they choose. Point out that a portfolio will help students track their progress through the year.

Name _____ Date _____

Personal Narrative

	YES	NO
Ideas		
Do I write about a real event in my life?		
Do I tell the events in time order?		
Organization		
Does the narrative have a beginning?		
Does the narrative have a middle?		
Does the narrative have an ending?		
Voice		
Do I use the words *I, me, we,* and *us*?		
Word Choice		
Do I use colorful adjectives?		
Do I use time words?		
Sentence Fluency		
Do my sentences include strong verbs?		
Conventions		
Do I use correct grammar?		
Do I use correct spelling?		
Do I use correct punctuation and capitalization?		
Presentation		
Is my paper neat?		
Do I use the same margins and spacing throughout?		
Do I include photos or illustrations?		
Additional Items		

Name _____

Date _____ Score _____

Personal Narrative

	POINTS
Ideas	
topic relating a real event	
events in time order	
Organization	
a beginning	
a middle	
an ending	
Voice	
the writer's point of view, using *I, me, we,* and *us*	
Word Choice	
colorful adjectives	
time words	
Sentence Fluency	
strong verbs	
Conventions	
correct grammar and usage	
correct spelling	
correct punctuation and capitalization	
Presentation	
neatness	
consistent margins and spacing	
photos or illustrations	
Additional Items	
Total	

©LOYOLAPRESS.

CHAPTER FOCUS

LESSON 1: What Makes a Good How-to Article?

LESSON 2: Parts of a How-to Article

- **GRAMMAR:** Nouns
- **STUDY SKILLS:** Dictionary Meanings
- **WRITING SKILLS:** The Four Kinds of Sentences
- **WORD STUDY:** Compound Words
- **SPEAKING AND LISTENING SKILLS:** How-to Talks
- **WRITER'S WORKSHOP:** How-to Article

SUPPORT MATERIALS

Practice Book
Writing, pages 137–141

Assessment Book
Chapter 2 Writing Skills, pages 43–44
How-to Writing Prompt, pages 45–46

Rubrics
Student, page 285y
Teacher, page 285z

Test Generator CD

Grammar
Section 2, pages 27–52

Customizable Lesson Plans
www.voyagesinenglish.com

How-to Articles

WHAT IS HOW-TO WRITING?

How-to writing is a form of exposition, an avenue for providing information. It can offer guidance and direction for accomplishing a task or goal, such as assembling an outdoor grill or making chili.

Good how-to writing includes the following:

- ☐ Logical steps organized in list form
- ☐ A clear purpose stated in the introduction
- ☐ A complete What You Need list
- ☐ Detailed, accurate instructions in the body
- ☐ Ideas expressed in step-by-step order
- ☐ A conclusion that summarizes the finished task
- ☐ Clear imperative sentences
- ☐ Compound words

LiNK Use the following titles to offer your students examples of well-crafted how-to writing:

Are You a Butterfly? by Judy Allen

How to Behave and Why by Munro Leaf

The Kids' Multicultural Cookbook by Deanna F. Cook

> **❝I am always doing that which I can not do, in order that I may learn how to do it.❞**
>
> —Pablo PIcasso

WRITER'S WORKSHOP TIPS

Follow these ideas and tips to help you and your class get the most out of the Writer's Workshop:

- Review the traits of good writing. Use the chart on the inside back cover of the student and teacher editions.
- Provide a variety of games with directions written in a how-to article format. Have students play the games and discuss the effectiveness of the directions.
- Make a bulletin board display of how-to pamphlets, brochures, recipe cards, and craft articles.
- Suggest that students hide an item in the classroom and write directions for a partner, telling him or her how to find it without mentioning the object.
- Have students make up or find a favorite recipe and compile their recipes into a book.
- Have students create inventions and write directions on how to make or use their inventions.

CONNECT WITH GRAMMAR

Throughout the Writer's Workshop, look for opportunities to integrate nouns with writing how-to articles.

- ☐ Have students identify common and proper nouns in their titles.
- ☐ During the prewriting and drafting steps, emphasize that a What You Need list will consist of nouns.
- ☐ Challenge students to identify words that can be used as nouns and as verbs in their published how-to articles.

SCORING RUBRIC

How-to Article

Point Values
0 = not evident
1 = minimal evidence of mastery
2 = evidence of development toward mastery
3 = strong evidence of mastery
4 = outstanding evidence of mastery

	POINTS
Ideas	
ideas expressed in logical, step-by-step order	
Organization	
a clear purpose stated in the introduction	
a complete What You Need list	
detailed, accurate instructions in the body	
a summarizing conclusion	
Voice	
imperative sentences	
Word Choice	
compound words used correctly	
Sentence Fluency	
four kinds of sentences	
steps that are complete sentences	
Conventions	
correct grammar and usage	
correct spelling	
correct punctuation and capitalization	
Presentation	
neatness	
consistent margins and spacing	
easy-to-read instructional graphics	
Additional Items	
Total	

Full-sized, reproducible rubrics can be found at the end of this chapter.

CHAPTER 2
How-to Articles

INTRODUCING THE GENRE

Ask students to tell about a time that they read how to do or make something. Explain that writing that teaches people how to do or make something is called how-to writing or a how-to article. Discuss the kinds of activities that people might learn from a how-to article.

Point out the following characteristics of a how-to article:

- A how-to article tells what the reader will do or make
- The directions are given in step-by-step order.
- A how-to article includes a title, an introduction, a What You Need list, the steps, and a conclusion.

Reading the Literature Excerpt

Have volunteers read aloud the recipe for cheesy quesadillas. Ask students to point out why this is a good example of how-to writing. Have students discuss other how-to writing they have encountered.

How-to Articles

LiNK The Kids' Multicultural Cookbook

The excerpts in Chapter 2 introduce students to published examples of how-to articles. The recipe for cheesy quesadillas is a strong example of a how-to article because it does the following:

- Tells what the reader will do or make
- Gives directions in step-by-step order
- Includes a title, an introduction, a What You Need list, the steps, and a conclusion

The excerpts in this chapter provide the opportunity to discuss different kinds of nouns. You may wish to point out nouns in the recipe, including the proper noun *Mexicans*.

LiNK **The Kids' Multicultural Cookbook**
by Deanna F. Cook

Cheesy Quesadillas

If you're a fan of grilled cheese sandwiches, then you will love this Mexican version. Instead of melting the cheese between sliced bread, northern Mexicans melt cheese in a flour tortilla. You can buy tortillas in the refrigerator section of most grocery stores.

What You Need

Pat of butter	1/4 cup grated cheese
1 flour tortilla	Salsa

1. In a frying pan, melt the butter over medium heat.
2. Set the tortilla in the pan and sprinkle half of it with the grated cheese. Fold the other half over the cheese to form a half circle.
3. Cook for about 2 minutes or until the tortilla browns. Then, use a spatula to flip the tortilla over. Cook it for another 2 minutes or until it browns. If you want, you can dip the quesadilla in salsa.

Makes 1 Mexican grilled cheese sandwich.

> This recipe has the characteristics of a how-to article. It has an introduction that tells what you will make or do, directions in step-by-step order, and a conclusion.

248

Reading the Student Model

Choose volunteers to read aloud the how-to article for making paper stained glass. If possible, provide materials for the activity and invite students to make paper stained glass by following the directions. Display students' paper stained glass around the classroom. Remind students to put the paper stained glass near a window to catch the sunlight.

As students work, ask them to point out the five parts of a how-to article: title, introduction, What You Need list, steps, and conclusion. Have students discuss their experience of making paper stained glass. Ask the following questions:

- Were the directions easy to follow?
- Were all the materials mentioned in the What You Need list?

TEACHING OPTIONS

Scavenger Hunt

Have small groups search the classroom and the school library for examples of how-to articles. Make a list on the board of the how-to articles students found. Discuss the characteristics of how-to articles. Compare examples and discuss why some are easier to follow than others.

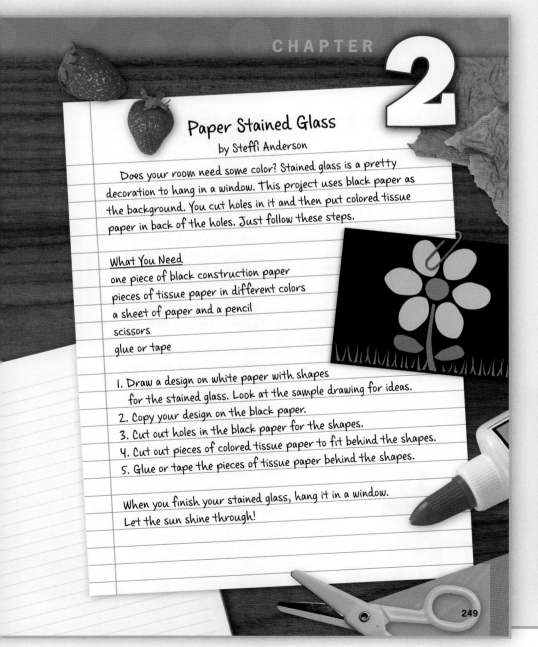

CHAPTER 2

Paper Stained Glass
by Steffi Anderson

Does your room need some color? Stained glass is a pretty decoration to hang in a window. This project uses black paper as the background. You cut holes in it and then put colored tissue paper in back of the holes. Just follow these steps.

What You Need
one piece of black construction paper
pieces of tissue paper in different colors
a sheet of paper and a pencil
scissors
glue or tape

1. Draw a design on white paper with shapes for the stained glass. Look at the sample drawing for ideas.
2. Copy your design on the black paper.
3. Cut out holes in the black paper for the shapes.
4. Cut out pieces of colored tissue paper to fit behind the shapes.
5. Glue or tape the pieces of tissue paper behind the shapes.

When you finish your stained glass, hang it in a window. Let the sun shine through!

249

For Tomorrow

Ask students to collect examples of how-to writing at home. Suggest that they look for directions for games, instructions for building something, or recipes for cooking or baking. Bring in your own example to share.

OBJECTIVES

- **To understand what makes a good topic for a how-to article**
- **To understand the proper order of a how-to article**

WARM-UP

Read, Listen, Speak

Share your example of how-to writing from yesterday's For Tomorrow homework. Invite small groups to share their examples of how-to writing. Ask students to discuss how they know the examples are how-to writing and whether the steps are easy to follow.

GRAMMAR CONNECTION

Take this opportunity to talk about common and proper nouns. You may wish to have students point out common and proper nouns in their Read, Listen, Speak examples.

TEACH

Read aloud the opening paragraph. Invite volunteers to discuss a time when they have followed written directions. Ask the volunteers how their experience was similar to or different from following the directions for making paper stained glass.

Have a volunteer read aloud the first paragraph of the Topic section. Ask students to name the topic of the model how-to article on page 249. Ask for other topics from how-to articles students have read.

Read aloud the second paragraph. Ask students why it is important to pick a topic that can be explained in a few short steps. Then ask why it is important to pick a topic they know about. *(They will already know the steps of the directions.)*

Have a volunteer read aloud the last paragraph. Invite students to discuss topics that interest them and things they would like to learn. Write their responses on the board. Guide students to understand which of their suggestions might be a topic for a how-to article.

PRACTICE

ACTIVITY A

After students have completed the activity, ask volunteers to suggest why each topic is or is not appropriate for a how-to article. Ask students what words in items 1, 5, 6, 7, and 9 indicated that each was a how-to article topic.

ACTIVITY B

Encourage students to write their answers in complete sentences. Ask volunteers to discuss their answers. Then tally on the board the number of students who would like to learn more about each topic. Discuss what made certain topics more appealing than others.

What Makes a Good How-to Article?

A how-to article tells how to do something. A how-to article might be a recipe for how to make peanut butter cookies. A how-to article might be directions to a party or rules for a game. A how-to article might teach you how to do something, like braid your hair or fly a kite. A how-to article might teach you how to make something, like the how-to article on page 249. Here are some things to remember when you write a how-to article.

Topic

Before you write a how-to article, you need to decide what the article will be about. The topic of a how-to article is what the reader will learn to make or do.

It is important to pick a topic that you can explain in a few short steps. It is also important to pick a topic that you know about. A how-to article about how to build a real-life castle would be too long and difficult. A better topic might be how to build a sandcastle.

Try to pick a topic that you think people will want to learn about. What topics interest you?

APPLY

WRITER'S CORNER

Allow time for students to finish their lists. Ask volunteers to name one snack from their lists and to explain where they learned to make the snack. Ask students to save their lists for the next Writer's Corner. Students should demonstrate an understanding of good topics for how-to articles.

TechTip You may wish to provide specific recipe Web sites. Ask students to print and read aloud their recipe choices and evaluate whether the directions are clear and easy to follow.

ASSESS

Note which students had difficulty understanding what makes a good topic for a how-to article. Use the Reteach option with those students who need additional reinforcement.

TEACHING OPTIONS

Reteach

Write on one side of note cards appropriate topics for how-to articles, such as *how to brush your teeth, how to draw a rainbow,* and *how to set a table.* Distribute one card to each student. Ask students to write on the back of the card one reason why this is a good topic for a how-to article and to write what the article might include. When students have finished, have them pass the card to another student and repeat the activity. Have volunteers share the information from the backs of several cards.

How-to Contents

Have small groups design a table of contents for a how-to book. Explain that a table of contents lists all the topics included in a book. Encourage groups to discuss general topics (*how to play games*) and then topics for six individual articles (*how to play tag, how to play soccer, how to play baseball, how to play hide-and-seek*). Display the finished tables of contents in the classroom.

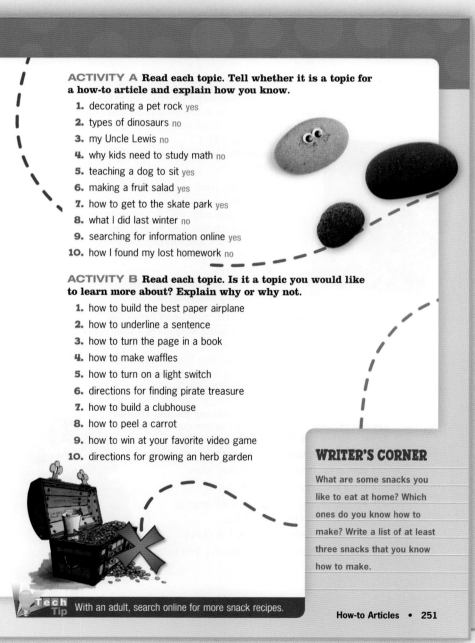

ACTIVITY A Read each topic. Tell whether it is a topic for a how-to article and explain how you know.

1. decorating a pet rock yes
2. types of dinosaurs no
3. my Uncle Lewis no
4. why kids need to study math no
5. teaching a dog to sit yes
6. making a fruit salad yes
7. how to get to the skate park yes
8. what I did last winter no
9. searching for information online yes
10. how I found my lost homework no

ACTIVITY B Read each topic. Is it a topic you would like to learn more about? Explain why or why not.

1. how to build the best paper airplane
2. how to underline a sentence
3. how to turn the page in a book
4. how to make waffles
5. how to turn on a light switch
6. directions for finding pirate treasure
7. how to build a clubhouse
8. how to peel a carrot
9. how to win at your favorite video game
10. directions for growing an herb garden

Tech Tip With an adult, search online for more snack recipes.

WRITER'S CORNER

What are some snacks you like to eat at home? Which ones do you know how to make? Write a list of at least three snacks that you know how to make.

How-to Articles • 251

For Tomorrow

Ask students to find an example of a how-to article at home and to copy only a part of it. Tell students to be ready to explain what information needs to be added to make it a complete how-to article. Bring in your own incomplete how-to article to share.

WARM-UP

Read, Listen, Speak

Read aloud your example of an incomplete how-to article. Ask students to listen carefully and to tell what is missing. Then have small groups share their incomplete how-to articles. Ask students to discuss what kind of information is needed to complete each article.

GRAMMAR CONNECTION

Take this opportunity to talk about singular and plural nouns. You may wish to have students point out singular and plural nouns in their Read, Listen, Speak examples.

TEACH

Invite a volunteer to read aloud the first paragraph of the section Order. Ask students why it is important that steps be written in the order the reader will do them.

Have volunteers read aloud the second paragraph and the steps for growing marigolds. Invite volunteers to read the steps in random order and to discuss what would happen if someone tried to follow the mixed-up steps. Then read the last paragraph aloud. Emphasize the importance of checking the order of steps when writing a how-to article.

PRACTICE

ACTIVITY C

Have partners complete the activity. Ask a volunteer to read the steps in the correct order. Challenge students to offer suggestions for other steps that could be added to the directions. *(Cook the noodles.)*

ACTIVITY D

Suggest that students reread the steps for their topic to be sure no steps are missing. Then ask volunteers to read aloud their steps. Encourage students to explain why they believe it would be important for an alien creature living on Earth to know how to do one of these things.

ACTIVITY E

Bring in the items needed to complete the task. Ask a volunteer to read aloud the steps while another completes them. Then ask the class what step is missing.

LiNK Read aloud the directions. Discuss the importance of order. Have partners create a pop-up card.

Order

A how-to article gives directions in step-by-step order. When you write a how-to article, put the steps in the same order that you want the reader to do them. Then number your steps, starting with 1.

Here are the steps for growing marigolds in an egg carton.

1. Put plastic wrap in each cup of an egg carton.
2. Fill the cups with soil.
3. Plant a marigold seed in each cup.
4. Pour a little water on the soil.
5. Close the egg carton to keep the seeds warm.
6. Give the seeds time to sprout. Then plant them outside.

Be sure that you put the steps in the right order before you number them. Imagine if steps 1 and 2 were in the wrong order. The reader might put the soil in the egg carton before putting in the plastic wrap. What a mess! You also have to be careful not to leave out an important step. Imagine if step 4 was left out. The plants wouldn't grow because they had no water.

ACTIVITY C **These steps for making colored noodles are out of order. Copy the steps in the right order. Then number the steps 1, 2, 3, 4, 5, and 6.**

3 • Swish the noodles in the bag until they are colored.

5 • Repeat the above steps with other colors.

4 • Place the noodles on paper towels to dry.

1 • Pour some food coloring and a few drops of rubbing alcohol into a plastic bag.

2 • Add some noodles and zip the bag closed.

6 • Use the different-colored noodles in a craft project.

APPLY

WRITER'S CORNER

Ask students to take out the lists they made in the last Writer's Corner. Remind students to choose one snack recipe and write the steps in the correct order. When students have finished, ask volunteers to share their work with the class. Ask students to tell if the directions are complete and in the correct order. Students should demonstrate the ability to write in the correct order steps for a how-to article.

Grammar in Action. Have students identify the nouns as common or proper and singular or plural.

ASSESS

Note which students had difficulty understanding how to give directions in step-by-step order. Use the Reteach option with those students who need additional reinforcement.

Practice Book page 137 provides additional work with the characteristics of an effective how-to article.

TEACHING OPTIONS

Reteach

Help students write step-by-step directions for how to play tic-tac-toe. Encourage partners to play the game carefully and to take notes that might help to write the directions. Tell students to number each step. When students have finished, have volunteers play the game by using the directions. If necessary, encourage students to edit the directions to improve them.

Follow the Steps

Write step-by-step directions for an activity for the class to complete, such as *how to make a paper heart*, *how to make a paper-bag puppet*, *how to make egg-carton tulips*, or *how to make paper-plate animals*. Distribute the directions and materials to small groups. Allow time for each group to follow the directions and make the item. Have groups present their completed activity to the class. Encourage students to discuss any steps that caused problems. Have students offer suggestions about how to improve the directions to make them easier to follow.

For Tomorrow

Ask students to give to a family member their steps for making a snack and to ask him or her to make or pantomime making the snack. Tell students to ask the family member if the steps were easy to follow. Have a friend or family member make a snack for which you provide directions and get feedback to share with students.

ACTIVITY D Imagine you have to explain how to do something simple to an alien creature. Pick a topic. Write the steps you would need to explain the topic to the alien creature.

1. how to make chocolate milk
2. how to do laundry
3. how to study spelling words
4. how to climb a tree
5. how to make a bed
6. how to play dodgeball
7. how to care for a hamster
8. how to use a digital camera

LiNK

Happy Pop-Up Card

1. Fold [a sheet of] paper in half to make a card.
2. Cut a thin strip of paper. Fold it back and forth to make the pop-up spring.
3. Use markers to make a decoration. Cut it out.
4. Paste one end of the spring to the inside of the card. Paste the other end to your decoration.
5. Write your message in the card.

Jill Frankel Hauser

Activity E
The missing step is where to put the knife.

ACTIVITY E There is something missing in these steps for how to set a dinner table. Read the steps and tell what is missing.

1. Get a plate, a fork, a knife, a napkin, and a glass for each person.
2. Put a plate at each place.
3. Put a fork to the left of the plate.
4. Fold the napkin and put it next to the fork.
5. Put a glass to the top right-hand side of the plate.
6. Do this for each person.

WRITER'S CORNER

Choose a snack from the list you made for the Writer's Corner on page 251. Write three steps for making that snack.

Grammar in Action. Circle all the nouns in your snack recipe.

How-to Articles • 253

OBJECTIVES

- **To recognize the parts of a how-to article**
- **To know what to include in a how-to article**

WARM-UP

Read, Listen, Speak

Tell students about your own experience giving a family member or friend snack-making directions. Emphasize mistakes or oversights as well as what worked. Have small groups discuss how well their family members were able to follow students' directions. Ask students to discuss what their family members said about their directions.

GRAMMAR CONNECTION

Take this opportunity to talk about plurals of nouns ending in *y*. You may wish to have students point out any plurals of nouns ending in *y* in their Read, Listen, Speak examples.

TEACH

Read aloud the opening paragraph. Then have a volunteer read aloud the Title callout. After the Title callout is read, tell students that in a how-to article, the title is the topic of the article. Have a volunteer read aloud the Introduction callout. Then ask students what the article says is the reason for making a banana milk shake. *(It is tasty.)* Have a volunteer read aloud the What You Need callout. Ask students to discuss why this part comes before the steps. *(It tells what the reader needs to gather to complete the steps.)* Discuss what would happen if all the materials needed were not listed. *(The reader would not be prepared to complete all the steps.)* Have a volunteer read aloud the Steps callout. Remind

students that the steps are always written in the order they should be done. Read aloud the Conclusion callout. Ask students what the writer says in the conclusion of the how-to article. *(The conclusion says that the banana milk shake is done and encourages the reader to experiment.)*

PRACTICE

ACTIVITY A

Tell students to use the example on page 254 as a guide while completing this activity. Then invite volunteers to write on the board the parts in the correct

order. Ask students what the introduction says is the reason to follow the directions of the how-to article *(to have healthy teeth).*

ACTIVITY B

Tell partners to read silently the model how-to article before working together to answer the questions. Then ask a volunteer to write on the board what the readers will learn to make. Invite a volunteer to write on the board the first sentence of the introduction. Continue this procedure for the remaining questions.

Parts of a How-to Article

A how-to article has five parts: the title, the introduction, the What You Need list, the steps, and the conclusion. Read what each part does in the example below.

Title
The title tells what the article is about.

What You Need
What You Need is a list of all the things the reader will need. Sometimes this part is called Materials.

Conclusion
The conclusion tells what readers made or did. You might give tips for other ways to do the activity. You might tell readers why what they learned will help them.

Make a Banana Milk Shake

A banana milk shake is tasty. It's so easy to make, you can enjoy it any time!

What You Need
1 scoop of vanilla ice cream
1/2 cup of milk
1 ripe, peeled banana
blender

Steps
1. Ask an adult to help you slice the banana.
2. Put ice cream in the blender. Add milk and the banana.
3. Place the lid on the blender. Have an adult turn on the blender.
4. When the ingredients are mixed, have an adult turn off the blender.
5. Pour the milk shake into a glass.

You've now made a tasty banana milk shake. Try using other fresh fruit to come up with flavors of your own!

Introduction
The introduction tells what you will make or do. It might also give a reason to make or do something.

Steps
The steps list what to do. Numbers show the order of the steps.

APPLY

WRITER'S CORNER

When students have finished, encourage volunteers to share their answers with the class (game pieces, checkerboard, and a timer). Accept any answers students can justify. Students should demonstrate an understanding of the parts of a how-to article.

ASSESS

Note which students had difficulty understanding the parts of a how-to article. Use the Reteach option with those students who need additional reinforcement.

ACTIVITY A This how-to article is mixed up. Copy the parts of the how-to article. As you copy the article, put the parts where they belong.

What You Need 3

toothbrush
toothpaste
water

Conclusion 5

Remember to brush at least twice a day. Try to brush after eating sugary snacks. And remember to floss!

Title 1

How to Brush Your Teeth

Introduction 2

Healthy teeth help you chew. They help you look your best. Follow these steps for healthier teeth.

Steps 4

1. Wet the toothbrush.
2. Squeeze the toothpaste onto the toothbrush.
3. Brush your teeth for three minutes. Use gentle strokes.
4. Rinse with cool water.

Activity B

1. a stained-glass artwork
2. first paragraph
3. one sheet of black construction paper, pieces of tissue paper in different colors, a sheet of paper and a pencil, scissors, glue or tape
4. 5
5. last paragraph

ACTIVITY B Read the how-to article "Paper Stained Glass" on page 249. Work with a partner to answer the following questions.

1. What will the readers learn to make?
2. Which part is the introduction?
3. What items are listed in the What You Need part?
4. How many steps are there?
5. Which part is the conclusion?

WRITER'S CORNER

Imagine that you are writing a how-to article about playing checkers. Write what you would list in the What You Need part.

How-to Articles • 255

Read, Listen, Speak

Share your steps from yesterday's For Tomorrow homework. Have small groups who have chosen common topics share their steps and discuss the differences.

GRAMMAR CONNECTION

Take this opportunity to talk about irregular plural possessives. You may wish to have students point out any irregular plural possessives in their Read, Listen, Speak examples.

TEACH

Invite a volunteer to read aloud the section Including What You Need. Ask students why it would be a good idea to do the activity before they begin writing.

Write on the board the What You Need list from the model on page 249. Read aloud the steps from the model. Have students circle each item from the list when it is mentioned in a step.

Read aloud the first paragraph of the Unneeded Information section. Have volunteers read the steps aloud. Then ask students to identify which step is unneeded and explain their reasoning. Invite a volunteer to read aloud the last two paragraphs. Discuss how unneeded information can confuse the reader.

PRACTICE

ACTIVITY C

Have a volunteer write the What You Need list on the board. While another volunteer is reading the steps, have the first volunteer circle the materials as they are mentioned and write the number of the steps in which they appear. Ask a volunteer to tell what item is missing from the list *(milk)*.

ACTIVITY D

Tell students to read all the steps before deciding which step is not needed. Challenge students to explain why step 3 is not needed. *(The step does not give any information for making a peanut butter and jelly sandwich.)*

ACTIVITY E

Ask volunteers to write the items without the item numbers on sentence strips. Then have seven students choose a sentence strip and hold it so the class can read it. Ask volunteers to arrange the strip-holding students in the correct order.

Including What You Need

When you write a how-to article, be sure to include everything needed to do the steps. Try doing the activity yourself to make sure you haven't left out any materials.

Unneeded Information

Adding unneeded information to a how-to article can confuse the reader. Look at these steps about how to make a penny bank.

How to Make a Penny Bank

Steps
1. Clean an old coffee can.
2. Cover the outside with white paper.
3. Use markers or paint to decorate it.
4. Don't ever tell your brother or sister where you keep your pennies.
5. Ask an adult to cut a slit in the center of the lid. Place the lid on the container.
6. Use your bank to collect spare pennies or other coins.

Do you see an unneeded step? If you said step 4, you are right. It might be a good idea to keep your penny bank secret, but this information is not needed to make a penny bank.

Always check that you have included only the information you need in your steps.

ACTIVITY C **Read this What You Need list. Then read the steps. What is missing from the list?** milk

What You Need	Steps
bowl	1. Pour cereal into the bowl.
spoon	2. Add milk to the cereal.
cereal	3. Use a butter knife to slice the banana.
banana	4. Drop the sliced banana into the cereal.
butter knife	5. Stir and eat.

APPLY

WRITER'S CORNER

When students have finished, ask them to draw a map of the route from the playground to the classroom. Consider having them create their map on a computer with a drawing program and type their directions. Have students exchange their directions and maps with partners and check that the map and the written directions match. Students should demonstrate the ability to write steps in order.

Grammar in Action. Remind students that common nouns are general and proper nouns are specific and capitalized. Point out that the names of streets, schools, parks, and businesses are proper nouns.

ASSESS

Note which students had difficulty understanding what to include in the steps of a how-to article. Use the Reteach option with those students who need additional reinforcement.

Practice Book page 138 provides additional work with the parts of a how-to article.

ACTIVITY D Read these steps for making a peanut butter and jelly sandwich. Tell which step is not needed. step 3

Making a Peanut Butter and Jelly Sandwich

1. Spread peanut butter on one slice of bread.
2. Spread jelly on the other slice of bread.
3. Some people call this a PB and J sandwich.
4. Place the slices together so that the peanut butter and the jelly are inside the sandwich.

Activity E
1. Conclusion
2. 3
3. Introduction
4. 2
5. 4
6. 1
7. 5

ACTIVITY E The following sentences are from a how-to article about making a bird feeder. Decide which sentence is the introduction and which is the conclusion. Then arrange the steps in order.

1. Enjoy watching birds flock to your bird feeder.
2. Steady the pinecone by holding it from the loop and spread cream cheese or soy butter on it.
3. Making a bird feeder is simple and fun.
4. Loop a piece of yarn around the top of the dried pinecone.
5. Roll the covered pinecone in birdseed.
6. Get a large pinecone and let it dry.
7. Hang the finished pinecone on a tree branch.

WRITER'S CORNER

Imagine that you have to give directions from the playground to your classroom. Close your eyes and picture the steps you have to take. Write the steps. Then read what you wrote to check for unneeded information.

Grammar in Action. Circle all the common nouns and underline all the proper nouns in your directions.

How-to Articles • 257

Reteach

Write on note cards materials lists and directions for several simple activities. For each activity include one piece of unneeded information or leave out an item in the materials that is necessary to complete the activity. Distribute the cards. Have students put the materials and steps in the correct order. Ask students to identify if materials are missing or if unneeded information was provided. Have volunteers read aloud the materials and steps in the correct order and point out unneeded steps and missing materials.

Party Time

Have students imagine that they are planning a party at school. Have small groups choose one of the following tasks: choosing the menu, decorating, planning party activities, making a guest list, and making invitations. Ask each group to write the steps in order for how to accomplish their task. Have groups share their party-planning steps with the class. Discuss suggestions for improving the steps to complete each task.

For Tomorrow

Ask students to write the steps they would do to make a greeting card. Tell them to make a list of the materials they would need. Write your own steps and materials list to share with the class. Bring in the materials on the list.

OBJECTIVE

- **To understand and be able to use dictionary entries to find word meanings**

WARM-UP

Read, Listen, Speak

Provide the materials on the list you made for yesterday's For Tomorrow homework. Read aloud your directions and have a volunteer perform the steps as you read them. Ask students to tell if any steps or materials are missing or unneeded. Have students share the steps they wrote for how to make a greeting card. Ask small groups to share the easiest and clearest directions with the class.

GRAMMAR CONNECTION

Take this opportunity to talk about singular possessive nouns. You may wish to have students point out any singular possessive nouns in their Read, Listen, Speak examples.

TEACH

Encourage students to discuss when and why they have used a dictionary. Invite a volunteer to read aloud the first paragraph.

Tell students that they will come across words in their reading that will have more than one meaning. Have students look up *gold* in a dictionary. Then ask a volunteer to read the meanings aloud. Discuss the different meanings of *gold*. Ask a volunteer to tell which meaning is a color.

Read aloud the second paragraph. Ask students why they think that learning new meanings will help them become better readers, writers, and speakers. *(The more meanings you know, the more word choices you have to use when you need a strong verb or colorful adjective.)*

Have a volunteer read aloud the third paragraph and the definitions of the word *quill*. Ask students which of these meanings they already knew. Have volunteers use *quill* in a sentence for each meaning.

PRACTICE

ACTIVITY A

Review guide words and alphabetical order. Complete the first item with the class. When students have finished, ask them if any words were unfamiliar and if they were surprised at the number of meanings for each word.

ACTIVITY B

Have partners complete this activity. Ask volunteers to read the correct meanings for each word to the class.

Dictionary Meanings

A dictionary is a book of words and their meanings. A word is listed in the dictionary in an entry. An entry lists the word, its pronunciation, and what it means. If a word has more than one meaning, each different meaning is listed with a number.

Learning new meanings for words can be fun. Learning new meanings can also help you become a better reader, writer, and speaker.

In this entry the word *quill* has three meanings. Can you find them?

> **quill** (kwil) **1.** a large, stiff feather. **2.** a writing pen made from the hollow stem of a feather. **3.** one of the sharp, stiff spines of a porcupine.

ACTIVITY A Use guide words and alphabetical order to find these words in a dictionary. Tell how many meanings each word has.

1. find
2. grade
3. steam
4. safe
5. phantom
6. family
7. drive
8. trunk
9. land
10. character

APPLY

WRITER'S CORNER

Tell students to pick a word that has more than one meaning. Invite volunteers to read their sentences to the class and tell the meaning of the word they did not know. Students should demonstrate the ability to use a dictionary to find multiple word meanings.

ASSESS

Note which students had difficulty with multiple meanings in dictionary entries. Use the Reteach option with those students who need additional reinforcement.

TEACHING OPTIONS

Reteach

Write multiple-meaning words on note cards. Have students choose cards, look up the word in a dictionary, and write a few meanings on the back of the card. Ask students to use the words in complete sentences. Have volunteers identify the meaning of the word as it was used in the sentence. Have the student read aloud another meaning of the word from the back of the card. Ask volunteers to use the word in a different sentence that illustrates another meaning.

My Little Dictionary

Have students choose five words to use to make a mini-dictionary. Instruct students to look up each word in a dictionary and write its meanings on a separate sheet of paper. Direct students to put the words in alphabetical order. Encourage students to illustrate the words and to write sample sentences using the words. Allow time for students to design covers for their mini-dictionaries. Display the dictionaries in the class reading corner or on a bulletin board.

ACTIVITY B These words have more than one meaning. Under each word there are three meanings. Two meanings are correct. Use a dictionary to choose the two meanings of each word.

1. safe
   a. a steel box for storing money or jewels
   b. in baseball, reaching a base without being out
   c. the dried leaves of a plant

2. crane
   a. a large box made of wood
   b. a machine for lifting heavy objects
   c. a large bird with long legs

3. flurry
   a. a brief, light snowfall
   b. a type of musical instrument
   c. a sudden burst of activity

4. cinch
   a. a strong strap for fastening a saddle on a horse
   b. something that is easy to do
   c. a cup-shaped object used to store water

5. substantial
   a. underwater
   b. strongly made
   c. large or important

6. stock
   a. a large fort
   b. a share in a company
   c. items in a store that people can buy

WRITER'S CORNER

Open a dictionary to any page. Find a word that you do not know. Read the meanings of the word. Then write a sentence that shows one meaning of the word.

For Tomorrow

Ask students to search books, newspapers, or magazines at home for three words of more than 10 letters. Have students write the words and their meanings and write a sentence using each word. Bring in your own list of words, their meanings, and a sentence using each.

How-to Articles • 259

WARM-UP

Read, Listen, Speak

Share your words, definitions, and sentences from yesterday's For Tomorrow homework. Invite small groups to share their words and sentences. Challenge groups to use in a single sentence two or more of the words they found.

GRAMMAR CONNECTION

Take this opportunity to talk about plural possessive nouns. You may wish to have students point out any plural possessive nouns in their Read, Listen, Speak examples.

TEACH

Have students discuss the information a dictionary entry can provide *(the pronunciation of the word, the spelling of the word, the different meanings of the word)*. Then ask students how they know a word has more than one meaning. *(If a word has more than one meaning, it will have numbered definitions within the entry.)* Invite students to discuss why it is a good idea to learn different meanings of a word *(to more clearly understand what they are reading, writing, or hearing)*.

PRACTICE

ACTIVITY C

Have students first write one meaning for each word. Then have students meet with a partner and compare and combine their lists of meanings. Tell students to use a dictionary to find out how many other meanings each word has.

ACTIVITY D

Allow time for students to write the meaning for each word. Then challenge volunteers to use each word in a sentence.

ACTIVITY E

Have partners complete the activity. When students have finished, ask volunteers to read aloud their answers.

ACTIVITY F

Read aloud all the meanings for *press*. Tell students to read each sentence carefully and then decide which meaning of *press* matches the sentence.

ACTIVITY G

Tell students that in this exercise they will use the dictionary as a scientific reference tool. Emphasize that Mercury in the

---

ACTIVITY C Write one meaning you know for each word below. Then look up each word in a dictionary. Tell how many other meanings there are.

1. blank
2. land
3. sharp
4. shell
5. double
6. pocket
7. party
8. train
9. rule
10. brand

ACTIVITY D Look up each word in a dictionary. Write one meaning of the word.

1. appliance
2. knoll
3. demolish
4. nocturnal
5. heron
6. cleaver
7. grime
8. bard
9. glacier
10. hush
11. pace
12. quest

ACTIVITY E Use a word from Activity D to complete each sentence.

1. The soldiers walked up the ___knoll___ to the castle.
2. Ziggy built a special ___appliance___ for making fruit smoothies.
3. It was difficult to keep up with the runner's fast ___pace___.
4. The rain washed the ___grime___ off the sidewalk.
5. I watched a wrecking ball ___demolish___ the old dance hall.
6. My dad uses a ___cleaver___ to chop steaks.
7. The bell rang and a ___hush___ fell over the entire auditorium.
8. Bats are my favorite ___nocturnal___ animals.
9. The ___bard___ sang a beautiful song for the king.
10. Scientists tell us that a large ___glacier___ created the Great Lakes.
11. The knight went on a ___quest___ to kill the dragon.
12. A large ___heron___ crossed the pond.

example is the planet closest to the sun, so students do not have to look up that name. Ask volunteers to draw on the board the planets in the proper order.

APPLY

WRITER'S CORNER

When students have finished making their flashcards, have small groups meet to quiz one another. Students should demonstrate the ability to use a dictionary to find multiple meanings of words.

 TechTip Provide an online dictionary Web site and help students to use the search, browse, and pronunciation tools.

ASSESS

Note which students had difficulty using dictionaries. Use the Reteach option with those students who need additional reinforcement. **Practice Book** page 139 provides additional work using dictionaries.

Practice Book page 139

Reteach

Assign partners a page in a dictionary. Have them choose three entry words from the page. Ask students to read aloud the entries and discuss the definitions. Then have partners write one sentence for each word they chose.

Word Detectives

Tell students to imagine that they are word detectives. Write on the board a list of multiple-meaning words. Have students choose five words from the list. Encourage students to use a dictionary to do the following:

1. Write the page number on which they find each word.

2. Find and write the guide words for each entry.

3. Write at least two definitions for each word.

4. Use each word in a sentence.

Have students share their detective work with the class.

ACTIVITY F Look carefully at the meanings for *press*. Tell which sentence goes with each meaning.

> **press** (w) *verb* **1.** to push something with steady force. **2.** to make something smooth with a hot iron. **3.** to hold someone or something close to you; hug. **4.** to keep asking somebody to do something.

1. My dad presses his shirts every morning so that he doesn't go to work with wrinkled clothes. 2
2. Dahlia pressed a tack into her wall. 1
3. Theodore pressed his teddy bear to his chest. 3
4. Mrs. Brown pressed her students to stop talking during the film. 4

Activity G
1. Mercury
2. Venus
3. Earth
4. Mars
5. Jupiter
6. Saturn
7. Uranus
8. Neptune

ACTIVITY G Look up the names of the planets in our solar system in a dictionary. Use the definitions to put the planets in order from the sun. The first planet has been done for you.

EXAMPLE   **1. Mercury**

Mars	Jupiter
Saturn	Neptune
Uranus	Earth
Venus	

WRITER'S CORNER

Make word flash cards with a partner. Find a word in a dictionary that you do not already know. Write the word on the front of the card and the meanings of that word on the back. You and your partner should each make three cards.

Tech Tip With an adult, use an online dictionary.

How-to Articles • 261

For Tomorrow

Ask students to open an encyclopedia or a textbook, close their eyes, and point to the page. Tell students to pick the longest word near their finger. Ask them to use a dictionary to look up the word and then make a riddle for the word they chose. Write your own riddle to share with the class.

- **To recognize and use the four kinds of sentences**

WARM-UP

Read, Listen, Speak
Read aloud your riddle from yesterday's For Tomorrow homework. Ask students to guess the word. Then read aloud the word's definition in a dictionary. Ask students to share their riddles with small groups. Have students determine the answer to the riddle.

GRAMMAR CONNECTION
Take this opportunity to talk about irregular plural possessive nouns. You may wish to have students point out any irregular plural possessive nouns in their Read, Listen, Speak examples.

TEACH

Read aloud the first paragraph. Ask volunteers to write on the board the names of the four kinds of sentences. Invite students to guess what each type of sentence does based on its name.

Ask a volunteer to read aloud the section Statements. Tell students that statements are the kind of sentence they use most often when speaking. Invite a volunteer to write an example statement next to the word *statement* on the board.

Have a volunteer read aloud the section Questions. Tell students that this kind of sentence is used to find out information. Encourage students to suggest other words that might start a question (*why, how, when*). Invite a volunteer to write an example question next to the word *question* on the board.

LiNK Have a volunteer read aloud the excerpt from *Learning How: Karate.* Ask a volunteer to perform the steps as they are read. Then ask students to tell what kind of sentences the first two are *(statements).*

PRACTICE

ACTIVITY A
Tell students to look for the sentences asking for information. Remind students that those will be questions. When students have finished, invite volunteers to tell how they identified the kind of sentence for each item.

ACTIVITY B
Remind students that a complete sentence has a subject and a predicate. Invite volunteers to read aloud their answers.

ACTIVITY C
Tell students to consider what kind of information they would like to find out about each statement. Have students work with partners. Then have partners share their questions with the class. Encourage volunteers to answer the questions or suggest where answers may be found.

The Four Kinds of Sentences

Writers can use sentences to say just about anything. There are four kinds of sentences. Each of them has a different purpose. The four kinds of sentences are statements, questions, commands, and exclamations.

Statements
Some sentences tell. Telling sentences are called statements. Statements end with a period. Here are four statements.

> **Mushrooms grow in warm, soggy places.**
> **A clean dog is a healthy dog.**
> **Your skateboard looks new.**
> **Many students enjoy music class.**

Questions
Some sentences ask. Asking sentences are called questions. Questions often begin with words such as *who, what, when, where, do,* and *is.* Questions end with a question mark. Here are four questions.

> **Do you like to paint?**
> **Where can I buy wind chimes?**
> **Is it going to rain today?**
> **What did you do over summer vacation?**

LiNK

Learning How: Karate

As a beginning karate student, you will learn four basic blocks. A *rising block* blocks a punch to the face. With your right fist facing up and resting on your right hip, raise your right arm in a bent position above your head. This upward motion deflects an opponent's punch to the face.

Jane Mersky Leder

APPLY

WRITER'S CORNER

When students have finished, ask a volunteer to write the nine question words on the board with large spaces between the words. Ask volunteers to write sentences on the board, using the question words as the first word of the sentence. Invite volunteers to write answers next to the questions. Students should demonstrate the ability to recognize and write statements and questions.

ASSESS

Note which students had difficulty recognizing and writing statements and questions. Use the Reteach option with those students who need additional reinforcement.

TEACHING OPTIONS

Reteach

Explain that we use questions and statements in conversations throughout the day. Ask students to think of situations in which they might have to ask or answer a question. *(What would you like for breakfast? How was school today? What are you doing after school?)* Have students write five questions and statements they would use to answer the questions. Remind students to use the correct punctuation mark for each sentence.

Interview a Friend

Have partners interview each other. First, have them write questions they want to know about each other. *(When is your birthday? Where were you born? What do you want to be when you grown up?)* Then have students take turns interviewing each other, writing questions and answers in different colors. Invite volunteers to read aloud their questions and answers. Have volunteers identify each sentence as a statement or a question.

For Tomorrow

Have students write three questions to ask a family member and then write the answers. Bring in your own questions and answers to share with the class.

ACTIVITY A Read each sentence. Tell whether the sentence is a statement or a question. Put the correct punctuation mark at the end of each sentence.

1. Is that a brown bear outside the tent? question
2. This tire would make a good swing. statement
3. Where can I find a ring like that? question
4. Kiki likes to watch the fish in the pond. statement
5. That apple has a worm in it. statement
6. Did that spy escape? question
7. Puppets scare my little sister. statement
8. Did you say he lives in the jungle? question
9. What is a diamond? question
10. A can of blue paint was spilled on the grass. statement

ACTIVITY B Read each question. Write a statement that answers the question. Put the correct punctuation mark at the end of each sentence.

1. What kinds of books do you like to read?
2. What is your favorite food?
3. When did you start going to school?
4. What do you like to do on the weekends?

ACTIVITY C Read each sentence. Write a question about the statement. Begin each question with a question word. Put the correct punctuation mark at the end of each question.

1. Charlotte and Wilbur are characters in *Charlotte's Web*.
2. Police officers help protect us.
3. Mumbai is in India.
4. We celebrate Memorial Day on the last Monday in May.

WRITER'S CORNER

Here are some other words that begin questions. Choose three words. Use each to write a question.

Has	Are	Did
Does	Was	Am
How	Which	Why

How-to Articles • 263

WARM-UP

Read, Listen, Speak

Read aloud your statements from yesterday's For Tomorrow homework. Have students guess the questions. Invite small groups to share the statements they wrote. Encourage students to guess the questions that were asked.

GRAMMAR CONNECTION

Take this opportunity to talk about collective nouns. You may wish to have students point out any collective nouns in their Read, Listen, Speak examples.

TEACH

Write on the board the names of the four kinds of sentences: *statement, question, command, exclamation.* Invite volunteers to write an example statement and an example question on the board next to the words *statement* and *question.*

Have a volunteer read aloud the section Commands. Ask students when they might hear a command used *(when a teacher or parent asks or tells a child to do something).* Have students turn to the model on page 249. Invite volunteers to identify examples of commands. Ask students why command sentences might be important in a how-to article *(because you are telling someone to do something).* Remind students that most commands begin with a verb. Invite a volunteer to write an example command on the board next to the word *command.*

Ask a volunteer to read aloud the first paragraph and examples of the section Exclamations. Invite a volunteer to write an example exclamation on the board next to the word *exclamation.* Have students read aloud the examples of the four types of sentences.

PRACTICE

ACTIVITY D

Remind students that commands tell the reader to do something. When students have finished, have volunteers share their answers with the class. Invite students to discuss why items 3, 5, and 6 are not commands.

ACTIVITY E

Have students work with a partner to complete this activity. When students have finished, ask them to discuss why certain kinds of sentences are in certain parts of a how-to article. *(Commands are in the steps because the reader is being told what to do.)*

ACTIVITY F

Ask a volunteer to read aloud the example statement and question. Tell students to think of themselves as Keri when writing their sentences. Then have students complete the activity with partners. Invite volunteers to read aloud their sentences.

Commands

Sentences that tell or ask readers to do something are called commands. Game directions and steps in a how-to article direct people to do something. Many commands begin with a verb. Here are three commands.

> **Go to the red square.**
> **Glue the yarn to the mask.**
> **Unwrap your gift.**

Exclamations

Sentences that express strong feelings are exclamations. Exclamations end with an exclamation point. Here are three exclamations.

> **What a great party!**
> **There's a spaceship over my house!**
> **I'm so happy to see you!**

Can you name the four kinds of sentences?

> A **George Washington was our first president.**
> B **Who was our second president?**
> C **Think about it for a minute.**
> D **It was John Adams, of course!**

You are right if you said that A is a statement, B is a question, C is a command, and D is an exclamation.

ACTIVITY D Tell which sentences are commands. Put a period at the end of each command. If the sentence is not a command, put the correct punctuation mark at the end.

1. Listen to the whistle. command
2. Sprinkle sugar on the berries. command
3. Can you hear the crickets? question
4. Wash the dishes. command

APPLY

WRITER'S CORNER

Remind students that an introduction tells the reader what he or she will make or do. Tell students that asking a question in an introduction is a good way to interest the reader. Encourage volunteers to read aloud their sentences. Have the class identify the kinds of sentences that were used. Students should demonstrate the ability to recognize and use statements and questions.

Grammar in Action Remind students that possessives are formed by adding an apostrophe and an -s to a word.

ASSESS

Note which students had difficulty understanding commands and exclamations. Use the Reteach option with those students who need additional reinforcement.

Practice Book page 140 provides additional work with the four kinds of sentences.

5. How scary that was! exclamation
6. Are there going to be clowns? question
7. Show me your new bike. command

ACTIVITY E Read the how-to article "Paper Stained Glass" on page 249. Work with a partner to find a statement, a question, a command, and an exclamation. Write the four sentences you find. Then write which part of the how-to article each sentence comes from.

ACTIVITY F Read these statements about things that Keri said. For each statement write a sentence telling what you think Keri actually said. Use questions, commands, and exclamations as your answers.

EXAMPLE   **Keri asked if I wanted to go to the park.**

Do you want to go to the park?

1. Keri asked what time it is.
2. Keri told me to take out the garbage.
3. Keri shouted for me to shut the door.
4. Keri told me to take the dog for a walk.
5. Keri asked what I had learned at school.
6. Keri yelled that she was glad it was Friday.
7. Keri told me to turn off the TV and read a book.
8. Keri asked when Mom would be home.
9. Keri asked if I had heard a noise upstairs.
10. Keri said she was excited to be going to California.

Activity E
Statement: various examples in introduction, steps, and conclusion
Question: *Do your windows need some color?* introduction
Command: various examples in introduction, steps, and conclusion
Exclamation: *Let the sun shine through!* conclusion

Activity F
1. What time is it?
2. Take out the garbage.
3. Shut the door!
4. Take the dog for a walk.
5. What did you learn at school?
6. I'm glad it's Friday!
7. Turn off the TV and read a book.
8. When will Mom be home?
9. Did you hear a noise upstairs?
10. I'm excited to be going to California!

WRITER'S CORNER

Read the steps for making a penny bank on page 256. Write three sentences for an introduction. Make at least one sentence a statement and one a question.

Grammar in Action Include one possessive noun in your introduction.

How-to Articles • 265

TEACHING OPTIONS

Reteach

Invite students to look in first-grade readers to find examples of exclamations. Then have students identify commands in this lesson. Ask students to take turns reading aloud one of the commands and one of the exclamations. Encourage students to use a different tone of voice for each kind of sentence.

English-Language Learners

Make punctuation flash cards for the four kinds of sentences (period, question mark, exclamation point). Review the punctuation used for statements, questions, commands, and exclamations. Say different types of sentences and have students hold up the correct punctuation mark.

Meeting Individual Needs

Kinesthetic Bring in a yoga or exercise video for children. Have students perform the movements. Ask them to point out different types of sentences as they are spoken.

For Tomorrow

Ask students to write a conclusion for the steps for making a penny bank on page 256. Ask them to make one sentence a command and one an exclamation. Write your own conclusion to share with the class.

OBJECTIVE
- **To recognize and use compound words**

WARM-UP
Read, Listen, Speak
Read aloud your conclusion from yesterday's For Tomorrow homework, using your voice to emphasize the kinds of sentences you used. Invite small groups to take turns reading aloud their conclusions. Encourage students to use their voices to emphasize each kind of sentence.

GRAMMAR CONNECTION
Take this opportunity to talk about nouns as subjects. You may wish to have students point out nouns as subjects in their Read, Listen, Speak examples.

TEACH
Ask volunteers to read aloud the first paragraph and the list of compound words. Encourage volunteers to say the two words that make up each compound word in the list.

Have a volunteer read aloud the next paragraph. Tell students that thinking about the words that make up the compound word can help them figure out the meaning. Ask students to write a sentence using a compound word. Then invite volunteers to read their sentences aloud.

Have students brainstorm a list of compound words. Start by explaining that the word *brainstorm* is a compound word. Have them tell what *brain* and *storm* mean. Then have them tell what *brainstorm* means and look up the word in a dictionary to verify the meaning. List on the board compound words students generate and leave the list on the board during the lesson.

PRACTICE

ACTIVITY A
Suggest that students create an equation for each word. Have them draw a picture of a horse with a +, a picture of a shoe, an =, and a picture of a horseshoe. When students have finished, discuss the pictures of the words and explore together how the drawings would look if they were combined.

ACTIVITY B
Tell students that if they are unsure of their answer for any item, they should imagine what each compound word might be, such as *bookstare, bookmark,* and *bookcheck* for item 1. Explain that using their imaginations might help students picture a familiar compound word. Then ask volunteers to share their answers with the class. Have students check each answer in a dictionary.

Compound Words

A compound word is one word that is made by putting two words together. Look at these compound words. Can you name the two words in each compound word?

lighthouse	bluebird
fingernail	bookcase
raincoat	watermelon
hairbrush	junkyard

The compound word *lighthouse* is made by putting together the words *light* and *house*. Each part of a compound word tells something about what the whole compound word means. A lighthouse is a kind of house built to shine a bright light. A hairbrush is a brush made for your hair.

ACTIVITY A **Name the two words that make up each compound word. Draw a picture of each of the two words. Then draw a picture of the compound word.**

1. horseshoe
2. houseboat
3. goldfish
4. ladybug
5. football
6. wheelchair
7. handshake
8. flowerpot

266 • Chapter 2

APPLY

WRITER'S CORNER

Ask students to think of two words that together make a new compound word that describes something real *(suncloudy to describe a partly sunny day)*. When students have finished writing a sentence with their word, have them draw a picture of what their word means. Students should demonstrate the ability to form and use compound words.

ASSESS

Note which students had difficulty understanding how compound words are formed. Use the Reteach option with those students who need additional reinforcement.

Reteach

Have partners look through a dictionary for compound words. Tell students that they will recognize compound words because they are made up of two smaller words. When students find a compound word, have them write the definition of the compound word and then look up the words that make up the compound word to compare the meanings.

Compound Charades

Invite small groups to play charades. Explain that each student should mimic actions for the two individual words that make up a compound word. Tell those watching to guess the compound word.

ACTIVITY B **Make a compound word by choosing the correct word from each list.**

1. book_____
   a. stare
   b. mark ☑
   c. check

2. camp_____
   a. tree
   b. burger
   c. fire ☑

3. shoe_____
   a. lace ☑
   b. stone
   c. shirt

4. ship_____
   a. horn
   b. wipe
   c. wreck ☑

5. door_____
   a. hand
   b. mat ☑
   c. hammer

6. sand_____
   a. plan
   b. floor
   c. storm ☑

7. tug_____
   a. boat ☑
   b. rope
   c. coast

8. steam_____
   a. cup
   b. rabbit
   c. ship ☑

9. arrow_____
   a. bow
   b. grass
   c. head ☑

10. black_____
    a. bird ☑
    b. tire
    c. bend

11. mail_____
    a. card
    b. box ☑
    c. paper

12. sky_____
    a. light ☑
    b. near
    c. stick

WRITER'S CORNER

Make a new compound word by putting two words together, such as *noseball*. Tell a partner what your new compound word means. Write a sentence that uses your new word.

How-to Articles • 267

For Tomorrow

Ask students to write five compound words they see throughout their day—in books, ads, menus, and so on. Challenge students to use the words within each compound word to form new compound words. Bring in your own list of compound words to share with the class.

WARM-UP

Read, Listen, Speak

Read aloud your compound words from yesterday's For Tomorrow homework. Tell students where you found each word. Then share the new words you made from your list. Invite small groups to share their lists of compound words. Encourage students to discuss where they discovered their compound words and to share the new compound words they made.

GRAMMAR CONNECTION

Take this opportunity to talk about words used as nouns and as verbs. You may wish to have students point out any words that can be used as nouns and as verbs in their Read, Listen, Speak examples.

TEACH

Have each student write three compound words. Ask volunteers to explain how the definition of the compound word is different from the definitions of the words that make up the compound word. Invite volunteers to write their compound words on the board. Have students determine the meanings of the compound words.

PRACTICE

ACTIVITY C

Tell students first to write the words in column A, then make the compound words that students know. Suggest that students use a dictionary to help them make compound words with the remaining words. Ask volunteers to read aloud their answers. Invite students to give the definitions of the compound words.

ACTIVITY D

Tell students to read quietly each item to help them think of the compound word. Then ask students to draw a picture of the meaning of each compound word. Have volunteers read aloud their questions and answers. When students read the answers, ask them to display their pictures.

ACTIVITY E

Have students complete this activity with a partner. Tell students to read aloud each possible compound word (*earthworm, earthfly, earthfighter*). Ask students to choose the compound words that they know are actual words. Encourage students to use a dictionary if they need help.

ACTIVITY C Make compound words by matching each word in column A with a word in column B.

Column A	Column B
1. junk___yard___	room
2. bird___house___	ball
3. table___cloth___	storm
4. class___room___	yard
5. air___plane___	house
6. thunder___storm___	guest
7. night___gown___	water
8. house___guest___	gown
9. basket___ball___	cloth
10. under___water___	plane

ACTIVITY D Answer each question with a compound word. Each compound word is started for you.

1. I am at the end of a fishing line. What am I? a fish___hook___
2. I bring printed news and information to people every day. What am I? a news___paper___
3. I leave my mark on wet sand. What am I? a foot___print___
4. I work at beaches and swimming pools, and I save lives. Who am I? a life___guard___
5. I make your dishes clean and sparkling. What am I? a dish___washer___
6. I hold your clothes when you go on vacation. What am I? a suit___case___
7. I am the place where you play or watch a baseball game. What am I? a ball___park___
8. I am a red and black-spotted insect. What am I? a lady___bug___

268 • Chapter 2

APPLY

WRITER'S CORNER

Have partners take turns reading the page aloud. Tell students who do not find any compound words on the first page to read a second page. Have students write their sentences independently. Then challenge students to include several of both partners' compound words in one sentence. Students should demonstrate the ability to recognize and use compound words in sentences.

TechTip You may wish to direct students to specific child-friendly online magazines or newspapers.

ASSESS

Note which students had difficulty understanding how compound words are formed. Use the Reteach option with those students who need additional reinforcement.

Practice Book page 141 provides additional work with compound words.

TEACHING OPTIONS

Reteach

Write on note cards individual words that can be used to make compound words. Shuffle the cards and lay them facedown on a table. Have students play a matching game by turning over two cards at a time and determining if the two words can be used to make a compound word. If so, tell students to keep the cards. Explain that if the words do not form a compound words the student should turn the cards facedown again. Challenge students to continue playing until all the cards are matched.

Compound Commercial

Have small groups make up three new compound words related to the same topic. Then have each group create a commercial to sell the three new words to a dictionary publisher. Direct students to include in their commercials the meaning of each word, the two words that make up each new compound word, and how the compound word is useful. Have the groups present their commercials to the class.

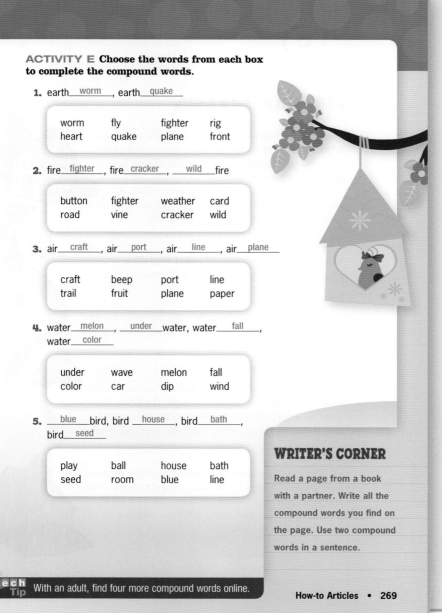

ACTIVITY E Choose the words from each box to complete the compound words.

1. earth___worm___, earth___quake___

| worm | fly | fighter | rig |
| heart | quake | plane | front |

2. fire___fighter___, fire___cracker___, ___wild___fire

| button | fighter | weather | card |
| road | vine | cracker | wild |

3. air___craft___, air___port___, air___line___, air___plane___

| craft | beep | port | line |
| trail | fruit | plane | paper |

4. water___melon___, ___under___water, water___fall___, water___color___

| under | wave | melon | fall |
| color | car | dip | wind |

5. ___blue___bird, bird___house___, bird___bath___, bird___seed___

| play | ball | house | bath |
| seed | room | blue | line |

WRITER'S CORNER

Read a page from a book with a partner. Write all the compound words you find on the page. Use two compound words in a sentence.

Tech Tip With an adult, find four more compound words online.

How-to Articles • 269

For Tomorrow

Ask students to list five items at home that name a compound word (*fireplace, coffeepot, bookshelf*). Bring in your own list of compound words for household items.

OBJECTIVES

- **To know the parts of a how-to talk**
- **To prepare, practice, and present a how-to talk**

WARM-UP

Read, Listen, Speak

Write on the board your list of compound words from yesterday's For Tomorrow homework. Have students name and define the two words that make up the compound words. Ask small groups to read aloud their lists of compound words. Have students define each word and tell the two words that make up each compound word.

GRAMMAR CONNECTION

Take this opportunity to review nouns. You may wish to have students point out nouns in their Read, Listen, Speak examples.

TEACH

Have a volunteer read aloud the first paragraph. Ask a volunteer to tell about a time he or she told someone how to do something. Then read aloud the second paragraph. Invite students to name the parts of a how-to article *(title, introduction, What You Need list, steps, conclusion).*

Ask a volunteer to read aloud the section Title. Invite students to suggest possible titles for a how-to talk. After each title is suggested, ask the class to decide if the title tells what the talk will be about—what the reader will learn to do. Have a volunteer read aloud the section Introduction. Remind students that the introduction might give a reason for making or doing something.

Invite volunteers to read aloud the section What You Need. Ask students what is included in a What You Need list *(everything to be used in the project).* Have a volunteer read aloud the section Steps. Tell students to include each step in the correct order. Discuss what might happen if the steps were given in the wrong order. Remind students that if they act out the steps, they should act out all the steps.

Read aloud the section Conclusion. Tell students to be ready to answer audience questions at the end of their talks. Explain that if their steps are clear, the audience may not need to ask any questions.

Have a volunteer read aloud the section Choosing a Topic. Tell students to choose topics they know well and are appropriate for a classroom setting.

PRACTICE

ACTIVITY A

Ask students to discuss topics that would be hard to act out in school. Then have students complete the activity independently. Invite volunteers to share their answers with the class.

How-to Talks

Imagine that you are telling a friend how to get to school from your house. That is a how-to talk. Any time you tell someone how to do something, you are giving a how-to talk.

A how-to talk is a lot like a how-to article. A how-to talk has all the parts of a how-to article. Can you remember what these parts are?

Title

The title of a how-to talk tells what the talk is about. Start your how-to talk by telling your audience the title.

Introduction

The beginning of a how-to talk is the introduction. In the introduction tell your audience what you are going to teach them.

What You Need

During your how-to talk, say what the audience will need for the activity. You might write the What You Need list on a poster and read it to the audience. If you can, show the audience the items they will need.

Steps

Explain the steps to the audience. You might even act out how to do each step. If you can't show the steps to your audience, you might draw pictures. Use time words, such as *first, then,* and *after that.* Time words help listeners follow the steps.

270 • Chapter 2

ACTIVITY B

Read aloud each title and ask students to tell which option *(acting out or drawing pictures)* is best for each and why. Then have students tell what kinds of actions or pictures would be helpful in explaining the topic.

APPLY

SPEAKER'S CORNER

Be sure that students choose topics about which they can speak knowledgeably. Guide students toward topics that are appropriate for school. When students have finished, ask them to display their posters in the classroom. Save the posters for the next Speaker's Corner. Students should demonstrate the ability to choose a topic and create a What You Need list for a how-to talk.

ASSESS

Note which students had difficulty understanding the parts of a how-to talk. Use the Reteach option with those students who need additional reinforcement.

Conclusion

The conclusion is the ending of your how-to talk. You might show what you made. You might tell other ways listeners could do the activity. When you finish, ask if anyone has questions.

Choosing a Topic

Some topics may be good for a how-to article, but they may not be very good for a talk. They may have too many steps. They may be useful, but they may not be very interesting to listeners. For example, explaining how to play a board game may be very long and hard to follow. The information may not be very interesting unless the listeners are planning to play the game.

Some topics may be good if you use pictures or put on a demonstration. For example, if you are explaining how to make an object by doing origami, which is the art of paper folding, it would be a good idea to demonstrate making the object.

ACTIVITY A Read each topic. Do you think it good for a how-to talk? Explain why or why not.

1. using a scooter safely
2. how to play chess
3. how to memorize a poem
4. how to play basketball
5. how to jump rope
6. how to ride a skateboard

ACTIVITY B Read the titles of these how-to talks. For which topics might you act out the steps? For which ones might you draw pictures?

1. Make Clay Beads
2. How to Do the Butterfly Stroke
3. Starting a School Club
4. Learn to Make Apple and Graham Cracker Sandwiches
5. Tips for Making Paper Boats
6. Playing Chinese Checkers

SPEAKER'S CORNER

Choose a topic for your how-to talk. Make a poster that shows everything your audience will need to complete the activity.

How-to Articles • 271

WARM-UP

Read, Listen, Speak

Read aloud your notes from yesterday's For Tomorrow homework. Ask students to draw conclusions about what is useful to include in a how-to talk. Invite small groups to discuss the notes students took while observing how-to talks. Encourage students to list points to remember when giving a how-to talk by finishing this sentence starter: "A good how-to talk . . ."

TEACH

Have volunteers read aloud the section Get Ready. Tell students to write only one step on each note card. Explain that the note cards for the introduction and the conclusion should have only words or phrases to help students remember what to say. Ask students to turn to the model on page 249. Have students suggest ideas about what to write on note cards if students were presenting this how-to article.

Ask volunteers to read aloud the section Practice. Demonstrate for students a brief how-to talk about how to put their names and the date on a sheet of paper. Use a clear, moderately paced speaking voice. Then allow time for students to practice their how-to talks with one another.

Invite volunteers to read aloud the section Listening Tips. Ask pairs of students to practice listening as their partner presents his or her how-to talk. When partners have finished, ask students to retell what they remember about the steps.

PRACTICE

ACTIVITY C

Have partners take turns speaking and listening. Allow time for the speakers and the listeners to finish listening and drawing. Display students' drawings around the room.

ACTIVITY D

When students have finished, have them meet with a partner and read aloud their steps. Ask students to tell their partners about any steps they notice that might be missing or out of order.

ACTIVITY E

Have students complete this activity independently. Encourage partners to share their ingredient lists and to think of names for their sandwiches.

ACTIVITY F

Review the Listening Tips and encourage partners to suggest improvements for the how-to talks. Have a volunteer give a how-to talk while you demonstrate the listening tips from the list.

Get Ready

Get the materials that you need for your how-to talk. Then list the steps needed to make or do your topic. Write the steps on note cards. If you are not using a poster to list what readers will need, write another note card with that list. Write one note card each for the introduction and the conclusion. Use the note cards during your how-to talk. They will help you remember what you want to say.

Practice

Practice your how-to talk several times. Use your note cards. Remember to speak clearly. Try not to talk too fast. Show each step slowly. Then practice with a partner. Make sure that your partner can see and hear what you are doing. After you have finished your presentation, discuss these questions with your partner:

- Were my steps easy to understand?
- Did I forget any steps or use unneeded steps?
- Did I forget anything for my What You Need list?
- Was my voice loud enough?

Listening Tips

It is important to be a good listener. Here are some ways to be a good listener.

- Pay attention. Sit quietly.
- Watch what the speaker does. Imagine that you are doing the same thing.
- Wait until the how-to talk is over before asking questions.
- When the speaker has finished, say one thing that you liked about the presentation.

APPLY

SPEAKER'S CORNER

Allow time for students to practice their how-to talks. Tell students to focus on the pacing and clarity of their partners' speaking voices. Encourage volunteers to present their talks to the class. Invite students to ask questions after each how-to talk. Students should demonstrate the ability to give a how-to talk and use good listening skills.

💡 **TechTip** Remind students that podcasts do not lend themselves to visuals. Suggest that they practice with a partner who should listen with closed eyes to ensure clarity.

ASSESS

Note which students had difficulty giving a how-to talk and using good listening skills. Use the Reteach option with those students who need additional reinforcement.

After you have reviewed Lessons 3–5, administer the Writing Skills Assessment on pages 43–44 in the **Assessment Book.** This test is also available on the optional **Test Generator CD.**

TEACHING OPTIONS

Reteach

Have students refer to the checklist they wrote in their notebooks for preparing a how-to talk in the Reteach option on page 271. Ask partners to use the checklist as a guide to prepare a how-to talk about how to pack a lunch for a school field trip. Encourage partners to write note cards for the materials they would need and for each part of the talk. Have partners share their work with another pair of students.

Show Time

Have the groups that worked on the Cooperative Learning option on page 271 prepare to present the how-to talks they planned. Remind students to have their materials ready and to prepare note cards to use. Encourage groups to assign parts of the talk to different students so that each group member has an opportunity to present part of the talk. Emphasize that each student should practice his or her presentation.

Have groups present their how-to talks to the class. Allow time for the class to ask questions about each presentation.

ACTIVITY C Think of something you like to draw. Then teach a partner how to draw the same thing without drawing it yourself.

ACTIVITY D Make a list of the steps you would use to teach someone how to do these everyday activities.

1. washing your hands
2. drawing a picture of a house
3. tying a shoe
4. making a bed
5. blowing a bubble
6. folding a T-shirt

ACTIVITY E Think about how to make your favorite sandwich. Write each step you take when you make that sandwich. Then read through your steps and make a What You Need list.

ACTIVITY F Reread the steps and the What You Need list that you wrote for Activity E. Then practice a how-to talk with a partner on how to make the sandwich. Reread the Listening Tips on page 272. When your partner practices his or her talk, remember to use the Listening Tips.

SPEAKER'S CORNER

Use the poster that you made for the Speaker's Corner on page 271 to practice and present your how-to talk. Practice it with a partner. Think of ways to improve your how-to talk.

🔧 **Tech Tip** Make a podcast of your how-to talk.

How-to Articles • 273

OBJECTIVES

- **To select a topic for a how-to article**
- **To list the steps of a how-to article in the proper order**

PREWRITING AND DRAFTING

Tell students that in this Writer's Workshop they will write a how-to article. Review the seven steps of the writing process—prewriting, drafting, content editing, revising, copyediting, proofreading, and publishing.

Ask a volunteer to read aloud the opening paragraph. Discuss things students know how to make and things they know how to do.

Prewriting

Ask students to read aloud this section. Tell students they will be reading about Kai, a third grader, who is writing a how-to article, but who hasn't decided what her topic will be. Tell students she will use prewriting as a time to explore ideas and to choose a topic.

Choosing a Topic

Invite a volunteer to read aloud the first paragraph of this section. Ask students if they have ever thought about all the things they know how to do. Tell students to read aloud the chart that Kai made about the things she can do. Ask students why they think Kai made a chart to list what she knows how to do. Guide students to understand that the chart can help Kai see and think about topics she might choose.

Invite volunteers to read aloud the next two paragraphs. Ask students to explain how Kai chose her topic. Tell students that Kai chose something that she knew

how to do and enjoyed doing. Point out that Kai also chose something she thought other kids would like to learn to do.

Tell students that their topic idea should be clear, interesting, and informative.

Your Turn

Invite a volunteer to read aloud this section. Tell students to make a chart like Kai's. Then ask students to fill in the chart with things they know how to do. Ask students to review their charts to decide on one activity that would be both fun and easy to teach.

Tell students that if their topic is something that they know well, their personality and confidence will come through in their writing.

Listing Steps

Invite a volunteer to read aloud the first paragraph. Ask volunteers to read aloud Kai's list. Encourage students to suggest other things that could go into the time capsule and to explain why.

Invite volunteers to read aloud the last two paragraphs. Ask students to name other ways to hide a time capsule. Write their suggestions on the board.

Writer's Workshop

How-to Articles

Prewriting and Drafting

What do you know how to make or do? Can you fly a kite? Can you make a tasty snack? These can be topics for a how-to article.

Prewriting

Kai's third-grade class was writing how-to articles, so she started by prewriting. Prewriting is what you do before you start writing. Kai knew that this was the time to plan the ideas that would go into her article.

Choosing a Topic

Ideas   Kai was having trouble choosing a topic. She decided to make a chart of things she can do.

Kai looked at the chart she made. She was surprised at how much she knows how to do. She asked herself what her classmates might like to learn about. She also asked herself what had been fun for her to learn.

Last summer Kai's older brother, Lono, taught her how to make a time capsule. It had been a lot of fun. Kai couldn't wait until next summer, when she and Lono would open it. She thought that other kids in her class might like to make time capsules too.

Things I Can Do

School	reading adding fractions
Dance and Sports	hula soccer goalie kickball
Arts and Crafts	making a time capsule using watercolors making friendship bracelets acting in plays
Other Skills	playing the guitar magic tricks making cookies

Your Turn

Make a chart like Kai's to help you think of topics. What can you do? How do you have fun? Fill in each column with as many things as you can think of. What things on your list were fun to learn? What would be easy to teach? Choose a topic that seems fun and interesting.

Voice

Your Turn

Invite a volunteer to read aloud this section. Ask students to make a list of the steps to complete their activity. Encourage students to trade their written steps with a partner and to check each other's work. Have students ask each other questions about steps they do not understand.

Organizing Ideas

Have volunteers read aloud the paragraph and Kai's notes. Encourage volunteers to answer the question Kai had about her introduction. Have students offer suggestions for adding details to the conclusion.

Tell students that how-to articles should be organized by steps. Ask students what would happen if they organized a how-to article differently.

Your Turn

Invite a volunteer to read aloud this section. Then have students go back over each direction and answer each question. Ask volunteers to read aloud what they wrote. Discuss the answers and make suggestions to help students better organize each part of their how-to articles.

TEACHING OPTIONS

Teaching Tip

Students may benefit from rereading the how-to articles on pages 248–249. Use the models to review the importance of writing steps in order and the parts of a how-to article (title, introduction, What You Need list, steps, and conclusion).

How-to Recipes

Tell students that their how-to articles are like recipes for making things, such as puffed-rice treats. Bring in some simple recipes and have students label the parts of a how-to article in each recipe. Discuss the parts not included in the recipes. Then have students write an introduction and a conclusion for one recipe.

Listing Steps

Kai knew to list all the steps for making the time capsule. She thought about what she and Lono did to make their time capsule.

1. Cover shoe box with construction paper. Write name and date on shoe box. Decorate shoe box.
2. Put fun things in time capsule.
3. Tape up time capsule. Find hiding place for time capsule.

Kai wanted to tell what could go in the time capsule. She and Lono had included coins, stamps, and pictures. She added those things to the second step.

Kai showed her list to Lono. He told her to tell kids how to hide a time capsule. Lono once buried a time capsule. Kai thought the extra tip would be good in the conclusion.

Your Turn

- Make a list of the steps needed to complete the activity you will write about.
- Read the steps again. Did you leave anything out? Are the steps in the right order? Do you see places where you can add information to make the steps clearer?

Organizing Ideas

Kai wanted to make sure that she didn't leave anything out. She wrote the five parts of a how-to article. Then she wrote notes about each part. Sometimes she thought of a question that she should answer. Here are Kai's notes.

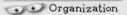

Title
   A Buried Surprise
Introduction
   Why would a kid want to make this?
What You Need
   shoe box, construction paper, coins,
   stamps, pitchers
Steps
   See new list of steps.
Conclusion
   stuff about burying time capsule

Your Turn

- Write the five parts of a how-to article.
- Look at your list of steps. What do you need to add to your What You Need list to complete the steps? What do you want to say in the introduction and the conclusion?
- Write your ideas.

Prewriting · Drafting · Content Editing · Revising · Copyediting · Proofreading · Publishing

Writer's Workshop   How-to Articles

• **To draft a how-to article**

Drafting

Ask a volunteer to read aloud the paragraph. Discuss how Kai's prewriting activities might have helped her write her draft.

Direct students' attention to Kai's draft. Invite a volunteer to read aloud the title, the introduction, and the What You Need list. Point out the materials Kai included in her list. Have students turn to page 275 to see which materials from her notes Kai included in her draft.

Have volunteers read aloud the steps. Point out the kind of information Kai included in her steps *(directions for covering the shoe box, for writing your name and date on the paper, for putting materials in the box, for hiding the box).*

Point out that Kai numbered the steps of her how-to article. Explain that she did this to help readers see how the steps were to be followed.

Invite a volunteer to read aloud Kai's conclusion. Challenge students to explain what the conclusion of a how-to article should do *(tell readers what they just made or did, suggest another way to do what was taught, or tell how readers might use what they have learned).*

Drafting

A draft is your first chance to put your prewriting notes in order. Kai used the notes she wrote during prewriting to write her first draft. She had written her ideas and steps in the correct parts of a how-to article. She then found that it was easy to write the details. Kai double-spaced her draft so that she would have room to make changes later.

A Buried Surprise

A time capsule is fun to make. George Washington even put one in the cornerstone of the Capitol building. But it has never been found.

<u>What You Need</u>

shoe box	stamps
construction paper	pitchers
coins	tape

<u>Steps</u>

1. Cover the shoe box in construction paper. The box will be the time capsule. Write your name and the date in big letters on the lid. Decerate the box any way that you want. You can ask friends to sign their names, or you can draw pitchers.

2. You can put anything in the time capsule. Put in coins from this year. You can add pretty stamps. You can also place pitchers of you and your friends in the time capsule.

3. Tape the time capsule closed. Then hide it in a closet or under your bed.

Your Turn

Invite a volunteer to read aloud this section. Before students begin writing their drafts, ask them to act out the steps they need to include in their how-to articles. Then tell students to write their drafts, using their prewriting notes as a guide. Remind students to include a title, an introduction, a What You Need list, a list of numbered steps written in complete sentences, and a conclusion. Tell students to double-space their drafts so that there will be room for revisions later.

Writer's Tip Tell students that commands are the clearest and most direct way to give instructions. Write on the board examples of commands. Have students suggest other commands.

You can even put your time capsule in a plastic bag and bury it in your yard. If you do, make a map so that you don't forget where you put it remember to ask an adult to help you bury your time capsule. Don't open your time capsule for a long, long time. Try to wait at least one year!

Prewriting | Drafting | Content Editing | Revising | Copyediting | Proofreading | Publishing

Your Turn

- Look at your notes.
- Use your notes to write your first draft.
- Remember to double-space your draft so you have room to make corrections later.

Writer's Tip Make sure you use commands in the directions.

OBJECTIVE

- **To content edit a how-to article**

CONTENT EDITING

Tell students that content editing how-to articles means checking that the steps are in order and are easy to understand. Remind students that the What You Need list should be complete and that the introduction and conclusion should be effective.

Invite volunteers to read aloud the first two paragraphs and the Content Editor's Checklist. Ask students to explain what each question asks.

Invite a volunteer to read aloud the paragraph that follows the checklist. Discuss why Kai asked Emily to read the draft. Point out that Emily might catch mistakes that Kai missed.

Invite volunteers to read aloud the next two paragraphs and each of Emily's comments. Point out that Emily's comments are helpful and said in a kind way. Ask students if they can add anything to Emily's comments.

Challenge students to find something that Emily missed. *(Kai's title does not tell what the reader will make or do.)* Ask volunteers how they might tell Kai about the problem with the title.

Editor's Workshop

How-to Articles

Content Editing

Kai knew that if she edited her draft for content, the draft would be better. She knew that content editors check to make sure that a reader can understand the article. They also check to make sure that all the important information is included.

Kai used this checklist to content edit her draft.

Kai knew that asking someone else to content edit her draft would be a big help. Kai asked her best friend, Emily. Emily was one of the best readers in the class. Kai knew that Emily would tell her good changes she could make.

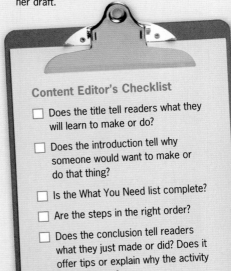

Content Editor's Checklist

- ☐ Does the title tell readers what they will learn to make or do?
- ☐ Does the introduction tell why someone would want to make or do that thing?
- ☐ Is the What You Need list complete?
- ☐ Are the steps in the right order?
- ☐ Does the conclusion tell readers what they just made or did? Does it offer tips or explain why the activity will help them?
- ☐ Does the article stay on the topic?

Have a volunteer read aloud the last paragraph of this section. Explain that Kai will think about what Emily said as Kai makes changes.

Your Turn

Invite a volunteer to read aloud the first two bulleted items in this section. Ask partners to read one another's drafts several times, checking each time for one item on the checklist.

Ask volunteers to read aloud the remaining bulleted items. Discuss how to give positive feedback. Encourage students to make at least one positive comment about the article they are reading. Then have partners talk quietly about what they read.

TEACHING OPTIONS

Do the How-to

Explain that one way to be sure that all the steps of a how-to article are included is to have another person act out the steps, one by one. Ask the content editors to act out the steps in the drafts. Tell students that having another reader follow the directions in the how-to article is a good way to find out whether all the necessary steps have been included.

Emily carefully read Kai's how-to article a few times. She answered the questions on the Content Editor's Checklist about Kai's draft. She also wrote notes about things that she liked in the draft. When Emily had finished, she and Kai met to talk about Emily's ideas.

First, Emily told Kai that making a time capsule sounded like fun. Then Emily showed Kai her ideas.

- The introduction says that making a time capsule is fun. Can you tell kids why it is fun?
- What can kids use to draw on the time capsule? It is not in your What You Need list.
- The steps are easy to follow. I like them.
- I like how you give kids another way of hiding their time capsules.
- I don't think the part about George Washington is about making a time capsule. You should delete it.
- I like how you tell kids what they can put in the time capsule. Maybe they can also put in newspaper articles.
- Can you tell kids what you put in your time capsule?

Kai liked what Emily said about her draft. Emily caught some things that Kai had missed. Even though Kai didn't agree with all Emily's ideas, she knew that her draft would be better because of Emily's help.

Your Turn

- Read your draft and answer the questions on the Content Editor's Checklist.
- Try to answer yes to each question. Don't try to check all the questions at once. Check for one question at a time.
- After you have edited your draft for content, trade drafts with a partner. Give your partner ideas to make the draft better. Be sure that you use the Content Editor's Checklist.
- Talk to your partner about your ideas. Remember to tell your partner what you liked.
- You do not have to make all the changes your partner tells you. But you should think carefully about each one.

Prewriting
Drafting
Content Editing
Revising
Copyediting
Proofreading
Publishing

OBJECTIVE
- **To revise a how-to article**

REVISING

Tell students that revising happens when writers make changes to improve what they have written. Explain that these changes can come from the content editor or they can come from the writer. Point out that in Kai's case, she incorporated edits from Emily and used ideas of her own to make her how-to article better.

Invite volunteers to read aloud Kai's revised how-to article. Remind students to read the parts that Kai added and not read the parts she deleted. Then read aloud the sentence following Kai's revised draft. Ask volunteers to read aloud and discuss each question in the bulleted list. After each point has been read, have volunteers find the answer in Kai's revised how-to article.

Encourage volunteers to say why they agree or disagree with Kai's decisions.

- She added a sentence in the introduction about why making a time capsule is fun.
- The information about George Washington was unrelated to the how-to process.
- She added markers or crayons.
- She added it to her steps and her What You Need list.

- The how-to article wasn't supposed to be about her own time capsule. Kai wants her readers to come up with their own ideas when filling their time capsules.
- Emily forgot to check for a title that reflected what was going to be explained in the how-to article.
- She added "The longer you wait, the more fun it will be when you open it."

Writer's Workshop
How-to Articles

Revising

This is Kai's revised draft.

Making a Time Capsule
~~A Buried Surprise~~

When you are older, you can open the time capsule and remember what
A time capsule is fun to make. ~~George Washington even put one in~~
it was like when you were in third grade.
~~the cornerstone of the Capitol building. But it has never been found.~~

What You Need

shoe box	stamps
construction paper	pitchers
coins	tape
markers or crayons	news paper articles

Steps

1. Cover the shoe box in construction paper. The box will be the time capsule.

   Write your name and the date in big letters on the lid. Decerate the box

   any way that you want. You can ask friends to sign their names, or you can

   draw pitchers.

2. You can put anything in the time capsule. Put in coins from this year. You can

   News paper articles are good too.
   add pretty stamps. You can also place pitchers of you and your friends in the

   time capsule.

3. Tape the time capsule closed. Then hide it in a closet or under your bed.

Your Turn

Have a volunteer read aloud this section. Be sure students understand that they do not have to use each of their content editor's suggestions. Tell students to use only what they think makes their how-to article better. When students have finished revising, have them look at the Content Editor's Checklist to see if they can answer yes to all the questions.

Writer's Tip Remind students that an editor can suggest changes, but that the writer is ultimately responsible for the information he or she publishes. Tell students that their editor's suggestions should always be checked for accuracy.

Grammar in Action. Guide students to find the missing period between *it* and *remember*. Point out that *remember* will then need to be capitalized.

Handwriting Counts

Explain that editors should write legibly so that the writers knows what changes should be made to a draft. Tell students that editing marks should be written so that the writer knows what changes are suggested, without having to explain them verbally.

Write on the board the following:

did you see the dog running down the road

Have partners work together to revise the sentence. Ask students to use proofreading marks in a different pencil color to make *dog* plural, begin the sentence with a capital letter, and end the sentence with a question mark. Remind students to use small, neat, and readable letters to make suggested changes. Then have students write the new sentence correctly, using the proofreading marks to make the changes.

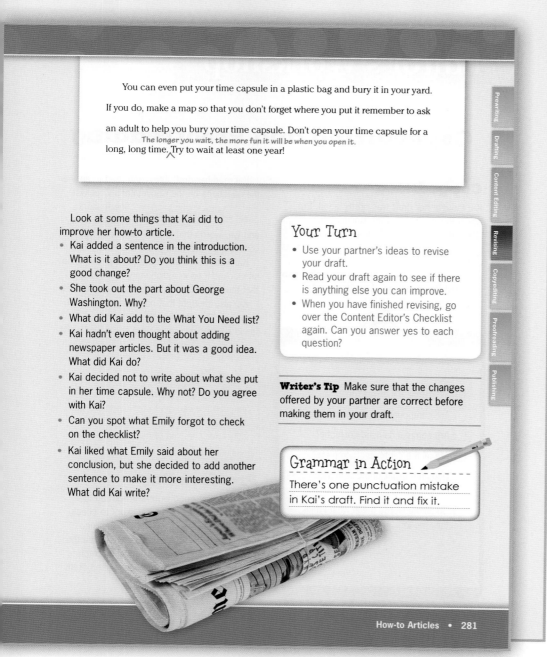

You can even put your time capsule in a plastic bag and bury it in your yard.

If you do, make a map so that you don't forget where you put it remember to ask

an adult to help you bury your time capsule. Don't open your time capsule for a

The longer you wait, the more fun it will be when you open it.

long, long time. Try to wait at least one year!

Look at some things that Kai did to improve her how-to article.

- Kai added a sentence in the introduction. What is it about? Do you think this is a good change?
- She took out the part about George Washington. Why?
- What did Kai add to the What You Need list?
- Kai hadn't even thought about adding newspaper articles. But it was a good idea. What did Kai do?
- Kai decided not to write about what she put in her time capsule. Why not? Do you agree with Kai?
- Can you spot what Emily forgot to check on the checklist?
- Kai liked what Emily said about her conclusion, but she decided to add another sentence to make it more interesting. What did Kai write?

Your Turn

- Use your partner's ideas to revise your draft.
- Read your draft again to see if there is anything else you can improve.
- When you have finished revising, go over the Content Editor's Checklist again. Can you answer yes to each question?

Writer's Tip Make sure that the changes offered by your partner are correct before making them in your draft.

Grammar in Action

There's one punctuation mistake in Kai's draft. Find it and fix it.

OBJECTIVES

- **To copyedit a how-to article**
- **To proofread a how-to article**

COPYEDITING AND PROOFREADING

Copyediting

Remind students that content editing is making ideas clearer and better. Tell students that the next step in the writing process is called copyediting. Explain that when students copyedit, they should make sure their words and sentences are strong and correct.

Invite a volunteer to read aloud the first paragraph of this section. Ask students to recall using a checklist when they copyedited their personal narratives. Tell students they will also use a checklist to copyedit their how-to articles.

👀 Suggest that students read their drafts to a partner. Point out that sentences should vary in length to give their writing a natural-sounding flow.

Invite a volunteer to read aloud the Copyeditor's Checklist. Have a volunteer read aloud the paragraph after the checklist. Challenge students to find the mistakes that Kai found in her draft. Remind students that they will have an easier time finding the mistakes if they read their drafts looking for one kind of mistake at a time.

👀 Suggest that students choose the most descriptive words they can think of and that they are words that their audience will understand.

Ask volunteers to read aloud the last two paragraphs. Encourage students to check a dictionary for the spelling of compound words.

Your Turn

Read aloud this section. Tell students to answer each question by looking at their drafts. Allow time for students to copyedit and make changes to their drafts.

Tell students to use the Copyeditor's Checklist to edit their how-to articles. Remind students to check for one kind of mistake at a time.

Proofreading

Invite a volunteer to read aloud the first paragraph in this section. Remind students that sometimes when they fix one part of their writing, they might accidentally make a new mistake. Point out that proofreading is a time to check for new mistakes that students might have made while revising and copyediting.

Editor's Workshop   How-to Articles

Copyediting and Proofreading

Copyediting

Kai thought her draft was pretty good. But she wanted it to be great. Kai used the Copyeditor's Checklist to make sure her 👀 **Sentence Fluency** sentences were complete and that they made sense. She also checked the meanings of words that she was not sure about.

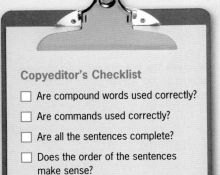

Copyeditor's Checklist

- ☐ Are compound words used correctly?
- ☐ Are commands used correctly?
- ☐ Are all the sentences complete?
- ☐ Does the order of the sentences make sense?
- ☐ Do all the words mean what I think they mean?

Kai read her draft again and tried to answer the questions on the Copyeditor's Checklist. 👀 **Word Choice** She found a misused word and two words that should have been one compound word. Can you find them?

Kai wasn't sure about the word *pitchers*, so she looked it up in a dictionary. She realized that the word she wanted to use was *pictures*.

Kai also thought that *news paper* might be incorrect. She checked the dictionary and found out that *newspaper* is a compound word.

Your Turn

Read your revised draft carefully. See if you can answer yes to the questions on the Copyeditor's Checklist. Remember to check for one kind of mistake at a time.

Proofreading

Kai knew that good writers proofread their 👀 **Conventions** work to check for spelling, punctuation, and capitalization. Kai used the Proofreader's Checklist to help her catch these types of mistakes in her revised draft.

Tell students that strong writing is free of mistakes in punctuation, capitalization, and grammar.

Review the proofreading marks on the inside back cover. Read aloud the Proofreader's Checklist.

Invite volunteers to read aloud the next two paragraphs. Point out that Lono might catch mistakes that Kai missed because he had not read Kai's how-to article yet.

Read aloud the last paragraph. Have students find the mistakes Lono found while proofreading Kai's draft. *(The first word of the third sentence of the conclusion is not capitalized. Decorate is misspelled decerate.)*

Your Turn

Read aloud this section. Have students proofread their drafts by answering one question on the checklist at a time. Invite partners to proofread one another's drafts and to share any mistakes they find.

TEACHING OPTIONS

Using the Dictionary

Tell students that a dictionary is a necessary tool for copyediting and proofreading. Explain that a dictionary will help determine whether a word is written as one compound word or as two separate words.

Encourage students to look up any unfamiliar words or any words they are unsure how to spell.

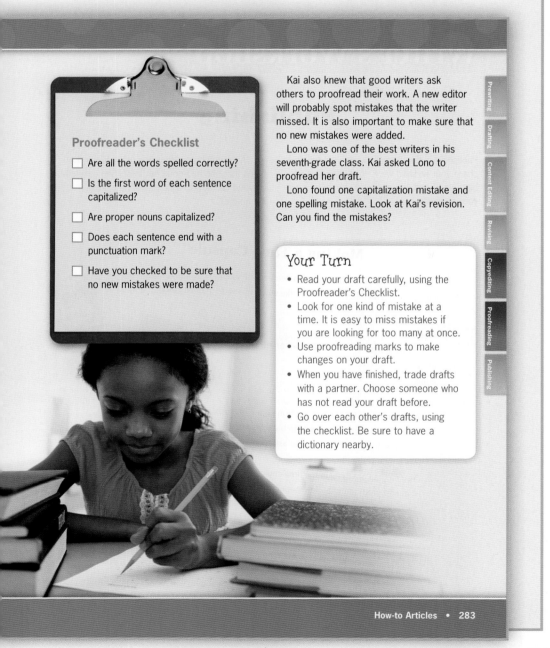

Proofreader's Checklist

☐ Are all the words spelled correctly?

☐ Is the first word of each sentence capitalized?

☐ Are proper nouns capitalized?

☐ Does each sentence end with a punctuation mark?

☐ Have you checked to be sure that no new mistakes were made?

Kai also knew that good writers ask others to proofread their work. A new editor will probably spot mistakes that the writer missed. It is also important to make sure that no new mistakes were added.

Lono was one of the best writers in his seventh-grade class. Kai asked Lono to proofread her draft.

Lono found one capitalization mistake and one spelling mistake. Look at Kai's revision. Can you find the mistakes?

Your Turn

- Read your draft carefully, using the Proofreader's Checklist.
- Look for one kind of mistake at a time. It is easy to miss mistakes if you are looking for too many at once.
- Use proofreading marks to make changes on your draft.
- When you have finished, trade drafts with a partner. Choose someone who has not read your draft before.
- Go over each other's drafts, using the checklist. Be sure to have a dictionary nearby.

Prewriting
Drafting
Content Editing
Revising
Copyediting
Proofreading
Publishing

Writer's Workshop
How-to Articles

OBJECTIVE
- **To publish a how-to article**

PUBLISHING

Ask students what it means to publish a piece of their writing. *(Publishing happens when a writer openly shares his or her work with readers.)* Invite a volunteer to read aloud the first two paragraphs of this section. Ask volunteers why Kai was careful when she wrote her how-to article on a new sheet of paper. *(Kai didn't want to make any mistakes.)* Tell students that Kai was careful because she knew that any mistakes might confuse her readers while they were trying to make their own time capsules.

Have volunteers read aloud the published version of Kai's how-to article. Encourage students to reread the first draft of Kai's how-to article. Ask volunteers how Kai's writing changed.

Ask a volunteer to read aloud the many ways students might publish their writing.

Remind students that the presentation of their article is the way it looks. Tell them that a published piece should be as neat as possible, with consistent margins and clear graphics, maps, or other visuals.

Publishing

Publishing is the moment when you decide to share your finished work. You know it is your best work, and you are ready to share it with your audience.

After editing and revising many times, Kai felt that she had done her best. She carefully typed her how-to article on a new sheet of paper.

Making a Time Capsule

A time capsule is fun to make. When you are older, you can open the time capsule and remember what it was like when you were in third grade.

What You Need

shoe box	stamps
construction paper	newspaper articles
markers or crayons	pictures
coins	tape

Steps

1. Cover the shoe box in construction paper. The box will be the time capsule. Write your name and the date in big letters on the lid. Decorate the box any way that you want. You can ask friends to sign their names, or you can draw pictures.

2. You can put anything in the time capsule. Put in coins from this year. You can add pretty stamps. Newspaper articles are good too. You can also place pictures of you and your friends in the time capsule.

3. Tape the time capsule closed. Then hide it in a closet or under your bed.

You can even put your time capsule in a plastic bag and bury it in your yard. If you do, make a map so that you don't forget where you put it. Remember to ask an adult to help you bury your time capsule. Don't open your time capsule for a long, long time. The longer you wait, the more fun it will be when you open it. Try to wait at least one year!

284

Your Turn

Invite volunteers to read aloud the paragraph and the first two bulleted items in this section. Then have students work on the final draft of their how-to articles. Tell students to be careful not to add any new mistakes.

Have a volunteer read aloud the final bulleted item.

ASSESS

Have students assess their finished how-to article using the reproducible Student Self-Assessment on page 285y. A separate How-to Article Scoring Rubric can be found on page 285z for you to use to evaluate their work.

Plan to spend tomorrow doing a formal assessment. Administer the How-to Article Writing Prompt on **Assessment Book** pages 45–46.

TEACHING OPTIONS

Portfolio Opportunity

Remind students to keep a copy of their finished how-to articles in their portfolios. Point out that having a portfolio will help students keep track of the progress they are making with their writing.

Classroom Publisher

Bind students' how-to articles together and make copies available for students to take home. Encourage students to think of illustrations that could be placed on the cover and a title for the collection.

 **Presentation** Publishing is the moment when writers share their finished work. However you publish, be sure the final work is neat and organized. There are lots of ways you can publish your how-to article.

 Film it. Use your how-to article as a script and videotape yourself. You might ask some of your friends to help you.

 Do a PowerPoint presentation of your how-to article. Add clip art for items, such as your materials and the finished product.

 Create a song out of it (like the "Hokey Pokey"). Choose a popular tune and write new lyrics, or create an entirely new how-to song.

 Post it to an online how-to manual. You might also take digital photos of each step and include the images with your article.

Your Turn

Remember, when you publish a how-to article, your goal is to share what you know with others. To publish, follow these steps:

- Make sure you have not left out any important steps.
- Use your best handwriting or a computer to make a final copy of your how-to article.
- Proofread your copy one more time for correct spelling, grammar, capitalization, and punctuation.

Prewriting · Drafting · Content Editing · Revising · Copyediting · Proofreading · Publishing

How-to Articles • 285

Name _____ Date _____

How-to Article

	YES	NO
Ideas		
Do I include ideas in logical step-by-step order?		
Organization		
Does the article have a clear purpose stated in the introduction?		
Does the article have a complete What You Need list?		
Does the article have detailed, accurate instructions in the body?		
Does the article have a summarizing conclusion?		
Voice		
Are many sentences commands?		
Word Choice		
Did I use compound words correctly?		
Sentence Fluency		
Do I use the four kinds of sentences?		
Are the steps complete sentences?		
Conventions		
Do I use correct grammar?		
Do I use correct spelling?		
Do I use correct punctuation and capitalization?		
Presentation		
Is my article neat?		
Do I use consistent margins and spacing?		
Are the instructional graphics easy to read?		
Additional Items		

CHAPTER 2 TEACHER'S SCORING RUBRIC

Name ______________________________

Date ______________________ Score __________

POINT VALUES

0 = not evident
1 = minimal evidence of mastery
2 = evidence of development toward mastery
3 = strong evidence of mastery
4 = outstanding evidence of mastery

How-to Article

	POINTS
Ideas	
ideas expressed in logical, step-by-step order	
Organization	
a clear purpose stated in the introduction	
a complete What You Need list	
detailed, accurate instructions in the body	
a summarizing conclusion	
Voice	
imperative sentences	
Word Choice	
compound words used correctly	
Sentence Fluency	
four kinds of sentences	
steps that are complete sentences	
Conventions	
correct grammar and usage	
correct spelling	
correct punctuation and capitalization	
Presentation	
neatness	
consistent margins and spacing	
easy-to-read instructional graphics	
Additional Items	
Total	

CHAPTER FOCUS

LESSON 1: What Makes a Good Description?

LESSON 2: Writing a Description

- **GRAMMAR:** Pronouns, Verbs
- **WRITING SKILLS:** Sensory Words
- **STUDY SKILLS:** Five-Senses Chart
- **WORD STUDY:** Synonyms
- **SPEAKING AND LISTENING SKILLS:** Oral Descriptions
- **WRITER'S WORKSHOP:** Descriptions

SUPPORT MATERIALS

Practice Book
Writing, pages 142–146

Assessment Book
Chapter 3 Writing Skills,
  pages 47–48
Description Writing Prompt,
  pages 49–50

Rubrics
Student, page 323y
Teacher, page 323z

Test Generator CD

Grammar
Sections 3 and 4, pages 53–79

Customizable Lesson Plans
www.voyagesinenglish.com

Descriptions

WHAT IS A DESCRIPTION?

A good description creates a vivid picture for the reader. Sensory words bring to life the thing being described. The focus is sharp and clear on its topic so that the reader knows what is being described.

A good description includes the following:

- ☐ An informative beginning that names the topic
- ☐ A middle with logical connections
- ☐ A summarizing ending
- ☐ Space order
- ☐ Sensory words
- ☐ Well-chosen synonyms

LiNK Use the following titles to offer your students examples of well-crafted descriptive writing:

The Curious Garden by Peter Brown

Harry Potter and the Sorcerer's Stone by J.K. Rowling

James and the Giant Peach by Roald Dahl

> **There is no way in which to understand the world without first detecting it through the radar-net of our senses.**
>
> —Diane Ackerman

WRITER'S WORKSHOP TIPS

Follow these ideas and tips to help you and your class get the most out of the Writer's Workshop:

- Review the traits of good writing. Use the chart on the inside back cover of the student and teacher editions.

- Encourage students to keep a journal to record their impressions of interesting people, places, and things.

- Fill your classroom library with description-rich literature, including poetry, fiction, and science books.

- Create a bulletin-board display of descriptive marketing material, such as descriptions of new products or travel destinations.

- Post the Student Self-Assessment in poster form during each writing session.

- Remind students that good descriptions sometimes require research about the topic.

CONNECT WITH GRAMMAR

Throughout the Writer's Workshop, take opportunities to integrate pronouns and verbs with writing descriptions.

- [ ] In the revising stage, have students identify pronouns and distinguish between subject and object pronouns.

- [ ] In the content editing stage, suggest that students improve sentence fluency by combining sentences into compound subjects and objects.

- [ ] In the copyediting stage, have students check for agreement of pronouns and verbs.

- [ ] When discussing synonyms, have students find more vivid verbs in a thesaurus. Invite students to find as many synonyms as possible and to work with partners to choose the best one for their purposes.

SCORING RUBRIC

Description

Point Values
0 = not evident
1 = minimal evidence of mastery
2 = evidence of development toward mastery
3 = strong evidence of mastery
4 = outstanding evidence of mastery

Ideas	POINTS
a sharp, distinct focus on the topic	
details that enhance the description	
Organization	
an informative beginning that names the topic	
a middle with logical connections	
a summarizing ending	
space order	
Voice	
language that shows the writer's feelings about the topic	
Word Choice	
sensory words	
well-chosen synonyms	
Sentence Fluency	
varied sentence length	
compound subjects and objects	
Conventions	
correct grammar and usage	
correct spelling	
correct punctuation and capitalization	
Presentation	
neatness	
consistent margins and spacing	
Additional Items	
Total	

Full-sized, reproducible rubrics can be found at the end of this chapter.

Descriptions

INTRODUCING THE GENRE

Explain that Chapter 3 is about writing descriptions. Tell students that descriptions are used in almost every kind of writing. Explain that knowing how to write a good description can come in handy in school, in the future when students have jobs, or even if they just want to tell someone about their day.

Ask volunteers to name things that might be easy to describe. Write their suggestions on the board.

Elaborate on the following characteristics of a description:

- A description includes a beginning that reveals the topic.
- A description gives details in the middle. The details are given in time order or space order.
- A description uses vivid adjectives, adverbs, and sensory words.
- The ending retells the main idea, restates the topic, or leaves the reader with something to think about.

Tell students that good writers can use all their senses to describe something.

Reading the Literature Excerpt

Explain that a successful description will create a clear and complete mental picture of what is being described. Ask volunteers to read aloud the excerpt from *James and the Giant Peach*. Have students identify words and phrases that help create a vivid picture of the garden and the giant peach.

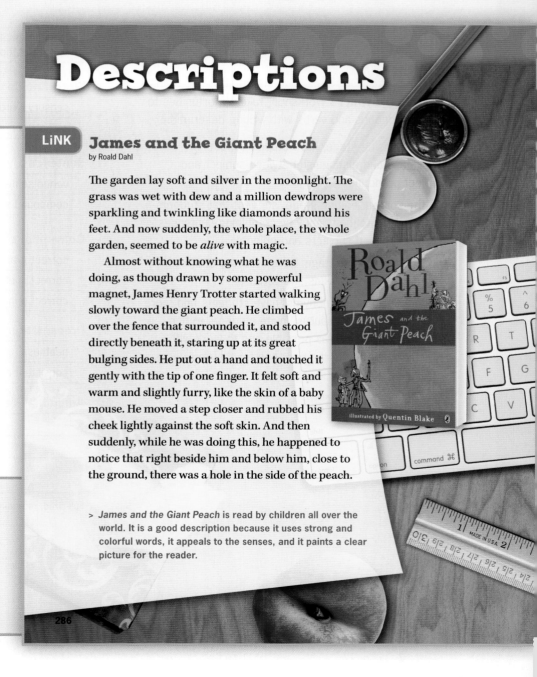

LiNK	**James and the Giant Peach**

The excerpts in Chapter 3 introduce students to published examples of descriptions. *James and the Giant Peach* is a strong example of a description because it does the following:

- Has a beginning that reveals the topic
- Gives details in space order
- Uses vivid adjectives, adverbs, and sensory words

The excerpts in this chapter also provide the opportunity to discuss pronouns. You may wish to point out the pronouns in this excerpt, including *he, his,* and *it.*

Descriptions

LiNK	**James and the Giant Peach**

by Roald Dahl

The garden lay soft and silver in the moonlight. The grass was wet with dew and a million dewdrops were sparkling and twinkling like diamonds around his feet. And now suddenly, the whole place, the whole garden, seemed to be *alive* with magic.

Almost without knowing what he was doing, as though drawn by some powerful magnet, James Henry Trotter started walking slowly toward the giant peach. He climbed over the fence that surrounded it, and stood directly beneath it, staring up at its great bulging sides. He put out a hand and touched it gently with the tip of one finger. It felt soft and warm and slightly furry, like the skin of a baby mouse. He moved a step closer and rubbed his cheek lightly against the soft skin. And then suddenly, while he was doing this, he happened to notice that right beside him and below him, close to the ground, there was a hole in the side of the peach.

> *James and the Giant Peach* is read by children all over the world. It is a good description because it uses strong and colorful words, it appeals to the senses, and it paints a clear picture for the reader.

286

Reading the Student Model

Tell students they are going to read a description written by a student. Have volunteers read aloud the model. Encourage students to listen for words that show that the author has heard, seen, smelled, or touched the thing being described.

Ask volunteers to name words that were used to describe the gorilla habitat. Then guide students to discuss how these words help readers create clear pictures of what is described.

Suggest new topics, such as the playground or the mall. Invite volunteers to give examples of words that writers might use to describe each topic.

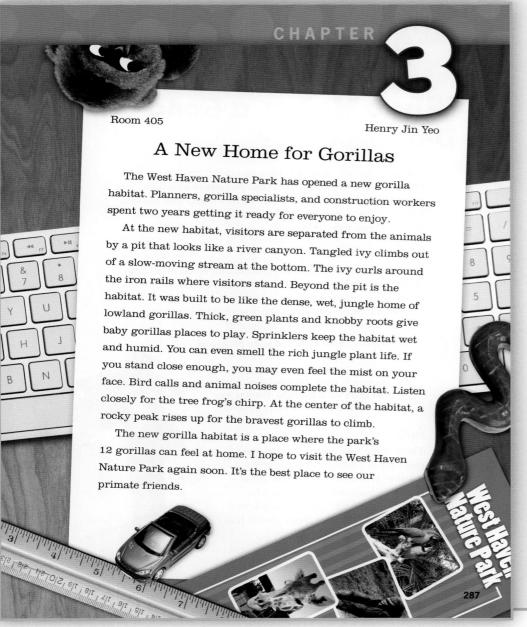

CHAPTER

3

Room 405   Henry Jin Yeo

A New Home for Gorillas

The West Haven Nature Park has opened a new gorilla habitat. Planners, gorilla specialists, and construction workers spent two years getting it ready for everyone to enjoy.

At the new habitat, visitors are separated from the animals by a pit that looks like a river canyon. Tangled ivy climbs out of a slow-moving stream at the bottom. The ivy curls around the iron rails where visitors stand. Beyond the pit is the habitat. It was built to be like the dense, wet, jungle home of lowland gorillas. Thick, green plants and knobby roots give baby gorillas places to play. Sprinklers keep the habitat wet and humid. You can even smell the rich jungle plant life. If you stand close enough, you may even feel the mist on your face. Bird calls and animal noises complete the habitat. Listen closely for the tree frog's chirp. At the center of the habitat, a rocky peak rises up for the bravest gorillas to climb.

The new gorilla habitat is a place where the park's 12 gorillas can feel at home. I hope to visit the West Haven Nature Park again soon. It's the best place to see our primate friends.

287

TEACHING OPTIONS

Scavenger Hunt

Have small groups search the classroom and the library for examples of descriptions. Ask students to explain what is being described in each example and to identify words that appeal to the five senses.

For Tomorrow

Ask students to find an example of a description in a fiction story. Tell students to be prepared to share their examples with the class. Bring in your own description to share.

OBJECTIVES

- **To choose strong and colorful words**
- **To recognize audience and space order in descriptions**

WARM-UP

Read, Listen, Speak

Read aloud your description from yesterday's For Tomorrow homework. Ask students to share specific pictures the description evokes for them. Have small groups share their descriptions. Ask students to explain how the description helps a reader picture what is being described.

GRAMMAR CONNECTION

Take this opportunity to talk about pronouns and subject pronouns. You may wish to have students point out any pronouns and subject pronouns in their Read, Listen, Speak examples.

TEACH

Write on the board the words *farmer, zebra, library,* and *banana.* Ask students to imagine that they are describing these things to someone who knows nothing about them. Ask volunteers to write on the board a sentence that describes one of the words. Have students identify the descriptive words. Point out the word choices that different writers make to describe the same thing.

Invite a volunteer to read aloud the first paragraph. Remind students that sight, hearing, smell, touch, and taste are our five senses. Ask students to name some words that we use to describe the way something looks, sounds, smells, feels, or tastes.

Ask volunteers to read aloud the section Choosing Words. Explain that strong descriptions give more information about what is being described. Write the following example on the board:

The boy looked cold.

Ask students to suggest stronger descriptive sentences. *(The boy's lips were purple from the cold. The boy was shivering.)*

Have a volunteer read aloud the section Audience. Invite students to name things that they would describe differently to their parents than to their friends. Encourage students to think about their audience whenever they are writing descriptions.

PRACTICE

ACTIVITY A

Have students complete this activity independently. Then have students share their answers with a partner. Encourage volunteers to point out the strong and colorful words they found.

ACTIVITY B

Have partners complete the activity and ask volunteers to name their strong and colorful words. Have several students give their answers for each item. Discuss the different choices of strong and colorful words.

What Makes a Good Description?

A description tells about a person, an animal, a place, or an object. Good descriptions form clear pictures in a reader's mind. Great descriptions tell not only how things look but also how they might sound, smell, feel, or even taste. What is the description on page 287 about?

Choosing Words

Choose words carefully. Strong and colorful words make clear pictures in a reader's mind. Pick words that help readers think about sight, sound, smell, touch, and taste.

Read the two descriptions. What words in the second description help you see and feel the gift?

A The box on the table had silver paper and a red ribbon.

B The enormous box on the table was covered in shiny, smooth, silvery paper that sparkled in the light. The box was tied with a bright red, velvety ribbon.

Audience

Think about who is going to read your description. Will it be your parents or a teacher? Will it be your friends? What does your audience know about what you are describing? Thinking about your audience will help you choose words that they will understand.

LiNK Have a volunteer read aloud the excerpt from *James and the Giant Peach*. Ask students to point out strong and colorful words. Then challenge students to replace the word *delicious* with other strong and colorful words.

APPLY

WRITER'S CORNER

Point out some items in the classroom that students might use for their descriptions. When students have finished, invite volunteers to read aloud their descriptions. Challenge volunteers to add sentences to each description. Students should demonstrate the ability to choose strong and colorful words.

ASSESS

Note which students had difficulty understanding how to choose strong and colorful words. Use the Reteach option with those students who need additional reinforcement.

TEACHING OPTIONS

Reteach

Display an object for students to describe, such as an orange or another common item. Discuss ways in which students might describe the object. Ask questions that draw attention to the five senses. List on the board the questions. *(What color is it? How big is it? What does it feel like? What do you think it will taste like? How does it smell?)* Encourage students to write the questions in their notebooks and to refer to them when writing descriptions.

English-Language Learners

Invite students to describe their favorite food without naming it. Ask students to tell how the food might look taste, smell, feel, and what sounds they might hear as it is being prepared or eaten. Encourage students to think about the ingredients in the dish as they formulate their oral descriptions. Have other students identify the food being described. Ask volunteers to offer suggestions to enhance the description.

For Tomorrow

Ask students to choose an outdoor location and to write a list of five strong and colorful words that describe the location. Bring in your own list of words to describe an outdoor location.

ACTIVITY A Which description uses strong and colorful words? Tell which words in the description help you imagine the scene.

1. My Cat

    I really like my cat. She is black and white and very cute. Her name is Tippy. She chases insects. She catches a fly. She doesn't like it, so she spits it out. It flies away.

2. Tippy's Snack

    My cat Tippy is a ball of black and white fur. She likes to leap at flies. Oh, no, she's eaten one! Her pink nose wrinkles, and her mouth opens. The fly hurries out and buzzes away.

ACTIVITY B Replace the underlined word in each sentence with a strong and colorful word. You can use more than one word. Imagine that your classmates are your audience.

1. What a nice view of the mountains!
2. That was a good dinner.
3. We can't burn the leaves because they make a bad smell.
4. The skater moved across the ice.
5. Our new puppy cries at night.
6. My room was clean.
7. The clouds were pretty.
8. I really liked that movie.
9. We saw a large building.
10. The child was happy on the water slide.

LiNK

James and the Giant Peach

The tunnel was damp and murky, and all around him there was the curious bittersweet smell of fresh peach. The floor was soggy under his knees, the walls were wet and sticky, and peach juice was dripping from the ceiling. James opened his mouth and caught some of it on his tongue. It tasted delicious.

Roald Dahl

WRITER'S CORNER

Choose an item in your classroom. It might be a toy, a desk, or your backpack. Then write four sentences describing the item. Use strong and colorful words.

WARM-UP

Read, Listen, Speak

Write on the board your list of descriptive words from yesterday's For Tomorrow homework. Use the words in sentences describing the location. Have small groups discuss the word lists they wrote. Encourage students to talk about their outdoor locations and to explain how they might use their listed words in a description.

GRAMMAR CONNECTION

Take this opportunity to talk about object pronouns. You may wish to point out students' use of object pronouns in their Read, Listen, Speak discussions.

TEACH

Have volunteers read aloud the first two paragraphs. Ask students to give examples of things that could be described by using time order (a vacation, a baseball game, a day at school).

Invite volunteers to read aloud the section Space Order. After each example, ask volunteers to name things that might be described by using that kind of space order (top to bottom—a picture, a building; side to side—a room, a desk; near to far—a field, a garden). Explain that by using one of these kinds of space order, students can write more accurate descriptions.

LiNK Have a volunteer read aloud the excerpt from *James and the Giant Peach*. Ask students to draw a picture of the scene, based on the description. Then discuss the words the author used while describing the scene in space order (directly across, next to, On a sofa nearby).

PRACTICE

ACTIVITY C

Have students complete this activity with partners. Invite volunteers to share their answers with the class. Then ask students to list the words in each description that help determine the kind of space order used.

ACTIVITY D

Have students complete this activity independently. When students have finished, ask volunteers to share their descriptions with the class. Challenge students to name the kind of space order used by the writer.

James and the Giant Peach

LiNK

There was an Old-Green-Grasshopper as large as a large dog sitting on a stool directly across the room from James now. And next to the Old-Green-Grasshopper there was an enormous Spider. And next to the Spider, there was a giant Ladybug with nine black spots on her scarlet shell. . . . On a sofa nearby, reclining comfortably in curled-up positions, there was a Centipede and an Earthworm.

Roald Dahl

A good description gives a picture of what is being described. Using a clear order will help your reader follow your description without getting lost.

When you use time order, you tell about events in the order that they happened. Here is another way to order a description.

Space Order

There are many kinds of space order. When you write a description from top to bottom, from side to side, or from near to far, you are using space order. Space order can help a reader see things the way that you do. Look at these examples of space order.

top to bottom

My cousin Micha has dark, curly hair. He has big, bushy eyebrows like Grandpa's. His eyes are almost black. His nose is just like mine. It is square at the tip. He has the same cheery smile my mom has.

side to side

My collections are on the shelf above my bed. On the left are my comic books. In the middle are my baseball cards. Then there are my dragon models. I keep my bowling trophies on the right side of the shelf.

near to far

The first thing you'll see by the park entrance are some picnic tables. Past the picnic tables are groups of trees. In the middle of all the trees is a duck pond. From there you can see the other end of the park.

What other things might you describe from top to bottom, from side to side, or from near to far?

APPLY

WRITER'S CORNER

Discuss the kind of details students might use to help describe a person, such as hair and eye color, facial features, and clothing. When students have finished, have them exchange descriptions with partners. Ask students to list the descriptive words and draw a picture of the person based on the description. Students should demonstrate the ability to use space order.

Grammar in Action. Challenge students to use at least one subject pronoun and one object pronoun.

ASSESS

Note which students had difficulty using space order. Use the Reteach option with those students who need additional reinforcement.

Practice Book page 142 provides additional work with the characteristics of descriptions.

TEACHING OPTIONS

Reteach

Choose three pictures that can be described by using the three different kinds of space order (a statue, a room, a forest). Discuss each picture. Encourage students to list strong and colorful words for each picture. Then ask students to think about what kind of space order they might use to describe each picture. Help students determine the best kind of space order to use for each description.

Space Order Race

Assign each student one of the following kinds of space order: top to bottom, side to side, near to far. Ask volunteers to explain each type of space order. Then have students write a brief description of a location, using their assigned space order. Divide the class into teams. Read aloud students' descriptions and have teams decide which kind of space order is being used. The team with the most correct answers wins the Space Order Race.

Activity C
1. near to far
2. top to bottom
3. side to side
4. near to far

ACTIVITY C What kind of space order is used in each of the descriptions below?

1. Just ahead, the trees grew dense and wild. The pine branches beyond were thick and prickly. I could see a wooden lookout station in the distance.

2. The veil floated around Mara's head like smoke. Her face was hidden. Her white dress was almost blinding. A long train with tiny pearls on the edges flowed behind her.

3. Father Elephant led the colorful circus parade. Mother Elephant gripped his tail with her trunk and followed. Baby Elephant tried to keep up. He held on to his mother's tail and trotted along after them.

4. The entrance hall to the museum was huge. Near the main entrance was a ticket booth. There was a long line of people waiting to buy tickets. Behind them was the information area. It had a big, round desk at which people were sitting. They could answer your questions and give out maps. In the background, towering over all, was a skeleton of a huge dinosaur—a *Tyrannosaurus rex*.

ACTIVITY D Write a short description of one of the items below. Write the description from top to bottom, from side to side, or from near to far.

- a birthday cake
- a classroom
- a table full of food
- a snow-covered mountain
- a model train
- a view of the ocean
- a parrot

WRITER'S CORNER

Picture someone you know well. Write five details you could use to describe that person. Then write one sentence for each detail. Put the sentences in space order from top to bottom.

Grammar in Action. Use at least two different pronouns in your descriptive sentences.

For Tomorrow

Ask students to draw a picture of a room they imagine might be in a castle. Draw your own picture to share with the class.

Descriptions • 291

OBJECTIVES

- **To choose a topic for a description**
- **To recognize the parts of a description**

WARM-UP

Read, Listen, Speak

Display your picture from yesterday's For Tomorrow homework. Then describe it for the class. Ask students to tell what order you used to describe your drawing. Have small groups share their pictures. Ask students to describe what they have drawn. Encourage students to use side-to-side space order or near-to-far space order in their descriptions.

GRAMMAR CONNECTION

Take this opportunity to talk about possessive pronouns. You may wish to point out students' use of possessive pronouns in their Read, Listen, Speak descriptions.

TEACH

Have a volunteer read aloud the first paragraph. Help students understand the importance of imagining the thing being described while writing about it. Then ask a volunteer to read aloud the section Choosing a Topic. Ask students to name some topics that can be described by using most or all of the five senses. List their responses on the board.

Invite a volunteer to read aloud the section Beginning. Discuss some ways to create a strong beginning (clear writing, strong and colorful words, an attention-grabbing first sentence).

Read aloud the section Middle. Tell students to look for the main details in the middle, as well as for the order of the description.

Invite a volunteer to read aloud the section Ending. Explain that a good ending ties the description together and makes it complete. Ask students to explain why a strong ending is important to a description.

PRACTICE

ACTIVITY A

You may wish to have students review the student model before beginning this activity. Read aloud the questions and have volunteers answer them.

ACTIVITY B

Have a volunteer read aloud the description. Then ask students to complete this activity independently. Have partners compare their drawings. Encourage students to talk about how the same information might lead different readers to imagine the market stall differently.

ACTIVITY C

Tell students to be sure they write complete sentences. When students have finished, ask them to read their descriptions aloud to the class.

Writing a Description

A good description helps readers feel like they are part of the story. When you write a description, think about and imagine what you are describing. Use words that help a reader easily follow your description.

Choosing a Topic

The topic of your description is the thing you are describing. Anything that you can see, hear, smell, touch, or taste can be the topic of a description.

Beginning

The beginning of a description tells what you will describe. A good beginning makes the reader want to read more.

Middle

The middle of a description tells about what is being described. In the middle the topic is described using either space order or time order.

Ending

The ending often retells what was said in the beginning and the middle of the description. The ending might explain why the thing being described is important. A good ending might leave the reader with something to think about.

Silverback gorilla

APPLY

WRITER'S CORNER

Have a volunteer read aloud the middle of the student model. Discuss other things students might see in a gorilla habitat. Remind students to use strong and colorful words and to describe the things by using their five senses. Invite volunteers to read aloud their sentences. Students should demonstrate the ability to write parts of a description.

ASSESS

Note which students had difficulty writing the parts of a description. Use the Reteach option with those students who need additional reinforcement.

TEACHING OPTIONS

○ Reteach

Ask students to imagine a favorite outdoor place (a park, a beach, the mountains, their own backyard, a campground, a lake). Have students draw three large boxes and label them Beginning, Middle, and Ending. Have students write in each box one sentence that begins each part of a description of that place. Encourage students to choose strong, colorful words for each part of their description.

○ Cooperative Learning

Have small groups work together to choose a place they have all visited, decide which space order to use to describe it, and write a beginning, middle, and an ending for their description. Direct students to choose different group members to perform each task. Encourage students to put the different parts of the description together and to revise it so that it flows from one section to another. Have volunteers read aloud their completed descriptions.

For Tomorrow

Have students write a new ending for "A New Home for Our Gorillas" on page 287. Write your own ending to share with the class.

Activity A

1. a new gorilla habitat
2. Answers will vary.
3. Answers will vary.
4. Possible answers: tangled, slow-moving, dense, wet, humid, chirp, rocky
5. near to far
6. Answers will vary.

ACTIVITY A Answer the questions below about "A New Home for Gorillas" on page 287.

1. What is the topic?
2. Does the beginning make you want to read more? Why or why not?
3. What words in the middle help paint a clear picture of what is being described?
4. What words appeal to your sense of sight, sound, smell, and touch?
5. What kind of space order is used in the middle?
6. Does the ending make sense? Why or why not?

ACTIVITY B Read the description below. Imagine what the market stall looks like and draw a picture of it, using the description as a guide.

The stall at the farmer's market had many boxes of colorful fruits and vegetables. At the left was a large box of peppers in three colors—some dark green, some bright red, and some light yellow. Next was a small box of light green grapes, followed by a small box of nectarines. At the right was a large box of red tomatoes with parts of their dark green stems and vines still attached.

ACTIVITY C Write a short description of a thing such as your favorite toy. Exchange your description with a partner. Read your partner's description and draw it. Then discuss how your drawings compare to the descriptions and the actual things.

WRITER'S CORNER

Look at the middle of "A New Home for Gorillas" on page 287. Write two sentences describing something else that could be in the gorilla habitat.

Descriptions • 293

WARM-UP

Read, Listen, Speak

Read aloud your new ending from yesterday's For Tomorrow homework. Ask students to tell how your ending changes the description. Have small groups share their endings. Then have students explain how each ending makes the description complete.

GRAMMAR CONNECTION

Take this opportunity to talk about possessive adjectives. You may wish to have students point out any possessive adjectives in their Read, Listen, Speak examples.

TEACH

Remind students that the topic of a description can be anything that they can see, hear, smell, touch, or taste. Then write these headings on the board: *Beginning, Middle, Ending.*

Guide students to talk about what each of these parts of a description does and why each part is important. Write students' responses under the appropriate headings. Encourage students to use the information on the board to help them remember what should be included in each part of a description.

PRACTICE

ACTIVITY D

Tell students to describe each topic in as much detail as possible. Have them imagine that they are giving hints about the topic but not revealing it.

ACTIVITY E

Ask students to complete this activity independently. Encourage students first to review the beginning of "A New Home for Our Gorillas" on page 287 for an example of a good beginning. Invite volunteers to read aloud their completed beginnings.

ACTIVITY F

Tell partners to take turns reading aloud the descriptions. Ask students to list the strong and colorful words in each middle. Ask volunteers to share their answers with the class.

ACTIVITY G

Point out that strong endings leave a reader with something to think about. Have small groups complete this activity. Tell students to take turns reading aloud the endings. Then have students decide which ending is stronger. When students have finished, invite volunteers to explain their choices.

ACTIVITY D Write two sentences that describe each topic below. Use strong and colorful words that help readers think about each topic.

1. a flock of pigeons
2. a bonfire
3. a newborn baby
4. a racehorse
5. a castle
6. a sunset
7. a firefly
8. a tree
9. a farm
10. a beach
11. a rainy day
12. a birthday party

ACTIVITY E Choose one of the topics from Activity D. Write the beginning of a description of that topic. Remember to tell readers something that will make them want to read more.

ACTIVITY F Read each middle of a description. Name the topic of each.

1. His nose is crooked because of a flying hockey puck years ago. His shoulders are so broad that he looks like he is still wearing his hockey shoulder pads. hockey player
2. The banana swims in gooey fudge along the bottom of the dish. Vanilla ice cream melts slowly over the banana, threatening to drown everything. Whipped cream forms three gentle peaks at the top, each holding a shiny, perfect cherry. banana split
3. The smell of bacon frying tickles my nose. I hear the pop of the toaster and the hiss of spattering butter. I know that the sound of cracking eggs is coming next. I am up before the eggs are scrambled. breakfast

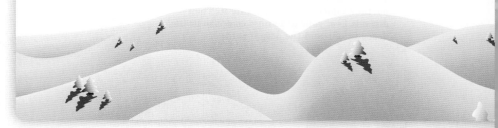

294 • Chapter 3

LiNK Have a volunteer read aloud the excerpt. Ask students to point out the most descriptive words in the passage. Ask if the description is in time order or space order.

APPLY

WRITER'S CORNER

Encourage students to reread the stronger endings from Activity G for models. Invite students to share their work. Students should demonstrate the ability to write an effective ending for a description.

ASSESS

Note which students had difficulty writing the parts of a description. Use the Reteach option with those students who need additional reinforcement.

Practice Book page 143 provides additional work with the parts of a description.

Reteach

Have students choose and write the middle from a description in Activity F. Discuss the characteristics of beginnings and endings in descriptions. Direct students to write on another sheet of paper a beginning for the middle they have chosen. Then have students trade papers with a partner. Have the partner write on another sheet of paper an ending for the description. Have students trade the three pages of their descriptions with another pair. Encourage students to put the descriptions in the correct order.

Go With the Flow

Assign small groups the beginning, middle, or ending of a description. Ask students to choose a topic with which they are all familiar, such as the playground. Then have students write only their assigned part without discussing the rest of the description. When students have finished, encourage them to read their parts aloud. Discuss whether the parts fit together. Point out the importance of a description that flows well from one part to the next.

ACTIVITY G Read the pairs of endings below. Which ending in each pair is stronger? Why do you think so?

1. a. My bedroom isn't fancy or neat, but that's OK. It's cozy, colorful, and comfortable. It's filled with lots of my favorite things. When I go into my bedroom, I can relax and be myself.
   b. My bedroom is my favorite room in the house. You could say it's two rooms, actually, because there's also a closet. I keep my clothes in there.

2. a. Grandma's gingerbread house makes me hungry. I sometimes want to break off a piece and eat it. Grandma would probably get mad if I did.
   b. Grandma's gingerbread house looks both beautiful and delicious. The candy canes, gumdrops, and peanut brittle somehow form a perfect house. I almost want to stop by for a visit and take a bite while I'm there!

3. a. Our backyard garden is an amazing sight. A few little seeds have sprouted into tomatoes, carrots, and beans. I can't wait to eat our homegrown vegetables.
   b. Our backyard garden is full of vegetables, not flowers. The flowers are in the front yard. Flowers are nice to look at, but vegetables are better to eat.

LiNK

James and the Giant Peach

And now the peach had broken out of the garden and was over the edge of the hill, rolling and bouncing down the steep slope at a terrific pace. Faster and faster and faster it went, and the crowds of people who were climbing up the hill suddenly caught sight of this terrible monster plunging down upon them and they screamed and scattered to the right and left as it went hurtling by.

Roald Dahl

WRITER'S CORNER

Choose a middle from Activity F and imagine that you wrote it. Write an ending for it. You might retell what was said in the beginning and the middle, or you might explain why the topic was important.

For Tomorrow

Tell students to choose a weaker ending from Activity G. Have them rewrite the ending, using strong and colorful words. Rewrite one of the endings yourself to share with the class.

Descriptions • 295

OBJECTIVE

• **To identify sensory words**

WARM-UP

Read, Listen, Speak

Read aloud your rewritten ending from yesterday's For Tomorrow homework. Ask students to tell what you changed and why it is better. Have small groups share their rewritten endings. Guide students to talk about why strong endings are important. Ask students to discuss what might happen if a description used strong and colorful words but had a boring ending.

GRAMMAR CONNECTION

Take this opportunity to talk about pronoun-verb agreement. You may wish to have students point out any pronoun-verb agreement in their Read, Listen, Speak examples.

TEACH

Ask a volunteer to read aloud the first paragraph. Write *flower shop* on the board and invite students to answer the question about which senses they would use to describe a flower shop. Then ask students to suggest words that describe a flower shop.

Have a volunteer read aloud the second paragraph. Explain that both the reader and the writer use their imaginations to experience the object of a description. Tell students why using sensory words in a description is important. *(Sensory words help the reader imagine what is being described. Sensory words help the reader feel like part of the story.)*

Read aloud the rest of the page. Ask students to name sensory words that make sentence B stronger than sentence A. Have students list other sensory words that could be used in sentence B.

PRACTICE

ACTIVITY A
Read aloud each item. Ask students to tell which sense each thing appeals to and to tell which words indicate that sense.

ACTIVITY B
Have students complete this activity independently. Then have partners compare their answers. Encourage students to list other words that might describe the words in Column B.

ACTIVITY C
Have small groups complete this activity. Encourage students to list words that relate to more than one of the five senses. Invite volunteers to read aloud their words. Have students guess the topic being described.

Sensory Words

People have five senses: sight, sound, smell, taste, and touch. What senses might you use to describe a flower shop?

Descriptions include words that tell what the writer sees, hears, smells, tastes, and feels. These sensory words help the reader imagine what is being described.

Read these two sentences. Both sentences tell what happened. Which sentence helps you imagine the swing?

A The swing swayed in the wind.

B The rusty, old swing creaked and groaned as the wind pushed it about.

In sentence A the writer writes only about what he or she saw. In sentence B the writer uses more senses to describe the scene. Sentence B forms a clearer picture in the reader's mind.

ACTIVITY A Tell which sense is used to describe the thing in each sentence.

1. Grandpa's homemade ice cream is sweet and nutty.
2. The rooster's ear-splitting crow woke us up at dawn.
3. The spaghetti sauce's spicy scent made my mouth water.
4. Becca buried her face in the soft, warm towels just out of the dryer.
5. The stormy sky was thick with clouds that were gray, purple, and muddy brown.
6. The roaring engine of the huge truck was deafening as it rumbled down the street.

Activity A
1. taste
2. sound
3. smell
4. touch
5. sight
6. sound
7. sight
8. smell

APPLY

WRITER'S CORNER

Tell students to use their imaginations as they complete this activity. When students have finished, invite them to share their sentences in small groups. Have students tell which sense the sentence appeals to. Students should demonstrate the ability to use sensory words in descriptions.

ASSESS

Note which students had difficulty using sensory words in descriptions. Use the Reteach option with those students who need additional reinforcement.

TEACHING OPTIONS

Reteach

Display an assortment of items that are can be described by using touch, smell, and hearing (sandpaper, tape, a cup of sand, a scented candle, a lemon, a bell). Have partners take turns wearing blindfolds. Tell students to choose an item and to place it in their partner's hands. Ask the blindfolded students to use their senses to describe the item. Encourage students to use strong, colorful words that can help paint a mental picture of each item. Then have students guess the item they are describing.

Describe Your Dream Machine

Tell students to imagine that they are taking a trip to a distant land in a whimsical car, train, bus, plane, or truck. Encourage them to think about the dream machine they might use to get to that place. Have students draw a picture of their dream machine. Then ask them to write a description of the vehicle and their imaginary journey, using sensory words. Have students share their pictures and descriptions in small groups.

For Tomorrow

Tell students to write brief descriptions of a snack they like without directly stating what it is. Write your own description of a snack to share with students.

7. The fireworks burst into expanding blooms of red, blue, green, and white in the sky.

8. The lilacs' strong, sweet fragrance spread from the garden into our house.

ACTIVITY B **Match the sensory words in Column A to what the words describe in Column B.**

Column A	Column B
1. sour smoke, blue flame, rough wood, sharp crack e	**a.** a teakettle
2. bumpy walnuts, crunchy vegetables, sweet berries c	**b.** a slide
3. cool metal, creaky steps, swooshing sounds b	**c.** a salad
4. sharp thorns, soft petals, sweet smell, dark red color f	**d.** a window
5. whistling steam, hot metal, blue flames beneath a	**e.** a match
6. dusty curtains, smooth glass, tinkling wind chimes, gray screen d	**f.** a rose

ACTIVITY C **Choose three topics below. Imagine the scene. List at least five sensory words.**

1. a birthday party
2. a carnival
3. a baseball game
4. lunch in the school cafeteria
5. a family reunion
6. a picnic
7. a parade
8. a thunderstorm

WRITER'S CORNER

Choose two senses: sight, sound, smell, taste, and touch. Then choose one of your favorite things, such as a food, a hobby, or a sport. Write two sentences, each using one of the senses you chose. Use strong and colorful words.

Descriptions • 297

Read, Listen, Speak

Read aloud your description from yesterday's For Tomorrow homework. Have students guess what snack you described and tell how they knew. Have small groups share the descriptions they wrote for homework. Encourage the listeners to guess what is being described.

GRAMMAR CONNECTION

Take this opportunity to talk about *I* and *me*. You may wish to have students point out any uses of *I* and *me* in their Read, Listen, Speak examples.

TEACH

Write on the board the following column headings: *Sight, Hearing, Smell, Taste, Touch*. Invite volunteers to list sensory words for each sense. Write students' suggestions in the appropriate columns. Then write a descriptive sentence using some of the words listed. Ask volunteers to write additional sentences using the other words listed. Emphasize that a good description uses as many of the five senses as possible.

LiNK Have a volunteer read aloud the excerpt from *James and the Giant Peach*. Ask students to point out the sensory words in the description and to tell to which sense they appeal. Write those words in the appropriate column of the chart on the board.

PRACTICE

ACTIVITY D

Refer students to the chart on the board. Have small groups complete this activity. When students have finished, invite them to write the sensory words for each item under the correct column heading.

ACTIVITY E

Have students complete this activity with partners. Tell them to imagine the thing that they are describing and think about what senses each item appeals to. When students have finished, invite volunteers to read aloud their sentences.

ACTIVITY F

Have partners work together to list the sensory words in the paragraph. When students have finished, invite them to share their answers with the class.

ACTIVITY G

When students have finished, review the answers by having volunteers read aloud each sentence in the paragraph. Have students identify other sensory words in the paragraph and tell which sense they appeal to.

ACTIVITY H

Point out that each word could appeal to more than one sense. (Smoky *could describe a smell, a taste, or even a sound or voice.*) Then have small groups compare their sentences and tell which senses they appeal to.

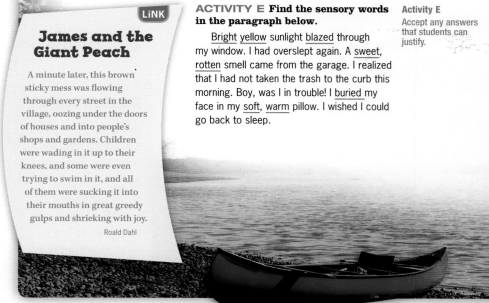

ACTIVITY D Which sense is used to describe the thing in each sentence below? Which words give you clues?

1. People always say that Kyle's <u>laugh</u> is like the <u>hee-haw</u> of a donkey.
2. Jo's dress is such a wild shade of <u>red</u> it hurts your <u>eyes</u> to <u>look</u> at it.
3. Sleeping on a featherbed is like <u>cuddling</u> on a <u>cloud</u>.
4. The <u>buttery</u>, <u>salty-sweet</u> <u>scent</u> drew us to the caramel corn.
5. At first Amanda didn't like the <u>tangy flavor</u> of mangos.
6. Gary's pet rabbit's fur was <u>smooth</u> and <u>soft</u> under my fingers.
7. The air in a rain forest can be <u>heavy</u> and <u>humid</u>.
8. The <u>deep red</u>, <u>juicy-looking</u> seeds of the pomegranate seemed tasty.
9. In the garden the <u>perky</u>, <u>yellow</u> tulips waved their heads in the breeze.
10. As we paddled our canoes, the water of the stream <u>whooshed</u> and <u>gurgled</u> over the stones.

Activity D
1. sound
2. sight
3. touch
4. smell
5. taste
6. touch
7. touch
8. sight
9. sight
10. sound

LiNK

James and the Giant Peach

A minute later, this brown sticky mess was flowing through every street in the village, oozing under the doors of houses and into people's shops and gardens. Children were wading in it up to their knees, and some were even trying to swim in it, and all of them were sucking it into their mouths in great greedy gulps and shrieking with joy.

Roald Dahl

ACTIVITY E Find the sensory words in the paragraph below.

Bright <u>yellow</u> sunlight <u>blazed</u> through my window. I had overslept again. A <u>sweet</u>, <u>rotten</u> smell came from the garage. I realized that I had not taken the trash to the curb this morning. Boy, was I in trouble! I <u>buried</u> my face in my <u>soft</u>, <u>warm</u> pillow. I wished I could go back to sleep.

Activity E
Accept any answers that students can justify.

ACTIVITY I
Challenge students to use unexpected sensory words. Ask volunteers to read aloud their sentences and write the sensory words in the correct columns of the chart on the board.

APPLY

WRITER'S CORNER
Guide students to describe specific things, such as food, the sky, or people. Students should demonstrate the ability to write sentences with sensory words.

Grammar in Action. Write on the board subject pronouns. Have students read their sentences and tell which subject pronouns they used and why.

ASSESS
Note which students had difficulty writing sentences with sensory words. Use the Reteach option with those students who need additional reinforcement.
Practice Book page 144 provides additional work with sensory words.

TEACHING OPTIONS

Reteach
Have students look around the classroom and choose three items that can be described by using sensory words. Direct students to write on note cards four words that can be used to describe each item. Have students tape their cards to the items. Then have students use the words to write sentences describing the items. Keep the cards on the items for students to refer to as they write other descriptions.

Picture This
Have students write four sentences to describe a person or an animal. Tell students to choose a family member, a friend, a pet, or a zoo animal. Explain that the descriptions should be so clear that another person could draw a picture after reading the description. When students have finished, have them trade papers with a partner. Allow time for students to draw pictures of their partners descriptions. Then have partners discuss whether the drawings are a reasonable representation of what was described.

For Tomorrow
Ask students to write three sentences describing a family member or friend. Encourage students to describe both the way the person looks and how the person acts. Bring in your own three-sentence description to share.

ACTIVITY F Complete the paragraph below with sensory words from the word box.

| smoky | buttery | hot | blue | cry |

I like to go to the beach with my family. As soon as we get there, I run across the hot sand and jump into the __blue__ water. Then I lie on my towel and soak up the __hot__ sun. I close my eyes and listen to the seagulls __cry__. When the __smoky__ smell of roasting corn tickles my nose, I know that it is time for lunch. I can't wait for the first __buttery__ bite.

ACTIVITY G Write one sentence that describes each item below. Include as many sensory words as you can.

1. a kitten
2. an old radio
3. fresh-baked bread
4. a new bicycle
5. a band concert
6. a cow
7. a snowstorm
8. a muddy puddle
9. a bouquet of flowers
10. a bowl of soup

ACTIVITY H Look at the words in the word box in Activity F. Write one item that each word might describe. Then write a sentence describing each item you listed. Use the words in the word box in your sentences.

ACTIVITY I Reread the paragraph from Activity F. List your own sensory words for each blank.

WRITER'S CORNER
Imagine a picnic. What do you see, hear, and smell? What can you touch and taste? Write five sentences describing the picnic. Use a different sense in each sentence.

Grammar in Action. Replace the subjects in your sentences with subject pronouns.

Descriptions • 299

OBJECTIVES
- **To create a five-senses chart**
- **To use a five-senses chart to write descriptions**

WARM-UP
Read, Listen, Speak
Read aloud your description of a person from yesterday's For Tomorrow homework. Ask students to raise their hands when they hear sensory words. Have small groups share the descriptions students wrote for homework. Ask students to talk about whether the descriptions use strong and colorful words.

GRAMMAR CONNECTION
Take this opportunity to talk about compound subjects and objects. You may wish to have students point out any compound subjects and objects in their Read, Listen, Speak examples.

TEACH
Ask a volunteer to read aloud the first paragraph. Explain that students will be learning how to use charts that will help to write strong, detailed descriptions.

Have a volunteer read aloud the next two paragraphs. Allow students to examine the five-senses chart about Elizabeth's favorite snack. Ask students to determine what Elizabeth's favorite snack is *(nachos)*. Discuss what students imagine when they think about the sensory words in the chart. Read aloud the paragraph above the second chart.

Direct students' attention to the second five-senses chart. Point out that the information in both charts is the same. Then draw a two-column five-senses chart on the board. Invite volunteers to suggest topics for the five-senses chart *(a day at camp, a hockey game, a restaurant)*. Select one topic and write it as a title. Then have students list words for filling in the five-senses chart. Write their suggestions in the chart.

PRACTICE
ACTIVITY A
Have partners complete this activity. Encourage them to take turns reading aloud the questions to each other. When students have finished, ask volunteers to share their answers with the class.

Five-Senses Chart

Using sensory words will help you write a clear, interesting description. Sensory words help the reader imagine what you describe.

A five-senses chart can help you remember details about what you are describing. It can also help you think of sensory words that you can use in your description.

Here is a five-senses chart that Elizabeth made on a computer about her favorite snack.

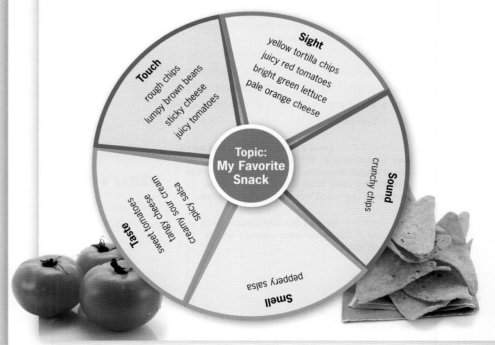

Sight
yellow tortilla chips
juicy red tomatoes
bright green lettuce
pale orange cheese

Touch
rough chips
lumpy brown beans
sticky cheese
juicy tomatoes

Sound
crunchy chips

Taste
sweet tomatoes
tangy cheese
creamy sour cream
spicy salsa

Smell
peppery salsa

Topic: My Favorite Snack

APPLY

WRITER'S CORNER

Invite volunteers to read aloud their sentences. Tell students that they can make their own five-senses charts to help write descriptions in the future. Students should demonstrate the ability to use a five-senses chart to write descriptions.

ASSESS

Note which students had difficulty understanding how to use five-senses charts to write descriptions. Use the Reteach option with those students who need additional reinforcement.

TEACHING OPTIONS

Reteach

Have students draw their own five-senses chart with the headings *Sight, Sound, Touch, Smell,* and *Taste.* Ask students to look at the student model "A New Home for Our Gorillas" on page 287. Direct students to find sensory words from the model and to write them in the appropriate sections of their charts. Explain that the writer of the model may have used a similar chart when planning to write his or her description. Encourage students to add to their charts additional sensory words that could have been used in the model.

Environment Charts

Take students on a nature walk. Have students bring notebooks to record their observations. Tell students they will be filling in a five-sense chart about their nature walk. Point out that students will not be able to taste anything on the walk. Challenge them to imagine things they might taste from nature such as berries or water from a stream. Allow time for students to complete their charts. Display the completed charts in the classroom.

Elizabeth might have also used a two-column five-senses chart. It might have looked like this.

Topic: My Favorite Snack

Sight	yellow tortilla chips, juicy red tomatoes, bright green lettuce, pale orange cheese
Sound	crunchy chips
Smell	peppery salsa
Taste	sweet tomatoes, tangy cheese, creamy sour cream, spicy salsa
Touch	rough chips, lumpy brown beans, sticky cheese, juicy tomatoes

Activity A
1. nachos
2. lettuce
3. crunchy chips
4. peppery
5. sweet
6. rough

ACTIVITY A Look at Elizabeth's charts and answer the questions below.

1. What is Elizabeth's favorite snack?
2. What did the writer see that was bright green?
3. What sound did the writer hear?
4. What word does the writer use to describe the smell of salsa?
5. What word does the writer use to describe the taste of tomatoes?
6. What word does the writer use to describe how the chips feel?

WRITER'S CORNER

Imagine that you wrote one of Elizabeth's five-senses charts. Write three sentences describing nachos, using the sensory words from the charts.

For Tomorrow

Tell students to make a circular five-senses chart about what they had for lunch. Make your own chart, using sensory words to describe your lunch.

Descriptions • 301

WARM-UP

Read, Listen, Speak

Write on the board your chart from yesterday's For Tomorrow homework. Ask students to tell what words were most vivid in describing your lunch. Have small groups share their five-senses charts. Encourage students to discuss how the words in the charts helped them to imagine each food.

GRAMMAR CONNECTION

Take this opportunity to review pronouns. You may wish to point out pronouns in students' Read, Listen, Speak discussions.

TEACH

Review the five-senses charts on pages 300–301. Ask students to explain how writers can use a five-senses chart to write descriptions. Tell students that writers use their imaginations to write strong descriptions. Point out that a five-senses chart helps to organize what a writer imagines. Encourage students to use five-senses charts whenever they write descriptions.

PRACTICE

ACTIVITY B

Have small groups complete this activity. Invite volunteers to share and explain their answers.

ACTIVITY C

Have students complete this activity independently. Invite volunteers to share their completed sentences in small groups. Challenge students to name additional words that might describe a day at camp. Ask students to explain why a five-senses chart with many words might help write a better description.

ACTIVITY D

Have partners complete this activity. Encourage students to imagine being at a picnic and at a bakery. Ask students what they might see, smell, hear, feel, and taste at these places. After students have completed the activity, invite them to share with the class the words they added to the chart.

ACTIVITY E

Have students complete this activity independently. Give them time to draw their charts. Tell students to write the topic *Getting Ready for School* at the top of their charts. Encourage students to write two or three items for each sense.

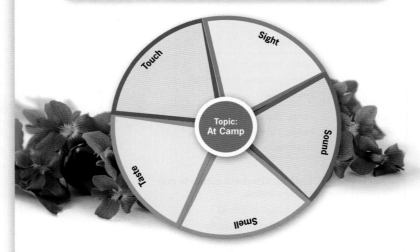

ACTIVITY B Copy the five-senses chart below. Write the words from the word box where they belong on the chart.

burnt marshmallows	sparkling lake	prickly grass
colorful wildflowers	laughing kids	sticky crafts
sharp pine scent	gritty sand	salty popcorn

Touch Sight Taste Smell Sound

Topic: At Camp

Activity B
Accept any answers students can justify.

ACTIVITY C Use the words from the word box in Activity B to complete these sentences from a description.

1. As I reached the campfire, I could smell the _____ and feel the _____ brush against my legs.
2. I lay back in my chair beside the _____ and dug my feet into the _____.
3. On my hike I saw the _____ in the fields and breathed in the _____ in the woods.
4. Outside at the picnic tables, _____ were enjoying making _____.

Activity C
1. burnt marshmallows, prickly grass
2. sparkling lake, gritty sand
3. colorful wildflowers, sharp pine scent
4. laughing kids, sticky crafts

302 • Chapter 3

Ask students how they might use their charts to write a description.

APPLY

WRITER'S CORNER

Tell students to use the words that were in their charts as well as any new words that they think of. When students have finished, invite volunteers to read aloud their sentences. Have students keep a tally of the senses used in each description. Then discuss which sense was most widely used and why. Students should demonstrate the ability to use a five-senses chart to write descriptions.

ASSESS

Note which students had difficulty writing descriptions by using five-senses charts. Use the Reteach option with those students who need additional reinforcement.

Practice Book page 145 provides additional work with five-senses charts.

Reteach

Write on the board a completed version of the chart from Activity B. Have students write one sentence for each sense, using the words from the chart. Work with students to choose sentences to write a complete description of the camp. Have students supply sentences for the beginning, middle, and ending of the description. Write the description on chart paper and have a volunteer read it aloud.

Mix Up Your Senses

Have students think of things that are easily described by one particular sense (*watching a sunset, tasting a juicy orange*). Then have students describe that thing by using a different sense. Encourage students to write sentences to describe how yellow might smell or how an orange might sound. Have students write their sentences. Ask volunteers to share their descriptive sentences.

ACTIVITY D **Look at the five-senses charts below. Imagine that you went to these places. Write two more items for each sense.**

1. Topic: Picnic in the Park

Sight	bright sunshine, fluffy white clouds, pale blue sky
Sound	chirping birds, gently rustling trees
Smell	freshly cut grass, flower blossoms
Taste	tangy grilled chicken, buttery corn, sour lemonade
Touch	soft blanket, cool grass

2. Topic: Bakery

Sight	gleaming glass display cases, pies with glossy brown crusts in crisscross patterns
Sound	chattering of bakery workers, clicking sound of silverware against cups
Smell	smell of freshly baked bread, smell of brewing coffee
Taste	sweet frosting on cakes, tangy blueberry pie
Touch	warm muffin, hot coffee cup

ACTIVITY E **Draw a two-column five-senses chart. Think about getting ready for school this morning. What are some things you saw, heard, smelled, tasted, and touched? Use your ideas to fill in the chart.**

WRITER'S CORNER

Use your five-senses chart from Activity E. Write a sentence for each sense. Include any new sensory words that come to mind.

For Tomorrow

Have students write five-senses charts describing their favorite after-school activities. Ask students to then write a beginning for a description of that activity. Write your own beginning based on a five-senses chart describing an after-school activity.

Descriptions • 303

OBJECTIVE

- **To identify synonyms**

WARM-UP

Read, Listen, Speak

Write on the board your five-senses chart and read aloud your beginning without revealing the topic. Ask students to tell what your topic is and how they know. Have small groups share the five-senses charts and beginnings they wrote. Guide students to identify words in each beginning that made the description easier to imagine.

GRAMMAR CONNECTION

Take this opportunity to review pronouns before administering the formal assessment. You may wish to have students point out any pronouns in their Read, Listen, Speak examples.

TEACH

Have a volunteer read aloud the first paragraph and the synonym pairs. Ask volunteers to explain what each synonym means. Then write the following on the board:

near	rock
tired	friend
small	smart

Ask students to name a synonym for each word (*close, sleepy, tiny, stone, pal, intelligent.*)

Invite a volunteer to read aloud the next paragraph. Allow time for students to suggest some synonyms for the word *happy* (*glad, joyful, gleeful, excited*). Tell students that most words have synonyms. Explain that writers use synonyms to add variety to their writing.

Have a volunteer read aloud the next paragraph and the pairs of example sentences. Ask why the second sentence in each pair is more interesting (*because* sprinted *and* enormous *are stronger and more colorful that* ran *and* big).

PRACTICE

ACTIVITY A

Have students complete this activity independently. Then have students compare their answers with partners. When students have finished, tell them to choose a synonym and to write a sentence using that synonym. Invite volunteers to share their sentences with the class.

ACTIVITY B

Have small groups complete this activity. When students have finished, ask volunteers to share their answers with the class. Then have groups write synonyms for each of the words that did not have synonyms. Ask volunteers to read aloud their new synonyms.

Synonyms

Synonyms are words that have the same or almost the same meaning. You probably use synonyms when you speak and write. Here are some pairs of synonyms you might know.

happy	glad
talk	speak
gift	present
store	shop
begin	start
hunt	search
fast	quick
big	large

Writers use synonyms to make their writing more interesting. They use synonyms to replace words that are used over and over. What are some other synonyms for the word *happy*?

Look at the sentences below. Which sentence in each pair is more interesting?

The runners *ran* **across the finish line.**
The runners *sprinted* **across the finish line.**

The giant wore *big* **shoes.**
The giant wore *enormous* **shoes.**

APPLY

WRITER'S CORNER

Allow time for students to think of synonyms or use a dictionary or thesaurus. Encourage students to choose strong and vivid synonyms. When students have finished, invite volunteers to share their synonyms with the class. Students should demonstrate the ability to identify synonyms in description.

💡 **Tech Tip** Tell students to find synonyms for their words and to choose the most vivid and appropriate synonym.

ASSESS

Note which students had difficulty identifying synonyms. Use the Reteach option with those students who need additional reinforcement.

TEACHING OPTIONS

Reteach

Have students choose five words from the lesson and write them on separate note cards. Direct students to write on the cards at least three synonyms for each word. If students cannot think of synonyms encourage students to use a thesaurus. Have students make up additional cards for words they overuse in their own writing (*great, nice, happy*).

Synonym Memory Game

Have small groups choose five simple words such as *good, funny, small,* and *pretty*. Tell students to write each word on a separate note card. Then have them write a synonym for each word on a separate note card. Have groups shuffle their cards and lay them out facedown on a table. Direct students to play a memory game by turning over two cards to try to match each word with its synonym.

Activity A
1. h
2. a
3. e
4. b
5. c
6. d
7. g
8. j
9. i
10. f

ACTIVITY A Match each word in Column A to its synonym in Column B.

Column A	Column B
1. cry	a. kids
2. children	b. angry
3. ill	c. mend
4. mad	d. paste
5. fix	e. sick
6. glue	f. journey
7. hurt	g. damage
8. polite	h. weep
9. pale	i. colorless
10. trip	j. respectful

ACTIVITY B Tell whether the words in each pair are synonyms.

1. hurry	scary	no
2. draw	bring	no
3. smile	grin	yes
4. wide	narrow	no
5. thin	skinny	yes
6. yummy	tasty	yes
7. teach	guide	yes
8. own	possess	yes
9. grow	expand	yes
10. shout	whisper	no
11. purchase	buy	yes
12. bright	dull	no

WRITER'S CORNER

Look at "A New Home for Gorillas" on page 287. List five words that you could replace with synonyms. Then work with a partner to think of a synonym for each word.

Tech Tip With an adult, use an online thesaurus.

For Tomorrow

Have students write three words of their choice from a newspaper or magazine article and think of an appropriate synonym for each word. Ask students to bring their articles and synonyms to class. Bring in your own article and synonyms to share with students.

Descriptions • 305

WARM-UP

Read, Listen, Speak

Share with students your list of words and synonyms from yesterday's For Tomorrow homework. Read aloud the original sentences from the article and then substitute the synonyms. Discuss the change in meaning. Invite small groups to share their lists. Tell students to suggest other words in their articles that might be replaced with synonyms.

GRAMMAR CONNECTION

Take this opportunity to talk about action verbs. You may wish to have students point out any action verbs in their Read, Listen, Speak examples.

TEACH

Ask a volunteer what synonyms are *(words that have the same or almost the same meaning)*. Write the following words on the board:

car	shut	cold
nice	big	fast

Have students write on the board synonyms for each word *(automobile, close, freezing, pleasant, large, quick)*. Point out that writers use synonyms to make their writing more interesting.

PRACTICE

ACTIVITY C

Have small groups complete this activity. Tell students to take turns writing the sentences after the group has determined the appropriate synonym. Then invite volunteers to share their answers with the class.

ACTIVITY D

Tell students to complete this activity with a partner. If students need help, guide them to use a thesaurus to locate synonyms.

ACTIVITY E

Have partners complete this activity. Tell students to take turns reading aloud the rhymes. Have partners work together to determine the correct word for each blank. When students have finished, invite volunteers to read aloud each rhyme with the correct word.

ACTIVITY F

Remind students to write complete sentences. Then invite volunteers to share their sentences with the class.

ACTIVITY C Use a synonym from the word box to replace each underlined word.

pick	hunt	shop	buddy	kind
chats	gift	giant	rush	carry

1. The <u>nice</u> guard showed us the way out. kind
2. Did you <u>choose</u> a book about the planets? pick
3. My parents <u>search</u> for the car keys every morning. hunt
4. My <u>friend</u> Taye won the three-legged race. buddy
5. Mrs. Torres <u>talks</u> with her friends on her front porch. chats
6. Kylie bought a chess set at a new <u>store</u> on Maple Street. shop
7. Did you <u>take</u> the garden tools into the house? carry
8. The <u>huge</u> pumpkin is sure to win first place. giant
9. There was a little <u>present</u> on my pillow. gift
10. Guy is always in a <u>hurry</u>. rush

ACTIVITY D Write a synonym for each word below.

1. see	6. calm	11. quiet
2. glad	7. meal	12. chair
3. yell	8. find	13. rock
4. start	9. fast	14. finish
5. story	10. path	15. hard

APPLY

WRITER'S CORNER

Have students write their synonym pairs independently. Then allow partners to complete the activity. Have students list any correct synonyms that their partners guess. Encourage students to save their lists and to refer to them when they need help finding synonyms. Students should demonstrate the ability to identify synonyms.

ASSESS

Note which students had difficulty identifying synonyms. Use the Reteach option with those students who need additional reinforcement.

Practice Book page 146 provides additional work with synonyms.

Reteach

Read aloud a passage from a story students have recently read as students follow along. Tell students to look for words for which they know synonyms. Have students list the words and their synonyms. Invite volunteers to read aloud the passage, substituting the synonyms for the original words.

Synonym Circles

Have students work in small groups. Ask one student to write a sentence. Then ask students to pass the sentence around the group. Have each student rewrite the sentence, replacing one word with a synonym. Invite students to read aloud what they wrote. Discuss how the sentence changed from beginning to end.

ACTIVITY E Read the rhymes below. Complete each rhyme with a correct synonym for the underlined word. Use the words from the word box.

old	town	like	bright	tiny	delighted	say	rip

1. The <u>city</u> bus goes up and down,
   Then moves on quickly to the next __town__.

2. A <u>tear</u> in your paper you don't want to see.
   If you're not careful, a __rip__ there will be.

3. <u>Shiny</u> stars fill the sky at night.
   They glow in the dark and look so __bright__.

4. My new baby brother is very <u>small</u>.
   His __tiny__ fingers can't hold a ball.

5. My older sister has a lot to __say__.
   She <u>speaks</u> on the phone all day.

6. That table is weak and really __old__.
   It's <u>ancient</u>, or so I'm told.

7. I <u>enjoy</u> spinach, and prunes that are stewed.
   Actually, I __like__ almost any food!

8. The <u>happy</u> child saw the toys in the store.
   He was so __delighted__ with one that he wanted more.

ACTIVITY F Choose three synonyms you thought of for Activity D. Use each synonym in a sentence.

WRITER'S CORNER

Make a list of five pairs of synonyms. Then work with a partner. Say one of the words in each pair and see whether your partner can think of the synonym you wrote. Try to guess the synonyms your partner wrote.

For Tomorrow

Ask students to search a thesaurus to find five unfamiliar words. Have students write a synonym for each word. Bring in your own list of five synonyms to share with the class.

Descriptions • 307

OBJECTIVES

- **To understand the characteristics of an oral description**
- **To present an oral description**
- **To listen actively to an oral description**

WARM-UP

Read, Listen, Speak

Read aloud your list of words and synonyms from yesterday's For Tomorrow homework. Ask students to offer different synonyms for the words. Invite small groups to share their lists. Have students write a sentence using two synonyms.

GRAMMAR CONNECTION

Take this opportunity to talk about being verbs. You may wish to have students point out any being verbs in their Read, Listen, Speak examples.

TEACH

Have a volunteer read aloud the first paragraph. Explain that an oral description is spoken. Ask students to name something that they have described orally in the past few days. Then ask students to imagine the robot that was mentioned in the paragraph. Invite volunteers to suggest a sentence that describes the robot.

Have a volunteer read aloud the second paragraph and the first bulleted item. Ask students to name the three kinds of space order that they read about in this chapter (*top to bottom, side to side, near to far*). Ask students to imagine the robot again and to offer descriptions of the robot, using one kind of space order.

Have a volunteer read aloud the second bulleted item. Remind students that an oral description of an event might include words related to all five senses. Ask students to imagine getting the robot as a gift from a family member and how they might describe the event in time order. Then read aloud the last sentence.

Have a volunteer read aloud the section Visual Aids. Ask students to name visual aids that might help describe people (*photographs, cards, letters*). Explain that an audience uses the sense of sight while looking at visual aids. Tell students to try to use all five senses when giving an oral description.

Have volunteers read aloud the section Prepare and Practice. Tell students that it is OK to make notes about things in an oral description, but that it is not necessary to write the whole description.

Discuss reasons to practice before giving an oral presentation. Then have volunteers reread the bulleted items. Explain that speaking too loudly or too softly, moving around, and talking too fast make it difficult for the audience to pay attention to what a speaker is saying. Encourage students to keep these things in mind when giving an oral description.

LESSON **6**   SPEAKING AND LISTENING SKILLS

Oral Descriptions

Imagine that you opened a present and found a walking, talking robot. Suppose that the robot was too big to bring to school. How would you describe it to your friends? If you told your friends about the robot, you would be giving an oral description.

Here are some tips on giving oral descriptions.

- If you are describing something you saw, try to remember what you thought and felt when you first saw it. Use space order to talk about it so that your listeners can imagine it.
- If you are describing something that happened, try to remember how you felt and what you thought both before and after it happened. Use time order to tell what happened so that your listeners can imagine it happening to them.

Remember that a description forms a clear picture in the listener's mind.

Visual Aids

Sometimes when we describe something to someone else, it helps if we show what we are talking about. A picture, drawing, map, or poster that you might show is called a visual aid. Visual aids help your audience imagine what you are describing. Anything that your audience can look at is a visual aid.

PRACTICE

ACTIVITY A

Encourage students to name their alien planets and some of the places that they visited. Tell students to save their work.

APPLY

SPEAKER'S CORNER

Tell students to make their maps large enough to include labels. Encourage students to make their maps as detailed as possible and to use their maps to describe the classroom to their families. Students should demonstrate the ability to present an oral description.

TechTip Have students use a drawing program to design their maps. Encourage students to use color and a variety of shapes and fonts.

ASSESS

Note which students had difficulty understanding what to include in oral descriptions. Use the Reteach option with those students who need additional reinforcement.

TEACHING OPTIONS

Reteach

Point out that an oral description has the same characteristics as a written description. Remind students that descriptions should have a beginning, a middle, and an ending. Explain that students may wish to use a certain space order in their oral descriptions. Encourage students to use sensory words as well. Have students think about a place that they really like and write notes that would help describe the place. Then have students number their notes in the order in which they would use them for an oral description.

Listen Up!

Tell partners to describe to each other a place in school or on the playground, without directly saying what the place is. Explain that the student listening should guess what the place is by the description his or her partner gives.

Prepare and Practice

Think of something you want to describe. Close your eyes and imagine how it looks or how it happened. Try to remember with all five of your senses. You may want to make a five-senses chart to help you. Write what you remember thinking and feeling. Use what you write to decide what you will say and what order you will use.

After you decide what you will say, try it out. Practice your description many times so that you will remember all you want to say. You might want to write notes on cards to help you remember the most important parts. As you practice, think about these things.

- Speak loudly enough for your audience to hear but do not shout.
- Stand up straight and try not to move around too much.
- Remember to breathe. Try pausing between sentences so you do not talk too fast.

ACTIVITY A Imagine that alien creatures took you to their home planet and gave you a tour. Close your eyes and try to imagine what their planet might be like. Are the rocks purple? Are there bubbles popping in the sky? Are there pools of green lava? Draw a picture of your imaginary alien planet. Then make a list of sensory words that describe your planet.

SPEAKER'S CORNER

Imagine that you were asked to give an oral description of your classroom to a family member. Draw a map of your classroom. Label your visual aid with the important parts of the classroom that you would want to describe.

Tech Tip Use a computer to design your map.

Descriptions • 309

For Tomorrow

Tell students to imagine that they are describing a typical school day to a younger student or sibling. Tell them to write notes for the description. Encourage students to use time order and to include sensory details. Bring in your own description of a typical day.

WARM-UP

Read, Listen, Speak

Use your notes from yesterday's For Tomorrow homework to describe your typical school day. Invite small groups to share their notes. Encourage students to use their notes to present the descriptions of their school day.

GRAMMAR CONNECTION

Take this opportunity to talk about helping verbs. You may wish to have students use helping verbs in their Read, Listen, Speak descriptions.

TEACH

Have a volunteer read aloud the first paragraph of the section Listening Tips. Tell students that listening is a skill just as speaking is a skill. Ask students to describe how they feel when a person isn't listening to something that they are saying. Then ask students to explain how they can tell when a person isn't listening.

Have volunteers read aloud the bulleted items. Discuss each item. Emphasize the importance of not laughing if the speaker makes a mistake. Point out that even the most experienced singers, speakers, and sports stars make mistakes. Then ask students to name additional tips for being a good listener *(being quiet, taking notes, looking at the speaker).*

LiNK Have volunteers read aloud the excerpt from *James and the Giant Peach.* Ask students to tell if the description uses time order or space order *(time order).* Ask students which senses the description appeals to.

PRACTICE

ACTIVITY B

Encourage students to keep in mind the listening tips. Then have students complete the activity. Have partners tell what sensory words were most helpful in guessing which animal was described.

ACTIVITY C

Allow time for students to practice and prepare their presentations. When students have described their drawings, invite volunteers to name parts of their partner's descriptions that were most clear.

ACTIVITY D

Before students begin, have them think of their cartoon characters independently. Then have small groups describe their characters. Have students point out which sensory words were most helpful in guessing the character.

ACTIVITY E

Allow time for students to complete their charts. When students have finished, invite volunteers to describe their chores to the class. Remind students to use time order or space order.

Listening Tips

Practicing can make it easier for you to tell an oral description to an audience. When you are a good listener, you can make it easier for someone else who is talking. Here are some things you can do to be a better listener.

- Listen to hear whether the speaker is talking about something that he or she saw or something that happened.
- Try to figure out whether the speaker is using space order or time order.
- Look at the visual aids the speaker uses to help you imagine.
- Try to imagine what it would feel like to see or do what the speaker is talking about.
- Don't laugh if the speaker makes a mistake.

LiNK

James and the Giant Peach

SMACK! [The peach] hit the water with a colossal splash and sank like a stone. . . . But a few seconds later, it came up again, and this time up it stayed, floating serenely upon the surface of the water. . . . The sun was shining brightly out of a soft blue sky and the day was calm. The giant peach, with the sunlight glinting on its side, was like a massive golden ball sailing upon a silver sea.

Roald Dahl

ACTIVITY B Work with a partner. Choose an animal to describe, but don't tell your partner what it is. Take turns describing what you chose so your partner can guess what it is. Use sensory words so that your partner knows what the animal might look, feel, or sound like. If it has a smell, describe that too.

ACTIVITY C Use the drawing you made for Activity A on page 309 to describe your alien planet to a partner. Point to things in your drawing as you describe them. Use your list of sensory words to tell your partner what you think a person might see, hear, and smell on that planet.

ACTIVITY F

Ask students to record the words their partners use to describe the objects. Encourage students to explain why those words were effective for quickly describing what the objects were.

APPLY

SPEAKER'S CORNER

Invite volunteers to present their oral descriptions to the class. Students should demonstrate the ability to present an oral description and to listen actively.

TechTip Remind students that they should speak clearly and appeal to their audience's senses of sight and sound.

ASSESS

Note which students had difficulty presenting an oral description. Use the Reteach option with those students who need additional reinforcement.

After you have reviewed Lessons 3–5, administer the Writing Skills Assessment on pages 47–48 in the **Assessment Book.** This test is also available on the optional **Test Generator CD.**

TEACHING OPTIONS

Reteach

Have students write a checklist of the listening tips from the lesson. Have listeners follow their checklists as other students present oral descriptions. After the speaker is finished, direct students to check the listening tips they followed. Discuss how well students were able to follow the listening tips. Have students tell if any were difficult to follow and why.

Who Am I?

Cut out pictures of famous people or characters with whom students are familiar and place them facedown at four stations around the classroom. Assign each of four groups to a station. Have students choose a picture from their station and describe to their group the appearance of the person or character, without naming him or her. Encourage students to guess who is being described. Be sure students use only physical descriptions. When students have described all the people and characters at their station, encourage them to rotate to a new station.

ACTIVITY D Work in small groups. Think of a cartoon character from television or from a movie. Picture the character and try to remember some things that he or she does and says. Then take turns describing your character without saying the character's name. Describe the way the character looks from top to bottom. Describe the way the character sounds or things the character says. After your description ask your classmates to guess who your character is.

ACTIVITY E Think of a chore you do at home for your family, such as washing dishes or dusting. Draw a five-senses chart and write the chore as your topic. Then try to describe your chore, using each sense. Use your chart to help you describe the chore to a partner.

ACTIVITY F Make a list of 10 things in the classroom that you could describe. Trade lists with a partner. Choose items from your partner's list and describe each one. See how quickly your partner can guess each item. Have your partner do the same with your list.

SPEAKER'S CORNER

Look at the map of your classroom you drew for the Speaker's Corner on page 309. Read the parts you labeled. Then meet with a partner. Pretend that your partner is a family member who has not seen your classroom before. Describe your classroom to your partner. Use sensory words. Try to use more than one sense to describe the classroom.

Tech Tip Do a podcast or a video of your oral description.

Descriptions • 311

PREWRITING AND DRAFTING

Have a volunteer read aloud the opening paragraph. Ask students for examples of sensory words for each of the five senses. Then ask students to tell about times they have described a person, a place, an animal, or an object.

Prewriting

Have a volunteer read aloud this section. Ask students to think about what makes a place special. Have volunteers offer some ideas.

Choosing a Topic

Read aloud the first paragraph. Have volunteers read aloud each place on the bulleted list. Then read aloud the next paragraph. Ask a volunteer to read aloud Georgia's list. Explain that Georgia began her prewriting by thinking about places that were special for different reasons and that all the places are interesting to describe.

👓 Tell students that the idea they choose should be clear. Suggest that students include unusual details about their chosen topic.

Have a volunteer read aloud the last paragraph. Ask students why it might be important for Georgia to choose a place she spends a lot of time in and knows well. *(Since Georgia spends so much time there, she knows that she could write a strong description of the place.)*

Your Turn

Have a volunteer read aloud this section. Encourage students to write the first place that comes to mind for each item on the list. Allow time for students to complete their lists. After students have completed their lists, tell students to select the place that they can describe the best or would like to describe the most, using all five senses. Remind students to select a place where they have spent a lot of time so they can do a complete job of describing.

Using a Five-Senses Chart

Read aloud the first paragraph. Tell students that the five-senses chart will help Georgia organize her ideas. Direct students' attention to Georgia's five-senses chart. Have volunteers read aloud the words in the chart. Encourage students to talk about which sense might be the hardest for Georgia to write about for her description.

Have volunteers read aloud the next paragraph. Explain that Georgia put as many details as possible into her chart so that she would have plenty of sensory words from which to choose. Then

---

Writer's Workshop Descriptions

Prewriting and Drafting

Descriptions can tell about people, places, animals, or objects. A description uses sensory words to form a clear picture in the reader's mind. You will be writing a description of a place that is special to you.

Prewriting

Georgia is a third grader who wrote a description for class. Her teacher asked the class to write descriptions of places that are special to them. Georgia was eager to get started, but first she needed to think of a topic.

Choosing a Topic

👓 **Ideas** Georgia's teacher gave the class this list to help them think of topics.

- a place that I visit with my family
- an exciting place
- the prettiest place I have ever seen
- a place that makes me calm and peaceful
- a place that I dream about
- a place that amazes me
- a place that scares me

Georgia sat in a quiet corner of the school library and used her teacher's list to help her choose a topic. Here is part of Georgia's list.

a place that makes me calm and peaceful
—window seat at home where I read
a place that I dream about
—beach near Uncle Thad's house
a place that amazes me
—Empire State Building
—lighted fountain in the park
a place that scares me
—empty building on Peeling Street

Georgia decided to write about the window seat at home. She read there almost every day, so she knew it well. There were also lots of things outside the window to describe.

Your Turn

- Use the list Georgia's teacher gave her to help you think of topics for your description.
- Think of one or more places for each item on the list.
- When you have finished, circle the place that you most want to write about.

read aloud the last paragraph. Ask students why they think Georgia chose to order her description from near to far. *(If readers were at the window seat with Georgia, they would most likely see the nearest things first.)*

Tell students that organization is the structure of a piece of writing. Point out that for a description of a place, the best structure is probably space order. Suggest that students think about whether top to bottom, side to side, or near to far is the best way of organizing their descriptions.

Your Turn

Invite a volunteer to read aloud this section. Tell students to fill their charts with as much information as they can. Encourage students to imagine that they are at their special places and to think about each sense, one at a time. Point out that students won't have to use everything that they put in their five-senses chart when they write their descriptions.

Allow time for students to complete their five-senses charts and to decide how to order their descriptions. Encourage students to discuss their charts and chosen order with a partner.

TEACHING OPTIONS

Tell Me About It

Have students meet with partners if they need help thinking of sensory words for their five-senses chart. Ask students to tell their partner for one minute what they have chosen to write about. When they have finished, have students write what they remember. Explain that talking about their places might help students think about those places differently. Point out that students might also be better able to think of sensory words for their descriptions.

Using a Five-Senses Chart

Georgia decided to use a five-senses chart to **Organization** help her think of things that appeal to each of her five senses. Here is Georgia's chart.

Topic: My Window Seat

Sight	cars in street, bus, dogs, people, Mr. Deimos
Sound	squeaky snack cart, traffic, barking, airplanes
Smell	popcorn, smoky bus, cut grass
Taste	lemonade
Touch	warm sunlight, smooth glass, curtains tickle my arm

When she was finished, Georgia read her chart. She was surprised by how many senses she could write about by just looking out a window. But she also knew that she needed to stay on the topic. She wanted to write about the taste of lemonade because she drinks lemonade while she reads. But it didn't really fit with what was outside the window. The feel of the smooth glass or the curtains that tickle her arm didn't fit either. She knew she wouldn't be able to use everything in her chart. But by making a chart, she had plenty of ideas to choose from.

Georgia decided that space order would be best for her description. She could describe the things nearest to her window first and the farthest things last.

Preediting · Drafting · Content Editing · Revising · Copyediting · Proofreading · Publishing

Your Turn

Make a five-senses chart like Georgia's. When you have finished, look at your chart. Think about how best to organize the details in your description.

Drafting

Invite a volunteer to read aloud the paragraph above Georgia's draft. Tell students that Georgia used the information from her five-senses chart to write the middle of her description. Then ask volunteers to read aloud Georgia's draft.

Ask students to tell how Georgia organized the middle of her description. *(Georgia used near-to-far order. She first talked about the sunlight and the window seat. Then she described the street below. She finished by describing the dogs across the street.)* Ask a volunteer to point out the ending of the draft *(the second paragraph).*

Ask volunteers to read aloud the paragraph after the draft. Have volunteers write on the board the sensory words from Georgia's draft. Tell students that Georgia left extra space between the lines so she could make changes later.

👀 Remind students to choose sensory words that help the reader experience their chosen place. Explain, for example, that "my treehouse is cozy" does not communicate their feeling about the place as well as "the soft pillows in the corner and the umbrella of leaves and branches."

Your Turn

Read aloud this section. Remind students that if they have put a lot of information in their five-senses chart, they should choose only the details that are important to describe their place clearly. Remind students that Georgia felt that the sense of taste wouldn't add anything to her description. Ask students to look through this chapter and to name additional things to consider while writing their drafts. *(Use strong and colorful words. Use synonyms to avoid repetition.)* Then allow time for students to complete their drafts.

Drafting

First, Georgia wrote the beginning of her description. It told what she was going to describe. Then she wrote the middle in space order. She described things nearest to her window first, and she described the things far away last. She finished by writing an ending that told readers to try to find a special place like hers. Here is Georgia's draft.

A Warm, Sunny Spot

My favrite place is a window seat. I love the sights, sounds, and smells outside my window. They get me ready to read my book. The sunlight on the window seat. The street has cars parked along both sides. When I open the window, I smell popcorn from Mr. deimos's snack cart. I hear his bell ringing as he pushes his squeaky cart down my sidewalk. A bus drives by at four o'clock every day. People and dogs play across the street. barking dogs and quiet dogs chase tennis balls in the green grass. The crazy dogs always make me laugh.

After I enjoy what I see, hear, and smell, I am ready to read. It is the perfect way to calm down after a day at school. Everyone should try reading at a window seat.

Similes

Read aloud the section title to demonstrate the word's proper pronunciation. Have a volunteer read aloud the first paragraph. Explain that similes are useful when writing descriptions. Then read aloud the next paragraph. Tell students that similes are helpful because they describe things by comparing one thing to another. Discuss the example of the man with the blue sweater. Then invite volunteers to suggest similes about the color of something in the classroom.

 Tell students that their voice is their personality coming through in their writing. Encourage them to use sensory words and similes that show how students feel about their chosen place.

TEACHING OPTIONS

Stay in Focus

Tell students that it is easy to get off the topic while describing a place. Encourage them to stop after writing each part of a description and ask themselves, *Is what I wrote part of the topic I am describing?* As an example, tell students that if they were describing their bedroom, they would not tell about how their father painted the room green last summer.

While Georgia wrote, she tried to use some things she had learned in class about descriptions. She used sensory words to

Word Choice

make the picture clearer for her audience. She wrote about the things outside her window in space order, starting with the nearest things. She also made sure to write a beginning, a middle, and an ending. She left extra space between lines so she could write changes on her draft later.

Your Turn

- Write the first draft of your description. Make sure that you tell the reader in the beginning what you are describing.
- Use space order to give the reader a clear idea of how things are placed.
- Use sensory words that describe more than just what you see.
- Use your five-senses chart to remind you of different sensory words to put in your description.

Similes

A simile is something you can use to make a

Voice

clearer picture. When you use a simile, you compare things by using either the word *like* or the word *as*.

Imagine you are trying to describe a man at the park. He is wearing a blue sweater. You want to make a clear picture for the reader. What kind of blue is his sweater? Is it blue like a thundercloud? Or is it blue like a blueberry? If you tell your reader that the sweater is blue like a blueberry, you make the picture clearer. You also use a simile.

Prewriting · Drafting · Content Editing · Revising · Copyediting · Proofreading · Publishing

Descriptions • 315

OBJECTIVE

- **To edit a description for content**

CONTENT EDITING

Invite a volunteer to read aloud the first paragraph. Review the things that a content editor checks in a draft. Then have a volunteer read aloud the next paragraph. Ask students why Georgia chose Armand to edit the content of her draft. (*Armand lived in the same building and had a similar view outside his window. He could check whether the description was correct.*)

Have volunteers read aloud the checklist. Clarify any misconceptions that students may have. Point out the last item on the checklist. Tell students that readers should be able to imagine that they are actually in the place being described.

Invite a volunteer to read aloud the paragraph following the Content Editor's Checklist. Ask students why Armand might have read Georgia's description while sitting on his own window seat (*so he could check if her description was correct*).

Read aloud the next paragraph. Point out that Armand started sharing his ideas by telling Georgia what he liked about her draft. Ask students to name the two things that Armand liked most about Georgia's draft (*the sensory words, the ending*).

Have volunteers read aloud Armand's ideas. After each idea has been read, have students turn to Georgia's draft and reread the part to which Armand is referring. Ask students to explain why they agree or disagree with Armand's ideas. Discuss how Armand's ideas compare to the questions in the Content Editor's Checklist.

Editor's Workshop Descriptions

Content Editing

Georgia was happy with her first draft. But she knew she could make it better. A content editor would check that the ideas in Georgia's description made sense.

Georgia thought it would be best if she had someone else content edit her draft. Armand lived in Georgia's building. He could look out his own window and see the same things as Georgia saw. Armand could make sure that Georgia's description was clear for a reader. Armand used the Content Editor's Checklist below.

Armand read Georgia's description a few times. He even read it once sitting on his own window seat. Armand wrote ideas he had to improve Georgia's draft. Then he met with Georgia to share his ideas.

Content Editor's Checklist

☐ Do the title and beginning tell what is being described?

☐ Does the middle describe something by using space order?

☐ Does the ending leave the reader with something to think about?

☐ Are sensory words used to tell what the writer sees, hears, smells, tastes, and feels?

☐ Does the description make a clear picture for the audience?

316 • Chapter 3

Read aloud the last paragraph. Ask students to discuss why Georgia wanted to think about each of Armand's ideas before using them. Explain that Georgia does not have to use all Armand's ideas, only the ones with which she agrees.

Your Turn

Invite volunteers to read aloud this section. Have students show their partners where they are having difficulty when they exchange drafts. Allow time for partners to work on each other's drafts. Remind students to offer praise as well as specific suggestions for change.

Writer's Tip Remind students that thinking about an editor's suggestions is helpful in making their writing clearer and more effective.

What's in a Name?

Explain that readers will often read something if it has an interesting title. Tell students to start with a working title—a title to use while they are writing their description. Explain that they can finalize the title later on, just before publishing. Give students these two ideas for writing a title when they are finished writing their description:

1. Hint at something in the description, such as an important word, sentence, image, or character.

2. Summarize your feeling about the topic.

Be sure students understand that they can give any title to their descriptions. Explain that these are hints if students need ideas for writing a title.

Armand started by saying what he liked about Georgia's description. Armand liked the sensory words that Georgia used, such as *squeaky* and *barking*. He said that he could almost smell the popcorn in Mr. Deimos's snack cart. He also liked that Georgia told readers to try reading at a window seat. He thought that would give readers something to think about when they were finished reading. Then Armand shared these ideas.

- Could you make the beginning grab the reader's attention more? It's also not clear to me which part is the beginning and which part is the middle.
- I can tell you are using space order in your description. But something is out of place. You describe the cars in the street before you finish describing the sidewalk. The sidewalk is closer.
- You use lots of sensory words in your description. But maybe you could say something about the great bread that Mr. Deimos's wife makes at the bakery down the street.
- You should tell your audience that there is a dog park across the street. They probably don't know that.

Georgia thanked Armand for reading her draft. She thought his ideas were helpful. But she wasn't sure she wanted to use all of them. She wanted to think about the ideas and come up with ideas of her own before she revised her draft.

Your Turn

- Read your first draft. Use the Content Editor's Checklist to help make it better.
- Mark your corrections on the draft.
- Trade drafts with a partner and read each other's work.
- Use the Content Editor's Checklist while you read your partner's draft.
- Pay attention to only one question at a time.
- Write ideas you have for making your partner's draft stronger.
- Take turns talking about your drafts. Remember to start by saying what you liked about your partner's draft.

Writer's Tip Write your partner's ideas. Think about each one before you make any changes. Which ideas will make your description clearer and more colorful?

Prewriting | Drafting | Content Editing | Revising | Copyediting | Proofreading | Publishing

OBJECTIVE
- **To revise a description**

REVISING

Explain that during revising, a writer decides which changes to make. Tell students that ideas for changes come from both the writer and the content editor.

Read aloud the first paragraph. Tell students to look over Georgia's revised draft. Then have volunteers read aloud the bulleted list. After each item has been read, have students look back at the revised draft to find the change and answer the question. Then ask how that particular revision makes the draft stronger.

- She thought Armand was right that her beginning could grab the reader's attention more. Armand liked the way she told her audience to try reading at a window seat, so Georgia decided to add a first line that might make readers more interested in her favorite place.
- She started a new paragraph after the beginning. This would make it clearer what part is the beginning and what part is the middle.
- Armand had a good point when he said that most readers wouldn't know that there was a dog park across the street. Georgia hadn't been thinking of her audience. She added that information to the sentence.
- Mr. Deimos and the sidewalk are closer to Georgia's window than the street is. Georgia made sure to focus on Mr. Deimos and the sidewalk first.
- She added the adjectives *big* and *smoky* to describe the bus.
- Georgia also changed the word *drives* to *rumbles* because it tells how the bus sounds.
- The idea was not really about her topic because she couldn't smell the bread from her window.

Read aloud the last paragraph. Point out that Armand's praise of

---

Writer's Workshop

Descriptions

Revising

When Georgia revised her draft, it looked like this.

A Warm, Sunny Spot

Everybody likes a special place to read.
My favrite place is a window seat. I love the sights, sounds, and smells outside my window. They get me ready to read my book. ¶ The sunlight on the window seat. The street has cars parked along both sides. When I open the window, I smell popcorn from Mr. deimos's snack cart. I hear his bell ringing as he pushes his squeaky cart down my sidewalk. A bus ~~drives~~ big, smoky rumbles by at four o'clock every day. People and dogs ~~play~~ fill the dog park across the street. barking dogs and quiet dogs chase tennis balls in the green grass. The crazy dogs always make me laugh.

After I enjoy what I see, hear, and smell, I am ready to read. It is the perfect way to calm down after a day at school. Everyone should try reading at a window seat.

Georgia's draft made Georgia feel good and encouraged her to write an even stronger description. Ask students to look over Georgia's draft one more time. Have them name some strong and colorful words in Georgia's description.

Your Turn

Have volunteers read aloud this section. Encourage students to examine their own ideas for revisions and those suggested by their content editors. Tell students that they know what they are describing better than anyone else. Explain that they should only use suggestions that make their description stronger. After students have decided which revisions to make, allow time to incorporate the changes. Have students review their revised drafts one more time, looking for places to use similes or strong and colorful words.

Using All the Senses

Explain that students can make a description of something even stronger by using all five senses, not just the most obvious sense. Tell students that if they wanted to describe what a hamburger smells like, they could use more than just the sense of smell. Tell students they might describe the grill, the fire leaping around the hamburger, and the sounds made by the fire. By using more senses, the reader will be better able to imagine what is being described. Explain that there is a better chance that the reader will imagine the smell of the hamburger if the reader pictures it cooking.

Here are some things Georgia did to make her description clearer.

- Georgia changed the beginning of her description. What did she do? Why? How does the change help the reader understand the topic?
- Where did Georgia choose to start a new paragraph? Why do you think she did this?
- What information did Georgia add about the people and dogs across the street? How does this change help the reader?
- Georgia decided to move the sentence about the cars in the street to a different place. Why did she make this change? Do you agree with her change? Why or why not?
- Georgia still thought the sentence about the bus could be better. She added two adjectives to describe the bus. What were they?
- Georgia decided to change the word *drives* to a stronger word. What word did she choose? Do you agree with her word choice? Why or why not?
- Armand had said that Georgia should say something about the smell of Mrs. Deimos's bread. But Georgia decided not to make that change. Why do you think she did not make the change?

Georgia read her draft again. She was glad that Armand liked all the sensory words in her description.

Your Turn

- Read the ideas your partner had about ways to change your draft.
- Think about which of those ideas and which of your own ideas you would like to use. Remember that it is up to you whether you want to use your partner's ideas in your draft.
- Revise your draft.
- When you have finished, go over the Content Editor's Checklist again. See if you can answer yes to each question.

Prewriting
Drafting
Content Editing
Revising
Copyediting
Proofreading
Publishing

Descriptions • 319

Editor's Workshop
Descriptions

OBJECTIVES
- **To copyedit a description**
- **To proofread a description**

COPYEDITING AND PROOFREADING

Copyediting

Invite a volunteer to read aloud the first paragraph. Discuss the difference between content editing and copyediting. *(Content editing is making sure that the draft is well organized and presents the right information. Copyediting is making sure that the draft contains complete sentences and has correct word choices.)* Ask students to explain the importance of copyediting.

Have volunteers read aloud each item on the checklist. Answer questions that students might have about each item. After the third item has been read, discuss how using synonyms will make Georgia's description less repetitive and more enjoyable.

Ask a volunteer to read aloud the first paragraph after the checklist. Invite a volunteer to point out the incomplete sentence in Georgia's draft. *(The sunlight on the window seat.)*

Invite a volunteer to read aloud the next paragraph. Explain that Georgia changed the order of her sentences to finish telling about the sidewalk before telling what was on the street. Point out that her sentences now correctly follow space order.

Tell students to read aloud their drafts and their partner's drafts. Suggest that they vary sentence length and structure to make their writing sound less repetitive and more natural.

Have a volunteer read aloud the last paragraph. Point out that the third question in the Copyeditor's Checklist helped her to see that she had used the word *dog* too many times. Ask students what synonyms for *dog* Georgia used *(hounds, puppies).*

Writer's Tip Ask students to look up dog in a student thesaurus and read the synonyms. Ask what synonyms would change the meaning of the words used in Georgia's description *(cur, mongrel).*

Your Turn
Read aloud this section. Encourage students to change words only in places where they believe that they can make the writing stronger or clearer. Allow time for students to finish making their changes.

Proofreading

Invite a volunteer to read aloud the first paragraph. Ask students why it is helpful to ask someone who hasn't read their work to proofread their drafts. *(A proofreader might catch mistakes that the writer and content editors missed.)*

Remind students that conventions are the rules of writing. Tell students that conventions include spelling, capitalization, and punctuation.

Copyediting and Proofreading

Copyediting

Georgia liked the content editing changes. She thought her draft was much better. But Georgia knew that by copyediting her draft, she could make the sentences and words stronger. Georgia used this checklist to copyedit her description.

Copyeditor's Checklist
- ☐ Are all the sentences complete sentences?
- ☐ Do the sentences make sense one after the other?
- ☐ Have you checked for repeated words that could be replaced by synonyms?
- ☐ Do the words paint a clear picture?

Georgia checked each question one at a time. She found an incomplete sentence in the second paragraph. Do you see it? Georgia fixed the sentence and added a sensory word to describe what the sunlight felt like. What did she write?

Sentence Fluency

Georgia also changed the order of some sentences. They didn't follow space order. She thought that it might be clearer if she described the street first, then the bus.

When Georgia checked the third question on the checklist, she saw that she used the word *dogs* five times in one paragraph. She decided to replace a few with synonyms. Which words did Georgia choose to replace the word *dogs?*

Writer's Tip Make sure the synonym or more exact word you use doesn't change the meaning of the sentence.

Your Turn
Read your draft again, using the Copyeditor's Checklist. Remember to check only one question at a time.

Have volunteers read aloud the Proofreader's Checklist. Emphasize the importance of looking for new mistakes made while editing. Answer any questions students might have about the checklist.

Ask volunteers to read aloud the last paragraph. Have students turn to the revised draft on page 318. Ask students to find the sentence and the proper noun that didn't begin with capital letters *(the second to last sentence in the second paragraph and the first mention of Mr. Deimos).*

Your Turn

Have a volunteer read aloud the first bulleted item. Ask students

why they should check for only one kind of mistake at a time. *(You are focusing on one problem at a time and are more likely to catch the mistake you are looking for.)* Allow time for students to proofread their drafts. Read aloud the second bulleted item. Then have students trade papers and proofread a partner's draft. Tell students to use a different pencil color when making their proofreading corrections. Have a volunteer read aloud the last two bulleted items. Give students time to consider their partners' suggestions.

> **Grammar in Action.** The word *favorite* in the second sentence is misspelled.

Editing Center

Set up an editing center in the classroom with reference materials and supplies. Include dictionaries and a copy of the list of proofreading marks found on page 514. Encourage students to use the editing center when they check their drafts.

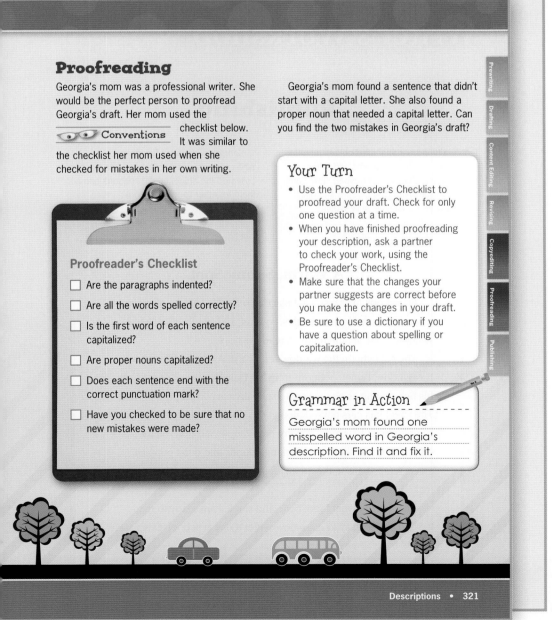

Proofreading

Georgia's mom was a professional writer. She would be the perfect person to proofread Georgia's draft. Her mom used the **Conventions** checklist below. It was similar to the checklist her mom used when she checked for mistakes in her own writing.

Proofreader's Checklist

- ☐ Are the paragraphs indented?
- ☐ Are all the words spelled correctly?
- ☐ Is the first word of each sentence capitalized?
- ☐ Are proper nouns capitalized?
- ☐ Does each sentence end with the correct punctuation mark?
- ☐ Have you checked to be sure that no new mistakes were made?

Georgia's mom found a sentence that didn't start with a capital letter. She also found a proper noun that needed a capital letter. Can you find the two mistakes in Georgia's draft?

Your Turn

- Use the Proofreader's Checklist to proofread your draft. Check for only one question at a time.
- When you have finished proofreading your description, ask a partner to check your work, using the Proofreader's Checklist.
- Make sure that the changes your partner suggests are correct before you make the changes in your draft.
- Be sure to use a dictionary if you have a question about spelling or capitalization.

Grammar in Action

Georgia's mom found one misspelled word in Georgia's description. Find it and fix it.

Tabs: Prewriting / Drafting / Content Editing / Revising / Copyediting / Proofreading / Publishing

Descriptions • 321

OBJECTIVE

- **To publish a description**

PUBLISHING

Read aloud the first two paragraphs. Emphasize the importance of Georgia's checking for spelling errors even though she may have used a computer's spell-checker. Tell students that if a word is the wrong word for the sentence but spelled correctly, the spell-checker will not catch that it is wrong.

Have volunteers read aloud Georgia's final draft. Ask students to compare her final draft with the previous drafts. Have volunteers point out the parts they find most improved in Georgia's final draft.

Read aloud the next paragraph and discuss the many ways students might publish their work.

Tell students that the presentation of a piece of writing is as important as its content. Emphasize that students' descriptions should be pleasing to the eye—handwriting or typing should be neat, the page should be clean, and the title and paragraphing should enhance the look of the piece.

Your Turn

Have volunteers read aloud the first two bulleted items. Ask students to look over all the revisions they have made to their drafts. Tell students to read their descriptions one more time, looking for any additional mistakes.

After students have completed their final drafts and drawings, ask students to name some places where descriptions are published *(magazines, encyclopedias, Web sites)*. Discuss the best way for students to share their written descriptions so that the entire class can enjoy them.

Writer's Workshop

Descriptions

Publishing

Georgia typed her final draft on her mom's computer. As she typed, she added the proofreading changes. She typed slowly and carefully. She wanted to be sure she didn't make any new mistakes while typing.

Georgia printed out her description. When she brought it to school, her teacher collected the students' descriptions and put them together to make a book.

A Warm, Sunny Spot

Everybody likes a special place to read. My favorite place is a window seat. I love the sights, sounds, and smells outside my window. They get me ready to read my book.

The sunlight on the window seat warms my skin. When I open the window, I smell popcorn from Mr. Deimos's snack cart. I hear his bell ringing as he pushes his squeaky cart down my sidewalk. The street has cars parked along both sides. A big, smoky bus rumbles by at four o'clock every day. People and dogs fill the dog park across the street. Barking hounds and quiet puppies chase tennis balls in the green grass. The crazy dogs always make me laugh.

After I enjoy what I see, hear, and smell, I am ready to read. It is the perfect way to calm down after a day at school. Everyone should try reading at a window seat.

ASSESS

Have students assess their finished description using the reproducible Student Self-Assessment on page 323y. A separate Teacher Scoring Rubric can be found on page 323z for you to use to evaluate their work.

Plan to spend tomorrow doing a formal assessment. Administer the Description Writing Prompt on **Assessment Book** pages 49–50.

TEACHING OPTIONS

Portfolio Opportunity

Remind students to keep a copy of their final descriptions in their portfolios. Point out that having a portfolio will help students keep track of the progress they are making with their writing.

New Focus

Have students choose a person, an object, or an animal that was mentioned in their descriptions. Then have them write the middle of a description about the person, object, or animal. When students have finished, ask them to display their original descriptions and their new descriptions. Invite students to read and compare both descriptions.

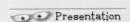 **Presentation** Publishing is the moment that you turn your work in to your teacher, read it aloud to your classmates, or post it on the bulletin board for others to read. Give these publishing ideas a try.

 Post your description on your classroom's wiki, blog, or Web site. Invite other students to review and comment on your work.

 Create a class magazine. Decorate the margins with small pictures of things representing the descriptions. Work with your classmates to decide on a cover.

 Film it. Videotape the person, place, or thing you described and add music. Narrate your video with your description.

 Submit your description to be published in your school's newspaper or literary magazine.

Whenever you publish your work, your goal is to share your thoughts and experiences with other people.

Your Turn

- Make a final copy of your description by writing it on a clean sheet of paper or by typing it on a computer.
- Make the proofreading changes that you decided to use. Try not to make any new mistakes while you fix the old ones.
- When you have finished your description, draw a picture of it. Read your description again to help you remember everything you will want to put in your picture.

Prewriting | Drafting | Content Editing | Revising | Copyediting | Proofreading | Publishing

Descriptions • 323

Name _____   Date _____

Description

Ideas	YES	NO
Do I have a sharp, clear focus on the topic?		
Do I include details that improve the description?		

Organization		
Do I have a beginning that names the topic?		
Do I have a middle that connects one idea to the next?		
Do I sum up my ideas in an ending?		
Do I use space order?		

Voice		
Does my tone show how I feel about the topic?		

Word Choice		
Do I use sensory words?		
Do I use well-chosen synonyms?		

Sentence Fluency		
Do I vary my sentence lengths?		
Do I use compound subjects and objects?		

Conventions		
Do I use correct grammar?		
Do I use correct spelling?		
Do I use correct punctuation and capitalization?		

Presentation		
Is my paper neat?		
Do I use consistent margins and spacing?		

Additional Items		

Name _____

Date _____ Score _____

POINT VALUES

0 = not evident
1 = minimal evidence of mastery
2 = evidence of development toward mastery
3 = strong evidence of mastery
4 = outstanding evidence of mastery

Description

Ideas   **POINTS**

    a sharp, distinct focus on the topic

    details that enhance the description

Organization

    an informative beginning that names the topic

    a middle with logical connections

    a summarizing ending

    space order

Voice

    language that shows the writer's feelings about the topic

Word Choice

    sensory words

    well-chosen synonyms

Sentence Fluency

    varied sentence length

    compound subjects and objects

Conventions

    correct grammar and usage

    correct spelling

    correct punctuation and capitalization

Presentation

    neatness

    consistent margins and spacing

Additional Items

_____

_____

_____

                                          Total

© LOYOLAPRESS.

CHAPTER FOCUS

LESSON 1: What Makes a Good Personal Letter?

LESSON 2: The Body of a Personal Letter

- **GRAMMAR:** Verbs
- **LITERACY SKILLS:** Personal E-Mails
- **WRITING SKILLS:** Compound Subjects
- **WORD STUDY:** Antonyms
- **SPEAKING AND LISTENING SKILLS:** Telephone Conversations
- **WRITER'S WORKSHOP:** Personal Letters

SUPPORT MATERIALS

Practice Book
Writing, pages 147–151

Assessment Book
Chapter 4 Writing Skills, pages 51–52
Personal Letter Writing Prompt, pages 53–54

Rubrics
Student, page 361y
Teacher, page 361z

Test Generator CD

Grammar
Section 4, pages 82–108

Customizable Lesson Plans
www.voyagesinenglish.com

Personal Letters

WHAT IS A PERSONAL LETTER?

Personal letters, perhaps the most common form of writing for most people, are unique in almost every way. While many genres speak to a wide audience, a personal letter is often meant to be read by one person or a small audience only. The purpose of a personal letter may be to inform, to persuade, to entertain, or to describe. Ideas in personal letters reflect a writer's own experience and often share sentiments that forge a personal connection between writer and reader.

A well-crafted personal letter includes the following:

- ☐ A clear focus on the writer's purpose
- ☐ A heading that gives the writer's address and the date
- ☐ A greeting that usually begins with *Dear* and the recipient's name
- ☐ A body that shares the writer's ideas
- ☐ An appropriate closing followed by the writer's signature
- ☐ Natural language
- ☐ The writer's personality
- ☐ Sentence variety, including some compound subjects

LiNK Use the following titles to offer your students examples of well-crafted personal letters:

First Year Letters by Julie Danneberg

Letters from Felix: A Little Rabbit on a World Tour by Annette Langen and Laura Lindgren

Yours Truly, Goldilocks by Alma Flor Ada

> **"** I consider it a good rule for letter-writing to leave unmentioned what the recipient already knows, and instead tell him something new. **"**
>
> —Sigmund Freud

WRITER'S WORKSHOP TIPS

Follow these ideas and tips to help you and your class get the most out of the Writer's Workshop:

- Review the traits of good writing. Use the chart on the inside back cover of the student and teacher editions.

- Have students bring in personal letters that they have received. Discuss the letters and their messages.

- Consider taking the class on a field trip to the local post office.

- Create a bulletin-board display of personal letters that you have received, including both e-mails and those sent by standard mail.

- Remind students that they should use the first-person point of view as they did when writing personal narratives.

- Create a file folder of addresses for celebrities that interest students. Invite students to write fan mail.

- Have students send e-mails to one another or to pen pals in another classroom or at another school.

CONNECT WITH GRAMMAR

Throughout the Writer's Workshop, look for opportunities to integrate verbs with writing personal letters.

- ☐ Encourage students to include past, present, and future tenses in their letters.

- ☐ In the copyediting stage, tell students to check for appropriate and consistent verb tenses.

- ☐ Have students check for correct use of irregular verbs.

- ☐ Challenge students to use helping verbs, being verbs, and action verbs in their letters.

SCORING RUBRIC

Personal Letter

Point Values
0 = not evident
1 = minimal evidence of mastery
2 = evidence of development toward mastery
3 = strong evidence of mastery
4 = outstanding evidence of mastery

	POINTS
Ideas	
a clear focus on the writer's purpose	
Organization	
a greeting that usually begins with *Dear* and the recipient's name	
a body that shares the writer's ideas	
an appropriate closing followed by the writer's signature	
Voice	
the writer's personality	
Word Choice	
natural language	
Sentence Fluency	
sentence variety, including some compound subjects	
Conventions	
correct grammar and usage	
correct spelling	
correct punctuation and capitalization	
Presentation	
neat handwriting or typing	
consistent margins and spacing	
a heading that gives the writer's address and the date	
Additional Items	
Total	

Full-sized, reproducible rubrics can be found at the end of this chapter.

CHAPTER 4
Personal Letters

INTRODUCING THE GENRE

Tell students that Chapter 4 is about personal, or friendly, letters. Ask students if they have ever written a letter to a friend or relative. Have volunteers describe what the letter was about and to whom it was sent. Discuss times students might write a personal letter *(to tell a friend or relative about their lives, to thank someone, to respond to a party invitation).*

Tell students that they will write personal letters throughout their lives.

Discuss the following characteristics of a personal letter:

- The letter is written to someone the writer knows.
- The heading has the writer's address and the date on which the letter was written.
- The greeting has the name of the person receiving the letter.
- The body gives the writer's message.

- The closing says good-bye to the receiver.
- The letter ends with the writer's signature.

Point out that the greeting shows that a message is beginning. Ask students to compare the heading to the closing, which shows the reader that the message has ended. Guide students to talk about how a personal letter might be different from a letter written to a business *(less formal, the writer knows the receiver, the letter includes more information about the writer).*

LiNK **Yours Truly, Goldilocks**

The excerpt from *Yours Truly, Goldilocks* is a good example of a personal letter because it has the following:
- A heading containing writer's address and the date
- A greeting with name of the person receiving the letter
- A body that gives the writer's message

As students read the excerpts of personal letters in this chapter, be sure to point out the characteristics of personal letters. Also be sure to point out verbs in the excerpts. Point out the helping verbs and the present progressive tense in the excerpt on this page.

Personal Letters

LiNK **Yours Truly, Goldilocks**
by Alma Flor Ada

Brick House
Woodsy Woods
April 7

Dear Goldilocks,

Thank you, thank you, thank you! The three of us had a great time at your birthday party.

It was a wonderful, wonderful, wonderful party. That is, all three of us think it was wonderful.

As you know, we have had a terrible time building our houses. Now that we are sure that no wolf can blow down our new house, no matter how hard he huffs and puffs, we would like to finally have a house warming party on April twenty-ninth. We would be very happy if you were our special guest. We are also sending invitations to Baby Bear, Little Red Riding Hood, and Peter Rabbit. We look forward to a wonderful day.

Love, love, love your three friends,
Pig One, Pig Two, and Pig Three

> This personal letter has five parts and states one topic at a time.

324

Reading the Literature Excerpt

Ask a volunteer to read aloud the literature model. Have students point out why it is a good example of a personal letter. Have students tell about other personal letters they have read or written.

Reading the Student Model

Have volunteers read the model aloud. Then discuss the following:

- Where in the letter is the sender's address located? *(It is in the top right-hand corner.)*
- To whom is the letter addressed? *(It is addressed to Mr. and Mrs. Ruiz.)*
- Who is the writer of the letter? *(Layne is the letter writer.)*
- What is the writer's message? *(The message is to thank them for hosting her and to tell what a good time she had at their cottage.)*

CHAPTER

4

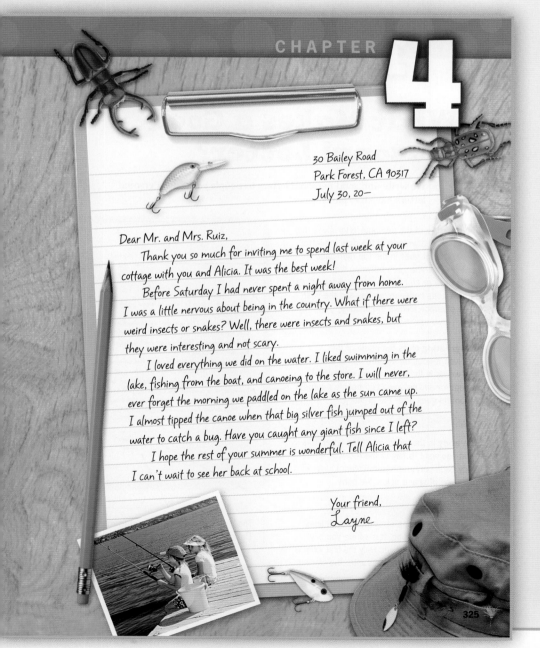

30 Bailey Road
Park Forest, CA 90317
July 30, 20—

Dear Mr. and Mrs. Ruiz,

Thank you so much for inviting me to spend last week at your cottage with you and Alicia. It was the best week!

Before Saturday I had never spent a night away from home. I was a little nervous about being in the country. What if there were weird insects or snakes? Well, there were insects and snakes, but they were interesting and not scary.

I loved everything we did on the water. I liked swimming in the lake, fishing from the boat, and canoeing to the store. I will never, ever forget the morning we paddled on the lake as the sun came up. I almost tipped the canoe when that big silver fish jumped out of the water to catch a bug. Have you caught any giant fish since I left?

I hope the rest of your summer is wonderful. Tell Alicia that I can't wait to see her back at school.

Your friend,
Layne

OBJECTIVE

- **To identify the parts of a personal letter**

WARM-UP

Read, Listen, Speak

Read aloud the letter you brought in for yesterday's For Tomorrow homework. Ask students how they know it is a personal letter. Have small groups share the letters they found. Guide students to discuss how they know that their examples are personal letters.

GRAMMAR CONNECTION

Take this opportunity to talk about *bring, buy, come,* and *sit.* You may wish to have students point out *bring, buy, come,* and *sit* if they exist in their Read, Listen, Speak examples.

TEACH

Invite volunteers to describe times when they have sent or received personal letters. Write on the board *heading, greeting, body, closing,* and *signature.* Read aloud the first paragraph. Ask volunteers to name people to whom they might send personal letters.

Have volunteers read aloud the heading and greeting callouts. Point out that the writer's address and the date are placed in the top right-hand corner. Have students notice the placement of the commas in the address and heading. Then draw students' attention to the greeting. Explain that greetings in personal letters often begin with *Dear* and always end with a comma.

Invite volunteers to read aloud the remaining callouts. Ask a volunteer to identify the first

and last words of the body. Tell students that the body of this letter has a beginning, a middle, and an ending. Ask students what other kinds of writing have a beginning, a middle, and an ending (*personal narratives, descriptions*). Then have a volunteer read the closing of the letter. Ask students to name other kinds of closings for personal letters (*Love, Sincerely, Yours truly*). Tell students that letters end with the writer's signature. Be sure students understand that a signature cannot be printed but must be written in cursive. Invite volunteers to write on the board examples of their own signatures.

PRACTICE

ACTIVITY A

Have students complete this activity independently. When they have finished, invite students to share their answers with the class.

ACTIVITY B

Have partners complete this activity. Encourage students to make up the information needed in the heading. Tell them to look at the model on page 325 if they need help identifying the type of missing information. Invite partners to share their answers with the class.

LESSON 1 PERSONAL LETTERS

What Makes a Good Personal Letter?

We write and send personal letters to people we know. Personal letters have five parts.

The **heading** of the personal letter gives the address of the writer and the date the letter was written. It goes in the top right-hand corner. A comma goes between the name of the town or city and the state. Another comma goes between the day and the year. A line of space follows the heading.

The **greeting** gives the name of the receiver. It goes on the left side of the letter. The words in the greeting are capitalized except for *and* between two people's names. A comma goes after the greeting.

The **body** is the message of the letter. It is what you want to say to the receiver. In the body each paragraph is indented. Leave an extra line of space below the body.

The **closing** comes after the body. It lines up under the heading. It is where you say good-bye to the receiver. Only the first word is capitalized. A comma goes after the closing.

The closing is followed by a **signature**. The signature is your written name.

> 30 Bailey Road
> Park Forest, CA 90317
> July 30, 20—
>
> Dear Mr. and Mrs. Ruiz,
> Thank you so much for inviting me to spend last week at your cottage with you and Alicia. It was the best week!
> Before Saturday I had never spent a night away from home. I was a little nervous about being in the country. What if there were weird insects or snakes? Well, there were insects and snakes, but they were interesting and not scary.
> I loved everything we did on the water. I liked swimming in the lake, fishing from the boat, and canoeing to the store. I will never, ever forget the morning we paddled on the lake as the sun came up. I almost tipped the canoe when that big silver fish jumped out of the water to catch a bug. Have you caught any giant fish since I left?
> I hope the rest of your summer is wonderful. Tell Alicia that I can't wait to see her back at school.
>
> Your friend,
> Layne

326 • Chapter 4

APPLY

WRITER'S CORNER

Have students complete this activity independently. Encourage students to write a closing that is different from the one in the letter on page 325. When students have finished, invite them to compare their work in small groups. Students should demonstrate the ability to identify parts of a personal letter.

ASSESS

Note which students had difficulty identifying the parts of a personal letter. Use the Reteach option with those students who need additional reinforcement.

ACTIVITY A Answer the questions below about the parts of the letter on page 325.

1. What city is Layne from? Park Forest
2. On what day did Layne write the letter? July 30
3. To whom did she write the letter? Mr. and Mrs. Ruiz
4. Why did Layne write the letter? to thank the Ruizes
5. What message did Layne want Alicia to know? She can't wait to see Alicia back at school.
6. How did Layne say good-bye in the letter? Your friend

Activity B

Possible answers:
1. Greencastle
2. MT
3. February
4. Hillenmeyer
5. Sincerely

ACTIVITY B Work with a partner to write the parts of the letter that are missing below.

955 _____(1)_____ Lane
Hoffman Lakes, _____(2)_____ 61049
_____(3)_____ 18, 20–

Dear Mrs. _____(4)_____,

   Please excuse Jason from class today. He is sick with the chicken pox and cannot come to school. On doctor's orders he will be missing a few days. Please send any work home with his sister, Kelly.

   I hope to see you at the next Open House. I always have a nice time talking with you about your adventures during the summer. You went to Peru this year, right?

_____(5)_____,

WRITER'S CORNER

Imagine that Layne wrote the letter on page 325 to you and that you would like to invite Layne to your home next summer. Write the heading, the greeting, the closing, and the signature for the letter.

Personal Letters • 327

Read, Listen, Speak

Show students your personal letter from yesterday's For Tomorrow homework. Demonstrate how you labeled the parts of the letter and ask students if any parts are missing. Invite small groups to share their letters. Ask students to talk about any parts of the letters that were missing.

GRAMMAR CONNECTION

Take this opportunity to talk about *eat*, *go*, and *see*. You may wish to have students point out *eat*, *go*, and *see* if they exist in their Read, Listen, Speak examples.

TEACH

Ask students to name some occasions on which they might send personal letters (*for a relative's birthday, to thank someone, to write to a friend who has moved*). Draw on the board five boxes to represent each part of a personal letter. Invite students to identify the five parts of a personal letter and to write the name of each part in the correct box (*heading, greeting, body, closing, signature*). Review the punctuation and capitalization in each of the five parts.

PRACTICE

ACTIVITY C

Have small groups complete this activity. Tell students first to copy the letter and then circle and label each of the five parts of the personal letter. When students have finished, invite volunteers to share their answers with the class. Ask a volunteer to explain why Luke wrote this letter.

ACTIVITY D

Tell students to use the letter on page 326 if they need help identifying the correct punctuation in each part. When students have finished, invite volunteers to share their answers with the class.

ACTIVITY E

Have partners complete this activity. When students have finished, invite volunteers to write the rearranged letter on the board.

ACTIVITY F

Tell students to look back at the letter on page 326 if they do not remember the correct capitalization and punctuation. When students have finished, invite volunteers to write their corrected items on the board.

ACTIVITY C Identify the parts of the letter below.

828 North Gunnison St.
Brazil, IL 60313
August 28, 20–

Dear Owen,

How are you doing, brother? How is college? I wanted to tell you that I heard that your favorite band, The Bowling Weevils, is going to be playing here on October 5. I was wondering if you were going to come home.

I hope you are having a good first week at school. Tell me if you are going to go to any football games. If you do, I will look for you on TV.

Yours truly,
Luke

Activity C
Heading, the address and date;
Greeting, Dear Owen;
Body, the message;
Closing, Yours truly;
Signature, Luke

ACTIVITY D Copy the headings, greetings, and closings below. Then add the correct punctuation.

1. Your best friend
2. March 28 20–
3. Dear Henry
4. Baltic ND
5. New Braunfels TX
6. Sincerely
7. Dear Uncle Marcos
8. Love
9. November 12 20–
10. Dear Mr. and Mrs. Hund
11. Des Plaines IL 60178
12. Yours truly

Activity D
1. Your best friend,
2. March 28, 20–
3. Dear Henry,
4. Baltic, ND
5. New Braunfels, TX
6. Sincerely,
7. Dear Uncle Marcos,
8. Love,
9. November 12, 20–
10. Dear Mr. and Mrs. Hund,
11. Des Plaines, IL 60178
12. Yours truly,

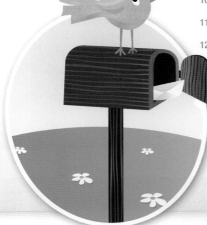

328 • Chapter 4

APPLY

WRITER'S CORNER

Help students with correct zip codes and the state abbreviation as they write their addresses. Remind students to write their signatures in cursive. Encourage volunteers to share their work in small groups. Students should demonstrate the ability to identify and write parts of a personal letter.

ASSESS

Note which students had difficulty identifying parts of a personal letter. Use the Reteach option with those students who need additional reinforcement.

Practice Book page 147 provides additional work with the parts of a personal letter.

ACTIVITY E The parts of the letter below are mixed up. Rewrite the parts in the correct order.

7   *Monique*

5   Yesterday I went with my neighbors Kat and Jack to a movie set. Kat works for a famous director. The movie is a big secret, but I can tell you it's about your favorite story.

4   Dear Leah,

2   Los Angeles, CA 90211

6   Your pen pal,

1   1823 La Casa Drive

3   October 3, 20–

Activity F

1. greeting; Dear Ali,
2. closing; Your grandson,
3. body; Did you hear Kelly won?
4. heading; May 23, 20–
5. heading; Toledo, OH 78791
6. greeting; Dear Kasey Johnson,
7. heading; 1984 Lisbon Avenue
8. closing; Best wishes,
9. heading; Miami, FL 33127
10. body; I will leave for Paris in one week.

ACTIVITY F Tell which part of a personal letter each item is from. Then rewrite the item with correct capitalization and punctuation.

1. dear ali.
2. your Grandson
3. did you hear kelly won.
4. may, 23 20–
5. toledo OH 78791
6. dear Kasey johnson
7. 1984 Lisbon avenue
8. best wishes
9. miami fl 33127
10. i will leave for paris in one week.

WRITER'S CORNER

Draw on a sheet of paper boxes where each part of a letter belongs. Then write the heading, greeting, closing, and signature as if you were writing the letter to a friend.

TEACHING OPTIONS

Reteach

Have students draw the outline of a person. Emphasize that the drawing should include a head, a face, arms, legs, and feet. Then have students label the person with all the parts of a personal letter. Guide students to label the head with the word *heading*, the mouth with the word *greeting*, the torso with the word *body*, the legs with the word *closing*, and the feet with the word *signature*. Discuss what should be included in each part of a personal letter.

A Welcoming Letter

Ask students to imagine what they might write in a letter to a pen pal from another country who is coming to their school next month. Work with students to compose a letter on poster board. Invite volunteers to write the heading and the greeting. Have students offer sentences for the body of the letter. Ask a volunteer to write a closing. Invite the class to sign their names to the letter. Work with students to label the parts of the letter. Display the poster in the classroom for reference.

For Tomorrow

Have students write one greeting and two closings that might have been used in the personal letter in Activity C. Bring in your own greeting and closings to share with the class.

OBJECTIVES

- **To identify the purposes of personal letters**
- **To understand the organization of a personal letter**

WARM-UP

Read, Listen, Speak

Write on the board your greeting and closings from yesterday's For Tomorrow homework. Have volunteers write on the board their greeting and closings. Discuss how the greeting and closings show that the writer knows the receiver. Encourage students to copy the different greetings and closings from the board and to save their lists.

GRAMMAR CONNECTION

Take this opportunity to talk about *take*, *tear*, and *write*. You may wish to have students point out *take*, *tear*, and *write* if they exist if they exist in their personal letter examples.

TEACH

Invite a volunteer to read aloud the opening paragraph. Explain that because a personal letter is like talking to someone on paper, the letter sounds like the writer's own voice. Tell students that a personal letter is written the way a writer would speak. Then read aloud the first paragraph of the section Purpose.

Invite a volunteer to read aloud the first item in the bulleted list. Ask students what other topics would be good for a personal letter. Have a volunteer read aloud the second bulleted item. Explain that this type of personal letter is about someone other than the writer. Invite a volunteer to read aloud the third bulleted item. Explain that students can write a personal letter to let someone know that they are grateful for something

that the receiver did for them. Ask volunteers to explain how a personal letter that tells news is different from a thank-you letter.

Have a volunteer read aloud the last bulleted item. Ask students to think of something that they want to know and the person to whom they would write to get that information. Encourage students to share appropriate responses.

LiNK Have a volunteer read aloud the excerpt. Ask students what the body of the letter and the closing tell about the relationship between the sender and receiver. *(The sender is the receiver's daughter.)*

PRACTICE

ACTIVITY A

Have students complete this activity independently. Encourage them to look at the bulleted list on page 330 for help. When students have finished, invite them to share their answers with the class. Have volunteers explain why the items that were not picked are not good for personal letters.

ACTIVITY B

Have partners complete this activity. Tell students to refer to the bulleted list on page 330 if they need help. Invite volunteers to share their answers with the class.

The Body of a Personal Letter

The body of a personal letter is where you write your message. Writing a personal letter is like talking on paper to someone you know.

Purpose

We write personal letters to someone we know. People write personal letters for different reasons. Here are some common reasons.

- People write personal letters to tell about something that happened to them. The topics can be anything. You might write about your day at school, your summer, or even a coyote you saw in your backyard.
- People write personal letters to share news or to tell a story about someone else. You might write to your grandpa about your sister's first day in acting class.
- People write personal letters to thank someone. On page 325 Layne wrote to Alicia's parents to thank them for letting her stay in their cottage.
- People write personal letters to find out information. You might write to your uncle to see what you need to bring when you go to the basketball championship with him.

LiNK

Dear Mother,

There is only room for me to send my love, and some pressed pansies from the root I have been keeping safe in the house for Father to see. I read every morning, try to be good all day, and sing myself to sleep with Father's tune. . . . Everyone is very kind, and we are as happy as we can be without you.

. . . Oh, do come home soon to your loving . . .

LITTLE BETH

APPLY

WRITER'S CORNER

Give students time to decide the purpose of their letter and who will receive it. Then have them look back at the letter on page 326 for help with writing the heading, greeting, closing, and signature. Students should demonstrate the ability to identify the purposes of personal letters.

ASSESS

Note which students had difficulty understanding the purposes of personal letters. Use the Reteach option with those students who need additional reinforcement.

TEACHING OPTIONS

Reteach

Discuss the different purposes of personal letters. Write on the board a four-column chart with the headings *To Share News About Yourself*, *To Share News About Someone Else*, *To Thank Someone*, and *To Ask for Information*. Have students write in the correct column examples of topics for each heading. Then have students choose a purpose from the board. Direct students to write two sentences that might be included in the body of a letter about their purpose. Have partners share their sentences.

Curriculum Connection

Invite students to write a letter to a historical figure they consider heroic. Have students use the person's first name in the greeting. Tell students the purpose of their letter should be to thank the person for one specific, important achievement. Suggest that students either research or make up their hero's address. Tell students that even their closing should express their gratitude to the person.

ACTIVITY A Pick which of the purposes below are for a personal letter.

1. to tell Aunt Rita you met the mayor of Chicago
2. to ask Luna Restaurant to help with the food drive
3. to talk about baseball with your friend in Miami
4. to tell your aunt that your brother won a swim meet
5. to complain to Street Team that the skateboard you bought from them broke after one ride
6. to thank your cousin for the gift card to your favorite store
7. to ask Paws Place Shelter if you can volunteer
8. to ask your friend what movie she would like to see with you when she visits

Activity B

1. to ask for information
2. to tell something that happened to the writer
3. to share news about someone else

ACTIVITY B Read the paragraphs from personal letters below. Decide the purpose of each personal letter.

1. Stephanie, the smartest kid in my class, told me about a new book about cheetahs that fly spaceships. Have you heard about this book? The main character is named Flip the Cheetah, and his friend is Donnie. She said the characters are funny. Do you know who wrote it?

2. Last Friday I had a chance to go to the museum to see the new exhibit about Rome. I got to pretend I was a gladiator in a show they had. Then we saw parts of old statues. You would have loved it, Mandy!

3. I wish you could have seen Kevin at the state spelling bee. He closed his eyes when he spelled each word. He finally won by spelling *individuality* correctly. We are so proud of him!

WRITER'S CORNER

Think of a family member to whom you would like to write a personal letter. Choose a purpose for your letter. Write the purpose and the person to whom you are writing. Then write the heading, greeting, closing, and signature.

For Tomorrow

Tell students to think of some news they would like to share with a relative. Ask students to write personal letters telling this news. Bring in your own letter to a relative to share with the class.

Personal Letters • 331

WARM-UP

Read, Listen, Speak

Read aloud your letter from yesterday's For Tomorrow homework. Identify the parts of the letter. Have small groups share the letters telling news that students wrote for homework. Ask students to read aloud the letters and check whether any parts of a letter are missing.

GRAMMAR CONNECTION

Take this opportunity to talk about the simple present tense. You may wish to have students point out the use of simple present tense in their Read, Listen, Speak examples.

TEACH

Review the purposes of personal letters. Read aloud the first two paragraphs. Explain that personal letters should be well organized and clearly written just like any other kind of writing.

Ask a volunteer to read aloud the first bulleted item. Explain that a letter that tells a story is similar to a personal narrative. Remind students that personal narratives are written in time order. Point out that students can use time order to organize a personal letter that is a story.

Have a volunteer read aloud the second bulleted item. Explain that writing about one idea at a time makes the letter easier to follow.

Invite a volunteer to read aloud the last bulleted item. Tell students that explaining why they want to know an answer can help the recipient more fully answer the question.

LiNK Have a volunteer read aloud the letter. Ask students to identify the purpose of the letter. Then ask volunteers to suggest additional sentences to add to the letter.

PRACTICE

ACTIVITY C

Suggest that students refer to the bulleted list on this page to match their topic to an appropriate order. Ask volunteers to share their answers with the class.

ACTIVITY D

Remind students that as in a personal narrative, the body of their letter should have a beginning, a middle, and an ending.

ACTIVITY E

Have partners complete this activity. Suggest that they begin by reading the letter aloud to determine what is out of order and what information is missing. Ask students to take turns adding the missing parts of the letter. Invite volunteers to share their revised letters with the class.

ACTIVITY F

Tell students that their letter should both give information about themselves and ask questions about the pen pal. Help students select the organization for their letters. Invite volunteers to share the bodies of their letters and organization choice.

Organization of a Personal Letter

A personal letter needs to be organized. In personal letters the writer writes about one topic at a time.

A personal letter will have a different order depending on your purpose.

- If the purpose of your personal letter is to tell a story about yourself or about someone else, write the events in the order they happened.
- If the purpose of your letter is to thank someone, write about one thing at a time. In Layne's letter she talked about many things she liked. But she wrote all her ideas about one thing before she wrote about the next.
- If the purpose of your letter is to find information, explain your questions one at a time. Then write why you want to know the answer.

Dear Pierre,

I am very happy you and I were matched up to be pen pals. You and your family sound very interesting.

In what part of France do you live? I could not find Fayence on my map. . . .

Your pen pal,
Eloise

ACTIVITY C Read the topics for personal letters below. Decide what the best way to organize each topic would be.

1. thanking your sister for the gifts from her vacation to Brazil
2. telling grandma about Dad getting chased by a dog
3. thanking your friend for a sleepover
4. telling your cousin about your first day of dance class
5. asking your friend to help you understand a difficult book
6. telling your grandfather what it was like to watch a dog show
7. asking your pen pal what her country is like
8. thanking your librarian for the books he found for you

Activity C

1. one thing at a time
2. the order the events happened
3. one thing at a time
4. the order the events happened
5. explaining one question at a time
6. the order the events happened
7. explaining one question at a time
8. one thing at a time

APPLY

WRITER'S CORNER

Have students match the purpose of their letter with the best type of organization from the bulleted list on page 332. When students have finished, have them exchange letters with partners. Encourage students to identify the type of organization their partners used. Students should demonstrate an understanding of organizing a personal letter.

Grammar in Action. Tell students that some action verbs have helping verbs *(were matched)*.

Suggest that students refer to the list of being verbs on page 76 to help identify the being verb in the excerpt *(am)*.

ASSESS

Note which students had difficulty organizing a personal letter. Use the Reteach option with those students who need additional reinforcement.

Practice Book page 148 provides additional work with the body of a personal letter.

TEACHING OPTIONS

Reteach

Write on the board the bulleted lists shown below. Explain that they will help students better understand how to organize their personal letters. Read aloud the lists and discuss them with the class.

To Tell a Story
- **This happened.**
- **Then this happened.**
- **Then this happened.**
- **And so on . . .**

To Thank Someone
- **thank you**
- **first whole topic**
- **second whole topic**
- **And so on . . .**

To Ask for Information
- **first question**
- **second question**
- **And so on . . .**
- **reason for questions**

Have students copy each list onto a separate note card. Emphasize that students should refer to the cards to help to organize their own personal letters.

ACTIVITY D Choose a topic for a personal letter. Think about the events you want to write about in the body of your letter. Tell the events in the order that they happened.

1. Your day at school
2. A friend's sporting event
3. A day spent with your family
4. A funny pet story

Activity E
Out-of-order sentences:
1. Using a wooden bat is going to be much easier than using a metal one.
2. Finally, the basketball is going to be fun too.
Accept any revisions students can justify.
Missing parts:
Greeting—Dear Uncle Andre, Closing—Love,

ACTIVITY E The personal letter below has two sentences out of order and two missing parts. Rewrite the letter in the right order. Add the missing parts.

1521 Agatite Ave.
Silvis, MI 90010
September 17, 20—

Thank you for the box of sports supplies, Uncle Andre! I love the baseball bat. The new baseball glove is great too. My old glove is too small for me now. Using a wooden bat is going to be much easier than using a metal one. The tennis racket is going to be great. I can go to tennis camp next summer. My little sister loves basketball, and now she won't bother me so much. Finally, the basketball is going to be fun too. Thank you once again!

Ricardo

ACTIVITY F Write the body of a letter to a new pen pal. Remember to tell your pen pal about yourself. Ask your pen pal at least one question.

Grammar in Action. Find one action verb and one being verb in the first sentence of the letter on page 332.

WRITER'S CORNER

Organize the personal letter you began in the Writer's Corner on page 331. Choose the organization that best fits the purpose of your letter. Then write the body of your letter.

Personal Letters • 333

For Tomorrow

Tell students to locate a personal letter they have brought in for a previous For Tomorrow. Have students identify the purpose of the letter and tell how it is organized. Be ready to model with one of your own letters.

OBJECTIVES

- **To understand the purpose of personal e-mails**
- **To recognize the parts of a personal e-mail**

WARM-UP

Read, Listen, Speak

Read aloud one of the letters you have brought in for homework. Tell students how you determined the letter's purpose and organization. Invite small groups to share the letters they brought. Ask students to discuss the purpose of their letters and how their letters are organized.

GRAMMAR CONNECTION

Take this opportunity to talk about the simple past tense. You may wish to have students point out any uses of the simple past tense in their Read, Listen, Speak examples.

TEACH

Invite a volunteer to read aloud the first two paragraphs. Ask students if they have sent personal e-mails.

Have a student read aloud the section Address. Explain that a character is a letter, number, or symbol that students can type.

Read aloud the section Subject Line. Ask students to suggest topics for e-mails and subject lines. Ask students how subject lines can be helpful.

Ask students how e-mails are similar to personal letters and how they are different.

PRACTICE

ACTIVITY A

Have partners complete the activity. Have students compare Lizzie's e-mail to the personal letter on page 326. Ask students to identify the parts of a personal letter and tell which part is missing in the e-mail. Ask students which part of an e-mail is the same as a heading. Then ask what part an e-mail has that a personal letter does not have *(subject line)*.

ACTIVITY B

Have students complete this activity independently. After they have completed the activity, challenge students to tell what kind of organization each e-mail might have. Suggest that they refer to the bulleted list on page 332.

Personal E-Mails

Some e-mails are like personal letters. People write e-mails to keep in touch with friends and family. People often write e-mails to share news and to get information quickly.

E-mails usually have fewer parts than letters you send through the post office.

Address

In an e-mail you need to type the receiver's e-mail address accurately, character by character. Otherwise, the person will not receive it, and the e-mail may bounce back to you.

The e-mail program automatically puts your e-mail address and date at the top of the e-mail. You do not have to type them. You do not have to type your street address at the top of an e-mail.

Subject Line

Subject lines are special to e-mails. They state the main topic of the e-mail in a few words. For example, if you are writing a thank-you e-mail, you might write "Thanks for the gift." Personal e-mails may have several topics, and people may sometimes use general headings such as "Checking in" or "What's new?" or "Touching base."

APPLY

WRITER'S CORNER

Review the bulleted list of purposes for personal letters on page 330. Tell students that their subject lines should tell about the main topic of the e-mail. Remind them that subject lines do not need to be written in complete sentences. Students should demonstrate the ability to understand the purpose of personal e-mails.

ASSESS

Note which students had difficulty understanding the purpose of personal e-mails. Use the Reteach option with those students who need additional reinforcement.

TEACHING OPTIONS

Reteach

Discuss that there are many different types of e-mail addresses, but that the basic format is _____@_____._____. Point out that e-mail addresses usually end in *.com*, *.net*, or *.org*. Stress that e-mail providers have a format for sending e-mails that includes an address line and a subject line. Have have students invent e-mail addresses. Then have students brainstorm possible subject lines for personal e-mails.

Super Subject Lines

Tell students that many people use the same subject lines in e-mails over and over again. Challenge small groups to come up with interesting subject lines that would grab a reader's attention for these e-mail topics: a thank-you note, keeping in touch with a family member, sharing news about a sporting event with a friend, a great summer trip.

For Tomorrow

Have students ask a family member to print out a personal e-mail for them to bring to school. Bring in your own printed e-mail to share with the class.

Activity A
1. Martina
2. March 22, 20–
3. My new cat!; Martina's new cat
4. the heading

ACTIVITY A Read the e-mail and answer the questions.

To:	martinaginetti@emailcentral.com
From:	lizziesanson@mailboxforme.com
Date:	March 22, 20–
Subject:	My new cat!

Dear Martina,

How are you? How are Aunt Anna and Uncle Will?

I am writing to tell you I got a cat yesterday from the shelter. His name is Leopold. He's a Siamese, and he's one year old.

Right now Leopold seems a little scared in his new home, but he already likes me to pet him. Soon he probably will be very friendly and even sleep in my bed.

I know that you have a cat. Can you suggest any good toys to get for Leopold? How about a cat DVD for my new cat to watch?

Please write back soon.

Your cousin,

Lizzie

1. Who is receiving the e-mail?
2. What is the date of the e-mail?
3. What are the words in the subject line? What is the topic of the e-mail?
4. Look back at page 326. Which part of a personal letter is missing from the e-mail?

Activity B
1. meeting someone at the train station on Friday
2. an invitation to a birthday party
3. request for a banana bread recipe
4. telling about a recent trip to an amusement park

ACTIVITY B Read the subject lines. **What is each e-mail about?**

1. See you at the train station on Friday
2. Birthday party!
3. Your recipe for banana bread
4. Amusement park trip

WRITER'S CORNER

Think of a topic for an e-mail that you would like to send a family member or a friend. Write the subject line and the person who will receive the e-mail. Do this for three different topics.

Personal Letters • 335

WARM-UP

Read, Listen, Speak

Read aloud the e-mail you brought in for yesterday's For Tomorrow homework. Invite students to suggest subject lines. Have partners work together to share their printed e-mails. Tell students to label the sender's e-mail address, the receiver's e-mail address, and the subject line.

GRAMMAR CONNECTION

Take this opportunity to talk about the future tense with *will*. You may wish to have students point out any uses of the future tense with *will* in their Read, Listen, Speak examples.

TEACH

Ask a volunteer to read aloud the section Body of an E-Mail. Discuss the purpose of the e-mail *(to tell a story)* and how the body is organized *(in time order)*.

Have a volunteer read aloud the Closing and Signature sections. Ask students to suggest other closings and how to decide on a good closing. Then give students time to practice their signatures. Remind students that a signature is written in cursive.

Read aloud the section E-mail Safety, stopping after each bulleted item to discuss its importance. Tell students that while the Internet is an easy and excellent way to communicate, it does have dangers, especially for children.

PRACTICE

ACTIVITY C

Emphasize that subject lines should show the purpose of the e-mail, but do not need to give information in complete sentences. Have students complete this activity independently. Ask partners to compare their subject lines.

ACTIVITY D

Have partners complete this activity. Tell students to invent an e-mail address and name for the sender. Ask students to determine the purpose of the e-mail and how it should be organized *(time order)*. Have volunteers share their answers with the class.

Body of an E-Mail

The body of an e-mail is like the body of a personal letter. E-mails are often written to tell personal stories, to share news, to thank someone, or to ask for information. Look back at page 332 for help on the organization of personal letters. How is the body of the e-mail on page 335 organized?

Closing

The closing of an e-mail is similar to that of personal letters. Some examples are *Your friend, Sincerely,* and *Best wishes.*

Signature

Some e-mail programs have a feature that lets you type your name once and then will automatically include it in your e-mails. Some allow you to include a handwritten copy of your signature. Does your e-mail account have a signature feature? Do you know how to use it?

E-mail Safety

It is important to follow some rules for using e-mail.
- Always get your parent's permission before going online.
- Keep the password for your e-mail account to yourself.
- Do not give out personal information on the Internet. There are people who try to get your personal information and use it for themselves.
- Remember that your e-mail may not stay private.
- Do not open e-mail for which you do not know the sender. Don't be fooled by subject lines such as "Remember me?"
- Do not download attachments from people you don't know. These attachments might have viruses that could harm your computer.

APPLY

WRITER'S CORNER

Help students brainstorm possible e-mail topics. Write them on the board. Remind students to include the receiver's e-mail address, the subject, a greeting, the body, a closing, and their signature. Ask students to identify the type of organization they chose and why. Students should demonstrate the ability to understand the purpose and recognize the parts of a personal e-mail.

TechTip Help students access the Internet and set up e-mail addresses through a school Web site.

ASSESS

Note which students had difficulty understanding the purpose and recognizing the parts of a personal e-mail. Use the Reteach option with those students who need additional reinforcement.

Practice Book page 149 provides additional work with writing e-mail.

Practice Book page 149

TEACHING OPTIONS

Reteach

Make up an e-mail puzzle by writing an outline of an e-mail with blank boxes for each part. Make copies for students and cut apart all the parts. Hand out one cut-up puzzle to each student. Have students put the e-mail puzzle back together and label each box with the following: *address, subject line, body, closing, signature.* Then have students fill in each part of the puzzle with information that should be included in that part of the e-mail.

Poster Power

Have small groups make posters about e-mail safety. Have groups make up or choose one rule from page 336 to use on their posters. Encourage students to make their posters colorful and eye-catching. Challenge students to come up with a catchy slogan or jingle to help people remember the rule. Have students share their posters with the class.

Activity C

Possible answers:
1. My poem won a prize!
2. Your backpack
3. My first hike
4. Thanks for the book

ACTIVITY C Write subject lines for these e-mails.

1. You are writing to your grandmother to tell her that your poem won a prize in a state poetry contest.
2. You are writing to a friend to ask where you can get a special backpack you know she has.
3. You are writing to a friend about your first time hiking.
4. You are writing to an aunt who sent you a book on knights for your birthday.

Activity D

Possible answers:
1. kevin@all-emails.com
2. Roberto Clemente card
3. Dear Dave,
4. Your friend,
5. Will

ACTIVITY D Complete the following e-mail. Then reorder the paragraphs of the body.

> **To:** daveb@worldwide.com
> **From:** _____(1)_____
> **Date:** November 11, 20—
> **Subject:** _____(2)_____
>
> _____(3)_____,
>
> 2 Here's what happened. I went to a garage sale with my mom, and I saw an old shoe box filled with baseball cards. I looked through the box carefully. Can you imagine my surprise when I saw a card for Roberto Clemente? And it only cost a dollar. I used some of my allowance to buy it.
>
> 3 The next time you come over, I can show it to you.
>
> 1 I am writing to tell you about my terrific find. I now own a Roberto Clemente baseball card! You know he's my favorite old-time player.
>
> _____(4)_____
> _____(5)_____

PITTSBURGH **PIRATES**

Roberto Clemente outfield

WRITER'S CORNER

Think of a topic for an e-mail you want to write to a friend. Write the e-mail, using the correct format.

For Tomorrow

Ask students to write an e-mail on paper to another student. Tell students to include all parts the of an e-mail. Bring in your own e-mail to share.

Tech Tip With an adult, go online and send your e-mail.

Personal Letters • 337

OBJECTIVE

- **To use compound subjects**

WARM-UP

Read, Listen, Speak

Read aloud your e-mail, leaving out one part. Ask students to identify the missing part. Then ask them to identify the purpose of the e-mail, as well as the receiver, the subject, the greeting, and the closing. Have students give their paper e-mails to the intended receiver. Ask the receiver to identify all the parts of the e-mail and compose a response.

GRAMMAR CONNECTION

Take this opportunity to talk about the future tense with *going to*. You may wish to have students point out the future tense with *going to* if it exists in their Read, Listen, Speak examples.

TEACH

Review subjects of sentences. Invite volunteers to offer sentences with the subject *actor. (The actor broke a leg. An actor is drinking green tea.)*

Have volunteers read aloud the first paragraph, the example sentence, and the second paragraph. Provide a sentence with three subjects. *(Todd, Ana, and Jim are in a play.)*

Have a volunteer read aloud the third paragraph and the example sentences. Ask students to name the predicate in each sentence *(dug for worms)*. Then have volunteers read aloud the last paragraph and the example sentence.

Write on the board *hopped across the beach*. Ask volunteers to write on the board two simple sentences that end with that predicate. Then ask students to explain how to combine the sentences into one sentence with a compound subject.

PRACTICE

ACTIVITY A

Complete this activity as a class. Remind students that the subject of a sentence is the person, place, or thing that performs an action. Ask volunteers to tell the subject of each sentence and what the subject does.

ACTIVITY B

Have partners complete this activity. Tell them to write each sentence on a separate sentence strip. Then have students underline the subject and write above it *single* or *compound*. Have students share their answers in small groups.

ACTIVITY C

Have small groups complete this activity. Ask students to circle each compound subject. When students have finished, invite them to share their answers with the class.

Compound Subjects

If two or more subjects in a sentence have the same predicate, they form a compound subject.

Chad and Nikki tied for first place.

In this sentence the compound subject is *Chad and Nikki*. You can use compound subjects to add variety to your writing. You can also use compound subjects to combine, or join, short, choppy sentences.

If two sentences have the same predicate, you can combine them.

Matt dug for worms. Curtis dug for worms.

These sentences have different single subjects. They are about two different people, Matt and Curtis. What is the same? The predicate is the same. Matt and Curtis did the same thing. They both *dug for worms*. The two sentences can be combined with the compound subject *Matt and Curtis*.

Matt and Curtis dug for worms.

ACTIVITY A **Find the subject in each sentence.**

1. <u>Kasey and Chris</u> planned a pet circus.
2. <u>Reggie</u> made posters.
3. <u>Mia and Miguel</u> rounded up the pets.
4. <u>The owners</u> trained their pets.
5. <u>Koren</u> announced the acts to the audience.
6. <u>My parrot</u> squawked.
7. <u>The puppies and kittens</u> ran into the crowd.
8. <u>The audience</u> laughed and clapped.

APPLY

WRITER'S CORNER

Help students find appropriate stories to read. When students have finished, invite volunteers to read aloud their sentences with compound subjects. Students should demonstrate the ability to use compound subjects.

Grammar in Action. Review the list of helping verbs on page 78. Tell students to make sure the verbs go with their compound subjects.

ASSESS

Note which students had difficulty using compound subjects. Use the Reteach option with those students who need additional reinforcement.

TEACHING OPTIONS

Reteach

Write on separate note cards subjects and predicates. Use both proper and common nouns as subjects. Place the subjects and predicates in two stacks facedown on a desk. Ask students to choose two subject cards and one predicate card. Ask a student to make up a sentence using both subjects and one predicate. Have students write the sentences on the board. Encourage volunteers to name the subjects and predicate in each sentence.

Two-Hat Sentences

Distribute two note cards to each student. Have students write on one note card their first name and on the other note card a predicate (*went fishing, are in a rock band, or fought a dragon*). Place the cards with students' names in one hat and the cards with the predicates in another hat. Have volunteers choose a name card and a predicate card. Challenge students to use the name they drew, their own name, and the predicate to write on the board a sentence with a compound subject.

ACTIVITY B Identify the subject in each sentence. Tell whether it is a single subject or a compound subject.

1. <u>Akimi</u> wanted to go skateboarding. single
2. <u>The skateboard</u> is black with many decals. single
3. <u>Akimi and Rex</u> performed a trick. compound
4. <u>The children</u> wore helmets. single
5. <u>Callie, Josh, and Carlos</u> got to the park late. compound
6. <u>The boys and girls</u> skated all day. compound
7. <u>The twins</u> learned a new trick. single
8. <u>Everyone</u> had a great time. single
9. <u>Kids and adults</u> enjoy the skate park. compound
10. <u>They</u> can't wait to go again next week. single

Activity C

1. José and Kiko played the piano.
2. The pencil and the pen fell off the desk.
3. The mad scientist and his assistant laughed.
4. Beth and Uncle George went to the capital.
5. Maria and the guide hiked the valley.
6. Paige and her mom washed the car.
7. Ben and Katie played soccer.
8. The fruit and the vegetables ripened.
9. Emilio and his sister moved away.
10. The flag and the branches swayed in the breeze.
11. The glass and the vase broke.
12. Tom and Marisol read a book.

ACTIVITY C Combine each pair of sentences into one sentence with a compound subject.

1. José played the piano. Kiko played the piano.
2. The pencil fell off the desk. The pen fell off the desk.
3. The mad scientist laughed. His assistant laughed.
4. Beth went to the capital. Uncle George went to the capital.
5. Maria hiked the valley. The guide hiked the valley.
6. Paige washed the car. Her mom washed the car.
7. Ben played soccer. Katie played soccer.
8. The fruit ripened. The vegetables ripened.
9. Emilio moved away. His sister moved away.
10. The flag swayed in the breeze. The branches swayed in the breeze.
11. The glass broke. The vase broke.
12. Tom read a book. Marisol read a book.

WRITER'S CORNER

Read a page from a story that tells about two or more characters. Write three sentences describing where the characters are and what they are doing. Use compound subjects in your sentences.

For Tomorrow

Ask students to write three sentences using compound subjects that tell what they did after school. Write your own sentences to share with the class.

Grammar in Action. Use at least two helping verbs in your sentences.

Personal Letters • 339

Read, Listen, Speak

Write on the board your sentences from yesterday's For Tomorrow homework. Ask volunteers to circle the compound subjects and underline the verbs in each sentence. Then have small groups share their sentences. Encourage students to tell what each sentence would be as two simple sentences.

GRAMMAR CONNECTION

Take this opportunity to talk about the present progressive tense. You may wish to have students point out any uses of the present progressive tense in their Read, Listen, Speak examples.

TEACH

Ask a volunteer to define a compound subject. Then invite volunteers to make up sentences with compound subjects.

Have volunteers read aloud the first paragraph and the example sentences. Ask which parts of these sentences are similar and which are different. *(The sentences have different subjects but similar predicates.)*

Ask a volunteer to read aloud the next paragraph. Invite volunteers to identify which predicate is more vivid and to explain why. Then read aloud the example sentence and the last paragraph. Ask students how *crept* makes a clearer picture than *went* in the sentence.

PRACTICE

ACTIVITY D

Encourage students to choose the predicate that gives readers a clearer picture. When students have finished, invite them to share their sentences with the class.

ACTIVITY E

Have partners complete this activity. Suggest that students read aloud the paragraph before choosing sentences that could be combined. Tell students to rewrite the paragraph with the new sentences. Invite students to read aloud their completed paragraphs.

ACTIVITY F

Have students complete this activity independently. Ask students to underline the compound subject in each sentence. When students have finished, invite volunteers to share their sentences with the class.

More Compound Subjects

Sometimes writers can combine subjects from sentences with different predicates. The predicates have to be close in meaning.

Olivia went upstairs silently. Kari crept upstairs silently.

Both predicates mean about the same thing. To make a sentence with a compound subject, choose one of the predicates to use. Which predicate would you use—*went upstairs silently* or *crept upstairs silently*? Use the predicate that makes a clearer picture.

Olivia and Kari crept upstairs silently.

Crept upstairs silently makes a clearer picture than *went upstairs silently.*

ACTIVITY D Combine each pair of sentences into one sentence with a compound subject.

1. A German shepherd went down the street. A dalmatian streaked down the street.
2. The president stepped out of the airplane. The Secret Service agents got out of the airplane.
3. Kim went across the lake in a kayak. I paddled across the lake in a kayak.
4. At the game Drew yelled a cheer. At the game Cameron and Lucy said a cheer.
5. Terrel went over the high jump. Randy leaped over the high jump.
6. Feng ran by. Ryan sprinted by.
7. Jared cleaned the roller coaster. Steve scrubbed the roller coaster.
8. The Cats were in the playoffs. The Squids played in the playoffs.

Activity D

1. A German shepherd and a dalmatian streaked down the street.
2. The president and the Secret Service agents stepped out of the airplane.
3. Kim and I paddled across the lake in a kayak.
4. At the game Drew, Cameron, and Lucy yelled a cheer.
5. Terrel and Randy leaped over the high jump.
6. Feng and Ryan sprinted by.
7. Jared and Steve scrubbed the roller coaster.
8. The Cats and the Squids played in the playoffs.

APPLY

WRITER'S CORNER

Help students brainstorm a list of monsters. Write them on the board. Tell students that they can write descriptions or brief stories. When students have finished, invite them to share their sentences in small groups. Students should demonstrate the ability to use compound subjects.

ASSESS

Note which students had difficulty writing sentences with compound subjects. Use the Reteach option with those students who need additional reinforcement.

Practice Book page 150 provides additional work with compound subjects.

TEACHING OPTIONS

Reteach

Write on the board the following predicate pairs:

1. **ran toward the house**
   scurried toward the house

2. **walked down the street**
   strolled down the street

Have students identify which predicate gives a clearer picture. Then ask students to write their own predicate pairs, making one more vivid than the other. Direct students to trade predicate pairs and identify which predicate is clearer. Have students write sentences using a compound subject and that predicate.

English-Language Learners

Have partners write on note cards predicates that can be pantomimed (*jumped rope, threw a ball, opened the door*). Collect the cards and mix them up. Have both students perform the action on the note card. Then have students write a sentence with a compound subject describing the action the students performed.

ACTIVITY E **Choose one of the paragraphs below. Combine short, choppy sentences into longer sentences with compound subjects.**

A. Carmen helped set the table. Her brother Tony helped set the table. Aunt Nora arrived at about 6:30. Aunt Julia came at about 6:30. Carmen was happy to see them. Tony was thrilled to see them. The chicken was grilled. The peppers were grilled. The guests enjoyed the tasty dinner. After dinner everyone went for a walk. Then Aunt Nora and Aunt Julia left. Carmen waved good-bye. Tony waved good-bye.

B. The farmer had spilled grain near the barn. The chicken pecked at the grain. The rooster ate the grain. The rooster flew to the roof. The chicken waddled across the yard. The chicks went across the yard. The barn in the yard was red. The wheelbarrow located in the yard was red. The day of work was finished. The chicken went to sleep. The chicks drifted off to sleep.

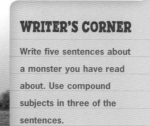

ACTIVITY F **Choose four sets of words below. Use each set in a sentence with a compound subject.**

A. squirrels, chipmunks, chattered
B. Jordan, Owen, painted
C. carrots, broccoli, grew
D. shark, seaweed, live
E. astronaut, alien, screamed
F. guide, hikers, photographed

WRITER'S CORNER

Write five sentences about a monster you have read about. Use compound subjects in three of the sentences.

Personal Letters • 341

For Tomorrow

Have students write three sentences for a letter or an e-mail. Tell students to use compound subjects in at least two of the sentences. Bring in your own three sentences with compound subjects.

OBJECTIVES

- To understand antonyms
- To use antonyms effectively in writing

WARM-UP

Read, Listen, Speak

Read aloud your sentences from yesterday's For Tomorrow homework. Ask students to identify the compound subjects. Then ask students to break the sentence into two simple sentences. Invite small groups to share their sentences. Tell students to discuss whether the sentences with compound subjects are written correctly.

GRAMMAR CONNECTION

Take this opportunity to talk about the past progressive tense. You may wish to have students point out any uses of the past progressive tense in their Read, Listen, Speak examples.

TEACH

Write on the board the words *easy, sick,* and *cold.* Invite volunteers to name synonyms for these words. Write the synonyms on the board. Then ask students to name words that have the opposite meaning. Write their responses on the board and explain that these words are antonyms of the first set of words.

Invite a volunteer to read aloud the first paragraph. Allow time for students to study the list of antonyms.

Read aloud the last paragraph. Ask volunteers to answer the question at the end of the paragraph.

PRACTICE

ACTIVITY A

Have students complete this activity independently. Tell students first to write all the words in Column A and then go back and choose the antonym in Column B that matches each word. When students have finished, invite volunteers to share their answers with the class.

ACTIVITY B

Have students complete this activity independently. When students have finished, challenge volunteers to take one of the words in each pair that is not an antonym and write an antonym for the word *(above, below; over, under).*

Antonyms

Antonyms are words that have opposite meanings. For example, *little* and *big* are antonyms. These words have opposite meanings of each other. Here are some other antonyms that you might know.

noisy	quiet
good	bad
in	out
happy	sad
thick	thin
first	last
up	down
fast	slow
come	go
weak	strong
messy	neat
forget	remember

Remember that writers use synonyms to make their writing interesting. Writers also use antonyms to make their writing interesting. They use antonyms to show the difference between people or things. What are some more antonyms for the word *good*?

APPLY

WRITER'S CORNER

Encourage students to try to write their sentences as part of a story. When students have finished, have them share their sentences in small groups. Students should demonstrate the ability to use antonyms in writing.

ASSESS

Note which students had difficulty identifying antonyms. Use the Reteach option with those students who need additional reinforcement.

TEACHING OPTIONS

Reteach

Have students write two sentences to describe today's weather, using two adjectives. Then ask students to exchange papers and rewrite the sentences using antonyms of the adjectives. Write the following examples on the board:

The weather is dry and sunny.

The weather is wet and cloudy.

Just the Opposite

Write on note cards words that have antonyms that are easy to pantomime. Have students choose a card and act out the antonym of the word. Challenge volunteers to say the antonym, being acted out. You can have students play as individuals or on teams. The team or person with the most correct responses wins the game.

ACTIVITY A Match each word in Column A with its antonym in Column B.

Column A		Column B
1. first	j	**a.** full
2. open	e	**b.** on
3. sick	i	**c.** day
4. new	d	**d.** old
5. off	b	**e.** closed
6. warm	g	**f.** little
7. sharp	h	**g.** cool
8. big	f	**h.** dull
9. empty	a	**i.** healthy
10. night	c	**j.** last

ACTIVITY B Tell whether the words in each pair are antonyms.

1. rough	smooth	yes	**7.** dark	bright	yes
2. above	over	no	**8.** many	few	yes
3. nasty	mean	no	**9.** straight	crooked	yes
4. hot	cold	yes	**10.** coarse	rough	no
5. win	lose	yes	**11.** wide	broad	no
6. near	close	no	**12.** tame	wild	yes

WRITER'S CORNER

Choose three pairs of antonyms from Activity A. Use each pair of antonyms in a sentence.

For Tomorrow

Have students find an article or a story and copy three sentences from it. Tell students to rewrite the sentences, substituting an antonym for at least one word in each sentence. Bring in your own rewritten sentences to share with the class.

Personal Letters • 343

Read, Listen, Speak

Read aloud your original sentences and your rewritten sentences from yesterday's For Tomorrow homework. Ask volunteers to identify the antonyms in each pair of sentences. Have students in small groups read aloud their original and rewritten sentences. Challenge students to identify the antonyms in each sentence pair.

GRAMMAR CONNECTION

Take this opportunity to talk about *is* and *are*, *was* and *were*. You may wish to have students point out any uses of *is* and *are*, *was* and *were* in their Read, Listen, Speak examples.

TEACH

Review the difference between antonyms and synonyms. Have students look over the list of antonyms on page 342. Guide students to understand that writers use synonyms to make their writing more interesting. Explain that knowing antonyms helps writers to make comparisons. Invite volunteers to write on the board pairs of antonyms.

PRACTICE

ACTIVITY C

Have partners complete this activity. When students have finished, ask them to write an additional pair of sentences using two of the antonyms from the word box. Ask volunteers to share their answers and new sentences with the class.

ACTIVITY D

Encourage students to read each sentence closely before deciding which antonym to use. Invite volunteers to read aloud their completed sentences.

ACTIVITY E

Have students complete the activity independently. Ask volunteers to read aloud their completed rhymes. Challenge students to write an additional pair of rhyming sentences using antonyms.

ACTIVITY F

Have partners complete this activity. Instruct students to take turns writing the antonym pairs. When students have finished, ask volunteers to share their answers with the class.

ACTIVITY C Complete each sentence with the antonym of the word that is underlined. Use an antonym from the word box.

soft	first	fast	down
old	laugh	last	never

1. December is the last month of the year. January is the __first__ month.
2. After Mom put the pictures up, one fell __down__.
3. Some pretzels are hard, and some are __soft__.
4. The tortoise finished the race first, and the hare finished __last__.
5. The snail was slow, but the dragonfly was very __fast__.
6. Dad bought me a new catcher's mitt because my __old__ mitt was falling apart.
7. My little sister wanted to cry when she fell, so I made funny faces to make her __laugh__.
8. I always set my alarm clock. I __never__ oversleep.

ACTIVITY D Complete each sentence with the antonym that best fits the sentence.

1. Be (careful careless) when you cross Main Street.
2. Only a (strong weak) person could carry that box.
3. I found a penny at the (bottom top) of the glass.
4. Please (open close) a new can of cat food for Zeus.
5. The (new old) rusty door hinge squeaked.
6. The (sleepy alert) guard did not notice the burglars.
7. Our car seems (roomy cramped) when all my brothers and sisters are in it.
8. The long, wooden table was (rough smooth), so Dad sanded it.

APPLY

WRITER'S CORNER

Allow time for students to write their lists of antonyms. Write on the board the words *little, nice,* and *slow*. After students have finished, have partners compare their lists. Write all the antonyms for each word in the appropriate column. Students should demonstrate an understanding of antonyms.

ASSESS

Note which students had difficulty using antonyms. Use the Reteach option with those students who need additional reinforcement.

Practice Book page 151 provides additional work with antonyms.

TEACHING OPTIONS

Reteach

Have students write a paragraph about an imaginary adventure. Tell them to use descriptive words in their paragraphs. Have students exchange paragraphs and rewrite the paragraphs using antonyms for as many words as possible. Tell students that they may have to make other changes to the sentences so that they make sense. Encourage students to use a classroom or online dictionary or thesaurus to find antonyms. Have volunteers read aloud each version of the paragraph.

Illustrated Antonyms

Have small groups play an antonym game. Direct students to write on note cards words that have antonyms. Have students mix up the cards and place them facedown on a desk. Ask one student at a time to choose a card and draw on the board a picture of an antonym for the word. Have students guess the antonym from the picture.

For Tomorrow

Tell students to choose a page in a book or children's magazine and copy three sentences. Ask students to rewrite the sentences, replacing some of the words with antonyms. Bring in your own three rewritten sentences with antonyms to share with the class.

ACTIVITY E Read these rhymes. Complete each rhyme with an antonym of the word that is underlined. Choose words from the word box.

in	sad	thin	bad	clean	mean

1. When the weather is <u>good</u>, we don't feel ___bad___.
   When a clown is <u>happy</u>, she isn't ___sad___.

2. When the dog is <u>out</u>, he won't come ___in___.
   I like my pancakes <u>thick</u>, not ___thin___.

3. When my room looks <u>messy</u>, I need to make it look ___clean___.
   With my friends and family I am <u>nice</u>, not ___mean___.

ACTIVITY F Think of an antonym for each word below. Write the antonym pairs. Possible answers below.

1. tall — short
2. easy — hard
3. late — early
4. end — beginning
5. push — pull
6. whisper — scream
7. here — there
8. young — old
9. find — lose
10. wrong — right

THE END

WRITER'S CORNER

How many antonyms can you think of for the words *little, nice,* and *slow*? Make a list with at least three antonyms for each word. Then compare your list with a partner's list.

OBJECTIVES

- **To understand the proper way to answer the telephone and to talk on the telephone**
- **To know how to take telephone messages**

WARM-UP

Read, Listen, Speak

Read aloud your original sentences and rewritten sentences. Tell students how antonyms changed the meaning of the sentences. Have small groups share their original sentences and rewritten sentences. Ask students to discuss how the antonyms changed the sentences.

GRAMMAR CONNECTION

Take this opportunity to talk about contractions with *not*. You may wish to have students point out any contractions with *not* in their Read, Listen, Speak examples.

TEACH

Invite a volunteer to read aloud the opening paragraph. Ask students how they would talk differently to a family member than to someone calling from a business.

Have volunteers read aloud the section Answering the Telephone. Explain that it is polite to turn down the radio or television when speaking on the phone to be able to give their attention to the person calling. Ask students to name other ways to be polite while on the phone *(not eating, answering questions with more than one word, letting the caller know if you are leaving the phone to get someone or something)*. Ask students how they usually answer the phone.

Have volunteers read aloud the section Talking on the Telephone. Ask students how they could show their feelings through their voices. Ask volunteers to say something showing that they are happy, surprised, or excited. Be sure students understand each bulleted item.

PRACTICE

ACTIVITY A

Have students complete this activity independently. Invite volunteers to share their answers with the class. Then ask volunteers why the other items are incorrect.

ACTIVITY B

Have partners complete this activity. Tell students to help each other think of the things that they would say for each situation. When students have finished, invite volunteers to perform their conversations for the class.

ACTIVITY C

Have partners work together to write a script, as in Activity B, for each item. Ask volunteers to perform their scripts for the class. Encourage students to tell what they liked about each conversation and what could be improved.

Telephone Conversations

Talking on the telephone is something that you might do every day. You might call someone or someone might call you. You might call a family member to catch up or a friend for help with math homework. A salesperson might call to speak to one of your parents. Your mom's boss might call.

Answering the Telephone

When the telephone rings, answer it right away. Before you answer it, turn down the radio or television. You can also leave a noisy room.

When you answer the phone, start by saying, "Hello." You might also say, "Hello, Peters' residence" or "Leah speaking, who's calling please?" Whatever you say, make sure it is how your parents want you to answer the telephone.

Talking on the Telephone

Be polite to anyone you talk to on the telephone, even if it is someone you don't know. Remember that the person you are talking to can't see you. Speak clearly and use your voice to show how you feel. The person on the other end won't be able to see you frown or smile.

Here are a few things that you need to remember.

- Pay attention to the person you are talking to.
- Don't talk to other people in the room.
- When you have finished, make sure you say good-bye.

APPLY

SPEAKER'S CORNER
Help students brainstorm conversation topics. Encourage partners not to look at each other while having their conversations. Then have volunteers present their calls to the class. Students should demonstrate an understanding of the proper way to answer and talk on the telephone.

ASSESS
Note which students had difficulty understanding the right way to answer and talk on the telephone. Use the Reteach option with those students who need additional reinforcement.

TEACHING OPTIONS

Reteach
Tell students you will be role-playing telephone conversations. If possible, begin with a ringing telephone. Explain that you will be the caller, but that you will not tell who you are before students answer the call. Dramatize the following situations: the school principal calling to speak with a parent, a telemarketer calling to sell something, a student from the class calling about a missing assignment. After role-playing each situation, discuss the call, point out appropriate things that were said, and help students make changes to statements that might not have been appropriate.

Telephone Safety
Discuss telephone safety at home or when using a cell phone. Then have small groups make a list of five telephone safety rules. Monitor groups to be sure their rules are appropriate. Have volunteers present their rules to the class. Display the lists on a bulletin board in the classroom.

ACTIVITY A Choose which sentences are good ways to answer the phone.

1. Hello, this is the Robinson residence.
2. Yeah, it's Jennifer.
3. Hi, Jon and Greta Calo's, how may I help you?
4. Hello, Theresa speaking.
5. Talk to me.
6. Who is this?

Hello?

Activity B
Students should speak clearly, be polite, and remember to say thank you and good-bye.

ACTIVITY B Tell what you would say in the following telephone conversation with your teacher.

(Telephone rings.)

Student: _____

Teacher: Hi (student's name). This is (teacher's name). I wanted to remind you that you are taking our class hamster home tomorrow. Do you have any questions?

Student: _____

Teacher: Okay. I will see you tomorrow.

Student: _____

Teacher: Good-bye.

ACTIVITY C Practice what you would say in these situations.

1. NoLeaks Roofers call and an adult can't come to the phone.
2. Your best friend calls to talk to you.
3. Your mother is at home, and her best friend calls to talk to her.
4. Your brother's boss at Grow 'em Garden Store calls, and your brother is in the backyard.
5. Your uncle calls to wish your sister a happy birthday. You are not sure if she is home, but your father is home.

SPEAKER'S CORNER
Meet with a partner and take turns "calling" each other. Show that you are happy, making a joke, worried, or sad by using only your voice.

For Tomorrow
Ask students to practice their telephone speaking skills by offering to answer the phone at home that evening. Tell students to answer the phone, using the skills they discussed in class. Take notes on your own telephone conversations to share with the class.

Personal Letters • 347

Read, Listen, Speak

Tell students about your telephone conversations from the previous evening. Note different levels of formality and how you avoided distractions. Have small groups discuss their experiences answering the phone. Ask students to share what they said and how the callers responded.

GRAMMAR CONNECTION

Take this opportunity to review verbs. You may wish to make students aware of verbs in their conversations.

TEACH

Invite a volunteer to read aloud the first paragraph of the section Taking a Message. Allow time for students to answer the question. Then read aloud the next paragraph. Ask students to share whether they have taken phone messages and what type of information they needed to write. Have a volunteer read aloud the bulleted list of questions. Explain that a good message includes answers to all these questions.

Ask a volunteer to read aloud the last paragraph. Point out that it is polite to thank the caller before hanging up. Guide students to understand that saying good-bye lets the caller know the conversation is over.

Have a volunteer read aloud the first paragraph of the section Making a Telephone Call. Ask volunteers to name some ways to find phone numbers *(online, in a telephone directory, in a personal address book)*. Have a volunteer read aloud the last paragraph. Tell students that they may want to say what day it is and when they can be reached when leaving a message on an answering machine. Guide students to understand that it is polite to leave a brief message. Explain that it is important to speak clearly and loud enough so that the person who listens to the message can understand it.

PRACTICE

ACTIVITY D

Have partners complete this activity. Tell them to take turns playing each part so that both students have a chance to write the message. When they have finished, invite volunteers to share their messages with the class.

ACTIVITY E

Tell partners to take turns as callers and receivers. Then have students practice leaving messages as one partner role-plays the answering machine by writing down everything the caller says.

Taking a Message

Suppose a caller wants to speak to your older brother. He's at work, and you ask if you can take a message. The caller says yes. What do you do to take a message?

Taking a message depends on what your parents want you to do. If they want only the name and phone number of the caller, that's all you ask for. Taking a message also depends on the caller. If a caller wants to give you a lot of information, write it down. Here are good questions to ask when taking a message.

- Who is calling?
- Who are you calling for?
- What is the message?
- What is your phone number?
- What would be a good time to return your call?

Be sure you have a pencil and paper near the phone. Also make sure to give the message to the person it is for. When you have finished taking a message, thank the caller. Then say good-bye and hang up.

Making a Telephone Call

What do you do when you make a telephone call? The first thing to do is to make sure that you have the right number. If you call the wrong number, don't hang up before saying you're sorry for calling the wrong number.

When someone answers the phone, say, "Hello," and tell who you are. Ask to speak to the person you called for. When that person answers, say, "Hello," and say your name again. If no one answers, leave a message on their voice mail or answering machine. Leave your name, number, and the reason for calling.

APPLY

SPEAKER'S CORNER

Encourage students to review the skills that they learned in this lesson. Suggest that students use the questions on page 348 as a guide for their messages. Invite volunteers to share their conversations with the class. Students should demonstrate the ability to leave and take a telephone message.

TechTip Have students listen to or watch one another's phone calls and tell if they answer the questions from page 348.

ASSESS

Note which students had difficulty taking and leaving telephone messages. Use the Reteach option with those students who need additional reinforcement.

After you have reviewed Lessons 3–5, administer the Writing Skills Assessment on pages 51–52 in the **Assessment Book.** This test is also available on the optional **Test Generator CD**.

Reteach

Bring in while-you-were-out message forms from a local office-supply store or make some of your own. Have students compare the information on the form with the questions in the Taking a Message section. Then have students take turns role-playing phone conversations as the caller and the person receiving the call. Direct the person receiving the call to use the form to take a message.

Playing Telephone

Play telephone two different ways. Have students sit in a circle. Begin the game by whispering quietly your name, phone number, and a brief message to one student. Have that student whisper the same information to the next student. Instruct students to keep relaying the message around the circle until each student has heard it. Ask the last student to say the information. Discuss how the message changed. Then repeat the game, but allow students to write notes about the message. Ask the last student to say the message. Discuss how writing the message assures that the information will be accurate.

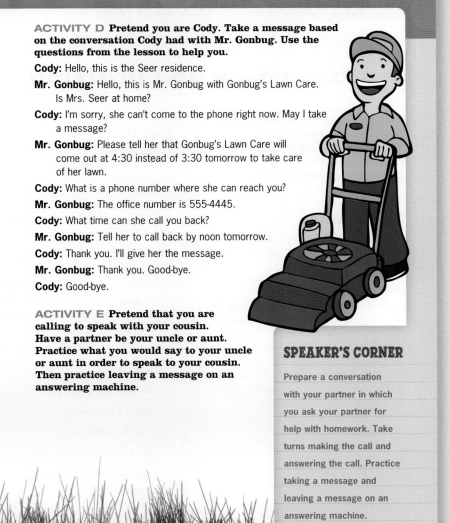

ACTIVITY D Pretend you are Cody. Take a message based on the conversation Cody had with Mr. Gonbug. Use the questions from the lesson to help you.

Cody: Hello, this is the Seer residence.

Mr. Gonbug: Hello, this is Mr. Gonbug with Gonbug's Lawn Care. Is Mrs. Seer at home?

Cody: I'm sorry, she can't come to the phone right now. May I take a message?

Mr. Gonbug: Please tell her that Gonbug's Lawn Care will come out at 4:30 instead of 3:30 tomorrow to take care of her lawn.

Cody: What is a phone number where she can reach you?

Mr. Gonbug: The office number is 555-4445.

Cody: What time can she call you back?

Mr. Gonbug: Tell her to call back by noon tomorrow.

Cody: Thank you. I'll give her the message.

Mr. Gonbug: Thank you. Good-bye.

Cody: Good-bye.

ACTIVITY E Pretend that you are calling to speak with your cousin. Have a partner be your uncle or aunt. Practice what you would say to your uncle or aunt in order to speak to your cousin. Then practice leaving a message on an answering machine.

SPEAKER'S CORNER

Prepare a conversation with your partner in which you ask your partner for help with homework. Take turns making the call and answering the call. Practice taking a message and leaving a message on an answering machine.

Tech Tip Videotape or record your conversation.

Personal Letters • 349

OBJECTIVE

- **To choose a topic, freewrite, and organize information**

PREWRITING AND DRAFTING

Read aloud the opening paragraph. Ask students to describe other purposes for writing personal letters besides thanking someone. Discuss things that students have read about in this chapter that will help to write personal letters *(the parts of a personal letter, different purposes for writing a personal letter, how to write sentences with compound subjects).*

Prewriting

Ask a volunteer to read aloud the paragraph. Explain that freewriting can help writers think of things to put in their letters. Tell students that organized freewriting notes will make drafting easier.

Choosing a Topic

Have a volunteer read aloud this section. Ask students to explain why Luis wanted to thank Alejandro for the guitar. Then ask how writing a letter to a cousin might be different from writing a letter to a grandparent. *(A letter written to a grandparent might be more formal.)*

👓 Tell students that having a clear idea and interesting, informative details will make their letter more enjoyable and more meaningful.

Your Turn

Read aloud this section. Help students think of things for which they might thank someone. Suggest that students think about friends, relatives, teachers, and coaches they might want to thank. Then allow time for students to choose a topic.

Freewriting

Invite volunteers to read aloud this paragraph. Explain that Luis freewrote a list of reasons so that he would have plenty of ideas to include in his letter. Then read aloud Luis's list. Discuss why Luis listed reasons that he liked the

guitar. *(By telling Alejandro specific reasons why he likes the guitar, Luis is showing why he appreciates the gift.)* Point out that Luis's list includes descriptions of the guitar that relate to different senses, such as sight and sound.

Your Turn

Read aloud this section. Explain that the more students freewrite, the more ideas they will have to include in their letters. Encourage students to list as many reasons as they can. If students are having difficulty, tell them to imagine that they are having a conversation with the person they want to

---

Writer's Workshop   Personal Letters

Prewriting and Drafting

There are many reasons to write thank-you letters. You might thank an uncle for helping you with your homework. You might thank a friend for a birthday present. When you write a thank-you letter, follow these steps.

Prewriting

Prewriting is the time to think about what you want to write. It is also the time to freewrite and to organize your ideas.

Choosing a Topic

Luis is a third grader. Luis's cousin Alejandro sent him a guitar last week. Luis likes playing the guitar, so he wanted 👓 **Ideas** to write Alejandro a letter to thank him. Luis wanted to tell his cousin that the guitar was the best gift he had ever received. He also wanted to tell Alejandro why the guitar was a great gift. Before Luis started writing his letter, he took time to think about what he wanted to write.

Your Turn

Brainstorm a list of people that you know and like. Then think about something you might thank them for. It can be something they did for you or something special they gave you. For example, you might want to thank someone for baking muffins for your class.

Freewriting

Luis freewrote to think of what to write in his letter. He knew that the guitar was the best gift he had ever received. Luis freewrote a list of reasons why he liked the guitar.

It is beautiful.

I was surprised when I got it.

It makes a cool sound.

I sit on the porch and play it.

It has a strap for my shoulder.

It has a picture of a sunset in a desert.

thank. Ask them what they would say to thank that person.

Organizing the Letter

Ask volunteers to read aloud the first paragraph. Explain that it is easier to organize the body of a letter if the ideas are listed in order of importance. Tell students that because Luis numbered his list, he can make sure that he includes in his letter the things he most wants to write. Have volunteers read aloud Luis's list.

Tell students that a personal letter, like any piece of writing, should have a logical organization. Tell students to decide how their ideas from freewriting relate to one another and in what order they want their reader to receive information.

Your Turn

Invite a volunteer to read aloud this section. Help students choose the strongest ideas from their freewriting lists. Then tell students to number their ideas just as Luis did. When students have finished, encourage them to share their lists with partners. Ask partners to talk about how they might use ideas from their lists in the body of their letters.

TEACHING OPTIONS

Thinking Like Someone Else

Write and photocopy a thank-you letter and distribute it to students. Ask them to imagine that they are the receiver of the letter. Have small groups to discuss how they might respond to the letter. Explain that if students put themselves in the place of the receiver, it will help them know what to write in their own thank-you letters.

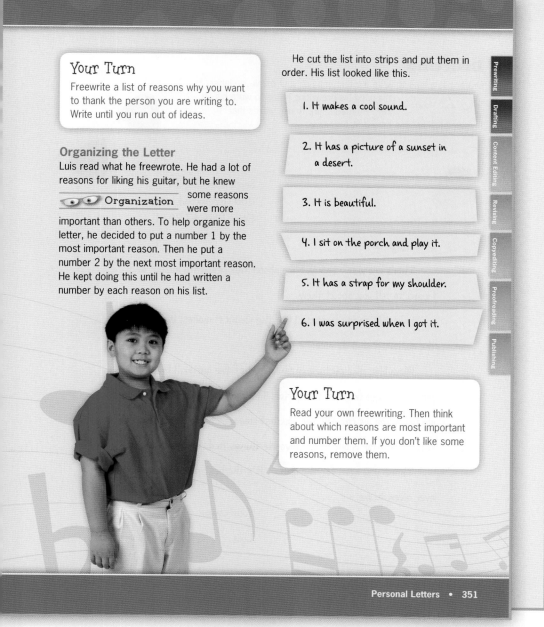

Your Turn

Freewrite a list of reasons why you want to thank the person you are writing to. Write until you run out of ideas.

Organizing the Letter

Luis read what he freewrote. He had a lot of reasons for liking his guitar, but he knew

Organization

some reasons were more important than others. To help organize his letter, he decided to put a number 1 by the most important reason. Then he put a number 2 by the next most important reason. He kept doing this until he had written a number by each reason on his list.

He cut the list into strips and put them in order. His list looked like this.

1. It makes a cool sound.

2. It has a picture of a sunset in a desert.

3. It is beautiful.

4. I sit on the porch and play it.

5. It has a strap for my shoulder.

6. I was surprised when I got it.

Prewriting · Drafting · Content Editing · Revising · Copyediting · Proofreading · Publishing

Your Turn

Read your own freewriting. Then think about which reasons are most important and number them. If you don't like some reasons, remove them.

Personal Letters • 351

Writer's Workshop Personal Letters

OBJECTIVE

- **To use prewriting notes to write a first draft**

Drafting

Ask a volunteer to read aloud the opening paragraph. Then read aloud Luis's first draft.

Have students compare Luis's list from prewriting with the body of his draft. Ask students what reasons Luis did not include from his list *(that the guitar has a shoulder strap, that he was surprised when he got the guitar).*

Guide students to understand that he did not include these reasons because they were not as important as the rest of the information in the letter. Then ask volunteers to suggest ways Luis might improve his draft.

 Tell students that their voice is their personality coming through in the writing.

Invite a volunteer to read aloud the paragraph following Luis's draft. Ask students to explain the purpose of Luis's letter.

Your Turn

Have a volunteer read aloud this section. Review the parts of a personal letter. Encourage students to look back at Lesson 1 to see where each part belongs. Explain that the bodies of students' letters should include the purpose and should include strong, descriptive writing.

Writer's Tip Explain that a draft is a work in progress, so leaving space for changes will help students when revising their drafts.

Drafting

Drafting is a time to write the first copy of your thank-you letter.

 Voice Luis used his prewriting notes to write his draft. He made sure to use words that sounded like he was talking to Alejandro.

> September 28, 20—
> 1100 Greenwood Lane
> Estes Park AZ 80711
>
> Dear Alejandro
>
> There are many things I like about this beautiful guitar, and I want to tell you about them.
>
> I like the guitar because I like the sound it makes. When I strum the guitar, it sounds nice.
>
> Mom likes the picture on the front of the guitar. I like the picture on the front of the guitar. The picture looks like the desert we saw when we came to see you last summer. Sitting on the porch with the guitar is one of my favorite things to do while playing it.
>
> Thank you agan for the guitar. It's the best present anyone has ever given to me.
>
> Your cousin,
>
> Luis

Telling More

Invite volunteers to read aloud this section. Discuss why descriptive sentences are important when writing personal letters. *(They help the reader picture what the writer is saying. They make the letter more interesting to read.)* Review some of the characteristics of descriptive writing from Chapter 3, such as using sensory words.

Tell students that word choice can make their writing more memorable and more meaningful. Remind students that a colorful synonym helps get their message and their voice across in their writing.

TEACHING OPTIONS

Letter Campaign

Tell students that sometimes personal letters can be used for a purpose other than communicating with a friend or relative. Explain that some people send letters to others to try to influence them. *(A group of students may send letters to their state's governor to try to get the ladybug designated their state's insect.)* Ask students what things they might like to write letters about. Then ask volunteers to name the people to whom the letters might be sent.

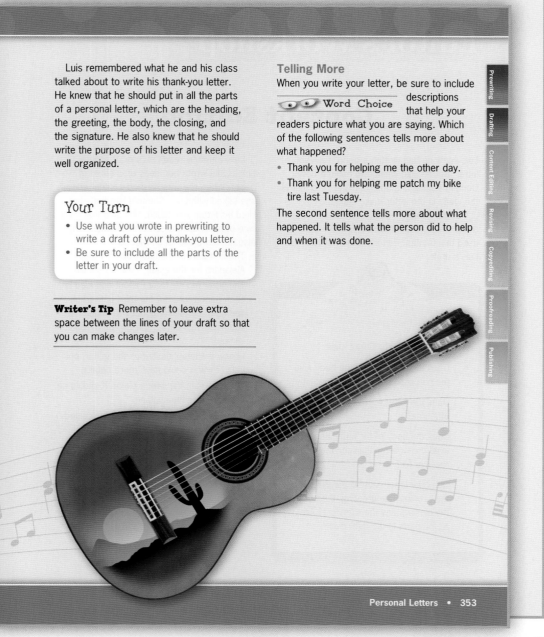

Luis remembered what he and his class talked about to write his thank-you letter. He knew that he should put in all the parts of a personal letter, which are the heading, the greeting, the body, the closing, and the signature. He also knew that he should write the purpose of his letter and keep it well organized.

Your Turn

- Use what you wrote in prewriting to write a draft of your thank-you letter.
- Be sure to include all the parts of the letter in your draft.

Writer's Tip Remember to leave extra space between the lines of your draft so that you can make changes later.

Telling More

When you write your letter, be sure to include **Word Choice** descriptions that help your readers picture what you are saying. Which of the following sentences tells more about what happened?

- Thank you for helping me the other day.
- Thank you for helping me patch my bike tire last Tuesday.

The second sentence tells more about what happened. It tells what the person did to help and when it was done.

Prewriting *Drafting* *Content Editing* *Revising* *Copyediting* *Proofreading* *Publishing*

Personal Letters • 353

OBJECTIVE
- **To edit a first draft for content**

CONTENT EDITING

Read aloud the first paragraph. Explain that a first draft often has mistakes that need to be fixed. Point out that Luis is content editing to make sure that his letter is well organized, contains important ideas, and is clearly written.

Have volunteers read aloud the next paragraph and the Content Editor's Checklist. Ask students to explain why Luis might want an editor to content edit his draft. *(An editor might find mistakes that Luis missed. The editor may have ideas that Luis had not thought about.)* Review the items on the checklist and clarify any misconceptions students may have. Tell students that when Lexy checks the parts of the letter, she will also check for the proper placement of the parts.

Ask volunteers to read aloud the next paragraph and Lexy's comments. Allow time for students to compare Lexy's suggestions with Luis's draft. For the third bulleted item, ask volunteers to suggest other ways that the guitar might have been described. Invite students to discuss how Lexy's suggestions might improve Luis's draft. Read aloud the last paragraph. Ask students if they agree with Lexy's suggestions.

Editor's Workshop
Personal Letters

Content Editing

Luis knew he had written a good thank-you letter. But he also wanted to make it better. Content editing is a time to make sure that all the ideas in the letter make sense.

To help content edit his letter, Luis asked a classmate, Lexy, to read his draft. Lexy used this Content Editor's Checklist to check Luis's draft.

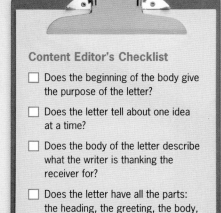

Content Editor's Checklist

☐ Does the beginning of the body give the purpose of the letter?

☐ Does the letter tell about one idea at a time?

☐ Does the body of the letter describe what the writer is thanking the receiver for?

☐ Does the letter have all the parts: the heading, the greeting, the body, the closing, and the signature? Are all the parts in the right place?

Lexy carefully read Luis's draft several times. She wrote her ideas on a sheet of paper. When she was finished content editing, she talked with Luis. She told him that she liked his letter very much. She said that it was nice of his cousin to send him a guitar. She also shared these ideas with Luis.

- The first part of the letter doesn't thank Alejandro for the guitar. I think it should.
- The letter mostly talked about one idea in each paragraph. But the third paragraph seems to be talking about two ideas. Can you make that paragraph two paragraphs instead?
- I know the letter describes the guitar, but I also think it could have more details.
- The date is in the wrong place. It should be moved under the heading.

Luis thanked Lexy for her ideas. He decided to think about her ideas before he made any changes.

Your Turn

Have volunteers read aloud this section. Instruct editors to use the Content Editor's Checklist to edit their drafts. Remind students to mark their changes carefully, using the proofreading marks on the inside back cover.

When students have finished, have them trade papers with a partner. Allow students time to content edit their partners' drafts, using the checklist. Then have students meet with their partners.

Remind editors to begin their suggestions by saying something positive about the draft. Then have students explain their ideas for improving the draft.

Allow time for students to talk about their suggestions. Tell students to think about each of their editor's suggestions, but to remember that the final decision about any change is up to the writer.

Your Turn

- Read your first draft. Use the Content Editor's Checklist to help you improve the draft. Answer each question on the checklist.
- Trade your draft with a partner. Use the Content Editor's Checklist as you edit. Read the draft once for each question on the checklist. Write your ideas as you edit.
- When you have finished, share your notes with your partner. Remember to start by telling your partner what you liked about the letter.

Prewriting

Drafting

Content Editing

Revising

Copyediting

Proofreading

Publishing

TEACHING OPTIONS

English-Language Learners

Group students whose primary language is the same. Ask students to trade letters with a partner. Have students evaluate their partner's letter, using the Content Editor's Checklist and writing their notes in English. When partners discuss their drafts, suggest that they do so in their primary language.

Guiding the Editor

Encourage writers to make notes in the margins of their drafts to guide their content editors. For example, writers might alert their editors that an incomplete section is "under construction" to prevent the editor from needlessly working on an incomplete paragraph. Tell writers to request feedback from their editors such as "Is this clear?" or "Do you understand this?" in different sections of their drafts.

OBJECTIVE
- **To revise a thank-you letter**

REVISING

Discuss previous writing projects that students have revised *(personal narratives, how-to articles, descriptions)*. Ask students to explain how revising their drafts made their writing better. Explain that editing and revising drafts help to make sure that the purpose of the letter is clear.

Read aloud the first paragraph. Then ask students to compare Luis's original draft with his revised draft. Invite volunteers to point to changes that Luis has made and to explain how he has used proofreading marks in his revised draft.

Read aloud the paragraph following the draft. Then ask volunteers to read aloud the bulleted list. After each item has been read, ask students to locate the change in the draft and to talk about how the change improves the letter.

- Luis added a sentence thanking Alejandro for the guitar.
- He made the last sentence in the third paragraph into a new paragraph.
- He described the picture on the front of the guitar.
- Luis moved the date so that it was in the right place, after the address.
- He added more details about playing the guitar on the porch. Luis also decided to add a detail about the way the guitar sounds.

Writer's Workshop | Personal Letters

Revising

Here is Luis's revised draft with his changes marked on it.

September 28, 20—
1100 Greenwood Lane
Estes Park AZ 80711

Dear Alejandro

Thank you for giving me your beautiful guitar.

There are many things I like about this ~~beautiful~~ guitar, and I want to tell you about them.

I like the guitar because I like the sound it makes. When I strum the guitar, it sounds nice. *like it is humming to me.*

Mom likes the picture *of the desert sunset* on the front of the guitar. I like the picture on the front of the guitar. The picture looks like the desert we saw when we came to see you last summer. Sitting on the porch with the guitar is one of my favorite things to do while playing it. *Mom can hear me inside the house. She tells me that I play well.*

Thank you again for the guitar. It's the best present anyone has ever given to me.

Your cousin,

Luis

Point out that Luis describes how the guitar both looks and sounds. Then ask students to suggest additional changes that might improve Luis's draft.

Your Turn

Read aloud this section. Encourage students to use their notes and their partner's suggestions to make changes that improve the content of their letter. Review what students have learned in this chapter that can help to create a

strong, well-written final letter *(understanding the parts of a letter, having a clear purpose, organizing a letter)*. Encourage students to use the proofreading marks on the inside back cover to mark their changes.

When students have finished, encourage them to double-check their content changes, using the Content Editor's Checklist. Emphasize the importance of making sure that the changes are clear and easy to understand.

Luis agreed with most of Lexy's ideas. Here are the changes he made to his draft.
- Luis added a sentence to the first paragraph. What did it say?
- He agreed with Lexy that the third paragraph should be made into two paragraphs. How did he do this?
- Luis thought that he should describe the guitar in more detail. What did he do?
- What change did Luis make to the heading?
- What details did Luis add to his letter?

Your Turn

- Use your ideas and your partner's ideas to revise your draft.
- Read your letter again. Use the Content Editor's Checklist to help you think of other ways to improve your letter.

Revising Do's

Share with the class the following tips for revising:

1. **It is okay to make mistakes**. You will write many drafts before you are finished. Give yourself plenty of time to revise. You may repeat content editing and revising several times before you are happy with your writing.

2. **Make your own choices.** Writing can be hard. You will make many choices as you write. That is what makes each person's writing special. Think about the ideas that other people have about your writing, but remember that you do not have to agree with all the ideas.

3. **Take a break.** Sometimes you have looked at a piece of writing for so long that you stop seeing your mistakes. Take a break from revising for a while. If you come back to it the next day, you can look at your work with fresh eyes.

Prewriting
Drafting
Content Editing
Revising
Copyediting
Proofreading
Publishing

OBJECTIVES
- **To copyedit a thank-you letter**
- **To proofread a thank-you letter**

COPYEDITING AND PROOFREADING

Copyediting

Have a volunteer read aloud the first paragraph. Help students understand that it was important for Luis to copyedit his work even though he was writing a letter. Tell students that it is important to check for clear writing and strong sentences whether they are writing something personal or something for school.

Ask a volunteer to read aloud the questions on the Copyeditor's Checklist. Clarify any confusion students may have about the items on the checklist.

Read aloud the paragraph following the Copyeditor's Checklist. Then have a volunteer read Luis's old sentence and his new sentence. Ask students whether they agree with Luis's decision to rewrite the sentence.

Read aloud the last paragraph. Ask students to find the sentences Luis might have combined to make a sentence with a compound subject *(the first two sentences of the third paragraph)*. Ask volunteers to suggest ways Luis might combine the two sentences.

Point out that when sentences are varied in length and structure, the writing has a more natural flow.

Your Turn

Invite a volunteer to read aloud this section. Then allow time for students to use the Copyeditor's Checklist to copyedit their letters. Help students to replace awkward or confusing sentences with sentences that are clearer or more descriptive. Emphasize the importance of checking for one kind of mistake at a time.

Writer's Tip Suggest that students read aloud their letters to a partner to make sure they are clear.

Proofreading

Read aloud the first two paragraphs. Ask students why Luis might have missed mistakes that Bobby might be able to find *(because Luis had looked at his draft so many times and might read what he wanted it to say, not what was actually on the draft).*

Editor's Workshop
Personal Letters

Copyediting and Proofreading

Copyediting

Luis made many content changes to his letter. But he knew that he could make his letter better by copyediting it. Copyediting means checking that all the sentences are strong and correct. It also means making sure the words in the letter make sense. Luis used this Copyeditor's Checklist to copyedit his letter.

Copyeditor's Checklist

- ☐ Are all the sentences complete sentences?
- ☐ Have you made sure that no sentences are awkward or confusing?
- ☐ Do all the words mean what you think they mean?
- ☐ Do subjects that use the same predicate make a compound subject?

Luis noticed that the first sentence of his new fourth Sentence Fluency paragraph was confusing. He decided to rewrite the sentence. Look at his revision.

Old Sentence: Sitting on the porch with the guitar is one of my favorite things to do while playing it.

New Sentence: One of my favorite things to do is sit on the porch and play the guitar.

Luis also found two sentences with subjects that had the same predicate. He combined those sentences to make one sentence with a compound subject. Can you find the two sentences that he might have combined?

Your Turn

- Carefully read your letter. Use the Copyeditor's Checklist to edit your draft.
- Be sure to check for one kind of mistake at a time when you copyedit your letter.

Have students read aloud each item on the Proofreader's Checklist. Then read aloud the last paragraph. Ask students to find the two missing commas *(between Estes Park and AZ in the heading and after Alejandro in the greeting).*

Tell students that conventions are the mechanics of good writing. They include spelling, punctuation, and capitalization.

Your Turn

Read aloud this section and tell students to proofread their letters. Encourage students to look for one kind of mistake at a time and to make sure that no new mistakes were introduced during previous revisions. Then allow time for students to trade their letters with partners and proofread each other's letters.

Grammar in Action. Invite a volunteer to find the misspelled word. *(Again is spelled* agan *in the last paragraph.)*

TEACHING OPTIONS

One at a Time

To improve their editing skills, encourage students to check one line at a time for each kind of mistake on the Proofreader's Checklist. Have students take two blank pieces of paper and place them on the page they are editing so that they can see only one line at a time.

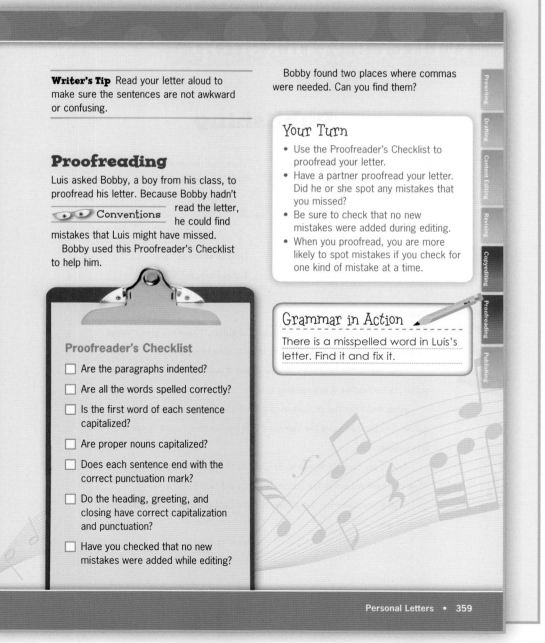

Writer's Tip Read your letter aloud to make sure the sentences are not awkward or confusing.

Proofreading

Luis asked Bobby, a boy from his class, to proofread his letter. Because Bobby hadn't ~~Conventions~~ read the letter, he could find mistakes that Luis might have missed.

Bobby used this Proofreader's Checklist to help him.

Proofreader's Checklist

☐ Are the paragraphs indented?

☐ Are all the words spelled correctly?

☐ Is the first word of each sentence capitalized?

☐ Are proper nouns capitalized?

☐ Does each sentence end with the correct punctuation mark?

☐ Do the heading, greeting, and closing have correct capitalization and punctuation?

☐ Have you checked that no new mistakes were added while editing?

Bobby found two places where commas were needed. Can you find them?

Your Turn

- Use the Proofreader's Checklist to proofread your letter.
- Have a partner proofread your letter. Did he or she spot any mistakes that you missed?
- Be sure to check that no new mistakes were added during editing.
- When you proofread, you are more likely to spot mistakes if you check for one kind of mistake at a time.

Grammar in Action

There is a misspelled word in Luis's letter. Find it and fix it.

Prewriting

Drafting

Content Editing

Revising

Copyediting

Proofreading

Publishing

Personal Letters • 359

OBJECTIVE
- **To publish a thank-you letter**

PUBLISHING

Have a volunteer read aloud the first paragraph. Invite volunteers to explain how Luis might go about mailing his thank-you letter to Alejandro *(typing or writing the letter, putting the letter in an addressed envelope, putting a stamp on the envelope, mailing the letter).*

Ask a volunteer to read aloud Luis's finished thank-you letter. Tell students to compare Luis's final draft with his first draft. Have volunteers point out all the changes that Luis has made. Then have students explain how the changes made the letter stronger. Ask students how the purpose of his letter has been accomplished. *(Luis thanked Alejandro and told Alejandro why he enjoyed the guitar.)* Discuss with students the many ways they might publish their writing.

 Tell students that presentation, including neatness and consistent margins and spacing, in a personal letter will affect the way it is received.

Your Turn

Have volunteers read aloud this section. Encourage students to proofread their letters one more time after they have printed or written in ink their final copies. Show students how to fold a letter so that it fits inside an envelope.

Writer's Workshop
Personal Letters

Publishing

Luis carefully wrote the finished draft of his thank-you letter. He also carefully made all the proofreading changes. Publishing his letter meant that he would mail it to his cousin Alejandro. Here is Luis's finished letter.

1100 Greenwood Lane
Estes Park, AZ 80711
September 28, 20—

Dear Alejandro,

Thank you for giving me your beautiful guitar. There are many things I like about this guitar, and I want to tell you about them.

I like the guitar because I like the sound it makes. When I strum the guitar, it sounds like it is humming to me.

Mom and I like the picture of the desert sunset on the front of the guitar. The picture looks like the desert we saw when we came to see you last summer.

One of my favorite things to do is sit on the porch and play the guitar. Mom can hear me inside the house. She tells me that I play well.

Thank you again for the guitar. It's the best present anyone has ever given to me.

Your cousin,

Luis

Point out that students should put the letter into the envelope with the first fold down so when the receiver unfolds the letter, it is not upside down.

Discuss how to address an envelope and where to place the stamp. Tell students to ask their parents for stamps and for help mailing their thank-you letters.

ASSESS

Have students assess their finished personal letter using the reproducible Student Self-Assessment on page 361y. A separate Personal Letter Scoring Rubric can be found on page 361z for you to use to evaluate their work.

Plan to spend tomorrow doing a formal assessment. Administer the personal letter Writing Prompt on **Assessment Book** pages 53–54.

TEACHING OPTIONS

Postal Challenge

Students may be unfamiliar with the postal two-letter state abbreviations. Provide students with a list of states and abbreviations. Have students find the postal abbreviation for their own state and for states with famous cities, landmarks, or parks.

Portfolio Opportunity

Remind students to keep a copy of their final thank-you letters in their portfolios. Point out that having a portfolio will help students keep track of the progress they are making with their writing.

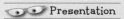 **Presentation** There are many ways you can publish your letter. However you decide to publish, make sure the message is clear.

 Mail or e-mail your letter. If you mail it, make sure to check the bulleted list at the right. Don't forget to sign your letter.

 Create a class display of all the situations in which people might send a personal letter. Include photos, drawings, and personal experiences.

 Post your letter on your classroom's wiki, blog, or Web site. You can receive comments about your letter and review others' work.

 Post your letter on a bulletin board along with your classmates' letters. Label the display "We Love Letters!"

Your Turn

Getting mail from someone you know can be exciting. A personal letter is like a gift. After your teacher reads your letter, mail it.

Follow these steps to finish your letter.

- Use a computer or a pen and paper to make a final copy of your letter.
- Proofread your letter one more time. Use your computer's spell-checker if you can.
- Write the address on an envelope. Check to make sure the address is correct.
- Fold your letter and place it in the envelope. See below.
- Seal the envelope and put a stamp on it.
- Ask a parent or your teacher to help you mail it.

Prewriting | Drafting | Content Editing | Revising | Copyediting | Proofreading | Publishing

1

2

3

Name _____ Date _____

Personal Letter

	YES	NO
Ideas		
Do I focus on my purpose for writing?		
Organization		
Do I include a greeting that begins with *Dear* and the reader's name?		
Does the body share my ideas?		
Do I end with a closing and my signature?		
Voice		
Does my personality shine through?		
Word Choice		
Do I use everyday words?		
Sentence Fluency		
Do I use different kinds of sentences, including those with compound subjects?		
Conventions		
Do I use correct grammar?		
Do I use correct spelling?		
Do I use correct punctuation and capitalization?		
Presentation		
Do I use neat handwriting or typing?		
Do I have consistent margins and spacing?		
Do I include a heading that gives my address and the date?		
Additional Items		

Name _____

Date _____ Score _____

POINT VALUES

0 = not evident
1 = minimal evidence of mastery
2 = evidence of development toward mastery
3 = strong evidence of mastery
4 = outstanding evidence of mastery

Personal Letter

Ideas

	POINTS
a clear focus on the writer's purpose	

Organization

a greeting that usually begins with *Dear* and the recipient's name	
a body that shares the writer's ideas	
an appropriate closing followed by the writer's signature	

Voice

the writer's personality	

Word Choice

natural language	

Sentence Fluency

sentence variety, including some compound subjects	

Conventions

correct grammar and usage	
correct spelling	
correct punctuation and capitalization	

Presentation

neat handwriting or typing	
consistent margins and spacing	
a heading that gives the writer's address and the date	

Additional Items

Total	

CHAPTER FOCUS

LESSON 1: What Makes a Good Book Report?

LESSON 2: Character and Plot

- **GRAMMAR:** Adjectives
- **STUDY SKILLS:** Parts of a Book
- **WRITING SKILLS:** Compound Predicates
- **WORD STUDY:** Prefixes
- **SPEAKING AND LISTENING SKILLS:** Oral Book Reports
- **WRITER'S WORKSHOP:** Book Reports

SUPPORT MATERIALS

Practice Book
Writing, pages 152–156

Assessment Book
Chapter 5 Writing Skills,
    pages 55–56
Book Report Writing Prompt,
    pages 57–58

Rubrics
Student, page 399y
Teacher, page 399z

Test Generator CD

Grammar
Section 5, pages 109–134

Customizable Lesson Plans
www.voyagesinenglish.com

Book Reports

WHAT IS A BOOK REPORT?

For students book reports are one of the most common forms of expository writing. A good book report begins with a thought-provoking book and an enthusiastic reader. Novels, rather than nonfiction works, are often the best subjects for classroom book reports. A good book report goes beyond recalling character, setting, plot, and theme; it also shows conclusions that the reader has drawn and judgments the reader has made. Good book reports are written in a confident, lively voice. They use exact words that make a book's plot understandable.

A good book report includes the following:

- [ ] A clear focus on the book
- [ ] Logical organization
- [ ] A beginning that identifies the title, the author, the characters, and the setting
- [ ] A middle that briefly describes the main events in time order
- [ ] An ending that sums up the writer's opinion of the book
- [ ] A variety of sentences, including those with compound predicates
- [ ] A confident, lively voice
- [ ] Exact words

LiNK   Use the following titles to offer your students examples of well-crafted book report topics:

Dawn Undercover by Anna Dale

Kids Review Kids' Books by Storyworks

The Mouse and the Motorcycle by Beverly Cleary

The Wheel on the School by Meindert DeJong

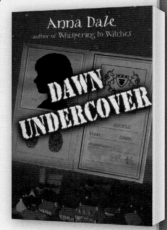

"Reading a book is like re-writing it for yourself."

—Angela Carter

WRITER'S WORKSHOP TIPS

Follow these ideas and tips to help you and your class get the most out of the Writer's Workshop:

- Review the traits of good writing. Use the chart on the inside back cover of the student and teacher editions.

- Fill your classroom library with a variety of quality fiction, including historical fiction, realistic fiction, science fiction, and fantasy.

- Create a bulletin-board display of popular book jackets that can be opened so that the inside flaps can be read. Inside each jacket, provide a two- or three-sentence summary of the book.

- Before writing begins, meet individually with each student about the book he or she has chosen. Guide the student to recount important information (characters, setting, problem, solution, conclusion) and express opinions and reading recommendations.

- Remind students that film adaptations of books often change important parts of the story, including character, plot, and theme.

- Play podcasts of book reviews and have students record their own book review podcasts to share.

CONNECT WITH GRAMMAR

Throughout the Writer's Workshop, look for opportunities to integrate adjectives with writing book reports.

☐ Challenge students to use adjectives as subject complements and compound subject complements when telling about their book.

☐ Have students use demonstrative adjectives when referring to the subjects of their book reports (this story, these characters).

☐ Have students highlight the adjectives in their drafts.

SCORING RUBRIC

Book Report

Point Values
0 = not evident
1 = minimal evidence of mastery
2 = evidence of development toward mastery
3 = strong evidence of mastery
4 = outstanding evidence of mastery

	POINTS
Ideas	
a clear focus on the book	
Organization	
a beginning that identifies the title, author, characters, and setting	
a middle that briefly describes the main events in time order	
an ending that sums up the writer's opinion of the book	
Voice	
confident, lively voice	
Word Choice	
carefully chosen adjectives	
Sentence Fluency	
a variety of sentences, including those with compound predicates	
Conventions	
correct grammar and usage	
correct spelling	
correct punctuation and capitalization	
Presentation	
neatness	
consistent margins and spacing	
Additional Items	
Total	

Full-sized, reproducible rubrics can be found at the end of this chapter.

CHAPTER 5
Book Reports

INTRODUCING THE GENRE

Tell students that Chapter 5 explains how to write a book report. Ask volunteers to name books that they have read recently. For each example ask students to tell what the book was about and whether or not they enjoyed the book. Explain that a book report is a way for students to tell about a book and their personal experience of reading the book.

Elaborate on the following characteristics of a book report.

- A book report provides information about a book and shares what the writer thinks of the book.
- The beginning includes the title of the book, the name of the author, the characters, and the setting.
- The middle tells what the book is about.
- The ending tells what the writer thought of the book and explains why.

Reading the Literature Excerpt

Ask volunteers to read aloud the book report. Have students explain why it is a good example. Ask students if the book report makes them want to read *Dawn Undercover*. Have students tell about book reports they have read or written.

Book Reports

LiNK   Dawn Undercover

The excerpt from Kristi Olson's book report on *Dawn Undercover* is a good example because it has the following:

- Information about a book and the writer's opinion of the book
- The title of the book and the name of the author
- An ending that tells what the writer thought of the book and explains why

As students read the excerpts of book reports in this chapter, be sure to identify the characteristics of book reports. Also be sure to point out adjectives in the excerpts, including the adjectives before nouns (*fun read, spy novel*), adjectives as subject complements (*adventurous, important, fun*), and proper adjectives (*British spying organization*) in this excerpt.

LiNK   *Dawn Undercover*
by Anna Dale
Reviewed by Kristi Olson

Would you love to be a spy? Doesn't it sound so adventurous, so important, and most of all, like a whole lot of fun? That's exactly why 11-year-old Dawn Buckle is so thrilled to be selected as a child spy for the British spying organization, S.H.H. (Strictly Hush-Hush) in the P.S.S.T. division (Pursuit of Scheming Spies and Traitors).

. . . Upon arriving at the P.S.S.T. headquarters, she is introduced to a quirky cast of spy-types who work hard to train her in the ins and outs of spying. . . . It seems that she has been made for spying and now will be put to the test on her first mission. The mission aims to track down a missing spy along with an evil criminal, Murdo Meek.

Dawn Undercover is a fun read with mystery and adventure—all good things a spy novel should possess. The character of Dawn Buckle is highly likeable . . . Though the book feels long at points, the ending is highly satisfying.

> This book report tells who the story is about, what happens in the story, and what the reader thought of the book.

362

Reading the Student Model

Explain that the book report is about *Sarah, Plain and Tall* by Patricia MacLachlan. Invite students to read aloud the book report. Then ask volunteers to identify the information that appears in the first paragraph *(title of the book, name of the author, details about the character and setting).*

Point out that the three paragraphs in the middle of the book report tell what the book is about. Review the three middle paragraphs. Invite volunteers to guess how the story might end.

Tell students that the last paragraph tells how the writer felt about the book. Ask students if this book report interested them in reading *Sarah, Plain and Tall.*

TEACHING OPTIONS

Scavenger Hunt

Have small groups search the classroom, the school library, and the Internet for examples of book reports. Encourage students to compare the book reports they find to the model.

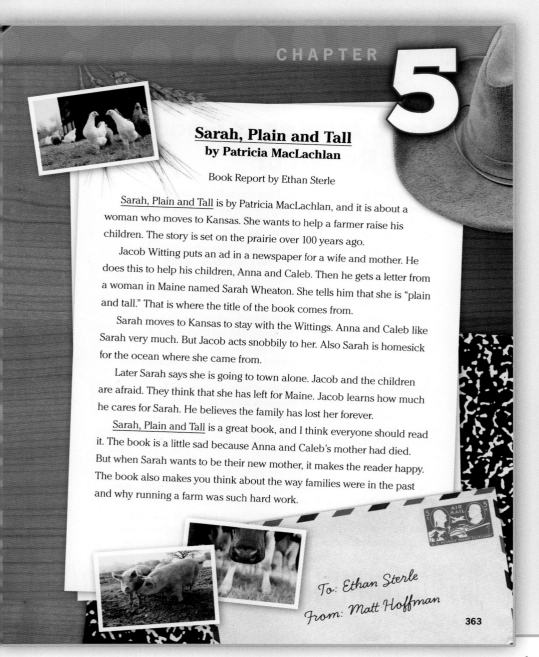

CHAPTER **5**

Sarah, Plain and Tall
by Patricia MacLachlan

Book Report by Ethan Sterle

Sarah, Plain and Tall is by Patricia MacLachlan, and it is about a woman who moves to Kansas. She wants to help a farmer raise his children. The story is set on the prairie over 100 years ago.

Jacob Witting puts an ad in a newspaper for a wife and mother. He does this to help his children, Anna and Caleb. Then he gets a letter from a woman in Maine named Sarah Wheaton. She tells him that she is "plain and tall." That is where the title of the book comes from.

Sarah moves to Kansas to stay with the Wittings. Anna and Caleb like Sarah very much. But Jacob acts snobbily to her. Also Sarah is homesick for the ocean where she came from.

Later Sarah says she is going to town alone. Jacob and the children are afraid. They think that she has left for Maine. Jacob learns how much he cares for Sarah. He believes the family has lost her forever.

Sarah, Plain and Tall is a great book, and I think everyone should read it. The book is a little sad because Anna and Caleb's mother had died. But when Sarah wants to be their new mother, it makes the reader happy. The book also makes you think about the way families were in the past and why running a farm was such hard work.

To: Ethan Sterle
From: Matt Hoffman

363

For Tomorrow

Tell students to find a book at home or at the library that they have read and might want to use for a book report. Ask students to record the title of the book and the name of the author. Bring in your own title and author to share.

OBJECTIVE
* **To recognize characteristics of a book report**

WARM-UP

Read, Listen, Speak

Share the title and author of your book from yesterday's For Tomorrow homework and tell why you chose it. Have small groups share the book information they recorded. Ask students to tell why they chose their books for a possible book report.

GRAMMAR CONNECTION

Take this opportunity to talk about adjectives before nouns. You may wish to have students point out any adjectives before nouns in their Read, Listen, Speak examples.

TEACH

Have a volunteer read aloud the first paragraph. Ask volunteers to name their favorite books. Use students' examples to illustrate the wide scope of time and place found in books. Then read aloud the next paragraph. Explain that book-report writers are authorities on their books, so they choose words that show they are confident about what they are saying.

Invite volunteers to read aloud the section Beginning. Ask students to explain why it is important to include the author and title in a book report *(to tell readers what book is being written about, to help readers who are interested in reading the book to find it on their own)*.

Ask a volunteer to read aloud the section Middle. Explain that book-report writers want to tell just enough to get a reader interested in reading the book. Name a familiar book that most students are likely to know. Help students to distinguish between parts that should be included in a book report and parts that should be left out.

Have a volunteer read aloud the section Ending. Point out that the ending of the book report on page 363 tells more than just whether or not the writer liked the book. Explain that the ending also describes some of the feelings that the writer had when reading the book. Ask students to name the feelings the writer of the book report had and to explain what it was in the book that caused the writer to feel that way *(sad, because Anna and Caleb's mother died; happy, because Sarah wants to be their new mother).*

PRACTICE

ACTIVITY A
Have partners complete this activity. When students have finished, invite volunteers to share their answers with the class.

ACTIVITY B
After students have completed the activity, ask volunteers to share their answers. Discuss additional information that might be included in a book report.

What Makes a Good Book Report?

Books are like magic carpets. They can take you anywhere you want to go. There is much to see and do in the world of books.

Writing a book report is one way to share what you have read. In a book report, include the title, the author, what the book is about, and what you think of the book. When you write a book report, use language that shows you know the book well. Write your opinions in a way that shows you are sure about how you feel.

Beginning

Book reports start with the title of the book and the name of the author. The title should be complete. The author's name should be spelled correctly.

The beginning of a book report should tell who the story is about. But readers want to know more than just the names of the people or animals in the book. Readers also want to know something about what the people or animals are like.

Sometimes the beginning describes the setting. The setting is when and where the story takes place. If the setting is important to the story, include it in your book report.

Middle

In the middle of a book report, you tell what happens in the story. Book reports tell just enough to make the audience want to read the book. You might tell about a problem a person in the book has, but don't tell how the problem was solved. Telling too much can spoil surprises for the reader. Don't tell the reader how the book ends!

APPLY

WRITER'S CORNER

Encourage students to find books that they might like to read. When students have found their books, invite them to share their titles and authors with the class. Have students tell how they made their choices. Students should demonstrate the ability to choose books for book reports.

ASSESS

Note which students had difficulty understanding what makes a good book report. Use the Reteach option with those students who need additional reinforcement.

TEACHING OPTIONS

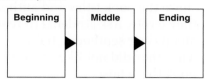

Reteach

Make copies of a graphic organizer like the one shown below for students to complete.

Beginning	Middle	Ending

Have students choose a favorite book about which to write notes. Explain that students should write in the appropriate boxes notes with their ideas for the beginning, middle, and ending of a book report about their chosen book. Have students tell why they included the information in each box of the organizer.

Book Mural

Have students choose a book to write about. Challenge students to illustrate a book cover for the book. Then have students write the title and author on the book cover. Ask students to write one sentence that tells why they liked the book. Have students glue their book covers onto a large sheet of paper to make a mural. Display the mural on a wall in the classroom.

Ending

The ending of a book report is where you tell what you think of the book. You should explain why you think the way you do. This is the place to tell about the parts of the book that you liked. It can also be the place to tell about the parts of the book that you did not like.

Activity A

1. *Sarah, Plain and Tall*
2. Patricia MacLachlan
3. over 100 years ago in Kansas
4. Jacob, Caleb, Anna, and Sarah
5. Answers will vary.
6. Answers will vary.
7. Answers will vary.

ACTIVITY A **Answer the questions about the book report on page 363.**

1. What is the title of the book?
2. Who wrote the book?
3. What is the setting?
4. Who are the people in the book?
5. What problems do the people have?
6. Why does the author think people will like this book?
7. After reading this book report, would you want to read the book? Why or why not?

Activity B

1. middle
2. beginning
3. ending
4. beginning
5. beginning
6. ending

ACTIVITY B **Tell whether each piece of information below would be found in the beginning, middle, or ending of a book report.**

1. A description of a character's problem
2. The title and the author's name
3. The reason why the writer liked or disliked the book
4. The names of the main characters
5. A description of the setting
6. A sentence telling people to read the book

WRITER'S CORNER

Find three books in the library. Write the titles of the books and the authors' names. Carefully check that you spelled the names and the titles correctly.

For Tomorrow

Ask students to search at home or in the library for a book they read but did not like or a book they read that had parts they did not like. Tell students to list the book's title and author and to write about something they did not like in the book. Bring in your own title, author, and reason for not liking a book.

WARM-UP

Read, Listen, Speak

Share the title and author and reason for not liking a book from yesterday's For Tomorrow homework. Have small groups share the book titles and authors they wrote. Ask students to read aloud their sentences, telling what they did not like about the book they chose.

GRAMMAR CONNECTION

Take this opportunity to talk about adjectives as subject complements. You may wish to have students point out any adjectives as subject complements in their Read, Listen, Speak examples.

TEACH

Create on the board a three-column chart with the headings *Beginning, Middle,* and *Ending.* Have volunteers list under each heading what is included in each part of a book report.

PRACTICE

ACTIVITY C

Have partners complete this activity. Encourage students to read their chosen paragraphs twice before writing. Ask students to make two columns and to write the time and place in one column and the clue words in the other. Ask volunteers to share their responses with the class.

ACTIVITY D

Have students read the paragraphs silently. Tell students to write why one book report is better than the others. When students have finished, invite volunteers to read aloud their answers. Encourage volunteers to offer suggestions for improving the other book reports.

LiNK Ask a volunteer to read aloud the excerpt from the book report on *Into the Land of the Unicorns.* Ask students to tell if the excerpt belongs in the beginning, middle, or ending of a book report and how they know *(middle, because it tells what happens in the story).* Then ask what the excerpt tells about the setting of the story *(that it takes place in a magical land).*

ACTIVITY C Read the following paragraphs from books. Choose one. Work with a partner and describe the time and place as fully as you can. What clue words let you know the setting?

A. A bright light flashed in the playground, and the drum noise burst out louder than ever. It spread all over the sky before curling away into nothingness. Polly Platt, who was easily frightened, bit her lip. Suddenly, there was an enormous cracking sound as though the walls of the school had split open. Bobby Briggs yelled and Polly Platt rushed toward Mr. Salt. But Mr. Salt didn't yell or rush anywhere. No, Mr. Salt smiled.

—*Summer Magic* by Margaret Nash

B. I'm beginning to see that Joe Feather was right not to try and find a way over the mountains for the wagons. They're much steeper than they look from the plains. Right now I'm on a patch of grass. But I can't be sure how the feed will be beyond. Before the sun went down, I checked the way ahead. . . .

In the morning I'll try the horses on one of the slopes and see if they can manage the climb.

—*The Climb* by Roger Carr

C. He took the path along the hedge towards the woods where he and his pals often played, hoping he might find somebody else to fool instead. At the very least, he thought, he could squirt them with his trusty water pistol that bulged from the back pocket of his jeans. But, in fact, what he did find in the middle of the woods made all thoughts of April Fools' Day fly right out of his head.

—*April Aliens* by Rob Childs

APPLY

WRITER'S CORNER

Tell students to include the title of the story and the name of the author. When students have finished, invite them to read aloud their work. Students should demonstrate the ability to form opinions about a book.

Grammar in Action. Have students use two adjectives before nouns and two adjectives as subject complements. Ask volunteers to read aloud their sentences and have students identify the adjectives.

ASSESS

Note which students had difficulty forming opinions about books. Use the Reteach option with those students who need additional reinforcement.

Practice Book page 152 provides additional work with the characteristics of a book report.

TEACHING OPTIONS

Reteach

Ask students to choose a book about which they have a strong opinion. Have students write five strong adjectives that describe the book. Then ask students to choose two of the words to write sentences that tell why that word describes the book.

Both Sides of the Story

Explain that book reviews are short book reports written in newspapers, online, or in magazines. Point out that book reviews tell what the book is about, but that they also give the writer's opinion of the book. Have students find a short book review that describes a book and also gives the writer's opinion of the book. Have students share their book reviews with a partner.

ACTIVITY D Read the following parts of book reports. Think about why the writer liked each book. Which book report is the best? Explain why.

1. In the book *Crow Boy* by Taro Yashima, I liked reading about Chibi. He was a young boy. The book was short, so I liked it. You will like reading this book too.

2. Young Ralph S. Mouse is the mouse in *The Mouse and the Motorcycle,* a story by Beverly Cleary. Ralph lives in room 215 of the Mountain View Inn, and people leave behind crumbs for him to eat. One day a boy named Keith stays in room 215. He brings along a toy motorcycle, just the right size for a mouse. Ralph borrows the motorcycle, and he gets trapped in a wastebasket. This story of adventure and friendship was funny. I read all of it without stopping. You probably will too.

3. I really enjoyed reading the book by Laura Ingalls Wilder. Laura's writing style was very clear and easy to follow. The stories she told about her life made me feel as if I was really there. She made me care very much about her and the other characters. The book made me want to learn more about life on the prairie.

LiNK

Into the Land of the Unicorns
by Bruce Coville

After leaping from a church steeple, Cara leaves her familiar world behind and lands in the mysterious land of Luster. At first, she can't believe her fairy tale-like surroundings. This strange, new world seems older than time itself. Filled with wonderful and not-so-wonderful creatures, she is attacked by delvers, rescued by a bearman, and healed by a rebellious young unicorn named Lightfoot . . . Together, Cara and her newfound friends, Lightfoot, Dimblethum, Thomas, and Squijim, must get to the Unicorn Queen before the mysterious person following them.

Reviewed by Tammy L. Currier

WRITER'S CORNER

Think of a story you read recently. Write four sentences telling what you think about the story. Then give two examples from the story to show why you liked it or did not like it.

Grammar in Action. Use at least four adjectives in your sentences. Circle each adjective.

Book Reports • 367

For Tomorrow

Have students write three sentences about a book they did not like. Tell students to include an example of something from the book that they did not like. Bring in your own example of why you did not like a book.

OBJECTIVES

- **To describe characters in a book report**
- **To describe the plot in a book report**

WARM-UP

Read, Listen, Speak

Read aloud the sentence you wrote for yesterday's For Tomorrow homework. Ask volunteers to share their sentences. Encourage students to discuss whether the example they wrote about supports their reason for not liking something about the book.

GRAMMAR CONNECTION

Take this opportunity to talk about adjectives in compound subject complements. You may wish to have students point out any adjectives in compound subject complements in their Read, Listen, Speak examples.

TEACH

Invite a volunteer to read aloud the first paragraph. Ask students to name their favorite story characters that are people and to describe these characters. Then ask students to explain what they like about these characters.

Have a volunteer read aloud the first paragraph of the section Character. Tell students to turn back to the book report on page 363. Ask students to describe the character Sarah. Encourage them to close their eyes and to imagine what Sarah looks like and sounds like. Then ask students to describe what they imagined about Sarah that is not mentioned in the book report.

Invite a volunteer to read aloud the second paragraph. Remind students of their favorite characters that were discussed earlier. Ask students to name and

describe their favorite characters that are not people. Point out that characters that are not people still act like people. Explain that a pencil that acts like a person can be a character in a story, but a pencil that is used for writing is not a character.

PRACTICE

ACTIVITY A

Ask students to imagine how these characters might look, sound, or act. Invite volunteers to share with the class how they imagine each character.

ACTIVITY B

Have partners complete this activity. Challenge students to write a sentence about each character.

ACTIVITY C

Have volunteers share their drawings with the class and explain what the character is doing. Encourage students to tell why they chose to have the character doing that particular thing. If any students drew the same character, have them compare their drawings.

Character and Plot

A character is a person, an animal, or a thing in a story. The plot of a story is what happens in the story.

Character

A character is not just a name in a story. A character is someone who seems real to you. You should be able to close your eyes and see the character and the action. When you write a book report, tell some important things about the character that you learned from the story.

The characters in stories can be kids just like you and your friends. Characters can also be people from times long ago and far away. They can be animals such as Ralph S. Mouse, Ribsy, or the Black Stallion. Characters can even be things like Thomas the Tank Engine, a talking train. Who or what are some of your favorite story characters?

ACTIVITY A Read these sentences from book reports. Give the name of each character. Tell whether the character is a person, an animal, or a thing.

1. On the planet Atara, there are no people or animals, just a robot named FIP-20.
2. Jonathan is a silly 10-year-old boy.
3. One of my favorite parts was when Sally tried to wash the spots off the dog.
4. The part about the dog Tatters being alone and hungry is sad.
5. What happens when Tony the Dinosaur gets a toothache?

Activity A
1. FIP-20, thing
2. Jonathan, person
3. Sally, person
4. Tatters, animal
5. Tony the Dinosaur, animal

APPLY

WRITER'S CORNER

Help any students who are having difficulty saying what they like or dislike about their character. When they have finished, invite volunteers to read aloud their sentences. Students should demonstrate the ability to describe characters in a book report.

TechTip You may wish to provide book review sites for students to search.

ASSESS

Note which students had difficulty describing characters in a book report. Use the Reteach option with those students who need additional reinforcement.

6. Mr. Baileymill, person
7. Ruff, thing
8. Moog, thing
9. Peter, person
10. Laura, animal

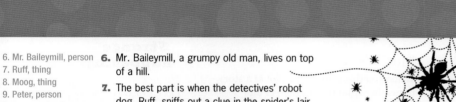

6. Mr. Baileymill, a grumpy old man, lives on top of a hill.

7. The best part is when the detectives' robot dog, Ruff, sniffs out a clue in the spider's lair.

8. The story really gets going when Moog, a talking tree, comes lumbering down the road.

9. Peter is a selfish boy who never wants to share his lunch with anyone.

10. When a ladybug named Laura gets swept down the river, she begins an amazing journey.

ACTIVITY B Imagine that the people and animals below are characters in books you have read. Give each character a name and think of three words that describe the character.

1. A neighbor
2. A friend
3. Your favorite animal
4. Your favorite athlete
5. A person in a movie or on TV
6. A wild animal

ACTIVITY C Draw a picture of a character you have read about. Show the character doing something he or she would normally do. At the bottom of the picture, write the name of the character and the book the character comes from.

WRITER'S CORNER

Write four sentences that tell why you like or do not like the character from Activity C.

Tech Tip With an adult, find and read a book report online.

Book Reports • 369

WARM-UP

Read aloud the description you wrote for yesterday's For Tomorrow homework. Have small groups share their character descriptions. Challenge students to explain how their descriptions match their characters' personalities.

GRAMMAR CONNECTION

Take this opportunity to talk about adjectives that compare. You may wish to have students point out any adjectives that compare in their Read, Listen, Speak examples.

TEACH

Review the terms *character* and *setting*. Ask students to name characters and settings of their favorite books.

Have a volunteer read aloud the first paragraph of the section Plot. Emphasize that the plot is the events that make up the story. Then ask a volunteer to read aloud the second paragraph. Invite volunteers to tell about some villains they have read about and to describe the villains.

Ask a volunteer to read aloud the last paragraph. Explain that many readers read a story to find out how the characters solve the problem in the story. Tell students that writing about a problem that needs to be solved might get readers interested in how the characters solve the problem.

LiNK Ask a volunteer to read aloud the excerpt from the book report of *Strange Happenings*. Ask students to identify the characters *(Tom, Charlie)*, their problems *(Tom is bored)*, and their goals *(Tom wants to sleep all day like Charlie)*.

PRACTICE

ACTIVITY D

Have students complete this activity independently. When students have finished, invite them to share their answers with the class and to explain how they decided on the correct order.

ACTIVITY E

Encourage partners to take turns reading aloud each sentence. Have students identify the character or characters in each sentence. Then have them tell which character has a problem and if that problem is their own or if another character caused the problem.

ACTIVITY F

Have students complete this activity in small groups. Tell students to read the paragraph silently and then to decide whether they would like to read the rest of the story. Be sure students give reasons to support their decisions.

Plot

When you think about the plot of a story, remember what the characters did. In most stories the characters have a problem that must be solved or a goal they want to reach.

Characters do things in the story to solve their problem. Sometimes villains work against the characters. This can make stories more exciting to read.

The ending of a book tells how the characters solved their problem or whether they reached their goal. A book report should tell only enough of the plot so the reader gets an idea of the beginning and middle of the story. A book report should not tell the ending of the story.

LiNK

Strange Happenings
by Avi

Tom is so bored he wishes he could sleep all day like his cat Charlie. Suddenly, this unusual feline starts talking to Tom and asks if he really would like to be a cat. Tom thinks he would, so Charlie takes him to a deserted building filled with cats. They are granted an audience with the wizard cat, who transforms Tom into Charlie and vice versa. For Tom, however, the experience isn't quite what he expected it to be.

Reviewed by Robert M. Oksner

ACTIVITY D Read each plot description from two different book reports. Put the events in the order that they happen so they make sense.

1. **Mystery Plot**
   a. You will never believe where they find Queenie!
   b. Then a detective is hired to help find Queenie.
   c. A champion show dog, Queenie, has been stolen from Jenny Clark.
   d. Jenny tells the police about her missing pet.

2. **Adventure Plot**
   a. The Miller family is enjoying a calm day of sailing.
   b. Mr. Miller has to make the decision for his family to stay on the boat or leave it.
   c. The boat is badly damaged, and dark, cold water quickly begins to fill the lower cabin.
   d. Suddenly, the boat hits a reef of sharp coral, and the family hears a loud, crashing noise.

Activity E
1. Mystery Plot: c, d, b, a
2. Adventure Plot: a, d, c, b

Grammar in Action Remind students that subject complements are adjectives that come after being verbs and describe nouns. Challenge students to use compound subject complements.

APPLY

WRITER'S CORNER

Encourage students to begin by thinking about the problem in the story. Suggest that they think about how the characters solved their problem. When students have finished, invite volunteers to read aloud their work. Students should demonstrate the ability to describe the plot of a story.

ASSESS

Note which students had difficulty writing about the plot in a book report. Use the Reteach option with those students who need additional reinforcement.
   Practice Book page 153 provides additional work with characters and plot.

TEACHING OPTIONS

Reteach

Discuss the characters and plots of familiar stories or fairy tales. Create a three-column chart with the headings *Character, Problem,* and *Solution.* Then choose three stories about which to complete the chart. Discuss similarities and differences between characters and their problems and solutions.

Map It Out

Have small groups choose a story with which they are all familiar, such as a story the class has recently read or a familiar fairy tale or folktale. Have students discuss the main events of the plot and the main problem. Then ask students to tell the solution to the story problem. Challenge students to design their own story map that shows the events in the order in which they happen, identifies the main story problem, and points out the solution to the problem. Have groups share their story maps with the class.

Activity F
1. character's problem
2. character's problem
3. villain tries to make a problem
4. villain tries to make a problem
5. character's problem
6. villain tries to make a problem
7. villain tries to make a problem
8. character's problem
9. villain tries to make a problem
10. villain tries to make a problem

ACTIVITY E The following sentences are from book reports. Which sentences tell about the character's problem? Which sentences tell how a villain tries to make a problem?

1. After that one little fib, life sure becomes harder for Junior!

2. It suddenly came to Emily that she had forgotten the item that no hiker should ever forget, water.

3. Fester can always get Bobo, the funny St. Bernard, into trouble.

4. Though the evil queen throws the key away, Tyrone finally finds it and opens the castle door.

5. Many kids are shy, but Cameron could not speak at all to his teacher.

6. After Antwan found the necklace, his brother hid it from him again.

7. Princess Alice knows that when she misbehaves, Lil will be punished.

8. Robert drove the go-cart to the other side of town during the storm.

9. While Penny was sleeping, her evil twin Margaret made a mess.

10. Jim flies to Europe to rescue his cat Sparks from the evil magicians.

ACTIVITY F Read the following paragraph. Describe what happens. Does the paragraph make you want to read more of the story? Explain why or why not.

   Tabitha took a deep breath and walked slowly down the basement stairs. Each step creaked and groaned under her weight. The more she tried to step lightly and quietly, the louder each sound seemed. With only a candle to light her way, Tabitha squinted through the darkness. Shadows jumped and danced across the walls. Then Tabitha felt something brush the back of her neck. She quickly spun around, but the breeze blew out the candle. Now Tabitha was in the cold, damp basement alone and in the dark. What was that odd sound? Was someone or something there? She felt as if she was not alone after all.

WRITER'S CORNER

Choose a book that you have read. Describe its plot in five sentences so that the reader would want to read the book. Think of ways to tell a little about the ending without telling the reader exactly how the book ends.

For Tomorrow

Have students write the title, author, and beginning of a book report on a book of their choosing. Remind students to describe the characters and the setting in their report. Write your own beginning with the title and author to share with the class.

Grammar in Action Use at least two subject complements in your plot description. See Section 5.3.

Book Reports • 371

OBJECTIVE
- **To identify parts of a book**

WARM-UP

Read, Listen, Speak

Share your beginning of a book report from yesterday's For Tomorrow homework. Ask students to exchange the beginnings of the book reports they wrote. Have students check if their partners forgot any necessary information.

GRAMMAR CONNECTION

Take this opportunity to talk about irregular adjectives that compare. You may wish to have students point out any irregular adjectives that compare in their Read, Listen, Speak examples.

TEACH

Display a variety of books, such as paperbacks, hardcovers, fiction, nonfiction, and textbooks. Have students look through the books. Read aloud the first paragraph after students examine the books.

Invite a volunteer to read aloud the section Cover and Spine. Ask a volunteer to show one of their book covers. Point out the spine on a textbook. Explain that a publisher gets a book ready to be sold. Ask what needs to be completed before a book can be sold. *(It needs to be written and printed.)*

Have a volunteer read aloud the section Title Page. Ask students to turn to the title page of one of their books.

Have a volunteer read aloud the section Contents Page. Guide students to understand that a contents page tells where each part of the book starts.

Ask a student to read aloud the section Glossary. Explain that a glossary is like a dictionary for important words in a book and that a glossary is found in the back of a book. Show students a glossary from one of the textbooks on display. Tell students that not all books have a glossary.

Ask a student to read aloud the section Index. Point out that an index is like a road map of information that is found in the book. Explain that an index guides readers to pages where information about a topic can be found. Ask students how an index is different from a book's contents page. *(The contents page tells where parts of the book begin. The index tells where to find topics.)*

PRACTICE

ACTIVITY A
Have students complete this activity independently. Then have partners compare their answers.

ACTIVITY B
Point out that a publisher's name is the name of a company, not a person. Ask students what other information they found on their title page.

ACTIVITY C
Encourage students to select words that are unfamiliar. Have volunteers read aloud their work.

LESSON **3** STUDY SKILLS

Parts of a Book

Most books have the same parts. Look around your classroom. A textbook, a book about making tree houses, and a book about volcanoes probably have the same parts.

Cover and Spine

The cover has the title of the book and often the author's name. The cover might have a picture or design.

The part of the cover that connects the front and the back is called the spine. The spine often shows the title of the book, the author's name, and the name of the publisher.

Title Page

The title page has the title of the book, the author's name, and sometimes the illustrator's name. It might also have the name of the company that published the book.

Contents Page

The contents page tells the name of each chapter. It also tells the page where the chapter starts.

Glossary

The glossary is a list of important words in the book and what they mean. The words are listed in alphabetical order. A book about volcanoes might have the word *magma* in its glossary. A book that tells a story won't have a glossary.

APPLY

WRITER'S CORNER

When students have finished, ask them where they found the answers to each question. Have them share their interesting topics. Students should demonstrate the ability to identify parts of a book and use an index.

ASSESS

Note which students had difficulty identifying parts of a book. Use the Reteach option with those students who need additional reinforcement.

Index

The index is a list of the topics found in the book. The topics are listed in alphabetical order with the page numbers where the topics can be found.

Page numbers connected with a dash tell readers that the pages between the numbers have information about that topic. If the page numbers are 8–11, you should look on pages 8, 9, 10, and 11.

ACTIVITY A Match each part of a book in Column A to its description in Column B.

Column A		Column B
1. index	d	**a.** a page with the title and the author's name
2. contents page	c	**b.** the outside of a book
3. glossary	e	**c.** a list of the chapters and the page numbers on which the chapters start
4. cover	b	**d.** a list of a book's topics in alphabetical order with page numbers
5. title page	a	**e.** a list of the meanings of important words in a book

ACTIVITY B Copy a title page from a book in your classroom. Then label each item, using the labels below. Trade your title page with a partner. Check to make sure the labels are in the correct place.

- Title
- Author's name
- Illustrator's name
- Publisher's name

ACTIVITY C Find a book that has a glossary. Write three words and their meanings from the glossary. Use each word in a sentence.

WRITER'S CORNER

Find a book that has an index. What is the title of the book? Who is the author? How many chapters does the book have? Write those facts. Then find an interesting topic from the index and look it up.

Book Reports • 373

TEACHING OPTIONS

Reteach

Have students form five small groups. Ask students to imagine that they are writing a book about a typical day in their classroom. Have each group design a different part for the book—cover/spine, title page, contents page, glossary page, and index page. Work with each group to be sure that students include the correct kind of information for their book part. Ask volunteers to tell why they chose to include each piece of information.

English-Language Learners

Have students make four bookmarks by cutting a sheet of paper into four strips. Tell students to write each of the following on a bookmark: *Title Page*, *Contents Page*, *Glossary*, and *Index*. Ask students to find a book in the classroom or library and place each bookmark in the appropriate place.

For Tomorrow

Have students draw a picture of the cover of an imaginary book they have written. Ask students to write the title of the book and their name on the cover. Then have them draw a picture on the cover that shows what the book is about. Bring in your own made-up book cover to share.

WARM-UP

Read, Listen, Speak

Display your book cover from yesterday's For Tomorrow homework. Ask students to identify the title and author and tell what they think the book is about based on the title and cover. Ask small groups to share their covers. Challenge students to put their hands over the titles and see if others can guess what the books are about based only on the pictures.

GRAMMAR CONNECTION

Take this opportunity to talk about adjectives that tell how many. You may wish to have students point out any adjectives that tell how many in their Read, Listen, Speak examples.

TEACH

Review the parts of a book. Invite a volunteer to point out the cover and spine of a book. Then have a volunteer point out and explain the purpose of the title page. *(The title page contains the title of a book, the author's name, and sometimes the illustrator's name. The publishers name might also be included.)*

Ask a volunteer to describe the contents page of a book. Have a volunteer point out the glossary and index of a book. Ask a volunteer to explain how glossaries and indexes are organized and used.

PRACTICE

ACTIVITY D

Have partners complete this activity. When students have finished, invite volunteers to share their answers with the class. Ask a volunteer to explain how to figure out the answer to question 7. *(Because the index starts on page 49, the glossary includes page 48 as well as page 47, the page number listed on the contents page.)*

ACTIVITY E

Have students complete this activity in small groups. Encourage students first to determine the subject of each question and then to look for that subject in the index. Point out that for question 9, there are two sets of pages *(space travel, International Space Station)*. After students have answered the questions, invite volunteers to share their answers with the class.

ACTIVITY D Use this contents page to answer the questions.

Contents

Chapter	Page
1 The Red Planet	1
2 Life on Mars	15
3 Temperature	26
4 Flights to Mars	30
5 Surface	39
6 Satellites	43
Glossary	47
Index	49

1. What is this book about? Mars
2. How many chapters are in this book? 6
3. On what page does Chapter 6 start? 43
4. On what page does the information about the temperature of Mars start? 26
5. On what page does the index start? 49
6. What is the title of Chapter 4? Flights to Mars
7. On what pages could you find the meanings of important words in the book? 47–48
8. On what page would you begin to look to find out if plants grow on Mars? 15
9. What chapter starts on page 39? Chapter 5: Surface
10. To what page would you turn to learn about flights to Mars? 30

APPLY

WRITER'S CORNER

Brainstorm with students a list of people, places, and symbols important to their state. When students have finished, invite them to share their book covers with the class. Students should demonstrate an understanding of parts of a book.

TechTip You may wish to direct students to specific Web sites to find facts about their state. You may also wish to have students copy images and paste them into a drawing program to create their book covers.

ASSESS

Note which students had difficulty understanding parts of a book. Use the Reteach option with those students who need additional reinforcement.

Practice Book page 154 provides additional work with parts of a book.

Reteach

Have students find library books with glossaries and indexes. Ask students to write six words from the indexes. Help students see if they can find any of their words in their books' glossaries. Point out that the words in the glossary are words the reader might not know, but that the index lists all the topics in the book.

A Book About Me

Invite students to create a contents page for a book about themselves. Encourage students to think about how their lives could be divided into chapters. Point out that students might divide the book according to ages, dates, or special events. Have students decide what they would call these parts of their lives. Ask students to write their chapter titles in the contents page. Invite volunteers to share their contents pages with the class.

Activity E
1. 26–29
2. Mars rover *Opportunity*
3. 8–11
4. 13–14
5. 47
6. 43
7. 13
8. plant life
9. 30–38 and 47–48
10. pages 39–42
11. space travel
12. 2–6
13. space travel

ACTIVITY E Use this index to answer the questions.

Index

International Space Station, 47–48	planets, 2–6
magnetic fields, 8–11	plant life, 17–21
Mars rover *Opportunity*, 35–36	satellites, 43–46
Milky Way, 10–13	space travel, 30–38
moons, 43	surface, 39–42
orbit, 13–14	temperature, 26–29

1. On which pages would you learn how hot and how cold it is on Mars?
2. What topic is on pages 35–36?
3. Which pages tell about magnetic fields?
4. Which pages tell how long it takes Mars to orbit the sun?
5. On which page does the information about a space station start?
6. On which pages would you learn how many moons Mars has?
7. Which page is the last page to learn about the Milky Way?
8. What is the topic that starts on page 17?
9. On which pages would you learn how people live in outer space?
10. Where could you find what the ground on Mars is like?
11. Which topic appears first in the book—*space travel* or *moons*?
12. Which pages tell about all the planets?
13. Which topic has the greatest number of pages?

WRITER'S CORNER

Imagine you are writing a book about the state you live in. Design a book cover with a picture, the title of the book, and your name.

Tech Tip With an adult, find facts about your state online.

Book Reports • 375

For Tomorrow

Ask students to write a list of names of people who would be included in a book about their own lives. Bring in your own list of names to share with the class.

OBJECTIVE

• **To identify and use compound predicates**

WARM-UP

Read, Listen, Speak

Share your list of names from yesterday's For Tomorrow homework. Invite small groups to share the names they listed. Have students choose one person and write a sentence explaining why this person would be included in their book.

GRAMMAR CONNECTION

Take this opportunity to talk about articles. You may wish to have students point out articles in their Read, Listen, Speak examples.

TEACH

Review subjects and predicates. Write these sentences on the board:

My uncle sent me a birthday card.

Marie washed her car.

Invite volunteers to underline the subject of each sentence. Then ask volunteers to circle the predicate of each sentence.

Ask volunteers to read aloud the first paragraph and the two example sentences. Invite a volunteer to name the subject of each sentence. Then have a volunteer read aloud the second paragraph and example sentence. Point out that a compound predicate has more than one verb. Invite volunteers to name the two verbs in the example sentence *(sits, watches)*.

Read aloud the third paragraph. Point out that the first two sentences about the tabby cat

sounded more like a list than a part of a paragraph. Read aloud the last paragraph. Have volunteers read aloud the example sentences. Have students identify the subject and predicate of the last sentence. Then ask students to identify both verbs in the compound predicate.

Invite volunteers to write on the board two simple sentences with the same subject. Show students how the sentences can be combined into one sentence with a compound predicate.

PRACTICE

ACTIVITY A
Remind students that verbs are action words. Suggest that students look for the word after *and* to find the second part of the compound predicate.

ACTIVITY B
Have students complete this activity independently. When students have finished, invite small groups to compare their answers.

Compound Predicates

Two sentences can often give information about the same subject. When sentences have the same subject, you can join the predicates to make one sentence. Read these sentences. Can you see how they can be joined to make one sentence?

My tabby cat sits in the sun.
My tabby cat watches the birds.

These sentences tell about the same subject—*My tabby cat.* The predicates are different—*sits in the sun* and *watches the birds.* You can make one smooth sentence by joining the predicates with the word *and.*

My tabby cat sits in the sun *and* **watches the birds.**

Writers use compound predicates so they don't have a row of choppy sentences. Writers often turn short, choppy sentences into smoother sentences by joining predicates.

Look at these sentences. You can join the predicates by using the word *and.*

Babies sleep at night.
Babies cry at night.
Babies sleep *and* **cry at night.**

APPLY

WRITER'S CORNER

Help students find appropriate books or magazines. Invite volunteers to read aloud their sentences and to identify each compound predicate. Students should demonstrate the ability to identify compound predicates.

Grammar in Action. Guide students to find the compound predicate in the second sentence by first identifying the subject *(Cara)* and

verbs *(leaves, lands)*. Ask a volunteer to read aloud the compound predicate *(leaves her familiar world behind and lands in the mysterious land of Luster)*.

ASSESS

Note which students had difficulty identifying compound predicates. Use the Reteach option with those students who need additional reinforcement.

TEACHING OPTIONS

Reteach

Whisper to a student instructions for two actions. After the student has performed the actions, ask a volunteer to describe in one sentence what he or she did. *(Paul walked across the room and sat in a chair.)* Write the sentence on the board. Have students identify the two verbs that make up the compound predicate. Repeat the activity with different students and different actions. Have volunteers write on the board each sentence. Ask students to underline the verbs that make up the compound predicate in each sentence.

So Many Things to Do

Have students write four sentences that describe what they like to do after school. Direct students to begin each sentence with the word *I*. Have students exchange sentences with a partner and join sentences to make two sentences with compound predicates. Ask volunteers to write their sentences on the board and to read them aloud.

For Tomorrow

Have students write two sentences telling something that a person does, using compound predicates in each sentence. Encourage students to choose a character from a book that they have talked or written about in this chapter. Bring in your own sentences to share with the class.

ACTIVITY A Each of the following sentences has a compound predicate. Find the two verbs in each compound predicate.

1. An airplane <u>speeds</u> down the runway and <u>lifts</u> off with its nose up.
2. The lion <u>leaped</u> from behind a bush and <u>ran</u> after the zebra.
3. Tim <u>shovels</u> snow in the winter and <u>mows</u> lawns in the summer.
4. Joe <u>argued</u> with his mother and <u>pouted</u> in his room.
5. After the party, I <u>waved</u> good-bye and <u>walked</u> away.
6. My dog, Sparky, <u>rolls</u> over and <u>plays</u> dead.
7. A crow <u>swooped</u> down and <u>landed</u> on the fence.
8. Uncle Roberto <u>wrote</u> and <u>illustrated</u> a children's book.
9. Yolanda <u>moved</u> the chair and <u>set</u> the table.
10. Wendy <u>answered</u> the phone and <u>took</u> the message.
11. The car <u>turned</u> the corner and <u>zoomed</u> away.
12. A hammer <u>pounds</u> nails and <u>pulls</u> them out.
13. Selina <u>thought</u> about the answer and <u>gave</u> it.
14. Ivan <u>moved</u> his chess piece and <u>smiled</u> at me.
15. Dad <u>brought</u> a pot of coffee and <u>poured</u> a cup.

ACTIVITY B Add two different verbs to each sentence to make a compound predicate.

1. The famous ballerina _____ and _____.
2. Miranda _____ her shoe and _____.
3. The fans _____ and _____ for their team.
4. Kyle _____ the car and _____ to the radio.
5. The photographer _____ his camera and _____ pictures of us.

WRITER'S CORNER

Look in a book or a magazine. Find two sentences that have compound predicates. Write the sentences. Then underline each verb.

Grammar in Action. Name the compound predicate in the first sentence of the page 367 excerpt.

Book Reports • 377

WARM-UP

Read, Listen, Speak

Read aloud the two sentences about a character that you wrote for yesterday's For Tomorrow homework. Ask students to identify the compound predicates in your sentences. Have small groups read aloud their sentences. Ask volunteers to identify the compound predicate in each sentence.

GRAMMAR CONNECTION

Take this opportunity to talk about demonstrative adjectives. You may wish to have students point out any demonstrative adjectives in their Read, Listen, Speak examples.

TEACH

Review compound predicates. Write on the board two short sentences with the same subject but different predicates. Have volunteers join the sentences into one with a compound predicate. Tell students that sentences with compound predicates have more than one verb. Use the sentence *The car is old and dirty* as an example of a sentence that has the word *and* in it but does not have a compound predicate. Point out that it has a compound subject complement.

PRACTICE

ACTIVITY C

Have partners complete this activity. Challenge students to change sentences 1, 3, 7, and 10 so that they have compound predicates. When students have finished, invite volunteers to share their answers.

ACTIVITY D

Encourage students to look at the example sentences on page 376 for help joining these sentences. When students have finished, invite volunteers to read aloud their sentences with compound predicates.

ACTIVITY E

Have students complete this activity independently. Encourage students to use a different subject for each sentence. When students have finished, invite them to share their sentences with the class.

ACTIVITY F

Ask partners to each choose one topic and then together choose a third topic. When students have finished, invite them to read their sentences aloud.

LiNK Invite a volunteer to read aloud the excerpt from the book report on *Bats at the Library*. Have students tell what the story is about. Ask if the book review writer liked the story.

ACTIVITY C Find the predicate in each sentence. Tell whether it is a compound predicate.

1. Dana and Reese made dinner last night.
2. My two sisters dusted the dining room and set the table.
3. They served salad, steak, and baked potatoes.
4. Every dish looked appealing and tasted delicious.
5. We all laughed and chatted during dinner.
6. Then Dana and Reese looked at each other and made an announcement.
7. Uncle Harry had sold them his old car.
8. Dad choked on his food and turned red as a beet.
9. Reese patted Dad's back and handed him a glass of water.
10. Dad finally got used to the news.

ACTIVITY D Join each pair of sentences into one sentence with a compound predicate.

1. The elephant flapped its big ears. The elephant flicked its scruffy tail.
2. Leigh and Cal played basketball after school.
   Leigh and Cal rode bikes after school.
3. Jim played games at the carnival.
   Jim rode the roller coaster at the carnival.
4. The lion stretched out on a rock. The lion took a nap.
5. The monkey ate four bananas.
   The monkey threw the peels over its shoulder.
6. Kiki goes to the mall. Kiki parks in the same spot.
7. Dr. Harmon washed the dishes.
   Dr. Harmon dried the dishes.
8. Hank bought fresh corn.
   Hank grilled fresh corn.
9. Rosa made a piñata.
   Rosa stuffed it with candy.
10. I earned money by babysitting.
    I spent most of it before I got home.

Activity C
Sentences 2, 4, 5, 6, 8, and 9 are compound predicates.

Activity D
1. The elephant flapped its big ears and flicked its scruffy tail.
2. Leigh and Cal played basketball and rode bikes after school.
3. Jim played games and rode the roller coaster at the carnival.
4. The lion stretched out on a rock and took a nap.
5. The monkey ate four bananas and threw the peels over its shoulder.
6. Kiki goes to the mall and parks in the same spot.
7. Dr. Harmon washed and dried the dishes.
8. Hank bought and grilled fresh corn.
9. Rosa made a piñata and stuffed it with candy.
10. I earned money by babysitting and spent most of it before I got home.

378 • Chapter 5

APPLY

WRITER'S CORNER

Encourage students to look over their previous work on compound predicates. Invite volunteers to read aloud their sentences. Students should demonstrate the ability to write sentences with compound predicates.

ASSESS

Note which students had difficulty writing sentences with compound predicates. Use the Reteach option with those students who need additional reinforcement.

Practice Book page 155 provides additional work with compound predicates.

TEACHING OPTIONS

Reteach

Distribute to each student two sentence strips and a note card with the word *and* written on it. Have students write simple sentences with the same subject on each strip. Then ask students to cut and glue the strips onto poster board to make one sentence with a compound predicate.

One-on-One Interview

Have partners interview each other about what each did for his or her last birthday or holiday. Encourage students to take notes on their partners' responses. Then have students use their notes to write two sentences with compound predicates. Invite volunteers to share the sentences they wrote, without identifying the interviewee. Have the class guess who the sentences are about.

ACTIVITY E Choose three of the following pairs of verbs. Write a sentence for each pair that uses both verbs as a compound predicate.

A. run, jump
B. chuckle, grin
C. mix, pour
D. study, learn
E. train, perform
F. draw, paint
G. enter, climb
H. wash, scrub
I. paddle, swim
J. camp, hike

ACTIVITY F Choose three of the following topics. For each topic write a sentence with a compound predicate.

A. pets you have known
B. planets and stars
C. homework every day
D. younger brothers or sisters
E. long vacations
F. favorite desserts
G. learning new things
H. keeping a journal
I. chores around the house
J. best friends

LiNK

Bats at the Library
by Brian Lies

It's bat night at the library, as one librarian forgot and left a window ajar! Bats from all around, near and far make their way inside for an unforgettable night of fun and adventure with books and library equipment . . . This book gives readers a different look at what the library holds as we're seeing it from a bat's-eye view rather than the human eye. The rhyming text is very attractive to the tongue and mind, and children will definitely be laughing at this one!

Reviewed by Katie Harvey

WRITER'S CORNER

Work with a partner. Choose one pair of verbs in Activity E that you did not use. Write a sentence that uses the verbs as a compound predicate. Then write another sentence about the same subject. Use a compound predicate in that sentence too.

For Tomorrow

Ask students to write three sentences describing what a pet or an animal does. Tell students to include compound predicates in their work. Bring in your own sentences with compound predicates to share with the class.

Book Reports • 379

OBJECTIVE
- **To use the prefixes *re-* and *un-***

WARM-UP
Read, Listen, Speak
Read aloud your sentences from yesterday's For Tomorrow homework. Identify the compound predicates. Have small groups share their sentences. Ask students to work together to rewrite the sentences with compound predicates into two separate sentences.

GRAMMAR CONNECTION
Take this opportunity to talk about proper adjectives. You may wish to have students point out any proper adjectives in their Read, Listen, Speak examples.

TEACH

Write *tell, name,* and *place* on the board. Ask volunteers to read aloud the words.

Add *re-* to each word. Ask students to tell what the new words mean. Guide students to understand how the meaning of a word changes when a prefix is added.

Have a volunteer read aloud the first paragraph. Invite volunteers to share any words they know that begin with the prefixes *re-* and *un-*.

Have volunteers read aloud the section *Re-*. Allow time for students to study the examples. Point out that a prefix by itself has a hyphen but that the hyphen is dropped when the prefix is added to a word.

Ask volunteers to read aloud the section *Un-*. Ask a volunteer to tell how the prefixes *re-* and *un-* are different and how they are alike. (*Re- means "again" or "back." Un- means "not." Both prefixes come at the beginning of a word.*)

Guide students to understand that not all words that begin with the letters *un* or *re* have *un-* or *re-* as a prefix. Write *read* and *uncle* on the board as examples.

PRACTICE

ACTIVITY A
Have students complete this activity independently. When students have finished, ask volunteers to share their answers with the class.

ACTIVITY B
Have partners complete this activity. Ask students to take turns reading the words aloud as their partners find the definitions. Invite volunteers to share their answers with the class.

ACTIVITY C
Have partners complete this activity. Ask volunteers to read aloud their sentences. Then have students read the sentence again, substituting the meaning from Column B for the word with the prefix.

LESSON **5** WORD STUDY

Prefixes

A prefix is a word part added to the beginning of a word. Prefixes change the meaning of a word. Sometimes a prefix changes the meaning of a word to its opposite. Two common prefixes are *re-* and *un-*.

Re-
Re- is a prefix that means "again." Read the example below. The prefix *re-* is added to the word *paint*.

> **re- + paint = repaint**

Repaint means "to paint again." *Re-* can also mean "back." Read the example below. The prefix *re-* is added to the word *pay*.

> **re- + pay = repay**

Repay means "to pay back." What other words do you know that have the prefix *re-*?

Un-
The prefix *un-* means "not." This prefix usually changes a word's meaning to its opposite. Read the example below.

> **un- + happy = unhappy**

Un- means "not," so *unhappy* means "not happy." *Unhappy* is the opposite of *happy*. What other words do you know that have the prefix *un-*?

APPLY

WRITER'S CORNER

Ask students to bring books from home to complete this activity. Tell students to write the dictionary definitions below their own definitions. When students have finished, encourage volunteers to share their words and definitions with the class. Students should demonstrate an understanding of the prefixes *re-* and *un-*.

💡 **TechTip** You may wish to direct students to a specific online dictionary. Point out that students can type in their word to search for the definition. Suggest that students browse the online dictionary to find other words that begin with the prefixes *re-* and *un-*.

ASSESS

Note which students had difficulty identifying the prefixes *re-* and *un-*. Use the Reteach option with those students who need additional reinforcement.

TEACHING OPTIONS

Reteach

Have students fold a sheet of paper in half. Then have them write the word *washed* on the left side. Instruct them to draw a picture that shows the meaning of the word. For example, students might draw a picture of a clean car. On the right side, have students write the word *unwashed*. Instruct them to draw a picture of the same item that illustrates the meaning of *unwashed*. Have volunteers share their pictures. Have a volunteer identify the prefix and tell how it changed the meaning of the word.

Expanding Prefix Knowledge

Write on the board some common prefixes to form the headings of a three-column chart (*bi-, pre-, dis-, anti-, di-, mis-*). Have partners write on the board under the correct heading words with the prefixes. Allow students to use dictionaries to find words. Discuss the meaning of the prefixes on the chart.

ACTIVITY A Find the prefix in each word. Then write the meaning of each word.

1. redo
2. resend
3. unable
4. redraw
5. reappear
6. rewrite
7. unbeaten
8. uncomfortable
9. uncertain
10. rejoin

ACTIVITY B Match the words with prefixes in Column A with their meanings in Column B. Check your answers in a dictionary.

Column A		Column B
1. unbelievable	h	a. build again
2. unusual	b	b. not usual
3. reread	i	c. apply again
4. rebuild	a	d. not safe
5. unwashed	e	e. not washed
6. uncertain	j	f. sell again
7. reapply	c	g. not remarkable
8. unsafe	d	h. not believable
9. unremarkable	g	i. read again
10. resell	f	j. not certain

ACTIVITY C Choose three words from Column A in Activity B. Use each word in a sentence. Underline the prefix in each word.

WRITER'S CORNER

Find four words with the prefixes *re-* or *un-* in a book you have read. Write what you think the meanings of the words are. Then check your answers in a dictionary.

Tech Tip With an adult, use an online dictionary.

For Tomorrow

Ask students to write three sentences that describe a villian from a book or movie, using at least three words with the prefixes *re-* or *un-*, such as *repay, unkind, and unbelievable*. Bring in your own sentences to share.

WARM-UP

Read, Listen, Speak

Read aloud the sentences you wrote for yesterday's For Tomorrow homework. Identify the words with prefixes and tell what they mean. Have small groups share the sentences they wrote. Invite volunteers to read their sentences aloud, tell which words have the prefixes *re-* or *un-*, and tell what they mean.

TEACH

Have the class compile a list of words that begin with *re-* and *un-* that they discussed in their small groups. After a volunteer has said a word, have another volunteer give a sentence with that word. Remind students that in words such as *red, read, uncle,* and *under, un* and *re* are not prefixes.

PRACTICE

ACTIVITY D

Have students complete this activity independently. Invite volunteers to share their answers with the class.

ACTIVITY E

Suggest that partners discuss which word would best complete each sentence. When students have finished, invite volunteers to read aloud their answers.

ACTIVITY F

Have students complete this activity independently. Encourage students to draw a picture for one of their sentences and share it with the class.

ACTIVITY G

Have small groups complete this activity. Tell one student in each group to read aloud the paragraph as the other students find the words with *re-* and *un-*. Encourage students to write what they think the words mean and then to look up the definitions in a dictionary. When students have finished, have them read aloud their answers.

ACTIVITY D Complete each sentence with a word from the word box.

unhappy	unbeaten	reheat	unwise
rerun	rewrite	unfortunate	unclog

1. The end of summer makes me __unhappy__.
2. Taking a test without studying is __unwise__.
3. When writers __rewrite__ a paper, they try to improve it.
4. I missed the TV show, but they will __rerun__ it.
5. The dinner is cold, so I will __reheat__ it.
6. It is __unfortunate__ that only a few people came to our band concert.
7. The championship team finished the season with an __unbeaten__ record.
8. Dad spent an hour trying to __unclog__ the bathtub drain.

ACTIVITY E Work with a partner. Complete each sentence with a word that has the prefix *re-* or *un-*. Use a dictionary if you need help.

1. What color would you like to _____ the house?
2. Jamal wrote neatly so that he would not have to _____ his draft.
3. Taking off a coat is much easier when you _____ it.
4. This hot weather is simply _____!
5. No matter how hard I try, I'm _____ to do more than 10 push-ups in a row.
6. My shoelaces were loose, so I had to _____ them.
7. When I arrived at Grandma's house, the first thing I did was _____ my suitcase.
8. I have to _____ the batteries in my flashlight.

Activity E
Answers will vary.
Possible answers:
1. repaint
2. rewrite
3. unbutton
4. unbearable
5. unable
6. retie
7. unpack
8. replace

382 • Chapter 5

APPLY

WRITER'S CORNER

Encourage students to think about their story before they write. Remind students that a plot has characters, a problem, and a solution. When students have finished, invite volunteers to share their work with the class. Students should demonstrate the ability to use words with the prefixes *re-* and *un-*.

ASSESS

Note which students had difficulty using words with the prefixes *re-* and *un-* in writing. Use the Reteach option with those students who need additional reinforcement.

Practice Book page 156 provides additional work with prefixes.

TEACHING OPTIONS

Reteach

Write on the board the following equations:

   re- + open = ?

   un- + sure = ?

Have two volunteers complete the equations and tell the meaning of the words with and without the prefixes. Then write on the board the following words: *write, friendly, loved, new.* Have partners write equations for each of the words, using the prefixes *re-* and *un-.* Have volunteers tell the meaning of the words with and without the prefixes.

Prefix Hunt

Have students look through books, newspapers, and magazines for words with prefixes. Have students make a list of the words and underline the prefixes *re-* and *un-.* Challenge students to define each prefix that they find. Then have students make up their own matching game by writing in random order one column with the prefixes they found and another column with the words that go with the prefixes. Have students exchange papers and draw a line to match each word with its prefix.

ACTIVITY F **Choose two of the following topics. Write a sentence about each topic. Use a word with the prefix *re-* or *un-* in each sentence.**

A. writing a story

B. wacky inventions

C. sailing around the world

D. an exciting sports match

E. a day you'll never forget

F. your earliest memory

G. your favorite CD

H. something you did to make money

I. something you do well

J. something you'd like to do better

ACTIVITY G **Read the sentences below and find the words with the prefixes *re-* or *un-*. Write the meaning of each word. Use a dictionary if you need help.**

My family's vacation started early in the morning. After the car was loaded, my mom saw many shirts lying <u>untouched</u> on the bed. She would have to <u>repack</u> two suitcases. She told my dad to <u>unload</u> the car.

First, he had to <u>untie</u> a knot he made to get to the suitcases. Then he had to <u>rearrange</u> things around the suitcases. When Mom opened the suitcases, she was <u>unable</u> to fit anything else in. She decided to just <u>replace</u> the shirts during our trip. We finally pulled out of the driveway around noon!

WRITER'S CORNER

Imagine you are writing a mystery book. Write one paragraph about the plot of your book. Use the words *reappear* and *unknown.*

For Tomorrow

Ask students to write two sentences about a book they have read. Tell students to include a word with the prefix *re-* or *un-* in each sentence. Write your own sentences about a book to share with the class.

Book Reports • 383

OBJECTIVES

- **To identify characteristics of an oral book report**
- **To write, practice, and present an oral book report**

WARM-UP

Read, Listen, Speak

Read aloud your sentences from yesterday's For Tomorrow homework. Invite small groups to share their sentences. Encourage students to talk about the books they have read.

GRAMMAR CONNECTION

Take this opportunity to review adjectives. You may wish to have students point out adjectives in their Read, Listen, Speak examples.

TEACH

Have a volunteer read aloud the first paragraph. Ask students to describe the purpose of a book report *(to share what you have read with others)*. Then ask students to name things that should be included in a book report *(title, author's name, setting, characters, plot)*. Explain that an oral book report is similar to a written book report.

Ask volunteers to tell what information goes in the beginning of a written book report *(book title, author's name, characters, setting)*. Then have a volunteer read aloud the section Beginning. Point out that students should begin their oral book report by telling the audience the book's title and author's name. Ask students why they might want to show the book to the audience.

Have volunteers read aloud the section Middle. Review that the middle of a book report tells about the plot, but does not give away the ending. Tell students that they might want to read aloud one or

two short parts from the book during their oral book report.

Have a volunteer read aloud the section Ending. Point out that an oral book report, just like a written book report, tells whether readers might like the book and explains why or why not.

Have a volunteer read aloud the section Prepare. Ask students to tell why note cards might be helpful *(to remember important information)*. Ask students what kinds of information they might write on note cards for an oral book report *(book title, name of the author, characters, plot, examples that show what the speaker thought about the book)*.

PRACTICE

ACTIVITY A

Encourage students to include three or four books on their lists. Tell students to save their completed lists.

ACTIVITY B

Ask students to describe the books they listed. Have students discuss their chosen books.

ACTIVITY C

Remind students that the plot of their story includes the main character's problem and solution.

Oral Book Reports

Have you ever read an interesting book that you wanted to share with friends? Giving an oral book report is one way to tell others about a book that you have read.

Beginning

Begin your talk by stating the name of the book and its author. Bring the book to show to your audience. Give your listeners an idea of what the book is about.

Middle

In the middle of your talk, tell what happens in the book. You may want to read a short part from the book. Reading from the book gives your listeners a chance to hear the words the author uses. Don't give away the ending! Let readers find out for themselves how the book ends.

Ending

End your talk by telling your audience what you thought of the book. You could say that you did not like the book. Or you could say that it was one of your favorites. Make sure that you tell your audience why you liked or did not like the book.

Prepare

After you choose a book for your talk, look through the book and write on note cards the important parts of the plot. If the book has pictures, look at them too. You might show the pictures in your talk.

ACTIVITY D

Ask volunteers to read aloud the parts that they chose and to explain why they might want to read these parts in an oral book report.

APPLY

SPEAKER'S CORNER

Observe students as they write their note cards and help those who are having trouble. Encourage students to include detailed information about the setting, plot, and characters. Students should demonstrate the ability to identify characteristics of an oral book report.

ASSESS

Note which students had difficulty understanding oral book reports. Use the Reteach option with those students who need additional reinforcement.

ACTIVITY A Talk with a partner about books that you have read. Write the titles and authors. Tell your partner what each book is about, who the characters are, and what the setting is. Then talk with your partner about whether or not you liked each book.

ACTIVITY B Talk with a partner about the books you wrote in Activity A. Which book is the most fun to talk about? Which book do you think your class would like to hear about? Choose one of the books for your book report. Then ask your partner to choose a book from his or her list. Tell your partner which book you would be most interested in hearing about.

ACTIVITY C Look through your book to help you remember the story. Write on note cards information about the characters, setting, and plot that you want to share with your listeners. If your book has a contents page, look at it to help you find information in the book. Use the note cards when you give your talk.

ACTIVITY D Look through your book and find a place that you would like to read aloud to your audience. Put a bookmark at the page so you can find it quickly when you give your talk.

SPEAKER'S CORNER

Write on note cards the three best events from the book you chose in Activity B. Then write what you thought of the book. Look through your book to help you remember the characters and the plot.

Book Reports • 385

TEACHING OPTIONS

Reteach

Have students prepare a two-minute advertisement to sell a book to the class. Encourage students to include the title, author, plot, and their own reaction to the book. Tell students they may use illustrations from the book or make up a visual of their own to add interest to their presentation. Point out that students may also use other props that will help sell the book (*a fire hat for a book about a firefighter, a stuffed dog for a book about a puppy*). Encourage students to offer constructive criticism after each presentation.

10 Facts

Have students choose a book and write 10 facts about it. Point out that writing 10 simple facts about a book is a good way to prepare for an oral presentation about a book. Have students write the title of the book and the 10 facts on a sheet of poster board. Have students illustrate their 10 facts. Ask volunteers to share their 10-fact posters. Display the completed posters in the classroom.

For Tomorrow

Have students practice with a family member reading aloud from a book. Ask students to bring the book to class. Bring in your own book to read aloud.

Read, Listen, Speak

Read aloud from your book from yesterday's For Tomorrow homework. Explain why you chose the book. Have small groups discuss why they chose their books. Ask volunteers to read aloud the part they practiced at home. Ask students how practicing the reading helped them read better today.

TEACH

Ask a volunteer to read aloud the first paragraph of the section Tone of Voice. Invite volunteers to speak in the different tones of voice that are mentioned in the paragraph. Have a volunteer read aloud the next paragraph. Ask students to describe the tone of voice that would be good for a book report. Point out that students might want to use an excited tone of voice when they tell how they feel about the book. Tell students that they may also want to use an excited tone of voice when they tell about the plot because that will help listeners to get excited about the story.

Read aloud the third paragraph. Invite volunteers to demonstrate different voices they could use to describe different moods. Then ask volunteers to read aloud dialogue from a book, using the tone of voice the characters might use.

Have volunteers read aloud the section Practice. Ask students to tell why looking at notes for help might be better than reading the notes to the class.

Invite volunteers to read aloud the section Listening Tips. Explain that good listening skills help the speaker to feel comfortable while giving an oral report. Tell students that good listening skills can also help listeners follow the oral book report and help them to avoid getting confused.

PRACTICE

ACTIVITY E

Have students complete this activity with partners. Encourage students to help their partners gather the appropriate information about their authors. Invite volunteers to share the information they found and to explain why it might add to their book reports. Tell students to decide if they want to include this information in their oral book reports.

ACTIVITY F

Encourage students to reread the last paragraph of the book report on page 363 for an example. Tell students to write at least three reasons on their note cards.

ACTIVITY G

Point out that if students practice reading several times, it will be easier to look at the audience occasionally and then look back at the book without losing their place. Encourage students to consider their partners' suggestions for making their reading more interesting.

Tone of Voice

Think about the times you've told your friends or family about something that you really liked. Did you tell people by using a quiet tone of voice? Or did you sound excited by using a lively tone of voice? Which way would make someone interested in what you have to say?

Use your tone of voice to show your feelings about your book. Speak lively, even if you did not like the book. Your audience wants to know what you think.

When you read aloud from your book, speak in a way that shows the mood of the story. Use a more excited voice if you are reading an exciting part. Use a deeper or slower voice if you are reading a spooky part. If you read dialogue from a character, use the tone of voice that you think the character would use.

Practice

Practice giving your talk. Ask a partner to listen to it. Ask your partner for ways to make your talk better. Remember to do these things.

- Introduce the book by telling its title and author. Hold up the book so everyone can see it.
- Speak loudly, clearly, and slowly. Tell your audience about the characters in the book. Tell what the book is about. Use your tone of voice to show your feelings about the book.
- Look at your audience. If you have notes, look at them, but do not simply read them aloud.
- Tell why you liked or did not like the book.

APPLY

SPEAKER'S CORNER

Have students practice their book reports with a partner. Encourage partners to give constructive feedback. Then have students form small groups and present their oral book reports. Students should demonstrate the ability to present an oral book report.

ASSESS

Note which students had difficulty presenting an oral book report. Use the Reteach option with those students who need additional reinforcement.

After you have reviewed Lessons 3–5, administer the Writing Skills Assessment on pages 55–56 in the **Assessment Book.** This test is also available on the optional **Test Generator CD.**

Reteach

Choose a book the class has recently read. Present an oral book report on the book as a model for students. During your presentation, stop and ask questions about important information you have included and about the organization of your oral report. Continue your presentation, stopping in strategic places to point out your tone of voice and word choice. After you have completed your report, allow time for students to provide feedback and comments about how your report compared to what they have learned in this lesson.

English-Language Learners

Have partners choose a fairy tale or movie they both know. Allow time for partners to work together to prepare an oral report on their fairy tale or movie. Encourage partners to divide the speaking parts and to be open to each other's suggestions. Encourage students with different opinions about the book or movie to tell their opinions separately at the end. Have volunteers present their oral reports to the class.

Book Report Comic Strips

Have students make a simple comic strip about a book of their choice. Tell students to use one frame to tell the author and title. Instruct them to use two frames to describe the plot and use the final frame to tell what they liked about the book. Challenge students to use their comic strip to give a short oral book report.

Listening Tips

Listen to your classmates' book reports. You might hear about a book you would want to read. Do these things while you listen.

- Look at the person giving the talk. Pay attention to what he or she is saying.
- Picture the characters and setting in your mind. Think about what happens in the book.
- If you have read the book the speaker is talking about, think about what you liked or didn't like about the book. Does the speaker talk about what you remember? Do you agree with the speaker?
- Don't interrupt the speaker. Wait until he or she is finished before raising your hand to ask a question.

ACTIVITY E Use the library or the Internet to look up information about the author of your book. You might share what you learned about the author during your talk.

ACTIVITY F Think about why you liked or did not like your book. Write on note cards some of the reasons why you feel that way. Use the note cards when you give your talk.

ACTIVITY G Take turns reading to a partner a short part from your book. Do it more than once so you feel comfortable looking up from your book. Ask your partner to suggest ways that you can change the tone of your voice to make it more interesting to your listeners.

SPEAKER'S CORNER

Practice and present the book report you chose in Activity B. Use the tips you learned to help give your talk.

Book Reports • 387

OBJECTIVES

- **To choose a book for a book report**
- **To organize information for a book report**

PREWRITING AND DRAFTING

Have a volunteer read aloud the first paragraph. Discuss books students may have recommended to friends or relatives. Encourage students to tell about books they have read. Explain that a book report is a chance to share feelings about a book.

Prewriting

Have a volunteer read aloud this section. Tell students that a book report can be about a book the writer liked or about a book that the writer disliked. Ask students if they would rather write about a book they liked or a book they disliked. Encourage students to consider the advantages and disadvantages of both choices.

Choosing a Book

Have a volunteer read aloud the first paragraph. Ask students why Callie might have wanted to pick a book that other students in her class had not read. Then ask why it might be important for Callie to pick a book she remembers well.

👀 Point out that choosing a book other students have not read will maintain audience interest in their book reports.

Read aloud the second paragraph. Ask students to list Callie's reasons for choosing *Abel's Island*. Encourage volunteers to name things they enjoy in the books they have read, such as certain kinds of characters, settings, or plots.

Your Turn

Read aloud the section. Suggest that students pick a book that they have read recently or that they remember well. Explain that a book that students have at home or that is available in the library might be a good choice.

Planning the Book Report

Have volunteers read aloud the first paragraph and Callie's plan. Review character and plot.

Writer's Workshop
Book Reports

Prewriting and Drafting

Have you ever told someone about a book you liked or about a book you didn't like? Writing a book report is a way to tell many people about a book. In a book report, you share what you thought about the book. If you really enjoyed a book, this is a way to tell other people how much you enjoyed it.

Prewriting

Callie is a third grader who wrote a book report for class. Callie needed to choose a book before she could write her book report. She wanted to pick her book carefully and plan her book report before she started writing.

Choosing a Book

Callie wanted to write a book report about a book that she enjoyed. She thought about 👀 **Ideas** the books that she had recently read. Callie wanted to pick a book that no one else in her class had read. She also wanted to pick one that she remembered well.

Callie remembered reading *Abel's Island* by William Steig. Abel, the main character, is a mouse. He has many funny and exciting adventures. Callie thought she would do well writing about this book because she enjoyed thinking about it.

Your Turn

Choose a book that you remember well and that you would like to write about. Or choose a new book that you really want to read now and report on that.

Planning the Book Report

Now that Callie knew what book she was 👀 **Organization** going to write about, she started to plan her book report. This is Callie's plan with some information already filled in.

Have a volunteer read aloud the last paragraph. Ask students why Callie might have used circles, squares, and triangles to divide her plan *(to help her organize her ideas)*.

 Tell students that the organization of their book report is the way the book report is arranged. Explain that Callie's book organization is based on the parts of a book report *(beginning, middle, ending)*.

Your Turn

Invite a volunteer to read aloud this section. Have students make a plan like Callie's, filling in the plan with information about the books they selected. Point out that students should spend most of their time writing about the last three items.

When students have finished their plans, allow them to meet with a partner to discuss their plans and why they did or did not like the book they are writing about. Encourage students to write any new ideas they have as they talk.

○ Books in Space

Allow time for students to double-check information on the books they chose to write about. Guide students to a Web site for a public library or commercial bookseller. Show students how to use the Web site to locate information on the author and title of their book. Explain that some Web sites tell what the books are about and might give the characters' names and the setting. Tell students that looking up a book can help them be sure that their information is correct and can also help refresh their memories.

My Plan

- Ⓑ Book Title: Abel's Island
- Ⓑ Author: William Steig
- Ⓑ Main character: Abel
- Ⓑ Setting: A deserted island
- Ⓜ Plot:

- △Ⓔ What I thought about the book:

- △Ⓔ Why I thought that way about the book:

Callie completed the plan. She wrote a circled Ⓑ beside the ideas that would go in the beginning. She then drew a square around an Ⓜ by the ideas for the middle, and a triangle around an △Ⓔ by the ideas for the ending. It was easy to see where the information went in the book report. She knew it was now easier to write the first draft of her book report.

Your Turn

- Write a plan like the one that Callie used for her book report.
- Complete the plan with the information about your book.
- Talk with a partner about the parts that will go into your book report.

Prewriting | Drafting | Content Editing | Revising | Copyediting | Proofreading | Publishing

Book Reports • 389

OBJECTIVE
- **To draft a book report**

Drafting

Invite a volunteer to read aloud the first paragraph. Ask students to explain why it is important not to give away the ending of a book. Then ask volunteers to read aloud Callie's draft.

Tell students that Callie wrote her draft, using her prewriting notes. Ask students to locate the following information in Callie's draft: the book's title, the author's name, the characters' names, the setting, a description of the plot, and how Callie felt about the book. Point out that Callie wrote why she liked the book and not just whether or not she liked it. Ask volunteers to tell why Callie liked *Abel's Island*.

Your Turn

Read aloud this section. Remind students to use their prewriting notes as they write their drafts. Tell students to use examples from their books to support whether they liked or did not like the books. Then allow time for students to write their first drafts.

Writer's Tip Tell students that extra space between lines will give them room to edit, as well as making their draft easier to read.

Drafting

Now it was time for Callie to write her draft. She used her plan from prewriting to help her. First, she wrote a beginning to tell about Abel and the setting of the book. Then she wrote in the middle what happens to Abel. Callie made sure not to give away the ending of the book. She finished the book report with an ending that told what she thought about *Abel's Island*.

Abel's Island
by William Steig

Abel's Island by William Steig is a wonderful book. It is a story about Abel Flint the mouse. The book is set in 1904 on a desserted island and Abel is a spoiled mouse who is trying to get home to his wife. Abel is on a picnic by a river with his new wife, Amanda. I thought the story of Abel was something that people could like if they have spent a lot of time on their own in the country.

When he chases it because Amanda's scarf blows away. He falls into the river. He is swept downstream, and he washes up on an island. He hopes to be saved, but that doesn't happen. He must learn to live alone on an island about 12,000 tails long. It is just like if I measured my house using my own feet! Abel is used to the comforts of home. But on the island he has adventures just trying to do everyday things. He has to find a place to live! He also has to find food to eat. He has to try not to be eaten himself. To make things harder. Through many adventures Abel learns to live in nature. Slowly he starts to try to find a way to get home to Amanda.

Using Examples

Ask a volunteer to read aloud this section. Point out where in Callie's draft she used examples that show why she thought the book was funny. Ask students what example tells why Callie couldn't stop reading the book. *(Abel fights so hard to live so he can see Amanda again.)* Invite volunteers to name something from their books that made them feel a certain way. Ask those volunteers to tell the class about what happened in the book and how it made them feel.

Starting in the Middle

Tell students that all the parts of a piece of writing are important but that in many forms of writing, the middle is the most important part. Tell students that the middle usually has the most information. Explain that in a book report, the middle tells the plot of the book. Suggest that students write the middle part of their book report first. Tell students that what they write in the middle might help them write the beginning and the ending later.

<u>Abel's Island</u> is filled with exciting adventures. I won't forget the funny characters. They made me laugh because they are animals that talk, dress, and act like people. I couldn't stop reading about how Abel fights so hard to live so he can see Amanda again.

Prewriting · *Drafting* · *Content Editing* · *Revising* · *Copyediting* · *Proofreading* · *Publishing*

Your Turn

- Write the first draft of your book report. Make sure to start with the title of the book and the name of the author.
- Write the beginning. Tell the reader about the main characters and the setting of the book. The setting of the book tells the reader when and where the story happens.
- Write the middle of the book report. Tell the reader what happens, but don't give too much away.
- Write the ending. Write what you thought about the book. Give examples in your book report to show whether or not you liked the book.

Writer's Tip When you write your book report, leave extra space between the lines. That way you will have room to make changes later.

Using Examples

In your book report, support what you say. If something is sad, explain why it is sad, using examples from the book. If something is funny, tell why you think it is. In Callie's book report, she said that the book is funny. She shows why it is funny by saying that the animals acted like people.

OBJECTIVE

- To edit a book report for content

CONTENT EDITING

Ask students to explain what it means to content edit a piece of writing *(to check that the ideas are clear and in the right order).* Then ask students to predict what they might find on a content editor's checklist for a book report.

Invite volunteers to read aloud the first two paragraphs. Ask students to explain why Callie might want someone else to content edit her draft. *(A different reader can tell if the ideas are clear.)*

Have volunteers read aloud the Content Editor's Checklist and discuss each item. Invite a volunteer to read aloud the first paragraph after the checklist. Ask students to explain why it might be helpful to use a content editor who has already read the book. *(The content editor can check that the book has been described correctly.)* Ask students why it might also be helpful to use a content editor who has not read the book. *(The content editor can read the book report to see if it will be clear to people who have not read the book.)*

Editor's Workshop Book Reports

Content Editing

Callie wanted to make her draft better. She knew that there were parts of her report she didn't like. She hoped that she would improve her book report by editing it for content.

Callie thought it would be a good idea to ask someone she trusted to content edit her book report. Callie decided to ask Selma. She is a friend of Callie's who lives nearby. Selma would check whether the ideas made sense. She used the Content Editor's Checklist.

Content Editor's Checklist

- [ ] Does the writing stay on the topic?
- [ ] Are the characters and setting introduced in the beginning?
- [ ] Is the plot discussed in the middle?
- [ ] Did you make sure not to give away the ending of the book?
- [ ] Does the ending tell what you think of the book?

392 • Chapter 5

Have volunteers read aloud the bulleted items. Then ask volunteers to explain why they agree or disagree with each of Selma's ideas.

Read aloud the last paragraph. Remind students that a content editor's suggestions are valuable only if they improve the writing. Tell students to think about each suggestion they receive before they decide to make a change.

Writer's Tip Tell students that if their partners did not understand what they were trying to say, they have the chance to make it clear when they revise.

Your Turn

Invite a volunteer to read aloud this section. Then have students trade drafts. Encourage students to discuss difficulties they had writing their book reports. Allow time for partners to content edit each other's drafts. Remind students to begin their discussion with what they liked about their partner's book report.

TEACHING OPTIONS

Different Opinions

Remind students that the ending of a book report is where writers tell why they liked or disliked the book. Explain that some people may feel differently about the same book because people enjoy different kinds of books. Suggest that when students disagree with someone about a book, they could talk about it to learn why they feel differently. Point out that students should show respect to people who disagree with them.

Selma told Callie that she liked the way that the main character and the setting were introduced in the beginning. This would help the reader understand the part about the plot in the middle. Then Selma told Callie these ideas.

- You have information about the plot in the beginning. It should be in the middle.
- The last sentence of the beginning is interesting, but it is what you think about the book. That sentence should be in the ending.
- The part about measuring your house with your feet was funny, but off the topic. It was not a part of the book.
- Why don't you say how Abel starts to find a way to get home to Amanda?

Callie thanked Selma for her help. She was glad Selma liked her book report. But she wasn't sure she was going to use all of Selma's ideas.

Writer's Tip Remember to write your partner's ideas. Think about each one. Make the changes that will make your book report more useful for your readers.

Your Turn

- Work with a partner and read each other's book reports.
- Pay attention to one question in the checklist at a time.
- When you have finished, take turns talking about each other's drafts.

Prewriting
Drafting
Content Editing
Revising
Copyediting
Proofreading
Publishing

394 • Chapter 5

OBJECTIVE

- **To revise a book report**

REVISING

Ask students to read Callie's revised draft silently. Review any proofreading marks that give students difficulty. Then have students read aloud the sentence below Callie's draft and the bulleted items. After each question, ask a volunteer to find the change that Callie made in her draft.

- Callie moved the sentence about the plot to the middle of the draft. It became the first sentence of the middle.
- Callie took the sentence out.
- Callie took out the part about measuring the ranch because it didn't have anything to do with the book.

Writer's Workshop   Book Reports

Revising

This is how Callie revised her draft.

Abel's Island
by William Steig

<u>Abel's Island</u> by William Steig is a wonderful book. It is a story about Abel Flint the mouse. The book is set in 1904 on a desserted island and Abel is a spoiled mouse who is trying to get home to his wife. ⟨Abel is on a picnic by a river with his new wife, Amanda.⟩ ~~I thought the story of Abel was something that people could like if they have spent a lot of time on their own in the country.~~ when he chases it because Amanda's scarf blows away. He falls into the river. He is swept downstream, and he washes up on an island. He hopes to be saved, but that doesn't happen. He must learn to live alone on an island about 12,000 tails long. ~~It is just like if I measured my house using my own feet!~~ Abel is used to the comforts of home. But on the island he has adventures just trying to do everyday things. He has to find a place to live! He also has to find food to eat. He has to try not to be eaten himself. To make things harder. Through many adventures Abel learns to live in nature. Slowly he starts to try to find a way to get home to Amanda.

Have a volunteer read aloud the last paragraph. Ask a volunteer to read aloud from Callie's revised draft the sentence she added to the ending. Ask students to explain whether they think the sentence improves the ending.

👓 Tell students that their words can show that a real person is speaking and that that person cares about the message.

Your Turn

Read this section aloud. Remind students to think about each idea they have and each idea their content editor gave them before they put it in their drafts. Tell students to ask themselves if the change will make their drafts clearer. After students have decided which changes to make, allow time for them to make the changes.

Everything in Its Place

Tell students that the beginning, the middle, and the ending of a book report each does a special job. Suggest that before students add new information, they check that they are adding it to the right part of the book report. Point out that they can use the circles, squares, and triangles they used in prewriting to mark their list of ideas.

Abel's Island is filled with exciting adventures. I won't forget the funny characters. They made me laugh because they are animals that talk, dress, and act like people. I couldn't stop reading about how Abel fights so hard to live so he can see Amanda again. The book makes you think about what people can do if they want something badly enough.

Prewriting

Drafting

Content Editing

Revising

Copyediting

Proofreading

Publishing

Here are some things that Callie did to improve her book report.

- Callie agreed that the sentence about the plot didn't belong in the beginning. Where did she move the sentence?
- What did Callie do to the last sentence of the beginning? Do you agree with this change?
- Callie took out the part about measuring her house. Why?

As Callie looked at her book report again, she saw that her ending didn't seem complete. Callie thought about adding how Abel tries to find a way home. But she kept it out because it would give away the ending 👓 Voice of the book. Callie wanted her ending to tell how she felt about the book. What did Callie do?

Your Turn

- Use your ideas and your content editor's ideas to revise your draft.
- Look at the Content Editor's Checklist again. Answer each question while reading your book report.

Book Reports • 395

OBJECTIVES
- **To copyedit a book report**
- **To proofread a book report**

COPYEDITING AND PROOFREADING

Copyediting

Tell students that revising a piece of writing in steps is like using a checklist. Explain that each step covers a special thing to do. Then ask a volunteer to explain what copyediting is *(checking that the draft has complete sentences and good word choices).*

Have volunteers read aloud the first paragraph and the items on the checklist. Elaborate on items that may cause students difficulty.

Ask a volunteer to read aloud the two paragraphs following the checklist. Ask students how Callie could make the fourth sentence of the second paragraph more clear. *(He hopes to be saved, but he isn't.)*

Have a volunteer read aloud the last paragraph. Help students find the incomplete sentence. *(To make things harder.)* Ask students why the sentence is incomplete. Invite volunteers to suggest ways to fix the incomplete sentence.

Tell students that sentence fluency is the rhythm and flow of their writing. Explain that breaking up longer sentences and varying the length of sentences makes their writing more clear and natural.

Your Turn

Read aloud this section. Tell students to use the Copyeditor's Checklist to check their work. Have students check only one item at a time. When students have finished, encourage them to read aloud their drafts quietly to see if any sentences could be improved.

Suggest that students look for opportunities to add descriptive adjectives in their writing.

Proofreading

Invite a volunteer to read aloud the first paragraph. Ask students to explain the difference between copyediting and proofreading. *(Copyediting is checking that sentences and words are clear. Proofreading is checking that punctuation, capitalization, and spelling are correct.)* Have students read aloud the Proofreader's Checklist. Point out the final question. Explain that because students have revised their drafts several times, they may have added or taken out a lot. Tell students that the final question will help to remind them to look for new mistakes they might have added when they revised.

Editor's Workshop

Book Reports

Copyediting and Proofreading

Copyediting

Callie knew that her book report was much stronger. Selma suggested that Callie copyedit her book report. By copyediting, Callie could check whether all the sentences and words were used correctly. Callie used this checklist to copyedit her book report.

Copyeditor's Checklist

- ☐ Are all the sentences complete sentences?
- ☐ Do the sentences make sense?
- ☐ Do the sentences make sense one after the other?
- ☐ Are compound predicates used correctly?
- ☐ Have exact words been used?

Callie found three sentences that she thought needed some work. The third sentence in the first paragraph seemed too long. **Sentence Fluency** When she read it again, she realized that the sentence was about both the character and the setting. She wanted to make a sentence about each. What could Callie do with the sentence?

The next problem was the second sentence of the second paragraph. Callie didn't think the sentence made sense. How could she fix it?

Finally, Callie found an incomplete sentence near the end of the second paragraph. Can you find it? How would you fix it?

Your Turn

Copyedit your book report. Look for **Word Choice** only one kind of mistake at a time. If you have problems with a sentence or word, ask someone for help. Look for ways to make your words and sentences clearer.

Ask volunteers to read aloud the next two paragraphs. Tell students that exclamation points can be useful in writing but they should not be overused.

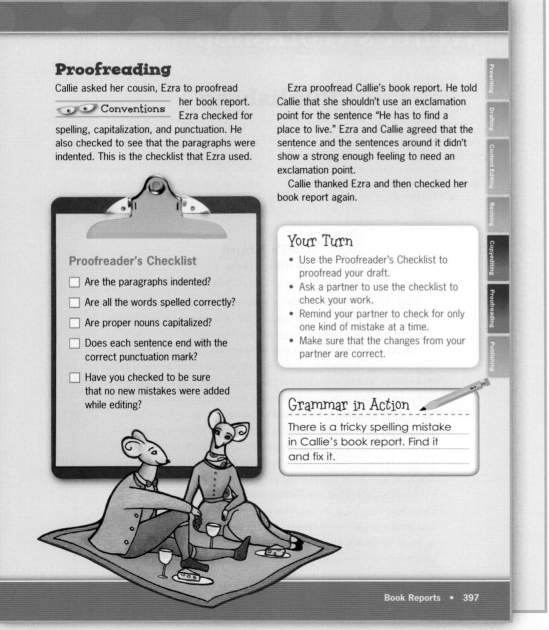 Explain that writing conventions include spelling, punctuation, and capitalization. Encourage students to keep these conventions in mind during every step of the writing process, especially during proofreading.

Your Turn

Read aloud this section. Tell students to check for one kind of mistake at a time, using the Proofreader's Checklist. Allow time for students to proofread their drafts. Then have students trade drafts and proofread a partner's draft. Encourage students to check that their partner's changes are correct before making the changes.

Grammar in Action. Guide students to find the spelling mistake. *(The word* desserted *was spelled wrong. The correct spelling is* deserted.*)* Write the words *dessert* and *desert* on the board. Explain that it is easy for writers to confuse these words. Tell students that they can tell which word is correct if they remember to imagine that in *dessert* the extra *s* stands for *sweet.*

TEACHING OPTIONS

Three More Proofreading Tips

Share the following proofreading tips with the class:

1. **Work in a quiet place.** Try to get rid of any noise that might distract you, such as music or TV.

2. **Slow down when you read.** Pay attention to each word, letter, and punctuation mark.

3. **Always proofread on a written or printed copy.** Mistakes are easier to spot on paper than on a computer screen.

Proofreading

Callie asked her cousin, Ezra to proofread her book report. **Conventions** Ezra checked for spelling, capitalization, and punctuation. He also checked to see that the paragraphs were indented. This is the checklist that Ezra used.

Ezra proofread Callie's book report. He told Callie that she shouldn't use an exclamation point for the sentence "He has to find a place to live." Ezra and Callie agreed that the sentence and the sentences around it didn't show a strong enough feeling to need an exclamation point.

Callie thanked Ezra and then checked her book report again.

Proofreader's Checklist

☐ Are the paragraphs indented?

☐ Are all the words spelled correctly?

☐ Are proper nouns capitalized?

☐ Does each sentence end with the correct punctuation mark?

☐ Have you checked to be sure that no new mistakes were added while editing?

Your Turn

• Use the Proofreader's Checklist to proofread your draft.

• Ask a partner to use the checklist to check your work.

• Remind your partner to check for only one kind of mistake at a time.

• Make sure that the changes from your partner are correct.

Grammar in Action

There is a tricky spelling mistake in Callie's book report. Find it and fix it.

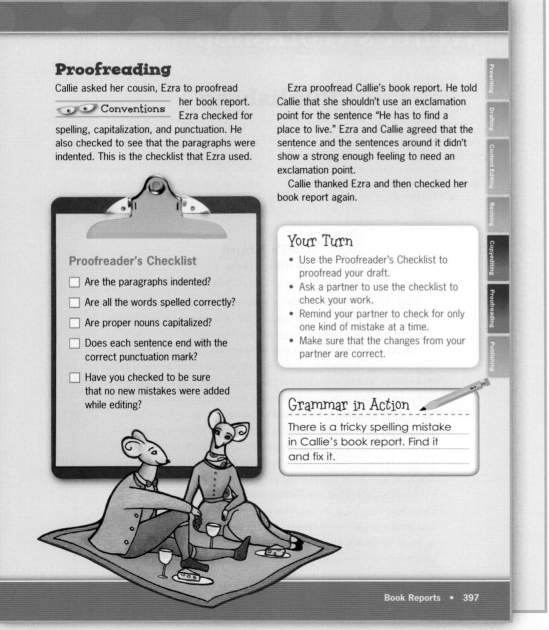

Tabs: Prewriting, Drafting, Content Editing, Revising, Copyediting, Proofreading, Publishing

OBJECTIVE
- **To publish a book report**

PUBLISHING

Have a volunteer read aloud the first paragraph. Point out that Callie enjoyed writing about *Abel's Island* because she liked the book and wanted others to read it. Explain that when students enjoy a book, there are many ways they can explore more about it. Tell students that Callie decided to read more about mice.

👀 Remind students that presentation is the look of their book report. Tell them their book report should look neat and welcoming to the reader.

Have volunteers read aloud Callie's final draft. Ask students to compare the final draft to the first draft. Discuss ways that Callie improved her draft each time she revised.

Discuss the many ways students might publish their book reports.

Your Turn

Ask volunteers to read aloud the bulleted items. Tell students to look over all the revisions that they have made to their drafts. Tell students to read their book reports one more time, looking for any additional mistakes.

Ask students to name things in their books they might like to read more about. Ask students what other topics Callie might have chosen to learn more about. Share with students the following ways that they might further explore a book, a character, or an author.

Writer's Workshop   Book Reports

Publishing

Publishing is sharing your work with an audience. Callie carefully typed the final draft of her book report. Since she wrote a book report, she knew that many people would be reading it to learn about the book. Callie liked the book *Abel's Island*. Reading it had made 👀 **Presentation** her want to learn more about mice, so she included some pictures and facts about mice with her book report.

Abel's Island
by William Steig

Book Report by Callie O'Sullivan

<u>Abel's Island</u> by William Steig is a wonderful book. It is a story about Abel Flint the mouse. The book is set in 1904 on a deserted island. Abel is a spoiled mouse who is trying to get home to his wife.

Abel is on a picnic by a river with his new wife, Amanda. When Amanda's scarf blows away, he chases it. He falls into the river. He is swept downstream, and he washes up on an island. He hopes to be saved, but that doesn't happen. He must learn to live alone on an island about 12,000 tails long. Abel is used to the comforts of home. But on the island he has adventures just trying to do everyday things. He has to find a place to live. He also has to find food to eat. To make things harder, he has to try not to be eaten himself. Through many adventures Abel learns to live in nature. Slowly he starts to try to find a way to get home to Amanda.

<u>Abel's Island</u> is filled with exciting adventures. I won't forget the funny characters. They made me laugh because they are animals that talk, dress, and act like people. I couldn't stop reading about how Abel fights so hard to live so he can see Amanda again. The book makes you think about what people can do if they want something badly enough.

- Check whether the book is part of a series. Many series feature the same characters.
- Find other books by the same author. Many authors write in a particular way, and students may enjoy other books written by the same author.
- Read nonfiction about parts of the book, such as the setting, characters, or historical period.
- Ask a librarian. Librarians can provide recommendations for further reading. Students can tell a librarian about the book they enjoyed and ask for other books that are similar.

ASSESS

Have students assess their finished book report using the reproducible Student Self-Assessment on page 399y. A separate Book Report Scoring Rubric can be found on page 399z for you to use to evaluate their work.

Plan to spend tomorrow doing a formal assessment. Administer the Book Report Writing Prompt on **Assessment Book** pages 57–58.

There are many ways you can publish your book report.

 Post your report to a Web site that publishes children's book reports. Work with an adult to find an appropriate site and share your report with the world.

 Make a classroom newsletter. Include all of your classmates' book reports so that the class can learn about books they might be interested in.

 Mail or e-mail your report to a local newspaper or to a children's magazine. If it gets printed, be sure to save a copy or two for your scrapbook.

 Make a poster with a picture and facts about what you have read. Display your book report and your poster.

Whenever you publish your work, your goal is to share your thoughts and experiences with other people.

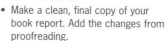
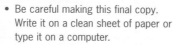

Your Turn

- Make a clean, final copy of your book report. Add the changes from proofreading.
- Be careful making this final copy. Write it on a clean sheet of paper or type it on a computer.
- People are going to read this book report to see whether or not they want to read the book. If you want people to follow your opinion, your book report will have to be written well.
- When you have finished, choose one thing from the story to read more about. If your book is set in the rain forest, you might choose to read about the Amazon rain forest.

Name _____   Date _____

Book Report

	YES	NO
Ideas		
Did I focus on the book?		
Organization		
Do I have a beginning that names the title, author, characters, and setting?		
Does the middle describe the main events in time order?		
Does the ending sum up my opinion of the book?		
Voice		
Does my voice seem lively and confident?		
Word Choice		
Do I use carefully chosen adjectives?		
Sentence Fluency		
Do I use different kinds of sentences, including those with compound predicates?		
Conventions		
Do I use correct grammar?		
Do I use correct spelling?		
Do I use correct punctuation and capitalization?		
Presentation		
Does my report look neat?		
Do I use consistent margins and spacing?		
Additional Items		

Name ______________________________

Date ______________________ Score __________

POINT VALUES

0 = not evident
1 = minimal evidence of mastery
2 = evidence of development toward mastery
3 = strong evidence of mastery
4 = outstanding evidence of mastery

Book Report

	POINTS
Ideas	
a clear focus on the book	
Organization	
a beginning that identifies the title, author, characters, and setting	
a middle that describes the main events in time order	
an ending that sums up the writer's opinion of the book	
Voice	
confident, lively voice	
Word Choice	
carefully chosen adjectives	
Sentence Fluency	
a variety of sentences, including those with compound predicates	
Conventions	
correct grammar and usage	
correct spelling	
correct punctuation and capitalization	
Presentation	
neatness	
consistent margins and spacing	
Additional Items	
Total	

CHAPTER FOCUS

LESSON 1: What Makes Good Persuasive Writing?

LESSON 2: Beginning, Middle, and Ending

- **GRAMMAR:** Adverbs and Conjunctions
- **STUDY SKILLS:** Idea Webs
- **WRITING SKILLS:** Compound Sentences
- **WORD STUDY:** Suffixes
- **SPEAKING AND LISTENING SKILLS:** Persuasive Speeches
- **WRITER'S WORKSHOP:** Persuasive Writing

SUPPORT MATERIALS

Practice Book
Writing, pages 157–161

Assessment Book
Chapter 6 Writing Skills,
   pages 59–60
Persuasive Writing Prompt,
   pages 61–62

Rubrics
Student, page 437y
Teacher, page 437z

Test Generator CD

Grammar
Section 6, pages 135–156

Customizable Lesson Plans
www.voyagesinenglish.com

Persuasive Writing

WHAT IS PERSUASIVE WRITING?

Persuasive writing is used to convince the reader of a writer's position. Good persuasive writing prompts the reader to thought and action. Persuasive writing can take many forms, including letters, speeches, advertisements, and articles.

Persuasive articles focus on one topic that can be viewed in different or opposing ways. All the ideas in good persuasive articles work toward convincing the reader to share the author's viewpoint.

The beginning of a persuasive article often clearly states the writer's opinion while engaging the reader. The middle of a persuasive article provides practical reasons for agreeing with the position statement. These reasons are supported with factual evidence using language that appeals to the reader's emotions. The ending often summarizes the position statement and calls on the reader to think or act.

Good persuasive articles are often organized so that each reason is covered in a separate paragraph, making the writing clear and easy to read. A well-crafted persuasive article includes the following:

- ☐ A focus on one viewpoint regarding a specific topic
- ☐ A beginning with a position statement
- ☐ A middle with reasons that support the stated position
- ☐ An ending that summarizes the position statement
- ☐ A persuasive voice
- ☐ A variety of sentences, including compound sentences
- ☐ Opinion words such as *should, ought, must,* or *believe*

LiNK Use the following titles to offer your students examples of well-crafted persuasive writing:

Advertising by Bess Milton

If Everybody Did by Jo Ann Stover

Why Should I Recycle? by Jen Green

"The persuasion of a friend is a strong thing."

—Homer

WRITER'S WORKSHOP TIPS

Follow these ideas and tips to help you and your class get the most out of the Writer's Workshop:

- Review the traits of good writing. Use the chart on the inside back cover of the student and teacher editions.

- Create a bulletin-board display that includes persuasive direct mail from political candidates or advocacy groups, letters to the editor, advertisements, and persuasive articles from magazines and newspapers.

- Hold a classroom debate about a current school topic. Point out student examples of effective arguments that support their position on the topic. Explain how these kinds of arguments can translate into students' writing.

- Discuss ideas such as bias and propaganda. Be sure to help students avoid this kind of persuasive writing.

- As students consider writing topics, encourage them to ask themselves the following questions: *Do I feel strongly about it? Do I know enough about it? Am I willing to do what I suggest to the readers?*

- Meet with each student during the drafting stage. Create open dialogue by asking questions such as *How can I help you?* or *What is most challenging for you right now?*

CONNECT WITH GRAMMAR

Throughout the Writer's Workshop, look for opportunities to integrate adverbs and conjunctions with writing a persuasive article.

- ☐ During the drafting stage, suggest that students use adverbs that tell how, when, where, and how often in their persuasive articles.

- ☐ When revising, suggest that students create compound sentences, using coordinating conjunctions.

- ☐ In the copyediting stage, have students check that *good* and *well*; *to, too,* and *two*; and *their* and *there* are used correctly.

SCORING RUBRIC

Persuasive Writing

Point Values
0 = not evident
1 = minimal evidence of mastery
2 = evidence of development toward mastery
3 = strong evidence of mastery
4 = outstanding evidence of mastery

Ideas	POINTS
a focus on one viewpoint about a specific topic	
an attempt to convince the reader to share a viewpoint	
reasons backed by research	
Organization	
a beginning with a position statement	
a middle with reasons that support the stated position	
an ending that summarizes the position statement	
Voice	
a persuasive voice	
Word Choice	
opinion words such as *should, ought, must,* or *believe*	
Sentence Fluency	
a variety of sentences, including compound sentences	
Conventions	
correct grammar and usage	
correct spelling	
correct punctuation and capitalization	
Presentation	
neatness	
consistent margins and spacing	
Additional Items	
Total	

Full-sized, reproducible rubrics can be found at the end of this chapter.

Persuasive Writing

INTRODUCING THE GENRE

Tell students that Chapter 6 is about persuasive writing. Explain that if students have ever tried to convince their parents to let them do something, they were persuading. Tell students that persuasive writing tries to convince readers to agree with the writer. Share some age-appropriate forms of persuasive writing (*letters to the editor, TV and radio commercials, magazine and newspaper advertisements*).

Discuss what each example is and what it might persuade an audience to believe or to do.

Elaborate on the following characteristics of persuasive writing:

- The beginning of a persuasive article includes a topic sentence, which states what the writer wants the audience to do.
- The middle of a persuasive article gives reasons why people should agree with the writer. The reasons are usually researched.

- The ending of a persuasive article reminds readers what the writer wants them to do. It also might tell readers what they can do to change something.

Reading the Literature Excerpt

Ask a volunteer to read aloud the persuasive article. Have students explain why it is a good example of persuasive writing. Ask students what the writer wants the reader to think or do (*drink tap water*).

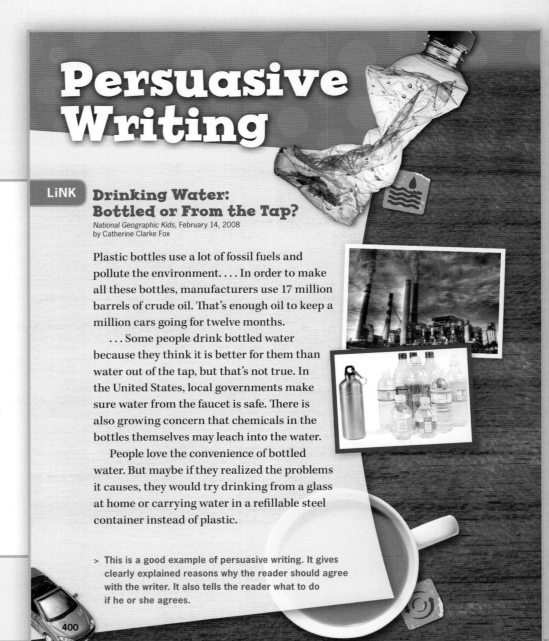

Persuasive Writing

LiNK Drinking Water: Bottled or From the Tap?

This excerpt is a good example of persuasive writing because it has the following:
- A clear topic
- Reasons why people should agree with the writer
- An ending that reminds readers what the writer wants them to do

As students read the excerpts of persuasive writing in this chapter, be sure to point out the characteristics of persuasive writing. Also, be sure to point out the adverbs and conjunctions in the excerpts. For example, point out the negative word (*not*) and the coordinating conjunction (*or*) on this page.

LiNK Drinking Water: Bottled or From the Tap?

National Geographic Kids, February 14, 2008
by Catherine Clarke Fox

Plastic bottles use a lot of fossil fuels and pollute the environment. . . . In order to make all these bottles, manufacturers use 17 million barrels of crude oil. That's enough oil to keep a million cars going for twelve months.

. . . Some people drink bottled water because they think it is better for them than water out of the tap, but that's not true. In the United States, local governments make sure water from the faucet is safe. There is also growing concern that chemicals in the bottles themselves may leach into the water.

People love the convenience of bottled water. But maybe if they realized the problems it causes, they would try drinking from a glass at home or carrying water in a refillable steel container instead of plastic.

> This is a good example of persuasive writing. It gives clearly explained reasons why the reader should agree with the writer. It also tells the reader what to do if he or she agrees.

400

Reading the Student Model

Invite volunteers to read aloud "Faster Library Computers." Ask a volunteer to identify the topic of the article. Tell students that the topic will be a statement that people might agree with. *(We need new computers at our public library.)* Then ask students to identify reasons the writer gives to support the topic. *(Computers at the library would give people who don't have computers a way to use the Internet. Computers would make it easier to find books.)*

Point out that the reasons in a persuasive article are often found in separate paragraphs.

Draw students' attention to the last paragraph. Ask them to identify words and phrases that end the letter in a convincing way. Ask students whether the writer convinced them to support getting computers at the library.

TEACHING OPTIONS

CHAPTER 6

Faster Library Computers

by Jeb Nealson

Have you ever worked on a computer at the Quincy Public Library? You search the Internet for the information you need, but then you give up waiting for the Web site to appear on your screen. These computers are slow. Quincy has extra money in its budget to spend at the library. I believe the money should go to creating a new computer lab.

More and more people are relying on the library's computers for information. They come here to check the Internet for news and to get e-mail from their family and friends. Adding faster computers would give people who don't have computers a way to use the Internet.

The librarians want new computers too. Computers make it easier to find books. The electronic catalog the library has now is slow and hard to figure out. Most libraries have updated computers with faster, easy-to-use electronic catalogs. They are also easier to update.

The citizens of Quincy want and need new computers at the library. If you want new computers there too, please go to the next town meeting.

401

For Tomorrow

Have students find a piece of persuasive writing. Tell students that they should be able to tell what the writer wants readers to do. Bring in your own piece of persuasive writing to share with the class.

OBJECTIVE
- **To understand the characteristics of persuasive writing**

WARM-UP

Read, Listen, Speak

Read aloud from your example from yesterday's For Tomorrow homework. Tell students how you know it is persuasive writing and what its purpose is. Have small groups share their examples of persuasive writing. Ask students to explain how they know each piece is persuasive writing. Then invite students to explain the writer's purpose for each article.

GRAMMAR CONNECTION

Take this opportunity to talk about adverbs and adverbs that tell when or how often. You may wish to have students point out any adverbs and adverbs that tell when or how often in their Read, Listen, Speak examples.

TEACH

Read aloud the first paragraph. Review what the writer of the article on page 401 wants the readers to do.

Have a volunteer read aloud the section Topic. Ask students to list other things they might ask their parents to agree with (*a later bedtime, to let the student see a movie or go to a party, to buy a toy*). Tell students that these requests might be topics for a persuasive article. Then guide students to name things that might be topics of persuasive articles that affect their community, the country, or the environment.

Ask a volunteer to read aloud the section Reasons. Discuss why the reasons listed might be strong reasons for buying a computer.

Have a volunteer read aloud the section Research. Tell students that a fact, such as that computers help kids learn, is a much stronger reason than an opinion, such as that computers are cool. Explain that to find good reasons, students may have to research reasons to support their topic. Tell students that they can do their research on the Internet or in books or magazines. Guide students to understand that a persuasive article with strong reasons will be more likely to persuade an audience.

PRACTICE

ACTIVITY A
Complete this activity as a class. Encourage students to find examples in the article that support their answers.

ACTIVITY B
Suggest that students choose at least one topic with which they agree and at least one with which they disagree. Have partners brainstorm reasons for their positions. Ask volunteers to read aloud their sentences.

What Makes Good Persuasive Writing?

Persuasive writing asks readers to believe something or to do something. A letter to the editor of a newspaper is an example of persuasive writing. The article on page 401 was written to persuade readers that the library needs a new computer lab.

Topic

A persuasive article needs to have a topic. The topic is what you want the reader to believe or do. Imagine that you want your parents to buy you a new computer. You could write a persuasive article to get your parents to agree. The topic of your article might be why it is a good idea for your parents to buy the computer.

Reasons

Reasons help your audience understand why they should do something. When you write a persuasive article, give at least two reasons why people should agree with you. For example, computers help kids learn by giving them practice in reading and writing. Kids can also play learning games. If you give your audience good reasons, they might agree with you.

Research

When you write a persuasive article, you should know a lot about your topic. You need to give reasons for your readers to agree with you. Research can help you find the reasons. For an article

APPLY

WRITER'S CORNER

Tell students to think of a reason that the audience would be likely to agree with. Help students who are having difficulty think about such ideas as using the computers for school assignments and checking books in and out more easily. Students should demonstrate an understanding of the characteristics of persuasive writing.

Grammar in Action Remind students that adverbs tell when, where, or how something happens and that many adverbs end in *ly*.

ASSESS

Note which students had difficulty identifying the characteristics of persuasive writing. Use the Reteach option with those students who need additional reinforcement.

about buying a computer, you might read on the Internet about ways computers can help kids learn. Or you might ask a teacher how computers help kids learn. The more you know about your topic, the more willing your audience will be to agree with you.

Activity A
1. why the library needs a new computer lab
2. go to the next town meeting
3. The old computers are slow.
4. Answers will vary.
5. Answers will vary.

ACTIVITY A Answer these questions about the article on page 401.

1. What is the topic?
2. What does Jeb ask people to do in the ending of his letter?
3. Why does Jeb think the library needs new computers?
4. Imagine Jeb wrote that the town should add computers so he could play video games. Why do you think his audience might not agree?
5. If you lived in Jeb's town, would you go to the town meeting? Why or why not?

ACTIVITY B Read each topic and decide if you agree or disagree. Choose three topics. Then write one sentence about each topic to tell why you agree or disagree.

1. making the school day longer
2. eight o'clock bedtime
3. no hats in school
4. dogs being the best pets
5. no chewing gum in class
6. having year-round school
7. using cell phones at school
8. taking a second language
9. summer being the best season
10. no homework on Fridays
11. having more field trips
12. a computer for each student

WRITER'S CORNER

Look at the article on page 401. Work with a partner. Write two more reasons why people might disagree with the topic of the article.

Grammar in Action Include two adverbs in your reason. Review Section 6.1.

Persuasive Writing • 403

WARM-UP

Read, Listen, Speak

Share your topics and reasons from yesterday's For Tomorrow homework. Invite small groups to share their topics and reasons. Then have students work together to name one additional reason for each topic.

GRAMMAR CONNECTION

Take this opportunity to talk about adverbs that tell where. You may wish to have students point out any adverbs that tell where in their Read, Listen, Speak examples.

TEACH

Review the sections Topic, Reasons, and Research on pages 402–403. Ask students to name possible topics for persuasive articles. Then invite volunteers to suggest reasons for the topics. Ask students to explain why doing research can be helpful when writing a persuasive article.

Invite volunteers to read aloud the section Audience. Explain that students should think about what reasons the audience might agree with. Write the following on the board:

Reasons

• Many families have computers.

• Computers help kids learn to read and write.

Ask students which reason a parent might agree with and why. Guide students to understand that the reasons in a persuasive article are more effective if the audience can see how agreeing with the writer might help them.

LiNK Ask volunteers to read aloud the excerpt from "Why Exercise Is Cool." Ask students to tell the excerpt's topic and reasons. Then ask students to tell who the intended audience is and how they know.

PRACTICE

ACTIVITY C

Have students complete this activity in small groups. Ask students to talk about how they know whether the sentences are asking them to believe something or to do something. When students have finished, invite volunteers to share their answers with the class.

ACTIVITY D

Ask students to complete this activity independently. When students have finished, have them read aloud their answers. Ask students to explain how they knew which audience went with each topic.

ACTIVITY E

Remind students to keep their audience in mind as they write their reasons. When students have finished, have them talk about the topics they chose. Ask students whether they agree with each reason, and if they disagree, ask volunteers to explain why.

LiNK

Why Exercise Is Cool

It feels good to have a strong, flexible body that can do all the activities you enjoy—like running, jumping, and playing with your friends. It's also fun to be good at something, like scoring a basket, hitting a home run, or perfecting a dive.

But you may not know that exercising can actually put you in a better mood. When you exercise, your brain releases a chemical called **endorphins** (say: en-**dor**-funz), which may make you feel happier. It's just another reason why exercise is cool!

Mary L. Gavin, M.D., kidshealth.org

Audience

When you think of reasons, keep in mind who is going to read your article. Who will be your audience? Think of reasons that interest them. For example, what reasons would interest your parents if you asked them to buy you a computer? Your parents might not agree if you said that you wanted a computer to e-mail your friends. But they might agree if you said that a computer would help you with your homework.

ACTIVITY C Tell which sentences are asking you to believe something or to do something.

1. I like my cousin's cottage in Michigan. no
2. Many people may disagree, but recess is an important part of the school day. yes
3. We have no choice but to vote Mel Ross out of office for stealing money from the city. yes
4. Margaret's goldfish is more of a red color. no
5. Kids should be allowed to decorate their bedrooms any way they want. yes
6. Do clowns scare you as much as they scare me? no
7. Let Homer play for the baseball team because he tries hard. yes
8. Come and support the high school band as they try for their third state championship. yes

APPLY

WRITER'S CORNER

Help students brainstorm topics that are important to them. When students have finished, invite them to share their topics and explanations with the class. Students should demonstrate an understanding of the characteristics of persuasive writing.

ASSESS

Note which students had difficulty considering the audience when writing a persuasive article. Use the Reteach option with those students who need additional reinforcement.

Practice Book page 157 provides additional work with the characteristics of persuasive writing.

Practice Book page 157

TEACHING OPTIONS

Reteach

Have partners choose two different audiences to whom they might write a persuasive article. Then have partners choose a topic for a persuasive article. Ask partners to write two reasons they would use to persuade each of their audiences of their opinion. Have partners read aloud their reasons.

Buy This!

Point out that advertising is a form of persuasion. Brainstorm with students things that popular advertisements try to persuade people to do *(taking a trip, buying a product, or learning something new)*. Distribute to small groups advertisements from magazines or newspapers. Have students identify the topic of each ad and the reasons given to persuade the readers to use the product or service. Have volunteers share their work with the class. Allow time for students to discuss other popular ads and reasons why the ads are persuasive.

ACTIVITY D Match each topic in Column A to an audience in Column B.

Column A

1. I should have a later bedtime. b
2. The public library should have more DVDs. d
3. Everybody in our school should play this video game. a
4. Schools should allow soft-drink machines. c

Column B

a. friends
b. parents
c. school board
d. librarian

ACTIVITY E Choose one of the following topics. Work with a partner to write two reasons for someone to agree with the topic.

A. Students should not have to do any homework.
B. Summer vacation should be longer than three months.
C. All students should wear school uniforms.
D. Third graders should decide how much TV they watch.
E. Students should not be able to sit wherever they want in class.
F. Students should not receive grades for their work.
G. No students should be allowed at parent-teacher conferences.

WRITER'S CORNER

Write three topics that you have strong feelings about. After each topic write a sentence explaining why it is important to you.

Persuasive Writing • 405

For Tomorrow

Have students interview someone at home about something they would like to see changed in their community. Ask students to write the reasons the person gives for the desired change. Conduct your own interview and bring in the reasons to share with the class.

OBJECTIVES

- **To include a topic sentence in the beginning**
- **To include reasons in the middle**
- **To retell the topic in the ending**

WARM-UP

Read, Listen, Speak

Read aloud your interview notes from yesterday's For Tomorrow homework. Model for students how you know that the reasons you shared are persuasive. Invite small groups to share their interview notes. Encourage students to decide which reasons given are persuasive. Ask students to tell how the proposed changes might affect their community.

GRAMMAR CONNECTION

Take this opportunity to talk about adverbs that tell how. You may wish to have students point out any adverbs that tell how in their Read, Listen, Speak examples.

TEACH

Read aloud the first paragraph. Review what students know about beginnings, middles, and endings in writing.

Invite a volunteer to read aloud the section Beginning. Tell students that the topic sentence of a persuasive article is what the writer wants the reader to do. Explain that the topic sentence states the writer's position.

Ask volunteers to read aloud the section Middle. Explain that while the first example shows a way that a swimming pool might make things better, the way a pool might do this is not explained clearly. Ask students to explain why the second example is more persuasive.

Invite a volunteer to read aloud the first paragraph of the section Ending. Explain that when a writer tells the reader what to do to change things, it is a "call to action." Tell students that persuasive articles often include a call to action. Have a volunteer read aloud the rest of the section. Ask students what the call to action is asking readers to do.

PRACTICE

ACTIVITY A

Have partners complete this activity. Tell students to think about whether they agree or disagree with what is being asked in each question. Encourage students who are having difficulty to review the definition of a topic sentence on page 406. When students have finished, encourage volunteers to share their topic sentences with the class.

LESSON **2** PERSUASIVE WRITING

Beginning, Middle, and Ending

Most kinds of writing need a beginning, a middle, and an ending. In persuasive writing each part has a special job to do.

Beginning

The beginning of a persuasive article has a topic sentence. The topic sentence tells exactly what the topic is. It tells readers what you want them to do or to think. Look at this topic sentence.

> **A swimming pool at school would help students in many ways.**

Middle

The middle gives the reader reasons to agree with you. Write more than one sentence to support each reason. Clearly explained reasons are more likely to persuade a reader. Look at this reason from a persuasive article.

> **A swimming pool will help students become healthier.**

This is a good reason. But it could be explained better.

> **A swimming pool will give students a fun way to exercise. Exercise will help keep students healthy.**

Give each reason its own paragraph. Let the reader clearly see each reason you give.

APPLY

WRITER'S CORNER

Remind students that a reason with support is more convincing than a reason without support. When students have finished, have volunteers share their reasons with the class. Students should demonstrate the ability to use reasons to support a topic sentence.

TechTip Help students use a spreadsheet or table to create a graph of the survey results.

ASSESS

Note which students had difficulty with writing topic sentences. Use the Reteach option with those students who need additional reinforcement.

Ending

The ending retells the topic of a persuasive article. Remind the reader what you want him or her to believe or to do. Try to say it in a different way. You might say what the reader can do to change things if he or she agrees with you. Use opinion words such as *should, ought, must,* or *believe* to show that you feel strongly about your topic.

This sentence tells the reader what to do if he or she agrees that there should be a swimming pool at school.

> If you believe that a swimming pool at school is a good idea, you should write a letter to Principal Pak today.

ACTIVITY A Read this list of questions. Choose three questions you feel strongly about. Decide what you believe about each one. Write a topic sentence for it.

A. Should every student have a computer at school?

B. Should people on bicycles have to wear helmets?

C. Should there be bowling alleys in schools?

D. Should students be able to wear in-line skates in school?

E. Should schools be open on Saturdays?

F. Should students be able to attend online school?

G. Should students be allowed to bring pets to school?

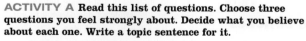

WRITER'S CORNER

Imagine that you are writing a persuasive article about going to school all year long. Your topic sentence is "Students should not have to go to school all year long." Write two reasons why readers should agree with your topic sentence.

 Tech Tip Graph a survey of your classmates' reasons.

Persuasive Writing • 407

Reteach

Explain that a persuasive article tries to get readers to respond in a certain way. Point out that before students write a topic sentence, they should decide how they want their readers to respond. Help students brainstorm a list of topics for persuasive articles. Have students choose a topic and think about the following questions: *What do I believe about this topic? How do I want the readers to respond?* Then have students write a topic sentence. Emphasize that a good topic sentence sets the tone for a strong persuasive article.

The Flip Side

Have students choose a question from Activity A. Direct them to write a topic sentence that introduces the opposite point of view about the topic from the one they wrote. Ask students to draw a poster illustrating the new topic and point of view. Have them use their new topic sentences as the slogans on their posters. Encourage volunteers to share their posters with the class. Discuss the importance of thinking about different points of view.

For Tomorrow

Ask students to imagine that they have invented a new healthy snack food. Tell students to draw a picture that they could use for an advertisement for their food. Bring in your own picture to share with the class.

WARM-UP

Read, Listen, Speak

Display your picture from yesterday's For Tomorrow homework. Model for students by explaining how the picture makes your invented snack food appealing. Invite small groups to share their drawings. Ask students to tell how the drawings might persuade someone to try their healthy snack.

GRAMMAR CONNECTION

Take this opportunity to talk about negative words. You may wish to have students use negative words in their Read, Listen, Speak discussion.

TEACH

Write on the board the column headings *Beginning, Middle,* and *Ending.* Ask students to recall what should be included in the beginning of a persuasive article *(a topic sentence).* Have a volunteer write an example topic sentence under the heading *Beginning.*

Ask students to explain what should be included in the middle of a persuasive article *(reasons that the reader should agree with the writer).* Invite volunteers to write in the *Middle* column two reasons that support the topic sentence.

Have students explain what should be included in the ending of a persuasive article *(a retelling of the topic, what the reader should do).* Ask a volunteer to write in the *Ending* column what the topic is and what the reader should do.

LiNK Ask volunteers to read aloud the excerpt from "School Lunches." Have students identify what the writer wants the reader to do *(read the cafeteria menu to decide if the lunch being offered is healthy).*

PRACTICE

ACTIVITY B

Invite small groups to complete this activity. When students have finished, ask in which part of a persuasive article students can find the topic sentence *(beginning),* where they can find the reasons *(middle),* and where to find what readers should do *(ending).*

ACTIVITY C

Have partners complete this activity. Tell students to explain whether each reason might persuade readers. When students have finished, invite volunteers to share their answers with the class.

ACTIVITY D

Have small groups complete this activity. When students have finished, ask which topic sentences in Column A students agree with and which they do not. Then invite volunteers to share their answers with the class.

ACTIVITY B **Read this persuasive article. Find the topic sentence. Then tell the two reasons the writer uses to persuade readers. Tell what sentence gives readers something to do if they agree with the writer.**

It's 12:00, and the bell rings. Everybody marches into the lunchroom. The lunchroom worker puts gravy on a square of mystery meat. Something green and slimy is supposed to be a vegetable. We need a change. Kids should decide what gets served in the lunchroom.

Most kids don't get to make grown-up decisions. Their families or the school decides what they eat. If kids get to decide what is served at lunch, they will get practice making grown-up decisions.

It could also be a chance to learn. Kids could learn more about food. They could find out where vegetables grow. They could find out about different kinds of fruits and grains.

Everyone agrees that our school lunches are bad. Instead of just buying different food, we should let students decide what to eat. If you think this is a good idea, go to Mrs. Silva's classroom and sign my petition.

ACTIVITY C **Read these reasons why people should recycle. Tell which reasons you think are good reasons.**

1. We're running out of room for trash. Recycling helps keep trash out of landfills.

2. Recycling is something that cool movie stars do. I want to be like my favorite movie stars.

3. Recycling turns trash into new stuff. I think it's a good idea.

4. Recycling can save more of our natural resources. When you recycle, people can cut down fewer trees, forests, and jungles.

Activity B

Topic sentence:
Kids should decide what gets served in the lunchroom.

Reasons:
Answers will vary.
Possible answers:
If kids get to decide what is served at lunch, they will get practice making grown-up decisions. Kids could learn more about food.

What readers should do:
If you think this is a good idea, go to Mrs. Silva's classroom and sign my petition.

LiNK
School Lunches

The typical school lunch is still higher in fat than it should be, according to a recent study. That doesn't mean you shouldn't buy your lunch, it just means you might want to give the cafeteria menu a closer look. Read the cafeteria menu the night before. Knowing what's for lunch beforehand will let you know if you want to eat it! Bring home a copy of the menu or figure out how to find it on the school website.

kidshealth.org

APPLY

WRITER'S CORNER

Remind students that endings restate the topic sentence and often tell the reader to do something. When students have finished, invite them to share their persuasive article endings with partners. Encourage students to tell their partner whether they found the endings persuasive. Students should demonstrate the ability to write an ending for a persuasive article.

ASSESS

Note which students had difficulty with beginnings, middles, and endings. Use the Reteach option with those students who need additional reinforcement.

Practice Book page 158 provides additional work with beginning, middle, and ending.

Reteach

Have students choose a toy or game they would like to have. Ask them to write a topic sentence and three reasons why they want the item. Discuss students' topics and reasons. Then encourage students to write a strong sentence they could use to end their persuasive article.

Convincing Comics

Invite students to choose a topic for a persuasive article. Ask them to write a topic sentence, two reasons to support it, and an ending sentence that tells the reader to do something. Then have students use each sentence to create a four-panel comic strip. Encourage students to use their sentences as the captions for each panel. When students have finished, display the comic strips. Allow time for students to read their classmates' comic strips.

Activity D

1. b, h
2. a, d
3. c, f
4. e, g

ACTIVITY D Match each topic sentence in Column A with two reasons that support it in Column B.

Column A

1. Hurting pets should be a serious crime.
2. People should get free medicine when they need it.
3. Students should not have to go to recess.
4. The school day should be longer.

Column B

a. Giving medicine to people who need it would mean fewer sick people passing their germs around.

b. Pets are best friends for some people. Hurting a pet is like hurting someone's best friend.

c. Some students like drawing pictures inside better than playing outside.

d. Some countries already give free medicine to people. It works well in those countries.

e. A longer school day would give teachers more time to help with schoolwork.

f. Some students can get hurt playing at recess.

g. Other countries have longer school days. Students in those countries score high on tests.

h. People who hurt pets might hurt people too.

WRITER'S CORNER

Choose a topic sentence from Activity D. Write an ending for a persuasive article on that topic.

For Tomorrow

Ask students to choose a persuasive topic and to write a beginning for the article. Remind students to include a strong topic sentence. Choose your own topic for a persuasive article and write a beginning to share with the class.

Persuasive Writing • 409

OBJECTIVE

- **To use an idea web to generate and organize ideas**

WARM-UP

Read, Listen, Speak

Read aloud the beginning you wrote for yesterday's For Tomorrow homework. Model for students how you were able to identify your topic sentence. Invite small groups to share the beginnings they wrote. Ask students to identify the topic sentence in each beginning. Then invite them to tell why a reader might agree or disagree with what the writer says in each beginning.

GRAMMAR CONNECTION

Take this opportunity to talk about *good* and *well*. You may wish to have students point out any uses of *good* and *well* in their Read, Listen, Speak examples.

TEACH

Bring a road map of your state to class. Point out major cities and the roads that connect them. Explain that idea webs work in a similar way. Tell students that idea webs can show the connection between ideas in writing, just like a road map shows the connections between cities.

Invite a volunteer to read aloud the opening paragraph. Then read aloud the first paragraph of the section Making an Idea Web. Direct students' attention to Jason's idea web. Allow time for students to examine it.

Have volunteers read aloud the next two paragraphs. Guide students to understand how each reason is connected to the topic, how reasons support the topic, and how ideas develop the reasons.

PRACTICE

ACTIVITY A

Have students complete this activity with partners. When students have finished, have volunteers share their answers with the class. Encourage several volunteers to answer question 3. Ask each volunteer to explain why their reason is the best.

ACTIVITY B

Have students complete this activity independently. Encourage students to think of additional reasons for their idea webs. Invite volunteers to draw their idea webs on the board and to explain them to the class.

LESSON **3** STUDY SKILLS

Idea Webs

If you get lost, a map can help you find where you are. When you are writing, you can use a map to find where your ideas are. We call this kind of map an idea web. An idea web looks a little like a spider web. It helps catch all your ideas.

Making an Idea Web

This is Jason's idea web for a persuasive article.

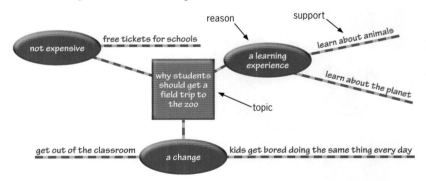

To get started, Jason wrote his topic. Then he drew a square around it. The topic of his article was why students should get a field trip to the zoo.

He wrote his reasons around the topic and drew ovals around each one. Then he drew lines from his topic to each of his reasons. He drew lines off of each reason. He wrote on each line ideas to support that reason.

APPLY

WRITER'S CORNER

Have partners discuss how an idea web can help them think of more ideas and organize their thoughts. Ask volunteers to read aloud their sentences. Students should demonstrate an understanding of the function of idea webs.

ASSESS

Note which students had difficulty writing idea webs. Use the Reteach option with those students who need additional reinforcement.

Reteach

Draw on a large sheet of paper a blank idea web. Ask a volunteer to write in the topic section *Having an Extended Recess*. Have partners work together to write two reasons in the idea web. Then tell students to interview other students and teachers to find ideas that support each reason. Have students fill in the reasons on the idea web. Discuss students' experiences gathering information about their topic. Ask how students might use their reasons in a persuasive article about having a longer recess.

What's the Big Idea?

Have students make an idea web for a persuasive article. Tell students to use different pencil colors for each reason and to write their ideas to support that reason in the same color. Then have students use the idea web to write on the bottom of the paper a topic sentence for their article. Display the idea webs in the classroom.

Activity A

1. not expensive, a change, a learning experience
2. learn about animals, learn about the planet
3. Answers will vary.

ACTIVITY A Answer these questions about Jason's idea web on page 410.

1. What are the three reasons students should get a field trip to the zoo?
2. What are two ideas that support the reason that going to the zoo would be a good learning experience?
3. Which reason do you think is best? Why?

ACTIVITY B Use the following to make your own idea webs.

1. **Topic A: why I deserve more allowance**

   Reason 1: I do more chores now.
   Support: sweep porch
   Support: do breakfast dishes
   Support: clean my room once a week

   Reason 2: Jamie got a raise.
   Support: be fair to your children
   Support: consider what each chore is worth

   Reason 3: The cost of everything has risen.
   Support: can't afford gum anymore
   Support: want to be able to buy things for myself

2. **Topic B: why living in the city is the best**

   Reason 1: many things to see and do
   Support: visit museums and stores
   Support: see monuments and play in big parks
   Support: plays, concerts, and sporting events

   Reason 2: many places to eat
   Support: try different kinds of food
   Support: find a restaurant for any occasion

   Reason 3: easy to get around
   Support: buses going anywhere
   Support: many trains and taxis

WRITER'S CORNER

Write three sentences that tell how you think an idea web can help you improve your writing. Share your sentences with a partner.

For Tomorrow

Ask students to make idea webs for taking a family vacation. Tell students to include at least two reasons to support their topic. Make your own idea web to share with the class.

Read, Listen, Speak

Write on the board your idea web from yesterday's For Tomorrow homework. Tell students how the ideas are connected. Invite small groups to share their idea webs. Encourage students to identify one more reason for each idea web.

GRAMMAR CONNECTION

Take this opportunity to talk about *to*, *too*, and *two*. You may wish to have students describe their idea webs using the words *to*, *too*, and *two*.

TEACH

Review idea webs and ask volunteers to name possible topics for persuasive articles. Have a volunteer write on the board one of the topics and circle it to start an idea web. Ask students to suggest reasons and fill in the idea web. Have volunteers explain how they might use the idea web to write a persuasive article.

Invite a volunteer to read aloud the section Phrases or Sentences. Guide students to understand that writing phrases for reasons is all right when making an idea web. Be sure students understand that phrases are groups of words without capitalization or punctuation. Explain that an idea web is a tool to help writers organize their ideas and to see how ideas are connected to one another.

PRACTICE

ACTIVITY C

Have partners complete this activity. Tell students to discuss possible reasons and to choose what they agree to be the strongest reasons for the idea web. When students have finished, ask volunteers to share their answers with the class.

ACTIVITY D

Have partners complete this activity. Tell students to choose the most important words and ideas when writing their phrases. When students have finished, have small groups compare their answers.

ACTIVITY E

Have students complete this activity in small groups. Then have volunteers share their work with the class. Ask students to justify their answers.

ACTIVITY F

Encourage students to review the idea web on this page before they begin. Then have students complete the activity independently. When students have finished, invite them to write their idea webs on the board. Ask volunteers to suggest additions.

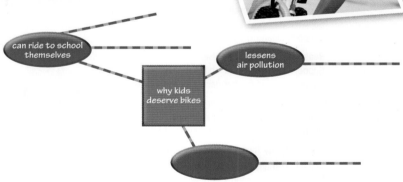

Phrases or Sentences

When you make an idea web, it is OK if you do not write complete sentences. You can write phrases, or groups of words. You can use only important words and not worry about capital letters or periods. Or you can write in complete sentences if you choose.

ACTIVITY C Copy this idea web. Fill in the missing blanks and ovals with your own ideas.

- can ride to school themselves
- lessens air pollution
- why kids deserve bikes

ACTIVITY D These sentences are topics and reasons to be used in a persuasive article. Rewrite each sentence as a phrase, or group of words, to put in an idea web.

1. Topic: Kids should spend at least an hour a day outside.
   Reason 1: Exercise is good for everyone.
   Reason 2: There are lots of fun games to play outside.

2. Topic: Parents and kids should shop for clothes together.
   Reason 1: Parents don't know all the latest fashions.
   Reason 2: Kids should try on the clothes to see if they fit.

APPLY

WRITER'S CORNER

Have students share their middles in small groups. Encourage students to offer feedback on whether or not they agree with the writer. Ask students to suggest additional reasons to add to one another's middles. Students should demonstrate the ability to use an idea web to write the middle of a persuasive article.

ASSESS

Note which students had difficulty making idea webs. Use the Reteach option with those students who need additional reinforcement.

Practice Book page 159 provides additional work with idea webs.

TEACHING OPTIONS

Reteach

Have students write at the top of a sheet of paper the following: *We Need a School Crossing Guard.* Then have students write *Who?, What?, Where?, When?, Why?,* and *How?* below the sentence. Have partners write two answers to each question and make an idea web using their list of answers. Encourage students to choose what they think are the strongest reasons to include in their idea webs. Invite volunteers to draw their idea webs on the board and to explain how they chose the information.

Check the Facts

Have students use one of the idea webs they made. Encourage students to find information about their topic on the internet or in the library. Challenge students to find two additional reasons from their research to add to their webs. Then have students trade idea webs with a partner. Have students use the Internet or the library to check that the information on their partner's idea web is accurate. Tell students to discuss any incorrect information and to find factual information to use in its place.

ACTIVITY E Each set of phrases is from an idea web. Identify which phrase is the topic, the reason, and the support.

1. **a.** better math scores support
   b. will do better in school reason
   c. why kids should have calculators topic
2. **a.** why bedtime should be later topic
   b. homework harder in third grade support
   c. will have more time for homework reason
3. **a.** will always know what time it is reason
   b. won't be late for school support
   c. why all kids should have watches topic
4. **a.** teamwork good for building trust support
   b. why gym class should teach soccer topic
   c. will teach kids teamwork reason

ACTIVITY F Choose one of the topics below. Make an idea web for the topic.

A. why the school day should be shorter
B. why the school day should be longer
C. why every kid should have a pet
D. why kids should not have pets
E. why students should be able to use calculators for math tests
F. why students should not be able to use calculators for math tests
G. why the school gym should be open all summer
H. why the school gym should not be open all summer

WRITER'S CORNER

Use the idea web you made in Activity F to write the middle of a persuasive article.

For Tomorrow

Have students look at the idea web on page 410. Tell them to write a paragraph that explains a reason given in the web. Write your own paragraph explaining one reason to share with the class.

Persuasive Writing • 413

OBJECTIVES
- **To make compound sentences using conjunctions**
- **To identify conjunctions**

WARM-UP
Read, Listen, Speak
Read aloud your paragraph from yesterday's For Tomorrow homework. Discuss the reason and how you explained it. Have small groups share their paragraphs. Ask students to identify the reason in each paragraph.

GRAMMAR CONNECTION
Take this opportunity to talk about *their* and *there*. You may wish to have students point out any uses of *their* and *there* in their Read, Listen, Speak examples.

TEACH
Invite volunteers to read aloud the opening paragraph and the two example sentences. Ask students how to determine which is the compound sentence *(two sentences combined with* and*)*.

Invite volunteers to read aloud the first paragraph in the section Making a Compound Sentence and the bulleted items. Help students identify how the two example sentences show the bulleted changes. *(The second example is one sentence. It has a comma and the word* and. *The word* another *begins with a small letter.)*

Ask a volunteer to read aloud the last paragraph. Explain that the example sentences share the same idea, which is what the musicians were doing, so the sentences make a good compound sentence. Write on the board the following:

> One clown juggled six balls. A lion in Africa roared.

Ask students to explain why these two sentences would not make an effective compound sentence *(because the ideas do not go together).*

PRACTICE
ACTIVITY A
Have students complete this activity independently. Then ask volunteers to share their answers with the class. Have volunteers write on the board the two sentences that were used to make each compound sentence.

ACTIVITY B
Have partners complete this activity. If students have difficulty, tell them to look back at the example compound sentence on page 414. When they have finished, invite volunteers to write the corrected sentences on the board.

Compound Sentences

You can join two sentences to make a compound sentence by using words such as *and, or,* and *but.* These words are called conjunctions. Compound sentences can make your writing more interesting. Can you find the compound sentence below?

> **One musician played a bass. Another musician played a trumpet.**

> **One musician played a bass, and another musician played a trumpet.**

Making a Compound Sentence
Sometimes you might find two sentences in your writing that are related to each other. Do these three things to join two sentences into one compound sentence.

- Change the period after the first sentence to a comma.
- Choose the word that best fits between the sentences. Use *and, or,* or *but.* Put that word after the comma.
- Change the capital letter at the beginning of the second sentence to a small letter. If the first word is the word *I* or a proper noun, don't change it. A proper noun and the word *I* always begin with a capital letter.

Check that both sentences are complete before you join them. Also be sure that the ideas go together. It's possible to join any two sentences, but not all sentences belong together as a compound sentence.

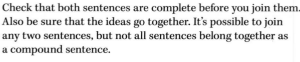

414 • Chapter 6

APPLY

WRITER'S CORNER

Help students brainstorm a list of after-school activities *(soccer practice, homework, play date)*. Encourage students to use the list for ideas. When students have finished, have partners check to make sure that the compound sentences include the correct punctuation, conjunctions, and capitalization. Students should demonstrate the ability to write compound sentences.

ASSESS

Note which students had difficulty writing compound sentences. Use the Reteach option with those students who need additional reinforcement.

TEACHING OPTIONS

Reteach

Have students find a page of fiction writing that has several examples of compound sentences. Help students to identify the conjunctions *and, or,* and *but.* For each sentence they identify, ask students to determine whether there is a complete sentence on each side of the conjunction. Explain that if there is a complete sentence on either side of the conjunction, the sentence is a compound sentence. Ask students to think about a topic for a persuasive article and write a compound sentence with reasons that support their topic.

Compound Challenge

Arrange the class into two teams. Write on the board a topic sentence. Have one member from each team write a sentence about the topic. Then challenge both students to combine the sentences into a compound sentence and write the compound sentence on the board. Award a point to the team that correctly writes the compound sentence first. Repeat the game as time allows. The team with the most points wins the game.

For Tomorrow

Ask students to write a paragraph that contains compound sentences. Tell students to underline the compound sentences and to circle the conjunctions *and, or,* and *but.* Write your own paragraph with compound sentences to share with the class.

ACTIVITY A **Read these compound sentences. Tell which conjunction was used to make the compound sentence: *and, or,* or *but.***

1. Tyler bought baseball cards, <u>and</u> Milo bought comic books.
2. Milo paid with dollar bills, <u>but</u> Tyler paid with quarters.
3. The clerk gave Milo his change, <u>and</u> he stuffed it in his pocket.
4. Milo and Tyler could take the bus home, <u>or</u> they could walk.
5. It started raining, <u>and</u> Milo and Tyler took the bus.
6. Tyler thought the bus smelled funny, <u>and</u> Milo agreed.
7. Milo could go to Tyler's house, <u>or</u> he could go home.
8. Tyler wanted Milo to stay, <u>but</u> Milo decided to leave.

Activity B
1. missing comma
2. capital letter for *The*
3. capital letter for *And*
4. period instead of comma
5. missing comma
6. small letter for *Sam*
7. missing comma
8. comma in the wrong place
9. capital letter for *Or*
10. comma after *but*

ACTIVITY B **Find the mistake in each compound sentence. Look for correct punctuation marks and capital letters.**

1. All of the Casos play musical instruments and they play tennis too.
2. I like big dogs, but The little ones scare me.
3. The clowns ran out of the tent, And the lions ran after them.
4. My best friend is a magician. but he is not a very good one.
5. Stevie the Mole is a character in a book but I wish he were real.
6. Evan has a pet iguana, but sam doesn't like it.
7. We were late but Mom made us change our clothes.
8. The horn sounded to start the game and, John scored a goal right away.
9. I can buy a new bike, Or I can keep saving my money.
10. Remove the roast from the oven, but, be sure to use pot holders.

WRITER'S CORNER

Write one sentence about something you did after school yesterday. Then write a sentence about something you did after that. Rewrite the two sentences as a compound sentence using the word *and.*

WARM-UP

Read, Listen, Speak

Read aloud your paragraph from yesterday's For Tomorrow homework. Have students raise a hand when they hear a conjunction. Tell students how you chose each conjunction. Reread those sentences and tell students if they are compound. Invite small groups to share their paragraphs. Encourage students to name the sentences on either side of the conjunction in each compound sentence.

GRAMMAR CONNECTION

Take this opportunity to talk about coordinating conjunctions. You may wish to have students point out coordinating conjunctions in their Read, Listen, Speak examples.

TEACH

Read aloud the first paragraph. Then have volunteers read aloud each conjunction, how it is used, and the example sentence. After each example sentence is read, ask students to explain how each conjunction shows the relationship between the two ideas. *(And shows how two things are the same; but shows how two things are different; or shows a choice.)* Invite volunteers to suggest their own examples of sentences that use each conjunction.

LiNK Have volunteers read aloud the excerpt from "Be a Fit Kid." Ask students to tell the topic of the excerpt. Then ask them to give the reasons. Ask what the author wants readers to think or do.

PRACTICE

ACTIVITY C

Have partners complete this activity. When students have finished, invite volunteers to write on the board the compound sentences and to explain how the conjunction shows the relationship between the sentences.

ACTIVITY D

Have partners complete this activity. Then have students check that the sentences were written correctly. Invite volunteers to share their answers with the class.

ACTIVITY E

Have small groups complete this activity. Tell students to choose two or three items to rewrite. Ask volunteers to read aloud each item and to tell why each conjunction was chosen to connect the sentences.

Conjunctions

Conjunctions have different meanings. When you write a compound sentence, be sure to use the correct conjunction. Here is how you can use some conjunctions.

CONJUNCTIONS	
and	shows how two things are the same or belong together
	Judy will wash the dishes, *and* I will dry.
but	shows how two things are different
	Max plays the piano, *but* Keene plays the guitar.
or	shows that one of two things might happen
	Tamera can go to the zoo, *or* she can go to the museum.

LiNK

Be a Fit Kid

You may have a favorite food, but the best choice is to eat a variety. If you eat different foods, you're more likely to get the nutrients your body needs. Taste new foods and old ones you haven't tried for a while. Some foods, such as green veggies, are more pleasing the older you get. Shoot for at least five servings of fruits and vegetables a day—two fruits and three vegetables.

kidshealth.org

ACTIVITY C Use the conjunction in parentheses to combine each pair of sentences into a compound sentence.

1. You painted the wall a pretty color. You missed a spot. (but)

2. Tito is taking a bus to the mall. Renaldo is riding his bike. (and)

3. The skate park is closed. I don't want to go home. (but)

4. Jada likes Mexican food. She might eat all these tacos. (and)

5. Oranges can be sweet. Oranges can be sour. (or)

6. I want to go to the monkey house. My sister doesn't like monkeys. (but)

7. Roberta is learning math. Jake is learning science. (and)

Activity C

1. You painted the wall a pretty color, but you missed a spot.

2. Tito is taking a bus to the mall, and Renaldo is riding his bike.

3. The skate park is closed, but I don't want to go home.

4. Jada likes Mexican food, and she might eat all these tacos.

5. Oranges can be sweet, or oranges can be sour.

6. I want to go to the monkey house, but my sister doesn't like monkeys.

7. Roberta is learning math, and Jake is learning science.

416 • Chapter 6

APPLY

WRITER'S CORNER

Encourage students first to write sentences with related ideas and then to rewrite the sentences as compound sentences. When students have finished, invite volunteers to write their sentences on the board. Have students check punctuation and capitalization, make sure each conjunction is used correctly, and check that the words on both sides of the conjunction have a subject and a predicate. Students should demonstrate the ability to use conjunctions in compound sentences.

Grammar in Action. Guide students to the first sentence and have a volunteer read it aloud. Ask students to identify the conjunction *(but)* and tell why it is the appropriate conjunction for the sentence *(because it shows how two things are different).*

ASSESS

Note which students had difficulty using conjunctions in compound sentences. Use the Reteach option with those students who need additional reinforcement.

Practice Book page 160 provides additional work with compound sentences.

Practice Book page 160

Reteach

Write the conjunctions *and, or,* and *but* on separate note cards. Have students take turns choosing a card and writing on the board the beginning of a compound sentence using the conjunction. Ask volunteers to complete the compound sentences. Discuss how the meaning of each conjunction fits the sentence.

English-Language Learners

Have students draw two pictures on one sheet of paper, showing their favorite sport, animal, or activity. Have students trade papers with a partner and write on separate sheets of paper compound sentences about the drawings. Continue having students trade with different partners until four compound sentences have been written about each picture. Have students compare all the sentences. Check that all the sentences are written correctly as compound sentences.

Activity E

1. Kim read the map, and Keith drove the truck.
2. Jerry can swim in the lake, and he can hike the trails.
3. My family will visit the country, or we will go to the city.
4. Kara must take the test, and she will study with Lucy.
5. The author read from his book, and he talked about the characters.
6. We wanted to have a picnic, but it rained all afternoon.
7. Levi's sister will dance on the stage, and she will design the programs.
8. Mrs. White planted bushes on the side of the house, and they grew up to her window.
9. Melissa broke her foot, and the doctor put it in a cast.
10. The phone was ringing loudly, but I could not answer it.

ACTIVITY D Complete these compound sentences.

1. Teresa draws pictures at the table, and _____.
2. _____, but Allen wants to go home.
3. Jesse's car has a flat tire, and _____.
4. _____, or you can see a movie.
5. Ivan and Tess want to buy that dollhouse, but _____.
6. _____, but Uncle Gilberto lost his fishing pole.
7. Elaine found a skunk in her yard, and _____.
8. Frieda can go camping this weekend, or _____.
9. I had planned to go sailing, but _____.
10. Michael got on his bike, and _____.

ACTIVITY E Write a sentence that contains the conjunction *and, or,* or *but* to connect each pair of sentences.

1. Kim read the map. Keith drove the truck.
2. Jerry can swim in the lake. He can hike the trails.
3. My family will visit the country. We will go to the city.
4. Kara must take the test. She will study with Lucy.
5. The author read from his book. He talked about the characters.
6. We wanted to have a picnic. It rained all afternoon.
7. Levi's sister will dance on the stage. She will design the programs.
8. Mrs. White planted bushes on the side of the house. They grew up to her window.
9. Melissa broke her foot. The doctor put it in a cast.
10. The phone was ringing loudly. I could not answer it.

WRITER'S CORNER

Write one compound sentence using each of these conjunctions: *and, or,* and *but.*

Grammar in Action. Find the compound sentence in the page 416 excerpt. Name the conjunction.

Persuasive Writing • 417

For Tomorrow

Have students write five sentences persuading someone at home to make a favorite meal. Tell students to include three or more compound sentences. Bring in your own persuasive compound sentences to share with the class.

OBJECTIVE

- **To use the suffixes -er and -less**

WARM-UP

Read, Listen, Speak

Write on the board the sentences you wrote for yesterday's For Tomorrow homework. Write on the board the compound sentences and identify the conjunction and the subjects and predicates. Have small groups share the sentences they wrote and identify the compound sentences. Ask students to check that each compound sentence has a subject and predicate on either side of the conjunction.

GRAMMAR CONNECTION

Take this opportunity to review adverbs and conjunctions. You may wish to have students point out any adverbs and conjunctions in their Read, Listen, Speak examples.

TEACH

Have a volunteer read aloud the first paragraph. Ask students to tell what they remember about prefixes. Review the prefixes *re-* and *un-*. Explain that suffixes are word parts just like prefixes, but unlike prefixes, suffixes are at the end of words.

Have volunteers read aloud the section *-er*. Then write on the board the words *sing, train,* and *play.* Invite volunteers to come to the board to add the suffix *-er* to each word. Explain how the suffix changes the words. Ask students to name other words that end with *-er.* Use the examples to help students distinguish between words that end in *-er* but do not have the suffix *-er,* such as *corner, meter,* or *flower.*

Have a volunteer read aloud the first paragraph of the section *-less.* Encourage students to suggest words that end with the suffix *-less.* Write their responses on the board. Have volunteers identify the words to which the suffix was added. Ask students what they think the suffix *-less* means. Then have a volunteer read aloud the last paragraph.

PRACTICE

ACTIVITY A

Have students complete this activity independently. After students have finished, ask volunteers to tell what they think each word means.

ACTIVITY B

Have partners complete this activity. Ask students to write what they think each word means. Then ask volunteers to read aloud the definition of each word from a dictionary.

ACTIVITY C

Complete this activity as a class. Ask volunteers to read aloud each sentence and try both suffixes to determine which is correct.

Suffixes

A prefix is a word part that you can add to the beginning of a base word to change its meaning. A suffix is a word part that you can add to the end of a base word to change its meaning. It is useful to learn suffixes. Knowing suffixes can help you figure out what words mean.

-er

One suffix is *-er.* If you add *-er* to the end of the word *teach,* it changes the meaning of the word. Look at the example below. *Teach* is the base word, and *-er* is the suffix.

teach + -er = teacher

Each suffix has its own meaning. The suffix *-er* means "one who." So when you add *-er* to the end of the word *teach,* you change it to mean "one who teaches." A teacher is "a person who teaches." Many words use this suffix. A *farmer* is a person who farms. A *painter* is a person who paints. Can you think of other words that use the suffix *-er*?

-less

Another suffix is *-less.* Can you think of words that end with the suffix *-less*? What do you think this suffix means?

One example is the word *hopeless.* The word *hopeless* means "without hope." The suffix *-less* means "without."

APPLY

WRITER'S CORNER

Help students brainstorm topics for the words in Activity A. When students have finished, invite volunteers to write their sentences on the board. Ask students to identify the words that have the suffixes -er or -less in each sentence. Students should demonstrate the ability to identify base words and use words with the suffixes -er and -less in sentences.

Grammar in Action Guide students to the word with the suffix -er (container). Ask students to identify the base word and tell how the suffix changes the meaning of the base word.

ASSESS

Note which students had difficulty identifying words with the suffixes -er and -less. Use the Reteach option with those students who need additional reinforcement.

TEACHING OPTIONS

Reteach

Help students brainstorm a list of words that might be base words and can be used with the suffixes -er or -less. Then have students look up the words in a dictionary to discover whether -er or -less can be added to them to make new words. Have students write on the board any new words they find. Discuss the meanings of each new word.

Suffix Spies

Have students choose three words from Activity B with which to write sentences. The have students trade papers with a partner and find the word with the suffix in each sentence. Have students identify the base word and tell the meaning of the word. Encourage students to use the base word in a sentence.

ACTIVITY A Find the suffix in each word.

1. binder
2. helpless
3. careless
4. thoughtless
5. seller
6. brainless
7. timeless
8. leader
9. trainer
10. climber
11. doubtless
12. buyer

Activity B
1. one who plays
2. without wind
3. without shoes
4. one who sings
5. one who cleans
6. one who paints
7. without word
8. without thought
9. one who drifts
10. one who sends
11. one who pitches
12. without end

ACTIVITY B These words have the suffix -er or the suffix -less. What does each word mean?

1. player
2. windless
3. shoeless
4. singer
5. cleaner
6. painter
7. wordless
8. thoughtless
9. drifter
10. sender
11. pitcher
12. endless

ACTIVITY C Add the suffix –er or –less to the base word in parentheses to correctly complete each sentence.

1. The owner fed the tiny __helpless__ puppy. (help)
2. Wishing for a chance to take the test again was __hopeless__. (hope)
3. Coach Bill is a very good batting __teacher__. (teach)
4. The __worker__ started her day planting flowers. (work)
5. My __worthless__ coin was just an old, rusty piece of metal. (worth)
6. A __builder__ looked at the blueprints for the new library. (build)
7. The losing __player__ called to the champion for a rematch. (play)
8. All the food we ate at the party was bland and __tasteless__. (taste)

WRITER'S CORNER

Write a sentence using one of the words from Activity A. Underline the base word in the word you used. Then write another sentence using just the base word.

Grammar in Action Find the word with the suffix -er in the page 400 excerpt.

Persuasive Writing • 419

For Tomorrow

Ask students to search a favorite book for words that use the suffixes -er or -less. Have students choose two words, identify the base word, and write each word with a suffix in a separate sentence. Bring in your own words with suffixes to share with the class.

WARM-UP

Read, Listen, Speak

Write on the board your words from yesterday's For Tomorrow homework. Ask students to identify the base words and tell how the suffixes change the meanings of the words. Have small groups share the sentences they wrote. Encourage students to discuss how often they use words with the suffixes *-er* and *-less.*

GRAMMAR CONNECTION

Take this opportunity to talk about adverbs and conjunctions. You may wish to have students point out any adverbs and conjunctions in their Read, Listen, Speak examples.

TEACH

Review the suffixes *-er* and *-less.* Read the following words aloud one at a time. Have volunteers write each word on the board.

butter   buyer   bitter

boxer   blubber   beeper

Ask students to tell which words have the suffix *-er. (boxer, buyer, beeper)* Have students tell what each base word is.

Using the same procedure, have students write the following words on the board:

hairless   wireless   flawless

unless   fruitless

Ask students to tell which words have the suffix *-less (wireless, fruitless, flawless, hairless).* Have students identify each base word.

PRACTICE

ACTIVITY D
Have partners complete this activity. When students have finished, ask volunteers to share their answers by using each word in a sentence.

ACTIVITY E
Have students complete this activity independently. When students have finished, have them share their answers in small groups. Ask students to explain their choices.

ACTIVITY F
Have small groups complete this activity. Point out that two sentences *(items 2 and 8)* need plural forms to make sense in the sentence.

ACTIVITY D Write a word with the suffix *-er* or the suffix *-less* to fit each definition.

1. without hair hairless
2. person who follows follower
3. person who farms farmer
4. without hope hopeless
5. without color colorless
6. without speech speechless
7. person who teaches teacher
8. person who owns owner
9. person who supports supporter
10. without noise noiseless
11. person who reports reporter
12. person who builds builder

ACTIVITY E Complete each sentence with an *-er* or *-less* word from the word box.

| singer | buyer | trainer | skinless | spotless |

1. He learned to tread water from a swimming ___trainer___.
2. Colby is looking for a ___buyer___ for her old tuba.
3. Jacob only eats ___skinless___ chicken.
4. With such a beautiful voice, she should be a ___singer___.
5. Have you noticed that Austin's bedroom is always ___spotless___?

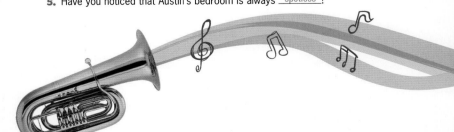

420 • Chapter 6

APPLY

WRITER'S CORNER

After students have finished, have partners share their work. Encourage students to identify each base word and then discuss how their sentences are similar or different. Students should demonstrate the ability to use the suffixes *-er* and *-less*.

ASSESS

Note which students had difficulty using the suffixes *-er* and *-less*. Use the Reteach option with those students who need additional reinforcement.

Practice Book page 161 provides additional work with suffixes.

ACTIVITY F Complete each sentence with a word that has the suffix *-er* or *-less*.

1. If you have a __hairless__ cat, you can see the wrinkles that are usually covered by fur.
2. Dozens of __climbers__ make their way up Mt. Everest every year.
3. It's a __timeless__ movie that never seems to get old.
4. The __cleaner__ dusted the desks and swept the floor.
5. The clear blue sky was __cloudless__ and full of sunlight.
6. He is such a __tireless__ worker that I've never seen him take a break.
7. The __buyer__ didn't have enough money to pay for the Oriental rug.
8. If it weren't for __teachers__, students would have recess all day.
9. Without his Super Power Bands, the hero was __helpless__.
10. I wonder which __speaker__ is giving the speech.
11. Jennie is a great soccer __player__.
12. At recess we played follow the __leader__.
13. The __pitcher__ threw a fast ball.
14. The doctor promised the shot would be __painless__.
15. A sailboat won't go anywhere on a __windless__ day.
16. Meg spilled the milk all over the table because she was __careless__.

WRITER'S CORNER

Write five sentences using the words from the word box in Activity E.

Persuasive Writing • 421

OBJECTIVES

- To understand the characteristics of a persuasive speech
- To understand how to be an active listener

WARM-UP

Read, Listen, Speak

Write on the board your sentence from yesterday's For Tomorrow homework. Have small groups share their sentences. Ask students to identify the words with suffixes, their base words, and their meanings. Have students identify what each base word means and to explain how the suffix changes the meaning of the word.

GRAMMAR CONNECTION

Continue with Day 2 of the Writing lesson. Administer the Section 6 Assessment tomorrow.

TEACH

Read aloud the first paragraph and invite volunteers to answer the questions. Encourage students to name specific things that they like about their favorite commercials. Then discuss the differences between TV and radio commercials. (*TV commercials use persuasive images and persuasive language. Radio commercials use only persuasive language.*)

Ask volunteers to read aloud the section Audience. Remind students that audience members will be more likely to agree with the speaker if they understand how it might benefit them.

Have a volunteer read aloud the section Voice and Body Language. Explain that body language is the movements and gestures people make, such as using facial expressions, to help get meaning across to others. Point out that a speaker who moves around too much or who looks down at the floor will appear less persuasive than a speaker who stands straight and looks at the audience. Tell students that other ways to project confidence when giving a persuasive speech are to make eye contact with audience members and to speak clearly.

Ask a volunteer to read aloud the section Visual Aids. Brainstorm with students topics for persuasive speeches and visual aids that might be used.

PRACTICE

ACTIVITY A

Have students complete this activity with partners. When students have finished, invite volunteers to share their answers with the class. Encourage students to explain why each thing is best matched to each audience.

ACTIVITY B

Have partners discuss the audience and topic for each item. Tell them to role-play and try out different voices and gestures to determine which is most effective.

LESSON **6** SPEAKING AND LISTENING SKILLS

Persuasive Speeches

You can hear persuasive speech any time you turn on the TV. A commercial is a kind of persuasive speech. The people who make the commercials are trying to persuade you to buy something. Do you have a favorite commercial? What do you like about it?

Audience

When people make commercials, they have an audience in mind. Have you ever noticed that commercials for toys almost always have kids in them? That's because the audience for those commercials is kids.

When you give a persuasive speech, you should keep your audience in mind. Who will be listening to you? How old is your audience? Will they be interested in your topic?

Voice and Body Language

Speak calmly when you are trying to persuade people. Try not to use sounds and words such as *um, uh,* and *you know.* Stand straight. Use your hands to make what you are saying come alive.

Visual Aids

When you give a persuasive speech, include visual aids such as pictures, charts, or maps. You can also use objects. Even costumes can be good visual aids.

ACTIVITY C

Have students refer to the list of visual aids on page 422. Ask students to compare their answers with a partner.

APPLY

SPEAKER'S CORNER

Help students brainstorm a list of possible inventions, such as a pen that does homework by itself or a computer that can tell what will happen tomorrow. Encourage students to use their imaginations as they describe their inventions.

Tell students to help their partners further develop their invention descriptions. Students should demonstrate the ability to generate topics for a persuasive speech.

ASSESS

Note which students had difficulty understanding the characteristics of a persuasive speech. Use the Reteach option with those students who need additional reinforcement.

TEACHING OPTIONS

Reteach

Point out that TV commercials are good examples of persuasive speech. Discuss some of students' favorite TV commercials. Emphasize the audience, tone of voice, and body language used in commercials. Ask students to tell what words, phrases, or other things are used in the commercials to get the viewers' attention. Have students make a list of things that make the commercials persuasive. Point out that students can use these same ideas when they make their own persuasive speeches.

Start Off Strong

Explain that a strong beginning in a speech is important to get the audience's attention. Ask students to choose a persuasive article topic from earlier in the chapter and to write the beginning of a persuasive speech. Tell students that, just like a persuasive article, a persuasive speech should have a strong topic sentence. Have students practice the beginnings of their speeches with a partner.

For Tomorrow

Ask students to talk to their parents about something they recently bought because of a commercial. Tell students to take notes about what made the commercial persuasive. Prepare to discuss an example of something you purchased because of a commercial.

ACTIVITY A Match the things in Column A to the possible audience in Column B.

Column A		Column B
1. swing set	b	a. men
2. prom clothes	e	b. kids
3. car rental company	c	c. grown-ups
4. mustache comb	a	d. women
5. perfume	d	e. teenagers

FOR RENT

ACTIVITY B Imagine you are talking to each audience below. Use your voice and body language to persuade your audience to agree with you.

1. **Audience:** friend
   Topic: You want to go to a different movie than your friend does.
2. **Audience:** brother or sister
   Topic: You want to switch after-school chores.
3. **Audience:** neighbor
   Topic: You want him or her to be your team's new soccer coach.
4. **Audience:** teacher
   Topic: You want to learn more about dinosaurs.

Activity C
Answers will vary.
Possible answers:
1. chart showing the number of children who cross the street each day
2. photographs of all the dogs who would use it
3. wear a costume worn by that person
4. brochures showing points of interest
5. equipment needed to play the sport

ACTIVITY C Imagine you are trying to persuade an audience to do the following things. Name a visual aid that you think would help you get your message across.

1. Add a crossing guard near the school.
2. Create a dog park in your neighborhood.
3. Assign a special day to honor the person your school is named after.
4. Visit a nearby large city.
5. Play a new sport in gym class.

SPEAKER'S CORNER

Imagine you invented something for kids your age, such as a flying bicycle. What is it called? What does it look like? What does it do? Write a four-sentence description of your invention. Then talk about it with a partner.

Persuasive Writing • 423

WARM-UP

Read, Listen, Speak

Discuss your example from yesterday's For Tomorrow homework. Explain what about the commercial was persuasive. Then invite small groups to discuss the notes they took. Have students compare notes and work together to create a list of things that make a commercial persuasive.

GRAMMAR CONNECTION

After you administer the Section 6 Assessment, be sure to continue on to the Writer's Workshop on pages 426–437.

TEACH

Invite a volunteer to read aloud the first paragraph and the first bulleted item. Explain that persuasive speeches often present only one side of the topic to convince the audience. Suggest that students carefully think about the information in a speech and consider the other side to what the speaker is saying.

Ask a volunteer to read aloud the second bulleted item. Explain that if students disagree with what a speaker says, they should think about why they disagree.

Invite a volunteer to read aloud the third bulleted item. Tell students that speakers cannot cover everything about a topic, so most speakers want listeners to be curious and ready to ask questions. Explain that if students do not understand something in a persuasive speech, they can ask questions after the speech is over.

PRACTICE

ACTIVITY D

Encourage students to look back at the section Voice and Body Language for tips as they read each sentence. Ask partners to talk about the differences between the two readings of each sentence.

ACTIVITY E

Give students time to brainstorm reasons why people should buy the product they chose. Then have partners discuss their lists. Encourage students to use their lists to practice persuading their partners.

ACTIVITY F

Remind students of the importance of keeping the audience in mind when deciding which visual aids to use. Then have students discuss with their partners how they think the visual aid might help persuade people to buy the product.

ACTIVITY G

Encourage students to think about characters, settings, and costumes that might be featured in their commercials. Have partners offer feedback about each other's ideas.

Being an Active Listener

When you listen to persuasive speech, be an active listener. Think about whether you agree with the speaker. Keep these things in mind for active listening.

- Think about whether the speaker's reasons are true.
- Decide if you agree with the speaker.
- Politely ask the speaker questions if you don't understand something.

ACTIVITY D Work with a partner. Take turns reading each of these sentences in different ways. First, read the sentence in a calm voice. Then read the sentence the way you might if you wanted to persuade someone to agree with you. Practice using your hands with each reading.

1. We should change the way our desks are arranged.
2. We should not have to wear uniforms to school.
3. Our class should go on more field trips.
4. We should have no homework.
5. We should have different kinds of food at lunchtime.
6. Science is one of the most important subjects.
7. We should have a two-hour lunch on Wednesdays.
8. First graders can learn a lot from third graders.
9. There should be a TV in the lunchroom.
10. We should have 15 minutes each day to read whatever we want.

APPLY

SPEAKER'S CORNER

Have volunteers present their commercials to the class. Discuss what seemed most persuasive about the commercials. Ask students if the commercials would get them to buy the products. Students should demonstrate the ability to give a persuasive speech.

TechTip Encourage students to consider visual aids that will show up clearly on video. Help students post their videos on the school Web site for other students and parents to view.

ASSESS

Note which students had difficulty giving a persuasive speech. Use the Reteach option with those students who need additional reinforcement.

After you have reviewed Lessons 3–5, administer the Writing Skills Assessment on pages 59–60 in the **Assessment Book.** This test is also available on the optional **Test Generator CD.**

TEACHING OPTIONS

Reteach

Have students make up a brief oral presentation for their parents about why they should be able to get a new pet. Direct students to practice their presentation with a partner. Ask partners to use the listening tips on page 424. Then have partners offer suggestions for how to improve the presentation. If they cannot think of any improvements, have partners tell what were the most persuasive points in the presentation. Allow time for students to practice and critique the presentations.

Stellar Speakers

Display picture books about famous persuasive speakers, such as Martin Luther King Jr. or President John F. Kennedy. If possible show students a video of one of the person's speeches. Discuss characteristics that made each speaker so powerful. Point out parts of specific speeches that might help students understand these characteristics.

ACTIVITY E Think of something that you use or like. List reasons why someone should buy it. Then meet with a partner. Tell your reasons. Here are some things you might talk about.

- toys
- clothes
- video games
- cereal
- books

ACTIVITY F Imagine that you are making a commercial for the thing you invented for the Speaker's Corner on page 423. List two visual aids that you might use in an oral presentation about your invention. Discuss with a partner how you might use the visual aids in your commercial.

ACTIVITY G Write a commercial for your invention. Tell the reasons people should buy it. Try to use at least one of the visual aids that you listed in Activity F.

SPEAKER'S CORNER

Practice with a partner the commercial that you wrote in Activity G. Then give your partner helpful feedback about his or her commercial. Present your commercial to your classmates. Talk about what you liked about each commercial.

Tech Tip Videotape the commercial for your new invention.

Persuasive Writing • 425

Writer's Workshop

OBJECTIVES
- **To choose and research a topic for a persuasive article**
- **To organize ideas for a persuasive article**

PREWRITING AND DRAFTING

Have a volunteer read aloud the opening paragraph. Tell students to think about times that they tried to get others to agree with them about something. Ask volunteers to tell how they tried to get people to agree with their idea.

Prewriting

Read aloud the first paragraph. Tell students that they are going to be reading about Jake as he writes a persuasive article. Explain that Jake's prewriting includes choosing and researching a topic. Tell students that he will then organize the information from his research.

Choosing a Topic

Have volunteers read aloud this section. Guide students to understand that Jake chose a topic that he felt strongly about. Point out that Jake used an experience from his past to help him think of something he would like to see changed in the future.

👓 Tell students that ideas should include their main topic and the supporting details for their persuasive article.

Your Turn

Invite a volunteer to read aloud the first paragraph. Have students think of topics based on their own experiences. Tell students that it is better to choose a topic about which they feel strongly. Ask students why this might be true. *(It is easier to convince a person to feel the way you do if you feel strongly about the topic.)*

Have volunteers read aloud the next sentence and the bulleted items. Tell students to answer the questions for each topic they think they might want to write about. Allow time for students to answer the questions. Guide students to choose topics dealing with something they want to change.

Researching the Topic

Have volunteers read aloud this section. Ask students what sources Jake used for his research *(the Internet and the Brownsville Recycling Center)*. Then invite volunteers to share other possible sources for Jake's research *(videos, DVDs, encyclopedias)*. Ask volunteers what Jake did with the research he found. *(He took notes on what he learned.)*

Your Turn

Read aloud the bulleted items. Encourage students to take their information from several sources. Tell students that supporting a position with research makes the position stronger and easier for readers to accept. Then have students begin researching their own topics.

Writer's Tip Tell students idea webs can help to visualize how

---

Writer's Workshop
Persuasive Writing

Prewriting and Drafting

People write persuasive articles when they want someone to agree with them. What do you want people to agree with you about? Is it something that others might disagree with? How might you persuade them to agree with you?

Prewriting

Prewriting is the time you plan what you are going to say in a persuasive article. Read about how Jake, a third grader, planned his persuasive article.

Choosing a Topic

When Jake was in second grade, his sister Amelia took him to a special Earth Day event. 👓 Ideas He learned about the importance of recycling. Now Jake wants to help the environment. Amelia said that he should start a recycling program at his school. To do that, Jake would need a lot of help. So he wrote a persuasive article to send to his town newspaper.

Your Turn

Choose your own topic. Think about something you want people to do. You might look back through this chapter, or you might ask your family for ideas. Make a list of topics that you find interesting.

Ask yourself these questions to help you decide which topic to choose:
- What do I want to happen?
- Will some people disagree with me?
- What do I know about my topic?
- Can I find out more about my topic?

Researching the Topic

Jake had learned a lot about recycling when he went to the Earth Day event. But he wanted to know more. So he did some research at the library, using books, magazines, and the Internet.

Jake found out that many things can be recycled. He learned that recycling paper saves trees from being cut down. He took notes on some of the things he learned.

their ideas are connected so that they can organize ideas easily into paragraphs.

Organizing Ideas

Have a volunteer read aloud this section. Tell students that Jake will have an easier time writing his persuasive article if he has his ideas organized in an idea web. Have students look at the idea web and notice the different ideas Jake planned to use to support his topic. Ask volunteers why "work together" and "get paper ready" are grouped together. *(They are both reasons why recycling is a good after-school activity.)*

👀 Suggest that students use their idea webs to organize their persuasive articles. The beginning of their article can come directly from the center of the web, and the supporting details in the middle can come from the ovals (reasons) and lines (support).

Your Turn

Read aloud the bulleted items. When students have finished their webs, have them meet with a partner. Have students discuss how they organized their idea webs and how they are planning to persuade their reader. Ask partners to suggest further support.

TEACHING OPTIONS

Let's Discuss It

Before students select their topics, have them discuss their topic ideas with you. Help students to select appropriate topics for their persuasive articles. Tell students to stay away from topics that might exclude or offend others. Encourage students to write about current topics that directly affect their lives. Guide students to understand that persuasive articles deal with today or the future, not with the past. *(Students should not write an article about why we should attempt to go to the moon. However, they might write about traveling to Mars or colonizing the moon.)*

Jake called the Brownsville Recycling Center. He was able to find out information about how to start a recycling program. Jake thought he might be able to use the information in his article.

Your Turn

- Write the things that you know about your topic.
- Do research online or in the library.
- Read articles and Web sites about your topic.
- If you read something that might make your persuasive article stronger, write it on a note card. You might be able to use the information in your article.

Writer's Tip Idea webs can help you organize your thoughts and research.

Organizing Ideas

Jake's head was buzzing with ideas. He wasn't sure where to start his article. So 👀 **Organization** Jake made an idea web to help organize his thoughts. Look at Jake's idea web below.

Your Turn

- Make your own idea web. Write the topic of your article in the square.
- Write your reasons in ovals around your topic.
- Write ideas that support your reasons.

Prewriting / Drafting / Content Editing / Revising / Copyediting / Proofreading / Publishing

recycling bins — is easy
recycling center collects paper
why our school needs a recycling program
is a good after-school activity
work together
get paper ready

WE RECYCLE

Writer's Workshop   Persuasive Writing

OBJECTIVE
- **To write a draft of a persuasive article**

Drafting

Read aloud the opening paragraph. Encourage students to look back at Jake's idea web on page 427. Then have volunteers read aloud Jake's draft. Have students look for the reasons Jake uses to tell readers why they should start a recycling program at Brownsville Grade School. Ask volunteers to name those reasons. (*Trees are important for animals and for our*

air. Recycling is easy. Recycling is a good after-school activity. Recycling not only saves trees, but it also saves water.) Discuss why Jake did not use the reason "Amelia thinks it is a good idea." (*It is an opinion that is not supported with reasons that the audience might agree with.*) Remind students that when they write persuasive articles, they should support their opinions with researched reasons.

Your Turn

Have a volunteer read aloud the first paragraph. Then read aloud each bulleted item, pausing after each to clarify any misconceptions students may have.

After you have read the second item, review the importance of writing sentences that support each reason.

After you have read the third item, tell students that in the ending they should tell what they want the audience to do. Point out that if the audience agrees with the topic of the article, they will want to know what the author wants them to do.

Read aloud the last item. Remind students that the purpose of a first draft is to organize ideas in paragraph form. Tell them that they will have time later to make additions and changes. Then have students write their drafts for their persuasive articles.

Drafting

Jake carefully looked over his prewriting notes and his idea web. Then he used his notes and idea web to write his persuasive article.

Why Brownsville Grade School Needs a Recycling Program

Every week Americans throw away a lot of paper. That's like throwing away trees. These trees are homes for animals. They also clean the air we breathe. Trees are very important. We should all do our part to protect our trees. Brownsville Grade School can do its part by starting a recycling program.

Recycling paper is very easy. We would have to put recycling bins around the school. Students and teachrs can put all the paper that they might throw away into the bins. the Brownsville Recycling Center will collect the paper every friday.

Recycling is also a good after-school activity. Students and teachrs can work together to bag up the paper and get it ready to be picked up. One ton of recycled paper saves 3,700 pounds of lumber and 7,000 gallons of water. That's like saving at least 7 trees from being cut down.

Respecting Your Audience

Have volunteers read aloud this section. Tell students that the words used in a persuasive article should be the same kinds of words that they would use in a polite conversation. Ask students why they wouldn't use hurtful words in a conversation. *(Using hurtful words may cause your audience not to listen to anything you have to say.)* Explain that persuading someone does not mean forcing the person to believe what you believe. Tell students that a strong, convincing argument has reasons and facts, not hurtful or insensitive words.

Tell students that their voice is their personality coming through in their writing. Point out that a friendly, confident voice will be more persuasive than a whiny or self-righteous voice. Suggest that students read aloud their writing to hear their writing voice.

Your Turn

Use your notes and your idea web to write your draft. As you write, remember the following points.

- Write a clear topic sentence in the beginning.
- Make sure that you have at least two reasons that tell why people should agree with your topic sentence. Write each reason in a separate paragraph.
- Say what your topic is again in the ending. If you can, tell your audience what you want them to do.
- Remember to leave extra space between the lines of your draft. That way you can make changes later.

Respecting Your Audience

You probably believe strongly in your topic. You might use strong words when you write your reasons. But not everyone will agree with you. Remember, when you write a persuasive article, you want to persuade people to agree with you. You don't want to make them angry. So choose your words carefully. Don't use words like *stupid, silly,* or *crazy.* You want your personality to shine through, but you should also respect your audience.

Prewriting
Drafting
Content Editing
Revising
Copyediting
Proofreading
Publishing

TEACHING OPTIONS

A Call to Action

Ask students to come up with an idea for what they want their audience to do in response to their persuasive articles. Be sure students understand that this should be something the readers will be able to do. Explain that students need to keep the goals within their audience's reach. Tell students to imagine that they are trying to get their school to start a recycling program, just like Jake. Ask them to think of what they would tell the audience to do. Ask students to make a list of possible ways to end their article. Tell students that they can write new persuasive articles to build on the success of their previous articles. *(First, Jake asks people to start recycling in his school. If this works, he can later ask the whole school district to do so and then perhaps all the schools in his state.)*

Persuasive Writing • 429

OBJECTIVE

- **To edit the first draft of a persuasive article for content**

CONTENT EDITING

Invite volunteers to read aloud the first two paragraphs. Ask a volunteer to explain what content editing is *(checking the draft to make sure that the ideas make sense)*. Read aloud the Content Editor's Checklist. After each item, ask students if they have any questions.

Have volunteers read aloud the next two paragraphs. Ask students why Jake asked someone else to content edit his draft even though Jake had edited it for content himself. *(A different person might find things Jake had missed.)* Explain that since Jake wrote the article, he knows what he meant to say. Tell students that since Charlie didn't write the article, he might catch mistakes that Jake didn't notice.

Writer's Tip Tell students to ask themselves basic questions when editing, such as *who, where, when, why,* and *how* about a topic.

Read aloud the next two paragraphs. Then ask volunteers to read aloud Charlie's comments. After each comment is read, tell students to find and read the part to which Charlie is referring in Jake's draft. After the first item, ask students why Charlie might want to remove the "stuff about trees."

Ask a volunteer to read aloud the last paragraph. Encourage volunteers to discuss how they would use Charlie's comments to improve Jake's draft.

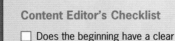

Editor's Workshop   Persuasive Writing

Content Editing

Jake liked what he had written so far. But he wanted his article for the newspaper to be his best work. He didn't want to have mistakes for the whole town to read!

Jake knew that the first thing he should do was content edit his draft. By content editing, he would be sure that the ideas in his draft made sense. He used this checklist to content edit his draft.

Content Editor's Checklist

- ☐ Does the beginning have a clear topic sentence?

- ☐ Does the middle include at least two reasons that are well supported?

- ☐ Are the reasons clear and fully explained?

- ☐ Does the ending retell what the topic is?

- ☐ Are opinion words used?

Jake read over his draft carefully, answering each question on the checklist. He knew that if the ideas in his draft were clear, he would have a better chance of persuading people to agree with him.

Then Jake asked his friend Charlie to content edit his draft. Jake knew that Charlie was good at content editing. He also knew that Charlie would make good suggestions for making the draft better.

Writer's Tip Try to put yourself in the reader's place. Imagine that you don't know anything about the topic. That will help you figure out what to add and what might be confusing.

Your Turn

Have volunteers read aloud the bulleted items. Have students content edit their drafts and then read and comment on their partner's drafts. Encourage students to start by commenting on what they liked about their partner's persuasive articles.

Be sure students understand that they do not have to use all their partner's ideas. Tell students that they are trying to persuade others with this article. Remind them that they should not use any of their partner's suggestions that change the position they are taking on the topic of the article.

In Your Own Words

Explain that plagiarism is using the exact words from a person, book, or online source without giving the source credit for the words. Tell students that when they are content editing their own drafts, they should be sure they wrote everything in their own words. Explain that although it is important to use reasons that support their topic, the reasons should be written in their own words, not taken word-for-word from a source.

Charlie read Jake's draft carefully. He used the Content Editor's Checklist to edit the draft. He wrote a list of his comments so he wouldn't forget any of his ideas.

When Charlie was finished, he and Jake met to talk about the draft. Here are Charlie's comments.

- Your topic sentence is good. But maybe in the beginning you should take out the stuff about trees being homes for animals and cleaning the air.
- The first reason in the middle looks OK. But people might wonder what the school will need to buy. The school might not have the money.

- You should explain your second reason more. Why would kids want to recycle after school?
- The stuff about recycling in the ending is good. But you didn't retell what your topic is. And you didn't use any opinion words to show how strongly you feel.

Jake liked what Charlie said about the draft. The article would be better because of Charlie's help.

Your Turn

- Content edit your draft.
- Trade drafts with a partner. Use the Content's Editor's Checklist to give your partner ideas to make the draft better.
- When you have finished, meet with your partner to talk about your ideas.
- When it is your turn to share your ideas, remember to use polite words.
- Think carefully about each of your partner's ideas before you decide if you will use them. You do not have to use all the ideas. It is up to you to decide what will make your writing better.

Prewriting · Drafting · Content Editing · Revising · Copyediting · Proofreading · Publishing

Persuasive Writing • 431

OBJECTIVE
- **To revise a persuasive article**

REVISING

Read aloud the introductory sentence. Ask volunteers to read aloud the draft. Then give students time to look carefully at Jake's revised draft. Ask students to find some of the changes that Jake made to his draft.

Read aloud the paragraph after the draft. Then have volunteers read aloud the bulleted items. After each item, ask volunteers to point out where the change occurs in the draft.

- Jake took this information out of his draft.
- Jake included in his article the information from the recycling center.
- He added a sentence about why recycling might be a good after-school activity.
- He added a sentence that retold his topic and a sentence telling the reader to help save the trees. The new sentences make the ending stronger.
- He included the opinion words *must* and *should* to show how strongly he felt about recycling.

Point out that Jake had to do more research to support his reason in the second paragraph. Tell students that in the third paragraph, Jake didn't have to do research to support his reason. Instead, Jake supported his reason by coming up with ideas on his own. Explain that Jake's persuasive article, like many persuasive articles, is a combination of information found by researching and by using his own ideas.

After the last two items, ask students what Jake told his readers he wants them to do. *(He wants*

Writer's Workshop | Persuasive Writing

Revising

Here is Jake's revised draft.

Why Brownsville Grade School Needs a Recycling Program

Every week Americans throw away a lot of paper. That's like throwing away trees. ~~These trees are homes for animals. They also clean the air we breathe.~~ Trees are very important. We should all do our part to protect our trees. Brownsville Grade School can do its part by starting a recycling program.

Recycling paper is very easy. ~~We would have to put~~ All need to do is buy recycling bins to put around the school. Students and teachrs can put all the paper that they might throw away into the bins. the Brownsville Recycling Center will collect the paper every friday. It won't cost the school any money to have the paper collected.

Recycling is also a good after-school activity. Students and teachrs can work together to bag up the paper and get it ready to be picked up. This will be a good way for kids to make friends who are interested in helping our planet. One ton of recycled paper saves 3,700 pounds of lumber and 7,000 gallons of water. That's like saving at least 7 trees from being cut down. We should start a recycling program. We must do our part to help save our trees.

them to save trees by starting a recycling program.) Have students silently read the last paragraph.

Your Turn

Ask a volunteer to read aloud this section. Remind students to use only the suggestions that they feel make their draft better. Encourage students to take their time revising their drafts. When students have finished revising, have them answer the questions in the Content Editor's Checklist again.

TEACHING OPTIONS

Meet Again

After students have finished revising their drafts, have them meet again with their content editors. Have students show their content editors how they incorporated their suggestions. Also have students explain why they did not choose some of their content editor's suggestions.

Jake made a lot of changes after he met with Charlie. Look at some of the things he did to improve his persuasive article.

- Jake liked the facts about trees being homes for animals and cleaning the air. But he thought Charlie was right. They made the beginning confusing. What did Jake do?

- He agreed that people might wonder what the school would need to buy. So he called the recycling center. How did Jake use this new information?

- Jake thought about Charlie's suggestion to explain the second reason more. He added a sentence. What is it about?

- He also added two sentences to the ending. Do you think they make the ending stronger? Why or why not?

- Jake also included opinion words. Which ones? Why?

Jake was happy with the changes that he had made. He thanked Charlie for his help.

Your Turn

- Use your partner's suggestions to revise your draft.
- Read your draft again and look for more ways to improve it.
- Try to answer the questions on the Content Editor's Checklist again. Can you answer yes to each question?

Prewriting

Drafting

Content Editing

Revising

Copyediting

Proofreading

Publishing

Persuasive Writing • 433

OBJECTIVES

- **To copyedit a persuasive article**
- **To proofread a persuasive article**

COPYEDITING AND PROOFREADING

Copyediting

Ask volunteers to read aloud the first paragraph. Tell students that Jake knew that his words and sentences had to make sense for his readers to understand and form an opinion on his topic and reasons.

Tell students that in persuasive writing strong word choice can change the way a reader sees the topic.

Have volunteers read aloud the Copyeditor's Checklist. Then read aloud the paragraph following the checklist. Ask students to point out the place where sentences could be joined to make a compound sentence. Tell students to look for the two short sentences that Jake combined. *(The compound sentence that Jake made is "Trees are very important, so we should all do our part to protect them.")* Emphasize that combining sentences was Jake's choice and that other sentences might also have been combined.

Tell students that sentence fluency is the way the writing sounds in the reader's mind. Tell students that when they read aloud, they can tell when too many sentences are the same length or structure. Explain that good writing has variety.

Your Turn

Ask a volunteer to read aloud this section. Tell students to answer the questions on the Copyeditor's Checklist one at a time. Remind students that using compound sentences is a choice. Explain that compound sentences offer variety to the writing and can help with sentence fluency.

Proofreading

Have volunteers read aloud the first paragraph. Ask volunteers why people would not take Jake seriously if he had mistakes in spelling, capitalization, or punctuation. *(It distracts readers from the ideas. It looks as if someone who doesn't know the rules of writing wrote it. Doing it properly shows that the writer cares about what he or she is writing.)* Have volunteers read aloud the Proofreader's Checklist.

Editor's Workshop   Persuasive Writing

Copyediting and Proofreading

Copyediting

Jake was sure that the ideas in his article were good. Now he wanted to make sure that the sentences were complete and that they made sense. He also wanted to make sure

Word Choice

that all the words were used correctly. So he decided to copyedit his draft. He used this Copyeditor's Checklist.

Jake read his draft again and answered the questions on the Copyeditor's Checklist. He found in his beginning two sentences he could

Sentence Fluency

join to make a compound sentence. Can you guess which sentences he joined?

Copyeditor's Checklist

- ☐ Are compound sentences used correctly?
- ☐ Are words with suffixes used correctly?
- ☐ Are the sentences complete?
- ☐ Does the order of the sentences make sense?
- ☐ Do all the words mean what you think they mean?

Your Turn

- Read your revised draft carefully.
- Can you join any sentences to make compound sentences?
- Have you used words with suffixes correctly?
- Make sure that you can answer yes to all the questions on the checklist.

Tell students that conventions are the agreed-upon rules people use to communicate in writing, including spelling, punctuation, and capitalization. Compare these rules to the rules of a game, such as soccer, football, or chess.

Read aloud the last paragraph. Ask a volunteer to point out the capitalization mistake in Jake's persuasive article. *(The* is not *capitalized at the beginning of a sentence in the second paragraph.)*

Your Turn

Have volunteers read aloud this section. Ask students to proofread their own draft before asking a partner to proofread. Tell students to check for one kind of mistake at a time. Be sure students look for new mistakes that might have been added during editing when they receive their drafts back from their proofreaders.

Grammar in Action. Guide students to find the incorrect suffix in Jake's draft *(teachr)* and help them fix it *(teacher)*. Review the meaning of the suffix *-er (one who).*

TEACHING OPTIONS

Copyediting Tips

Read aloud the following tips:

1. **Slow down.** When you are copyediting, don't read as fast as you might if you were reading a book. Slowing down can help you catch mistakes.

2. **Cut out wordiness.** Sometimes writers use wordy sentences, which can make the meaning of the sentence confusing. Look in your draft for places where long phrases can be replaced by shorter, more direct ones.

3. **Know your mistakes.** Every writer has mistakes that he or she makes over and over. Talk to your teacher about what your usual writing mistakes are. Be on the lookout for those mistakes when you copyedit. Provide your copyeditor with a list of your usual mistakes so that he or she can look for them in your work.

Proofreading

Jake wanted people to take his persuasive article seriously. If his article had mistakes **Conventions** in spelling, capitalization, or punctuation, people wouldn't take him seriously. Jake used the Proofreader's Checklist to catch these kinds of mistakes. He also checked to make sure that he hadn't left out anything when he revised his article.

Jake knew that a different proofreader would spot mistakes that he missed. Jake asked his teacher, Mrs. Wu, to proofread his draft. Mrs. Wu found one capitalization mistake and one word misspelled several times. Can you find these mistakes?

Your Turn

- Read your draft carefully, using the Proofreader's Checklist.
- Look for only one kind of mistake at a time.
- Use the proofreading marks from page 245 to mark changes on your draft.
- When you have finished, trade drafts with a new partner. Go over each other's drafts, using the checklist.
- Use a dictionary to look up any words that might be misspelled or used incorrectly.

Proofreader's Checklist

- ☐ Are all the words spelled correctly?
- ☐ Is the first word of each sentence capitalized?
- ☐ Are proper nouns capitalized?
- ☐ Does each sentence end with the correct punctuation mark?
- ☐ Have you checked to be sure that no new mistakes were made while editing?

Grammar in Action

Jake used an incorrect suffix twice. Find it and fix it.

Prewriting · Drafting · Content Editing · Revising · Copyediting · Proofreading · Publishing

OBJECTIVE
- **To publish a persuasive article**

PUBLISHING

Have volunteers read aloud the first paragraph. Tell students that Jake is typing his persuasive article because it will look more professional to the person at the newspaper who will read his article. Then tell students that Jake checked his final draft, using the Proofreader's Checklist because he wanted his article to be the best that it could be.

Explain that presentation is the look of a piece of writing. Tell students that neatness and consistency will make their writing more inviting for readers and will strengthen the effect of their persuasive writing.

Invite volunteers to read aloud Jake's final version. After it has been read, ask students to look back at Jake's first draft. Ask students if they think that Jake's article is better now than it was before and to explain how.

Read aloud the paragraphs following the draft. Discuss with students the many ways they might publish their writing.

Writer's Workshop
Persuasive Writing

Publishing

Jake typed the final copy. He checked his final copy one more time. He used the Proofreader's Checklist to make sure that he didn't make any new mistakes while he typed. Here is Jake's final persuasive article.

Why Brownsville Grade School Needs a Recycling Program

Every week Americans throw away a lot of paper. That's like throwing away trees. Trees are very important, so we should all do our part to protect them. Brownsville Grade School can do its part by starting a recycling program.

Recycling paper is very easy. All we need to do is buy recycling bins to put around the school. Students and teachers can put all the paper that they might throw away into the bins. The Brownsville Recycling Center will collect the paper every Friday. It won't cost the school any money to have the paper collected.

Recycling is also a good after-school activity. Students and teachers can work together to bag up the paper and get it ready to be picked up. This will be a good way for kids to make friends who are interested in helping our planet.

One ton of recycled paper saves 3700 pounds of lumber and 7,000 gallons of water. That's like saving at least 7 trees from being cut down. We should start a recycling program. We must do our part to help save our trees.

Your Turn

Ask volunteers to read aloud this section. Have students prepare a final copy of their persuasive article. Remind them to work slowly when copying or typing their work. Then tell students to use the Proofreader's Checklist a second time. Be sure they know to check for mistakes introduced during editing and copying or typing.

When students have finished with their persuasive articles, ask volunteers to read aloud their work.

ASSESS

Have students assess their finished persuasive article using the reproducible Student Self-Assessment on page 437y. A separate Persuasive Writing Scoring Rubric can be found on page 437z for you to use to evaluate their work.

Plan to spend tomorrow doing a formal assessment. Administer the Persuasive Writing Prompt on **Assessment Book** pages 61–62.

See It Through

Encourage students to find the next step of seeing through what they proposed. In Jake's case he might have asked his teacher if he could talk to the principal or the student council. Tell students that writing is the first step, but that action often leads to success.

Portfolio Opportunity

Remind students to keep a copy of their final persuasive articles in their portfolios. Point out that having a portfolio will help students keep track of the progress they are making with their writing.

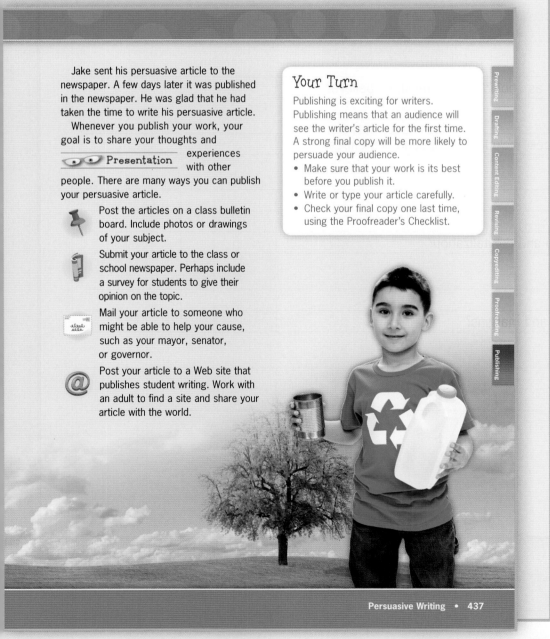

Jake sent his persuasive article to the newspaper. A few days later it was published in the newspaper. He was glad that he had taken the time to write his persuasive article.

Whenever you publish your work, your goal is to share your thoughts and experiences with other people. There are many ways you can publish your persuasive article.

Presentation

Post the articles on a class bulletin board. Include photos or drawings of your subject.

Submit your article to the class or school newspaper. Perhaps include a survey for students to give their opinion on the topic.

Mail your article to someone who might be able to help your cause, such as your mayor, senator, or governor.

Post your article to a Web site that publishes student writing. Work with an adult to find a site and share your article with the world.

Your Turn

Publishing is exciting for writers. Publishing means that an audience will see the writer's article for the first time. A strong final copy will be more likely to persuade your audience.

- Make sure that your work is its best before you publish it.
- Write or type your article carefully.
- Check your final copy one last time, using the Proofreader's Checklist.

Prewriting · Drafting · Content Editing · Revising · Copyediting · Proofreading · Publishing

Name _____ Date _____

Persuasive Writing

	YES	NO
Ideas		
Do I focus on one viewpoint for my topic?		
Does the piece convince readers to share my viewpoint?		
Are my reasons backed by research?		
Organization		
Do I have a beginning that tells my position?		
Do I have a middle with reasons that support my position?		
Do I have an ending that summarizes my position?		
Voice		
Do I use a persuasive voice?		
Word Choice		
Do I use opinion words such as *should, ought, must,* or *believe*?		
Sentence Fluency		
Do I use a variety of sentences, including compound sentences?		
Conventions		
Do I use correct grammar?		
Do I use correct spelling?		
Do I use correct punctuation and capitalization?		
Presentation		
Is my paper neat?		
Do I use consistent spacing and margins?		
Additional Items		

Name _____

Date _____ Score _____

POINT VALUES

0 = not evident
1 = minimal evidence of mastery
2 = evidence of development toward mastery
3 = strong evidence of mastery
4 = outstanding evidence of mastery

Persuasive Writing

Ideas

	POINTS
a focus on one viewpoint about a specific topic	
an attempt to convince the reader to share a viewpoint	
reasons backed by research	

Organization

a beginning with a position statement	
a middle with reasons that support the stated position	
an ending that summarizes the position statement	

Voice

a persuasive voice	

Word Choice

opinion words such as *should*, *ought*, *must*, or *believe*	

Sentence Fluency

a variety of sentences, including compound sentences	

Conventions

correct grammar and usage	
correct spelling	
correct punctuation and capitalization	

Presentation

neatness	
consistent spacing and margins	

Additional Items

Total	

CHAPTER FOCUS

LESSON 1: What Makes Good Realistic Fiction?

LESSON 2: Characters

- **GRAMMAR:** Punctuation and Capitalization
- **WRITING SKILLS:** Dialogue
- **WORD STUDY:** Contractions
- **WRITING POETRY:** Lines That Rhyme
- **SPEAKING AND LISTENING SKILLS:** Skits
- **WRITER'S WORKSHOP:** Realistic Fiction

SUPPORT MATERIALS

Practice Book
Writing, pages 162–166

Assessment Book
Chapter 7 Writing Skills,
   pages 63–64
Creative Writing: Realistic Fiction
   Writing Prompt, pages 65–66

Rubrics
Student, page 475y
Teacher, page 475z

Test Generator CD

Grammar
Section 7, pages 157–182

Customizable Lesson Plans
www.voyagesinenglish.com

Creative Writing

WHAT IS REALISTIC FICTION?

Realistic fiction is a genre of narrative fiction. Realistic fiction can take many forms, including plays, novels, or short stories. Topics and themes for realistic fiction vary greatly. Mysteries, adventure stories, and historical fiction can all be realistic fiction.

A well-written realistic-fiction story has an organized pattern of events giving it good plot structure. Good writers of realistic fiction use informal language for a natural voice, vivid words to create realistic images or for impact, and correct conventions.

Good realistic fiction includes the following:

- ☐ Realistic characters and events
- ☐ A beginning that introduces the characters and setting
- ☐ A middle that describes a realistic problem or situation
- ☐ An ending that solves the problem or brings the situation to a close
- ☐ Events told in time order
- ☐ Dialogue that uses informal language for a natural voice
- ☐ A variety of sentences, including dialogue to move the story along
- ☐ Vivid words

LiNK Use the following titles to offer your students examples of well-crafted realistic fiction:

Amber Brown Is Not a Crayon by Paula Danziger

Fly Away Home by Eve Bunting

Island of the Blue Dolphins by Scott O'Dell

" Truth is stranger than fiction; fiction has to make sense. "

—Leo Rosten

WRITER'S WORKSHOP TIPS

Follow these ideas and tips to help you and your class get the most out of the Writer's Workshop:

- Review the traits of good writing. Use the chart on the inside back cover of the student and teacher editions.
- Display posters from family movies that are in the genre of realistic fiction, such as *Parent Trap, Cheaper by the Dozen,* and *The Sandlot.*
- Bring in podcasts of radio stories that are realistic fiction.
- Pass around exceptional writing samples by former students to give students real-life examples of quality, age-appropriate realistic-fiction writing.
- Conduct an interview with each student before the drafting stage to be certain that he or she has a clear, coherent plot.

CONNECT WITH GRAMMAR

Throughout the Writer's Workshop, look for opportunities to integrate punctuation and capitalization with writing realistic fiction.

- ☐ Have students use direct quotations to indicate dialogue in their stories.
- ☐ During revising suggest that students combine simple sentences into compound sentences using commas.
- ☐ Tell students to use a personal title for characters, when thinking of characters' names.
- ☐ During copyediting and proofreading, have editors check that each sentence begins with a capital letter and has the appropriate end punctuation.

SCORING RUBRIC

Creative Writing: Realistic Fiction

Point Values
0 = not evident
1 = minimal evidence of mastery
2 = evidence of development toward mastery
3 = strong evidence of mastery
4 = outstanding evidence of mastery

Ideas	POINTS
realistic characters and events	
Organization	
a beginning that introduces the characters and setting	
a middle that describes a problem or situation	
an ending that solves the problem or brings the situation to a close	
events told in time order	
Voice	
dialogue that uses informal language for a natural voice	
Word Choice	
vivid words	
Sentence Fluency	
a variety of sentences, including dialogue to move the story along	
Conventions	
correct grammar and usage	
correct spelling	
correct punctuation and capitalization	
Presentation	
neatness	
consistent margins and spacing	
Additional Items	
Total	

Full-sized, reproducible rubrics can be found at the end of this chapter.

Creative Writing

INTRODUCING THE GENRE

Tell students that Chapter 7 explains how to write realistic fiction. Ask volunteers to name books that they have read recently. For each example ask students to tell what the book is about. Then ask each volunteer to tell whether he or she thinks the book is realistic and whether the characters, setting, and events in the book could happen in real life.

Explain that realistic fiction contains characters and settings that come from the real world. Guide students to understand that realistic fiction does not contain characters such as talking dinosaurs and is not set in magical places such as Peter Pan's Neverland. Tell students that realistic fiction does not include magical or fantastic elements.

Elaborate on the following characteristics of realistic fiction:

- Characters in realistic fiction are usually people.
- The setting of realistic fiction must be a place that exists today or existed at a time in the past. It cannot exist in the far future or in make-believe places.
- Realistic fiction has a beginning, a middle, and an ending.
- Realistic fiction has dialogue that gives the exact words that the characters use.

Creative Writing

LiNK Fly Away Home

Fly Away Home is a good example of realistic fiction because it has the following:

- People as main characters
- A realistic setting
- Dialogue that gives the characters' exact words.

As students read the excerpts of realistic fiction in this chapter, be sure to identify how punctuation and capitalization are used. For example, on this page you may wish to point out apostrophes in the two contractions in the second sentence (*that's, don't*), the quotation marks showing dialogue in the third paragraph, and the capitalization of proper nouns (*Dad, Delta, TWA, Northwest, Continental*).

LiNK Fly Away Home
by Eve Bunting

My dad and I live in an airport. That's because we don't have a home and the airport is better than the streets. We are careful not to get caught.

. . . Dad and I try not to get noticed. We stay among the crowds. We change airlines.

"Delta, TWA, Northwest, we love them all," Dad says.

He and I wear blue jeans and blue T-shirts and blue jackets. . . . Not to be noticed is to look like nobody at all.

Once we saw a woman pushing a metal cart full of stuff. She wore a long, dirty coat and she lay down across a row of seats in front of Continental Gate 6. The cart, dirty coat, the lying down were all noticeable. Security moved her out real fast.

> *Fly Away Home* is a good example of realistic fiction. It has characters that readers care about, and there is a problem the characters need to solve.

Reading the Literature Excerpt

Ask volunteers to read aloud the excerpt from *Fly Away Home.* Have students explain why it is a good example of realistic fiction. Ask students if the excerpt makes them want to read the entire story and why or why not.

Reading the Student Model

Ask volunteers to read aloud the story. Point out the parts of the story that let the reader know that it is realistic fiction. Direct students' attention to the objects the characters use in the story and the setting of the story. Ask students if they have seen these kinds of things and this type of place before. Point out that these objects and the setting are not magical or fantastic, but are realistic and familiar.

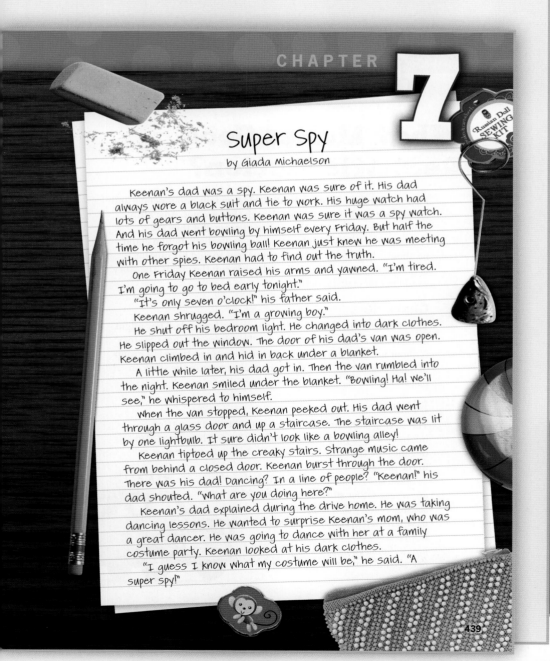

CHAPTER 7

Super Spy
by Giada Michaelson

Keenan's dad was a spy. Keenan was sure of it. His dad always wore a black suit and tie to work. His huge watch had lots of gears and buttons. Keenan was sure it was a spy watch. And his dad went bowling by himself every Friday. But half the time he forgot his bowling ball! Keenan just knew he was meeting with other spies. Keenan had to find out the truth.

One Friday Keenan raised his arms and yawned. "I'm tired. I'm going to go to bed early tonight."

"It's only seven o'clock!" his father said.

Keenan shrugged. "I'm a growing boy."

He shut off his bedroom light. He changed into dark clothes. He slipped out the window. The door of his dad's van was open. Keenan climbed in and hid in back under a blanket.

A little while later, his dad got in. Then the van rumbled into the night. Keenan smiled under the blanket. "Bowling! Ha! We'll see," he whispered to himself.

When the van stopped, Keenan peeked out. His dad went through a glass door and up a staircase. The staircase was lit by one lightbulb. It sure didn't look like a bowling alley!

Keenan tiptoed up the creaky stairs. Strange music came from behind a closed door. Keenan burst through the door. There was his dad! Dancing? In a line of people? "Keenan!" his dad shouted. "What are you doing here?"

Keenan's dad explained during the drive home. He was taking dancing lessons. He wanted to surprise Keenan's mom, who was a great dancer. He was going to dance with her at a family costume party. Keenan looked at his dark clothes.

"I guess I know what my costume will be," he said. "A super spy!"

OBJECTIVE

- **To recognize the characteristics of realistic fiction**

WARM-UP

Read, Listen, Speak

Share your example of realistic fiction from yesterday's For Tomorrow homework and tell what makes it a good example of realistic fiction. Invite students to share their examples of realistic fiction and to explain what makes their examples realistic fiction.

GRAMMAR CONNECTION

Take this opportunity to talk about end punctuation and capitalization. You may wish to have students point out end punctuation and capitalization in their Read, Listen, Speak examples.

TEACH

Have a volunteer read aloud the first paragraph. Tell students that everything in realistic fiction—especially the characters, settings, and events—could actually exist and happen. Explain that realistic fiction doesn't have talking animals or fantastic things such as flying brooms. Tell students that realistic fiction has people and animals doing things that people expect them to do.

Read aloud the section Characters. Ask students to name their favorite characters from realistic fiction stories. Encourage students to describe why they think these characters are interesting.

Have a volunteer read aloud the section Setting. Ask students to describe settings in fiction that would not be realistic *(a beach on Mars, a dragon's cave).*

Invite volunteers to read aloud the section Problem. Ask students to identify the problem that the character solved in the story on page 439. *(He wanted to find out whether his dad was a spy.)* Point out that problems in stories could be things that need to be done or goals that need to be reached.

Have a volunteer suggest a realistic story topic. Then ask students to change the topic to make it unrealistic.

PRACTICE

ACTIVITY A

Have small groups complete this activity. Direct each student to choose two or three settings and then write their sentences. Ask volunteers to share their answers with the class. Discuss how different students wrote different sentences for the same setting. Explain that each student imagines the character differently. Tell students to save their work for the Writer's Corner on page 443.

What Makes Good Realistic Fiction?

Fiction is a made-up story. Realistic fiction tells about people and events that could be real, even though they are not. Adventure stories and mysteries can be realistic fiction. But they are realistic only if they could really happen. Realistic fiction could be about a boy sneaking into a circus tent to find his missing dog. If he discovered that talking lizards run the circus, the story would not be realistic fiction.

Characters

The characters in realistic fiction are usually people. They might be teachers, singers, or taxi drivers. The character that the story is about is called the main character. Sometimes there is a group of main characters. Who is the main character in the story on page 439?

Setting

The setting is the time and place of the story. The setting might be a backyard or an airport in China. The setting also includes the time. Realistic fiction takes place in the past or in the present.

Some stories could happen almost anywhere. Other stories need a special setting. A story that happens at a baseball diamond will be different from a story that happens in a jungle. Some characters will fit with one setting but not with another.

APPLY

WRITER'S CORNER

Discuss fiction books that students have read. Suggest that students choose a title and think about the setting and one of the characters. When students have finished, ask them to read their descriptions to partners. Students should demonstrate the ability to identify setting and character.

Grammar in Action. Ask students to tell which end punctuation expresses strong feelings *(exclamation point)*. Have students read aloud their sentences and tell what end punctuation was used.

ASSESS

Note which students had difficulty identifying the characteristics of realistic fiction. Use the Reteach option with those students who need additional reinforcement.

TEACHING OPTIONS

Reteach

Write on the board a two-column T-chart like the one below. Discuss the characteristics of realistic fiction. Ask students to give examples of characters and settings that would be found in realistic fiction and that would not be found in realistic fiction.

Realistic Fiction

Is	Is Not
a girl from Miami	a girl who can grow smaller
an old barn	a barn that flies

Bookmark Basics

Have students make bookmarks to use to review the characteristics of realistic fiction. Cut strips of poster board and distribute them to students. Direct them to make bookmarks that include sections for characters, setting, and problem. Then have students list the characteristics of each. Encourage students to illustrate their bookmarks. Tell students to use their bookmarks to remind them of the characteristics of realistic fiction.

Problem

Fiction is interesting when characters have a problem they need to solve. One character might need to learn to do a flying judo kick for a contest. Another might have a noisy pet that bothers the neighbors. Another might be trapped in a snowstorm. What is the main character's problem in the story on page 439?

Readers become interested because they want to see how the character solves the problem. A story about a character walking to school might be boring. But if the character has to get past a bully to get there, then the story gets interesting.

ACTIVITY A Write a sentence describing a realistic character you might find in each of these settings. Be sure to give your character a name.

1. in a cornfield
2. at a swimming pool
3. at a toy store after it is closed
4. in an airplane over Montana
5. at a pond in the woods
6. in a rose garden at sunrise
7. at a parade on Thanksgiving Day
8. in an elevator going to the top of a skyscraper
9. on the soccer field during the championship game
10. in a dunk tank at the school carnival
11. in a bike race
12. at a pet shop

WRITER'S CORNER

Think of a fiction book you have read. Then write four sentences to describe the setting and one character.

Grammar in Action. Include one sentence that expresses a strong feeling. Circle all the end punctuation.

Creative Writing • 441

For Tomorrow

Have students find a piece of realistic fiction and record the main characters, the setting, and the problem the characters try to solve. Bring in your own example to share with the class.

WARM-UP

Read, Listen, Speak

Share the information from yesterday's For Tomorrow homework. Tell students why the characters and setting are realistic. Invite small groups to share their work. Ask them to explain how they know their characters and settings are realistic.

GRAMMAR CONNECTION

Take this opportunity to talk about abbreviations. You may wish to have students point out any abbreviations in their Read, Listen, Speak examples.

TEACH

Review the sections Characters, Setting, and Problem from pages 440–441. Discuss how the characters can influence the story. Ask students to explain why the setting is often important in realistic fiction. Then have volunteers name examples of problems that characters might face in a realistic-fiction story. Encourage students to describe problems they have read about in realistic-fiction books.

Have a volunteer read aloud the first paragraph of the section Plot. Ask a volunteer to summarize the plot of a book that students have read in class. Guide students to understand that the plot is what happens in a story.

Invite volunteers to read aloud the rest of the section. Remind students that personal narratives also have beginnings, middles, and endings. Explain that, just like personal narratives, the events in a realistic-fiction story are told in time order.

LiNK Invite a volunteer to read aloud the excerpt. Then ask students what the excerpt tells about the setting and plot.

PRACTICE

ACTIVITY B

Have partners complete this activity. Suggest that students first identify the problem introduced in each item. Then have them discuss possibilities for what might happen next in a realistic-fiction story. When students have finished, invite volunteers to share their answers with the class.

ACTIVITY C

Review the model on page 439. When students have finished, ask volunteers to read aloud their answers.

ACTIVITY D

Have small groups complete this activity. Encourage students to review the section Problem on page 441 if they need help. After students have selected the problems that might make good realistic stories, have volunteers share their explanations with the class. Challenge students to explain why items 1, 3, 8, and 9 would not make good problems for realistic stories.

LiNK

Fly Away Home

Everything in the airport is on the move—passengers, pilots, flight attendants, cleaners with their brooms. Jets roar in, close to the windows. Other jets roar out. Luggage bounces down chutes, escalators glide up and down, disappearing under floors. Everyone's going somewhere except Dad and me. We stay.

Eve Bunting

Plot

The plot is what happens in a story. It tells what the characters do to solve a problem. A plot is the events that happen in the beginning, middle, and ending of a story.

The beginning of a story tells the reader about the characters and the setting. The plot begins when the characters face a problem that they must solve. Readers will be interested if they know what the problem is right away.

The middle tells what the characters do to solve their problem. The middle can be one paragraph or many paragraphs. It can have one event or many events. One event usually leads to the next.

The ending of the story tells whether the characters solved their problem. It finishes the story. Sometimes it tells what happens to the characters after the problem is solved.

ACTIVITY B Write three sentences telling what might happen next in these plot descriptions. Choose something that might happen in realistic fiction.

1. Austin sees a white monkey loose in the monkey house at the zoo. He tells his parents, but they don't see the monkey. Then he sees a brown monkey. It peeks its head out from a trash can. He tells a zookeeper, but the zookeeper doesn't see the monkey either.

2. Sydney hears a strange machine noise from her neighbor's house one night. She goes to her neighbor's yard. A bright light shines in the basement. She hears her neighbor whistling in the basement. Then the machine noise roars again.

3. All day long the new student stared at Deborah. Once, the student tried to get her attention, but Deborah's friend Maria caught her attention first. At last the new student found Deborah at the end of the school day. "I think this is yours," the student said.

APPLY

WRITER'S CORNER

Have students take out the work they did for Activity A on page 441. Encourage students to select realistic problems for their characters. Ask volunteers to share their sentences with the class. Students should demonstrate an understanding of plot in realistic fiction.

ASSESS

Note which students had difficulty understanding plot. Use the Reteach option with those students who need additional reinforcement.

Practice Book page 162 provides additional work with the characteristics of realistic fiction.

○ Reteach

Discuss realistic-fiction stories students have read recently. Encourage students to identify the beginning, middle, and ending of each story. Have students choose one story to fill out the graphic organizer below.

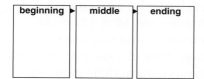

beginning ▶	middle ▶	ending

○ What's Happening?

Bring to class realistic pictures of people doing some type of action. Have students tell partners a story about the person, based on what the person is doing in the picture. Encourage students to focus their stories on a problem the person could be trying to solve. Tell students to be sure the characters and the setting are realistic.

---

4. As Kyle leaves for school, he notices a big hole that has been dug under the top step to his house. He knows that the hole wasn't there the day before. He is running late, so he doesn't have time to tell his mom about it. Kyle thinks about the hole all day at school. When he gets home, his dog runs out to greet him, but immediately turns around and starts barking at the hole.

Activity C

1. Keenan and his father
2. He wants to find out whether his father is a spy.
3. Everything that happens in the story could happen in the real world.
4. Keenan pretends to go to bed early. He hides in his father's van. He follows his father. He bursts in on his father's dance lesson.

ACTIVITY C Answer these questions about the story on page 439.

1. Who are the characters in the story?
2. What is Keenan's problem in the story?
3. How do you know the story is realistic fiction?
4. What are the events in the middle of the plot?

ACTIVITY D Tell which of these you think would make a good problem for a realistic story. Explain your answers.

1. Kelven gets a real dragon for his birthday. no
2. Teresa has a treasure map and wants to find the treasure. yes
3. Fergus is riding a school bus that starts to fly. no
4. Jude loses her mother's new cell phone. yes
5. Michael is trying to win a pie-eating contest. yes
6. Holly is throwing a surprise birthday party for her mom. yes
7. Lyle moves away to another town. yes
8. David finds a lost unicorn in his backyard. no
9. Jason's grandfather leaves him a crystal ball that lets him see the future. no
10. Elizabeth discovers that she is locked in her school for the night. yes

WRITER'S CORNER

Pick one character you made up for Activity A on page 441. Imagine what that character's life is like. Write three sentences about a problem that character might have to solve.

Bearded dragon

For Tomorrow

Have students draw pictures that represent the beginning of a realistic-fiction story. Encourage students to have family members or friends as characters in the story. Bring in your own picture to share with the class.

Creative Writing • 443

OBJECTIVES
- **To reveal characters by using appearance and dialogue**
- **To develop characters through action**

WARM-UP

Read, Listen, Speak

Display your picture from yesterday's For Tomorrow homework. Model how the picture could show the beginning of a story. Have small groups share their pictures. Encourage students to discuss ways their pictures tell the beginning of a story.

GRAMMAR CONNECTION

Take this opportunity to talk about personal titles and initials. You may wish to have students use personal titles in their Read, Listen, Speak discussion.

TEACH

Review the meaning of the term *realistic fiction*. Invite volunteers to name and describe the different characteristics that make up a good realistic fiction story (*characters, setting, problem, plot*).

Ask a volunteer to read aloud the first paragraph. Have volunteers name some characters from realistic fiction. Write on the board the names of the characters. Then have volunteers read aloud the section Appearance. Invite the volunteers who named their favorite characters to write on the board descriptive words and phrases about their characters.

Have a volunteer read aloud the first paragraph of the section Dialogue. Then ask two students to read aloud the example sentences. Encourage students to read with the appropriate expression. Have volunteers tell what they think Ava feels in each example. Ask students to tell how they know what Ava is feeling. Point out each sentence's punctuation. Tell students that writers can use punctuation in dialogue to show how a character feels. Have students make up dialogue for the characters described on the board. Then read aloud the last paragraph.

PRACTICE

ACTIVITY A

Encourage students to imagine how their character looks and acts. Then have students answer the questions, using words and phrases instead of complete sentences.

ACTIVITY B

Have small groups complete this activity. For each item suggest that students choose a different writer to record the group's sentence of dialogue. Allow time for students to share their sentences with the class.

Characters

In realistic fiction, readers care about the main characters. You can help readers care about your characters by telling what the characters are like.

Appearance

Readers can picture your characters when you tell how they look. Does your character have curly hair or straight hair? Does your character wear smelly, old sneakers or shiny, new boots? Readers like to know how the characters in a story look. Good descriptions can help readers picture the characters more clearly.

Dialogue

Dialogue is what the characters say in a story. Dialogue also tells readers about the characters. A character who is excited talks differently than a character who is nervous. What is Ava's mood in these examples?

> **"Yippee! School is closed today!" Ava shouted.**
> **"Oh, no, school is closed today," Ava groaned.**

One line of dialogue shows Ava is happy that school is closed. The other example shows she is sad that school is closed.

APPLY

WRITER'S CORNER

Tell students to use their answers from Activity A while writing their descriptions. When students have finished, have them share their descriptions with partners. Make sure students save their descriptions for the Writer's Corner on page 447. Students should demonstrate the ability to reveal characters by using appearance.

ASSESS

Note which students had difficulty describing characters. Use the Reteach option with those students who need additional reinforcement.

ACTIVITY A **Think of a character you might like to put in a story. Decide if it is a boy or a girl. Give your character a name. Then write answers for these questions about your character.**

1. Where does your character live?
2. What kinds of books does your character read?
3. What is your character's hobby?
4. How old is your character?
5. How does your character dress for school?
6. What is your character's favorite food?
7. What is something your character might say?
8. Who lives with your character?
9. Where does your character like to visit?
10. What three words best describe your character's appearance?

ACTIVITY B **Write one sentence each character might say.**

1. Mrs. Charles, a school bus driver with loud children on her bus
2. Timeka, a girl who is lost in the woods
3. Hanna, a third grader about to play a piano concert
4. Mr. Conner, a teacher who is surprised with a gift from his class
5. Kasey, a fifth grader about to win a big prize
6. Horace, a firefighter trying to get a cat out of a tree
7. Delia, an older sister who dares her brother to knock on a door
8. Gina, a first grader meeting her baby brother for the first time
9. Mrs. Day, a principal who sees an older student crying by her locker
10. Jay, a boy greeting his dog who has just been sprayed by a skunk

WRITER'S CORNER

Write three sentences that describe the appearance of the character you thought of for Activity A.

For Tomorrow

Have students find two stories or poems with character names in the titles. Bring in your own titles to share with the class.

Creative Writing • 445

WARM-UP

Read, Listen, Speak

Share your titles with character names from yesterday's For Tomorrow homework. Model for students an explanation of the titles and what they tell about the characters and stories. Have students discuss their titles and what they say about the characters and their stories.

GRAMMAR CONNECTION

Take this opportunity to talk about titles of books and poems. You may wish to have students write on the board the titles of their Read, Listen, Speak examples.

TEACH

Have volunteers name characters that they have read about in realistic fiction. Ask students to describe some of the things these characters do. Encourage students to discuss how a character's actions might influence what a reader thinks of that character.

Ask volunteers to read aloud the section Actions. Have students respond to the questions. Reinforce that a character's actions can help the reader to understand the character better.

Have students turn back to the model on page 439. Ask students to identify the actions that Keenan takes in the story. *(He sneaks out of his bedroom, hides in the van, and follows his dad to dance class.)* Discuss what kind of character students think Keenan is, based on his actions in the story *(brave, curious, suspicious)*.

LiNK Ask a volunteer to read aloud the excerpt. Have students tell what action takes place in this part of the story. Ask students to refer to the previous excerpts to tell who the narrator is and what the narrator sees in this excerpt *(a bird trapped in the airport)*. Ask how the bird compares to the narrator. *(Both are trapped.)*

PRACTICE

ACTIVITY C

Have groups of three each choose a character and take turns answering the questions about their character. Have students share their answers with the class.

ACTIVITY D

Have students complete this activity with partners. Ask volunteers to read aloud the story beginning. When students finish answering the questions, ask students to write what they think happens when Kari gets to the farm.

Actions

Readers learn about characters from the things they do. Different characters might choose different ways to solve a problem. Suppose that a character needs money for a new comic book. What are some different ways he or she could get the money? What would you think about that character, based on the way he or she got the money?

Characters might also act differently when something happens. Suppose that a boy falls off his bike in front of two characters. One character might walk away. Another character might try to help. What would you think about each of these characters?

LiNK

Fly Away Home

Once a little brown bird got into the main terminal and couldn't get out. It fluttered in the high, hollow spaces. It threw itself at the glass, fell panting on the floor, flew to a tall, metal girder, and perched there, exhausted.

Eve Bunting

ACTIVITY C **Pick one character from the word box. Then answer the questions about that character.**

> police officer   bank robber   librarian

1. Your character is trapped in an elevator with a woman and her young daughter. What does your character say?
2. Your character finds a wallet at the beach. What does your character do?
3. Your character needs money for a new car. How does your character get the money?
4. Your character goes to the video store, but the movie your character wanted isn't there. What does your character do?
5. Your character is asked to give money to help buy new equipment at the local school. What does your character say and give if anything?

APPLY

WRITER'S CORNER

Tell students to think about a problem for their character. Encourage students to use dialogue to reveal their character. When students have finished, ask volunteers to read aloud their sentences. Students should demonstrate an understanding of how a character's actions reveal his or her personality.

ASSESS

Note which students had difficulty understanding how a character's actions reveal his or her personality. Use the Reteach option with those students who need additional reinforcement.

Practice Book page 163 provides additional work with characters.

Reteach

Write on the board the following character traits: *smart, generous, stingy, lazy*. Have students think of an action that a character might take that illustrates each trait. Then have students write each trait and under the trait, write a description of the actions the character takes that illustrate the trait. Allow time for students to discuss each trait and how the character's actions relate to the traits.

English-Language Learners

Have students work together to role-play a scene in which a character has a problem to solve. Help students brainstorm situations (*a lost dog, getting home late for dinner*). Assign one student to play an angry character and another to play a cheerful character for each situation. Encourage students to use gestures and tone of voice to emphasize the emotions of each character. When students have finished, discuss how the emotions of the characters affected their words and actions.

Activity D

1. Kari

2. She has long brown hair, brown eyes, and likes to wear a ripped green jacket and sunglasses.

3. yes; Kari's father and Kari

4. "Let's get this over with," she groaned at the mirror. "I can come home if I hate it, right?" Kari finally asked.

5. Kari's arms crossed over her chest, Kari not talking to her father for an hour

ACTIVITY D Read the story beginning below. Then answer the questions.

Kari did not want to live at her Aunt Lynn's farm for two months. Kari was a city girl. She was used to cars and buses. She was used to people and noise. She liked having stores she could walk to. Working on a quiet farm was not her idea of a summer vacation.

"You'll love it once you get used to it," Kari's father promised. "My sister and I had a lot of fun growing up there."

Kari packed her jeans and T-shirts in her suitcase. She put her long brown hair in a ponytail and then took one last look around her room. She put on her ripped green jacket with the army patches. Then she slid her sunglasses over her brown eyes. "Let's get this over with," she groaned at the mirror.

Kari reluctantly got into the car with her father. She put her earphones in right away. She crossed her arms over her chest. There was silence in the car for over an hour. "I can come home if I hate it, right?" Kari finally asked.

Her father looked at Kari and smiled. "Give this a little time. You won't hate it," he replied. "You'll see."

1. Who is the main character?

2. What do you know about Kari's appearance?

3. Is there dialogue in the story? Who says it?

4. What lines of dialogue tell you that Kari doesn't want to go to the farm?

5. What actions tell you that Kari is angry about going to the farm?

WRITER'S CORNER

Think about the character you described in the Writer's Corner on page 445. Write four sentences about what that character would do if he or she was going on a long trip.

For Tomorrow

Ask students to write about a good character, describing actions that show the character is good. Write your own description of a good character to share with the class.

Creative Writing • 447

OBJECTIVES

- To understand how to write dialogue
- To understand how to use dialogue tags

WARM-UP

Read, Listen, Speak

Share your character description from yesterday's For Tomorrow homework. Ask students to identify the actions that show the character is good. Have small groups discuss their characters. Encourage students to suggest other actions the characters could do to show that they are good.

GRAMMAR CONNECTION

Take this opportunity to talk about commas in a series. You may wish to have students point out commas in a series if they exist in their Read, Listen, Speak examples.

TEACH

Read aloud the first paragraph and the two example sentences. Then have volunteers answer the questions about these sentences. Ask volunteers to describe how they know that one sentence is dialogue and the other is not.

Have a volunteer read aloud the first paragraph of the section Using Dialogue. Help students identify the quotation marks and the dialogue tag in the example sentence above.

Ask volunteers to read aloud the rest of the section. As each rule is read, illustrate the rule by pointing out how it works in the example sentences. Invite volunteers to write on the board examples of dialogue. Then have students turn back to the model on page 439. Point out that the dialogue between Keenan and his dad is separated into paragraphs.

PRACTICE

ACTIVITY A

Review that quotation marks show the words a character says. Tell students first to identify what the person said in each sentence and then put quotation marks around the spoken words. When students have finished, invite volunteers to write the dialogue examples on the board.

ACTIVITY B

Have small groups complete this activity. Encourage students to review the examples in the lesson to check their work. When students have finished, have volunteers write their sentences on the board.

Dialogue

Dialogue lets readers know the exact words a character says. Which of these is dialogue? Which is more interesting?

Mr. Fielding told the kids to get out of his barn.

"Hey! You get out of my barn right now!" Mr. Fielding shouted.

Using Dialogue

Quotation marks show which words a character said. A dialogue tag tells the reader which character said the words. Can you tell which part of the example sentence above was spoken by a character? Which part is the dialogue tag?

There are three rules to remember when writing dialogue.

- Spoken words have quotation marks before and after the words.
- The first word of each spoken part is capitalized.
- Spoken words are separated from the dialogue tag by a comma. If the dialogue tag comes first, the comma goes after it.

Jared said, "But we lost our ball in your barn!"

If the spoken part comes first, the comma goes after the last word before the quotation marks.

"I guess I'll help you kids find your ball," Mr. Fielding said.

APPLY

WRITER'S CORNER

Guide students to name appropriate movies or books. Review the rules for dialogue on page 448. After students have written their lines of dialogue, ask volunteers to read aloud their work. Students should demonstrate the ability to write dialogue.

TechTip You may wish to suggest appropriate movie or book review Web sites.

ASSESS

Note which students had difficulty writing dialogue. Use the Reteach option with those students who need additional reinforcement.

TEACHING OPTIONS

Reteach

Have volunteers say one sentence to describe something they did last night. Write on the board the sentence as dialogue, but omit all the capitalization and punctuation. Instruct students to add the correct capitalization and punctuation to show that the sentence is an example of dialogue. Then ask students to rewrite each sentence in a different way by changing the dialogue tag or adding an exclamation point to show stronger emotion. Remind students to change the punctuation when they change the dialogue.

Everyday Dialogue

Have partners write dialogue for a conversation they might have at lunchtime or during recess. Tell students to include at least two sentences for each speaker. Remind students to check their dialogue for correct punctuation and capitalization. Encourage students to use questions and exclamations. Have partners read aloud their dialogue, using appropriate tone to show emotions and to indicate questions.

The third rule changes with questions and exclamations. A character's question ends with a question mark, not a comma. An exclamation ends with an exclamation point.

"Do you see it in that horse stall?" Jared asked.

"What a beautiful horse!" Maya exclaimed.

Readers can follow dialogue better if you write a new paragraph for each speaker. Every time a different character speaks, indent the sentence and start it on a new line.

ACTIVITY A Rewrite the sentences. Add the missing quotation marks around the dialogue.

1. "Airplanes fly over my house all night long," Jerome said.
2. Julianna asked, "Where are my shoes?"
3. Karl yelled, "Someone just stole my bike!"
4. "Lexi is short for Alexis," the girl explained.
5. Someone in the audience stood and said, "This show stinks!"
6. "Jeanne says that she is going home after school," said Veronica.

ACTIVITY B Rewrite the sentences. Add the missing quotation marks to the dialogue. Add capital letters where they are needed.

1. Gary said, this book is about a family in Alaska.
2. he is looking out a window at the hospital, she whispered.
3. He stood up and said, let's head for that hill.
4. She asked, what's the big idea?
5. the fishing is great today, the old captain said.
6. Her brother shouted, now this is a party!
7. did you bring your lunch? asked Ashley.
8. Pat cried, she's going to trip over her shoelace!
9. Craig asked, what time is it?
10. Ming whispered, who wants to go first?

Activity B

1. Gary said, "This book is about a family in Alaska."
2. "He is looking out a window at the hospital," she whispered.
3. He stood up and said, "Let's head for that hill."
4. She asked, "What's the big idea?"
5. "The fishing is great today," the old captain said.
6. Her brother shouted, "Now this is a party!"
7. "Did you bring your lunch?" asked Ashley.
8. Pat cried, "She's going to trip over her shoelace!"
9. Craig asked, "What time is it?"
10. Ming whispered, "Who wants to go first?"

WRITER'S CORNER

Write two lines of dialogue you remember from a book or movie. Be sure to use dialogue tags to tell who said each line. Have a partner check that you followed all three rules for writing dialogue.

Tech Tip With an adult, research your book or movie online.

Creative Writing • 449

For Tomorrow

Ask students to write three lines of dialogue from a conversation they had during dinner. Write your own three lines to share.

WARM-UP

Read, Listen, Speak

Share your lines of dialogue from yesterday's For Tomorrow homework. Have small groups share their dialogue. Ask students to identify the dialogue tags in each sentence and the exact words the person says. Encourage them to work together to add more lines of dialogue. Tell students to check for correct use of dialogue tags, quotation marks, and punctuation.

GRAMMAR CONNECTION

Take this opportunity to talk about commas in direct address. You may wish to have students point out commas in direct address if they exist in their Read, Listen, Speak examples.

TEACH

Review the correct way to write dialogue. Have volunteers write on the board examples of dialogue with correct punctuation and capitalization. Make sure that students include exclamations and questions. Then read aloud the first paragraph of the section Dialogue Tags. Ask volunteers to read aloud the two examples of dialogue. Have students tell how the examples are different.

Have a volunteer read aloud the second paragraph. Invite four volunteers to take turns reading the examples, using different feelings.

Ask students to explain how each dialogue tag changes the way the sentence is spoken. Then ask a volunteer to read aloud the last paragraph. Explain that a strong dialogue tag is one way that writers can show how a character is speaking.

LiNK Ask a volunteer to read aloud the excerpt. Have students point out dialogue and dialogue tags. Ask students to give suggestions for other appropriate dialogue tags and discuss how they might alter the meaning.

PRACTICE

ACTIVITY C

Complete this activity as a class. Invite volunteers to write on the board the revised dialogue. Encourage students to determine whether the revisions are correct.

ACTIVITY D

Read aloud the example. Ask if there is another way to rewrite this sentence *(by putting the dialogue tag* Silvio said *at the beginning of the sentence)*. Have partners complete this activity. Encourage students to use dialogue tags at the beginning of at least two sentences. When students have finished, have small groups check for correct punctuation and capitalization.

ACTIVITY E

Encourage students to use a variety of dialogue tags so that

LiNK

Fly Away Home

"Don't stop trying," I told [the bird] silently. "Don't! You can get out!"

For days the bird flew around, dragging one wing. And then it found the instant when a sliding door was open and slipped through. I watched it rise. Its wing seemed OK.

"Fly, bird," I whispered. "Fly away home!"

Though I couldn't hear it, I knew it was singing. Nothing made me as happy as that bird.

Eve Bunting

Dialogue Tags

Dialogue tags tell who spoke a line of dialogue. Dialogue tags can also tell how the character spoke the line.

> **"It's just a grass stain," said Maria.**
>
> **"A grass stain doesn't come out!" Tori shouted.**

The dialogue tags *said Maria* and *Tori shouted* tell you who said that dialogue. The second example also tells that Tori shouted when she spoke. Dialogue tags can tell a reader how a character is feeling. Each example below tells a different feeling by using dialogue tags.

> **"This is not mine," Robbie said.**
>
> **"This is not mine," Robbie sobbed.**
>
> **"This is not mine!" Robbie shouted.**
>
> **"This is not mine," Robbie whispered.**

Dialogue tags help readers learn more about the characters. Dialogue tags also keep readers interested in the story. Follow the "just right" rule about using the word *said*. Don't use *said* too many times or too few. If everyone in your story is screaming and shouting and crying, your story won't seem realistic.

ACTIVITY C Rewrite this dialogue, using correct punctuation and capitalization.

Tippy gave her little brother a dirty look. get out of my bedroom she growled.

but I like being in here Malcolm wailed.

Tippy said you are such a pain.

I'll play any game you want Malcolm begged.

Tippy felt sorry for her brother. fine, let's play checkers she said and smiled at him.

Activity C

Tippy gave her little brother a dirty look. "Get of my bedroom," she growled.

"But I like being in here!" Malcolm wailed.

Tippy said, "You are such a pain."

"I'll play any game you want," Malcolm begged.

Tippy felt sorry for her brother. "Fine, let's play checkers," she said and smiled at him.

each line differs. When students have finished, invite volunteers to share their answers with the class.

APPLY

WRITER'S CORNER

Display a photo of a llama or have a volunteer describe a llama. After they have written their dialogue, have small groups share their sentences. Tell students to check that the dialogue tags are written using appropriate punctuation and capitalization. Students should demonstrate the ability to write dialogue and use dialogue tags.

Grammar in Action Remind students that in direct address the speaker uses the name of the person to whom he or she is speaking.

ASSESS

Note which students had difficulty writing dialogue tags. Use the Reteach option with those students who need additional reinforcement.

Practice Book page 164 provides additional work with dialogue.

TEACHING OPTIONS

Reteach

Help students brainstorm different ways of speaking to express different feelings. List on the board students' suggestions. Then have students come up with a list of verbs that can be used as dialogue tags to illustrate the feelings listed on the board (*shouted, yelled, exclaimed, whispered, cried, sobbed*). Ask students to choose three words from the list with which to write lines of dialogue. Remind students to check their writing for correct capitalization and punctuation. Have volunteers read aloud their dialogue, using their voices to show the emotion being conveyed.

Make the Picture Come Alive

Display a picture of two people talking from a magazine or newspaper. Have students write at least six lines of dialogue for the picture. Encourage students to vary the position of their dialogue tags, use verbs that express characters' emotions, and include questions and exclamations in their dialogue. Have volunteers read aloud their dialogue.

For Tomorrow

Ask students to write four lines of dialogue about what they might say while on a trip to the beach with their family or friends. Bring in your own four lines of dialogue to share with the class.

Activity D

1. "Stop giggling," said Mrs. Donovan.
2. "Would you please not skate in the store?" the clerk asked.
3. "Will you come to my party?" Jackie asked.
4. "Get off my bike!" Marco shouted.
5. "I hate my red shirt," said Anamaria.
6. "I'm coming home soon," Darcy said.
7. "I scraped my knee," said Bindi.
8. "Get out of my garden!" Mr. Britt shouted.
9. "Would you show me a book?" Jill asked.

Activity E

Answers will vary.

ACTIVITY D Rewrite these sentences as dialogue.

EXAMPLE Silvio said that he was going to be late for soccer practice.

"I'm going to be late for soccer practice," Silvio said.

1. Mrs. Donovan told her class to stop giggling.
2. The clerk asked the kids not to skate in the store.
3. Jackie asked her friend to come to her party.
4. Marco told his sister to get off his bike.
5. Anamaria said she hates her red shirt.
6. Darcy told her brother she was coming home soon.
7. Bindi said she scraped her knee.
8. Mr. Britt told the dog to get out of his garden.
9. Jill asked the librarian to show her a book.

ACTIVITY E Rewrite each line of dialogue. Make up a character name for each line. Add a dialogue tag to tell how each line is said.

1. "Does this water taste strange?"
2. "I guess we'll just go home early."
3. "That was the best movie I ever saw!"
4. "Our picnic is ruined."
5. "This package is for you and me."
6. "Bedtime is nine o'clock and no later."
7. "Jump in! The water isn't cold at all!"
8. "I can't find my homework!"
9. "May I please go with you?"
10. "Don't put your dirty shoes on the couch!"

WRITER'S CORNER

Imagine that your teacher brought a llama to class. Write three sentences of dialogue your classmates might say.

Grammar in Action Remember to use commas correctly in direct address. See Section 7.7.

Creative Writing • 451

OBJECTIVE

- **To use contractions**

WARM-UP

Read, Listen, Speak

Read aloud your dialogue from yesterday's For Tomorrow homework. Ask students whether the dialogue sounds the way people actually speak. Invite small groups to share their lines of dialogue. Encourage students to discuss whether the dialogue sounds real and whether it is punctuated and capitalized correctly.

GRAMMAR CONNECTION

Take this opportunity to talk about commas in compound sentences. You may wish to have students point out any commas in compound sentences in their Read, Listen, Speak examples.

TEACH

Have volunteers read aloud about contractions through the paragraph following the example *let's*. As students read, invite volunteers to answer the questions. Ask volunteers to say sentences with each of the contractions they just read. Then invite students to read aloud the next paragraph and examples. Have volunteers say sentences using each of the contractions.

Have volunteers read aloud the next paragraph and the examples of contractions with *have*. Discuss what is similar in each contraction with *have* (*'ve*).

Ask a volunteer to read aloud the last paragraph. Explain that people often use contractions when speaking. Write on the board the following sentences:

I am in third grade.

I'm in third grade.

Have students read aloud both sentences. Ask which sentence students might say to a friend.

PRACTICE

ACTIVITY A

Have students complete this activity independently. Suggest that students refer to the lists of contractions in the lesson for help. When students have finished, invite volunteers to write their completed equations on the board.

ACTIVITY B

You may wish to complete the first riddle as a class. Have partners complete this activity. Tell students to take turns asking and answering the riddles. Ask volunteers to share their answers with the class.

LESSON **4** WORD STUDY

Contractions

A contraction is a short way to write two words. The words are joined into one word with an apostrophe. The apostrophe replaces the letters that are left out.

it + is = it's

The words *it* and *is* are joined to make the contraction *it's*. An apostrophe takes the place of the letter *i*.

do + not = don't

The words *do* and *not* are joined to make the contraction *don't*. Which letter is replaced by the apostrophe?

Look at this contraction.

let's

Which two words are joined to make *let's*? What letter is replaced by the apostrophe?

Here are some contractions with *am, are,* and *is.*

I + am = I'm	**she + is = she's**
you + are = you're	**we + are = we're**
he + is = he's	**they + are = they're**

Here are some contractions with *have.* In these contractions an apostrophe replaces the two letters *h* and *a.*

I + have = I've	**we + have = we've**
you + have = you've	**they + have = they've**

> Let's ride that roller coaster!

> I'm not sure. It looks scary.

> We'll have fun! You'll see.

APPLY

WRITER'S CORNER

Suggest that students write their sentences about one topic. When students have finished, invite volunteers to read aloud their sentences. For each sentence ask a volunteer to say the sentence with the two words from which the contraction was made. Students should demonstrate the ability to use contractions.

Grammar in Action. Point out that apostrophes are used in contractions as well as to show possession. Challenge students to use apostrophes both ways in one sentence.

ASSESS

Note which students had difficulty using contractions. Use the Reteach option with those students who need additional reinforcement.

TEACHING OPTIONS

Reteach

Write the contractions from this lesson on separate note cards. Then write the corresponding contraction equations, without the answers, on other note cards (*have + not = haven't*). Shuffle the cards and guide students to play a game of Memory, matching each contraction to its equation.

Dream Poems

Have students write the following sentence starter five times on a sheet of paper:

Last night I dreamed about

Have students complete each sentence by telling some strange and imaginary things they might see only in a dream. (*Last night I dreamed about a lion with a fiery mane.*) When students have finished, ask them to cross out the sentence starter in each sentence. Then have students rewrite the sentences, beginning with a contraction from the lists on page 452. (*I'm a lion with a fiery mane.*) Tell students that these five lines make a dream poem. Invite students to share their dream poems with the class.

For Tomorrow

Have students write three sentences about their family or friends. Tell students to include one contraction in each sentence. Bring in your own three sentences to share wth the class.

Contractions make your writing sound more like the way people talk. Contractions can help you write dialogue that sounds real.

ACTIVITY A Write the missing word that makes up each contraction.

1. she + ____is____ = she's
2. we + have = ____we've____
3. ____you____ + have = you've
4. I + have = ____I've____
5. ____they____ + are = they're
6. we + are = ____we're____
7. they + ____have____ = they've
8. ____I____ + am = I'm
9. ____he____ + is = he's
10. you + ____are____ = you're

Activity B
1. She's at the circus.
2. I'm at a baseball game.
3. We're at school.
4. She's at the beach.
5. We're at the grocery store.
6. I'm at an amusement park.

ACTIVITY B Answer each riddle in a complete sentence. Use the contractions *I'm*, *we're*, or *she's* in each answer.

1. She sees animals and acrobats. Where is she?
2. I hear the crowd yell, "Home run!" Where am I?
3. We see books, desks, and friends. Where are we?
4. She swims and builds sand castles. Where is she?
5. We see shelves of fruits, vegetables, and cereal boxes. Where are we?
6. I ride roller coasters and bumper cars. Where am I?

WRITER'S CORNER

Pick two contractions from Activity A. Write two sentences. Use one contraction in each sentence.

Grammar in Action. Review the correct use of apostrophes in Section 7.9.

Creative Writing • 453

WARM-UP

Read, Listen, Speak

Read aloud your sentences from yesterday's For Tomorrow homework. Have students write the contractions. Then ask them to tell which two words are combined in each contraction. Invite small groups to share their sentences. Ask students to tell how they knew which letters in the contractions to replace with an apostrophe.

GRAMMAR CONNECTION

Take this opportunity to talk about apostrophes. You may wish to have students point out apostrophes in their Read, Listen, Speak examples.

TEACH

Review the contractions students read about on pages 452–453. Invite volunteers to write on the board sentences using these contractions.

Read aloud the first paragraph and the contractions with *not*. Ask students to write on the board some other contractions with *not* (*isn't, wasn't*). Invite volunteers to use the contractions on the board in sentences. Have a volunteer read aloud the next paragraph. Explain that the contraction *won't* is an unusual contraction because the first part of the contraction has a different spelling than the word it is made from. Read aloud the next paragraph and have students read aloud the remaining examples.

PRACTICE

ACTIVITY C
Have partners complete this activity. Tell students to read aloud each sentence to hear which words might be made into a contraction. When students have finished, invite volunteers to read their answers by having one student read aloud the original sentence and another student read aloud the sentence with the contraction.

ACTIVITY D
Complete the first question as a class. Then have partners complete this activity. When students have finished, read aloud the sentences and questions and have volunteers say their answers aloud.

ACTIVITY E
Have students complete this activity independently. When they have finished, have partners compare answers.

ACTIVITY F
Complete this activity as a class. Have volunteers read aloud the original sentence and the sentence with a contraction. Ask students to tell which letter or letters were replaced with apostrophes.

Here are some contractions with *not*.

can't	don't	won't
couldn't	shouldn't	wouldn't

The word *won't* is a contraction with *not*. But it is different from the others. The word *won't* is a contraction of *will* and *not*.

Here are some contractions with *will*.

I'll	she'll	he'll
we'll	you'll	they'll

ACTIVITY C Rewrite the sentences. Use contractions to make these sentences sound more like the way people talk.

1. Is not Jamal at camp this week? Isn't
2. Are not all the visitors gone yet? Aren't
3. Were not the stones nice and smooth? Weren't
4. Is not this a good night for stories? Isn't
5. Was not the boat rocking on the waves? Wasn't
6. You will see lots of stars here. You'll
7. The hikers are not camping in cabins. aren't
8. Some children could not swim. couldn't

ACTIVITY D Answer the questions. Write each answer in a complete sentence that starts with a contraction.

1. He is tall with a long neck and eats leaves from trees. What is he?
2. She is able to jump and carries her baby in a pouch. What is she?
3. They are legless and slither on the ground. What are they?
4. We are furry, eat bananas, and swing through trees. What are we?
5. She is fierce and white and lives near the North Pole. What is she?
6. He is a colorful bird who can talk. What is he?
7. They are using their trunks to spray water in the air. What are they?

Activity D
1. He's a giraffe.
2. She's a kangaroo.
3. They're snakes.
4. We're monkeys.
5. She's a polar bear.
6. He's a parrot.
7. They're elephants.

LiNK Invite a volunteer to read aloud the excerpt. Have students point out the contractions (*I'd, It's, isn't, It's, It's, It's, he's*). Ask students to tell which two words make up each contraction (*I would, it is, is not, it is, it is, it is, he is*).

APPLY
WRITER'S CORNER

When students have finished, invite volunteers to read their sentences to the class. Ask students to describe the difference between the dialogue with the contractions and the dialogue without the contractions. Students should demonstrate the ability to identify and use contractions in dialogue.

ASSESS

Note which students had difficulty using contractions. Use the Reteach option with those students who need additional reinforcement.

Practice Book page 165 provides additional work with contractions.

Reteach

Remind students that using contractions in dialogue makes it seem real. Have students search their previous writing to find examples of dialogue. Challenge students to find examples of words that can be changed into contractions. Then ask students to read aloud the dialogue first without the contractions and then again using contractions. Ask other students to tell which example sounds more realistic and more like something someone would really say in a normal conversation.

Contraction Caper

Invite volunteers to come up to the front of the room to be interviewed. Have the rest of the class write on a separate sheet of paper a list of all the contractions they hear during the interview. Ask the volunteers five questions about trips they have taken or things they like to do during the summer. Have students read aloud the list of contractions they heard. Discuss how often people use contractions in everyday conversation and how using contractions makes dialogue sound more realistic.

ACTIVITY E Match each word group in Column A with its contraction in Column B.

Column A		Column B
1. do not	d	a. we'll
2. I am	f	b. won't
3. we are	j	c. you're
4. we have	g	d. don't
5. they are	i	e. hasn't
6. could not	h	f. I'm
7. has not	e	g. we've
8. we will	a	h. couldn't
9. will not	b	i. they're
10. you are	c	j. we're

LiNK
Fly Away Home

"Will we ever have our own apartment again?" I ask Dad. I'd like it to be the way it was, before Mom died.

"Maybe we will," he says. "If I can find more work. If we can save some money." He rubs my head. "It's nice right here, though, isn't it, Andrew? It's warm. It's safe. And the price is right."

But I know he's trying all the time to find us a place.

Eve Bunting

Activity F
1. will not, won't
2. I am, I'm
3. should not, shouldn't
4. Do not, Don't
5. could not, couldn't
6. did not, didn't
7. would not, wouldn't
8. we will, we'll

ACTIVITY F Identify the two words in each sentence that can form a contraction. Then tell the contraction they form.

1. Kati will not climb the tree in her backyard.
2. "I am afraid," she said.
3. Whiskers, her cat, should not climb the tree.
4. "Do not go near that tree!" Kati tells Whiskers.
5. However, Whiskers could not resist chasing the squirrel up the tree.
6. Kati did not see Whiskers at first.
7. Then she would not let Whiskers be alone in the tree.
8. "I guess we will just climb this tree together," laughed Kati.

WRITER'S CORNER

Look at the story on page 439. Copy one sentence of dialogue that uses a contraction. What are the words that make up the contraction you found? Rewrite the sentence, using the two words instead of the contractions. Read both sentences aloud. Can you hear the difference?

For Tomorrow

Ask students to write four lines of dialogue for two friends who are planning a birthday party. Have students include contractions in all four lines. Write your own dialogue to share with the class.

Creative Writing • 455

OBJECTIVES
- **To recognize rhyming words**
- **To write rhyming couplets**

WARM-UP
Read, Listen, Speak
Ask a volunteer to read with you your dialogue from yesterday's For Tomorrow homework. Ask students to identify the characters' roles and the contractions in the dialogue. Have small groups read aloud their dialogue. Ask students how the two characters in each dialogue sound different.

GRAMMAR CONNECTION
Take this opportunity to talk about addresses. You may wish to have students point out any addresses in classroom books.

TEACH
Read aloud the first paragraph. Ask volunteers to say the first things that come to mind when you ask what poetry is. Encourage students to describe the differences between poetry and other forms of creative writing. Invite students to name their favorite poems. You may wish to read aloud examples of popular children's poetry.

Have volunteers read aloud the first paragraph of the section Rhyme and the example. Point out that the words start with different sounds but that they end with the same sound. Then read aloud the question and have volunteers write their answers on the board (*fair, mare, pear, dare, scare*).

Read aloud the next paragraph. Then have two volunteers alternate reading aloud the lines of the poem. Read aloud the last sentence. Explain that some poems rhyme to make them sound different from regular speech. Point out that poets write poems to give them a special sound that is like music.

PRACTICE

ACTIVITY A
Have students complete this activity independently. Some students may need to say the words aloud to identify which words rhyme. When students have finished, have them share their answers by reading aloud a word in Column A and having a volunteer read the rhyming word from Column B.

ACTIVITY B
Have partners complete this activity. Invite students to use a rhyming dictionary, if necessary. Encourage students to read aloud the lines to help think of an answer. When students have finished, invite volunteers to share their rhymes with the class.

Lines That Rhyme

Poetry is writing that expresses feelings or ideas in a special way. Poets use the sounds of words to create feelings in the reader. Do you have a favorite poem? Why do you like it?

Rhyme
Many poems rhyme. Words that rhyme start with different sounds but end with the same sound. Look at the example below.

share	*rhymes with*	hair
		care
		stare
		bear
		wear
		tear

Can you think of other words that rhyme with *share*?

Poets make patterns of rhyme in their poems. One way is to have the last word of each line rhyme with the last word of another line. Read this poem by Rachel Field.

> **In the morning very early,**
> **That's the time I love to go**
> **Barefoot where the fern grows curly**
> **And grass is cool between each toe.**

In this poem every other line rhymes.

APPLY

WRITER'S CORNER

Help students brainstorm the actions of animals. When students have finished, invite volunteers to act out their subjects and rhyming words for the rest of the class to guess. Students should demonstrate the ability to recognize and write rhyming words.

ASSESS

Note which students had difficulty identifying and using rhyming words. Use the Reteach option with those students who need additional reinforcement.

Reteach

Help students identify the letters that make two words rhyme. Give examples of words that rhyme and that are spelled similarly, such as *jiggle* and *wiggle*. Write the words on the board. Ask volunteers to underline the letters that sound the same and circle the letters that sound different. Continue with additional words that rhyme and that have similar spellings. Then explain that some words rhyme even though their spellings are different. Write on the board examples such as *said*, *bed*, and *thread*. Underline the letters in these words that share the same sound. Explain that it is the sound of the letters that make these words rhyme, not the spelling of the words.

Rhyme Time

Read aloud children's poems or nursery rhymes. As you read, omit the second of two rhyming words. Ask students to predict what the next word in the rhyme will be. Then challenge students to say and spell each rhyming word. Emphasize that many words that rhyme end in different spellings.

ACTIVITY A Match each word in Column A to its rhyming word in Column B.

Column A		Column B
1. creep	d	a. bed
2. hop	g	b. guest
3. care	f	c. stalk
4. walk	c	d. leap
5. said	a	e. wiggle
6. jiggle	e	f. share
7. test	b	g. plop

ACTIVITY B Complete each sentence with a word that rhymes with the underlined word in the sentence above.

1. Peacocks squawk.
   Parrots _talk_.

2. Panthers hunt.
   Piglets _grunt_.

3. Gerbils wiggle.
   Kids _giggle_.

4. Tigers roar.
   Eagles _soar_.

5. Toddlers fall.
   Babies _bawl_.

6. Lions track.
   Ducks _quack_.

7. Monkeys swing.
   Canaries _sing_.

WRITER'S CORNER

Look at Activity B. Think of other ways that animals move and act. Write two rhyming words that compare the animals.

For Tomorrow

Have students choose five words from Activity A. Tell students to list three words that rhyme with their chosen words. Bring in your own list of rhyming words to share with the class.

Creative Writing • 457

WARM-UP

Read, Listen, Speak

Read aloud your rhyming words from yesterday's For Tomorrow homework. Have small groups share their lists of rhyming words. Encourage students who chose the same word to compare lists and add any words they did not think of. Challenge students to use their rhyming words in dialogue between two characters.

GRAMMAR CONNECTION

Take this opportunity to talk about direct quotations. You may wish to have students point out direct quotations in their Read, Listen, Speak examples.

TEACH

Ask students what it means when you say you have a couple of tickets to the movies. *(It means you have two tickets.)* Explain that a couplet is two lines of a poem and that a rhyming couplet is two lines of a poem that rhyme at the end.

Have students read aloud the first paragraph and the poem. Ask students to count the rhyming couplets in the poem *(two)* and to explain what a rhyming couplet is *(two lines of a poem that rhyme at the end).*

Ask a volunteer to read aloud the last paragraph. Have a volunteer answer the question at the end of the paragraph *(bake, cake).*

PRACTICE

ACTIVITY C

Complete this activity as a class. Ask volunteers to read aloud the couplets. Challenge students to replace one of the rhyming words with a different rhyming word.

ACTIVITY D

Have partners complete this activity. Suggest that students first identify which lines contain rhyming words. When students have finished, ask volunteers to read aloud the couplets.

ACTIVITY E

Have small groups complete this activity. Encourage students to write their couplets as one poem of six lines. When students have finished, have volunteers read aloud their rhyming couplets.

ACTIVITY F

Have small groups complete this activity. Suggest that students first think of two rhyming words for each subject and then write their rhyming couplets.

Rhyming Couplets

A rhyming couplet is two lines of a poem that rhyme at the end. Read the poem below.

Late for Dinner

Ms. Seal was late, tripped on her shoelace.

Mr. Seal ate, kept stuffing his face.

There was nothing left of the famous fish bake.

But Ms. Seal ate sea scallop dessert cake.

In "Late for Dinner," the last words of the first two lines rhyme. The word *shoelace* rhymes with *face.* These lines together are a rhyming couplet. This poem has two rhyming couplets. What rhyming words are used in the second rhyming couplet?

ACTIVITY C Complete each rhyming couplet. Choose a word from the word box that rhymes with each underlined word.

book	hill	tree	dad

1. A duck with an orange <u>bill</u>
   Came running over the ___hill___.

2. In the yard the big oak ___tree___
   Provides a lot of shade for <u>me</u>.

3. In the doorway stood my ___dad___
   Uh-oh, he looks very <u>mad</u>!

4. While fishing in the leafy <u>brook</u>
   My brother found a golden ___book___

LiNK Ask a volunteer to read aloud the excerpt. Ask how the narrator feels and how his feelings change by the end of the excerpt and why.

TechTip You may wish to type the keywords *rhyming words* into a search engine and then direct students to age-appropriate rhyming dictionaries.

APPLY

WRITER'S CORNER

Help students brainstorm poem topics. Create a three-column chart with the headings *Something I Like, Someone I Care About,* and *How I Feel.* Tell students to list words that rhyme before beginning their poems. Invite volunteers to read aloud their completed poems. Students should demonstrate the ability to write rhyming couplets.

ASSESS

Note which students had difficulty writing rhyming couplets. Use the Reteach option with those students who need additional reinforcement.

Practice Book page 166 provides additional work with lines that rhyme.

TEACHING OPTIONS

Reteach

Write on the board a children's poem with rhyming couplets. Draw a blank for the last word in each line. Guide students to fill in the blanks with words that rhyme and that make sense in the poem. Encourage students to offer several suggestions. Discuss which rhymes are most effective.

Passing the Poetry

Have groups of six students sit around a table with a single sheet of paper and a pencil. Have one student write a line for a poem and pass the paper to the person on his or her right. Ask the second student to write a second rhyming line. Have students pass the paper again and write a third line that does not rhyme with the first two. Tell students to pass the poem again and write a fourth line that rhymes with the third line. Repeat this procedure for the fifth and sixth lines. Allow students to read their poems to the class.

ACTIVITY D **The following lines of poetry are mixed up. Match each line to its rhyme to form three pairs of rhyming couplets.**

a Last night I had a wonderful dream,

b My little brother is a pest.

c Time to clean, I guess!

b It's because he knows that I'm the best.

a of chocolate cake and vanilla ice cream.

c My bedroom is quite a mess.

ACTIVITY E **Choose three of the following word pairs. Then write rhyming couplets using each word pair.**

wonder/thunder	bark/shark
taste/paste	ditch/pitch
drum/plum	broken/spoken
dwell/shell	win/spin
candle/handle	sail/pail
doubt/shout	sour/power

ACTIVITY F **Write a rhyming couplet about each of these subjects.**

1. A farmer
2. A hairdresser
3. A veterinarian
4. A firefighter
5. A mail carrier
6. A dog groomer

LiNK

Fly Away Home

Sometimes I watch people meeting people.... Sometimes I get mad, and I want to run at them and push them and shout, "Why do *you* have homes when we don't? What makes *you* so special?...Sometimes I just want to cry. I think Dad and I will be here forever. Then I remember the bird. It took a while, but a door opened. And when the bird left, when it flew free, I know it was singing.

Eve Bunting

WRITER'S CORNER

Write a poem that uses three rhyming couplets. The poem might be about how you feel. It might be about something that you like or someone that you care about.

Tech Tip With an adult, search for rhyming words online.

Creative Writing • 459

For Tomorrow

Ask students to write two couplets that describe a scene in nature. Write your own couplets to share with the class.

OBJECTIVES

- **To develop characters and a plot for a skit**
- **To write, rehearse, and perform a skit**

WARM-UP

Read, Listen, Speak

Read aloud your couplets from yesterday's For Tomorrow homework. Ask students to name the rhyming words. Have small groups share their couplets. Ask students to identify the rhyming words in each couplet.

GRAMMAR CONNECTION

Take this opportunity to talk about punctuation and capitalization. You may wish to have students point out punctuation and capitalization in their Read, Listen, Speak examples.

TEACH

Encourage students to describe their experiences watching or acting in plays. Then have a volunteer read aloud the first paragraph. Explain that a skit is a story that is acted out for an audience, just as a play is.

Have volunteers read aloud the section Characters and Problems. Explain that being able to describe how characters act can give writers ideas for problems the characters might face. Ask students to name a problem that a character who is in third grade might have. Ask whether a character who is a police officer would have the same problem.

Have volunteers read aloud the section Plot. Explain that the audience learns the plot of a skit from what the characters say. Ask volunteers to give examples of things that actors might say or do to show that their characters are in various settings, such as sneaking into a circus tent, hacking through a steamy jungle, climbing an icy mountain, or running in a fierce thunderstorm. Record the examples to use in the Rehearse section on page 462.

PRACTICE

ACTIVITY A

Encourage students to imagine the character as you read aloud the character notes. Have small groups discuss ideas for story problems that Cuba might have. Invite students to share their ideas with the class.

Skits

A skit is a story acted out in front of an audience. A skit has characters, a problem, and a plot. A skit also has dialogue. The audience watches the actors in the skit. The actors move and talk as the characters would. The audience watches the skit to find out what happens.

Characters and Problems

A skit is mostly dialogue. Each character talks in a different way. If you think about your characters first, it will be easier to write dialogue for them.

Decide which characters you want in your skit. Then write notes about your characters.

- Write the characters' names.
- Draw or write what the characters look like.
- Write how the characters act.

When you know the characters, you can think about a problem for the skit. What kind of trouble can these characters get into? Sometimes the problem can be between the characters. Sometimes it can be a problem the characters have to work together to solve.

You might have an idea for a story's problem before you have an idea for the characters. Think about the problem for your story. What kind of characters might have that problem? Then write notes about your characters.

460 • Chapter 7

APPLY

SPEAKER'S CORNER

Have students work in the same groups as they did in Activity A. Tell students to choose one problem to write dialogue for. Have volunteers share their dialogue with the class. Students should demonstrate the ability to develop characters and a plot for a skit.

ASSESS

Note which students had difficulty developing characters and a plot for a skit. Use the Reteach option with those students who need additional reinforcement.

Plot

The plot is what happens in a skit. The beginning of the skit tells the audience what the problem is. The middle tells what the characters do to solve their problem. In skits the characters talk to one another about their problems. The listeners can hear about the problems and become interested in the story.

Sometimes the characters talk about what is happening in the skit. For example, if the characters are going into a spooky cave, they might talk about how spooky the cave is. The characters can also crawl or bend the way they would in a cave. Using your imagination, you can make your characters go anywhere.

The ending will show how the characters solve their problem. Write dialogue that lets them talk about what happened. When you have finished your skit, take a bow!

ACTIVITY A Read these character notes. Write a problem this character might have in a skit.

Name: Cuba Delmore

Appearance: Cuba is tall. He has short black hair. His eyes are brown. He wears a red cap when it is cold. His white shoes are clean. His favorite shirt is blue and gray with black buttons. At school he always wears a big silver watch his sister gave him.

What the character is like: Cuba is clumsy. He trips on things a lot. When he trips, his face turns red. If he falls on someone, he always says he is sorry. He is a good student. He plays the piano. His favorite game is chess.

SPEAKER'S CORNER

Look at the problem you wrote for Cuba in Activity A. Write three lines of dialogue that you think Cuba might say in a skit.

Creative Writing • 461

WARM-UP

Read, Listen, Speak

Read aloud your character description and dialogue from yesterday's For Tomorrow homework. Ask students what they know about the character from the line of dialogue. Have small groups discuss the shows they watched. Ask students to tell about the character they described and to read aloud their dialogue. Encourage students to say the line of dialogue the way the character said it in the show.

TEACH

Invite a volunteer to read aloud the first paragraph of the section Writing a Skit. Then have two volunteers read aloud the parts of Cuba and Martha. Ask students to explain how this dialogue is different from dialogue in a story. *(The dialogue in a skit does not have quotation marks or dialogue tags. The character's name and a colon show who is speaking the line.)* Have volunteers read aloud the last two paragraphs. Ask volunteers to rewrite on the board the example lines of dialogue as they would appear in a story.

Have volunteers read aloud the section Rehearse. Ask students to explain the importance of rehearsing a skit. Explain that professional actors sometimes rehearse for many weeks before performing for an audience. Tell students that actors also rehearse to memorize their lines and to try out different ways of saying them.

Ask students to describe some props and costumes that they have seen in skits or plays. Encourage students to suggest props and costumes that might be used in skits with the settings and situations you recorded from the Plot section on page 461.

Have volunteers read aloud the section Listening Tips. Emphasize the importance of being a good listener and showing respect for the actors performing the skit. Reinforce the importance of following the third listening tip. Remind students that everyone makes mistakes. Tell students that good listeners never laugh when someone makes a mistake.

PRACTICE

ACTIVITY B

Provide students with books in which they can find dialogue.

Have partners rewrite the dialogue as a skit. Allow volunteers to perform the dialogue they wrote. Encourage volunteers to act the way they think the characters would act.

ACTIVITY C

Ask students to imagine what is inside the package before acting out their feelings. Remind students to perform for their partner, without using any words or sounds. After the partner guesses the feeling that was acted out, ask the actor to share what he or she imagined was inside the package.

Writing a Skit

Skits are written for the actors to read. The written skit will help the actors know what to say and do when they perform. Dialogue for a skit is written differently than in a story. It looks like this.

Cuba:	Hey guys, look at this caterpillar!
Martha:	That's gross, Cuba.
Cuba:	It's orange and fat. Boy, is it climbing fast!

Write the name of the character who is speaking. Put a colon after the name. Then write what the character says.

Read your plot and character notes before you write dialogue for your characters. Be sure that the dialogue tells the audience what is happening in the skit.

Rehearse

When actors rehearse, they practice the skit together. Practice your skit. Try saying lines in different ways. Talk about what kinds of gestures and actions the characters might use. In the example above, Cuba might point at the caterpillar. He might wrinkle his nose, or he might do both.

When you decide how the characters will act, rehearse a few times. Try different ways of doing the skit. You might want to have a friend watch your skit before you perform for an audience. Your friend can tell you if something is confusing in the skit.

Think about costumes you might use. What would your characters wear? You can also use props. A book, a phone, or a chair could all be props. Using these props will make your skit more interesting.

APPLY

SPEAKER'S CORNER

Have students meet in the same groups as they did for the previous Speaker's Corner on page 461. Have students write character notes about their new characters before writing the dialogue. Encourage students to use the character notes in Activity A on page 461 as a model. Allow students to rehearse their skits and gather props and costumes. Have students perform their skits for the class. Students should demonstrate the ability to write, rehearse, and perform a skit.

TechTip Have students watch the rehearsals for clarity in plot and character.

ASSESS

Note which students had difficulty writing, rehearsing, and performing a skit. Use the Reteach option with those students who need additional reinforcement.

After you have reviewed Lessons 3–5, administer the Writing Skills Assessment on pages 63–64 in the **Assessment Book.** This test is also available on the optional **Test Generator CD.**

TEACHING OPTIONS

Reteach

Have small groups change the story on page 439 into a skit. Ask students to rewrite the story dialogue into skit dialogue. Remind students that in skit dialogue a colon follows the name of the character that is speaking and that quotation marks are not used. Have groups perform their skits, using appropriate expression and gestures.

Improvise a Skit

Help students brainstorm situations that would make good skits (*children offering to help a grumpy neighbor with some yard work, two siblings arguing over what to watch on TV, a person learning how to play tennis*). Write on the board students' ideas. Tell students that an improvised skit is one in which the actors make up dialogue as they go along. Challenge small groups to choose a situation from the list on the board to perform an improvised skit.

Listening Tips

Skits can be fun to watch. You can see people become the characters in the skit. You can imagine where the characters are. You can see how they solve their problems. Here are some tips for watching a skit.

- Do not talk during the skit.
- Think about whether the story could really happen. Would you act the way the characters do?
- Laugh at the funny parts. But don't laugh if someone makes a mistake. Think about how you would feel if people laughed at your mistakes.
- When the skit is over, clap to show that you enjoyed it.

ACTIVITY B Find five lines of dialogue in a book. Write the dialogue as a skit. Write the names of the characters at the top. Describe the characters. Then write their dialogue like the example on page 462. Practice reading your dialogue with a partner.

ACTIVITY C Imagine you got a package in the mail. You open the package. The thing inside makes you feel mad, scared, happy, or amazed. Pick one feeling. Without using words, act out opening the package for a partner. Use gestures and actions only. See if your partner can guess how you felt when you opened the package.

SPEAKER'S CORNER

Work in small groups. Make up characters for each member of your group. Write dialogue for all the characters. Then perform your skit for the class.

Tech Tip Record or videotape your rehearsal for review.

Creative Writing • 463

OBJECTIVES
- **To brainstorm ideas**
- **To plan a story**

PREWRITING AND DRAFTING

Ask students if they have ever made up a story by drawing pictures. Explain that writing a story in words is not that different from using pictures because writers make pictures in the readers' minds by using description and dialogue.

Have a volunteer read aloud the first paragraph. Invite students to share examples of stories or movies that have characters who are like students. Use students' examples to distinguish between realistic fiction and kinds of fiction that are not realistic, such as fantasy and science fiction.

Prewriting

Review the characteristics of realistic fiction *(character, setting, problem, plot, dialogue)*. Explain that the idea for a story can start with any of these things. Tell students that an idea for an interesting character can help writers come up with ideas for a plot or a setting. Explain that an interesting setting can give writers ideas for characters and a plot that go with that setting.

Have students read aloud this section. Ask volunteers to tell things they did recently. Write their suggestions on the board.

Help students make up "What if . . ." scenarios that might go with their suggestions. *(A boy went bowling with his father. What if the father's bowling ball never returned? Where did it go? What would they have to do to get it back?)*

Brainstorming

Have volunteers read aloud this section. Explain that Riley's character, Lauren, could have different kinds of problems. Ask students to name some problems that a girl in third grade might have.

Ask students why Riley made up the character of Lauren's little brother *(to make a problem for Lauren to solve in the story)*.

Tell students that their ideas are the main message and all the details of their writing. Point out that even though students' stories should be realistic, they can still be fun and unusual enough to maintain their readers' interest.

Your Turn

Read aloud this section. Encourage students to use the questions to help brainstorm ideas for their story. If students are having trouble, suggest that they draw pictures of their characters or settings. Guide students to use the pictures to develop written brainstorming notes about their ideas.

Writer's Workshop   Realistic Fiction

Prewriting and Drafting

Have you ever read a story or seen a movie about kids like you? Did you think the characters could be real? Were you interested in what happened to the characters? Realistic fiction has characters, settings, and plots that could be real, even though they are not.

Prewriting

Before writing realistic fiction, many writers brainstorm ideas. When writers brainstorm, they jot down ideas about the characters, the setting, and the plot. A good way to start brainstorming is to ask, what if? Did you ever wonder, What if *this* happened? For example, what if a lion got loose in a big city?

Brainstorming

Riley is a third grader. Her grandmother likes hearing the stories that Riley writes.

Ideas Riley wanted to write a new story for her grandmother. She began by brainstorming a list of characters. When she had finished, she read her list. She liked the name Lauren, so she decided that her main character would be a girl named Lauren.

Next, Riley brainstormed ideas for a plot. She had many ideas, but one interested her more than the others. She asked herself, What if Lauren had a little brother who gave her a problem? Riley thought more about what kind of problem Lauren's brother could give her. She decided that Lauren would fight with her brother over a clubhouse. That would be a good problem for her character to solve.

Your Turn

Take some time to brainstorm ideas. Start by listing possible characters, settings, and problems. If you get stuck, you can ask yourself the following questions:

- What setting would be fun to write about? A big city? A small town? A desert? An island? Which setting might lead to an interesting character or problem?
- What characters would be fun to write about? Are any of the characters like you? Are any like your best friend? What is special about these characters?
- What will happen in the story? What is the problem that must be solved?

Planning the Story

Read aloud the first paragraph. Then have volunteers read aloud Riley's plan. Point out that Riley described in her notes what her characters are like. Explain that she might not use all her notes, but that her notes will help her imagine the story as she writes it. Point out that Riley's plot tells step-by-step how Lauren solved her problem. Tell students that Riley's ending describes what happened afterward.

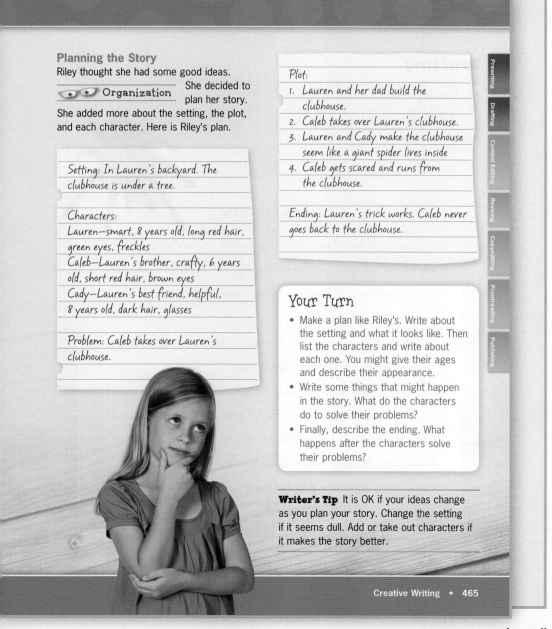 Tell students that Lauren's structure for note-taking is important, but that to organize their story, they may wish to create beginning, middle, and ending boxes as in the Reteach on page 443.

Your Turn

Ask volunteers to read aloud this section. Encourage students to use Riley's notes as a model for their own notes. Suggest that students number what happens in their plot to keep events in the right order.

Writer's Tip Remind students that revision is one of the most important parts of the writing process. Be sure students understand that they can change anything in their stories at any time before publishing.

Planning the Story

Riley thought she had some good ideas. **Organization** She decided to plan her story. She added more about the setting, the plot, and each character. Here is Riley's plan.

> Setting: In Lauren's backyard. The clubhouse is under a tree.
>
> Characters:
> Lauren—smart, 8 years old, long red hair, green eyes, freckles
> Caleb—Lauren's brother, crafty, 6 years old, short red hair, brown eyes
> Cady—Lauren's best friend, helpful, 8 years old, dark hair, glasses
>
> Problem: Caleb takes over Lauren's clubhouse.

> Plot:
> 1. Lauren and her dad build the clubhouse.
> 2. Caleb takes over Lauren's clubhouse.
> 3. Lauren and Cady make the clubhouse seem like a giant spider lives inside
> 4. Caleb gets scared and runs from the clubhouse.
>
> Ending: Lauren's trick works. Caleb never goes back to the clubhouse.

Prewriting · Drafting · Content Editing · Revising · Copyediting · Proofreading · Publishing

Your Turn

- Make a plan like Riley's. Write about the setting and what it looks like. Then list the characters and write about each one. You might give their ages and describe their appearance.
- Write some things that might happen in the story. What do the characters do to solve their problems?
- Finally, describe the ending. What happens after the characters solve their problems?

Writer's Tip It is OK if your ideas change as you plan your story. Change the setting if it seems dull. Add or take out characters if it makes the story better.

Creative Writing • 465

Drafting

Invite a volunteer to read aloud the paragraph above Riley's draft. Point out that Riley's notes helped her get started, but that Riley added new ideas as she imagined the story. Tell students that writers sometimes see or hear new things as they imagine the story. Then ask volunteers to read aloud Riley's draft.

Ask students to name the characters in Riley's story *(Lauren, Caleb, Cady).* Encourage students to describe what each character is like. Discuss how the characters' actions in the story give readers an idea of what the characters are like. Have students look back at Riley's notes about plot on page 465. Ask students to note which plot items Riley used in the story.

Tell students that their word choice will bring alive their writing and help their reader picture the story and care about the characters and what happens to them. Suggest that students use writing that shows instead of tells.

Your Turn

Read aloud this section. Encourage students to read their notes and to imagine that they are watching the story as it happens. Remind students that they might not use everything they wrote in their notes and that they might imagine new ideas as they write. Encourage students to have fun as they write their stories. Point out that the reader will be more likely to enjoy a story that a writer enjoyed writing. Then allow time for students to write their first drafts.

Drafting

Riley used her plan to write her first draft. As she wrote, she thought of new details and ideas to include. Riley used colorful words like *huge, ugly,* and *fuzzy.*

Word Choice

She decided to leave some ideas from her plan out of her story. Here is Riley's first draft.

The Clubhouse

Lauren and her dad built a clubhouse. Lauren was eight years old. She had red hair and green eyes. She had freckles. Lauren's clubhouse would be a place where she could hang out with her friends. She could also get away from her little brother, Caleb.

But the day Lauren was ready to move in, there was a problem Caleb had already moved his stuff into the clubhouse.

Lauren told her best friend, Cady, that she was angry at Caleb.

Lauren had a plan. Caleb was afraid of spiders. So one day Lauren and Cady sat under the tree in the backyard. They knew that Caleb could hear them. Lauren told Cady that a huge, ugly spider lived in the clubhouse. Lauren explained that the spider had spun a web in the corner of the clubhouse. It had big, fuzzy legs and ate anything that came near it.

Lauren knew that Caleb heard every word. Lauren and Cady waited

Something's Not Right

Have volunteers read aloud the first two paragraphs of this section. Help students brainstorm reasons that a soccer coach might get lost in the desert. Encourage students to name ideas that are realistic.

Have a volunteer read aloud the last paragraph. Brainstorm with students ideas for stories that would explain why a millionaire might wear a dirty, ripped jacket and no shoes. Ask volunteers to think of other character descriptions where something is "not right."

👀 Tell students that voice in writing is the writer's personality and feeling coming through. Point out that they should try to convey their feelings about the story to their readers. Tell students to work on communicating suspense, humor, or disappointment to their readers through word choice, character description, and dialogue.

TEACHING OPTIONS

Story Puzzles

Have students write three note cards, one with a brief description of a made-up character, one with a problem that the character might have in a story, and one with a specific setting for that character. Encourage students to be creative. Tell students to label the cards *Character*, *Setting*, and *Problem* as appropriate.

When students have finished, collect the note cards and group them by character, setting, and problem. Shuffle each stack and give each student a new character, setting, and problem card. Then have small groups share their cards. Ask students to brainstorm ideas for stories that explain how students' cards might go together.

until dark. Then they hid under the window of the clubhouse. They waited until Caleb went inside the clubhouse. Then Lauren sprayed silly string through the window at the back of Caleb's neck. A moment later Caleb ran out of the clubhouse, shouting that there was a giant spider inside.

Lauren finally had the clubhouse all to herself.

Prewriting | Drafting | Content Editing | Revising | Copyediting | Proofreading | Publishing

Your Turn

- Use your plan to help write your first draft.
- Add details as you write. Give more information about the characters and the setting.
- Include dialogue to bring your characters to life.
- Be sure that the events in your story make sense. Time order can help you be sure one event leads to the next.
- Use colorful words in your descriptions to make your story more interesting.

Something's Not Right

Sometimes you can make a story interesting by making something not right. You can put things together that don't seem to belong together.

You probably wouldn't find a soccer coach lost in a desert. But that could be an interesting beginning for a story. The reader would want to know how the soccer coach got there. The reader will want to know how the soccer coach is going to get out.

You can make something not right with a character too. You can describe a character wearing a dirty, ripped jacket and no shoes. Then you can tell that he's really a millionaire. Why is he dressed like that? The reader will want to know. If you are excited about your characters and story, it will come through for your readers.

👀 Voice

CONTENT EDITING

Invite volunteers to read aloud the first two paragraphs. Ask students to predict what might be checked when content editing a work of realistic fiction. Then have volunteers read aloud the Content Editor's Checklist. Point out the last item on the checklist.

Tell students that if a story is clear, readers will be able to see and hear the story happening in their imaginations.

Read aloud the next paragraph. Point out that because Riley read her draft with the checklist before she had someone else read it, she probably had ideas on how to improve her draft. Explain that since the story is in Riley's imagination, it might be helpful to have another person read the story to see if the words make the story she imagines clear to the reader.

Have volunteers read aloud the next two paragraphs. Discuss Evan's positive comments.

Have volunteers read aloud Evan's comments. Ask students whether or not they agree with Evan's comments and to explain why. After the last comment, ask students why dialogue might make Riley's draft better. Then read the last paragraph aloud.

Editor's Workshop   Realistic Fiction

Content Editing

Riley was happy with her story. She liked writing about Lauren. She also liked how Lauren solved her problem.

Riley knew that she could make her story better. The day after she wrote her draft, she read her story again. She read it aloud to hear how it sounded. Then she used this Content Editor's Checklist to edit her draft.

Content Editor's Checklist

☐ Does the beginning tell who the characters are? Does it tell the setting?

☐ Does the middle tell the plot? Is there a problem that must be solved?

☐ Does the ending tell whether the characters were successful?

☐ Are the characters realistic?

☐ Is dialogue used?

☐ Is the story clear and in order?

Using the checklist, Riley wrote ways she might improve her draft. But she knew that a different reader could help her with content editing. She decided to take her draft to the writing center at school. High school students there helped younger kids with reading and writing. Evan, one of the high school students, offered to content edit Riley's story.

Evan read Riley's story a few times. First, he wrote things he liked about the story. He used the checklist and wrote his suggestions. Then he and Riley talked about her draft.

Evan really liked the story. He told Riley that Lauren's problem got him interested. He also liked Lauren's trick to get Caleb out of the clubhouse. Evan thought that the characters were realistic. He told Riley that the order of the story was clear. Then he shared the following comments with Riley.

• You don't need a description of what Lauren looks like. You tell the reader a lot about her through what she does.

• Where is this story set? You don't say in the beginning.

Your Turn

Read aloud this section. Encourage students to take notes on ways to improve their drafts.

Have students trade drafts with a partner. Tell students to read their partner's draft twice. Ask students to read the draft the first time for enjoyment without taking any notes. Encourage students to read their partner's draft as if they were reading a story in a book.

Tell students to read their partner's draft a second time as content editors, using the Content Editor's Checklist. Encourage students to make notes if parts of the story seem unclear or confusing. Remind students to begin their comments about their partner's draft by telling what they liked about the story.

TEACHING OPTIONS

Speaking of Dialogue

Tell students that dialogue can make a story sound more real. Explain that the reader forms a picture of the character based on what he or she says and how he or she says it. Tell students that dialogue can also give readers an idea of how the character is feeling at that moment in the story. Point out that dialogue gives readers a chance to hear the characters interact with one another.

Review the use of punctuation and dialogue tags in writing dialogue. Encourage students to use dialogue at least once in their stories.

- In the middle you say that Lauren and Cady sit under the tree. Where was Caleb? How do they know that Caleb can hear them?
- Maybe you should add a description of Cady.
- The ending tells whether Lauren is successful. But maybe you could add something about Caleb. Readers might wonder whether he goes back to the clubhouse again.
- You don't have any dialogue. Dialogue might help readers learn more about the characters. Dialogue can make the story seem more real.

Riley thanked Evan for his help. Then Riley went through her story again to decide which of Evan's suggestions she would use.

Your Turn

- Read your draft again. Make sure that all the parts of realistic fiction are included. Then see if there are other ways you might improve your draft.
- Trade drafts with a classmate. Use the checklist to make suggestions about your partner's draft. Remember to write some things that you like about the story. Then take turns talking about your stories with your partner.
- Think about your partner's comments. Use the ideas that you think will make your draft better.

Creative Writing • 469

OBJECTIVE
- **To revise a draft for content**

REVISING

Explain that when students revise, they are deciding which changes to make from the notes they made and the notes they received from their content editors. Read aloud the first paragraph. Then have volunteers read aloud Riley's revised draft.

Read aloud the paragraph after Riley's revised draft. Have volunteers read aloud the bulleted questions. Ask students to find each of Riley's changes on her revised draft. Encourage students to explain how each change makes the draft stronger.

- Riley agreed with Evan that the description did not make her story better.
- She made it clear that the story takes place in Lauren's backyard.
- Riley added that Caleb is present when Lauren talks about the spider in the clubhouse.
- Answers will vary.
- She wanted to make sure readers knew that Caleb never went back to the clubhouse.
- She added dialogue about why she was annoyed with Caleb and turned the description of the spider into dialogue. The dialogue shows the reader more about Lauren as a character.
- She changed the title to "The Creepy-Crawly Clubhouse."

Ask students to explain how changing the title and adding dialogue to the story makes it stronger.

Writer's Workshop
Realistic Fiction

Revising

Read Riley's revised draft. Notice how she marked her changes.

Creepy-Crawly
The ^Clubhouse

in the backyard

Lauren and her dad built a clubhouse. ~~Lauren was eight years old. She had red hair and green eyes. She had freckles.~~ Lauren's clubhouse would be a place where she could hang out with her friends. She could also get away from her little brother, Caleb.

But the day Lauren was ready to move in, there was a problem Caleb had already moved his stuff into the clubhouse.

"He did'nt even help build it! And now he thinks it's his."
Lauren told her best friend, Cady, ~~that she was angry at Caleb.~~

Lauren had a plan. Caleb was afraid of spiders. So one day Lauren and

Caleb was in the clubhouse.
Cady sat under the tree in the backyard. They knew that Caleb could hear

Lauren said, "Cady, I'm scared of the huge spider in the clubhouse."
them. ~~Lauren told Cady that a huge, ugly spider lived in the clubhouse.~~

"I did see a large spider web in the corner," Cady said. Lauren said, "yes, it has big,
~~Lauren explained that the spider had spun a web in the corner of the~~

fuzzy legs and it eats anything that comes near it."
~~clubhouse. It had big, fuzzy legs and ate anything that came near it.~~

Lauren knew that Caleb heard every word. Lauren and Cady waited

Your Turn

Read aloud this section. Encourage students to look at their own notes and the notes they received from their content editors. Tell students that the story they are writing exists in their imagination and that they are trying to write it so that others can see it too. Explain that since the story is in their heads, only they can decide what will make the story clearer.

Tell students that as they revise, they might think of new ideas to add. Explain that every time writers imagine a story again, it gets stronger and more real. Tell students to add new descriptions and dialogue that they may think of while revising. Encourage students to be sure that any changes make the story stronger before adding them. Ask students to check their drafts against the Content Editor's Checklist again.

TEACHING OPTIONS

Making It More Real

Tell students that they can make their stories seem real by adding clear descriptions. Explain that descriptions in a story can help a reader picture the story. Point out that too many descriptions can be distracting. Tell students to be sure that their descriptions are important to the story. Write the following questions on the board:

- **Suppose my story was a skit.**
- **What props would I need?**
- **What costumes would my characters wear?**
- **How would the actors talk?**
- **What kind of gestures would the actors make?**
- **What would the stage look like?**

Ask students to imagine that their story is a skit as they respond to these questions. Tell students to use their responses to these questions to create descriptions in their story.

until dark. Then they hid under the window of the clubhouse. They waited until Caleb went inside the clubhouse. Then Lauren sprayed silly string through the window at the back of Caleb's neck. A moment later Caleb ran out of the clubhouse, shouting that there was a giant spider inside. ~~Caleb never went near the clubhouse again.~~

Lauren finally had the clubhouse all to herself.

Riley used a lot of Evan's ideas. She also found some other ways to make her story better. Here is what Riley did.

- Riley took out the description of what Lauren looks like. Why?
- She added information about the setting. What did she write?
- What information about Caleb did Riley add to the fourth paragraph? Why do you think she did this?
- Riley decided not to add a description of Cady. A description of Cady would not add anything to the story. Do you agree or disagree? Why?
- Riley added a sentence about Caleb to the ending. What did she add? Why?
- What dialogue did Riley add to the story? Do you like what she added? Why?
- Riley changed the title of her story. What is the new title? Do you like it better than the old title? Why or why not?

Your Turn

- Think about your content editor's ideas. Choose the ideas that you think will make your story better.
- Mark the changes neatly on your draft.
- When you have finished, read your draft again.
- Check your draft against the Content Editor's Checklist. Can you answer yes to each question?

Creative Writing • 471

OBJECTIVE
- **To copyedit and proofread a draft**

COPYEDITING AND PROOFREADING

Copyediting

Invite volunteers to read aloud the first two paragraphs. Point out that when students edited their stories for content, they checked that the story was clear. Explain that when students copyedit, they check that all the sentences are correct and easy to read.

Tell students that sentence fluency is the flow of language, the way it sounds when read aloud.

Point out that Riley changed *Lauren* to *she* in one place to make the sentences less choppy. Explain that people read fiction for enjoyment and that good sentence fluency helps make reading more enjoyable.

Have volunteers read aloud each item on the Copyeditor's Checklist. After the second item, point out that contractions are useful in dialogue. Ask students why this is true. *(Most people use contractions when they speak.)*

Read aloud the third paragraph. Ask a volunteer to find the capitalization mistake Riley made with the word *yes*. Have students identify where Riley needed to begin new paragraphs.

Your Turn

Read aloud this section. Encourage students first to read aloud their stories, underlining any sentences that cause trouble. Tell students to then look closely at the underlined sentences and to identify the problem. Have students read their drafts again, using the Copyeditor's Checklist. Tell students to check for one question at a time. Allow time for students to make changes.

Writer's Tip Tell students that reading aloud will help them hear mistakes and hear whether sentences flow smoothly.

Proofreading

Invite volunteers to read aloud the first two paragraphs and the Proofreader's Checklist. Tell students that writers often add new ideas throughout the writing process. Point out that the last question on the checklist reminds writers to check that no new mistakes were added during editing.

Ask a volunteer to read aloud the paragraph after the checklist. Ask students to find all the contractions in the story and to identify the one that is spelled incorrectly *(didn't)*.

Editor's Workshop   Realistic Fiction

Copyediting and Proofreading

Copyediting

Riley thought that her story was better because of her revisions. She especially liked the dialogue that she added.

Now Riley wanted to make sure that the sentences were clear and correct. Riley read her story aloud.

Sentence Fluency

Reading aloud would help her hear places in the story that sounded choppy. As she read aloud, she heard that she used Lauren's name a lot. She changed *Lauren* to *she* in one place. Then she read her story, using the Copyeditor's Checklist.

Riley saw that she should have capitalized *yes* when Lauren spoke back. She also remembered that she should have put Lauren's and Cady's dialogue into separate paragraphs when she revised.

Copyeditor's Checklist

- ☐ Does the dialogue include correct capitalization and punctuation? Is each speaker's dialogue in a separate paragraph?
- ☐ Are contractions used correctly?
- ☐ Are all the sentences complete?
- ☐ Does the order of the sentences make sense?
- ☐ Do all the words mean what you think they mean?

Your Turn

- Read your draft again, using the Copyeditor's Checklist.
- Make sure that you can answer yes to each question on the checklist.

Writer's Tip Read your story aloud as you copyedit.

Tell students that writing conventions are the correctness of the piece and include spelling, punctuation, and capitalization.

Your Turn

Have a volunteer read aloud the first paragraph. Allow time for students to proofread their drafts. Tell students to check for one kind of mistake at a time and to pay special attention to any writing they added since the first draft.

Have a volunteer read aloud the second paragraph. Ask students to trade papers and proofread a partner's draft. Tell students to use a different pencil color when making their proofreading corrections.

Grammar in Action Have students read the draft, one sentence at a time, until they find the sentence without end punctuation (*But the day Lauren was ready to move in, there was a problem*). Have students name the correct end punctuation (*period*) and tell why it is correct (*because it is a statement*).

Double-Check Drawing

Have students trade drafts with a partner. Ask students to read their partner's draft and to draw a picture of a part of their partner's story. When students have finished, have them share their pictures with their partner and describe what they put in their pictures.

Tell students that a story lives in their head, and that when they write fiction, they try to use precise words and clear sentences to share that story with a reader. Explain that the partners' drawings can show students what one reader saw. Tell students to compare the drawing they receive to the way that they imagine their story. Explain that seeing how others understand their story can help them revise to make the sentences in the story better match the story that lives in their head.

Proofreading

Riley had worked hard on her story. Content editing and copyediting had made the story much better. Now Riley had to do proofreading.

Riley knew that a new reader would catch mistakes that she might have missed. So she asked her best friend, Olivia, to proofread her draft. Olivia **Conventions** was good at spelling and grammar. Plus she liked to read Riley's stories. Olivia used this Proofreader's Checklist as she read Riley's story.

Proofreader's Checklist

- ☐ Are all the words spelled correctly?
- ☐ Is the first word of each sentence capitalized?
- ☐ Are proper nouns capitalized?
- ☐ Does each sentence end with the correct punctuation mark?
- ☐ Have you checked to make sure no new mistakes were made while editing?

Olivia read Riley's story several times. She found one contraction spelled incorrectly. Can you find it and correct it?

Your Turn

Read your draft and answer the questions on the Proofreader's Checklist. Remember to check for mistakes that you may have added as you revised your draft.

Next, trade drafts with a partner. Proofread each other's stories. Use the Proofreader's Checklist and answer the questions about your partner's draft. Then talk to your partner about what you found.

Grammar in Action

Riley forgot to add end punctuation to one of her sentences. Find it and fix it.

Prewriting
Drafting
Content Editing
Revising
Copyediting
Proofreading
Publishing

Realistic Fiction

OBJECTIVE

• **To publish a work of realistic fiction**

PUBLISHING

Read aloud the first paragraph. Ask students why Riley mailed her story to her grandmother *(to share her work with someone)*. Explain that this is the way Riley chose to publish her work. Discuss why students might enjoy writing fiction. Point out some of the following reasons that writers like to write fiction:

• to imagine what might happen if . . .
• to show readers what life is like for another person
• to share feelings
• to entertain readers
• to show readers something in the world that they may not have seen or experienced before
• because it is fun!

Have volunteers read aloud Riley's final copy. Then have students compare it to Riley's first draft. Ask students to tell how the story was improved. Discuss the many ways students might publish their writing.

Tell students that presentation, the way their writing looks, is important to how it will be received. Emphasize that neatness and consistent spacing, as well as illustrations are part of presenting students' work.

Your Turn

Have students read aloud this section. Invite volunteers to share the titles of their stories. Explain that a good title will make the reader want to read the story. Ask students to check their stories again for mistakes.

Writer's Workshop

Realistic Fiction

Publishing

After all her hard work, Riley was excited to publish her story. She printed out her story. Then she mailed it to her grandmother. Her grandmother thought it was great! Here is Riley's final copy.

The Creepy-Crawly Clubhouse

Lauren and her dad built a clubhouse in the backyard. Lauren's clubhouse would be a place where she could hang out with her friends. She could also get away from her little brother, Caleb.

But the day Lauren was ready to move in, there was a problem. Caleb had already moved his stuff into the clubhouse.

"He didn't even help build it! And now he thinks it's his," Lauren told her best friend, Cady.

Lauren had a plan. Caleb was afraid of spiders. So one day Lauren and Cady sat under the tree in the backyard. Caleb was in the clubhouse. They knew that Caleb could hear them.

Lauren said, "Cady, I'm scared of the huge spider in the clubhouse."

"I did see a large spider web in the corner," Cady said.

Lauren said, "Yes, it has big, fuzzy legs and eats anything that comes near it."

Lauren knew that Caleb heard every word. Lauren and Cady waited until dark. Then they hid under the window of the clubhouse. They waited until Caleb went inside the clubhouse. Then Lauren sprayed silly string through the window at the back of Caleb's neck. A moment later Caleb ran out of the clubhouse, shouting that there was a giant spider inside.

Caleb never went near the clubhouse again. Lauren finally had the clubhouse all to herself.

474

If time allows, have students draw pictures and make a cover for their stories. Encourage students to think about writing more stories for fun. Tell students they can write fantasy stories, science fiction stories, or any other kind of story. Suggest that if students liked the characters or setting of the story they wrote for class, they could write a series of stories with those same characters and setting.

ASSESS

Have students assess their finished realistic-fiction story using the reproducible Student Self-Assessment on page 475y. A separate Creative Writing Scoring Rubric can be found on page 475z for you to use to evaluate their work.

Plan to spend tomorrow doing a formal assessment. Administer the Creative Writing: Realistic Fiction Writing Prompt on **Assessment Book** pages 65–66.

Portfolio Opportunity

Remind students to keep a copy of their final realistic-fiction piece in their portfolios. Point out that having a portfolio will help students keep track of the progress they are making with their writing.

From Story to Stage

Have students meet in small groups to read one another's stories and to pick one that could be turned into a skit for the class. Encourage students to review the tips in Lesson 6 of this chapter. Have students make a stage and collect props as necessary. Help students develop their stories into a written skit. If some students are nervous about performing, suggest that they make sound effects or play the part of a narrator who reads from the written skit. Provide time for students to rehearse and to make any materials needed for their skits. Then ask students to present their skits to the class.

Whenever you publish your work, your goal is

👀 Presentation to share your thoughts and experiences with other people. There are many ways you can publish your story.

Create a book. Decorate the margins with small pictures that illustrate the story. You might choose to print the title and your name on a separate cover page and illustrate it with a scene from your story.

Film it. Ask friends to take parts and paint scenery. Add music. Do the narration as you film it.

Ask your school librarian if the book you created could be a checkout book for a limited time.

Create a classroom "Realistic Fiction" banner decorated with pictures of characters from the stories. Display the stories below the banner.

Your Turn

- Read your story one more time. If you typed your story on a computer, use the spell-checker to look for spelling mistakes. Make sure you have not added new mistakes as you revised.
- Check your title again. Does it still fit the story? If not, revise it.
- Use your best handwriting or a computer to make a final copy of your story.
- If you liked writing this story, think about writing more on your own. There are a lot of characters just waiting for you to tell their stories!

Prewriting

Drafting

Content Editing

Revising

Copyediting

Proofreading

Publishing

Lauren's Creepy-Crawly Clubhouse

Name _____ Date _____

Creative Writing
Realistic Fiction

	YES	NO
Ideas		
Does my story have realistic characters and events?		
Organization		
Is there a beginning that introduces the characters and setting?		
Is there a middle that describes a problem or situation?		
Is there an ending that solves the problem or brings the situation to a close?		
Are the events told in time order?		
Voice		
Do I use dialogue with informal language for a natural voice?		
Word Choice		
Do I use vivid words?		
Sentence Fluency		
Do I use a variety of sentences, including dialogue to move the story along?		
Conventions		
Do I use correct grammar?		
Do I use correct spelling?		
Do I use correct punctuation and capitalization?		
Presentation		
Is my story neat?		
Do I use consistent margins and spacing?		
Additional Items		

Name _____

Date _____ Score _____

POINT VALUES

0 = not evident
1 = minimal evidence of mastery
2 = evidence of development toward mastery
3 = strong evidence of mastery
4 = outstanding evidence of mastery

Creative Writing
Realistic Fiction

	POINTS
Ideas	
realistic characters and events	
Organization	
a beginning that introduces the characters and setting	
a middle that describes a problem or situation	
an ending that solves the problem or brings the situation to a close	
events told in time order	
Voice	
dialogue that uses informal language for a natural voice	
Word Choice	
vivid words	
Sentence Fluency	
a variety of sentences, including dialogue to move the story along	
Conventions	
correct grammar and usage	
correct spelling	
correct punctuation and capitalization	
Presentation	
neatness	
consistent margins and spacing	
Additional Items	
Total	

© LOYOLA PRESS.

CHAPTER FOCUS

LESSON 1: What Makes a Good Research Report?

LESSON 2: Facts and Notes

- **GRAMMAR:** Diagramming
- **STUDY SKILLS:** Library Skills
- **WRITING SKILLS:** Revising Sentences
- **WORD STUDY:** Homophones
- **SPEAKING AND LISTENING SKILLS:** Oral Biographies
- **WRITER'S WORKSHOP:** Research Reports

SUPPORT MATERIALS

Practice Book
Writing, pages 167–171

Assessment Book
Chapter 8 Writing Skills, pages 67–68
Research Report Writing Prompt, page 69–70

Rubrics
Student, page 513y
Teacher, page 513z

Test Generator CD

Grammar
Section 8, pages 183–208

Customizable Lesson Plans
www.voyagesinenglish.com

Research Reports

WHAT IS A RESEARCH REPORT?

A research report is an expository piece that provides information on a specific topic. The information is derived from a variety of sources found by the writer. A writer then interprets, analyzes, and draws conclusions from the information to develop a topic sentence and supporting ideas.

The writer of a research report often completes a process such as the following: choose a topic, form a preliminary topic sentence, locate sources, take notes on note cards, draft, revise, edit, and publish.

Good research reports include an introduction that states the topic, a body that supports the topic, and a summarizing conclusion. Throughout the piece the writer uses formal language, a variety of sentence styles and lengths, and correct conventions.

A good research report includes the following:

- ☐ A clear focus on one topic
- ☐ Factual information supported by research that was gathered as notes
- ☐ An introduction that includes a topic sentence
- ☐ A body that includes ideas supported by facts
- ☐ A summarizing conclusion
- ☐ A confident voice
- ☐ Formal language

LiNK Use the following titles to offer your students examples of well-crafted research writing:

First Space Encyclopedia by DK Publishing

Just the Facts: Writing Your Own Research Report by Nancy Loewen

Mountains by Seymour Simon

Stop the Copying with Wild and Wacky Research Projects by Nancy Polette

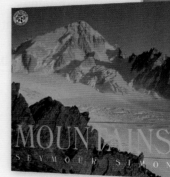

> **"Research is formalized curiosity.**
> **It is poking and prying with a purpose."**
>
> —Zora Neale Hurston

WRITER'S WORKSHOP TIPS

Follow these ideas and tips to help you and your class get the most out of the Writer's Workshop:

- Review the traits of good writing. Use the chart on the inside back cover of the student and teacher editions.

- Stock the classroom library with a variety of nonfiction works to spark topic ideas.

- Invite a guest speaker, such as a marketing executive or a scientist, to explain to the class why he or she writes research reports and how they are used.

- Encourage students to watch the local, national, or international news for topic ideas.

- Require students to meet with you at least once during the following steps of the writing process: prewriting, drafting, and revising.

CONNECT WITH GRAMMAR

Throughout the Writer's Workshop, look for opportunities to integrate diagramming with writing research reports.

- ☐ During drafting ask students to diagram their topic statements.

- ☐ During revising have students include and diagram sentences with compound subjects and compound predicates.

- ☐ During copyediting ask partners to choose a troubling sentence from their partner's research report to diagram. Then ask them if diagramming helped them decide how to revise the sentence.

SCORING RUBRIC

Research Report

Point Values
0 = not evident
1 = minimal evidence of mastery
2 = evidence of development toward mastery
3 = strong evidence of mastery
4 = outstanding evidence of mastery

Ideas	POINTS
clear focus on one topic	
factual information supported by research gathered as notes	
Organization	
an interesting introduction that includes a topic sentence	
a body that includes ideas supported by facts	
a summarizing conclusion	
Voice	
a confident voice	
Word Choice	
formal language	
Sentence Fluency	
varied sentence styles and lengths	
Conventions	
correct grammar and usage	
correct spelling	
correct punctuation and capitalization	
Presentation	
neatness	
consistent margins and spacing	
Additional Items	
Total	

Full-sized, reproducible rubrics can be found at the end of this chapter.

Research Reports

INTRODUCING THE GENRE

Tell students that Chapter 8 is about research reports. Explain that research reports contain facts about real people, places, things, or events. Emphasize that the topic is what the research report is about. Point out that when writers write research reports, they find facts in books, in magazines, in newspapers, or on the Internet and use those facts in their writing. Elaborate on the following characteristics of a research report:

- The introduction identifies the topic.
- The body gives information about the topic.
- Details that are alike are grouped together in paragraphs.
- The conclusion sums up information in the report.
- A research report includes reliable facts from different sources.

Reading the Literature Excerpt

Invite volunteers to read aloud from *Mountains* by Seymour Simon. Have students identify the topic *(mountain ranges)* and what information is included *(how they are formed, where they are formed)*. Ask why they think this is a good example of a research report.

Research Reports

LiNK Mountains

Mountains is a good example of a research report because it has the following:

- An introduction that identifies the topic.
- Facts from trustworthy sources.
- Information about the topic grouped by detail.

You may wish to have students diagram sentences from the excerpts in this chapter.

LiNK **Mountains**
by Seymour Simon

Mountain ranges do not arise just anyplace. Most are formed when *plates,* giant pieces of the earth's crust, push and pull against each other. The United States, Canada, Mexico, and part of the North Atlantic Ocean are on the North American plate. The Rockies and the coast ranges of the western United States and Canada were formed where the North American plate pushed against the Pacific plate.

The Mid-Atlantic Ridge, a 12,000-mile-long underwater mountain chain that stretches the length of the Atlantic Ocean, was formed where the North American plate pulled away from the Eurasian plate and the African plate. The islands of Iceland and Surtsey are actually the tops of volcanic mountain peaks reaching above the surface of the ocean, which covers most of the Mid-Atlantic Ridge.

> The book *Mountains* has many characteristics of a research report. It contains facts from reliable sources and is written in an organized way.

476

Reading the Student Model

Invite volunteers to read aloud the model. Ask students to identify the topic of the research report *(Callimico monkeys)*. Then ask what information is given about the topic in the body of the research report *(where Callimico monkeys are from, baby Callimicos, adult Callimicos, how Callimicos are like humans)*. Point out that in a research report, separate facts about the topic are often found in separate paragraphs. Ask students to identify how the writer sums up the information in the last paragraph. *(The writer invites readers to go to the zoo and learn more about Callimicos.)*

Ask students whether they knew any of this information about Callimico monkeys before reading the research report. Discuss what students know about Callimico monkeys now. Explain that research leads writers to learn more about a topic and to share that knowledge with others.

TEACHING OPTIONS

Scavenger Hunt

Have students search the classroom, the school library, and the Internet to find examples of research reports. Ask students to list the titles, topics, and authors.

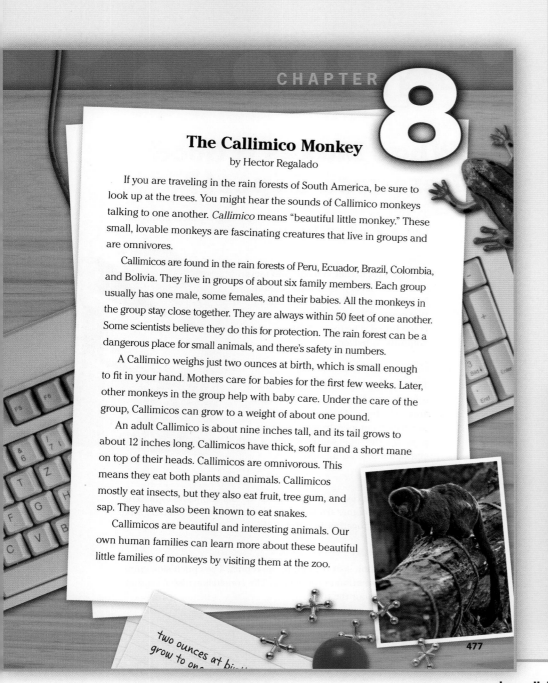

CHAPTER

8

The Callimico Monkey
by Hector Regalado

If you are traveling in the rain forests of South America, be sure to look up at the trees. You might hear the sounds of Callimico monkeys talking to one another. *Callimico* means "beautiful little monkey." These small, lovable monkeys are fascinating creatures that live in groups and are omnivores.

Callimicos are found in the rain forests of Peru, Ecuador, Brazil, Colombia, and Bolivia. They live in groups of about six family members. Each group usually has one male, some females, and their babies. All the monkeys in the group stay close together. They are always within 50 feet of one another. Some scientists believe they do this for protection. The rain forest can be a dangerous place for small animals, and there's safety in numbers.

A Callimico weighs just two ounces at birth, which is small enough to fit in your hand. Mothers care for babies for the first few weeks. Later, other monkeys in the group help with baby care. Under the care of the group, Callimicos can grow to a weight of about one pound.

An adult Callimico is about nine inches tall, and its tail grows to about 12 inches long. Callimicos have thick, soft fur and a short mane on top of their heads. Callimicos are omnivorous. This means they eat both plants and animals. Callimicos mostly eat insects, but they also eat fruit, tree gum, and sap. They have also been known to eat snakes.

Callimicos are beautiful and interesting animals. Our own human families can learn more about these beautiful little families of monkeys by visiting them at the zoo.

two ounces at bi...
grow to on...

477

For Tomorrow

Have students find one additional fact about monkeys. Tell students to look in an encyclopedia, on the Internet, or in books about monkeys. Ask students to be prepared to share what they have found during the next class. Bring in your own fact to share with the class.

OBJECTIVE

- **To understand the characteristics of a research report**

WARM-UP

Read, Listen, Speak

Share your fact about monkeys from yesterday's For Tomorrow homework and tell where you found it. Have small groups share the facts that they found. Ask students to discuss the new information they found and where they found it.

GRAMMAR CONNECTION

Take this opportunity to talk about diagramming subjects and predicates and possessives. You may wish to have students point out subjects and predicates and any possessives in their Read, Listen, Speak examples.

TEACH

Read aloud the first paragraph. Explain that in using formal language, students should not use slang words, such as *cool*. Tell students that they should also avoid using contractions. Then invite a volunteer to read aloud the section Topic. Discuss why a narrow topic is better than a broad topic. *(If the topic is too broad, the research report is harder to write.)*

Have volunteers read aloud the sections Introduction and Body. Guide students to understand that the information they find when they do research will be in the body of their research report.

Have a volunteer read aloud the section Conclusion. Point out that the conclusion of a research report usually leaves the reader with something to think about.

Read aloud the section Research. Explain that a research report uses information from trustworthy sources and that

the information is written in the writer's own words. Tell students that writers do not copy sentences or paragraphs from a source and then write them as their own.

PRACTICE

ACTIVITY A

Remind students that a topic should be narrow enough to cover in one or two pages. Have partners complete this activity. When students have finished, invite volunteers to explain their answers.

LiNK Have a volunteer read aloud the excerpt. Ask students to tell what the topic is *(magnets)* and what the excerpt tells about the topic *(how they work)*. Ask students to guess what else "Magnets" might tell about the topic *(how magnets are made, who discovered magnets and the science of magnets, what magnets and magnetism are used for)*. Ask students what part of a research report this excerpt comes from and how they know *(body; it gives an idea about the topic, supported by facts)*.

What Makes a Good Research Report?

A research report is a kind of writing that gives facts about one topic. A research report uses formal language.

Topic

Choose a topic that you can find facts about in a library. Your topic should be narrow enough to cover in one or two pages. The topic "sea animals" is too broad. The topic "bottle-nosed dolphins" is better.

Introduction

The introduction of the report should grab the reader's attention and tell about the topic. The topic is stated in a topic sentence. In the report on page 477, the topic sentence comes at the end of the first paragraph.

Body

The body of a research report gives details about the topic. The information comes from different sources. Details that are alike are grouped together in paragraphs.

Conclusion

The conclusion is at the end of the report. The conclusion sums up the information in the report. The conclusion also contains a comment about the topic.

APPLY

WRITER'S CORNER

Help students brainstorm weather terms. Remind students that a fact is a true statement that can be tested or proven. *(Tornadoes bring strong wind and rain.)* Invite small groups to share their facts and to tell how they know their sentences are facts. Students should demonstrate the ability to identify and write facts.

Grammar in Action. Remind students that a subject is what a sentence is about and a predicate tells what a subject is or does.

ASSESS

Note which students had difficulty understanding the characteristics of research reports. Use the Reteach option with those students who need additional reinforcement.

TEACHING OPTIONS

Reteach

Provide students with copies of a science or social studies article from a children's magazine. Allow time for students to read the article. Then have students answer the following questions:

- What is the topic sentence or sentences in the introduction?
- What two facts about the topic can you find in the body?
- What sentence or sentences sum up the information in the article?

Topic Time

Write on the board a four-column chart with the headings *Animal, Person, Place, Thing.* Have students copy the chart. Direct students to brainstorm topics for research reports. Have students write the topics in the appropriate columns on their charts. Encourage students to list under each topic questions they might research and facts they know. Explain that using a chart helps organize information when choosing a topic for a research report.

For Tomorrow

Have students find in a book or on the Internet one additional fact about the weather term they wrote about in the Writer's Corner. Tell students to rewrite the fact in their own words. Have students bring to class their fact and the name of the source that they used. Bring in your own weather fact to share.

Research

When writers do research, they first gather information from different sources. A source is any book, magazine, newspaper, encyclopedia, or Web site in which you can find information for your report.

After writers do research, they organize the facts and write them in their own words. Writing facts in your own words shows that you understand what you are reading.

ACTIVITY A Decide whether each idea below makes a good topic for a research report. Explain your answers.

1. my trip to the museum no
2. the history of Europe no
3. coral reefs yes
4. John Quincy Adams yes
5. mammals no
6. the cotton plant yes
7. the invention of the airplane yes
8. the future of space travel no
9. the parts of the eye yes
10. my favorite band's latest album no

Magnets

LiNK

A magnet works because of a natural force called magnetism. Magnetism is a force that you cannot see. . . . The force of magnetism pushes and pulls, causing a magnet to pull some metal objects. . . . Magnets also can push or pull other magnets. Each magnet has a magnetic field around it. This is the area where the force of magnetism can affect objects.

Jason Cooper

WRITER'S CORNER

Write two facts that you know about the weather. Be sure to write complete sentences.

Grammar in Action. After you write your weather facts, underline the subjects and circle the predicates.

Research Reports • 479

WARM-UP

Read, Listen, Speak

Read aloud the weather fact you found for yesterday's For Tomorrow homework. Read first the exact quote from the source and then the fact in your own words. Tell students the source for your fact. Then have small groups share the facts they found. Invite students to compare the facts and to discuss how the information is restated.

GRAMMAR CONNECTION

Take this opportunity to talk about diagramming adjectives. You may wish to have students point out any adjectives in their Read, Listen, Speak examples.

TEACH

Ask students to name reasons why knowing how to write a research report might be an important skill. Then review the characteristics of research reports.

Invite volunteers to tell what is found in the introduction, body, and conclusion in a research report. Ask students to compare each of these parts to the beginning, middle, and ending of a persuasive article and to note the similarities.

Point out the importance of doing research before writing a research report. Ask students to explain why a topic is researched *(so that writers can learn more about the topic; so that writers can share what they have learned with an audience)*.

PRACTICE

ACTIVITY B

Have partners complete this activity. Ask students to discuss which topic sentence in each item they think is the strongest. Ask volunteers to explain their answers.

ACTIVITY C

Have partners complete this activity. Ask them to decide which sentence they think is the best ending sentence. Invite volunteers to explain their answers.

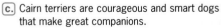

ACTIVITY B Read each research topic below. Choose the best topic sentence for a report about that topic.

1. **whitetail deer**
   a. Whitetail deer are well-known, large mammals in North America.
   b. I like deer, especially the whitetail deer.
   c. Bambi is the cutest whitetail deer.

2. **red pandas**
   a. I have a stuffed panda at home.
   b. Red pandas are shy animals that live in Nepal, Burma, and central China.
   c. There is a really good documentary about red pandas that everyone should watch.

3. **orcas**
   a. Orcas are warm-blooded mammals and one of the largest members of the dolphin family.
   b. Shamu is an orca.
   c. We had to do a report about animals, so I chose orcas.

4. **cairn terriers**
   a. Cairn terriers are dogs.
   b. I saw a cairn terrier at the park the other day and decided I want one.
   c. Cairn terriers are courageous and smart dogs that make great companions.

Cairn terrier

APPLY

WRITER'S CORNER

Tell students that they can look at a globe, in an atlas, in an encyclopedia, in a science textbook, or online to find a country they would like to know more about. Then allow time for students to write their questions and share them in small groups. Students should demonstrate the ability to generate a topic for a research report.

TechTip You may wish to suggest a specific online atlas or travel Web site for students to explore.

ASSESS

Note which students had difficulty writing introductions and conclusions. Use the Reteach option with those students who need additional reinforcement.

Practice Book page 167 provides additional work with the characteristics of research reports.

TEACHING OPTIONS

Reteach

Have small groups brainstorm topics for a research report. Then have groups choose a topic. Encourage students to discuss what is interesting or unusual about the chosen topic. Then have groups write several statements that might be used in an introduction. Have groups review the sentences and choose the ones they would use in a strong introduction. Ask groups to restate the sentences from the introduction to write a conclusion. Have volunteers share their introductions and conclusions.

English-Language Learners

Distribute copies of a simple research report. Ask students what the report is about. Then ask partners to work together to identify the topic sentence. Have students discuss how they know that the chosen sentence is the topic sentence. Then have partners identify a sentence in the conclusion that sums up the information in the report. Reinforce that the conclusion includes a restatement of the information in the introduction.

For Tomorrow

Have students write an introduction for a research report about their chosen country from the Writer's Corner. Bring in your own introductory paragraph for a research report on a country to share with the class.

ACTIVITY C Choose the best ending sentence that would be in a conclusion about each topic below. Tell why you chose that sentence.

1. **whitetail deer**
   a. Whitetail deer change colors in the fall.
   b. Whitetail deer can run very fast.
   c. Watch for these beautiful creatures in a field near you.

2. **red pandas**
   a. The red panda is a beautiful creature, and we should all do our part to save it.
   b. Red pandas live in forests and mountains.
   c. I really want to see a red panda.

3. **orcas**
   a. Orcas have teeth like sharp cones.
   b. Orcas are one of the most majestic creatures in the sea.
   c. Orcas are not fish, but are large mammals.

4. **cairn terriers**
   a. Cairn terriers are funny and furry.
   b. Now that I know so much about them, I want a cairn terrier as a pet.
   c. Cairn terriers are lovable creatures.

WRITER'S CORNER

Write the name of a country that you would like to know more about. List three questions that you might research about that country.

Red panda

Tech Tip With an adult, research your country online.

Research Reports • 481

OBJECTIVES

- **To understand how to find facts for a research report**
- **To learn how to take and organize notes**

WARM-UP

Read, Listen, Speak

Read aloud your introduction from yesterday's For Tomorrow homework. Tell students how you used your questions in your introduction. Have small groups read aloud their introductions. Ask students to discuss how they used questions about their country to write their introductions.

GRAMMAR CONNECTION

Take this opportunity to talk about diagramming adverbs. You may wish to have students point out any adverbs in their Read, Listen, Speak examples.

TEACH

Have a volunteer read aloud the first paragraph. Tell students that a library is a good place to find information about a topic.

Ask volunteers to read aloud the section Nonfiction Books. Tell students that a nonfiction book might be general and cover many parts of one topic or might be specific and cover only one part of a topic.

Have a volunteer read aloud the section Encyclopedias. Ask a volunteer how information is organized in an encyclopedia *(alphabetical order)*. Remind students that there are many reliable online encyclopedias. You may wish to refer students to specific Web sites.

Invite a volunteer to read aloud the section Magazines. Ask volunteers why magazines have the latest information.

(Magazines come out many times a year.) Explain that if students are researching tigers, they should search nature magazines, not sports magazines. Point out that most magazines are also published online and that back issues are often available on the magazines' Web sites.

Ask volunteers to read aloud the section Internet. You may wish to demonstrate how to use a search engine. Remind students that they should ask their parents for permission whenever they use the Internet.

PRACTICE

ACTIVITY A

Ask students to complete the activity independently. Have volunteers share their answers with the class. Then invite students to explain why the third source in each item is a poor source for information on the topic.

LESSON **2** RESEARCH REPORTS

Facts and Notes

After choosing a topic for your research report, you will need to find information about it. Your classroom and your school library are good places to start. If you need more information, go to your local library and do research on the Internet.

Finding Facts

Nonfiction Books

Nonfiction books are about real people, things, and events. Nonfiction books are usually about one topic. For example, a book about tigers would probably cover all the different kinds of tigers. It would discuss where tigers live, what they eat, and how they act toward one another.

Encyclopedias

Encyclopedias contain information about many different topics. For example, there would be an entry for "Tiger." The information would probably be more general than what you would find in a book about tigers.

Magazines

Magazine articles usually have the latest information about a topic. For example, a magazine article about tigers might tell about new ideas that scientists have about what tigers eat. Or the article might tell about new places in the wild where tigers have been seen.

APPLY

WRITER'S CORNER

Tell students to carefully evaluate the Web sites they use to conduct Internet research. You may wish to suggest specific, child-friendly science and astronomy Web sites, such as those from a planetarium or science magazine. Ask students to write a phrase or sentence that describes each Web site. Then have partners discuss the facts they found. Students should demonstrate the ability to find facts for a research report.

ASSESS

Note which students had difficulty using different sources for finding facts. Use the Reteach option with those students who need additional reinforcement.

Reteach

Tell students that they will be doing research about dinosaurs. Direct each student to find one fact about dinosaurs from each of three different types of sources. Remind students they may use nonfiction books, encyclopedias, magazines, or the Internet. Help students choose one fact with which to make a poster. Have students present their posters and display them in the classroom. Ask students to include the source of their fact on their posters.

Presidential Power

Ask half the class to research Thomas Jefferson and the other half to research Abraham Lincoln. Have partners write four facts about their presidents. Then have partners pair up with another pair of students who did research on the same president to compare their facts. Challenge the groups to combine their facts into one list. Have volunteers share their lists with the class.

Internet

You can search the Internet to find information about your topic. If you don't know how to use a computer, ask the librarian for help.

Be careful when choosing Web sites to use in your research. Not all the information on the Internet is correct. Look for sites written by experts or organizations. A site written by another student might not have the best facts. Ask an adult if you are not sure whether a Web site is reliable.

Be sure to tell your teacher or parents if you are doing research on the Internet. Never give information about yourself without first asking your teacher or parents.

Activity A

1. C would not be a good choice because the information is limited to surfing.
2. A would not be a good choice because it is a fictional movie.
3. C would not be a good choice because the Web site is not written by an expert.

ACTIVITY A Read each topic. Choose which two sources would have good information for a research report about that topic. Then tell why the third source would not have good information.

1. Los Angeles, California
   a. an encyclopedia, volume *C*
   b. the book *American Cities Travel Guide*
   c. *Surfer* magazine

2. tarantula
   a. the movie *Spiders from Mars*
   b. the Web site www.spiders.edu
   c. the book *The Life of Spiders*

3. the sun
   a. the book *Solar Flares Explained*
   b. the magazine *Astronomy Today*
   c. a student's Web site about the sun

WRITER'S CORNER

With an adult find information on the Internet about one of the planets. Write three Web site addresses that contain information about that planet. Then write one fact from each site.

For Tomorrow

Ask students to write two facts about cars. Tell them to get the facts from books or magazines. Have students record the facts and the sources the facts came from. Write two facts and sources to share with the class.

Research Reports • 483

WARM-UP

Read, Listen, Speak

Read aloud your two facts about cars from yesterday's For Tomorrow homework. Tell where you found your facts and why it is a good source. Ask small groups to share their facts about cars and to name their sources. Have a volunteer in each group keep a tally of the kinds of sources that were used.

GRAMMAR CONNECTION

Take this opportunity to talk about diagramming adjectives as subject complements. You may wish to have students point out any adjectives as subject complements in their Read, Listen, Speak examples.

TEACH

Have volunteers read aloud the section Taking Notes and the example note card. Tell students that notes are made during research but used during the planning and writing of a research report. Explain why students should put only one fact on each note card. *(It makes it easier to find the fact when you have many note cards.)*

Ask a volunteer to read aloud the section Organizing Notes. Tell students that sometimes there will be cards that do not fit into any pile. Point out that these notes might be used for an introduction or a conclusion. Explain that students don't have to use every fact they find and record in their research report.

PRACTICE

ACTIVITY B

Have students complete the activity independently. Then ask volunteers to read aloud the fact they found without saying the name of the animal. Invite the class to guess the animal.

ACTIVITY C

Have students look for facts that they did not find in Activity B. Invite volunteers to read aloud their facts and name the sources.

ACTIVITY D

Tell students to record on their note cards the full Web site address for the specific Web page where they found information— not just the home page of the Web site. Have students share their facts and source names with a partner.

ACTIVITY E

Tell students to keep the note cards that may not fit into the three piles in a fourth pile to use later. Then have small groups share their fourth piles.

Taking Notes

As you find facts in your sources, write them on note cards. Use your own words to write your notes. Write one fact on each note card. Also write the title of the source, the page number, and the author. Think about the information you are reading.

A note card might look like this.

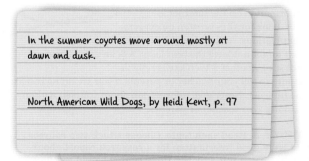

In the summer coyotes move around mostly at dawn and dusk.

North American Wild Dogs, by Heidi Kent, p. 97

Organizing Notes

After you have taken notes from your sources, you should put them in order. One way to organize your note cards is to put them into piles.

Suppose the topic of your report is the mongoose. You might want to make three separate piles of note cards. The first pile could be about what the mongoose looks like. The second pile could tell where it lives. The third pile could describe what the mongoose eats.

ACTIVITY B Choose an animal that interests you. Use an encyclopedia to find out one fact about the animal. Write the fact on a note card in your own words. Write the name, the volume, and the page number of the encyclopedia.

APPLY

WRITER'S CORNER

Suggest that students include a topic sentence that tells what the paragraph is about—what the animal eats, what it looks like, or where it lives—as well as sentences with the facts about the animal. When students have finished, invite volunteers to share their paragraphs with the class. Students should demonstrate the ability to take and organize notes from research.

ASSESS

Note which students had difficulty taking and organizing notes from research. Use the Reteach option with those students who need additional reinforcement.

Practice Book page 168 provides additional work with facts and notes.

Reteach

Discuss what needs to be included on note cards. Distribute note cards and have partners choose a topic for a research report and find a fact about their topic in an encyclopedia. Have partners work together to summarize the fact in their own words. Then ask students to write on a note card the title of their source and the page number. Have students share their facts and the source information.

Noteworthy Places

Have small groups choose a famous place as a topic for a research report. Have each group member find and write on note cards two facts about the place. Then ask students to look at all the note cards and to work together to organize them into separate piles. Have groups share their cards and describe how they decided to organize them.

ACTIVITY C Look in two nonfiction books to find information about the animal that you chose in Activity B. Write three facts on separate note cards. Find facts about what your animal looks like, where it lives, and what it eats. Write on the note card the source for each fact.

ACTIVITY D Go to one of the Web sites below to find facts about the animal that you chose in Activity B. Make note cards about what your animal looks like, where it lives, and what it eats. For each fact write the Web site address you used as the source.

Phoenix Zoo
www.phoenixzoo.org

Kids' Planet ESPECIES Animal Fact Sheets
www.kidsplanet.org

SeaWorld/Busch Gardens
www.seaworld.org

Western North Carolina Nature Center
www.wildwnc.org

ACTIVITY E Gather all the note cards that you wrote. Arrange them into three piles: what your animal looks like, where it lives, and what it eats.

Crested gecko

WRITER'S CORNER

Look over one of your piles of note cards from Activity E. Write a five-sentence paragraph using the facts in your notes.

Maroon clown fish and anemone

Research Reports • 485

For Tomorrow

Have students interview a parent or another adult about his or her job. Ask students to write on separate note cards three facts about the job. Interview a friend or colleague and write three facts about his or her job to share with the class.

OBJECTIVES

- **To understand how libraries are organized**
- **To learn how to search for a book, using an electronic catalog**

WARM-UP

Read, Listen, Speak

Write on the board the facts and source you found from yesterday's For Tomorrow homework. Tell why your source is knowledgeable and reliable. Have small groups read aloud their note cards. Ask students to explain how they know that their facts are accurate.

GRAMMAR CONNECTION

Take this opportunity to talk about diagramming compound subjects. You may wish to have students point out any compound subjects in their Read, Listen, Speak examples.

TEACH

Read aloud the section How Libraries Are Organized. Invite volunteers to share their experiences of looking for books in libraries. Ask how students found what they were looking for.

Have volunteers read aloud the sections Fiction Books, Nonfiction Books, and Reference Books. Tell students that a reference book is a collection of facts and information about a variety of subjects. Ask students what they would find in an atlas *(maps)*.

Have a volunteer read aloud the section Searching for Books. Explain that until recently all libraries used card catalogs. Point out that today most libraries have electronic catalogs on computers, but they can be searched in the same way—by title, by author, by subject, and sometimes by keyword.

PRACTICE

ACTIVITY A

Remind students how reference books, nonfiction books, and fiction books differ. When students have finished, ask volunteers how they knew which book fit in each category.

ACTIVITY B

Have students complete the activity independently. Then ask volunteers to answer the questions. Have students tell if the book is a nonfiction book, a reference book, or a fiction book and how they know.

Library Skills

How Libraries Are Organized

Finding useful information is a big part of writing a research report. Your school library and local library are good places to look for information.

Knowing how libraries are organized can help you find the information you need. Libraries separate fiction books from nonfiction books.

Fiction Books

Fiction books are organized alphabetically by the last name of the author.

Nonfiction Books

Nonfiction books are organized by subject, or what they are about. For example, books about whales can usually be found together in the same area of the library.

Reference Books

Reference books help you find information about different people, places, things, and events. Dictionaries, encyclopedias, and atlases are kinds of reference books.

Searching for Books

When searching for a book in a library, the first place to look is the library catalog. The library catalog is a complete list of all the books in a certain library or a group of libraries. The library catalog tells you exactly where to find the books you need. There are three ways that you can search for books in a library: by the title, by the author's name, and by the subject.

APPLY

WRITER'S CORNER

After students have finished, have partners discuss how they know that a book is fiction, nonfiction, or a reference book. Ask volunteers to share their book titles and reasons with the class. Students should demonstrate an understanding of how libraries are organized and how to search for a book.

ASSESS

Note which students had difficulty understanding how to find a book in the library. Use the Reteach option with those students who need additional reinforcement.

ACTIVITY A Tell whether each book is a fiction book, a nonfiction book, or a reference book.

1. *Trees of North America* nonfiction
2. *World Book* reference
3. *The Mousewife* fiction
4. *The Civil War* nonfiction
5. *Encyclopaedia Britannica* reference
6. *Prehistoric Animals* nonfiction
7. *The Adventures of Liam Leprechaun* fiction
8. *Webster's New World Student's Dictionary* reference
9. *The Life and Times of George Washington* nonfiction
10. *Atlas of the World* reference
11. *Mr. and Mrs. Moonbeam* fiction
12. *The Planets* nonfiction

ACTIVITY B Read the book cover below. Then answer the questions.

Bugs, an ANTcestry
by Beetrice Bloom

1. What is the title of the book? *Bugs, an ANTcestry*
2. Who is the author of the book? Beetrice Bloom
3. What is the subject of the book? bugs; insects

WRITER'S CORNER

Go to the library with a partner and find the following: two fiction books, two nonfiction books, and two reference books. Write all six titles.

Research Reports • 487

WARM-UP

Read, Listen, Speak

Tell students the categories you used to organize your books or magazines for yesterday's For Tomorrow homework. Have small groups discuss how they organized their books or magazines. Have students write a sentence about organizing their books or magazines.

GRAMMAR CONNECTION

Take this opportunity to talk about diagramming compound predicates. Have students point out any compound predicates in their Read, Listen, Speak examples.

TEACH

Have volunteers read aloud the first two paragraphs of the section Electronic Catalogs. Direct students' attention to the Catalog Search page. Help students identify the Search box and what it means to search by author, title, and subject. Tell students that looking for a book by subject in an electronic catalog is like looking for a certain topic, using a search engine on the Internet.

Ask a volunteer to read aloud the third paragraph. Invite students to describe what they see on the Search Results page. Be sure that students know that they should look at more than the first book in the list after completing a subject search. Tell students that just because the book is first does not mean that it is the best source for research.

Read aloud the section Call Numbers. Point out the importance of writing the call number correctly because the call number tells where the book is in the library.

PRACTICE

ACTIVITY C

Have partners complete this activity. When students have finished, invite them to share their books with the class. Tell students to explain how they found the books.

Electronic Catalogs

Although card catalogs are still used in some libraries, most libraries have electronic catalogs. You use a computer to search for books on electronic catalogs.

You usually start your search by typing a title, an author, or a subject into a search box. For a research report, type your topic into the box. Then click on a menu to tell the computer that you are looking for a subject. Press "Enter" or "Return" on the keyboard or click the button on the screen that starts the search.

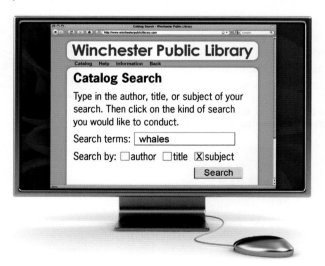

The computer will look for books about your topic and list them on the screen. Sometimes you may have to click on a book title to get more information about it. The screen will show the book's title, its author, and its call number. Sometimes electronic catalogs include a brief description of the book.

APPLY

WRITER'S CORNER

Allow time for students to complete this activity in the library. Then have partners share their information. Encourage students to discuss how they might use the information in a research report. Students should demonstrate the ability to find books in the library.

ASSESS

Note which students had difficulty with library skills. Use the Reteach option with those students who need additional reinforcement.

Practice Book page 169 provides additional work with library skills.

Reteach

Have students find three nonfiction books in the library, write the title and author of each book, and return the books to the shelves. Then have students trade lists with partners and use the electronic catalog to find the books from their partners' lists by doing a search by title. You may wish to have students search for the books by author and subject.

Learn from Your Librarian

Invite the school librarian to give a presentation that describes the electronic catalog and how to use it. Ask the librarian to include a section about online search engines and Internet safety. Encourage students to take notes about the main points of the presentation. Discuss the presentation with the class and have students use their notes to summarize the important facts they learned.

Winchester Public Library

Catalog   Help   Information   Back

Search Results

Your search for "whales" located 21 items.

1. Creatures of the Deep / Rachel Henderson / 599.524
2. Whales / Kwame Johnson / 599.513
3. Whale Stories / Ed. Seth Goldberg / 639.2 B23

Call Numbers

Every nonfiction book has a call number. The call number is like an address. It tells where the book can be found. Use the call number to find the books that you need.

Write the call numbers, authors, and titles of the books you want. Ask the librarian to help you find the books.

ACTIVITY C Choose three of the following topics. Use a library catalog to find one book about each topic. If you need help, ask a librarian.

outer space	Native Americans
American Revolution	glaciers
dinosaurs	whales
tornadoes	China

WRITER'S CORNER

Look at the books you found for Activity C. Write each book's title, the author's name, and the book's call number. Then write two facts from each book.

For Tomorrow

Tell students to choose a topic for a research report. Ask them to write keywords to type into a subject search for their topic in an electronic catalog. Choose your own topic and write keywords to share with the class.

- **To revise sentences by using exact words**
- **To understand how to combine sentences**

WARM-UP
Read, Listen, Speak

Share your topic from yesterday's For Tomorrow homework. Tell students the keywords you chose and why you chose them. Ask small groups to share their topics. Then have students share the keywords they wrote to use in the subject search. Invite volunteers to suggest other words that could be used in the search.

GRAMMAR CONNECTION

Take this opportunity to talk about compound complements. Have students fill in the following sentences based on their Read, Listen, Speak examples: *My keywords are _____ and _____.*

TEACH

Read aloud the first paragraph. Ask students why they might want to revise sentences to improve their writing. *(It makes the writing more interesting.)*

Ask a volunteer to read aloud the first paragraph of the section Exact Words. Point out that using exact words makes sentences colorful and more interesting.

Invite volunteers to read aloud the examples. After each example, ask students to explain how the revised sentences give the reader a clearer picture of the scene. Explain that the more clearly a writer describes a picture or an event, the better the reader can see and understand it.

Read aloud the last paragraph. Point out that exact nouns, stronger verbs, and colorful adverbs and adjectives are like different colors of paint students can use to make their writing more vivid.

PRACTICE

ACTIVITY A
Point out the colorful adjectives in the example *(hardworking, dazzling).* Have partners complete the activity. Then ask volunteers to explain their answers.

ACTIVITY B
Complete this activity as a class. For each item, help students brainstorm nouns, verbs, adjectives, and adverbs. Encourage students to evaluate each suggestion.

Revising Sentences

When you revise a sentence, you change words and combine ideas to improve your writing.

Exact Words

One way to make your sentences more interesting is to use exact words. Read the following sentences. Notice how the sentence becomes more interesting with a few changes.

> **The horse ran home.**

1. Change to tell what kind of horse.
   > **The mare ran home.**
   > **The pinto ran home.**

2. Change to tell how the horse ran.
   > **The mare galloped home.**
   > **The pinto trotted home.**

3. Change to describe where the horse ran.
   > **The mare galloped into the corral.**
   > **The pinto trotted into its stall.**

4. Use colorful adjectives and adverbs.
   > **The runaway mare galloped into the muddy corral.**
   > **The shivering pinto gladly trotted into its cozy stall.**

In each example the writer used exact nouns, stronger verbs, and colorful adjectives and adverbs to revise the sentence.

APPLY

WRITER'S CORNER

Suggest that students choose any piece of writing from their portfolios. Have them choose two or three sentences to revise. When students have finished, invite volunteers to read aloud their original and revised sentences. Discuss how exact word choices change the meaning of the sentences. Students should demonstrate the ability to revise sentences by using exact words.

TechTip You may wish to suggest a specific online thesaurus. Remind students that the biggest or most unusual word is not always the most exact word.

ASSESS

Note which students had difficulty revising sentences using exact words. Use the Reteach option with those students who need additional reinforcement.

TEACHING OPTIONS

Reteach

Help students use the four-step method described in the lesson to revise the following sentences:

The dog barked.

The cat meowed.

Write on the board several versions of the same sentences. Have students compare the sentences to the original sentence. Ask why the revised sentences are more interesting than the original.

English-Language Learners

Ask students to each say something that they ate yesterday (*pasta*). Ask them each what kind about what they ate (*linguine with clam sauce*). Then ask them to tell how it tasted (*fresh*). Then ask them to say a sentence describing the thing they ate. (*Yesterday, I ate fresh linguine with clam sauce.*)

For Tomorrow

Ask students to write two sentences that describe a family member or friend and then to revise the sentences by using exact words. Write your own two original and revised sentences to share with the class.

ACTIVITY A Read the following sentences. The first sentence is the original sentence. The second is the revised sentence. Tell what the writer did to revise each sentence.

EXAMPLE   **The third graders put on a show.**
The hardworking third graders put on a dazzling talent show.
used colorful adjectives

Activity A
1. used a stronger verb and an exact noun
2. used colorful adjectives
3. used a stronger verb
4. used stronger verbs
5. used colorful adjectives and an adverb

1. We saw many trees.
   We gazed at many redwoods.

2. Our family rode a train through a redwood forest.
   Our family rode an old, rickety train through a redwood forest.

3. Our guide said that some trees get to be 300 feet tall.
   Our guide said that some trees grow to be 300 feet tall.

4. Kenny did gymnastics, and Calvin jumped on the trampoline.
   Kenny performed gymnastics, and Calvin tumbled on the trampoline.

5. When the movie ended, everyone clapped.
   When the thrilling adventure movie ended, everyone clapped loudly.

ACTIVITY B Write an exact noun or a stronger verb in place of each underlined word. Add colorful adjectives and adverbs to make the sentences more interesting.

1. Jennifer <u>laughed</u> when she saw me water the plastic plant.
2. The <u>dog</u> rolled around in the mud.
3. The dish <u>broke</u> into pieces.
4. Mom put her necklace into a <u>box</u>.
5. The penguin <u>walked</u> toward the man.

WRITER'S CORNER

Look through a piece of your past writing. Find sentences that can be improved by using exact words. Revise those sentences.

 Tech Tip With an adult, use an online thesaurus.

Research Reports • 491

WARM-UP

Read, Listen, Speak

Read aloud your original and revised sentences from yesterday's For Tomorrow homework. Have students point out the exact words in the revised sentences and tell how they make the descriptions more vivid. Invite small groups to share their original sentences and revisions. Encourage students to suggest additional exact words that they could use in their sentences.

GRAMMAR CONNECTION

Take this opportunity to talk about compound sentences. You may wish to have students combine smaller sentences with a comma and a conjunction and then diagram the compound sentences from their Read, Listen, Speak examples.

TEACH

Have a volunteer read aloud the first paragraph of the section Combining Sentences. Ask how writing sentences of different lengths might improve the writing. *(It makes the writing less choppy.)* Explain that when trying to write sentences of different lengths, short sentences are needed just as much as long sentences are.

Have volunteers read aloud the second paragraph and the first set of example sentences. Ask why the two sentences about mules might be combined. *(Both sentences share the same subject—mules.)*

Have volunteers read aloud the next paragraph and the example sentences. Ask what two ideas are combined in the example *(two different ideas about mustangs).*

Read aloud the last paragraph and the example sentences. Tell students that *or* combines two ideas, but also shows a choice. *(The person in the sentence can ride either kind of saddle.)*

PRACTICE

ACTIVITY C

Remind students that subjects tell who or what a sentence is about and that predicates tell what the subject is or does. Have students complete this activity independently. Then have volunteers share their answers with the class.

ACTIVITY D

Complete the first item as a class. Have students first decide whether the two sentences have a subject or a predicate in common.

Remind students that they should choose the best conjunction for each combined subject or predicate. When students have finished, have volunteers share their sentences with the class.

ACTIVITY E

Have partners complete this activity. When students have finished, invite them to share their work with the class and tell why they chose to combine their sentences.

Combining Sentences

Too many short sentences together will make your writing sound choppy. That's why good writers write sentences of different lengths. One way to make sentences longer is by combining them.

You can use the word *and* to combine subjects or predicates. You can also use the word *and* to combine two short sentences that give information about the same idea. Read these examples. Notice how sentence parts can be combined.

> **Mules are dependable. They are sure-footed.**
> **Mules are dependable** *and* **sure-footed.**

And is not the only word that you can use to combine sentences. The word *but* can be used to combine two different ideas.

> **Mustangs are wild horses. Mustangs can be trained.**
> **Mustangs are wild horses,** *but* **they can be trained.**

The word *or* is used to show a choice.

> **I can ride with an English saddle. I can ride with a Western saddle too.**
> **I can ride with an English saddle** *or* **a Western saddle.**

ACTIVITY C In each item below, the first two sentences are choppy. The third sentence is a revision of those two sentences. Tell whether the writer combined subjects, predicates, or sentences in each.

1. Dale read funny poems. Christa read funny poems.
   Dale and Christa read funny poems.

2. Nancy played the piano. Ron played his drums.
   Nancy played the piano, and Ron played his drums.

3. Eve sang a song. Eve danced at the same time.
   Eve sang a song and danced at the same time.

Activity C
1. combined subjects
2. combined sentences
3. combined predicates

Activity D
1. I can ride the bus and drive my car.
2. Erin and Charlie played the violin.
3. The road was bumpy and had many turns.
4. I combed Ginger's mane and her tangled tail.
5. I could buy a new hat or new boots instead.
6. Harry returned the screwdriver and the nails.

APPLY

WRITER'S CORNER

Help students brainstorm a list of facts about carnivals and fairs. After students have combined their partner's sentences, have volunteers share their work with the class. Discuss how students combined the sentences. Students should demonstrate the ability to combine sentences.

ASSESS

Note which students had difficulty combining sentences. Use the Reteach option with those students who need additional reinforcement.

Practice Book page 170 provides additional work with revising sentences.

TEACHING OPTIONS

Reteach

Display pairs of pictures showing related but different activities, such as a person skiing and a person sledding. Write on the board one sentence for each picture. Ask volunteers to combine the two sentences for each pair of pictures into one sentence.

Conjunction Connections

Choose a book or short story the class has recently read. Discuss the characters and the plot. Invite volunteers to write on the board sentences about the book, comparing it to other books students have read. Challenge students to use the conjunctions *and, but,* and *or* to write longer, more interesting sentences.

7. Pam sees the sailboat on the water, but she cannot see Rich steering.
8. We put the party favors and the games away.
9. Jenny and Gretchen biked home.
10. Write the address and put a stamp on the envelope.

Activity E
The Fun Fair had finally begun, and everyone was excited. Kim worked at the popcorn booth, Mrs. Carter grilled hot dogs, and Linda sold raffle tickets. Mr. Palmer organized a softball game, and all the students had a chance to play. By the end of the day, we were tired, and everyone was ready to go home.

ACTIVITY D **Combine each of the following pairs of short sentences into a longer sentence.**

1. I can ride the bus. I can drive my car.
2. Erin played the violin. Charlie played the violin.
3. The road was bumpy. The road had many turns.
4. I combed Ginger's mane. I combed her tangled tail too.
5. I could buy a new hat. I could buy new boots instead.
6. Harry returned the screwdriver. He returned the nails.
7. Pam sees the sailboat on the water. She cannot see Rich steering the sailboat.
8. We put the party favors away. We put the games away.
9. Jenny biked home. Gretchen biked home.
10. Write the address on the envelope. Put a stamp on the envelope.

ACTIVITY E **Rewrite this paragraph. Combine the sentences that tell about the same idea.**

The Fun Fair had finally begun. Everyone was excited. Kim worked at the popcorn booth. Mrs. Carter grilled hot dogs. Linda sold raffle tickets. Mr. Palmer organized a softball game. All the students had a chance to play. By the end of the day, we were tired. Everyone was ready to go home.

WRITER'S CORNER

Write two sentences about a carnival or fair. Trade your sentences with a partner. Combine your partner's sentences into one longer sentence.

Research Reports • 493

For Tomorrow

Ask students to choose sentences from a favorite book that can be combined by using conjunctions. Encourage students to write at least two new sentences. Bring in your own combined sentences from a book to share with the class.

OBJECTIVE

- **To identify and use homophones**

WARM-UP

Read, Listen, Speak

Write on the board your original and revised sentences from yesterday's For Tomorrow homework. Ask students to tell what part of the sentences you combined and how. Have small groups share their sentences. Tell students to decide whether the sentences could be combined by using other conjunctions. Have students discuss how using other conjunctions changes the meaning of the sentence.

GRAMMAR CONNECTION

Take this opportunity to talk about diagrams. You may wish to have students diagram sentences from their Read, Listen, Speak examples.

TEACH

Have volunteers read aloud about homophones and the examples. After each homophone pair is read, invite volunteers to define both words. Ask a volunteer why writers should make sure that they use the right spelling when using a homophone. *(If they use the wrong spelling, the reader could be confused.)*

Remind students that they should use a dictionary if they are not sure how to spell a homophone.

PRACTICE

ACTIVITY A

Complete this activity as a class. Ask a volunteer to identify each correct homophone. Then ask another volunteer to say a sentence with the homophone that was not chosen.

ACTIVITY B

When students have finished, have them meet with a partner to check each other's work. Encourage students to use a dictionary if needed.

ACTIVITY C

When students have finished choosing the correct homophones, ask volunteers to read their sentences aloud. Tell students to say and spell the homophones when they reach them in the sentences.

Homophones

Homophones are words that sound alike but are spelled differently and have different meanings.

Here are some pairs of homophones:

deer/dear	meet/meat	ate/eight
be/bee	our/hour	here/hear
threw/through	write/right	your/you're
night/knight	plane/plain	son/sun

When you use homophones, make sure that you use the correct spellings.

Often you will know which spelling to use because you have seen the words before in your reading. If you aren't sure which spelling is correct, look up the words in a dictionary.

ACTIVITY A **Tell which word is correct in each sentence.**

1. The baby (<u>deer</u> dear) ran across the road.
2. Lions eat (meet <u>meat</u>).
3. Spiders have (ate <u>eight</u>) legs.
4. The (be <u>bee</u>) flew from flower to flower.
5. (<u>Our</u> Hour) class went on a field trip.
6. The coach (<u>threw</u> through) the ball to the player.
7. Turn (write <u>right</u>) when you get to the corner.
8. I (here <u>hear</u>) music playing from that house.
9. The woman's (<u>son</u> sun) bought her a new car.
10. We will board the (plain <u>plane</u>) in a few minutes.

APPLY

WRITER'S CORNER

Tell students to write their sentences before looking in a dictionary. Challenge students to write a fourth sentence that uses two or three of the homophones. Invite volunteers to share their sentences with the class. Students should demonstrate the ability to identify and use homophones.

ASSESS

Note which students had difficulty identifying and using homophones. Use the Reteach option with those students who need additional reinforcement.

ACTIVITY B Use a homophone in parentheses in place of the underlined word or words.

1. Jenna <u>pitched</u> the ball over the fence. (<u>threw</u> through)
2. The sun felt warm on my <u>uncovered</u> feet. (bear <u>bare</u>)
3. Let's <u>print</u> a report about eagles. (<u>write</u> right)
4. <u>You are</u> coming with me. (Your <u>You're</u>)
5. I am my parents' first <u>male child</u>. (<u>son</u> sun)
6. Owls don't hunt until <u>after sunset</u>. (<u>night</u> knight)
7. The startled bird <u>fluttered</u> away. (flu <u>flew</u>)
8. The burned toast had a <u>bad</u> smell. (<u>foul</u> fowl)
9. A <u>rabbit</u> hopped in the garden. (hair <u>hare</u>)
10. I had to <u>stop</u> and <u>watch</u>. (<u>pause</u> paws) (stair <u>stare</u>)

ACTIVITY C Choose the correct words from the word box to complete each sentence.

| here | hour | ate | meat | knight | right | you're |
| hear | our | eight | meet | night | write | your |

1. Ed can __write__ with his left hand or his __right__ hand.
2. I can __hear__ you whispering way over __here__.
3. __You're__ wearing __your__ new shoes today.
4. They __ate__ breakfast today at __eight__ o'clock.
5. We have one __hour__ before __our__ train leaves.
6. You can __meet__ the butcher when we buy our __meat__.
7. The __knight__ put on his armor and rode off into the __night__.

WRITER'S CORNER

Use a dictionary to look up the following homophones: *to, too,* and *two.* Use each word in a sentence that shows what it means.

Research Reports • 495

WARM-UP

Read, Listen, Speak

Read aloud the paragraph you wrote for yesterday's For Tomorrow homework. Ask students to raise their hands when they hear a homophone. Invite small groups to share their paragraphs. Have students identify the homophones in the paragraphs. Ask students to decide whether the homophones were used correctly.

GRAMMAR CONNECTION

Take this opportunity to talk about diagramming. You may wish to have students diagram sentences in their Read, Listen, Speak examples.

TEACH

Ask a volunteer to explain what homophones are *(words that sound alike but are spelled differently and have different meanings)*. Write on the board one word of a homophone pair. Ask a volunteer to write the other word that completes the pair.

PRACTICE

ACTIVITY D

Have students complete this activity independently. When they have finished, read aloud each sentence. At each blank have volunteers say and spell the correct homophone.

ACTIVITY E

Ask partners to complete this activity. Tell students that both words of each pair will be used. Suggest that students try to complete the activity without using a dictionary. Then tell students to use a dictionary to check their work.

ACTIVITY F

Have students complete this activity independently. When students have finished, ask them to choose two homophone pairs from the list and to write a sentence for each homophone. Invite volunteers to share their sentences with the class.

ACTIVITY G

Have partners complete this activity. Suggest that partners take turns reading aloud each sentence and identifying the incorrect homophone. Tell students to spell the correct homophone. Invite volunteers to share their answers with the class.

LiNK Ask a volunteer to read aloud the excerpt. Have students identify the topic *(foghorns in lighthouses)* and the facts about the topic.

ACTIVITY D Complete each sentence with the correct homophone from the word box.

steal	cent	hare	doe	creak
steel	scent	hair	dough	creek

1. The bridge we crossed was made of ___steel___.
2. In the fable the tortoise beats the ___hare___.
3. A ___doe___ is a female deer.
4. The stairs in the old house began to ___creak___.
5. A skunk's ___scent___ is easy to recognize.
6. Pizza crust is made out of ___dough___.
7. A penny is worth one ___cent___.
8. The raccoon will ___steal___ the apple from the picnic table.
9. Marcy can get her ___hair___ cut and styled tomorrow.
10. We put our feet in the cool ___creek___.

ACTIVITY E Complete each pair of sentences with the correct homophones. Use a dictionary if you need help.

1. (bough/bow)
   a. That tree has a strong ___bough___.
   b. The ship's ___bow___ cuts into the water.
2. (fur/fir)
   a. The campers slept under a ___fir___ tree.
   b. A thick coat of ___fur___ keeps a bear warm.
3. (yoke/yolk)
   a. The oxen were held by the ___yoke___ of the plow.
   b. Mix the egg ___yolk___ with the milk.

APPLY

WRITER'S CORNER

Tell students to use at least three homophone pairs in their poems. Suggest that students select the homophones they will use before they begin writing their poems. Tell students that the poem does not need to rhyme. Allow time for students to finish and then ask volunteers to read aloud their poems. Have students make a copy of their poems and save them for the For Tomorrow activity. Students should demonstrate the ability to use homophones.

Grammar in Action Help students find the homophones in the excerpt (*sites, its, air, two, high, be, heard, to*).

ASSESS

Note which students had difficulty using homophones. Use the Reteach option with those students who need additional reinforcement.

Practice Book page 171 provides additional work with homophones.

ACTIVITY F Match each homophone in Column A with its definition in Column B. Use a dictionary if you need help.

Column A		Column B
1. wait	e	**a.** listened to
2. weight	d	**b.** shelters made from cloth
3. tense	h	**c.** paddle
4. tents	b	**d.** heaviness
5. oar	c	**e.** stay
6. ore	g	**f.** group of animals
7. heard	a	**g.** rocks dug from the ground
8. herd	f	**h.** nervous
9. weak	j	**i.** seven days
10. week	i	**j.** not strong

Activity G
sent
deer
mail
write
plane
wait

ACTIVITY G The paragraph below includes several incorrect homophones. Rewrite the paragraph, using the correct homophones.

Today I <u>cent</u> a package to my grandma. It was a little statue of a baby <u>dear</u> and its mother. I walked to the post office to <u>male</u> it. The postal worker said that I should <u>right</u> my address on the package. She said the package would be put on a <u>plain</u> that evening and flown to Reno, where Grandma lives. I can't <u>weight</u> until she sees it!

LiNK

Beacons of Light

Today, at many lighthouse sites, foghorns give off warnings. Each foghorn has its own special sound and number of blasts. The *diaphone*, one of the best foghorns, uses compressed air to give off two tones, a high-pitched screech and a low grunt. The high sound can be heard for seven miles. The low tone travels farther. Lighthouses also use radio beacons to send warning signals.

Gail Gibbons

WRITER'S CORNER

Work with a partner to write a short poem using homophones. Use any of the homophones in this lesson. Use any other homophones that you can think of.

Grammar in Action Find the homophones in the excerpt on this page.

Research Reports • 497

TEACHING OPTIONS

Reteach

Read aloud some sentences from the lesson's activities. Have students act out what is happening in the sentences. Ask students how they knew the correct meaning of the homophone without seeing it written. Then ask students to write the homophone on the board. Explain that the context of a sentence can help determine which homophone is being used.

Homophone Challenge

Have students keep a list of homophones for the next week. Tell students to write homophone pairs they hear or read. When the week is up, the student with the most homophones wins.

For Tomorrow

Have students take home the poem they wrote in the Writer's Corner and replace one word with its homophone. Then tell students to change the poem so it makes sense with the new word added. Write your own poem and rewrite it, using homophones, to share with students.

OBJECTIVES

- **To identify the characteristics of an oral biography**
- **To understand how to use visual aids and audio aids in an oral biography**

WARM-UP

Read, Listen, Speak

Read aloud your original and rewritten poem from yesterday's For Tomorrow homework. Tell students how you changed the poem by using different homophones. Have small groups share their poems. Ask students to tell how they changed the poem by using a different homophone.

GRAMMAR CONNECTION

Take this opportunity to review diagramming. You may wish to have students point out different kinds of sentences to diagram in their Read, Listen, Speak examples.

TEACH

Read aloud the first two paragraphs. Ask students to name biographies they have read or seen. Explain that learning about the lives of others can help us see how a person can change the world.

Invite volunteers to read aloud the section Research. Have students brainstorm personality traits or achievements that might make someone an interesting subject for an oral biography *(someone who has done something significant or heroic)*. Point out that students should check their facts against other sources to make sure that the facts are true.

Have volunteers read aloud the section Prepare. Explain that note cards should contain dates, names, and important facts to use in students' oral biographies.

Invite volunteers to read aloud the section Visual Aids and Audio Aids. Ask students to list on the board visual aids and audio aids that could be used in an oral biography.

PRACTICE

ACTIVITY A

Help students brainstorm a list of possible subjects for an oral biography. Then have partners talk about the subjects they find interesting. After students have chosen a subject, ask partners to list a few things they want to know about their subject.

ACTIVITY B

Allow students time to complete this activity in the library. When students have finished, invite volunteers to share their facts with the class.

ACTIVITY C

Help students brainstorm a list of visual aids and audio aids. Help students find Web sites for royalty-free audio files and images.

Oral Biographies

An oral biography is a researched talk about the life of a famous person. The talk can be about almost anyone, but it should be about someone that you can research. For example, you can give a report about Abraham Lincoln or Martin Luther King Jr.

Keep these things in mind as you prepare your oral biography.

Research

After you have chosen a person for your oral biography, you should start researching that person's life. You will need to use your school or local library to find sources, just as you do for a written research report.

Use your own words to tell about your subject, or the person you are talking about. Using your own words shows that you understand the sources you used in your research.

Prepare

To prepare your report, gather information about your subject's life. Write your notes on note cards.

The next step is to organize your notes. One way to organize them is to put them into separate piles. One pile might be about the early years of the subject's life. A second pile might cover the middle years, and a third pile might be about the later years. A fourth pile might be about what we should remember about this person. Use your piles to plan the introduction, body, and conclusion of your biography.

"I have a dream . . ."

Dr. Martin Luther King Jr.

APPLY

SPEAKER'S CORNER

Allow time for partners to complete this activity. Encourage students to offer suggestions and feedback about what they might like to know about each topic. Students should be able to identify interesting facts about subjects for oral biographies.

ASSESS

Note which students had difficulty identifying subjects for oral biographies. Use the Reteach option with those students who need additional reinforcement.

TEACHING OPTIONS

Reteach

Work with students to list categories of famous people for subjects of oral biographies (*political figures, athletes, artists, authors, scientists, military leaders*). Then ask students to name people for each category. Ask where students might find information about these people.

The Value of Visuals

Have students gather or make visual aids to use in their oral biography presentations. Encourage students to look on the Internet or in the school library for photos and videos of their famous person. Ask students to think about props they might use to make their presentations more interesting. For example, if a student is doing a biography about Christopher Columbus, he or she might want to display a boat similar to one that Columbus sailed on. Encourage students to do research if they want to dress up as the subject of their oral biography. Remind students to prepare their visual aids and practice using them before their final presentations.

Visual Aids and Audio Aids

If possible, use visual aids, such as pictures and photos, to make your report livelier. Your audience will want to know what the person you're talking about looks like.

You can also play audio recordings or videos to help your audience get to know your subject. For example, if you are giving a report on President John F. Kennedy, you might want to play an audio recording of one of his speeches.

President John F. Kennedy

ACTIVITY A Choose a subject for your oral biography. If you need help thinking of ideas, look in your social studies book for famous people.

ACTIVITY B Look in the library for information about the subject for your oral biography. Write on a separate note card each fact that you learn. When you have finished, organize your note cards into piles. Think of an interesting introduction and a memorable conclusion for your report.

ACTIVITY C Think about visual aids that will help your audience understand your subject better. Make a list of pictures, videos, and audio recordings you want to include in your oral biography. Check with an adult to see if you need permission to use these visual aids and audio aids.

SPEAKER'S CORNER

Tell a partner at least five facts that you learned about the subject of your oral biography. Talk about which facts seem most interesting. Decide what other facts about the subject might be interesting to know.

For Tomorrow

Have students choose a foreign country and find one fact about a national hero from that country. Find your own fact about a hero to share with the class.

Research Reports • 499

WARM-UP

Read, Listen, Speak

Read aloud the fact you found for yesterday's For Tomorrow homework. Tell students why you chose that specific country and how your research on the country helped you find the hero. Encourage small groups to present their facts. Ask students how they might use the facts in an oral biography about their subject.

TEACH

Review what students know about preparing oral biographies. Then invite volunteers to read aloud the section Practice. Explain that the more students practice, the more comfortable they will be when they present their oral biographies. Tell students that practicing in front of family members is similar to having their writing edited by someone else. Explain that family members can offer feedback about the presentation and suggest ways in which students might improve.

Ask volunteers to read aloud the section Speaking Tips. Discuss each tip and clarify any questions students may have. Point out that speakers should speak slowly, make eye contact, and use body language.

Read aloud the first paragraph of the section Listening Tips. Tell students that because it is difficult for some people to give oral presentations, it is important that listeners be quiet and respectful. Then have volunteers read aloud the bulleted list. Encourage students to practice these tips as they listen to oral biographies.

PRACTICE

ACTIVITY D

Have partners help each other make an audio or a video recording of their oral biography. Then allow time for partners to study their presentations and help each other find ways in which they might improve their presentations. Suggest that students use the speaking tips as a checklist as they review their presentations. Have students practice their presentations again, incorporating their latest changes.

Practice

When you have written your note cards, practice giving your talk. Look at your notes to remind you what to say. Look up at the audience. Make your voice sound lively. Sound interested in your subject.

Find an audience to listen to your talk. Family members make good listeners. You can also take turns listening and speaking to classmates.

Speaking Tips

Here are some tips to make your oral biography go smoothly.

- Give your speech in front of a mirror before you give it to an audience. Know your information well enough to avoid pausing and using fillers such as "uh" and "um." Being familiar with your presentation will build your confidence.
- Make sure that everyone can hear you. Always talk loudly enough and clearly enough so that people who are sitting in the back can understand what you are saying.
- Speaking in front of others can be a little scary. Pick out two or three friendly faces around the room and pretend that you are speaking only to them.

APPLY

SPEAKER'S CORNER

Allow time for the presentations and for any questions that students may have. You may wish to make anonymous comment cards for students to offer feedback about each presentation. Include items such as these on the comment cards:

- Which part did you like best?
- Which part could be better?
- Did the person speak loudly enough?

Students should demonstrate the ability to present an oral biography.

ASSESS

Note which students had difficulty presenting an oral biography. Use the Reteach option with those students who need additional reinforcement.

After you have reviewed Lessons 3–5, administer the Writing Skills Assessment on pages 67–68 in the **Assessment Book.** This test is also available on the optional **Test Generator CD.**

TEACHING OPTIONS

Reteach

Ask students to put together a short summary about a person from a recent news story. Encourage students to choose people who have made positive changes in the world or who have done something heroic. Direct students to name the person, to tell what the person accomplished, and to include at least one visual aid. Remind students to speak clearly, to make eye contact with their audience, and to vary their tone of voice. Suggest that students practice at home to prepare for their classroom presentations.

Listen Up

Have students write the following information about themselves: birth date, place of birth, favorite color, favorite food, favorite after-school activity. Tell students to share the information with a partner. Encourage partners to practice good listening skills and to take notes. Then have students present the information back to their partners.

- Move your hands to make a point if you need to. Use a lively voice to keep your listeners interested.

Remember that giving an oral biography is like any other skill. The more you do it, the easier it gets.

Listening Tips

Show the speaker the same courtesy that you want when you give your oral biography.

- Be quiet while others are giving their talks. If you speak, you will disturb the speaker and the other people in the audience.
- Pay attention to the speaker.
- Listen to the talk for interesting parts of the biography. Listen for something in the talk that makes you want to know more about that person.
- Take notes while you listen to the speaker. Use these notes to ask questions about the subject when the speaker is finished giving the talk.
- Save your questions until the end of the talk. Raise your hand to ask your questions.

ACTIVITY D **Use a recorder or video camera to record yourself presenting your oral biography. Listen to or watch your presentation. Look for places where you think you can improve your oral biography.**

SPEAKER'S CORNER

Present your oral biography to your class. Use your visual aids or audio aids and your notes.

Research Reports • 501

Research Reports

PREWRITING AND DRAFTING

Read aloud the opening paragraph. Explain that writing a research report will bring together many of the things that students have discussed about writing during the year. Review what students know about research reports *(using formal language, stating the topic sentence in the introduction, giving details in the body, summing up information in the conclusion, using sources to research a topic, making notes on note cards, combining sentences).*

Prewriting

Invite volunteers to read aloud the first two paragraphs. Remind students that prewriting is a time to choose a topic, think of ideas, research facts, and organize their notes.

Choosing a Topic

Have volunteers read aloud this section. Tell students that Adil chose something from his life that he was curious about. Encourage students to think about things in their own lives that they may be curious about.

Tell students that their ideas are the main message and all the supporting details. Remind students to choose details that are interesting and informative. Explain that Adil would not include the detail that there are many elephants in zoos because his audience would already know that.

Your Turn

Read this section aloud. As students brainstorm their lists, remind them that a topic for a research report should also be something that interests the audience. Invite small groups to discuss their lists. Suggest that students take a vote in their group about the topics on their lists and choose a topic that is interesting both to themselves and to their classmates.

Researching

Have volunteers read this section aloud. Explain that because Adil already knew that he needed facts about Asian elephants, he was able to focus his research. Point out that Adil used the most recent sources that he found and that he was careful to use reliable Web sites. Discuss why Adil chose his sources carefully. *(Recent sources are more up-to-date. A zoo Web site is less likely to have mistakes.)*

Your Turn

Explain that asking questions about a topic is a good way of beginning to research, because finding the answers will give students information for their research reports. Brainstorm with students questions that they might ask themselves as they do their research. *(What do I know*

Writer's Workshop
Research Reports

Prewriting and Drafting

When you are interested in a topic, do you try to learn more about it? Writing a research report is a way to learn more about something you are interested in. It is also a way to share what you have learned with others.

Prewriting

Adil is a third grader. His class decided to make an encyclopedia. The encyclopedia would be made up of research reports.

Adil needed a topic to research before he could write a report. He would take time to choose a topic, research it, and organize the facts and ideas he found.

Choosing a Topic

Adil wanted to choose a topic he was interested in. He didn't want to get bored while he was researching his topic.

Adil was born in India. He and his parents moved to the United States when he was a baby. There were many pictures and statues of elephants in his home. He was curious about the animals, so he decided to research them. Adil did know one fact already. He knew that the elephants in the pictures were Asian elephants.

Ideas

Your Turn

- Think of topics that interest you. You might research an animal, a famous person, a special place, or an important event.
- Think of topics that you already know something about. Write a list of topics that interest you or that you know something about.
- Choose the topic that seems most interesting to you.

Researching

Adil went to the local library after school. He found in an encyclopedia information about Asian elephants. He also found books and Web sites about Asian elephants.

With the books and Web sites, Adil had many sources. He decided to look at the information that was most recent. He made sure the Web sites he used were from reliable sources. He used only Web sites from zoos.

about the topic? What do I want to know about the topic?) Then allow students time in the library to find sources. Help students who are conducting Internet research to choose appropriate Web sites.

Using Note Cards
Ask volunteers to read aloud the first two paragraphs and Adil's note card. Point out that Adil wrote facts in his own words.

Invite a volunteer to read aloud the last paragraph. Ask students why sorting the note cards into piles is a good way for Adil to organize his notes. *(Similar facts and ideas will be grouped together.)*

Tell students that their research report will likely follow the organization they make with their note card groupings.

Your Turn
Read aloud this section. Ask students why they should write only one fact on each note card *(so that they can easily organize their notes)*. Allow time for students to look through their sources for facts for their research reports. Help students who are having difficulty to write and organize their note cards.

TEACHING OPTIONS

More Topics
If students are having difficulty brainstorming a topic, suggest the following possibilities:

- a famous town or state landmark
- an important event in state or national history
- a family celebration or tradition
- an invention
- a historical figure

Charting Ideas
Students may benefit from using a KWL chart to help them write research reports. Write on the board a three-column chart with the column headings *What I Know, What I Want to Know,* and *What I Learned.* After students have selected a topic, encourage them to copy the chart and to write in the first column what they know about the topic. Then have students write in the second column questions that they have about the topic. Tell students to use the questions to guide their research and then to write in the third column the answers to their questions.

Your Turn
- Find sources that give information about your topic.
- Check in an encyclopedia for information about your topic. Don't rely on only one book or article. Instead, look in many different books and articles.
- Use the index and contents page of a book to search for information you need.
- You can also check Web sites for information. Ask your teacher or the librarian if the Web site has reliable information.

Using Note Cards
Adil began to find facts from his sources. After he found a fact he thought might be interesting, he wrote it on a note card. Adil wrote the facts in his own words. Then he made sure to write at the bottom of each card the name of the source and the author.

Here is a note card that Adil wrote about the eating habits of Asian elephants.

Adil had written many note cards. He decided to organize them into separate piles.

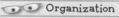 **Organization** Some were about how the elephants live or what they eat. Others were about why the elephants are endangered. He had note cards with other ideas too.

Your Turn
- Begin taking notes from your sources. Write on note cards facts you find interesting. Put only one fact on each note card.
- Remember to include at the bottom of the card the title of the source, the author, and the page number.
- Place the note cards in piles with other note cards about the same ideas.
- Put aside any note cards that don't fit with any of the other cards.

Prewriting | Drafting | Content Editing | Revising | Copyediting | Proofreading | Publishing

eats 330 to 350 pounds of food each day

Large Animals by Maxine Orwell, p.55

Research Reports • 503

Writer's Workshop   Research Reports

Drafting

Invite volunteers to read aloud the opening paragraph and Adil's draft. When students have finished, ask them to identify each of the following in Adil's research report: introduction, body, conclusion, and researched facts. Ask students to explain how Adil uses his research to support his topic.

Ask students what they think is effective about Adil's research report. Encourage volunteers to suggest ways in which Adil might improve his draft.

Your Turn

Have volunteers read aloud this section. Then allow time for students to write their drafts. As students work, explain that by rewriting facts in their own words, students show that they understand the topic. Help students who are having difficulty to rewrite facts in their own words.

Drafting

Now it was time for Adil to write his draft. He used the note cards he wrote during prewriting to help him. First, he wrote a title. Then he wrote an introduction that gives some general information about the Asian elephant. Next, he wrote the body. In the body Adil included information that he learned from his research. Adil finished his report with a conclusion.

The Asian Elephant

The Asian elephant lives in India, Srilanka, and Sumatra. Asian elephants are amazing creatures. They are intelligent. They are strong. But they are also endangered. This means that there are not many Asian elephants left. They need to be protected so that we all can enjoy them.

Asian elephants are endangered. The mane reason is that they are losing their forest home. People need more land. They cut down the forests that the elephants live in. There is another problem. Elephants are getting in trouble with people because elephants eat peoples crops. But some people are working to protect the Asian elephant. Large areas of forest are being saved. These are places for the elephants to live without fences or cages.

Asian elephants are large animals. They need to eat a lot of food. They will wash it all down with up to 30 gallons of water. In one day an Asian elephant will eat up to 350 pounds of food. How does all of that food and water get into the elephant. It uses its trunk. The trunk has a "finger" it uses like a hook. Not only are elephants

Encourage students to refer back to Lessons 1 and 2 to review the characteristics of research reports. Emphasize the importance of organizing their report by grouping similar ideas together. Work with students who need help writing clear topic sentences in their introductions.

 Remind students that even though a research report includes facts from other sources, the writer's voice should still come

through. Tell students that writing the facts in their own words will allow their personality to shine.

Writer's Tip Encourage students to communicate what first made them interested in their topic.

TEACHING OPTIONS

Which Facts Are Facts?

Tell students that when they research a topic on the Internet, they should double-check their information. Explain that because anyone can put information on the Internet, sometimes what one person believes to be true is presented as fact. Explain that students should confirm their facts on another site. Recommend that students use Web sites with domain names that end in .edu, .org, and .gov and to be careful when using public sites that end in .com.

interesting, but they are also smart. They can dig for food by using their tusks. They can talk to one another using their own language.

The Asian elephant is a special animal. It is smart and strong and can do amazing things. There are good ideas for how to protect it. But Asian elephants also need people to come up with new ideas to help them. I like Asian elephants.

Prewriting

Drafting

Content Editing

Revising

Copyediting

Proofreading

Publishing

Your Turn

- Write the first draft of your research report. First, write a title. Next, write your introduction. In your introduction tell your reader the topic of the research report. Give some general information about your topic.
- Write the body of the research report. This is where you present the information you found. Be **Voice** sure to use your own words and write with a confident voice. Group similar ideas together in the body.
- For the conclusion, sum up the information in the report. Also write a comment about your topic.
- When you write your research report, leave extra space between the lines. That way you will have room to make changes later.

Writer's Tip Catch the reader's attention with an interesting fact or question about the topic.

Research Reports • 505

OBJECTIVE
- **To edit a first draft for content**

CONTENT EDITING

Ask volunteers to explain what it means to content edit a draft *(to edit ideas to make sure they are clear)*. Explain that when students content edit a research report, they should pay attention to how well the facts support the topic of the report.

Invite volunteers to read aloud the first two paragraphs and the Content Editor's Checklist. Discuss the items on the checklist and clarify any misconceptions.

Have volunteers read aloud the third paragraph. Ask students to explain why Adil asked Henry to content edit his draft. *(Henry might catch mistakes that Adil missed. Henry can see if Adil's research supports his topic.)*

Have students read aloud Henry's suggestions. Ask students to identify ways in which Henry used helpful and positive language.

Then use Henry's suggestions to have students answer the following questions about Adil's draft:

- What did Henry like about Adil's draft?
- Do you agree with Henry's comment about the elephants' tusks? Explain why or why not.
- How might Adil improve his introduction?
- Do you agree with Henry's comment that it would be good to know more facts?
- How might Adil improve his conclusion?

Editor's Workshop

Research Reports

Content Editing

Now that Adil had finished his first draft, he wanted to make it better. He hoped to improve his research report by content editing.

Content Editor's Checklist

- [ ] Does the writing stay on the topic?
- [ ] Does the introduction state the topic and catch the reader's attention?
- [ ] Is the information in the body organized?
- [ ] Are there supporting facts?
- [ ] Does the conclusion sum up the topic and end with a comment?

Adil asked his classmate Henry to content edit his research report. Henry would check whether Adil's ideas made sense. Henry used the Content Editor's Checklist.

Henry read Adil's research report. He told Adil that he enjoyed learning about the Asian elephant. He said that he really liked learning about the "finger" on the end of the trunk. He had never heard of that before. Then Henry made these suggestions.

- The facts in the third paragraph are interesting, but the information about the elephants' tusks and how elephants talk doesn't fit with the rest of the ideas. The rest of the paragraph is about what they eat and how they use their trunk.
- Your report needs a more interesting introduction. Maybe you can add a fact or a question.

Ask a volunteer to read aloud the last paragraph. Have students name other ways that Adil might improve his draft.

Your Turn

Have students check their own drafts, using the Content Editor's Checklist. Then ask volunteers to read aloud this section. Have students trade drafts with partners and check the drafts against the Content Editor's Checklist. Remind editors to begin with positive comments and to

suggest specific ways for writers to improve their drafts. When students have finished, allow time for editors to explain their comments. Tell students that their editors are offering suggestions to improve their research reports, but that the final decision on what to change will be their own.

Teacher Conferences

Some students may benefit from a content-editing session with you. Take time to content edit the drafts of those students who need extra help. When you meet, help them determine ways to clarify the content of their drafts. Students may also benefit from additional research suggestions.

Looking Back

After students read one another's drafts for content, have editors reread the introduction and conclusion to be sure that they support the content of the body. Tell students that the introduction and conclusion do not need to mention everything covered in the body, but that they should provide a guide to what the report is about.

- It would be better to read about the elephants before reading about the problems that the elephants are having.
- It would be good to know more facts. How tall and how heavy are these elephants?
- The conclusion sums up the topic, but it doesn't include a comment on the topic. The last sentence is just your opinion.

Adil thanked Henry for his help. Adil liked what Henry said, but he didn't know if he agreed with everything. Adil needed to think about each idea before deciding to use it.

Your Turn

- Work with a partner and read each other's research reports. Pay attention to only one question on the checklist at a time. When you have finished, take turns talking about each other's drafts.
- Think about each of your partner's ideas. Make only the changes that seem right to you. You did the research, so you know the information best.

Prewriting / Drafting / Content Editing / Revising / Copyediting / Proofreading / Publishing

Research Reports • 507

OBJECTIVE
- **To revise a research report**

REVISING

Ask a volunteer to explain the purpose of revising *(to improve the writing and to make it clear)*. Discuss how the skills students learned in this chapter, such as using the library and the Internet to conduct research, have helped their writing. Tell students that writing is a process of many revisions and that they may revise several times before they are finished.

Ask students to look at Adil's revised draft. Point out how he marked his draft to add and to take out sentences and parts of sentences based on the comments he received from Henry. Read aloud the opening paragraph. Then have students look over Adil's revised draft.

Ask volunteers to read aloud the bulleted questions and locate the corrections in the draft.

- The two sentences give more information about the elephants.
- He wrote a question to grab the reader's attention.

- Adil switched the order of the two body paragraphs. He agreed that it would be better to learn general facts first.
- He added information on how tall and heavy an Asian elephant could get.
- "We must care for them before they are gone forever."

Discuss how each correction improves the draft. Then read aloud the last paragraph.

Writer's Workshop
Research Reports

Revising

This is how Adil decided to revise his research report.

The Asian Elephant

Did you know that elephants live in other places besides Africa?

^The Asian elephant lives in India, Srilanka, and Sumatra. Asian elephants are amazing creatures. They are intelligent. They are strong. But they are also endangered. This means that there are not many Asian elephants left. They need to be protected so that we all can enjoy them.

Asian elephants are endangered. The mane reason is that they are losing their forest home. People need more land. They cut down the forests that the elephants live in. There is another problem. Elephants are getting in trouble with people because elephants eat peoples crops. But some people are working to protect the Asian elephant. Large areas of forest are being saved. These are places for the elephants to live without fences or cages.

Some are as tall as 10 feet. Some are as heavy as 11,000 pounds.

Asian elephants are large animals. ^They need to eat a lot of food. They will wash it all down with up to 30 gallons of water. In one day an Asian elephant will eat up to 350 pounds of food. How does all of that food and water get into the elephant. It uses its trunk. The trunk has a "finger" it uses like a hook. Not only are elephants

508 • Chapter 8

Your Turn

Have a volunteer read aloud this section. Point out that if students rewrite large parts of their drafts, they should check the new writing against the Content Editor's Checklist carefully because the rewritten parts may present new information and ideas.

Explain that the skills students have learned in this chapter will help them write a strong research report. Then allow time for students to revise their drafts. Tell students to use a different pencil color to mark changes in their drafts.

Do Not Use *Don't*

Explain that it is important to use formal language in research reports because the audience will be more likely to take the writing seriously. Tell students that some ways to make their writing more formal include avoiding contractions and using exact words. Write these sentences on the board and have students make them more formal.

The cider mill has interesting things.

(More formal: The cider mill has interesting machines.)

The horses didn't always live on the island.

(More formal: The horses did not always live on the island.)

Lots of folks helped out during the Revolutionary War.

(More formal: Many people helped out during the Revolutionary War.)

---

interesting, but they are also smart. They can dig for food by using their tusks. They can talk to one another using their own language.

The Asian elephant is a special animal. It is smart and strong and can do amazing things. There are good ideas for how to protect it. But Asian elephants also need people to come up with new ideas to help them. ~~I like Asian elephants.~~

We must care for them before they are gone forever.

Here are some things that Adil did to improve his research report.

- Adil left in the two sentences about tusks and language. Why do you think he did this?
- He wrote a new sentence in the introduction. What kind of sentence did he write? Does it grab your attention? Why or why not?
- What did Adil do to the order of the two body paragraphs? Why?
- What new information did Adil add to the body? Do you think it's a good change? Why or why not?
- Adil wrote a new sentence in the conclusion. What did the sentence say?

Adil felt that he had learned a lot about the Asian elephant. He thought that other people would be interested in his topic too.

Your Turn

- Use your ideas and your content editor's ideas to revise your draft.
- Use the Content Editor's Checklist to check your draft again.

Prewriting · Drafting · Content Editing · Revising · Copyediting · Proofreading · Publishing

Editor's Workshop
Research Reports

OBJECTIVE
- **To copyedit and proofread a research report**

COPYEDITING AND PROOFREADING

Copyediting

Invite a volunteer to read aloud the first paragraph. Ask why Adil wants to copyedit his draft. *(In copyediting, Adil will check whether his sentences and words make sense.)* Then have volunteers read aloud the Copyeditor's Checklist. Ask if anything on the checklist looks unfamiliar or confusing and guide students to understand the meaning of those items.

Have a volunteer read aloud the first paragraph after the checklist. Ask how Adil combined the sentences in the new second paragraph *(by adding the conjunction* and*)*.

Read aloud the last paragraph. Ask students whether they agree with the correction and to explain why.

Remind students to choose the most precise and descriptive words they can. Tell students that they should define any unfamiliar words for their readers.

Remind students that sentence fluency is the way writing sounds to the ear, or the flow of writing. Explain that fluent writing uses different sentence lengths and styles.

Grammar in Action *(Mane should be spelled* main.*)* Ask students how Adil might have checked to make sure he used the correct word. *(He might have looked the word up in a dictionary.)*

Your Turn
Ask a volunteer to read aloud this section. Then allow time for students to use the Copyeditor's Checklist to improve their drafts. Emphasize that students should think about their word choice and carefully check the homophones in their drafts.

Proofreading
Have volunteers read aloud the first paragraph and the Proofreader's Checklist. Discuss why it is important to proofread any piece of writing before publishing it *(to make sure that there are no spelling, capitalization, or punctuation mistakes that might distract the audience from the topic).* Ask why Adil might have felt it would be a good idea to have Aunt Kamala proofread his draft. *(Aunt Kamala had not read Adil's research report before, so she might spot mistakes that Adil had missed.)*

Invite a volunteer to read aloud the first paragraph after the

---

Copyediting and Proofreading

Copyediting

Adil knew that his revisions had made his draft stronger. Now he needed to copyedit his research report. He wanted to check whether

Word Choice all the sentences and words were clear and correct. Adil used this checklist to copyedit his research report.

Copyeditor's Checklist
- ☐ Are all the sentences complete sentences?
- ☐ Do the sentences make sense?
- ☐ Do the sentences make sense one after the other?
- ☐ If sentences were combined, was it done correctly?
- ☐ Are all the words used correctly?

Adil decided to combine two sentences in the first paragraph to make the writing flow better. He wrote a new sentence, *They are intelligent and strong.* He also combined the sentences about how tall and heavy the elephants are. Can you explain how?

Adil found a sentence about what the elephants eat that he thought was out of

Sentence Fluency order. It made sense first to talk about how much food elephants ate and then to say that they drank a lot of water. Adil moved the two sentences about food next to each other.

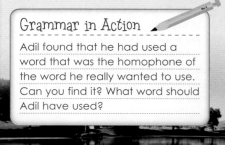

Grammar in Action

Adil found that he had used a word that was the homophone of the word he really wanted to use. Can you find it? What word should Adil have used?

checklist. Ask students to identify in the draft where Adil misspelled *Sri Lanka*.

Read aloud the next paragraph. Invite a volunteer to find the mistake in Adil's draft. *(The third sentence should end with a question mark.)*

Read aloud the last paragraph. Discuss why *peoples* is incorrect. *(Adil meant to write people's, the word that means "belonging to the people.")*

 Remind students that conventions of writing include spelling, punctuation, and grammar. Tell students that these conventions are as important as content in effective writing.

Your Turn

Read aloud this section. Point out that it is important to proofread a draft for one mistake at a time. Allow time for students to proofread their research reports, using the Proofreader's Checklist. When students have finished, allow time for them to trade drafts with a partner and to proofread each other's work. Have students discuss any mistakes they find during proofreading.

Writer's Tip Remind students that the final decision about each suggested edit is theirs.

TEACHING OPTIONS

A Proofreader's Proofreader

Before students incorporate their proofreader's changes, suggest that students have a second proofreader check their draft. Have the second proofreader check over the work of the first proofreader. *(If the first proofreader found a spelling mistake, have the second proofreader check that the first proofreader spelled the word correctly.)* If students have conflicting marks, guide them to choose the correct change.

Your Turn

- Copyedit your research report, using the Copyeditor's Checklist.
- Look for only one kind of mistake at a time.
- Pay special attention to words that are homophones.
- Try to make your sentences different lengths by combining them. Be sure your sentences still make sense.

Proofreading

Adil wanted someone to proofread his research report before he wrote a final draft. Adil decided to ask his Aunt Kamala. Here is the checklist that Aunt Kamala used.

Proofreader's Checklist

- [ ] Are all the paragraphs indented?
- [ ] Are all the words spelled correctly?
- [ ] Are all the proper nouns capitalized?
- [ ] Does each sentence end with the correct punctuation mark?
- [ ] Have you checked to be sure that no new mistakes were made while editing?

Aunt Kamala proofread Adil's research report. She found that the name of the country  **Conventions** Sri Lanka was spelled wrong. She told Adil that he needed to put a space between *Sri* and *lanka*. She also told him that he needed to capitalize the *L* in *Lanka*.

Aunt Kamala found that Adil had used a punctuation mark incorrectly. In the new second paragraph, one of the sentences asks a question but ends with a period. Can you find it?

In the new third paragraph, Aunt Kamala added an apostrophe. The word *peoples* needed an apostrophe. Can you explain why?

Your Turn

- Use the Proofreader's Checklist to proofread your draft.
- Trade drafts with a partner and proofread each other's drafts, using the Proofreader's Checklist.
- Check for one type of mistake at a time.
- Read over your draft again to make sure that none of the changes added a new mistake to your research report.

Writer's Tip Be sure you agree with each change you get from your proofreader.

Prewriting | Drafting | Content Editing | Revising | Copyediting | Proofreading | Publishing

OBJECTIVE
• **To publish a research report**

PUBLISHING

Read aloud the opening paragraphs. Ask students to explain why publishing is an important part of the writing process. *(It is the time that writers get to share their work with an audience.)*

Tell students that the look, or presentation, of their research report makes a difference in how it is received. Reinforce that neatness and consistent margins and spacing will make their report look clean, organized, and professional.

Invite volunteers to read aloud Adil's research report. Ask students to look back at the first draft and tell how Adil has made his research report better. Allow students time to point out parts of Adil's draft that they found informative or well written.

Discuss with students the many ways they might publish their work.

Writer's Workshop
Research Reports

Publishing

Adil worked on the final copy of his research report. He made sure to add his proofreading changes while writing. Here is Adil's finished research report.

Adil included a picture of an Asian elephant, and he made a map showing where Asian elephants live. He then presented his research report to the class. The class put together all the reports and pictures in their encyclopedia.

Presentation

The Asian Elephant

Did you know that elephants live in other places besides Africa? The Asian elephant lives in India, Sri Lanka, and Sumatra. Asian elephants are amazing creatures. They are intelligent and strong. But they are also endangered. This means that there are not many Asian elephants left. They need to be protected so that we all can enjoy them.

Asian elephants are large animals. Some are as tall as 10 feet and as heavy as 11,000 pounds. They need to eat a lot of food. In one day an Asian elephant will eat up to 350 pounds of food. They will wash it all down with up to 30 gallons of water. How does all of that food and water get into the elephant? It uses its trunk. The trunk has a "finger" it uses like a hook. Not only are elephants interesting, but they are also smart. They can dig for food by using their tusks. They can talk to one another using their own language.

Asian elephants are endangered. The main reason is that they are losing their forest home. People need more land. They cut down the forests that the elephants live in. There is another problem. Elephants are getting in trouble with people because elephants eat people's crops. But some people are working to protect the Asian elephant. Large areas of forest are being saved. These are places for the elephants to live without fences or cages.

Your Turn

Read aloud the first bulleted item. Tell students that it is always a good idea to proofread a draft one last time to make sure that no new mistakes have been made. Then allow students time to write or type their final copies.

Ask a volunteer to read aloud the last bulleted item. Encourage students to think of visual aids that might go with their research reports.

ASSESS

Have students assess their finished research report using the reproducible Student Self-Assessment on page 513y. A separate Research Report Scoring Rubric can be found on page 513z for you to use to evaluate their work.

Plan to spend tomorrow doing a formal assessment. Administer the Research Report Writing Prompt on **Assessment Book** pages 69–70. Have students choose a topic and conduct research prior to administering the Research Report Writing Prompt.

TEACHING OPTIONS

Curriculum Connection

Discuss how students can use the skills they have learned in this chapter to write research reports for other classes. Help students brainstorm topics about which they might write research reports for a science or social studies class.

Portfolio Opportunity

Remind students to keep a copy of their research reports in their portfolios. Point out that keeping a copy of their research reports in their portfolios will help students keep track of the progress they have made with their writing during the year.

The Year in Review

Ask volunteers to make a list on the board of the kinds of writing they did during the year. Discuss everyday ways in which students might use each of these kinds of writing. Then allow students time to look through their portfolios and determine how their writing has changed since Chapter 1.

The Asian elephant is a special animal. It is smart and strong and can do amazing things. There are good ideas for how to protect it. But Asian elephants also need people to come up with new ideas to help them. We must care for them before they are gone forever.

Whenever you publish your work, your goal is to share your thoughts and experiences with other people. There are many ways you can publish your research report. However you decide to publish, make sure the message is clear.

Your Turn

- Make a clean, final copy of your research report. Be careful copying or typing your report.
- Find visual aids that go with your research report. You can use pictures that you find or draw. You might make charts that show your research. If your report is about a certain place, you might want to include a map that shows the location.

Submit your report to an online magazine or newspaper that publishes student work. Add photos or illustrations that support your topic.

Film it. Make your own documentary. Narrate the report with a backdrop of photos, music, and illustrations. Interview someone who can add information to your topic.

Create a class encyclopedia by combining all the research reports under a single cover. Arrange the reports in alphabetical order and create a contents page.

Have your class encyclopedia on hand for Parents' Night. You might wish to present it as a PowerPoint presentation.

Prewriting | Drafting | Content Editing | Revising | Copyediting | Proofreading | Publishing

Research Reports • 513

Name _____ Date _____

Research Report

	YES	NO
Ideas		
Do I focus on one topic?		
Do I give factual information supported by research I gathered as notes?		
Organization		
Does the report have an introduction that includes a topic sentence?		
Does the report have a body that includes ideas supported by facts?		
Does the report have a summarizing conclusion?		
Voice		
Is my voice confident?		
Word Choice		
Do I use formal language?		
Sentence Fluency		
Do I use different kinds of sentences with different lengths?		
Conventions		
Do I use correct grammar?		
Do I use correct spelling?		
Do I use correct punctuation and capitalization?		
Presentation		
Is my research report neat?		
Are my margins and spacing consistent?		
Additional Items		

Name _____

Date _____ Score _____

Research Report

Ideas

POINTS

clear focus on one topic	
factual information supported by research gathered as notes	

Organization

an interesting introduction that includes a topic sentence	
a body that includes ideas supported by facts	
a summarizing conclusion	

Voice

a confident voice	

Word Choice

formal language	

Sentence Fluency

varied sentence styles and lengths	

Conventions

correct grammar and usage	
correct spelling	
correct punctuation and capitalization	

Presentation

neatness	
consistent margins and spacing	

Additional Items

Total	

Common Proofreading Marks

Use these proofreading marks to mark changes when you proofread. Remember to use a colored pencil to make your changes.

Symbol	Meaning	Example
¶	begin new paragraph	over. ¶ Begin a new
⊂⊃	close up space	close u p space
∧	insert	students think *should*
℘	delete, omit	that the ~~the~~ book
/	make lowercase	/Mathematics
∿	reverse letters	reve(sr)e letters
≡	capitalize	washington
∨ ∨	add quotation marks	I am, I said.
⊙	add period	Marta drank tea ⊙

Making a Time Capsule

A Buried Surprise

When you are older, you can open the time capsule and remember what it was like when you were in third grade. A time capsule is fun to make. George Washington even put one in the cornerstone of the Capitol building. But it has never been found.

What You Need

This chart from the student book is reproduced here for your convenience.

Grammar and Mechanics Handbook

Grammar

Adjectives

An adjective points out or describes a noun.

Adjectives That Compare

Adjectives can be used to make comparisons. To compare two people, places, or things, *-er* is often added to an adjective. To compare three or more people, places, or things, *-est* is often added to an adjective.

> A horse is **taller** than a deer.
> A moose is **bigger** than a horse.
> An elephant is the **largest** land animal.

Some adjectives that compare have special forms.

> Vanilla ice cream is **good**.
> Strawberry ice cream is **better** than vanilla.
> Chocolate ice cream is the **best** flavor of all.

> The girl had a **bad** cold on Sunday.
> The cold was **worse** on Monday.
> It was the **worst** cold she'd ever had.

Adjectives That Tell How Many

Some adjectives tell how many or about how many.

> Only **six** members came to the meeting.
> A **few** members were sick.

Some adjectives tell numerical order.

> I finished reading the **sixth** chapter.

The pages of the Grammar and Mechanics Handbook from the student book are reproduced here for your convenience.

Articles

Articles point out nouns. *The, a,* and *an* are articles. *The* points out a specific person, place, or thing. *A* and *an* point out any one of a group of people, places, or things. Use *a* before a consonant sound and *an* before a vowel sound.

The man ate **a** peach and **an** apple.

Demonstrative Adjectives

Demonstrative adjectives point out or tell about a specific person, place, or thing. The demonstrative adjectives are *this, that, these,* and *those.*

	Singular	Plural
Near	**This** flower is red.	**These** bushes are tall.
Far	**That** flower is yellow.	**Those** bushes are short.

Descriptive Adjectives

A descriptive adjective tells more about a noun. It can tell how something looks, tastes, sounds, feels, or smells. It can tell about size, color, shape, or weight.

A descriptive adjective often comes before the noun it describes.

A **tall** tree stood beside the **red** barn.

A descriptive adjective can follow a being verb as a subject complement. It describes the subject of the sentence.

The tree is **tall**.   The barn was **red**.

Possessive Adjectives

A possessive adjective shows who or what owns something. A possessive adjective is used before a noun. The possessive adjectives are *my, your, his, her, its, our,* and *their.*

I have **my** camera, and Lucy has **her** cell phone.

The pages of the Grammar and Mechanics Handbook from the student book are reproduced here for your convenience.

Proper Adjectives

Proper adjectives are formed from proper nouns. A proper adjective begins with a capital letter.

When we went to Mexico, I ate **Mexican** food.

Adverbs

An adverb tells more about a verb. Many adverbs end in *ly*.

Some adverbs tell when or how often an action takes place.

I went to the mall **yesterday**. I **sometimes** go to the toy store.

Some adverbs tell where an action takes place.

I went **outside** after dinner. I played **there** until it was dark.

Some adverbs tell how an action takes place.

My new skateboard goes **fast**. I ride it **gracefully**.

Negative Words

Some adverbs form negative ideas. Use *not, n't* for *not* in a contraction, or *never* to express a negative idea. Do not use more than one negative word in a sentence.

He will **not** be ready on time. He **can't** find his sneakers.
He **never** remembers where he left them.

Contractions

A contraction is a short way to write some words. An apostrophe (') is used to show where one or more letters have been left out of a word. Many contractions are formed with the word *not*.

do not = don't
cannot = can't
was not = wasn't
will not = won't

The pages of the Grammar and Mechanics Handbook from the student book are reproduced here for your convenience.

Coordinating Conjunctions

A coordinating conjunction joins two words or groups of words. The words *and, but,* and *or* are coordinating conjunctions.

My dad **and** I went to the pool. I can swim **but** not dive.
The pool is never too hot **or** crowded.

Nouns

A noun is a word that names a person, a place, or a thing.

Collective Nouns

A collective noun names a group of people or things.

My **class** saw a **herd** of buffalo.

Common Nouns

A common noun names any one member of a group of people, places, or things.

My **cousin** saw a **dog** run down the **street**.

Plural Nouns

A plural noun names more than one person, place, or thing.

The **boys** have some **puppies** and some **fish**.

Possessive Nouns

The possessive form of a noun shows possession or ownership.

A singular possessive noun shows that one person owns something. To form the singular possessive, add an apostrophe (') and the letter *s* to a singular noun.

friend   friend**'s** book report
baby   baby**'s** bottle
Tess   Tess**'s** soccer ball
woman   woman**'s** purse

The pages of the Grammar and Mechanics Handbook from the student book are reproduced here for your convenience.

A plural possessive noun shows that more than one person owns something. To form the regular plural possessive, add an apostrophe (') after the plural form of the noun.

friends   friends' book reports
babies   babies' bottles
the Smiths   the Smiths' house

To form the plural possessive of an irregular noun, add an apostrophe and *s* (*'s*) after the plural form.

women   women**'s** purses
mice   mice**'s** cheese

Proper Nouns

A proper noun names a particular person, place, or thing. A proper noun begins with a capital letter.

Meg saw **Shadow** run down **Pine Street**.

Singular Nouns

A singular noun names one person, place, or thing.

The **girl** has a **kite** and a **skateboard**.

Predicates

The predicate of a sentence tells what the subject is or does.

Complete Predicates

The complete predicate of a sentence is the simple predicate and any words that go with it.

Tom **rode his new bike**.

Compound Predicates

Two predicates joined by *and, but,* or *or* form a compound predicate.

Karen **got a glass and poured some milk**.

The pages of the Grammar and Mechanics Handbook from the student book are reproduced here for your convenience.

Simple Predicates

The simple predicate of a sentence is a verb, a word or words that express an action or a state of being.

The boys **ran** noisily down the street. They **were** happy.

Pronouns

A pronoun is a word that takes the place of a noun.

Personal Pronouns

A personal pronoun refers to the person speaking or to the person or thing that is spoken to or about. In this sentence *I* is the person speaking, *you* is the person spoken to, and *them* are the people spoken about.

I heard **you** calling **them**.

Object Pronouns

An object pronoun is used after an action verb. The object pronouns are *me, you, him, her, it, us,* and *them.* An object pronoun can be part of a compound object.

Karen will help **them**. Chris will help **her** and **me**.

Possessive Pronouns

A possessive pronoun shows who or what owns something. A possessive pronoun takes the place of a noun. It takes the place of the owner and the thing that is owned. The possessive pronouns are *mine, yours, his, hers, its, ours,* and *theirs.*

My cap is here, and **your cap** is over there.
Mine is here, and **yours** is over there.

Subject Pronouns

A subject pronoun can be used as the subject of a sentence. The subject pronouns are *I, you, he, she, it, we,* and *they.* A subject pronoun can be part of a compound subject.

She is a great tennis player. **She** and **I** play tennis often.
She and **Tom** like to play video games.

The pages of the Grammar and Mechanics Handbook from the student book are reproduced here for your convenience.

Sentences

A sentence is a group of words that expresses a complete thought. Every sentence has a subject and a predicate. Every sentence begins with a capital letter.

Commands

A command is a sentence that tells what to do. The subject of a command is *you.* The subject is not stated in most commands. A command ends with a period (.).

> Please wear your jacket.

Compound Sentences

Two sentences joined by a comma and *and, but,* or *or* form a compound sentence.

> Ming is eating, but Lili is sleeping.

Exclamations

An exclamation is a sentence that shows strong or sudden emotion. An exclamation ends with an exclamation point (!).

> How cold it is today!

Questions

A question is a sentence that asks something. A question ends with a question mark (?). A question often starts with a question word. Some question words are *who, when, where, what, why,* and *how.*

> Are you ready?   Where is your jacket?

Statements

A statement is a sentence that tells something. A statement ends with a period (.).

> Your jacket is in the closet.

The pages of the Grammar and Mechanics Handbook from the student book are reproduced here for your convenience.

Subject Complements

A subject complement is an adjective that comes after a being verb in a sentence. A subject complement describes or tells more about the subject. Two or more subject complements can be joined by *and, but,* or *or* to form a compound subject complement.

The sky is **blue**.   The clouds are **white** and **fluffy**.

Subjects

The subject of a sentence is who or what the sentence is about. The subject can be a noun or a pronoun.

Complete Subjects
The complete subject is the simple subject and the words that describe it or give more information about it.

The little gray kitten is playing.

Compound Subjects
Two or more subjects joined by *and* or *or* form a compound subject.

Bob and **Lisa** went to the movies. **Nora** or **I** will sweep the floor.

Simple Subjects
The simple subject is the noun or pronoun that a sentence tells about.

His little **dog** likes to chase the ball.   **It** runs very fast.

Tense

The tense of a verb shows when the action takes place.

Future Tense
The future tense tells about something that will happen in the future.

The pages of the Grammar and Mechanics Handbook from the student book are reproduced here for your convenience.

Grammar

One way to form the future tense is with a form of the helping verb *be* plus *going to* plus the present form of a verb.

I **am going to make** toast.   Dad **is going to butter** it.
They **are going to eat** it.

Another way to form the future tense is with the helping verb *will* and the present form of a verb.

We **will go** to the museum. The guide **will explain** the exhibits.

Past Progressive Tense

The past progressive tense tells what was happening in the past. This tense is formed with *was* or *were* and the present participle of a verb.

I **was feeding** the cat.   My parents **were reading**.

Present Progressive Tense

The present progressive tense tells what is happening now. The present progressive tense is formed with *am, is,* or *are* and the present participle of a verb.

We **are watching** TV.   I **am eating** popcorn.
My sister **is drinking** juice.

Simple Past Tense

The simple past tense tells about something that happened in the past. The past part of a verb is used for the past tense.

We **cooked** breakfast this morning.   Mom **fried** the eggs.
We **drank** orange juice.

Simple Present Tense

The simple present tense tells about something that is always true or something that happens again and again. The present part of a verb is used for the present tense. If the subject is a singular noun or *he, she,* or *it, -s* or *-es* must be added to the verb.

Prairie dogs **live** where it's dry.

A prairie dog **digs** a burrow to live in.

The pages of the Grammar and Mechanics Handbook from the student book are reproduced here for your convenience.

Verbs

A verb shows action or state of being. See TENSE.

Action Verbs

An action verb tells what someone or something does.

The girl **sings**.   Dogs **bark**.

Being Verbs

A being verb shows what someone or something is. Being verbs do not express action.

The girl **is** happy.   The dog **was** hungry.

Helping Verbs

A verb can have more than one word. A helping verb is a verb added before the main verb that helps make the meaning clear.

We **will** go to the movie.   We **might** buy some popcorn.

Irregular Verbs

The past and the past participle of irregular verbs are not formed by adding *-d* or *-ed.*

Present	Past	Past Participle
sing	sang	sung
send	sent	sent
write	wrote	written

Principal Parts

A verb has four principal parts: present, present participle, past, and past participle. The present participle is formed by adding *-ing* to the present. The past and the past participle of regular verbs are formed by adding *-d* or *-ed* to the present.

Present	Present Participle	Past	Past Participle
walk	walking	walked	walked
rake	raking	raked	raked

The pages of the Grammar and Mechanics Handbook from the student book are reproduced here for your convenience.

Grammar

The present participle is often used with forms of the helping verb *be*.

> We ***are walking*** to school. Carla ***was raking*** leaves.

The past participle is often used with forms of the helping verb *have*.

> We ***have walked*** this way before.
> She ***has raked*** the whole backyard.

Regular Verbs

The past and the past participle of regular verbs are formed by adding *-d* or *-ed* to the present.

Present	Past	Past Participle
jump	jumped	jumped
glue	glued	glued

The pages of the Grammar and Mechanics Handbook from the student book are reproduced here for your convenience.

Mechanics

Capitalization

Use a capital letter to begin the first word in a sentence.

Tomorrow is my birthday.

Use a capital letter to begin the names of people and pets.

Aunt **P**eg let me play with her ferret, **N**ibbles.

Use a capital letter to begin the names of streets, cities, states, and countries.

I live on **R**oscoe **S**treet. My cousin lives in **G**uadalajara, **M**exico.

Use a capital letter to begin the names of days, months, and holidays.

Veteran's **D**ay is on **W**ednesday, **N**ovember 11.

Use a capital letter to begin a proper adjective.

I like to eat **C**hinese food.

Use a capital letter to begin personal titles.

Mrs. Novak

Dr. Ramirez

Governor Charles Royce

Use a capital letter to begin the important words in the title of a book or poem. The first and last words of a title are always capitalized.

The **S**ecret **G**arden

"**S**ing a **S**ong of **C**ities"

The personal pronoun *I* is always a capital letter.

The pages of the Grammar and Mechanics Handbook from the student book are reproduced here for your convenience.

Punctuation

Apostrophes

Use an apostrophe to form possessive nouns.

> Keisha's skateboard
> the children's lunches
> the horses' stalls

Use an apostrophe to replace the letters left out in a contraction.

> didn't   can't   wasn't

Commas

Use a comma to separate the words in a series.

> Mark, Anton, and Cara made the scenery.
> They hammered, sawed, and nailed.

Use a comma or commas to separate a name in direct address.

> Carl, will you help me?
> Do you think, Keshawn, that we will finish today?

Use a comma when two short sentences are combined in a compound sentence.

> Dad will heat the soup, and I will make the salad.
> Dad likes noodle soup, but I like bean soup.

Use a comma to separate the names of a city and state.

> She comes from Philadelphia, Pennsylvania.

Use a comma or commas to separate a direct quotation from the rest of the sentence.

> "Hey," called Mario, "where are you going?"
> "I'm going to the movies," Juana answered.

Exclamation Points

Use an exclamation point after an exclamation.

> We won the game!

The pages of the Grammar and Mechanics Handbook from the student book are reproduced here for your convenience.

Periods

Use a period after a statement or a command.

The cat is hungry.

Please feed it.

Use a period after most abbreviations.

Sun.	Sept.	Mrs.
Ave.	gal.	Gov.

Question Marks

Use a question mark after a question.

Where are you going**?**

Quotation Marks

Use quotation marks to show the exact words a person says.

Nicole said, **"**I can't find my markers.**"**

"Where,**"** asked her mother, **"**did you leave them?**"**

Use quotation marks around the title of a poem. Underline the title of a book.

"Paul Revere's Ride**"**

<u>Dawn Undercover</u>

The pages of the Grammar and Mechanics Handbook from the student book are reproduced here for your convenience.

Index

A

Abbreviations, 162, 176, 529
Actions, of characters, 446
Action verbs, 74, 220, 525
Active listening, 424
Ada, Alma Flor, 324
Addresses, 162, 176
    e-mail, 334
Adjectives, 146, 150, 516
    as articles, 124, 517
    colorful, 224
    for comparing, 118, 120, 516
    defined, 110
    demonstrative, 126, 517
    descriptive, 112, 517
    diagramming, 188, 192, 198
    irregular, 120
    nouns used as, 130
    possessive, 62, 517
    proper, 128, 518, 527
    as subject complements, 114, 192, 198, 523
    for telling how many, 122, 516
Adverbs, 518
    defined, 136
    diagramming, 190
    negative words as, 144
    for telling how, 142
    for telling when or how often, 138, 518
    for telling where, 140, 518
Agreement, of pronouns and verbs, 64
Alphabetical order, in dictionaries, 228
Answering, of telephone, 346
Antonyms, 342
Apostrophes
    contractions and, 104, 452
    possessive nouns and, 38, 40, 42, 186, 519–20
    uses of, 174, 528
Appearance, of characters, 444
Are/is, 102
Articles (adjectives), 124, 517
Asking sentences. *See* Questions
Audience
    descriptions, 288
    oral personal narratives, 232
    persuasive speeches, 422
    persuasive writing, 404, 429
Audio aids, oral biographies and, 499
Avi, 370

B

Bats at the Library **(Lies),** 379
Beacons of Light **(Gibbons),** 497
Beginnings. *See also* Introductions
    book reports, 364
    descriptions, 292
    oral book reports, 384
    personal narratives, 216

    persuasive writing, 406
Being verbs, 76, 102, 192, 525
Biographies, oral, 498–501
Body. *See also* Middle
    e-mails, 336
    personal letters, 326, 330–33
    research reports, 478
Body language, persuasive speeches and, 422
Book reports, 362–63
    beginning, 364
    characters in, 368
    content editing, 392–93
    copyediting, 396
    drafting, 390–91
    ending, 365
    middle, 364
    oral, 384, 386–87
    plots in, 370
    prewriting, 388–89
    proofreading, 397
    publishing, 398–99
    revising, 394–95
    setting, 364
    Writer's Workshop, 388–99
Books
    in libraries, 486
    parts of, 372–73
    as sources, 479
    titles of, 166, 527
Brainstorming, 464
Bunting, Eve, 438, 442, 446, 450, 455, 459

C

Call numbers, of books, 489
Capitalization, 527
    in addresses, 176, 527
    of personal titles and initials, 164, 527
    of titles of books and poems, 166, 527
    uses of, 160, 527
Card catalogs. *See* Catalogs, library
Catalogs
    electronic, 488
    library, 486
Characters
    in book reports, 368
    in realistic fiction, 440, 444, 446
    in skits, 460
Chart, five-senses, 300–301, 313
Checklists
    content editor's, 240, 278, 316, 354, 392, 430, 468, 506
    copyeditor's, 244, 282, 320, 358, 396, 434, 472, 510
    proofreader's, 245, 282–83, 321, 359, 397, 435, 473, 511
Choosing words. *See* Word choice
Cities, commas with, 528

Closing
    e-mails, 336
    personal letters, 326
Collective nouns, 44, 519
Colorful adjectives, 224
Combining sentences, 20, 492
Commands, 8, 264, 522, 529
Commas
    in addresses, 176
    in compound sentences, 20, 172, 414
    in dialogue, 448
    in direct address, 170
    in direct quotations, 178
    in a series, 168
    uses of, 528
Common nouns, 30, 519
Comparisons, adjectives in, 118, 120, 516
Complete predicates, 2, 14, 16, 520
Complete subjects, 2, 14, 16, 523
Compound objects, 68
Compound predicates, 18, 196, 376, 520
Compound sentences, 20, 414, 416, 522
    commas in, 20, 172, 528
    conjunctions in, 414, 416
    defined, 20
    diagramming, 200
    making, 414
Compound subject complements, 116, 198
Compound subjects, 338, 340, 523
    combining, 18
    pronouns in, 68, 521
    in sentences, 194
Compound words, 266
Computers, searching electronic catalogs on, 488–89
Conclusions. *See also* Endings
    how-to articles, 254
    how-to talks, 271
    research reports, 478
Conjunctions
    in compound sentences, 414, 416
    coordinating, 152, 168, 519
Content editing
    book reports, 392–93
    descriptions, 316–17
    how-to articles, 278–79
    personal letters, 354–55
    personal narratives, 240–41
    persuasive articles, 430–31
    realistic fiction, 468–69
    research reports, 506–7
Contents page, 372
Contractions, 104, 174, 452–54, 518
Conventions. *See* Proofreading
Conversations, telephone, 346, 348
Cook, Deanna F., 248
Cooper, Jason, 479
Coordinating conjunctions, 152, 168, 519
Copyediting
    book reports, 396

The pages of the Index from the student book are reproduced here for your convenience.

descriptions, 320
how-to articles, 282
personal letters, 358
personal narratives, 244
persuasive articles, 434
realistic fiction, 472
research reports, 510
Couplet, rhyming, 458
Covers, of books, 372
Coville, Bruce, 367
Creative writing. *See* Realistic fiction

D

Dahl, Roald, 286, 289, 290, 295, 298, 310
Dale, Anna, 362
Dawn Undercover (Dale), 362
Days of the week, 162
Definitions, in dictionaries, 228
Demonstrative adjectives, 126, 517
Descriptions, 286–87
    audience, 288
    beginnings, 292
    content editing, 316–17
    copyediting, 320
    drafting, 314–15
    ending, 292
    middle, 292
    oral, 308–10
    prewriting, 312–13
    proofreading, 321
    publishing, 322–23
    revising, 318–19
    sensory words, 296
    space order of, 290
    topics, 292, 312
    word choice for, 288
    Writer's Workshop, 312–23
Descriptive adjectives, 112, 517
Diagramming
    adjectives, 188
    adverbs, 190
    compound predicates, 196
    compound sentences, 200
    compound subject complements, 198
    compound subjects, 194
    defined, 184
    possessives, 186
    practice, 202–5
    predicates, 184
    subject complements, 192
    subjects, 184
Dialogue, in realistic fiction, 444, 448–50
Dialogue tags, 448, 450
Dictionaries
    alphabetical order in, 228
    defined, 228
    guide words in, 230
    word meanings in, 258
Direct address, 170, 528

Direct quotations, 178, 528
Drafting
    book reports, 390–91
    descriptions, 314–15
    how-to articles, 276–77
    personal letters, 352–53
    personal narratives, 238–39
    persuasive articles, 428–29
    realistic fiction, 464–65
    research reports, 504–5
"Drinking Water: Bottled or From the Tap?"(Fox), 400

E

Editing. *See* Content editing; Copyediting
Electronic catalogs, 488, 489
E-mails, 334, 336
Encyclopedias, 482
Endings. *See also* Conclusions
    book reports, 365
    descriptions, 292
    oral book reports, 384
    personal narratives, 217
    persuasive writing, 407
End punctuation, 158
Entry words, in dictionaries, 228
-er (suffix), 418, 516
-es, **adding to form plural nouns,** 32, 34
Exact words, 490
Exclamation points
    as end punctuation, 158
    in exclamation sentences, 10, 449
    uses of, 529
Exclamations, 10, 264, 449, 522

F

Fact finding, 482–83
Fiction, realistic. *See* Realistic Fiction
Fiction books, 486
Field, Rachel, 456
Five-senses chart, 300–301, 313
Fly Away Home (Bunting), 438, 442, 446, 450, 455, 459
Fox, Catherine Clarke, 400
Freewriting, of personal letters, 350
Future tense, 523–24
    with *going to* as helping verb, 96, 524
    with *will* as helping verb, 94, 524

G

Gavin, Mary L., 404
Gibbons, Gail, 497
Glossary, 372
Going to, **future tense with,** 96
Good/well, 146
Grammar. *See* Adjectives; Adverbs; Capitalization; Conjunctions;

Diagramming; Nouns; Pronouns; Punctuation; Sentences; Verbs
Graphic Organizers
    five-senses chart, 300–301, 313
    idea web, 410, 412, 427
    storyboarding, 237
Greeting, in personal letters, 326
Guide words, in dictionaries, 230

H

Hauser, Jill Frankel, 253
Heading, in personal letters, 326
Helping verbs, 78, 525
    going to in future tense, 96, 524
    will in future tense, 94, 524
Homophones, 494
How-to articles, 248–85
    conclusions, 254
    content editing, 278–79
    copyediting, 282
    drafting, 276–77
    introductions, 254
    prewriting, 274–75
    proofreading, 282–83
    publishing, 284–85
    revising, 280–81
    step-by-step order in, 252, 254, 275
    titles, 254
    topics, 250, 274
    unneeded information in, 256
    what you need list (materials), 254, 256
    Writer's Workshop, 274–85
How-to talks, 270–72
Huynh, Quang Nhuong, 210, 214, 218, 221, 225

I

I (personal pronoun), capitalization of, 527
I/me, 66
Idea webs, 410, 412, 427
Index, 373
Initials, capitalization of, 164
Internet, research on, 483
Into the Land of the Unicorns (Coville), 367
Introductions. *See also* Beginnings
    how-to articles, 254
    how-to talks, 270
    research reports, 478
Irregular adjectives, 120
Irregular plural nouns, 36
Irregular plural possessive nouns, 42, 520
Irregular verbs, 82, 84, 86, 88, 525
Is/are, 102

J

James and the Giant Peach (Dahl), 286, 289, 290, 295, 298, 310

The pages of the Index from the student book are reproduced here for your convenience.

K

Kids' Multicultural Cookbook, The (Cook), 248

L

Leder, Jane Mersky, 262
-less (suffix), 418
Letters, personal. *See* Personal letters
Libraries, 486, 488–89
Library catalog, 486
Lies, Brian, 379
Listening tips
　how-to-talks, 272
　oral biographies, 501
　oral book reports, 387
　oral descriptions, 310
　oral personal narratives, 234
　persuasive speeches, 424
　skits, 462
-ly endings, 518

M

MacLachlan, Patricia, 363
Magazines, 482
Magnets (Cooper), 479
Me/I, 66
Messages, taking, 348
Middle. *See also* Body
　book reports, 364
　descriptions, 292
　oral book reports, 384
　personal narratives, 216–17
　persuasive writing, 406
Months of the year, 162
Mountains (Simon), 476

N

Negative words, 144, 518
Nonfiction books, 482, 486, 489
Not, contractions with, 104
Note cards
　how-to-talks, 272
　oral biographies, 498
　oral personal narrative, 234
　research reports, 484, 503
Note taking, 484
Nouns, 519–20
　as adjectives, 130
　collective, 44, 519
　common, 30, 519
　defined, 28
　diagramming, 184, 186
　irregular plural, 36
　irregular plural possessive, 42, 520
　plural, 32, 34, 519, 520

plural possessive, 40
possessive, 38, 40, 42, 186, 519, 520
proper, 30, 414, 520
singular, 32, 520
singular possessive, 38
as subjects, 14, 184
words used as verbs and, 48
Numerical order, adjectives for, 516

O

Object pronouns, 58, 68, 521
Objects
　compound, 68
　me as, 66
Opinion words, 407
Oral biographies, 498–501
Oral book reports, 384, 386–87
Oral descriptions, 308–10
Oral personal narratives, 232, 234
Order
　space, 290
　step-by-step, 252, 254, 270, 272, 275
　time, 212, 290
Organizing
　book reports, 388–89
　descriptions, 313
　how-to-articles, 275
　personal letters, 332, 351
　personal narratives, 237
　persuasive writing, 427
　realistic fiction, 465
　research notes, 484
　research reports, 503

P

Past participle, 80, 82, 525, 526
Past tense, 80, 82
　irregular verbs, 92
　progressive, 100, 524
　regular verbs, 92
　simple, 92, 524
Periods, 158
　abbreviations with, 162
　after commands, 8
　after statements, 4
　uses off, 529
Personal e-mails. *See* E-mails
Personal letters, 324–25
　body, 326, 330, 332
　closing, 326
　content editing, 354–55
　copyediting, 358
　drafting, 352–53
　greetings, 326
　headings, 326
　organization of, 332
　prewriting, 350–51
　proofreading, 359

publishing, 360–61
purpose of, 330–31
revising, 356–57
signature, 326
topics, 350
Writer's Workshop, 350–61
Personal narratives, 210–11
　beginning, 216
　content editing, 240–41
　copyediting, 244
　drafting, 238–39
　ending, 217
　middle, 216–17
　oral, 232–35
　point of view, 212
　prewriting, 236
　proofreading, 244–45
　publishing, 246–47
　revising, 242–43
　time order, 212
　title of, 218
　topics, 212, 236
　Writer's Workshop, 236–47
Personal pronouns, 521
　capitalization of *I*, 527
　defined, 54
　as objects, 58, 68
　as subjects, 54, 56, 68
Persuasive speeches, 422, 424
Persuasive writing, 400–401
　audience, 404
　beginning, 406
　content editing, 430–31
　copyediting, 434
　drafting, 428–29
　ending, 407
　middle, 406
　prewriting, 426–27
　proofreading, 435
　publishing, 436–37
　reasons in, 402, 406
　researching, 402–3, 426–27
　revising, 432–33
　topics, 402, 426–27
　Writer's Workshop, 426–37
Phrases, in idea webs, 412
Planning. *See also* Organizing
　book reports, 388–89
　oral personal narratives, 232
　realistic fiction, 465
Plot
　in book reports, 370
　in realistic fiction, 442
　in skits, 461
Plural nouns
　defined, 32, 519
　forming, 32, 34
　irregular, 36
　irregular possessive, 42
　possessive, 40, 520

The pages of the Index from the student book are reproduced here for your convenience.

Poetry
    rhyme in, 456
    rhyming couplets, 458
    titles of, 166, 527, 529
Point of view, 212, 232
Possession, apostrophes showing, 174, 528
Possessive adjectives, 62, 517
Possessive nouns, 519–520
    diagramming, 186
    irregular plural, 42
    plural, 40, 520
    singular, 38, 519
Possessive pronouns, 60, 521
Practicing
    how-to-talks, 272
    oral biographies, 500
    oral book reports, 386
    oral descriptions, 309
    oral personal narratives, 234
Predicates, 520–21
    combining subjects and, 18, 340
    complete, 2, 14, 16, 520
    compound, 18, 196, 376, 520
    defined, 2, 16
    diagramming, 184, 196
    simple, 16, 521
Prefixes, 380, 418
Preparing
    oral biographies, 498
    oral book reports, 384
    oral descriptions, 309
Presenting
    book reports, 398–99
    descriptions, 323
    how-to articles, 285
    oral descriptions, 309
    oral personal narratives, 234
    personal letters, 361
    personal narratives, 246
    persuasive writing, 437
    realistic fiction, 475
    research reports, 512–13
Present participle, 80, 525–526
Present tense, 64, 524, 525
    progressive, 98–99, 524
    simple, 90, 524
    of verbs, 80, 90, 94
Prewriting
    book reports, 388–89
    descriptions, 312–13
    how-to articles, 274–75
    personal letters, 350–51
    personal narratives, 236–37
    persuasive articles, 426–27
    realistic fiction, 464–65
    research reports, 502–3
Principal parts of verbs, 80, 525–26
Problem
    solving in fiction, 441
    solving in skits, 460
Progressive tenses, 98, 100, 524

Pronouns, 521
    agreement of verbs and, 64
    in compound subjects and objects, 68
    defined, 54
    object, 58, 68, 521
    personal, 54, 521, 527
    possessive, 60, 521
    subject, 56, 68, 184, 521
Pronunciations, in dictionaries, 228
Proofreading
    book reports, 397
    descriptions, 321
    how-to articles, 282–83
    personal letters, 359
    personal narratives, 244–45
    persuasive articles, 435
    realistic fiction, 473
    research reports, 511
Proofreading marks, 245, 514
Proper adjectives, 128, 518, 527
Proper nouns, 30, 414, 520
Publishing
    book reports, 398–99
    descriptions, 322–23
    how-to articles, 284–85
    personal letters, 360–61
    personal narratives, 246–47
    persuasive writing, 436–37
    realistic fiction, 474–75
    research reports, 512–13
Punctuation, 158. *See also* specific types
    of addresses, 176
    of compound sentences, 172, 414
    of dialogue, 448–49
    in direct address, 170
    of direct quotations, 178
    end, 4, 158
    of personal titles and initials, 164
    in a series, 168
    of titles, 166

Q

Question marks, 4, 158, 448–49, 529
Questions, 522, 529
    as asking sentences, 262
    defined, 6
    in dialogue, 449
Question words, 6
Quotation marks
    in dialogue, 448
    in direct quotations, 178
    in titles of books and poems, 166
    uses of, 529
Quotations, direct, 178, 529

R

Re- **(prefix),** 380
Realistic fiction, 438–39
    characters, 440, 444, 446

    content editing, 468–69
    copyediting, 472
    dialogue in, 444, 448–50
    drafting, 466–67
    plot, 442
    prewriting, 464–65
    problem in, 441
    proofreading, 473
    publishing, 474–75
    revising, 470–71
    setting, 440
    Writer's Workshop, 464–75
Reference books, 486
Regular verbs, 82, 526
Rehearsing, of skits, 462
Research, 479, 502
    for oral biographies, 498
    for persuasive writing, 402–3, 426–27
Research reports, 476–77
    body, 478
    conclusion, 478
    content editing, 506–7
    copyediting, 510
    drafting, 504–5
    finding facts for, 482–83
    introduction, 478
    note taking for, 484, 503
    oral biographies, 498–501
    prewriting, 502–3
    proofreading, 511
    publishing, 512–13
    researching, 479, 502
    revising, 508–9
    topics, 478, 482, 502
    Writer's Workshop, 502–13
Revising
    book reports, 394–95
    descriptions, 318–19
    how-to articles, 280–81
    personal letters, 356–57
    personal narratives, 242–43
    persuasive articles, 432–33
    realistic fiction, 470–71
    research reports, 508–9
Rhyme, 456
Rhyming couplet, 458–59
Run-on sentences, 22

S

Sarah, Plain and Tall **(MacLachlan),** 363
Sensory words, 296, 300
Sentence fluency
    book reports, 396
    descriptions, 320
    how-to articles, 282
    personal letters, 358
    personal narratives, 244
    persuasive writing, 434
    realistic fiction, 472
    research reports, 510

Index • 533

The pages of the Index from the student book are reproduced here for your convenience.

Sentences, 522. *See also* Compound
  sentences; Diagramming; specific kinds
  combining, 20, 492–93
  defined, 2
  in idea webs, 412
  kinds of, 12
  punctuation of, 158
  revising, 490–91
  run-on, 22–23
  subject pronouns in, 521
  topic, 406, 478
  using exact words in, 490
Series, commas in, 168, 528
-s/-es endings, for plural nouns, 32
Setting, 364, 440
Signature
  e-mails, 336
  personal letters, 326
Similes, 315
Simon, Seymour, 476
Simple predicates, 16, 184, 521
Simple subjects, 14, 184, 523
Simple tenses
  past, 92, 524
  present, 90, 524
Singular nouns, 32, 38, 519, 520
Skits, 460–63
Sources, books as, 479
Space order, 290
Speeches
  how-to talk, 270–73
  oral biographies, 498–501
  oral book report, 384, 386–87
  oral description, 308–10
  oral personal narrative, 232, 234
  persuasive, 422, 424
Spines, of books, 372
Statements, 4, 262, 522, 529
Step-by-step order, 252, 254, 270, 272, 275
Storyboarding, 237
Strange Happenings (Avi), 370
Strong verbs, 220
Subject complements, 114, 523
  compound, 116, 198
  diagramming, 192, 198
Subject lines, of e-mails, 334
Subject pronouns, 56, 68, 184, 521
Subjects, 523
  agreement of verbs and, 64
  combining predicates and, 18, 340
  of commands, 8
  complete, 2, 14, 16, 523
  compound, 18, 68, 194, 338, 340, 523
  defined, 2, 14
  diagramming, 184, 194
  I as, 66
  nouns as, 14, 184
  possessive pronouns as, 60
  pronouns as, 54, 56, 68, 184
  simple, 14, 184, 523

Suffixes, 418
Synonyms, 304

T

Telephone calls, 346, 348
Telling sentences. *See* Statements
Tenses, verb, 90–101, 523–24
  defined, 90
  future, 94, 96, 523–24
  progressive tenses, 98, 100, 524
  simple tenses, 90, 92, 524
Their/there, 150
Time order, 212, 290
Title pages, 372
Titles
  of books and poems, 166
  how-to articles, 254
  how-to talks, 270
  personal, 164, 527
  personal narratives, 218
Tone of voice, 386
Topics
  descriptions, 292, 312
  how-to articles, 250, 274
  how-to-talks, 271
  personal letters, 350
  personal narratives, 212, 236
  persuasive writing, 402, 426–27
  research reports, 478, 482, 502
Topic sentences, 406, 478
To/too/two, 148

U

Un- (prefix), 380
Underlining, for book titles, 166, 529
Units of measure, 162

V

Verbs, 525–26
  action, 74, 220, 525
  agreement of pronouns and, 64
  being, 76, 102, 192, 525
  defined, 16
  diagramming, 184
  helping, 78, 525
  irregular, 82, 84, 86, 88, 525
  as predicates, 16, 184
  principal parts of, 80, 525
  regular, 82, 526
  strong, 220
  tenses of, 90, 92, 94, 96, 98, 100
  words used as nouns and, 48
Visual aids
  oral biographies, 499
  oral descriptions, 308
  persuasive speeches, 422

Voice. *See also* Tone
  book reports, 395
  descriptions, 315
  personal letters, 353
  personal narratives, 243
  persuasive speeches, 422
  persuasive writing, 429
  realistic fiction, 467

W

Was/were, 102
Water Buffalo Days **(Huynh),** 210, 214, 218, 221, 225
Web sites, 483
Well/good, 146
What You Need list (Materials), 254, 256, 270
Who, what, when, where, why, how **(question words),** 6
"Why Exercise Is Cool" (Gavin), 404
Will, future tense with, 94
Word choice
  book reports, 396
  descriptions, 288, 315
  how-to articles, 282
  personal letters, 353
  personal narratives, 244
  persuasive writing, 434
  realistic fiction, 466
  research reports, 510
Words
  antonyms, 342
  beginning with capital letters, 160
  compound, 266
  exact, using in sentences, 490
  meanings in dictionaries, 258
  negative, 144, 518
  opinion, 407
  prefixes, 380, 418
  question, 6
  sensory, 296, 300
  suffixes, 418
  synonyms, 304
  used as nouns and verbs, 48
Writer's Workshop
  book reports, 388–99
  descriptions, 312–23
  how-to articles, 274–85
  personal letters, 350–61
  personal narratives, 236–47
  persuasive writing, 426–37
  realistic fiction, 464–75
  research reports, 502–13
Writing, skits, 462

Y

You, **as subject,** 8
Yours Truly, *Goldilocks* **(Ada),** 324

The pages of the Index from the student book are reproduced here for your convenience.

Acknowledgments

Literature

Loyola Press has made every effort to locate the copyright holders for the cited works used in this publication and to make full acknowledgment for their use. In the case of any omissions, the publisher will be pleased to make suitable acknowledgments in future editions.

Excerpt and cover from *Yours Truly, Goldilocks* by Alma Flor Ada. Text Copyright © 1998 by Alma Flor Ada. Reprinted by permission of Aladdin Paperbacks, an imprint of Simon & Schuster Children's Publishing Division.

Review of *Bats at the Library* used by permission of Katie Harvey. www.katiesliteraturelounge.blogspot.com

Excerpt from "Be a Fit Kid." Kidshealth.org. Copyright © 1995–2009 The Nemours Foundation. All rights reserved. Used by permission.

Excerpt and cover from *Fly Away Home* by Eve Bunting. Text copyright © 1991 by Eve Bunting. Published by Clarion Books, an imprint of Houghton Mifflin Company. All rights reserved.

Excerpt from *The Climb* by Roger Carr. Copyright © 2007. Reprinted by permission of Sundance/Newbridge LLC.

Excerpt from *April Aliens* by Rob Childs. Reprinted by permission of Harcourt Education, United Kingdom.

"Cheesy Quesadillas" from *The Kids' Multicultural Cookbook.* Copyright © 1995 by author Deanna F. Cook. Used by permission of Williamson Books, an imprint of Ideals Publication.

Excerpt from *Magnets* by Jason Cooper. Copyright © 2003 Rourke Publishing LLC. Used by permission.

Excerpt and cover from *James and the Giant Peach* by Roald Dahl. Copyright © 1961 by Roald Dahl. Text copyright renewed 1989 by Roald Dahl. Used by permission of Alfred A. Knopf, an imprint of Random House Children's Books, a division of Random House, Inc.

Review of *Dawn Undercover* used by permission of Kidsread.com. Copyright © 1998–2009 by Kidsread.com. All rights reserved.

Excerpt from "Drinking Water: Bottled or From the Tap?" *National Geographic Kids.* February 2008. Copyright © 2008 by National Geographic Society. Used by permission.

Excerpt from *Beacons of Light: Lighthouses* by Gail Gibbons. Copyright © 1990 by Gail Gibbons. Published by William Morrow & Company. All rights reserved. Used by permission.

Excerpt from *Easy Art Fun! Do-It-Yourself Crafts for Beginning Readers* by Jill Frankel Hauser. Copyright © 2002 by Jill Frankel Hauser. Used by permission of Williamson Books, an imprint of Ideals Publication.

Review of *Into the Land of the Unicorns* used by permission of Kidsread.com. Copyright © 1998–2009 by Kidsread.com. All rights reserved.

Excerpt from *Learning How: Karate* by Jane Mersky Leder. Copyright © 1992 by Bancroft-Sage Publishing. Used by permission.

Excerpt from *How to Write a Letter* by Florence D. Mischel. Copyright © 1957, 1988. Published by Franklin Watts. All rights reserved.

Excerpt from *Summer Magic (With a Pinch of Salt)* by Margaret Nash. Reprinted by permission of Harcourt Education, United Kingdom.

Excerpt and cover from *Water Buffalo Days* by Huynh Quang Nhuong. Copyright © 1997 by Huynh Quang Nhuong. Used by permission of HarperCollins Publishers.

Excerpt from "School Lunches." Kidshealth.org. Copyright © 1995–2009 The Nemours Foundation. All rights reserved. Used by permission.

Excerpt from *Mountains* by Seymour Simon. Copyright © 1994 by Seymour Simon. Published by William Morrow & Company. All rights reserved. Used by permission.

Review of *Strange Happenings* used by permission of Kidsread.com. Copyright © 1998–2009 by Kidsread.com. All rights reserved.

Excerpt from "Why Exercise Is Cool." Kidshealth.org. Copyright © 1995–2009 The Nemours Foundation. All rights reserved. Used by permission.

All other excerpts come from public-domain sources, including Project Gutenberg.

The Acknowledgments from the student book begin on page ii and continue here.

Scope and Sequence

E=Explored   **I**=Introduced   **T**=Taught   **M**=Mastered   **R**=Reviewed

Grammar — Grade Level	1	2	3	4	5	6	7	8
NOUNS								
common/proper	E	I	T	M	R	R	R	R
singular/plural	E	I	T	M	R	R	R	R
irregular plural			T	M	R	R	R	R
possessive			E	I	T	M	R	R
collective		E	I	T	M	R	R	R
as subjects			E	I	T	M	R	R
used in direct address			E	I	T	M		
words used as nouns and verbs			E	I	T	M	R	R
words used as nouns and adjectives			E	I	T	M		
as direct objects				E	I	T	M	R
as subject complements				E	I	T	M	R
as indirect objects					E	I	T	M
as objects of prepositions				E	I	T	M	R
concrete and abstract				E	I, T	T	M	R
showing separate and joint possession					E	I	T	M
as appositives						I	T	M
as antecedents						I	T	M
noun clauses							I, T	M
as prepositional phrases							I, T	M
as object complements							I, T	M
appositive phrases, restrictive and nonrestrictive					E	I	T	M
PRONOUNS								
singular/plural	E	I	T	M	R	R	R	R
subject	E	I	T	M	R	R	R	R
object	E	I	T	M	R	R	R	R
possessive			E	I	T	M	R	R
as compound subjects			E	I	T	M	R	R
agreement with antecedent			E	I	T	M	R	R
as direct objects				E	I	T	M	R
first/second/third person				E	I	T	M	R
in contractions				I	T	M		
as indirect objects					I	T	M	R
as objects of prepositions					I	T	M	R
as subject complements					I	T	M	R
intensive					I	T	M	R
reflexive					I	T	M	R
demonstrative					I	T	M	R
interrogative					I	T	M	R
indefinite					E	I	T	M
masculine/feminine/neuter					I	T	M	R
who and *whom*						I	T	M
relative							I, T	M
after *than* and *as*							I, T	M

Grammar

Grade Level	1	2	3	4	5	6	7	8
ADJECTIVES								
descriptive	E	I	T	M	R	R	R	R
comparative/superlative/positive	E	I	T	M	R	R	R	
articles			I	T	M	R		
demonstrative			E	I	T	M	R	R
that tell how many	E	I	T	T	M	R	R	R
common/proper			I	T	M			
as subject complements				E	I	T	M	R
position of				I	T	M	R	R
words used as nouns or adjectives				E	I	T	M	
little, less, least				E, I	T	T	M	R
few, fewer, fewest			E	I	T	T	M	R
definite/indefinite articles				I	T	M		
repetition of articles					I, T	M		
interrogative adjectives					E	I	T	M
adjective phrases					E	I	T	M
indefinite adjectives						I	T	M
adjective clauses							I, T	M
as object complements							I, T	M
participles as adjectives							I, T	M
comparisons with *as . . . as* and *so . . . as*							I, T	M
possessive						I	T	M
numerical					I, T	M		
ADVERBS								
manner		E	I	T	M	R	R	R
time			E	I	T	M	R	R
place			E	I	T	M	R	R
negation			E	I	T	M	R	R
-er/-est				E	I	T	M	R
double negatives				E	I	T	M	R
there is/there are				I	T	M		
more/most, less/least				E	I	T	M	R
adverbial phrases					E	I	T	M
adverbial clauses					E	I	T	M
affirmation						I	T	M
degree					E	I	T	M
words used as adverbs and adjectives						I, T	M	R
words used as adverbs and prepositions						I	T	M
interrogative							I, T	M
adverbial nouns							I, T	M
conjunctive							I, T	M
comparisons with *as . . . as* and *so . . . so*							I, T	M
comparative					I, T	T	T	M
superlative					I, T	T	T	M

Scope and Sequence

Grammar *Grade Level*	1	2	3	4	5	6	7	8
VERBS								
subject/verb agreement	E	I	T	M	R	R	R	R
action	E	I	T	M	R	R	R	R
being/linking	E	I	T	M	R	R	R	R
words used as nouns/verbs			E	I	T	M	R	R
regular/irregular	E	I	T	T	M	R	R	R
simple present	E	I	T	T	M	R	R	R
simple past	E	I	T	T	M	R	R	R
future with *will*			E	I	T	M	R	R
future with *going to*			E	I	T	M	R	R
helping (auxiliary verb)		E	I	T	M	R	R	R
principle parts			E	I	T	M	R	R
present progressive		E	I	T	M	R	R	R
past progressive		E	I	T	M	R	R	R
future progressive			E	I	T	M	R	R
verb phrases				E	I	T	M	R
present participle				E	I	T	M	R
past participle				E	I	T	M	R
present perfect				E	I	T	M	R
past perfect				E	I	T	M	R
future perfect				E	I	T	M	R
transitive/intransitive							I	T	M
active and passive voice							I	T	M
indicative mood							I	T	M
emphatic mood							I	T	M
imperative mood							I	T	M
subjunctive mood							I	T	M
modal auxiliaries							I	T	M
gerunds							I, T	M
infinitives							I, T	M
phrasal verbs							I, T	M
troublesome							I	T	M
PREPOSITIONS								
phrases used as adjectives					E	I	T	M
phrases used as adverbs					E	I	T	M
objects of					E	I	T	M
words used as adverbs or prepositions							I	T	M
phrases used as nouns							I, T	M
single and multi-word							I, T	M
CONJUNCTIONS								
coordinate				E	I	T	M	R	R
correlative							I, T	M
subordinate						I	T	M	R
conjunctive adverbs							I, T	M

Grammar — Grade Level	1	2	3	4	5	6	7	8
INTERJECTIONS								
common exclamations					E	I	T	M
SENTENCES								
declarative	E	I	T	T	M	R	R	R
interrogative	E	I	T	T	M	R	R	R
exclamatory	E	I	T	T	M	R	R	R
imperative	E	I	T	T	M	R	R	R
simple	E	I	T	T	M	R	R	R
compound (conjunctions)			E	I	T	M	R	R
natural/inverted word order					I	T	M	
compound (semicolon)					E	I	T	M
complex					E	I	T	M
compound-complex							I, T	M
PARTS OF SENTENCES								
subject and predicate		E	I	T	M	R	R	R
simple subject		E	I	T	M	R	R	R
simple predicate		E	I	T	M	R	R	R
compound sentence elements			E	I	T	M	R	R
subject complement			E	I	T	M	R	R
direct object				E	I	T	M	R
complete subject			E	I	T	T	M	R
complete predicate			E	I	T	T	M	R
indirect object					E	I	T	M
object complement							I, T	M
PHRASES								
verb				E	I	T	M	R
prepositional					E	I	T	M
adverb					E	I	T	M
adjective					E	I	T	M
infinitive							I, T	M
noun							I, T	M
participle							I, T	M
gerund							I, T	M
CLAUSES								
adverb					E	I	T	M
adjective							I, T	M
independent							I, T	M
dependent							I, T	M
restrictive							I, T	M
nonrestrictive							I, T	M
noun							I, T	M
as subjects							I, T	M
as direct objects							I, T	M
as objects of prepositions							I, T	M
as complements							I, T	M
as appositives							I, T	M

Scope and Sequence

E=Explored   I=Introduced   T=Taught   M=Mastered   R=Reviewed

Grammar — Grade Level	1	2	3	4	5	6	7	8
PUNCTUATION / CAPITAL LETTERS								
end punctuation	E	I	T	M	R	R	R	R
capital letters	E	I	T	M	R	R	R	R
periods/capital letters in abbreviations		E	I	T	M	R	R	
periods/capital letters in titles and initials			E	I	T	M	R	R
titles of books, stories, etc.			E	I	T	M	R	R
commas in series			E	I	T	M	R	R
commas in compound sentences			E	I	T	M	R	R
apostrophes	E	I	T	M	R	R	R	R
writing addresses			T	M	R	R	R	R
writing direct quotes			I	T	M	R	R	R
commas in direct address			I	T	M	R	R	R
commas after initial phrase			I	T	M	R	R	R
semicolons in compound sentences					I	T	M	R
colons						I	T	M
hyphens						I	T	M
italics					E	I	T	M
underlining	E	I	T	M	R	R	R	R
dashes							I, T	M
exclamation points	E	I	T	M	R	R	R	R
question marks	E	I	T	M	R	R	R	R
quotation marks			I	T	T	T	M	R
DIAGRAMMING								
subjects			E	I	T	M	R	R
predicates			E	I	T	M	R	R
possessives			E	I	T	M	R	R
adjectives			E	I	T	M	R	R
adverbs			E	I	T	M	R	R
adjective complements			E	I	T	M	R	R
compound sentence elements			E	I	T	M	R	R
compound sentences			E	I	T	M	R	R
direct objects				E	I	T	M	R
noun complements				E	I	T	M	R
indirect objects					E	I	T	M
prepositional phrases					E	I	T	M
adverb clauses					I, T	T	T	M
appositives						I	T	M
intensive pronouns						I	T	M
participles							I, T	M
gerunds							I, T	M
infinitives							I, T	M
noun clauses							I, T	M
adjective clauses							I, T	M
nouns in direct address							I, T	M
interjections					I, T	T	T	M

Writing

	Grade Level	1	2	3	4	5	6	7	8
GENRES									
Personal Narratives		✔	✔	✔	✔	✔	✔	✔	✔
Descriptions		✔	✔	✔	✔	✔	✔	✔	✔
Comparative Description							•	•	•
Description in Paragraph Form			•	•	•	•	•	•	•
Expository Writing		✔	✔	✔	✔	✔	✔	✔	✔
Book Report/Review		•	•	•		•		•	
How-to Articles		✔	✔	✔	✔	✔	✔	✔	✔
Business, Formal, and Friendly Letters		✔	✔	✔	✔	✔	✔	✔	✔
Business or Formal Letter					•	•	•	•	•
Friendly Letter		•	•	•					
Creative Writing				✔	✔	✔	✔	✔	✔
Prose									
Fable					•				
Fantasy								•	
Folk Tale							•		
Play/Script									•
Realistic Fiction				•					
Tall Tale						•			
Trickster Tale							•		
Poetry									
Free Verse									•
Haiku					•				
Limerick								•	
Nonsense Verse						•			
Rhyming Couplets				•					
Rhyming Stanzas							•		
Persuasive Writing			✔	✔	✔	✔	✔	✔	✔
Advertisement					•		•		•
Book Review			•					•	
Persuasive Article/Essay				•	•	•	•		•
Research Reports		✔	✔	✔	✔	✔	✔	✔	✔
GENRE SKILLS									
Plot Development				✔	✔	✔	✔	✔	✔
Organization		✔	✔	✔	✔	✔	✔	✔	✔
Ideas and Outlines		•	•	•	•	•	•	•	•
Spatial Order				•	•	•	•	•	•
Chronological Order		•	•	•	•	•	•	•	•
Comparing and Contrasting						•	•	•	•
Title		✔	✔	✔	✔	✔	✔	✔	✔
Topic		✔	✔	✔	✔	✔	✔	✔	✔
Introduction		✔	✔	✔	✔	✔	✔	✔	✔
Body		✔	✔	✔	✔	✔	✔	✔	✔
Conclusion		✔	✔	✔	✔	✔	✔	✔	✔
Audience		✔	✔	✔	✔	✔	✔	✔	✔

Scope and Sequence

✔ = Skill Taught   • = Subskill Taught

Writing — Grade Level	1	2	3	4	5	6	7	8
Purpose	✔	✔	✔	✔	✔	✔	✔	✔
Voice/Tone/Word Choice	✔	✔	✔	✔	✔	✔	✔	✔
Sentence Fluency	✔	✔	✔	✔	✔	✔	✔	✔
WRITING PROCESS								
Prewriting	✔	✔	✔	✔	✔	✔	✔	✔
Brainstorming	•	•	•	•	•	•	•	•
Free Writing	•	•	•	•	•	•	•	•
Organizing Ideas	•	•	•	•	•	•	•	•
Choosing a Topic	•	•	•	•	•	•	•	•
Drafting	✔	✔	✔	✔	✔	✔	✔	✔
Content Editing	✔	✔	✔	✔	✔	✔	✔	✔
Copyediting			✔	✔	✔	✔	✔	✔
Proofreading	✔	✔	✔	✔	✔	✔	✔	✔
Revising	✔	✔	✔	✔	✔	✔	✔	✔
Publishing	✔	✔	✔	✔	✔	✔	✔	✔
WRITING SKILLS								
Expanded Sentences			✔	✔	✔	✔	✔	✔
Varied Sentences			✔	✔	✔	✔	✔	✔
Revising Sentences			✔	✔	✔	✔	✔	✔
Rambling Sentences			•	•	•	•	•	•
Run-on Sentences			•	•	•	•	•	•
Redundant Words					•		•	•
Adjectives	✔	✔	✔	✔	✔	✔	✔	✔
Adjective Clauses							✔	✔
Adverb Clauses					✔	✔	✔	✔
Graphic Organizers	✔	✔	✔	✔	✔	✔	✔	✔
Five Senses Chart	•	•	•	•		•		
Venn Diagrams					•		•	•
Word Maps/Word Webs/Idea Webs			•	•	•	•	•	•
Time Lines			•	•			•	•
Expanding Sentences			✔	✔	✔	✔	✔	
Compound Subjects and Predicates			•	•	•	•	•	
Compound Direct Objects				•	•	•		
Compound Objects of a Preposition					•	•		
Combining Sentences			✔	✔	✔	✔	✔	✔
Verbs			✔	✔	✔	✔	✔	✔
Using Quotations				✔		✔	✔	✔
Dialogue, Monologue, and Asides			✔	✔	✔	✔	✔	✔
Noun Clauses							✔	✔
Sentence Types	✔	✔	✔	✔	✔	✔	✔	✔
Simple Sentences	•	•	•	•	•	•	•	•
Compound Sentences		•	•	•	•	•	•	•
Complex Sentences				•	•	•	•	•
Transition Words		✔	✔	✔	✔	✔	✔	✔

Writing — Grade Level	1	2	3	4	5	6	7	8
WORD STUDY LESSONS								
Prefixes			✔	✔	✔	✔	✔	✔
Number Prefixes				✔	✔	✔		
Antonyms	✔	✔	✔	✔	✔	✔		
Synonyms	✔	✔	✔	✔	✔	✔	✔	✔
Exact Words	✔	✔	✔	✔	✔	✔	✔	✔
Nouns	●	●	●	●	●	●	●	●
Verbs	●	●	●	●	●	●	●	●
Adjectives	●	●	●	●	●	●	●	●
Adverbs				●	●	●	●	●
Homophones	●	●	●	●	●	●	●	
Compound Words			✔	✔	✔			✔
Pluralizing Compounds								●
Turning Phrases into Compounds								●
Clipped Words								✔
Roots					✔	✔	✔	✔
Contractions	✔	✔	✔	✔	✔	✔	✔	✔
Figurative Language			✔	✔	✔	✔	✔	✔
Similes			●	●	●	●	●	●
Metaphors				●	●	●	●	●
Personification							●	●
Hyperbole					●		●	●
Cliches						●	●	●
Transition Words		✔	✔	✔	✔	✔	✔	✔
Suffixes	✔	✔	✔	✔	✔	✔	✔	✔
Noun and Adjective Suffixes	●	●	●	●	●	●	●	●
Adverb and Verbs Suffixes	●	●	●	●	●	●	●	●
Idioms, Slang, and Jargon								✔
Denotation and Connotation							✔	✔
Homographs						✔		✔
STUDY SKILLS LESSONS								
Dictionary	✔	✔	✔	✔	✔	✔	✔	✔
Syllabication				●	●	●	●	●
Pronunciation			●	●	●	●	●	●
Parts of Speech					●	●	●	●
Word Definition	●	●	●	●	●	●	●	●
Etymology					●	●	●	●
Online Dictionaries			●	●	●	●	●	●
Entry Words		●	●	●	●	●	●	●
Guide Words		●	●	●	●	●		
Thesaurus			✔	✔	✔	✔	✔	✔
Dictionary Thesaurus					●	●	●	●
Indexed Thesaurus					●	●	●	●
Online Thesaurus			●	●	●	●	●	●
Denotation						●	●	●
Connotation							●	●

Scope and Sequence

Writing — Grade Level	1	2	3	4	5	6	7	8
Taking Notes	✔	✔	✔	✔	✔	✔	✔	✔
Evaluating Web Sites			✔	✔	✔	✔	✔	✔
Determining Web Site Credibility			•	•	•	•	•	•
Conducting Research			•	•	•	•	•	•
Recording Internet Research			•	•	•	•	•	•
Library and Internet Sources	✔	✔	✔	✔	✔	✔	✔	✔
Parts of a Book	✔	✔	✔					
Time Lines			✔	✔	✔	✔	✔	✔
Citing Sources			✔	✔	✔	✔	✔	✔
LITERACY SKILLS LESSONS								
Advertisements				✔		✔		✔
Propaganda						•		•
Lost-and-Found Ads								•
Campaign Posters								•
Sales Ads								•
Analyzing Advertisements								•
Writing Advertisements								•
Summarizing								✔
Using Direct Quotations				✔				✔
Paraphrasing			✔	✔	✔			✔
Instructional Graphics					✔	✔	✔	✔
Flowcharts					•	•		
Diagrams					•	•	•	•
Outline				✔	✔	✔	✔	✔
SPEAKING AND LISTENING SKILLS								
Oral Personal Narratives			✔	✔	✔	✔	✔	✔
How-to Talks			✔	✔	✔	✔	✔	✔
Business Telephone Calls			✔		✔			✔
Oral Descriptions			✔	✔	✔	✔	✔	✔
Oral Book Reports			✔		✔			
Job Interview							✔	
Persuasive Speech			✔	✔	✔	✔		✔
Current-Event Reports				✔		✔		
Self-Help Presentations								✔
Storytelling				✔	✔		✔	
Oral Movie Review							✔	
Oral Science Reports							✔	
Congratulatory and Thank-You Speeches						✔		
Destination Guides							✔	
Telling a Trickster Tale						✔		
Reader's Theater								✔
Oral Reports				✔	✔			✔
Biographical Reports			✔			✔		
Skits			✔					
Oral Complaints and Conflicts				✔				